Microsoft 365 Administration Inside Out, Third Edition

Aaron Guilmette
Darryl Kegg
Ed Fisher

Microsoft 365 Administration Inside Out, Third Edition
Published with the authorization of Microsoft Corporation by:
Pearson Education, Inc.

ISBN-13: 978-0-13-790885-1
ISBN-10: 0-13-790885-7

Library of Congress Control Number: 2022951941

99 2024

Trademarks

Microsoft and the trademarks listed at http://www.microsoft.com on the "Trademarks" webpage are trademarks of the Microsoft group of companies. All other marks are property of their respective owners.

Warning and Disclaimer

Every effort has been made to make this book as complete and as accurate as possible, but no warranty or fitness is implied. The information provided is on an "as is" basis. The author, the publisher, and Microsoft Corporation shall have neither liability nor responsibility to any person or entity with respect to any loss or damages arising from the information contained in this book or from the use of the programs accompanying it.

Special Sales

For information about buying this title in bulk quantities, or for special sales opportunities (which may include electronic versions; custom cover designs; and content particular to your business, training goals, marketing focus, or branding interests), please contact our corporate sales department at corpsales@pearsoned.com or (800) 382-3419.

For government sales inquiries, please contact governmentsales@pearsoned.com.
For questions about sales outside the U.S., please contact intlcs@pearson.com.

Editor-in-Chief: Brett Bartow
Executive Editor: Loretta Yates
Sponsoring Editor: Charvi Arora
Development Editor: Rick Kughen
Managing Editor: Sandra Schroeder
Senior Project Editor: Tracey Croom
Project Editor: Charlotte Kughen
Copy Editor: Rick Kughen
Indexer: Johnna VanHoose Dinse
Proofreader: Sarah Kearns
Editorial Assistant: Cindy Teeters
Cover Designer: Twist Creative, Seattle
Compositor: Bronkella Publishing, LLC
Graphics: TJ Graham Art

Pearson's Commitment to Diversity, Equity, and Inclusion

Pearson is dedicated to creating bias-free content that reflects the diversity of all learners. We embrace the many dimensions of diversity, including but not limited to race, ethnicity, gender, socioeconomic status, ability, age, sexual orientation, and religious or political beliefs.

Education is a powerful force for equity and change in our world. It has the potential to deliver opportunities that improve lives and enable economic mobility. As we work with authors to create content for every product and service, we acknowledge our responsibility to demonstrate inclusivity and incorporate diverse scholarship so that everyone can achieve their potential through learning. As the world's leading learning company, we have a duty to help drive change and live up to our purpose to help more people create a better life for themselves and to create a better world.

Our ambition is to purposefully contribute to a world where:

- Everyone has an equitable and lifelong opportunity to succeed through learning.

- Our educational products and services are inclusive and represent the rich diversity of learners.

- Our educational content accurately reflects the histories and experiences of the learners we serve.

- Our educational content prompts deeper discussions with learners and motivates them to expand their own learning (and worldview).

While we work hard to present unbiased content, we want to hear from you about any concerns or needs with this Pearson product so that we can investigate and address them.

Please contact us with concerns about any potential bias at
https://www.pearson.com/report-bias.html.

Dedications

I'd like to dedicate this book to my kids, several of whom reminded me that I didn't include their names in my last book. Sorry for the oversight. I also want to thank my co-authors, without whom I would have had to write a lot more.

—Aaron Guilmette

I'd like to dedicate this book to my family for their support and understanding, and I'd like to thank my co-authors, a motley crew, for their willingness to collaborate. This book has been a labor of love, and I sincerely hope it can help others to learn and grow.

—Darryl Kegg

I dedicate this book to Connie, without whom this could not have happened and would not have mattered. Thanks for being my better half in every way. And to my partners in crime on this book: It's always a pleasure, gentlemen! And thank you to the great team at Pearson and The Wordsmithery for all your help and patience!

—Ed Fisher

Contents at a Glance

About the Authors

Aaron Guilmette is a Senior Program Manager for Customer Experience at Microsoft and provides guidance and assistance to customers adopting the Microsoft 365 platform, focusing on messaging, identity, automation, and security solutions. You can follow Aaron on LinkedIn at *aka.ms/aaronlinkedin*.

Darryl Kegg is a Senior Program Manager at Microsoft, dedicated to deploying Microsoft 365 and Azure technologies with a focus on identity, security, and access management. Darryl has been involved in deploying Microsoft 365 to government, education, healthcare, and commercial customers since its launch in 2011 and has helped migrate 15+ million users to Azure. You can follow Darryl on LinkedIn at *aka.ms/darrylkegg*.

Ed Fisher is a Technical Solution Leader-Security at Microsoft, focusing on helping customers evaluate, deploy, and adopt Microsoft 365 collaboration technologies, networking, and security solutions. His focus is on Microsoft's XDR and SIEM platforms and Microsoft Defender for Office. Find out more at *aka.ms/edfisher*.

Introduction

Microsoft's online offerings have continued to evolve since the first debut of the Live@Edu service in 2005. Four years later, in April 2009, Microsoft expanded its cloud services offering with the launch of Microsoft Business Productivity Online Services. Over the last 18 years, Microsoft has steadily rolled out new features to the service and paved the way for today's modern Microsoft 365 platform.

Microsoft 365 enables organizations as small as a single person or as large as the world's biggest multinational retailers and manufacturers to harness the power of cloud scaling, automation, and availability. Microsoft's online services currently enable over 200 million monthly active users to collaborate—whether they're in the same room, across the hall, or around the world.

The service is evergreen—built around the ideas of continuous improvement and feature release—to ensure that customers always receive the latest capabilities and enhance their ability to be more agile, productive, and secure. With the launch of the Microsoft 365 product suite in 2017, Microsoft added Windows platform, mobility, and enterprise security capability to the already popular Office 365 software-as-a-service offering.

Microsoft has a vision for a cloud-first, mobile-first future—built on the broad capabilities of Microsoft 365 and Azure. This book equips you with the knowledge you need to tackle the deployment of one of the largest transformational products available as well as insider tips that help you avoid the mistakes that might slow you down.

Who this book is for

This book is written for IT professionals responsible for deploying, migrating to, and managing some (or all) of an organization's Microsoft 365 environment. Microsoft 365 isn't just a single application or service; it's a suite of software-as-a-service tools that can touch every part of the business.

For some, Microsoft 365 might seem like just one more thing to learn. In reality, though, if you've been administering on-premises versions of Active Directory, Exchange, or SharePoint, you're already familiar with many of the core concepts you need to hit the ground running. The Microsoft 365 platform enables myriad hybrid capabilities, allowing your organization to adopt the cloud on its terms and timeline. There are a lot of compelling cloud-only features that you'll want to explore as well.

We at Microsoft believe that the Microsoft 365 platform is an extension of your own datacenter. The management patterns and practices you've built for your on-premises environment can be updated and adapted to the cloud, enabling you to achieve quicker results.

We've organized this book to try to take you from the very beginning through progressively more advanced concepts. However, you don't have to read it in order—you can skip around to the parts that address your most immediate needs. Our goal with this book is to help you at any stage of your cloud journey—whether you're a consultant looking for architecture and planning guidance or an IT pro tasked with deployment and management.

Conventions

This book uses special text and design conventions to make it easier for you to find the information you need.

Text conventions

The following conventions are used in this book:

- **Boldface type** is used to indicate text that you should type where directed.

- For your convenience, this book uses abbreviated menu commands. For example, "Click Tools > Track Changes > Highlight Changes" means you should click the Tools menu, point to Track Changes, and then click the Highlight Changes command.

- Elements with the Code typeface are meant to be entered on a command line or inside a dialog box. For example, "type cd \Windows to change to the Windows subdirectory" means that you should be entering cd \Windows with your keyboard or text input device.

- The first letters of the names of menus, dialog boxes, dialog box elements, and commands are capitalized—for example, the Save As dialog box.

- *Italicized type* indicates new terms.

Book features

In addition to the text conventions, this book contains sidebars to provide additional context, tips, or suggestions.

Inside OUT

These are the book's signature tips. In these tips, you'll get the straight scoop on what's going on with the software or service—inside information about why a feature works the way it does. You'll also find field-tested advice and guidance as well as details that give you the edge on deploying and managing like a pro.

READER AIDS

Reader aids are exactly that—Notes, Tips, and Cautions provide additional information on completing a task or specific items to watch out for.

Acknowledgments

We would like to thank the teams at Pearson and Microsoft Press for giving us the opportunity to share our knowledge, experiences, and lessons learned in this update. We'd also like to thank our coworkers and peers for content ideas, suggestions, and feedback during the writing and revising process. And, of course, we want to thank the countless engineers, programmers, and technical experts who tirelessly work behind the scenes to expand the capabilities of the platform, giving all of us the ability to achieve more.

Errata, updates, & book support

We've made every effort to ensure the accuracy of this book and its companion content. You can access updates to this book in the form of a list of submitted errata and their related corrections—at:

MicrosoftPressStore.com/365AdminInsideOut/errata

If you discover an error that is not already listed, please submit it to us at the same page.

For additional book support and information, please visit MicrosoftPressStore.com/Support.

Please note that product support for Microsoft software and hardware is not offered through the previous addresses. For help with Microsoft software or hardware, go to:

http://support.microsoft.com.

Stay in touch

Let's keep the conversation going! We're on Twitter: *twitter.com/MicrosoftPress.*

CHAPTER 1

It's hard to believe that it's been more than 11 years since Microsoft released Microsoft 365, and despite the millions of customers currently on the platform, we continue to add new ones daily. That said, no matter the number of Microsoft 365 tenants in production today, the planning and deployment of Microsoft 365 is not a simple task, and key decisions require review and planning before jumping into the cloud. Some decisions, like naming, are permanent, while others, like licensing, can be changed (with a change in costs). Still others could permanently change your internal IT infrastructure regarding mail routing, VPN, network, and firewall design. Each facet of the deployment process should be carefully reviewed, and each decision's long-term impact should be considered before proceeding to the next.

In the coming chapters, we will help outline each of those key changes, provide some detail about the downstream impact, and help you avoid some of the most common pitfalls associated with getting to the cloud.

Getting started

To start your journey to the cloud, open a new browser window and navigate to *https://www.office365.com* to select the plan that best suits your needs. Choosing a plan is the first of many decisions you'll have to make to get started on your journey to the cloud, and the licensing plan you pick will depend on several things you'll need to know before you can choose.

As shown in Figure 1-1, you can choose between Personal, Business, Enterprise, and Education.

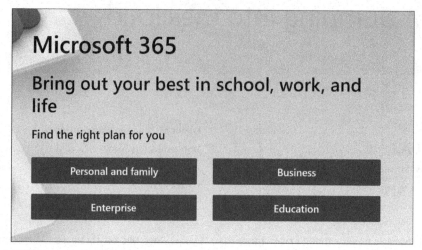

FIGURE 1-1   M365 plan selection options

If you are setting this up for yourself, Personal and Family is the best choice, and if you're setting up a subscription for your school, you will want to choose Education. However, things get a little more confusing if you're setting this up for your company because there are two plans (Business and Enterprise) that you'll need to choose between—and the differences might not be obvious.

Which plan is best for me?

The Business and Enterprise plans each have several packages you can choose from, so understanding each will help you decide what's right for you.

> **TIP**
>
> **Microsoft 365 is a new suite encompassing the previous Office 365 suite (Exchange Online, SharePoint Online, Office apps, and Skype for Business or Microsoft Teams), the Enterprise Mobility + Security Suite, and Windows 10 or Windows 11. This book covers the expanded suite offering instead of just the core productivity apps.**

Microsoft 365 Business consists of Basic, Standard, and Premium plans, each with its own per-user, per-month pricing that increases with each tier. Each of the Business packages includes the Web and Mobile versions of the Office suite, including Outlook, Word, Excel, PowerPoint, and OneNote, and inboxes come with a 50GB size limit, while OneDrive storage is capped at 1TB. Each of the Microsoft 365 Business plans also includes Microsoft Teams and the world-class Exchange Online protection for your email traffic. However, the main limitation is that Microsoft 365 Business plans—regardless of the tier—are limited to 300 total users. If your company has more than 300 users (or close to 300), you should look at Microsoft Enterprise.

Additional features in the Microsoft 365 Business Premium plan include Advanced Threat Protection, Rights Management, Exchange Online Archiving, as well as Intune for device management, so if your company has fewer than 300 users, you should check out the plans in more detail at *https://www.microsoft.com/en-us/microsoft-365/business*.

Inside Out

Counting your users

Microsoft 365 requires a license for Shared Mailboxes over 50GB, so be sure to keep that in mind when adding up the cost of a Microsoft 365 subscription or when deciding between Microsoft 365 Business and Microsoft 365 Enterprise.

Microsoft 365 Enterprise, just like Business, also has three different tiers: F3, E3, and E5:

- F3 is the most basic plan for *firstline* (previously called *kiosk*) workers with 2GB mailboxes and the web-only versions of the Office applications.

- E3 is like the Microsoft 365 Business plans, with the addition of things like BitLocker, Security and Compliance Center, and Azure Information Protection.

- E5 is the flagship Enterprise product and includes everything in the E3 plan but with even more features like eDiscovery, Customer Lockbox, Privileged Access Management, Data Governance, and more.

NOTE

Head over to *https://www.microsoft.com/en-us/microsoft-365/compare-microsoft-365-enterprise-plans* to review their differences and the Microsoft 365 Enterprise plan pricing.

Picking a tenant name

The second decision you must make when creating your Microsoft 365 tenant is your tenant's name. In fact, you will be prompted for this name during the first pages of your initial Microsoft 365 registration.

CAUTION

The name prompt is accompanied by very little fanfare and absolutely no warning that you are about to pass the point of no return. It is a deployment milestone representing a critical decision that cannot be undone when setting up Microsoft 365.

NOTE

For more detail on all the places where a tenant name is visible, refer to Chapter 2, "Preparing your environment for the cloud."

The tenant name selection occurs on the How You'll Sign In page, as shown in Figure 1-2, immediately after selecting your preferred Microsoft 365 subscription type and verifying your name, phone number, and email.

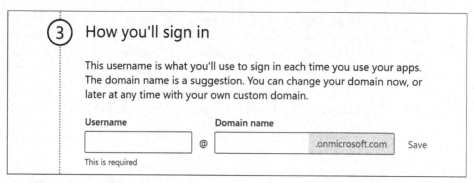

FIGURE 1-2   How You'll Sign In page

The Domain Name value provided during this process will become the tenant name used to set up your Microsoft 365 subscription and will be configured as a subdomain of the onmicrosoft.com namespace.

CAUTION

All Microsoft 365 and Azure tenants are subdomains of the onmicrosoft.com **namespace. This suffix cannot be changed and will be visible in any Microsoft 365 URLs, sharing invitations, and cloud logins.**

Your tenant name must be globally unique from all other Microsoft tenants. The selection process will tell you if the subdomain portion of the sign-in ID is already in use when you click Save and will not allow you to proceed if it is not unique, as shown in Figure 1-3.

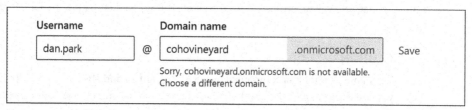

FIGURE 1-3   This tenant name is not available.

Once you have selected a valid Username and Domain name, click Next to start the subscription setup. Your new name will be set up across the Microsoft 365 tenant and will appear in several locations.

CAUTION

Once you have selected a tenant name, it cannot be changed. Before creating your Microsoft 365 tenant, you should discuss the ramifications of the name with all the appropriate resources (such as Legal or Marketing) in your company. If you are planning any merger, acquisition, or divestiture (MAD) activity, you should ensure the tenant name will remain relevant after that activity has concluded.

Adding your domain name to your tenant

Once you've completed the setup of your Microsoft 365 tenant, you will be directed to the Microsoft 365 admin center, as shown in Figure 1-4. In the Top Action For You Section is the Finish Setting Up Email option, where you can set up your email domain and add additional accounts. Make sure you choose this option to add your domain name to your Microsoft 365 tenant.

FIGURE 1-4   The Finish Setting Up Email option in Microsoft 365 admin center

If the domain name you entered already exists, the Microsoft 365 admin center will attempt to determine where the domain is registered and provide instructions for confirming your ownership of the domain. Typically, this is done by configuring either a TXT or MX DNS record for domain verification. In Figure 1-5, the domain name cohovineyards.us is registered at GoDaddy, and the step-by-step instructions link will guide you through setting up the correct records.

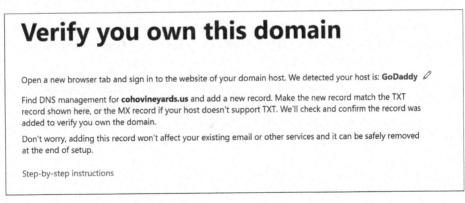

FIGURE 1-5   Verify You Own This Domain

Once you have followed the instructions to set up the correct MX or TXT record with your DNS host, click the Verify button to complete the addition of the domain name.

> ### TIP
>
> **Because of the nature of DNS, any changes you make with your domain registrar might take between 1 and 24 hours before the changes are replicated globally across the Internet. If you cannot verify the domain name immediately, the Microsoft 365 admin center will remember where you are in the process, and you can return later to complete the verification step.**

Once you have successfully added your domain name, you will be prompted to sign out of Microsoft 365 with your @onmicrosoft.com login you initially set up and sign back in with your registered domain name. Your password will remain the same, though your login will be name@yourdomain.com instead of name@yourtenant.onmicrosoft.com.

After successfully logging back in, you will be directed to the Microsoft 365 default landing page, where you can start using the Office Web Apps or install the desktop versions. However, to complete the email domain setup, you will need to click the app launcher (sometimes known as the *waffle*) icon in the upper-left corner of the screen, as shown in Figure 1-6.

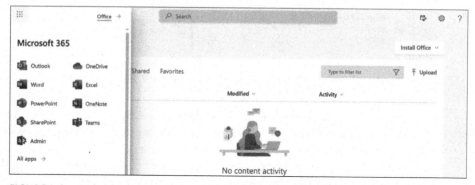

FIGURE 1-6   Navigating to the admin center from the default landing page using the app launcher

Clicking the App launcher will allow you to select the Admin menu option, which will return you to the Microsoft 365 admin center. From here, you can click Finish to finish setting up email, completing the addition of your domain name to the tenant.

The final step in the domain name setup is to create the remaining Microsoft 365 DNS records with your domain registrar. You will be prompted for the method you would like to use to create these records. As shown in Figure 1-7, the recommended approach is to allow Microsoft to add the DNS records for you automatically.

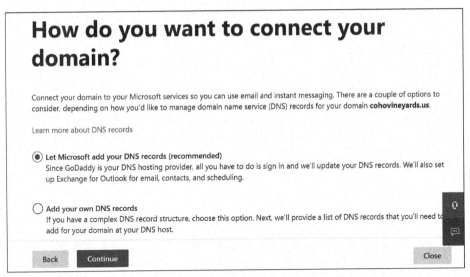

FIGURE 1-7   Choosing the method to add DNS records to your domain configuration

Clicking Continue will prompt you to sign in to your domain registrar's website, and the admin center will automatically make all the DNS record changes for you. Once complete, you will see a screen like the one shown in Figure 1-8. Click Done to complete the setup process and return to the Microsoft 365 admin center.

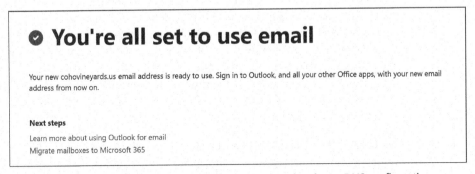

FIGURE 1-8   Confirmation that the admin center has completed your DNS configuration

So far, you have successfully selected your licensing plan and chosen your Microsoft 365 tenant name. These first steps represent the two largest and most impactful decisions you can make when setting up Microsoft 365. Additionally, you have linked your personal or company's domain name to your tenant, which means Microsoft 365 will now start handling your email and secure it using Exchange Online Protection (spam and antivirus protection). We will discuss Exchange Online setup and other security features in the coming chapters.

Before anyone else can utilize Microsoft 365 applications or email, you might need to add additional administrators to your tenant, so it is important to understand the different types of administrative roles when delegating access.

Delegating access to your tenant

By default, the user account that was used to set up the tenant will have Global Administrator privilege, which provides unrestricted access to all features of the tenant and the underlying Azure Active Directory. However, several additional Microsoft 365 administrative roles allow you to delegate additional levels of permissions to the service without needing to grant unrestricted access.

Currently, there are eight pre-built administrative roles:

- **Global Administrator**   The Global Administrator role has all rights within the Microsoft 365 subscription. It is much like the Domain Admin role in on-premises Active Directory and should be treated with the same vigilance. The number of Global Administrators in your Microsoft 365 tenant should be kept at a minimum, and their credentials should be protected. Like the on-premises Domain Admin role, Global Administrators can create any of the administrative roles, including another Global Administrator, and grant additional rights not delegated by default.

- **Exchange Administrator**   The Exchange Administrator role grants full access to Exchange Online administration. This includes the creation, deletion, and editing of mail-users, user mailboxes, and groups, as well as allowing the creation of service requests and reviewing Exchange Online service health. It is important to note that the Exchange Administrator role by itself cannot create a new user in the tenant. A User Administrator or Global Administrator account or the AAD Connect synchronization process must be used. Instead, an Exchange Administrator can only enable or disable users present in Azure Active Directory created by a Global Administrator, User Administrator, or via the directory synchronization process.

- **Global Reader**   The Global Reader role can view all settings in all the Microsoft 365 administration centers (such as Teams, SharePoint, Exchange, and so on) but cannot make any changes to any settings in the tenant. It is important to note that the Global Reader role can be added in addition to other administrative roles. For example, it is possible to assign the Teams and Exchange Administrator roles, along with Global Reader, to an administrator so that they can make changes to the Teams and Exchange admin center settings but only view other tenant settings.

- **Helpdesk Administrator**   The Helpdesk Administrator role can reset passwords, manage service requests, and monitor service health. Additionally, the Helpdesk Administrator role can force users to sign out and enforce re-authentication for all user roles and limited admin roles.

- **Service Support Administrator**   The Service Support Administrator can create service requests for Microsoft 365, Azure Active Directory, and the associated Microsoft 365 workloads, as well as monitor service health.

- **SharePoint Administrator**   The SharePoint Administrator has full access to the SharePoint Online service and can create Microsoft 365 Groups, manage service requests, and monitor service health.

- **Teams Administrator**   The Teams Administrator has full access to the Teams service, can manage Microsoft 365 groups, manage service requests, and monitor service health.

- **User Administrator**   The User Administrator can create and manage users and groups, reset passwords, manage service requests, and monitor service health. Also, User Administrators can assign licenses and update password policies.

NOTE

It is important to note that User Administrators can also manage user login names, delete and restore users, and force users to sign out, provided the selected user is not delegated another administrative role.

TIP

It is possible to delegate multiple administrative roles to a single user so that they can be responsible for more than one task (such as SharePoint and Exchange Administration) without granting too much access to your tenant.

Should I deploy in hybrid mode?

When deploying Microsoft 365, *hybrid* is one of the most common terms that you will hear discussed. In fact, the term hybrid will be used not only when discussing Exchange Online but also SharePoint Online, Teams, and even identity or directory synchronization.

Understanding what hybrid really means will help you decide if it is something you want to configure. Typically, this decision should be made before onboarding a service or workload, as it drives additional infrastructure and setup tasks.

Exchange Hybrid

When referring to Microsoft Exchange, *hybrid* is a configuration methodology that provides a seamless look and feel for a single organization between on-premises Exchange and Microsoft 365 for both administrators and end users. Exchange Hybrid offers a near-parity of features and experience between Exchange Online and Exchange on-premises by enabling things like cross-premises calendaring and mailbox migrations and allowing administrators to manage both environments from a single administrative interface. See Figure 1-9.

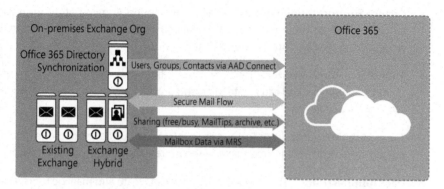

Figure 1-9 Exchange Hybrid architecture overview

An Exchange Hybrid configuration provides and uses the following features:

- Delegated authentication between on-premises Exchange and Exchange Online

- Enables free/busy information sharing, calendar sharing, and message tracking

- Allows administrators to manage both environments from a single Exchange Administrative Center (EAC)

- Allows for online mailbox moves

- Preserves the Microsoft Outlook profile and Offline Store (OST) file after a mailbox move

- Enables authenticated and encrypted mail flow between on-premises Exchange and Exchange Online

- Preserves Exchange mail headers during email transport between organizations

- Allows for a centralized transport to support compliance mail flow

TIP

Microsoft Exchange Hybrid requires additional configuration steps, which are outlined in detail in Chapter 14, "Exchange Online hybrid planning and deployment." Exchange Hybrid also requires several deployment prerequisites before running the Exchange Hybrid Configuration Wizard:

- Implementation of directory synchronization between on-premises and Microsoft 365

- Exchange AutoDiscover DNS records properly configured for each SMTP domain used

- A publicly trusted certificate from a third-party certification authority

- Additional TXT records in public DNS for Exchange federation

- Additional firewall and network configurations

- Internet-facing Exchange 2013 (or later) CAS/MBX roles

- Active Directory Windows Server 2003 forest-functional level or later

- Exchange Web Services and AutoDiscover published to the Internet and secured with a public certificate

TIP

The Exchange Hybrid configuration process is complex, and despite the simple appearance of the Hybrid Configuration Wizard (HCW), there are many pre- and post-setup tasks that must be performed to achieve a successful implementation.

SharePoint Hybrid

Hybrid for SharePoint refers to a configuration where organizational content is mixed between SharePoint Online and on-premises SharePoint. Unlike Exchange Hybrid, the SharePoint Hybrid configuration is much less complex, typically consisting of the two environments with a reverse-proxy configuration, which allows users to traverse links across the two environments.

There are three basic topologies when configuring SharePoint Hybrid.

One-way outbound

The on-premises SharePoint farm connects one-way, outbound, to SharePoint Online. Search is supported in this topology, as shown in Figure 1-10.

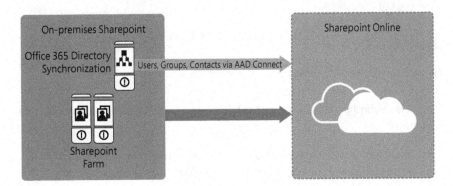

Figure 1-10   SharePoint Hybrid one-way outbound topology

One-way inbound

SharePoint Online connects to an on-premises SharePoint farm, one-way, inbound, via a reverse proxy; search is supported in this topology, as shown in Figure 1-11.

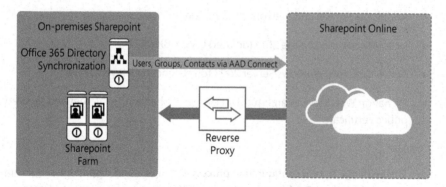

Figure 1-11 SharePoint Hybrid one-way inbound topology

Two-way hybrid

SharePoint Online and an on-premises SharePoint farm are connected to one another, utilizing a reverse proxy. Search and Business Connectivity Services (BCS) are both supported, as shown in Figure 1-12.

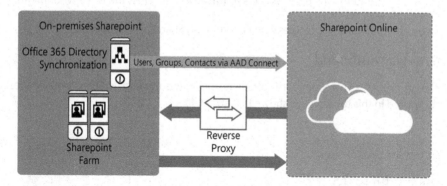

Figure 1-12 SharePoint Hybrid two-way inbound topology

SharePoint Hybrid provides a somewhat homogenous user experience, though there are several limitations:

- There is no combined navigation experience between the two environments; book-marked sites and links in one environment do not appear in the other.

- Document templates, branding, and content-type chaining are not shared across the two environments; they must be maintained separately.

- While search does work across the two environments, searches are done in two stages (first one environment, then the other), and the results from each search are displayed in separate result blocks.

- Unlike Exchange Hybrid, SharePoint Hybrid does not enable migrating content between on-premises and cloud environments.

Please refer to Chapter 27, "SharePoint Online hybrid configuration," for a detailed description and walkthrough of the SharePoint Hybrid configuration process.

As you can see, each of the hybrid scenarios outlined previously can create additional deployment tasks when implementing Microsoft 365. It is important to understand the benefits of each hybrid configuration and ensure that you have identified whether these scenarios are needed or wanted before beginning your Microsoft 365 deployment. Each will drive up the cost of deployment and increase the project timeline.

Most importantly, choosing a hybrid topology for one service or workload does not mean you have to choose it for all workloads. For example, you could decide to use Exchange Online Hybrid without configuring the hybrid features for SharePoint.

Is your Exchange environment ready?

When beginning any Microsoft 365 implementation that includes Exchange Online, reviewing your on-premises Microsoft Exchange environment is important. Your environment must meet the minimum requirements for deployment, and you must identify configurations that might require a change in deployment strategy. Lastly, you must identify any Exchange schema updates, additional network infrastructure, or mail flow changes that must be made.

These configurations include (but are not limited to) physical Exchange Server infrastructure, mail routing, spam and antivirus appliances, load balancers, proxy servers, intrusion detection appliances, and firewall rules.

Physical Exchange Server infrastructure

When evaluating your physical Exchange on-premises infrastructure, you should begin by reviewing the number of Exchange servers you have located within your enterprise and each of their roles.

The Mailbox Replication Service (MRS), which is responsible for mailbox migrations to Microsoft 365, will act as a proxy server for mailbox move requests on any existing (or additional) Exchange servers you designate during the Hybrid setup.

If your user mailboxes are distributed geographically in the enterprise, but your Hybrid servers—which are used to proxy the move requests—are in another physical location across wide-area network links, you will encounter additional latency during moves, increasing the possibility of timeouts or migration failures.

Depending on the distribution of mailboxes, it might be necessary to perform the migration in multiple stages. One such example might be moving mailboxes over the wide-area network to a mailbox server at the same site as the Exchange server configured as a migration endpoint before migrating the mailboxes to Exchange Online.

Depending on the geographic difference, this approach might make the process easier, despite adding additional steps, because the net impact to the users would be mitigated. The migration, internally between servers, would allow you to move the mailbox without any user downtime based on the way that Exchange handles in-progress MRS moves. The second step, while also non-invasive, would have a much lower failure risk because of latency concerns.

Mail routing

The next physical infrastructure component worth reviewing is the location of any Exchange Client Access (CAS) servers, which support mail exchanger (MX) records and answer auto-discover requests for Outlook and other email clients.

Depending upon the intended mail routing and the complexity of your environment, it might be necessary to add additional endpoints for mail routing, change the location of existing public-facing endpoints, or even remove endpoints, depending on your users' locations relative to their mailboxes.

Also, it is important to note that you cannot put any additional mail transport appliances between Exchange Online and the Exchange on-premises hub/transport servers used for hybrid routing between on-premises and Microsoft 365. Doing so will strip the Exchange verbs used in message headers. If additional mail transport is required, be prepared to install Exchange Edge servers.

Mailboxes

Physical infrastructure aside, the next item to consider (which relates both to migration duration and costs) is your mailboxes. The number of mailboxes in your environment will directly impact the project timeline. You will need to account for both the number of mailboxes and their sizes.

Additionally, any mailboxes with items that exceed the attachment limit (150MB when using MRS moves) will need those large attachments removed, or the mailbox migration will fail. There is an option to skip large items, though this results in the offending messages being automatically removed from the mailbox during migration.

Large items

Typically, the identification of large items must either be assigned to your users (asking them to create Outlook views to identify large items) or done with PowerShell or other utilities to create reports that will require additional action from your users to remove or archive. These tasks require lead-time and user interaction, lengthening your migration project timeline.

It can be advantageous to group your mailboxes by department and move them for people who interact with one another in a batch. Finally, when identifying mailboxes in your environment, it is recommended to sort them by type, which helps calculate the total number of licenses required. Remember, user mailboxes (and some shared mailboxes) require a license, while room and equipment mailboxes do not. Also, this will help you better understand how many mailboxes of each type exist in your environment. You will need this information when creating migration batches because moving groups of users and their resource mailboxes is customary.

Recipient types

One additional step that should be included when reviewing mailboxes is a review of each mailbox's recipient type compared to the intended purpose of the mailbox. In older versions of Microsoft Exchange, there were no room and equipment type mailboxes, so it was common practice to create user mailboxes and simply delegate access differently.

Mailboxes in this state will not cause issues in on-premises Exchange, though once they are migrated to Exchange Online, licensing requirements will apply. This means while a mailbox is considered a room or resource (based simply on its name or historical use), as soon as that mailbox is migrated to Microsoft 365, it will be deleted if it is not licensed within 30 days.

> ### TIP
> We recommend identifying shared, resource, and equipment mailboxes ahead of time and ensuring the recipient type is correctly configured before migration.

Proxy addresses and domains

Many Exchange environments evolve over time. As a result, you likely have email domains that have either been acquired and subsequently decommissioned or relegated to secondary addresses. There might also be domains purchased as part of special projects or divestiture efforts.

The migration to Microsoft 365 will require a house cleaning of sorts to ensure that the only remaining email domains are valid and supported domains in your enterprise.

When migrating to Microsoft 365, your users will be synchronized to Azure AD, and any mail-enabled or mailbox-enabled objects (users, resources, groups) will be created as mail-enabled objects in Exchange Online.

During this initial synchronization—and while the source mailbox remains in on-premises Exchange—Microsoft 365 does not care if the email addresses on the object are valid. In fact, many customers don't realize (until their very first pilot mailbox migrations) that they have invalid email domains configured for their users. This is because Exchange Online will allow a mail-enabled user object to be created in Exchange Online because it is simply there to allow for mail flow and a complete Global Address List experience with non-routable email domain suffixes in the proxy addresses array. However, the object will not be allowed to be converted to a mailbox during the migration unless all the user's email addresses are valid domains registered in Microsoft 365.

For this reason, it is recommended that reports of all mail-enabled objects and their email addresses are generated before starting mailbox moves. You might find that you have a lot of cleanup to do in Exchange before you can start migrating mailboxes.

Along with the cleanup of email addresses, you should review any email addressing policies (EAPs) in Exchange to ensure that legacy or unused domains are still not being automatically assigned to newly mail-enabled or mailbox-enabled objects in your Exchange organization.

> ### TIP
> Although they will not prevent the migration of mailboxes, email addresses that begin with prefixes like NOTES:, FAX:, and X400: are not synchronized to Exchange Online and will not exist on mailboxes in Exchange Online.

Delegating access between mailboxes does not work across the on-premises and cloud environments. Therefore, while any permissions existing before migration are retained, any new delegation can only occur if both the mailbox and the delegate exist in the same environment. So, when you are planning mailbox migration batches, it is advisable to identify any shared or delegated mailboxes within teams and departments in your organization and make sure that those mailboxes are moved to Exchange Online during the same migration batches to avoid any confusion or loss of functionality.

Public Folders

Public Folders are the next item in your on-premises Exchange infrastructure that warrant careful review. You can rest easy if you have no Public Folders in your organization or are only using Public Folders for free/busy data in support of legacy Outlook clients.

However, if you have Public Folders and require data to be migrated to Microsoft 365, you will want to know your options for co-existence and migration of Public Folder data, including mail-enabled Public Folders. See Chapter 17, "Migrating public folders to Exchange Online."

Load balancers, network configurations, proxy servers, and firewall rules

Finally, you will want to review your network configurations related to your Exchange environment:

- **Server placement** The Hybrid servers that will support the MRS role should be located as close to the public Internet as possible (directly exposed if possible). This ensures that network connectivity, latency, or other network devices (like stateful packet inspection appliances) do not interfere with mailbox moves. In fact, based on the distribution of mailboxes compared to the Exchange servers with the hybrid role configured, it is often recommended that multiple MRS endpoints are configured in an enterprise to allow for more efficient migration of mailboxes, particularly in geographically dispersed environments.

- **Load balancers** You should carefully review the placement of hybrid servers supporting MRS moves behind load balancers. Some load balancers might be configured to ignore or enforce a sticky state, and some might change header behavior, which could affect the speed at which mailbox migrations occur. Talk with your load balancer vendor and ensure it supports load balancing Exchange servers that will be used to perform MRS mailbox migrations.

- **Network configurations** Next, you should review the end-to-end network configuration of your Exchange servers relative to one another and Active Directory. If you are adding new Exchange servers to perform hybrid roles (as opposed to utilizing existing Exchange servers), ensure they are not separated from the rest of your infrastructure by firewalls or network devices that might otherwise limit or block traffic. While it is not possible to identify every device that might cause problems in your environment simply by looking at a network map or reviewing server roles, these exercises will help you become more familiar with your environment. This clarity will help you understand which configurations might require changes to accomplish mailbox migrations to Exchange Online.

- **Proxy servers** While not directly related to Exchange Online or Microsoft 365 roles, proxy servers are equally important. Before any mailboxes can be migrated to Exchange Online, your tenant directory must be fully populated via the directory synchronization tool. Proxy servers, particularly authenticated proxies, will cause issues with synchronizing identities to your tenant. Authenticated proxies are not supported for use with the Azure AD Connect synchronization tool, so they should have the proxy configurations either bypassed or changed to use non-authenticated proxy servers.

Inside Out

Setting up your network environment for success

If your network configuration is complex or you are unsure whether any network devices or their configurations might cause issues, you should be prepared to deploy at least one Exchange server with a direct NAT from the Internet through your firewall for testing purposes. Presenting an Exchange server directly to the Internet will allow you to prove or disprove whether network configurations are affecting connectivity or mailbox migration performance issues.

As you can see, there are many things that should be carefully reviewed when discussing the placement of mailbox migration infrastructure in your organization. In some cases, your environment can support a migration to Microsoft 365 with minimal effort. However, you need to include these activities in the project timeline if your environment requires changes to network routing, firewall, or load balancers (or even the deployment of new servers). These items will increase migration time and possibly drive the need for upgrades to other supporting technologies.

TIP

Plan time in your deployment schedule to review network and server configuration items with the appropriate teams in your organization and get them involved in Microsoft 365 planning meetings early. The best way to ensure success is to involve everyone responsible for your infrastructure.

Is your directory ready?

Once you have had an opportunity to review your Exchange infrastructure, similar activities must be performed in your on-premises Active Directory environment.

Your Active Directory environment impacts not only Exchange but all the services available in Microsoft 365 because your Active Directory identities are synchronized to Azure in most environments and form the foundation of all Microsoft 365 use cases.

User readiness

Unless your users are all cloud users (explained in more detail in Chapter 9, "Identity and authentication planning"), you will need to synchronize your Active Directory to Azure so your users can log in to Azure and consume Microsoft 365 services.

When synchronizing your users to Azure, many attribute values must be unique and meet certain requirements before they synchronize successfully. Often, synchronization errors are caused by invalid character values in key attributes or duplication of values between users (values that must be unique). These errors must be resolved before the object will exist in Azure.

TIP

Microsoft provides a free tool called IDFix (*http://aka.ms/idfix*) that can be run against your on-premises environment and will generate a report of all known error conditions present in your directory. The IDFix tool is not multi-forest aware, so it will need to be run against each Active Directory forest. Also, the results will need to be combined to provide a complete list of remediation activities.

UserPrincipalName

Because the UserPrincipalName attribute in Active Directory is primarily used for the user login name in Microsoft 365, it must meet several requirements before it is allowed to synchronize to Azure:

- The value must be unique within your environment. Two users cannot share the same UserPrincipalName value if this attribute is configured as your login name, even in multi-forest scenarios.

- The value must not contain any spaces.

- The value must not contain any special characters.

- The value must be in the format of prefix@suffix.xyz. Failure to create a UserPrincipalName value in this format will result in a user not synchronizing properly to Microsoft 365.

- A routable email domain suffix (the portion after the @ symbol) must be used.

- The UserPrincipalName cannot begin with the @ symbol.

- The UserPrincipalName cannot end with a period (.), ampersand (&), a space, or the @ symbol.

- The value must not exceed 79 characters. The maximum length is 30 characters on the left side of the @ symbol and 48 characters on the right side.

- The ampersand (&) character, when present in the value, will be replaced by an underscore (_).

TIP

Often, organizations will be required to make changes to some or all UserPrincipalName values in on-premises Active Directory to comply with Microsoft 365 requirements for synchronization. Before changing any values, you should ensure that no legacy applications in your environment use the UserPrincipalName value.

MailNickname

The MailNickname attribute, much like the UserPrincipalName attribute, must also meet several requirements:

- The value must not exceed 64 characters.

- The value cannot contain a space.

- The value cannot contain special characters.

- The value must be unique within each on-premises Exchange organization.

It is important to note that the MailNickname value is managed by Microsoft Exchange. If Exchange is the only mechanism allowed to create or modify the MailNickname value, there will be no cases where the value will violate any of the conditions listed previously. If, however, the value is set programmatically by PowerShell scripts or other third-party applications, the values should be reviewed to ensure uniqueness.

In a multi-forest environment, where more than one Exchange organization exists, it will be necessary to compare the two environments programmatically. Neither the IDFix application nor Microsoft Exchange will be able to evaluate both environments when searching for uniqueness across them.

SamAccountName

The SamAccountName attribute in Active Directory is equally as important as the UserPrincipalName attribute and must meet several requirements for a user to be synchronized to Azure:

- The value must not exceed 20 characters.

- The value cannot contain any special characters.

- If the SamAccountName value is invalid, but the UserPrincipalName value is properly formatted, the user account will successfully synchronize to Azure.

- If both the SamAccountName and UserPrincipalName values are invalid, the user account will not synchronize.

Invalid characters

Invalid characters include the following:

- { and }

- (and)

- [and]

- < and >

- \ and /

- Comma (,)

- Apostrophe (')

- Equals (=)

- Pound or hashtag (#)

- Ampersand (&)

- Dollar ($)

- Percent (%)

- Asterisk (*)

Forests and domains

When evaluating your Active Directory, care should be taken to review all Active Directory forests as well as any subdomains within each. This is particularly important as it could potentially reduce the total number of objects that you must synchronize to Azure and possibly the synchronization server configuration.

The Azure AD Connect synchronization engine can be configured during the installation process (and afterward), so only specific forests, domains, and their organizational units are synced to Azure. Understanding your directory structure, where objects are located, and what types of objects are synchronized to Azure will allow you to better prepare your environment for synchronization to Microsoft 365.

Forests

In some environments, it might be necessary to synchronize one or more Active Directory forests to your Microsoft 365 tenant. This might be because you have users in several forests or have a split-resource model (where mailboxes exist in one forest while the users exist in another).

In either case, it is important to review objects and their attributes to make sure they are unique and understand whether some (or even all) domains within the forest must be synchronized.

If you have a forest with multiple sub-domains, review each domain. In some cases, an empty forest root domain will either contain no objects or only administrative objects or accounts. Unless these accounts should be synchronized to Azure, the forest root can be removed from the synchronization scope.

Similarly, when reviewing each forest, ensure that the forest contains users, groups, contacts, or devices that should be synchronized to Microsoft 365. If the domain lacks any of these required object types, you should deselect the domain during the installation of the sync tool.

Domains

Finally, when reviewing domains and organizational units within your directory, note the locations of the user, group, contact, and devices in relation to the organizational units. In some organizational unit hierarchies—and depending on how your Active Directory was architected—you might find that all users, groups, contacts, and devices exist in organizational units specifically designed for each object type.

In cases like this, you can minimize the scope of synchronization by simply selecting the organizational units containing only these objects and deselecting all others, as shown in Figure 1-13.

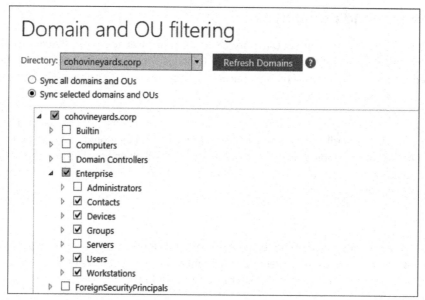

Figure 1-13   Selectively choosing organizational units that contain desired object types

However, if your organizational units are separated geographically or by business unit, team, or function, you might need to select organizational units that have objects in which objects of all types are kept together. These objects might contain things like servers and computers (which do not synchronize to Azure) that need to be read and evaluated by the synchronization engine, as shown in Figure 1-14.

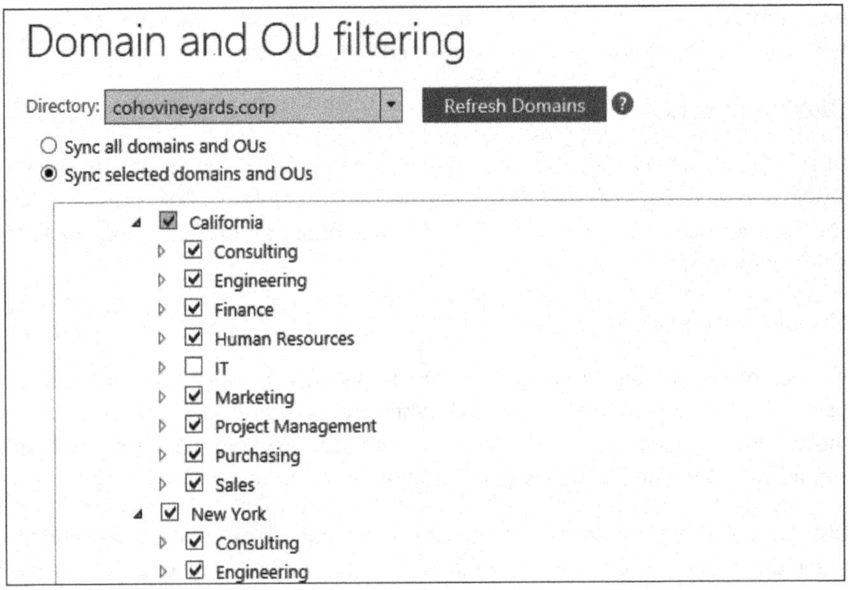

Figure 1-14   Choosing organizational units organized by location or function containing all object types

Stale or disabled users and empty groups

As a best practice, you should review your environment for stale or disabled users and empty groups before synchronization to Azure. These objects will add to the total object count synchronized to your tenant and increase synchronization time and overall clutter in your Microsoft 365 tenant.

Stale users

Stale users are unused user accounts still valid in Active Directory for an extended period without a current last login attempt. Depending on your company's requirements, or legal requirements based on your industry, user accounts for departed users might need to be retained for an extended period. However, few companies review the last login date for all user accounts and quarantine or review out-of-date accounts. At best, these accounts represent unnecessary data; at worst, they are a security risk. Therefore, we recommend that stale accounts be identified before synchronizing with Microsoft 365.

While synchronization of user accounts does not automatically consume licenses, if there are accounts that have not been used for a long time (for example, 90–180 days), we recommend you don't synchronize them to your Microsoft 365 tenant. This will minimize security risks. If known-stale accounts are synchronized to Microsoft 365, care should be taken not to delegate any administrative privilege to those accounts.

Understandably, some users might be on leave and require their accounts to remain active. However, if an account is pending deletion or is simply in a "held" state, we recommend you move these accounts to organizational units that are not within the scope of the synchronization solution (and, therefore, not synchronized with Microsoft 365).

Disabled users

Disabled users are like stale users, except they are security principals that are known to be invalid and should not be used. This is why disabled users should not be synchronized to Microsoft 365. Like stale users, they should be moved to organizational units that are not within the scope of the sync.

Unused or empty groups

It is recommended that your company's groups, security, and distribution alike be reviewed before synchronization to Microsoft 365. While unused groups do not represent a security threat, they do increase the object count synchronized to your tenant; this results in longer synchronization times and a larger synchronization server database.

Distribution groups should be evaluated, ensuring that they are still relevant and their membership is up-to-date. One of the best methods for auditing and evaluating groups and their validity is to task their owners to recertify the group and the membership. Often, groups are created for special projects or events (especially if users can create their own groups) and then forgotten once the project or event has ended. Requiring the recertification of distribution groups is a great way to keep groups and their membership current and accurate.

When referring to security groups, *unused groups* mean the resource to which the group was delegated access is no longer valid. Like distribution groups, security groups should be recertified and maintained regularly.

Inside Out

Unused security groups

Unused distribution and security groups add to the object counts, synchronization database size, synchronization size, and overall clutter in your tenant.

More importantly, however, unused security group memberships also mean that the Kerberos token size for your users is unnecessarily large. This is because each security group membership counts toward the Kerberos token for a user, and excessively large Kerberos tokens can cause other access issues. If a user belongs to more than 120 universal security groups, the default Kerberos maximum token size value might not create a large enough buffer to hold the data. Users might fail to authenticate to resources or find that Group Policy doesn't apply consistently. While not specifically a Microsoft 365 issue, it's important for the overall health of your Active Directory environment. For more information, see *https://bit.ly/3VWDlpd*.

Are your users ready?

While most of this chapter has been focused on the major deployment milestones and technical preparation of things like Exchange servers, network devices, firewalls, servers, and Active Directory, user readiness is one of the most important steps in the move to Microsoft 365. This not only includes the user's workstation and Office software but the users themselves.

A successful Microsoft 365 implementation includes user communication and setting clear expectations of the process, timing, and possible issues. Your users need to understand

- How the process works

- How their logins can change

- What type of problems to expect

- When each step in the process is happening

While these might all sound like common activities, some customers overlook the value of this level of detail, resulting in deployments that were longer than originally planned.

UPN versus email address

Typically, users are accustomed to logging in to their workstations using the standard `domain\username` format shown in Figure 1-15.

Figure 1-15   Sign in using the Domain\UserName format

Microsoft 365 sign-in prompts are very similar, though instead of expecting the Active Directory domain and the user's SamAccountname seen in Figure 1-15, they expect the user's UserPrincipalName, as shown in Figure 1-16.

Figure 1-16   Sign in using the UserPrincipalName format of first.last@domain.com

The UserPrincipalName value is a separate attribute altogether despite being formatted like the user's email address. Therefore, it might be confusing to your users if your environment is configured to use an alternate ID (AltId) or if your users have multiple email addresses they frequently use for email communication. See Chapter 9, "Identity and authentication planning," for more about using an alternate ID (AltId).

Therefore, it's important to educate your users about the UserPrincipalName value—meaning how it is the same as (or different than) their primary email addresses. They should also be instructed to use the UserPrincipalName whenever they are prompted for credentials, especially once you have deployed the Office applications and started sharing OneDrive and Share-Point content.

Multi-forest environments

Frequently, organizations with a complex architecture that consists of more than one Active Directory forest will choose to use the migration to Microsoft 365 as an opportunity to consolidate their directories. The migration of mailboxes to Microsoft 365 allows for the elimi-nation of on-premises Exchange infrastructure; in a multi-forest scenario where Exchange is separated from user accounts in a resource forest, there might also be a need to migrate user workstations as the resource forest is decommissioned.

If user workstations are migrated between forests during a Microsoft 365 migration, it is important to tell your users they might need to change the account used to log in to their workstations. Also, your users need to know they might receive additional login prompts when launching Microsoft Outlook.

> **NOTE**
>
> **To ensure the best user experience for multi-forest deployment and migration scenarios, refer to Chapter 12, "Advanced Azure AD scenarios."**

Office versions

Depending on the version of Microsoft Office installed on your users' workstations, it might be necessary to upgrade to a newer version before the client can successfully connect to Microsoft 365. This is because of how Microsoft Outlook authenticates to the Exchange Online environment.

One option to help with this issue is to enable Office licenses for your users before beginning migration of any Microsoft 365 workloads and instructing your users to use their Microsoft 365 login to authenticate to the service and download the latest version of the Office products, including Microsoft Outlook, before any mailbox migrations.

This approach will allow you to acclimate your users to the Microsoft 365 portal experience and ensure their mailbox migrations will not encounter client issues that can make the experience lengthy or unpleasant.

Updates

One common problem when migrating users to Microsoft 365, if they cannot be upgraded to the latest version of Microsoft Outlook, is confirming whether the latest Microsoft operating system updates (including Office updates) have been applied.

Updating workstations is strongly recommended for both security and functionality reasons. Additionally, we recommend you test, approve, and deploy patches well before the first mailbox moves.

CHAPTER 1

Inside Out

Getting current

As a rule, when connecting Office suite applications to Microsoft 365, you'll want to make sure you have the latest public update (PU) or Office Update (OU) available. After the initial release of Office 2013, Microsoft implemented Active Directory Authentication Library (ADAL) components to support modern authentication. For more information on obtaining the most recent Office updates, see *https://docs.microsoft.com/en-us/officeupdates/office-updates-msi*.

Delegation is the primary reason you want to make sure Outlook updates are in place before any mailboxes are migrated. The migrated mailbox will be inaccessible while the delegate's mailbox remains on-premises if a user mailbox is migrated to Exchange Online (but their delegate is not) and the delegate does not have a compliant version of Microsoft Outlook or the latest updates.

TIP

When using automated update deployment mechanisms, like the Windows Software Update Service (WSUS), make sure that the necessary updates are approved. When managing updates, ensure that any Microsoft Office or Microsoft Outlook updates are included in the approval process.

Mailbox cleanup

Earlier in this chapter, we discussed large items, their impact on mail migrations, and the likelihood of data loss if they are not addressed. The identification and remediation of large items is another item you can communicate to your users in advance of mailbox migrations.

Ask your users to sort their mailboxes, including subfolders and archives, and identify all messages with large attachments. Outlook folders can easily be sorted by message size by selecting the Size column in Microsoft Outlook, as shown in Figure 1-17.

From	Subject	Received	Size	Cate... Mention
Huge (10 - 25 MB)				
Pilar Ackerman	Valentines 2022 Winery Event Calendar	Mon 2/7/2022 12:34 PM	22 MB	
Very Large (5 MB - 10 MB)				
Pilar Ackerman	Winery and Vineyard schedules for Q2 2022	Mon 2/7/2022 12:20 PM	6 MB	
Medium (25 KB - 1 MB)				
Pilar Ackerman	Welcome to the COVID-19 Response team!	Mon 2/7/2022 12:23 PM	941 KB	
Pilar Ackerman	Misc Documentation	Mon 2/7/2022 12:22 PM	126 KB	
Pilar Ackerman	Latest delivery schedules	Mon 2/7/2022 12:24 PM	67 KB	
Pilar Ackerman	Softball team roster	Mon 2/7/2022 12:23 PM	53 KB	
Pilar Ackerman	Winter Olympics 2022 event schedule	Mon 2/7/2022 12:25 PM	41 KB	
Pilar Ackerman	Team outing next weekend	Mon 2/7/2022 12:22 PM	30 KB	
Pilar Ackerman	What time is lunch?	Mon 2/7/2022 12:25 PM	29 KB	

Figure 1-17   Microsoft Outlook Inbox sorted by message size

Once the mailbox has been sorted, users can delete any large items they do not wish to keep in their mailbox. Alternatively, you can right-click an email containing a large attachment, choose the attachment, and select Remove Attachment. After selecting that option, as shown in Figure 1-18, you will be prompted to remove the item. After removing the attachment, you will be prompted to save the update to the email.

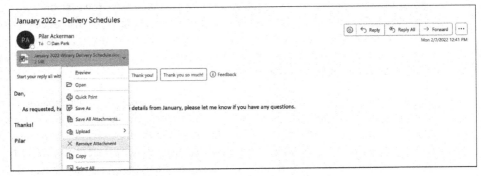

Figure 1-18   Removing an attachment from an Outlook email

Removing any large attachments but leaving the email intact will allow your users to maintain their email history without adding excessive bloat to their mailboxes. In fact, if your users are licensed for SharePoint Online, the attachments could be saved to a SharePoint team site or the user's personal OneDrive before they are removed from the mailbox, so the attachment is not lost.

Scheduling

If you have Exchange Hybrid configured to allow MRS mailbox moves, your users can continue to work while their mail is migrated. In fact, if mailbox migration batches are configured in Suspend When Ready to Complete (SWRC) mode, mailbox data migration might occur over several days, with a final cutover of the mailbox to Microsoft 365 after hours or over a weekend.

The MRS mailbox move process allows you to move user mailboxes in large batches during the business day without affecting your users, with the final cutover step happening at a more convenient time for your administrators. When the final cutover step occurs, your users will receive a pop-up in Microsoft Outlook, depicted in Figure 1-19, prompting them to close and re-open Outlook. This will be the only way your users will be affected by the migration.

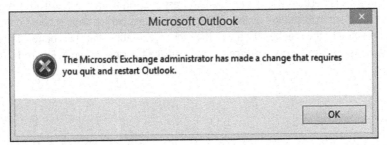

Figure 1-19   Pop-up dialog received once Microsoft 365 mailbox migration has been completed

CHAPTER 1

The Global Address List

Once your users have been migrated to Microsoft 365, one of the first things that might look different to them will be the Global Address List (GAL).

While their mailbox was on-premises, the Global Address List consisted of all mail-enabled user, group, resource, and contact objects present in Active Directory. However, once a user has been migrated to Microsoft 365, their Global Address List will comprise all mail-enabled user, group, resource, and contact objects in Azure. While they are similar, these lists might differ depending on what you have decided to synchronize from your on-premises environment or if you have additional mail-enabled, cloud-only objects.

As part of the initial configuration of your Microsoft 365 tenant, you will implement directory synchronization, which is discussed in detail in later chapters. However, it is important to understand that decisions made during the synchronization tool implementation will directly affect the contents of the Global Address List. Failure to include the correct organizational units from Active Directory or the manual creation of cloud-based users, groups, and contacts will both result in either too few or too many objects in your Exchange Online GAL. As a general rule, if a mail-enabled user doesn't see a recipient in the GAL, migrated and cloud users will be unable to send email to that recipient.

Therefore, it is strongly recommended that you create pilot groups for mailbox migrations so users can review the Exchange Online GAL and provide feedback about it when compared with the on-premises GAL before you start moving your users in bulk to Microsoft 365.

Replying to old emails

Once your users' mailboxes have been migrated to Microsoft 365 and the Global Address List is confirmed accurate, the look and feel of the Exchange Online experience should be identical to that of the on-premises Exchange experience. In fact, some customers have actually reported that their users had no idea they had been migrated to Microsoft 365 because the experience was identical.

After migrating to Microsoft 365, one of the most common issues is the occasional receipt of non-delivery errors when replying to some old emails or calendar appointments. While this does not happen frequently, it can be quite annoying for affected users.

This typically occurs because there is an x500 address missing from the proxy addresses list for the correct recipient in Exchange Online. If the x500 address (which should contain the Legacy-ExchangeDN value of the mailbox receiving the message) is absent and Exchange Online cannot deliver the message, the sender will receive an email like the one shown in Figure 1-20.

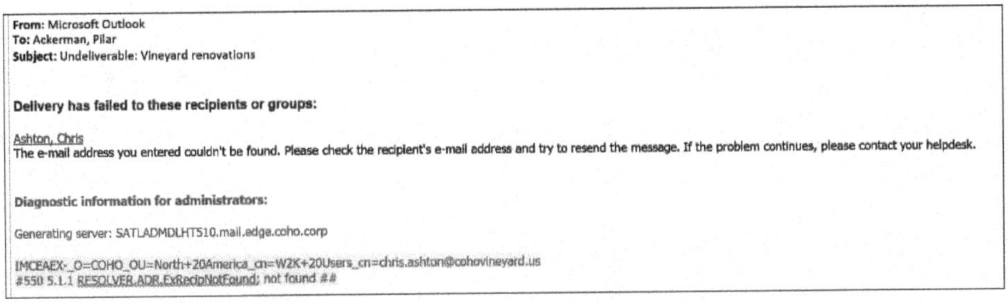

From: Microsoft Outlook
To: Ackerman, Pilar
Subject: Undeliverable: Vineyard renovations

Delivery has failed to these recipients or groups:

Ashton, Chris
The e-mail address you entered couldn't be found. Please check the recipient's e-mail address and try to resend the message. If the problem continues, please contact your helpdesk.

Diagnostic information for administrators:

Generating server: SATLADMDLHT510.mail.edge.coho.corp

IMCEAEX-_O=COHO_OU=North+20America_cn=W2K+20Users_cn=chris.ashton@cohovineyard.us
#550 5.1.1 RESOLVER.ADR.ExRecipNotFound; not found ##

Figure 1-20   A non-delivery report that includes the IMCEAEX error

The AAD Connect directory sync process typically handles synchronization of LegacyExchangeDN values from on-premises Active Directory for all mail-enabled objects to Azure AD. However, sometimes there are issues with missing LegacyExchangeDN values because of direct manipulation of the attribute. In those cases, the easiest way to resolve any NDR issues related to LegacyExchangeDN is to populate the on-premises object with the missing x500 address and allow it to synchronize to Microsoft 365 automatically. Subsequent emails will then deliver successfully.

> ### NOTE
> **The process for converting the IMCEAEX non-delivery report address to an x500 address can be found at *https://aka.ms/imceaex*.**

What's next?

Once you have successfully reviewed your infrastructure and identified any upgrades, new servers, or configuration changes, you are almost ready to start synchronizing your users and moving your services to Microsoft 365.

There is still a long road ahead, especially if you plan to implement any hybrid configurations. However, the steps in this chapter should give you sufficient information to start with each of those tasks. Additionally, major milestone activities (such as synchronization, hybrid, and mailbox migrations) are outlined in greater detail in Chapter 2, "Preparing your environment for the cloud."

You've learned about preparing for Microsoft 365 migration; in the next chapter, you'll learn about the deployment and configuration processes.

CHAPTER 1

Preparing your environment for the cloud

In the previous chapter, we identified some high-level tasks involved in a Microsoft 365 deployment. In this chapter, we will use your understanding of those tasks to

- Continue setting up your Microsoft 365 subscription

- Assign administrators

- Configure your network

- Run the IDFix tool to clean up your directory

- Update and install client software

- Start synchronizing your users to your tenant

Once these tasks are complete, you will be able to start using your Microsoft 365 subscription and migrating your users.

Setting up your subscription

If you have not already set up your Microsoft 365 subscription, that is the best place to start. Please review the steps in the previous chapter to select and begin a subscription. As discussed, the tenant name you select will become permanent and branded across your subscription, so choose carefully.

Finding your tenant name

Once the tenant name selection is complete, each of the services within your Microsoft 365 subscription (such as Exchange, SharePoint, or Teams) will be branded with the name you selected. As mentioned previously, this branding process is permanent, and the name will be visible in several locations—the Microsoft 365 service, your users, and external parties.

Exchange Online

Exchange Online uses your tenant name in the routing email address stamped on every mail-enabled object you create.

The Exchange Hybrid process (discussed in more detail in Chapter 15, "Exchange Online hybrid planning and deployment") configures a recipient policy in your Exchange on-premises organization that automatically assigns an email address suffix of `@tenantName.mail.onmicrosoft.com` for every mail-enabled object. This `@tenant.mail.onmicrosoft.com` address is typically referred to as the *service routing address*.

This service routing address is required for every mailbox that will be migrated to Exchange Online. It will not appear on cloud-only mailboxes because it is applied in an on-premises environment. However, within the Exchange Online service, there is another automatic email address assignment that is not optional and cannot be changed.

As seen in Figure 2-1, Exchange Online automatically assigns an email address ending in `@tenantName.onmicrosoft.com` to every mail-enabled object.

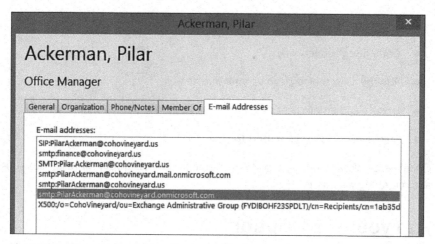

Figure 2-1   The tenant.onmicrosoft.com email address

The email address seen in the example above is only visible to your internal users when viewing the contact properties of another mail-enabled object. It is also important to note that this address does NOT contain the word *mail*, like in the service routing address mentioned above.

This additional `onmicrosoft.com` routing address is not visible outside your organization, nor is it present in the email header when sending messages to external recipients over the Internet.

TIP

The domain suffix `mail.onmicrosoft.com` **is not added automatically to the tenant during the Exchange Online setup; instead, this domain suffix is added to every mail-enabled object in on-premises Exchange via an email address policy added during the Exchange Hybrid setup.**

SharePoint Online

Of all the services in Microsoft 365, your tenant name appears most prominently in SharePoint Online. It is visible internally in site content URLs and in the shared URLs provided to external parties.

As shown in Figure 2-2, the tenant name is present in the URL for every external sharing request sent via email.

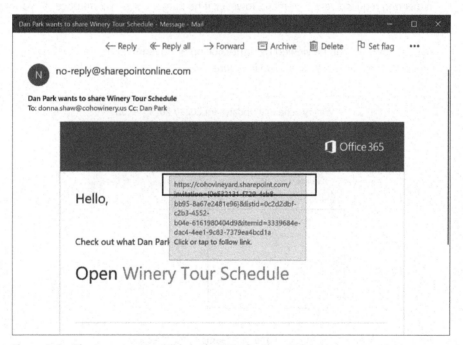

Figure 2-2   The tenant name visible in the URLs for SharePoint sharing requests

OneDrive for Business

Because OneDrive is part of the SharePoint Online service and takes the place of MySites in SharePoint Server, your tenant name will appear in any OneDrive URLs shared via email to internal or external recipients. Additionally, when OneDrive content is viewed when navigating between folders or stored files, it will display the tenant name in the URL (visible in the address bar at the top of the browser). See Figure 2-3.

Figure 2-3   The tenant name visible in OneDrive URLs

Microsoft Teams

In past versions, the tenant name in Microsoft Teams was visible when viewing the meeting URL in meeting requests sent via email. However, it no longer contains references to your tenant name.

The meeting URL can be viewed by right-clicking or hovering over the Join Teams Meeting hyperlink in email invites, as shown in Figure 2-4.

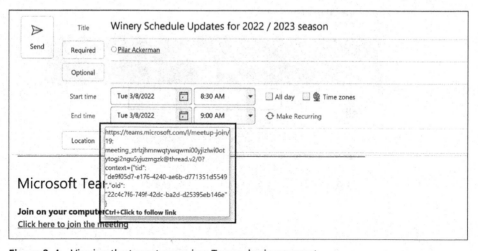

Figure 2-4   Viewing the tenant name in a Teams sharing request

Microsoft 365 Apps

The tenant name is not visible when viewing the properties of the Microsoft 365 Apps (formerly Microsoft Office 365 ProPlus) applications, nor is it visible in any of the additional licensed Office-suite applications like Visio or Project.

Office Online

Office Online applications automatically use OneDrive for Business as the default save location for newly created documents, as shown in Figure 2-5. This is visible to your user in the browser address bar, and if these documents are shared with external parties, the file's URL will contain the tenant name.

Figure 2-5   Tenant name visibility when using Office Online applications

Assigning administrators

Using the information you learned in Chapter 1, you can either create cloud accounts and delegate administrative privileges or wait until you've started synchronizing your users (discussed later in this chapter) and assigning permissions.

In either case, you might need to delegate permissions to one or more additional administrators. Keep in mind that the Global Administrator role has the right to create other Global Administrators, so you should limit administrative delegation to one of the other administrative roles discussed in Chapter 1 and avoid creating other Global Administrator accounts unless necessary.

Follow the steps below to create a new administrative account with User administration privileges:

1.   Navigate to the Microsoft 365 admin center (*https://admin.microsoft.com*).

2.   Select Add A User from the Home or Users views, as shown in Figure 2-6.

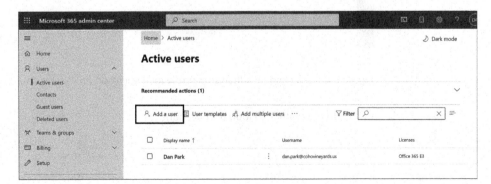

Figure 2-6   The Active Users view in the Microsoft 365 admin center

3. Enter the necessary First Name, Last Name, Display Name, and User Name in the boxes provided, as shown in Figure 2-7.

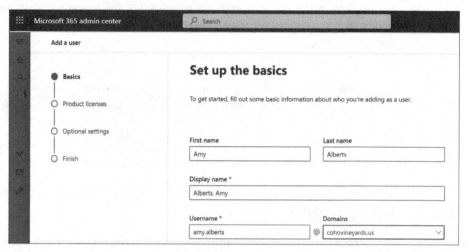

Figure 2-7   Creating a cloud user with administrative privilege

4. When creating the account, select the Roles dropdown under Optional Settings, select Admin Center Access, and check the User Administrator box, as shown in Figure 2-8.

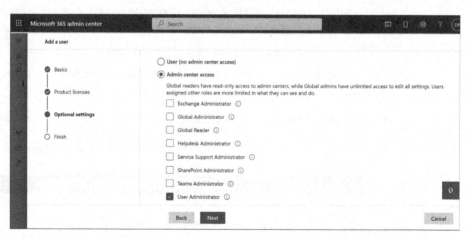

Figure 2-8   Selecting an administrator role for a Microsoft 365 user account

5. Click Add to create the cloud user account.

6. This process can be used to modify existing cloud accounts or even accounts that have been synchronized from on-premises Active Directory using the AAD Connect synchronization tool.

7. Once you have completed the creation of any administrator accounts in your new tenant, you can move on to creating DNS records to verify your domains, as well as any other services that you wish to add.

Configuring DNS, firewalls, and proxy servers

As discussed in Chapter 1, several network devices could affect your Microsoft 365 deployment, connectivity, and continued success with the services provided. Therefore, it is strongly recommended that all network devices be updated to their latest versions, and each device vendor should be contacted to ensure that your device supports Microsoft 365 connectivity.

Often, it is merely a matter of upgrading your existing devices to support Microsoft 365. However, this upgrade process can be time-consuming and disruptive if not done correctly. Therefore, it is strongly recommended that any infrastructure changes required to support Microsoft 365 be made before starting your Microsoft 365 deployment.

Public DNS records

The first necessary configuration changes will be to your public DNS records, which will allow you to verify any domain names and configure the necessary DNS records for things like mail exchange (MX), Exchange AutoDiscover, and Teams.

Proof of domain ownership

When setting up your domain name, as discussed in Chapter 1, the Microsoft 365 admin center configuration steps will walk you through making the necessary DNS changes with your registrar to provide domain ownership proof, typically in the form of a TXT record.

This TXT record can be removed once ownership is verified, and in many cases, the admin center configuration will automatically connect to your registrar and make the necessary addition if you provide credentials.

The network changes will need to be made manually by an authorized administrator if your public DNS infrastructure is managed internally or hosted on Microsoft Windows Server via the Domain Name Services role or another network appliance.

MX, SRV, and other DNS records

Once you have completed the setup process described previously using the Microsoft 365 admin center, your domain will automatically be registered in Microsoft 365, and it can be used as the domain suffix for the `UserPrincipalName` for the user login and Exchange Online mail routing. This is because the automated configuration process will add MX records to your DNS configuration, allowing email to be delivered to Microsoft 365 automatically.

Additionally, the Exchange AutoDiscover, Sender Policy Framework (SPF), and required Server Resource (SRV) records will exist in Microsoft 365 tenant's initial domain namespace (`tenant.onmicrosoft.com`). These will allow Outlook and mobile client connectivity to your tenant and Teams client. Also, they will allow you to send and receive email directly to or from your tenant or communicate using Instant Message (IM) and Voice Over IP (VOIP) communications via Teams.

TIP

If your existing domain name (`cohovineyards.us` in this chapter's examples) is already configured with MX, SIP, SMTP, CNAME, or SPF records in your public DNS and routing to your on-premises infrastructure, you will want to select the manual configuration options in the previous configuration process and make only the necessary changes to support your Microsoft 365 setup.

NOTE

Additional configuration changes for Exchange mail routing as part of the Exchange or Teams hybrid processes are covered in later chapters and can be performed later so as not to impact existing functionality.

Firewall configurations

Microsoft 365 is a cloud-based solution, so it is a requirement that your internal infrastructure can communicate with your tenant without any connectivity issues introduced by your networking infrastructure.

If your internal infrastructure cannot communicate with Azure, your Microsoft 365 experience will be impacted—possibly resulting in email delays. Also, this can prevent you from authenticating and using services or provisioning or licensing users. It can even prevent access to cloud data.

It is strongly recommended that all network devices responsible for packet filtering, load balancing, and network port access control be configured to allow unrestricted outbound traffic to the Microsoft datacenters.

The Microsoft datacenter IP ranges include all the Microsoft 365 services and are maintained on the Microsoft 365 support site. The IP ranges can be viewed and downloaded here: *https://aka.ms/M365_IPs*

Proxy servers

Traditionally, proxy servers are used to relay requests to the Internet via a single host, though this behavior can create issues when setting up certain services for Microsoft 365 connectivity.

Primarily, traffic to Microsoft 365 is outbound traffic. Some services, like Exchange AutoDiscover, AD FS authentication, and mail routing, might be an exception; however, it is important to understand that proxy server configurations can cause interruptions.

Many proxy servers or services rely on some form of user authentication (either explicit or implicit) to allow the infrastructure to track users and filter requests according to business requirements. This proxy authentication feature primarily impacts directory synchronization.

The directory synchronization process, performed by the AAD Connect tool, connects to Microsoft 365 every 30 minutes to synchronize any directory updates. Additionally, depending on the AAD Connect tool's configuration, it will retrieve password changes and other data. If the connectivity between AAD Connect and Microsoft 365 is affected, the synchronization might fail, resulting in incomplete data in Microsoft 365.

Therefore, we recommend the AAD Connect tool be exempted from any proxy server configurations and allowed to communicate with Azure without any proxy configuration.

CAUTION

The AAD Connect tool does not support authenticated proxy servers. Instead, you must bypass any authenticated proxy servers, or you will be unable to synchronize your directories with Microsoft 365.

If you cannot bypass proxy servers for the AAD Connect implementation, we recommend configuring both Internet Explorer and the shell to use the same proxy server. Both methods are used during the AAD Connect setup for communication with Microsoft 365, so failure to enable both might result in a failed installation.

To set up Internet Explorer on the server where the synchronization tool will be installed, you will need to do the following:

1. Launch Internet Explorer.

2. Select Tools and Internet Options from the Internet Explorer main menu.

3. Select Connections > LAN Settings from the Internet Options menu.

4. Make sure the Proxy Server box is checked and a proxy server and port are provided in the Address and Port fields, as shown in Figure 2-9.

CHAPTER 2

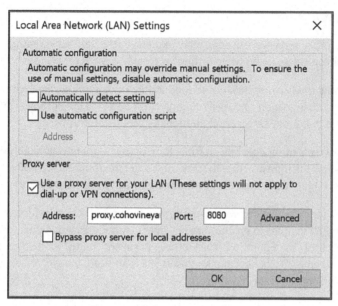

Figure 2-9   Configuring Internet Explorer proxy server

5.   Click OK to close the Local Area Network (LAN) Settings dialog box and OK again to close the Connections dialog box.

Once the proxy server has been properly configured in Internet Explorer, perform the following steps to configure the proxy server for the Windows Shell:

1.   Open an administrative command prompt by clicking Start, Run (or Win+R), typing CMD.EXE, and pressing Enter.

2.   Enter the netsh winhttp show proxy command and press Enter.

3.   If the command returns the Direct access (no proxy server) result, as shown in Figure 2-10, proceed to the next step to configure the proxy server.

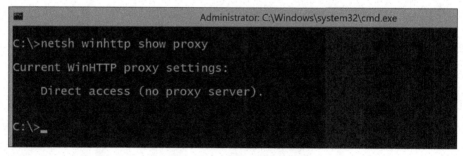

Figure 2-10   Displaying current WinHTTP proxy server configuration

4. Enter the `Netsh WinHTTP Import proxy Source=IE` command and press Enter.

5. If the command completes successfully, it should display the same proxy server that is configured in Internet Explorer, as seen in Figure 2-11.

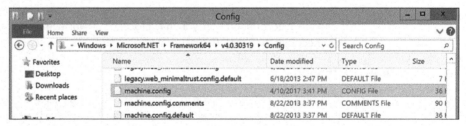

```
Administrator: C:\Windows\system32\cmd.exe

C:\>netsh winhttp import proxy source=ie

Current WinHTTP proxy settings:

    Proxy Server(s) :  proxy.cohovineyard.corp:8080
    Bypass List     :  (none)


C:\>_
```

Figure 2-11   Configuring Netsh proxy using Internet Explorer

6. Finally, in some circumstances, it might also be necessary to modify the `machine.config` file used by the `Windows.Net` configuration to also define the proxy server that should be used by any .Net applications.

If the AAD Connect setup fails to properly communicate with Azure—even after the settings in Internet Explorer and the Windows Shell have been configured—the .Net configuration file can be modified via the following steps:

1. On the AAD Connect server, navigate to `C:\Windows\Microsoft.Net\Framework64\v4.xxxxxxx\Config`, where `x4.xxxxx` is the `v4.0` or `v4.5` directory located under the Framework64 folder. This directory name will depend upon the .Net 4 version installed on your AAD Connect server.

2. Edit the `machine.config` file, shown in Figure 2-12, using Notepad.

Name	Date modified	Type	Size
legacy.web_minimaltrust.config.default	6/18/2013 2:47 PM	DEFAULT File	7
machine.config	4/10/2017 3:41 PM	CONFIG File	36
machine.config.comments	8/22/2013 3:37 PM	COMMENTS File	90
machine.config.default	8/22/2013 3:37 PM	DEFAULT File	36

Figure 2-12   The Microsoft .Net machine.config file location

CHAPTER 2

3. At the bottom of the file, insert the following block of text before the `</configuration>`
    line, substituting `<PROXYADDRESS>` with the name or IP address of your proxy server and
    `<PROXYPORT>` with the correct port number:

```
<system.net>
    <defaultProxy enabled="true" useDefaultCredentials="true">
      <proxy
      usesystemdefault="true"
      proxyaddress="http://<PROXYADDRESS>:<PROXYPORT>"
      bypassonlocal="true"
      />
    </defaultProxy>
  </system.net>
```

4. Save the updated file, as shown in Figure 2-13.

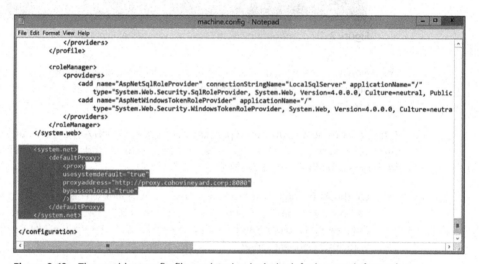

Figure 2-13   The machine.config file, updated to include default proxy information

5. Once the proxy server configurations have been made to Internet Explorer, the Windows
    Shell, and the .Net configuration, you may proceed with installing and configuring the
    AAD Connect tool for directory synchronization.

Network tracing

Occasionally, during the implementation or configuration of proxy server or network firewall
changes, it might be necessary to review the communication between your application and
Microsoft 365. Understanding the route that Microsoft 365 communication must take to reach
Azure will help troubleshoot network connectivity issues.

Other than mailbox moves, the synchronization process is the most common reason for connectivity tracing with Microsoft 365. Unless configured differently, the AAD Connect sync engine

will connect to Azure every 30 minutes to synchronize directory changes from on-premises to the cloud.

Depending on the additional features selected during installation, the AAD Connect engine might connect as frequently as every 1 to 2 minutes to retrieve password change and other authentication requests from the Azure service bus.

If you need to review traffic between your AAD Connect server and Microsoft 365, you can use tools like NetMon3, Fiddler, or WireShark to capture network traces from the server to ensure no other devices are preventing proper communication.

In the example below, we are using Fiddler to capture and import from the Microsoft 365 tenant using the AAD Connect tool. Fiddler is installed on the AAD Connect server and has been configured to decrypt HTTPS traffic.

The trace was captured by using the following steps:

1. Download and install Fiddler (*https://www.telerik.com/fiddler/fiddler-everywhere*).

2. Launch Fiddler and press F12, or select File and choose Capture Traffic.

3. Start the AAD Connect Synchronization Service Manager.

4. Select Connectors.

5. In the Connections window, select the Windows Azure Active Directory connector.

6. In the Actions pane, select Run.

7. Choose Full Import and click OK, as shown in Figure 2-14.

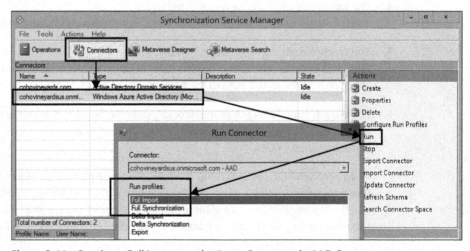

Figure 2-14   Starting a Full Import on the Azure Connector in AAD Connect

CHAPTER 2

8. Once the Full Import has been completed, review the results of the Fiddler trace, as shown in Figure 2-15.

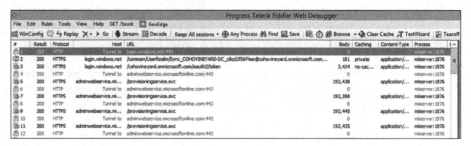

Figure 2-15   Fiddler trace of the AAD Connect Full Import run step

In the screen capture above, each line represents a packet in the communication between the AAD Connect server and Azure Active Directory. The packets are performing the following actions:

1. Communication is established between the synchronization engine and Azure via the login.windows.net URL over secure SSL port 443.

2. Home realm discovery is initiated using the Sync_COHOVINEYARD-DC_c8cd2f06f4ae@cohovineyard.onmicrosoft.com account. This account, discussed in detail in Chapter 4, is the account used to authenticate with Microsoft 365 for synchronization.

3. The home realm discovery process results in an authentication token with the cohovineyard.onmicrosoft.com tenant.

4. The synchronization engine is redirected to the adminwebservice.microsoftonline.com URL over secure SSL port 443.

5. The synchronization engine begins reading data from the adminwebservice.microsoftonline.com/provisioningservice.svc endpoint URL, which returns the tenant data to the sync engine.

6. The process continues until all the directory data has been read from the Microsoft 365 tenant into the Azure connector in the synchronization engine, at which point, communication ceases.

7. As you can see from the preceding example, despite the existence of a proxy server in the configuration, there was no effect on the traffic between the synchronization engine and the Microsoft 365 tenant. If there had been issues with the traffic, you would have experienced retransmissions or transmission failures like the example in Figure 2-16.

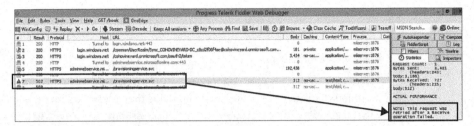

Figure 2-16 A transmission failure in a Fiddler trace

In the example shown in Figure 2-16, communication with Azure AD was initiated, and the sync account was authenticated properly. However, the transmission was interrupted, resulting in a retry operation, which failed and stopped the Import from Azure.

Tools like Fiddler and NetMon3 can be invaluable when you first set up the synchronization process because they ensure communication is working properly and none of your network devices are affecting performance or connectivity. Therefore, it is strongly recommended that you become familiar with the proper functionality of the synchronization process and any other service-related connectivity (such as mailbox moves and Office application activation) to ensure the best possible Microsoft 365 experience.

CAUTION

Network connectivity between the synchronization engine and Microsoft 365 is one of the most common troubleshooting areas, primarily related to proxy servers and any network devices that do packet inspection.

The synchronization engine connects in 30-minute intervals, and depending on the additional features, it can connect as frequently as every 2 minutes.

Make sure you understand the network path between the sync engine and Azure, eliminate devices if possible, and be familiar with traffic patterns and troubleshooting that communication.

ExpressRoute

ExpressRoute is a secure connection between your on-premises network and the Azure cloud. It provides managed connectivity to the Microsoft datacenters via a secure and private connection and eliminates the need to traverse the public Internet for your Microsoft 365–related traffic.

In addition to bypassing the public Internet for Microsoft 365 traffic, ExpressRoute provides a fast and reliable connection to Azure, making replication, high-availability, and data migration scenarios easier to implement.

Inside Out

Do I need ExpressRoute?

Microsoft 365 services are designed to work best over the Internet because the multi-pathing characteristics of the Internet provide the best service routes and reliability. Microsoft does not recommend using ExpressRoute to connect to Office 365 or Microsoft 365 services. Purchasing ExpressRoute for Microsoft 365 requires Microsoft approval. For more information, see *https://aka.ms/erguide*.

If you are considering ExpressRoute connectivity to the Microsoft cloud during your implementation of Microsoft 365, we strongly recommend implementation be done before the rest of your Microsoft 365 readiness milestones. An ExpressRoute implementation changes your network routing internally and affects things like load balancers, proxy servers, and firewalls. These changes will affect communication, so they should be made before establishing synchronization and starting mailbox migrations.

Preparing your directories

Much like preparing your network for a successful Microsoft 365 implementation, it is equally important to ensure that your on-premises directories are free from any issues that might impact a successful synchronization of users, groups, and contacts to your tenant.

Microsoft provides the IDFix tool, which will review your environment and highlight any problem areas or data inconsistencies. Follow these steps to install IDFix:

1. Download the IDFix setup media from *https://aka.ms/idfix* and launch it.

2. Launch the IDFix setup media and click Install, as shown in Figure 2-17.

3. If prompted with an Open File–Security Warning, as shown in Figure 2-18, click Run to proceed with the installation.

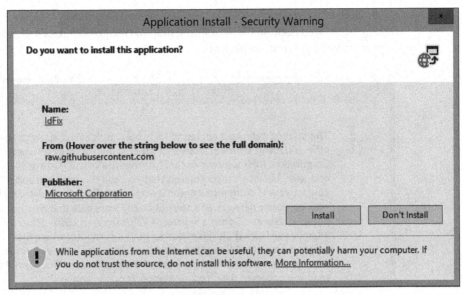

Figure 2-17 Application Install Security Warning dialog

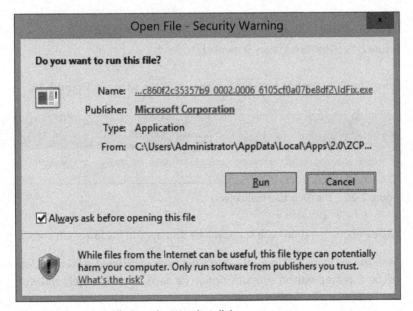

Figure 2-18 Open File Security Warning dialog

4. Click OK to proceed past the IdFix Privacy Statement dialog shown in Figure 2-19. This dialog is displayed because the IDFix application will review your data and provide reports containing sensitive information.

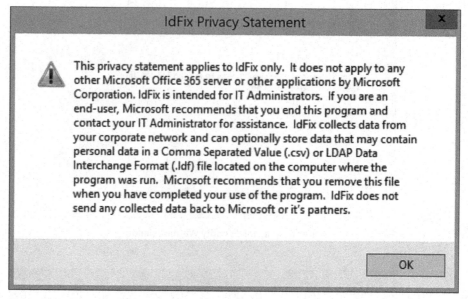

Figure 2-19   The IDFix Privacy Statement

5. Select the Query option from the topmost menu, as shown in Figure 2-20.

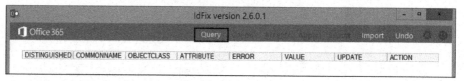

Figure 2-20   The IDFix tool main menu

6. While the query is running, a status will be displayed in the lower-left corner.

7. As shown in Figure 2-21, once the query has been completed, a list of all detected issues will be displayed with an error description for each. The total object and error counts will be displayed in the lower-left corner.

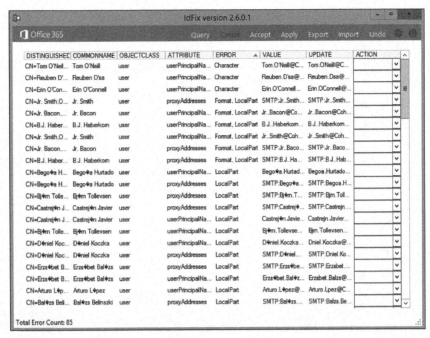

Figure 2-21   IDFix error report summary

8.   Selecting a single error will allow you to use the Action column to define the behavior that should be used to resolve it. As shown in Figure 2-22, you can choose to Edit, Remove, or Complete the object in question.

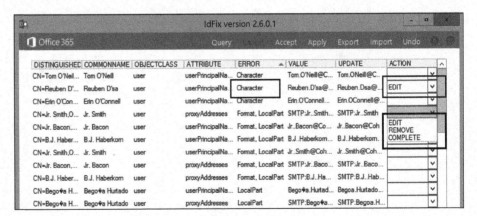

Figure 2-22   Selecting actions for error objects in IDFix

9.   Once you have selected the appropriate action for each object, selecting Apply at the top of the menu returns the confirmation dialog shown in Figure 2-23.

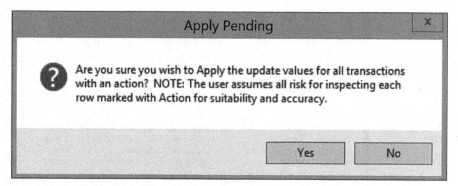

Figure 2-23   IDFix Apply Pending dialog

10. Click Yes to apply all selected updates.

11. Once complete, all updates that have been applied will be marked as Complete, as shown in Figure 2-24.

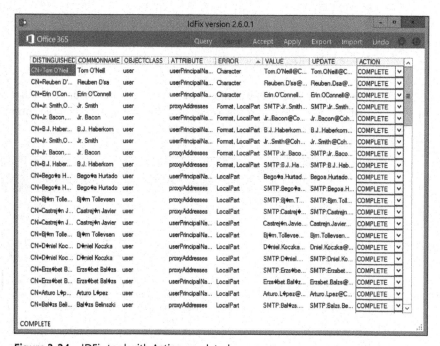

Figure 2-24   IDFix tool with Actions updated

12. Following are a few important notes:

    ■ When selecting Edit, you will not be allowed to edit the value in error manually. Instead, the IDFix tool will simply apply the update displayed in the Update column. You should review this new value below, allowing IDFix to make the change.

- Optionally, you can use the Accept option on the IDFix main menu to automatically apply the updated value shown in the Update column to each object in an error state, as shown in Figure 2-25.

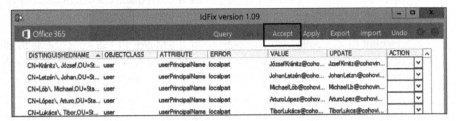

Figure 2-25   The IDFix Accept option

- Like the Apply option, the Accept option will also display a dialog warning that the changes being made represent a risk as they are changing data in your directory. See Figure 2-26.

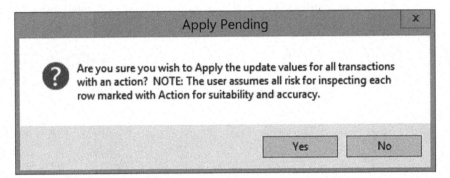

Figure 2-26   Apply Pending dialog

- Using the Accept All option in the Accept dropdown menu will simply change all Action fields to Edit, and it is then necessary to use the Apply option to make the changes.

13. Once the changes have been applied, select Query to re-run the IDFix process against your directory and confirm no additional changes are required.

Updating and deploying client software

Before migrating mailboxes to Microsoft 365, any machines with Microsoft Outlook installed must be updated to the latest public update (PU) so there is no interruption in the user experience after mailbox migrations have begun.

Even a mailbox that has not yet migrated to Exchange Online might experience connectivity issues or constant credential prompts if that mailbox is delegated permission to another mailbox that HAS been migrated to Microsoft 365. For this reason, it is strongly recommended that Microsoft Office and Windows updates be approved and applied in advance of the Microsoft 365 implementation.

Frequently, customers will choose to apply the Microsoft 365 Apps license to all users ahead of the mailbox moves (or even SharePoint Online and Teams deployments) so all Microsoft Office versions are current and support the Microsoft 365 workloads.

Installing Microsoft 365 Apps

Installation of the Microsoft 365 Apps software is straightforward:

1. Log in to the Microsoft 365 portal at *https://portal.office.com.*

2. When prompted, log in to Microsoft 365 using your username and password.

3. On the Microsoft 365 portal page shown in Figure 2-27, select Install Office in the upper-right corner.

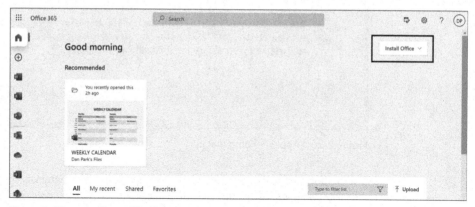

Figure 2-27   Installing Office from the Microsoft 365 portal

4. The Microsoft 365 portal will display additional information, as shown in Figure 2-28, which will assist in the Microsoft 365 Apps installation.

5. Click Run to begin the Microsoft 365 Apps installation.

6. If any conflicting software versions are already installed on the workstation, there is a lack of local disk space, or issues connecting to the Internet, you will receive a pop-up dialog showing the issue, as shown in Figure 2-29.

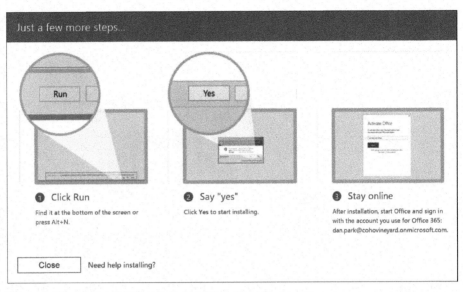

Figure 2-28   Microsoft 365 portal's Just A Few More Steps page

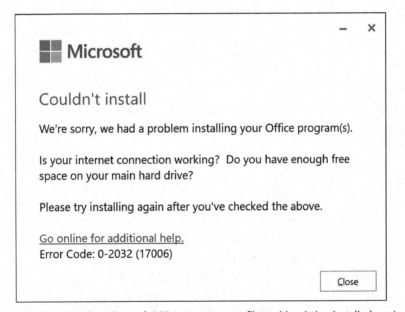

Figure 2-29   The Microsoft 365 Apps setup conflicts with existing installed versions

- If conflicting versions are already installed on the computer, you can click the I Understand box and select Install Anyway if you want to proceed with the installation. This will remove the conflicting software version(s) and proceed with the installation. Clicking I'll Wait will end the Office installation process.

7. As shown in Figure 2-30, once the installation has been completed, a new window will be displayed, indicating the installation is complete.

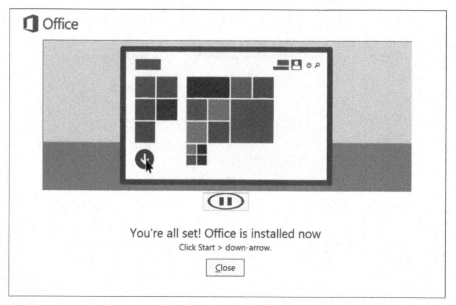

Figure 2-30   Microsoft 365 Apps installation completion page

8. Click Close to complete the installation process.

Once the installation is complete, the Office products will be available for use, and when applicable, you will be prompted to update any previous documents created in past versions of the applications.

Inside Out

Microsoft 365 Apps

Apps installed with the Microsoft 365 portal will be enabled for automatic updating. These updates will occur over the Internet, not via any internal automatic update services (such as Windows Server Update Services) configured in your organization. Microsoft also provides resources for centralized deployment of Microsoft 365 Apps using either Group Policy, System Center Configuration Manager, or Microsoft Endpoint Manger (Intune). You can learn more about additional deployment methods for Microsoft 365 Apps at *https://docs.microsoft.com/en-us/mem/intune/apps/apps-add-office365*.

Activation

Activation is the last step and is a process whereby the Office application will connect to Microsoft 365 to ensure that the user is properly licensed by the tenant to use it.

The good news is that activation is automatic. No additional action is required on the user's part to activate their Office installation. Activation does, however, require that the computer has Internet access available to complete the process.

TIP

As you've already learned, Microsoft 365 Apps are typically licensed in a per-user model. (A per-device model is available under some license agreements, but it is outside the scope of this book.) Each user is entitled to five desktop installations. If you have roaming or shared computer scenarios, you might find that each time a user logs into a new machine, they consume one of their five allotted licenses. To account for this, you can configure Shared Computer Activation for those computers. User logins for Shared Computer Activation won't count against the user's total count. A user still must be licensed for Microsoft 365 Apps for Shared Computer Activation. Shared Computer Activation can be enabled through the setup configuration file or Group Policy. For more information, see *https://docs.microsoft.com/en-us/deployoffice/overview-shared-computer-activation*.

Once Office is installed on a user's workstation, the system will try daily to reach the Microsoft Office Licensing Service activation endpoint on the Internet. If it is unsuccessful, it will retry daily for up to 30 days before the applications enter reduced functionality mode.

In reduced functionality mode, the software will remain installed on the workstation, though your users will only be able to view and print documents. Any features related to document editing or the creation of new documents will remain disabled until they either enter a product key or successfully authenticate with Microsoft 365.

If Office cannot reach the licensing service for more than 30 days, the reduced functionality mode will display a Product Deactivated dialog screen, as shown in Figure 2-31.

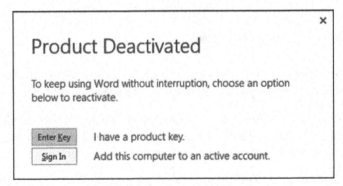

Figure 2-31   Product Deactivated dialog box

Synchronizing your users

The next step in your deployment of Microsoft 365 will be the synchronization of your users to Azure Active Directory.

Synchronization is performed using the Azure Active Directory Connect tool, typically referred to as Azure AD Connect or AAD Connect. AAD Connect is a free download from Microsoft for Microsoft 365 users and is based upon the Microsoft Identity Manager (MIM) product line.

While simple in theory, the directory synchronization process can be very involved when installing and configuring the AAD Connect tool. In addition to selecting objects and organizational units, the AAD Connect tool can also be configured to support features like pass-through authentication, group writeback, password writeback, Exchange Hybrid writeback, and device writeback.

Chapter 9, "Identity and authentication planning," and Chapter 10, "Installing AAD Connect," contain an in-depth look into directory synchronization, features, and installation options.

Once the synchronization engine has been installed, it is important to pay attention to the synchronization statistics for each of the run profile steps on the Operations tab of the AAD Connect tool, as shown in Figure 2-32.

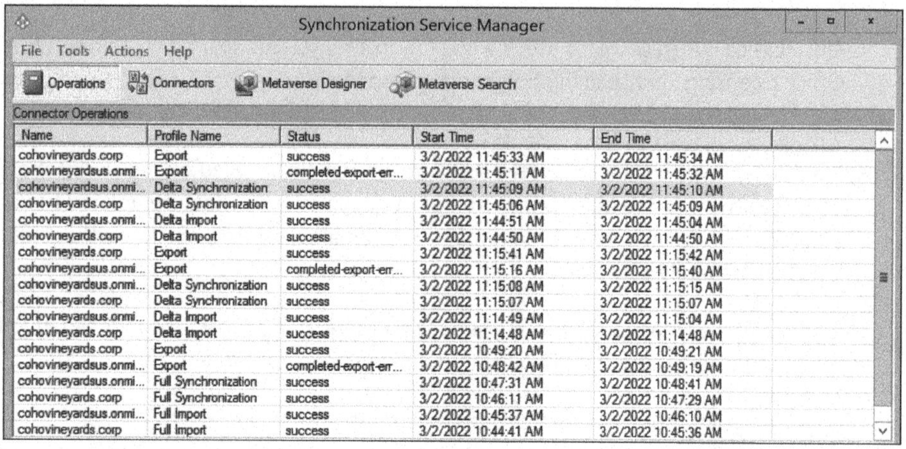

Figure 2-32   The Operations view in AAD Connect

While it is important to review all errors reported in the Status column, those operations for the Azure connector, typically named `tenant.onmicrosoft.com`, should be reviewed carefully.

Any errors on the Azure connector will mean either bad or missing data in Microsoft 365. In fact, if the IDFix tool has been run and all issues are resolved before installation of the AAD Connect tool, the Azure connector should not show any errors related to data problems.

If errors do appear in the synchronization statistics view, the data provided there might not be sufficient to diagnose the issue adequately. In those cases, we recommend reviewing the Application Event Log for more detail.

While it's not 100 percent inclusive of events returned by the AAD Connect engine (primarily because the tool is constantly evolving and maturing), this data represents the most common and important events that should be reviewed and included in any event log monitoring utilities.

Licensing your users

Once a cloud user has been created, and you have started synchronizing identities to your tenant, you will need to assign licenses to your users before they can begin consuming Microsoft 365 services.

Licensing plans and subscriptions were explained in detail in Chapter 1, though there are several methods available for licensing users in Microsoft 365. It is important to understand each available method so you can pick the best option for you. Currently, there are three primary methods for license assignment in Microsoft 365:

- Azure Active Directory group–based licensing

- PowerShell licensing cmdlets included in the MSOnline PowerShell module

- Manual licensing via the Microsoft 365 portal

Group-based licensing

One of the most popular features available for licensing in Microsoft 365 is group-based licensing, commonly referred to as GBL.

Group-based licensing is a feature that requires either Azure AD Premium Plan 1 or Azure AD Premium Plan 2. It is one of the quickest, easiest, and most effective ways to manage Azure AD licenses. As the name implies, group-based licensing uses Azure AD groups for the assignment of licenses to users.

Licenses are assigned to either security groups, which are synchronized to Azure via the Azure AD Connect tool, or to cloud-only groups created directly in Azure.

In the example shown in Figure 2-33, an on-premises security group and its membership has been synchronized to Azure AD, and the Exchange Online Enterprise E3 license is assigned (1 of 26 enabled services).

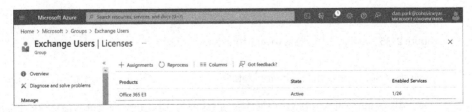

Figure 2-33 Group-based license assignment in the Azure portal

Additionally, dynamic groups can be created in the Azure portal and configured to define membership based on synchronized attributes. The creation of Azure AD dynamic groups, shown in Figure 2-34, requires an Azure AD Premium license.

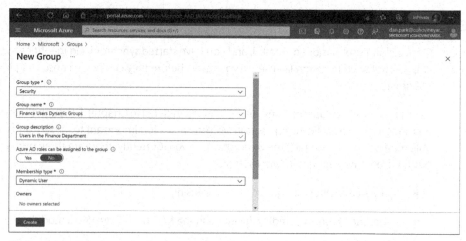

Figure 2-34   Creating a dynamic group in the Azure portal

Once a dynamic group has been created in the Azure portal, the group can then be used for automatic license assignment via group-based licensing, as shown in Figure 2-35.

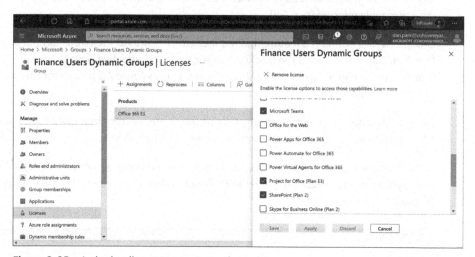

Figure 2-35   Assigning licenses to an Azure dynamic group

It is important to note the following details regarding Azure AD group-based licensing:

- All existing Microsoft Azure license types are supported by Azure AD group-based licensing.

- Group membership updates made in on-premises groups synced to Azure AD are effective within just a few minutes of a membership change.

- Users can be members of multiple groups, and licenses across groups are combined.

- If no licenses are available within the tenant, group-based licensing will be unable to assign licenses to a user, and no error will be returned.

- Licenses assigned via a group cannot be manually removed via PowerShell or the portal.

- Users can have licenses assigned via multiple groups or direct assignment (PowerShell and manual).

- Users can have licenses through multiple means, such as manual licensing applied through PowerShell or group-based licensing.

PowerShell licensing

The second licensing method is using the provided PowerShell cmdlets in the Azure Active Directory PowerShell for Graph module.

This Powershell module includes several cmdlets that can be used for user license assignment in Azure AD. These cmdlets can assign users SKUs and enable or disable specific plans under the SKU.

1. All users must have a Usage Location assigned to be licensed. Define the list of sub-plans that you wish to have disabled (not enabled) and assign the options directly to the user.

2. A user's Usage Location is set automatically via the AAD Connect tool, provided the msExchUsageLocation value in the on-premises Active Directory is populated with a valid two-digit ISO country code. If the value is not set, the AAD Connect tool can be customized to synchronize any other Active Directory attribute (such as CountryCode) as Usage Location, provided it is a valid two-digit ISO country code.

3. If the Usage Location is not set via AAD Connect, it can be set programmatically using the Azure Active Directory PowerShell for Graph cmdlets as follows:

```
Set-AzureADUser -ObjectID userUPN@domain.com -UsageLocation YY
```

In the example shown in Figure 2-36, the user Pilar Ackerman's Usage Location has been set to US.

```
Administrator: Windows Powershell
C:\ PS> Set-AzureADUser -ObjectId pilar.ackerman@cohovineyards.us -UsageLocation US
```

Figure 2-36   Setting UsageLocation via PowerShell

4. Next, it is necessary to retrieve a list of Subscribed SKUs available in the tenant; these can be identified using the following command:

```
Get-AzureADSubscribedSkus
```

5. As shown in Figure 2-37, the `Get-AzureADSubscribedSkus` command returns a list of the SkuIds and their ObjectIds for licenses available in the tenant.

Figure 2-37   Returning a list of Azure SKUs available in a tenant

6. Next, it is necessary to retrieve a list of service plans available for a particular SKU so they can be assigned to a user. The list of service plans available can be displayed using the following command:

```
Get-AzureADSubscribedSkus -ObjectID <ObjectID of the desired SKU>
```

7. In Figure 2-38, you can see that the `Get-AzureADSubscribedSkus` command is used in conjunction with a `Select` statement to return a list of service plans.

Figure 2-38   Returning a list of service plans from a SubscribedSku

8. Once a SubscribedSku Object ID and service plan name has been identified, the license can be assigned to a user with the following command:

```
Set-AzureADUserLicense -ObjectID <user UPN> -AssignedLicenses $LicenseObject
```

9. To create the `LicenseObject` needed for license assignment, it is necessary to create an Azure AD `License` object that can be applied to the user. In Figure 2-39, you can see the steps necessary to set the `License` and `LicenseObject`.

```
$License = New-Object -TypeName Microsoft.Open.AzureAD.Model.AssignedLicense
$License.SkuId = "SkuID of the license you wish to assign"
$Licenses = New-Object -TypeName Microsoft.Open.AzureAD.Model.AssignedLicenses
$Licenses.AddLicenses = $License
```

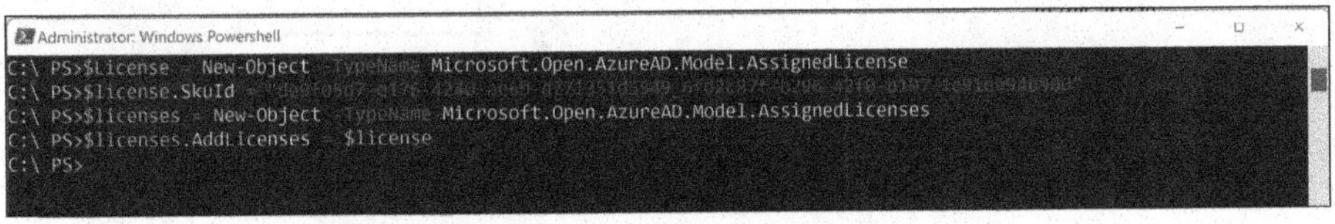

Figure 2-39   Creating a LicenseObject for user assignment

10. Finally, the `License` object created in the previous step can be used with the following command to assign the `License` object to the user, as shown below and in Figure 2-40:

```
Set-AzureADUserLicense -ObjectID <User UPN> -AssignedLicenses $Licenses
```

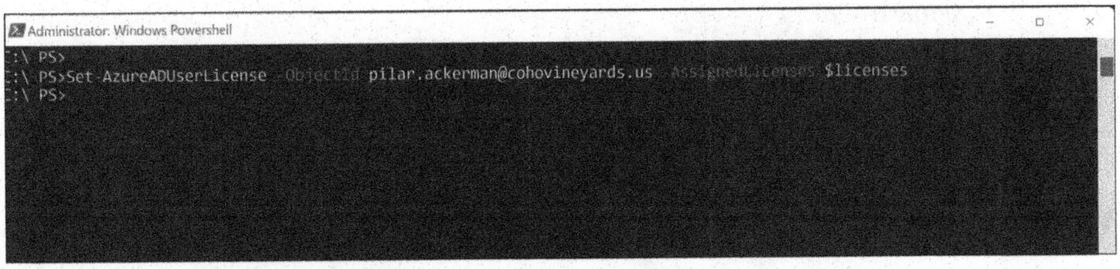

Figure 2-40   Assigning a license to a user with Powershell

Manual license assignment

The final method available for license assignment is using the Microsoft 365 portal to assign user licenses manually.

Manual license assignment can be done on an individual user basis by selecting the user and editing assigned licenses or by selecting multiple users, as shown in Figure 2-41.

CHAPTER 2

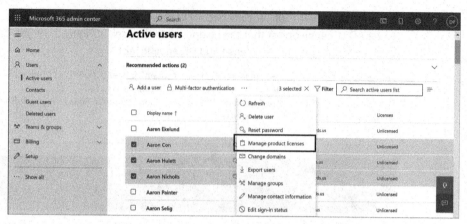

Figure 2-41   Bulk user license assignment via the Microsoft 365 portal

While the ability to assign user licenses is available via the Microsoft 365 portal for both indi-vidual and bulk assignment, it does not typically scale well for large organizations with many thousands of users. Also, it does not scale well with licensing requirements because doing so can create the need to assign licenses in various combinations based on role, location, or department.

This is why the manual assignment of licenses should be used on an ad-hoc basis and as a sup-plement to one of the other options for license assignment.

What's next?

Now that we have discussed the major milestones involved in your Microsoft 365 tenant setup and provided guidance on each of these steps, we will move on to discussing more advanced topics such as Federation, Directory Synchronization, Exchange Hybrid setup, and tasks that will be required to help you get the most from your Microsoft 365 experience.

Governance concepts

What is governance? In broad terms, it's a set of policies or a framework that describes how your organization will operate under a given set of circumstances or requirements. From a systems or data management perspective, governance typically focuses on topics such as how identities get provisioned or retired, how systems and data access are managed, and what data operations are audited and managed.

This chapter explores the types of governance planning activities and topics you should consider when approaching the Microsoft 365 platform.

Governance can take many forms, including written policies and procedures, approval workflows, audits, remediation activities, and automated processes. When assembled, these pieces lay out a framework to help the organization operate optimally.

Governance programs can also fail because of a number of circumstances, including:

- Incomplete policy documentation

- Failure to allocate resources to acquire tooling or implement policies

- Incomplete understanding of available technology policy controls and capabilities

- Lack of proper automated tooling to help compliance or governance efforts

- Poor understanding of business or applicable legal requirements

In addition to prescribing policy and standards, a governance program should also provide integrated guidance for addressing auditing and exception handling. It is also recommended that the governance program includes processes (either internal or external) that cover any tasks necessary to remediate out-of-compliance items.

Typically, governance controls and policies should be implemented for things that fall into these categories:

- Security, access controls, rights, or permissions

- Object provisioning and retirement

- Data management

- Compliance with regulations or reporting requirements

- Activities that could intersect with corporate policies (human resources, security, working hours, and so on)

- Activities that influence costs to the business

For example, an organization would likely be concerned about a governance policy covering the onboarding of contractor identity accounts or how to handle device encryption. A governance policy would most likely not be recommended for managing things like monitoring resolutions or how users organize Internet favorites.

In this chapter, we look at governance controls available in the Microsoft 365 platform for several key areas, including identity, Exchange Online, Microsoft Teams, SharePoint Online, data governance, and eDiscovery. By the end of this chapter, you should be able to discuss governance concepts. It's important to understand the kinds of questions you should be asking business stakeholders and how to start approaching governance discussions—either within your organization or with customers.

Identity and access management concepts

Azure Active Directory provides the security foundation for every service in the Microsoft 365 ecosystem. Modern *zero-trust*-based frameworks focus on securing identity as one of the primary ways to protect organizational resources. Identity governance addresses how you'll handle tasks such as onboarding and offboarding users, what identity provider (*IdP*) applications will use, and how and when access or privileges are granted (or removed).

From a standards perspective, the term *Identity and Access Management (IAM)* is frequently used interchangeably with the Authentication, Authorization, and Accounting (AAA) information technology framework:

- **Authentication** describes the method for verifying a unique identity linked to a person, group, or process.

- **Authorization** is the process that determines the level of privilege or access an identity has to a given resource.

- **Accounting** is logging and auditing data, detailing what actions a given identity has performed against a set of resources.

From an Azure AD perspective, identity governance should address the following three key areas:

- Identity lifecycle

- Access management lifecycle

- Secured privilege lifecycle

In the coming sections, we look at each of these areas in more detail.

Identity lifecycle

For most organizations, user identity is linked to employment or contractual working relationships. When a person is included in and given responsibility for business processes, they might need identity records in various systems such as human resources, Active Directory, Azure Active Directory, or other line-of-business (LOB) applications. These records (typically, a security principal or user account) can be used to store information about the person's job role or tasks and personalized information such as phone numbers, addresses, and other information. In the AAA framework, the identity lifecycle closely maps to the Authentication process.

In most organizations, provisioning an identity includes creating an identity in an on-premises Active Directory. Many human resources information systems (HRIS) can be integrated with Active Directory or Azure AD directly to help ensure an identity's existence is correctly managed throughout a user's relationship with the organization.

Identity provisioning covers the beginning of the identity lifecycle. It starts when a business process dictates a new account needs to be added to one or more systems. Depending on an organization's business process maturity level, this process can be as complex as a workflow initiated by a new employee resource being added to an HRIS or as simple as a manager putting in a service ticket for a new account. Typical identity provisioning governance topics include:

- Required account identification fields (first name, last name, office, phone number, and so on)

- Password requirements such as minimum password length or complexity

Correspondingly, the identity deprovisioning process covers the end of the identity lifecycle. Identity deprovisioning is triggered when an employee, contractor, or other account holder leaves an organization. Like identity provisioning, it can be initiated via an automated workflow or manually.

> ### NOTE
> It's important to note that identity lifecycles are not limited to internal users. Organizations might need to provision identities for partners, vendors, or other people external to their organization. An identity lifecycle process should include systems and applications where external users might need identities.

From a Microsoft 365 perspective, the identity provisioning process will include creating an object either in an on-premises Active Directory forest and synchronizing it via Azure AD Connect to Azure Active Directory or creating an object directly in Azure Active Directory. The deprovisioning process will work the same way—terminating the account either in an on-premises directory and synchronizing changes to Azure Active Directory or terminating the account directly in Azure Active Directory.

Access management lifecycle

While the identity lifecycle processes are typically run only once per user (once to provision or once to deprovision), the access management lifecycle (or access lifecycle) should be an iterative process. This process is responsible for identifying the resources an identity should be able to use while their job or task role requires it. Access management solutions and processes can be used to authenticate, authorize, and audit access to systems—including on-premises or cloud-based networking applications and services as well as physical building or room access. Access management is related to the Authorization process of the AAA framework.

The access management lifecycle is very closely integrated with the identity lifecycle. The first access lifecycle starts during (or immediately following) the identity provisioning process. The identity can be granted access to a broad list of resources, including both role-specific (such as accounting or engineering software) and broad (such as access to a human resources benefits web portal or a door-badging system). As people move throughout the organization, an access lifecycle process should be run to evaluate what role-specific resources need to be granted to or removed from a user.

For example, let's imagine someone is hired for a field sales role. During the identity provisioning process, a unique identity is created for them in the HRIS and Active Directory. During the first access lifecycle process, that person is granted rights to use both the internal employee human resources portal and a customer relationship database specific to field sales employees. After a few years, the person moves from sales to a marketing role. At this point, another access lifecycle process is triggered, during which their identity is granted access to the Marketing SharePoint site and deactivated in the CRM database.

In addition to governing the rights granted to a particular resource, the access management lifecycle processes can also include requirements or stipulations on *how* resources are accessed. For example, the governance policy might dictate that some applications require multifactor authentication or can only be accessed via a virtual private network (VPN) or from an on-premises network.

In the Microsoft 365 context, the rights-management aspect of access control can be achieved by granting direct permissions to an object, such as a mailbox or SharePoint site, to an identity. Or, the identity can be included in a group that has been granted permissions for an object. Additional access requirements, such as multifactor authentication or network locations, can be enforced with Conditional Access policies.

Inside Out

Secured privilege lifecycle

From a best-practices perspective, it's important to ensure that each identity only has the minimum rights necessary to allow the person to complete their tasks. This concept, known as *least privilege*, reduces the opportunity for malicious actors to gain access to resources and data.

Some organizations might wish to achieve this least privilege concept by using dedicated identities for administrative duties, while others might elect to use a rights management framework known as *Privileged Identity Management*. Privileged Identity Management (PIM) is a Microsoft 365 feature that allows people to request elevated access for a period of time to perform specific tasks. PIM is configured to be time-bound, meaning that people only have a limited amount of time to perform their tasks requiring elevation before those rights are revoked.

You can learn more about configuring Privileged Identity Management in Chapter 7, "Enterprise Mobility + Security," and Chapter 8, "Security Features of Enterprise Mobility + Security."

CHAPTER 3

Governance for core workloads and features

In this section, we'll examine some of the core Microsoft 365 workloads and start exploring service-specific concepts and controls in the Microsoft 365 environment.

Azure Active Directory

As you've seen so far throughout this book, Azure Active Directory provides the foundational identity-based security component for the entire Microsoft 365 suite. Azure Active Directory is tied to every service, including Exchange Online, SharePoint Online, OneDrive for Business, and Microsoft Teams.

Like on-premises Active Directory, Azure Active Directory includes objects representing users, groups, and devices. Azure Active Directory supports traditional user and device accounts and traditional security and distribution groups. However, it also supports additional types of objects—including guest user and Microsoft 365 groups.

Guest user accounts are external identities that have been invited into your organization's Azure Active Directory. These accounts are typically easy to identify because they are configured to use an external email address as their identity. Guest user accounts can be granted varying levels of access to resources in your environment, so it is important to ensure that there is a governance process to oversee both the lifecycle of a guest's access to your environment and which resources they can access.

Microsoft 365 Groups are an Azure Active Directory-specific construct that combines several familiar components, including a group, an Exchange Online mailbox, a SharePoint Online site, and a OneNote notebook, as shown in Figure 3-1.

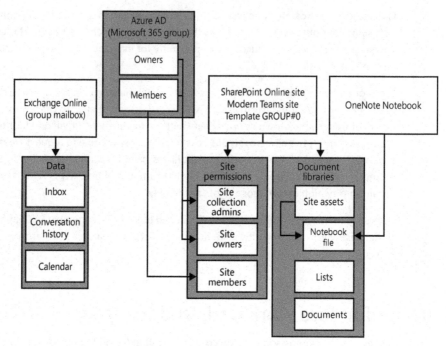

Figure 3-1   Microsoft 365 Group architecture

While administrators or power users may be delegated the rights to create and manage these users and groups, it's important to plan the governance of how those objects will be provisioned and deprovisioned, as well as what access controls will be used to secure resources.

Delegating rights in an on-premises Active Directory environment typically involves designing a forest, domain, and organizational unit structure that maps to geographic locations, business units, or other functions. In Azure Active Directory, however, all user, device, and group objects exist in a single flat directory. Azure Active Directory does provide a feature called Administrative Units, which is a role-based administrative control (RBAC) model that allows you to dynamically group objects for delegation.

A complete governance plan for Azure Active Directory will address:

- The source of authority for user, device, and group objects (cloud, synchronized from on-premises, or a mixture)

- The directory membership requirements for devices (Active Directory domain–joined, Azure Active Directory–joined, hybrid, or not joined)

- The identity provisioning lifecycle

- The access governance lifecycle

- The standardized naming conventions for user and group identities

- The group provisioning, renewal, and auditing controls

- Administrative delegation using technologies like Privileged Identity Management (PIM), Role-Based Access Control (RBAC), and Azure Active Directory administrative units

The most fundamental aspect of building governance for a Microsoft 365 deployment begins with ensuring you've established guidelines for Azure Active Directory.

Exchange Online

Exchange Online relies on identity stored in Azure Active Directory. Like its on-premises counterpart, several items and controls can be configured to meet specific security and functional requirements.

From an Exchange governance perspective, you'll want to focus on things like mailbox creation (both user and shared or resource mailboxes) and mailbox access policies, including allowed protocols and network location restrictions. You might also require governance around calendar sharing access with other organizations. You can learn more about inter-organizational calendar sharing in Chapter 18, "Managing Exchange Online."

Finally, tying back to identity, you might need to govern access controls for administering the Exchange Online service. You can use built-in roles like the Exchange Admin, create custom roles with limited feature sets, and a combination of Azure Active Directory administrative units and Exchange Online role-based access controls to restrict the scope of which administrators can manage which users.

SharePoint Online

SharePoint Online, like Exchange Online, also relies on securing resources using Azure Active Directory identity. Unlike Exchange Online, though, the role-based access controls aren't as granular, so SharePoint administrators cannot be restricted as easily to specific sites or site collections.

And, unlike Exchange Online, SharePoint Online content (including sites and site collections associated with SharePoint Online, Microsoft Teams, and OneDrive for Business) can be shared with people outside the organization. A thorough governance plan will account for how sharing controls are implemented and what (if any) restrictions are placed on either shared content or sharing recipients, both internal and external.

CHAPTER 3

SharePoint Online storage backs SharePoint site collections, Microsoft Teams file data, Microsoft 365 groups, and individual OneDrive for Business sites. File storage governance decisions will need to be applied to cover all workloads.

Microsoft Teams

Microsoft Teams also leverages Azure Active Directory identity to secure resources. Teams are built on top of Microsoft 365 Groups, so some governance policies may be reused. Teams also includes chat and conversation features, both of which can feature a mix of internal and external users. Governance topics include what level of access members and guests have to contribute to team files and conversations and whether features like GIFs and private channels are allowed.

Retention and data security

Not only does identity have a lifecycle, but data does, too. Many organizations have records management departments that specify the lifecycle of data, regardless of media type (audio, video, analog, or digital representations). Retention and data loss prevention are important concepts that dictate how organizations categorize, classify, preserve, and protect data.

Classification is a records management concept that categorizes data, typically based on business criteria or data elements. Data can be classified by any number of indicators that an organization feels help it meet specific regulatory guidelines or business directives. Common classification factors include

- Content age

- Storage medium (printed, electronic, or voicemail)

- Storage location (email, file server, or database)

- Whether it is project- or initiative-related

- Other structured data elements (custom forms, medical records, legal communications, or personally identifiable information)

Retention is another records management concept that addresses how long data should be preserved. Many organizations have internal policies on both the minimum and maximum amount of time to retain different types of information. Some other organizations might also need to comply with federal or local laws governing how long certain types of records are maintained, including

- Employment records and other human resources data

- Tax information

- Mortgages, loans, stocks, or other financial information

- Patient medical data

- Service plans, warranties, or contracts

- Product literature

- Departed employee data

As with classifications, retention might also be driven by a number of factors, including age, medium, or content. Retention is typically treated separately from data backups. Retention is more of a legal concept and frequently focuses on preserving the immutability of records if the data is requested for litigation purposes; backups are an operational concept, supporting the availability of work products.

Microsoft 365 provides labels, which allow organizations to classify their data. Labels have three functions:

- They can act as virtual sticky notes describing a document's classification.

- They can provide security instructions to applications, restricting access or limiting features.

- They can be used to drive retention policies.

While data security, content classification, and retention are typically different organizational functions, Microsoft provides unified tooling that enables content classification to inform both security and retention decisions. Security, classification, and retention features can also be used independently of each other.

A data governance policy should address the following questions:

- How will I classify my data?

- Will classifications be used to secure content by limiting sharing or enabling encryption?

- Do I have any requirements to retain data for a minimum period of time?

- Do I have any requirements to dispose of data after a maximum period of time?

- Do I have retention requirements based on content location, content age, or data elements inside the retained content?

NOTE

For more information on configuring eDiscovery, labels, and retention, see Chapter 6, "eDiscovery, labels, and retention."

CHAPTER 3

eDiscovery

eDiscovery, the process of finding documents and data matching certain query criteria for legal inquiries, has its own set of compliance and governance questions as well. While many organizations configure role-based access controls to limit the amount of data access administrators have during day-to-day management, eDiscovery presents a different challenge.

By default, people who have been granted access to eDiscovery can locate content across the Microsoft 365 tenant, regardless of any role-based access controls elsewhere in the tenant. For example, if someone has been granted the SharePoint Admin role and the eDiscovery Manager role group, that person can discover content across SharePoint, Exchange, and more.

Microsoft Purview's eDiscovery capabilities allow Microsoft 365 administrators to limit the scope of what content people can discover. If you have multiple business organizations or units inside a single tenant, it might be important to ensure people performing discovery activities are limited to only discovering and exporting content within their particular business unit.

Microsoft 365's roles control for eDiscovery also allows you to limit the scope of what content can be acted upon and the types of actions the person can take (search, review, export, and more).

Governance controls

Now that you know which areas need to have governance applied, it's time to look into some available controls. There are a number of ways to organize and categorize governance controls—such as by Microsoft 365 workload, control plane, or feature set. Along with defining the controls that need to be enabled, your governance plan will also need to include an operational schedule where you'll evaluate if new controls are necessary and if existing controls and procedures are being followed.

The tables in the following sections list potential control planes that should be included in your organization's governance strategy. While there are suggested review frequencies for control objects, your organization might choose to review those on a more or less frequent basis.

Azure AD

The Azure AD governance controls listed in Table 3-1 cover a broad array of features available to manage.

Table 3-1   Azure Active Directory governance decisions

Control, feature, or capability	Details	License	Review frequency
Source of authority for user device and group objects	Cloud, synchronized from on-premises, or a mixture.	N/A	Once
Authentication method for users	Cloud authentication, Azure Active Directory Password Hash Sync, Azure Active Directory Pass-Through Authentication, federation with AD FS, Ping, Okta, or other federated identity solution.	N/A	Once
Directory membership requirement for devices	Active Directory domain–joined, Azure Active Directory–joined, hybrid, or not joined.	N/A	Once
Identity provisioning lifecycle	The policy and procedure to determine what process will be used to create identities (such as integration with an HRIS application or manual creation) and terminate them.	N/A	Yearly
Access governance lifecycle	Manual or automated governance procedure for requesting, granting, tracking, and revoking access to resources. This can be performed with Azure AD Access Reviews.	Azure AD Premium P2	Quarterly
User naming policy	Determine how to compose user identity names.	N/A	Once
Group naming policy	Set standards for constructing group names, including blocked words.	Azure AD Premium P1	Once
Group expiration policy	Set time-based controls for group renewal and retirement.	Azure AD Premium P1	Yearly
Restricted group creation policy	Controls who can create groups, including everyone, a select a group of administrators, or service principals through an app template.	Azure AD Premium P1	Yearly
Per-group guest access controls	Allow or prevent team and group sharing with people outside the organization on a per-group or per-team basis.	Microsoft 365 E3 or E5	Quarterly
Administrative delegation using Privileged Identity Management	Use of just-in-time access to manage risk from standing administrative access.	Azure AD Premium P2	Quarterly
Administrative delegation using native Microsoft 365 administrative roles	Choose which roles to implement based on organizational size, administration distribution, and security requirements.	Microsoft 365 E3 or E5	Quarterly

CHAPTER 3

Administrative delegation using Azure AD Administrative Units	Scoped management of Azure AD objects.	Microsoft 365 E3 or E5	Quarterly
Conditional Access Controls	Control access to applications and administrative endpoints and interfaces.	Microsoft 365 E3 or E5	Quarterly
Azure AD Cross-tenant identity access	Allow external B2B collaboration.	N/A	Quarterly
Trust multifactor authentication from external Azure AD tenants	Allow users who authenticate via a multifactor authentication process in an external tenant to meet your organization's multifactor authentication requirements.	N/A	Yearly
Trust devices marked as compliant by external Azure AD tenants	Allow devices that have been marked as compliant in an external tenant to meet your organization's compliance requirements.	N/A	Yearly
Trust hybrid Azure AD-joined devices from external Azure AD tenants	Allow devices that have been marked as joined to an external tenant to meet your organization's compliance requirements.	N/A	Yearly
Configure the level of guest user access	Decide whether guests have the same access as members, limited access to properties and membership of directory access, or are restricted to only being able to view their directory objects.	N/A	Yearly
Configure guest inviters	Decide who can invite guests to the tenant, such as anyone, only specific admin roles, or no one.	N/A	Yearly
Guest invitation domain restrictions	Manage restrictions for Azure AD guest invitations, including allowed or blocked domains.	N/A	Quarterly
Self-service password reset	Enable self-service password reset, including the number of required authentication factors and the factors available to users.	Azure AD P1	Yearly
Allow users to consent to apps access data on their behalf	Choose whether you want to allow users to consent to third-party applications accessing organizational data.	Azure AD P1	Yearly

Exchange Online

While dependent on Azure AD for identity and access management, Exchange Online has its own set of unique controls and features that need to be governed. Table 3-2 details some of the core Exchange Online controls for which you should craft a governance policy.

Table 3-2   Exchange Online governance decisions

Control, feature, or capability	Details	License	Review frequency
User and shared mailbox provisioning lifecycle	Govern which types of mailboxes need to be created for a given business requirement and license acquisition and assignment.	Exchange Online (Any)	Yearly
Public folder provisioning lifecycle	Establish a process and governance cycle for provisioning, tracking, and retiring public folders.	Exchange Online (Any)	Yearly
Protocol availability	Determine which protocols and access methods will be enabled (MAPI/HTTP, Outlook on Web/Outlook Web Access, POP3, IMAP, ActiveSync, Exchange Web Services, and PowerShell).	Exchange Online (Any)	Yearly
Permitted mail applications	Determine what mail client applications will be permitted or supported, including native mobile email clients, Outlook for iOS/Android, Outlook perpetual license versions, and Microsoft 365 Apps versions.	Exchange Online (Any)	Yearly
Self-service distribution list management	Determine if your organization will allow, prevent, or restrict the creation and management of standard distribution lists in Exchange Online.	Exchange Online (Any)	Yearly
Inter-organization calendar and Free/Busy sharing	Specify permissions and visibility for cross-organization calendar sharing.	Exchange Online (Any)	Yearly
Inter-organization Global Address List Synchronization	Many organizations that collaborate and enable cross-organization calendar sharing also implement some level of Global Address List synchronization. Choose if and how that will be implemented and maintained.	Exchange Online (Any)	Yearly
Administrative delegation using built-in role groups	Determine administrative delegation for built-in management role groups.	Exchange Online (Any)	Yearly
Administrative delegation using custom management scopes	Determine administrative delegation for custom management scopes.	Exchange Online (Any)	Yearly
Email forwarding outside the organization	Set a policy to specify whether people can configure email to automatically forward to a recipient outside the organization.	Exchange Online (Any)	Quarterly

CHAPTER 3

SharePoint Online

While SharePoint Online also utilizes Azure AD for its identity store, several application-level governance controls must be considered. Because SharePoint Online is used as the storage medium for SharePoint sites, Microsoft 365 Groups, OneDrive personal sites, and Teams, some controls will affect those services, as shown in Table 3-3.

Table 3-3   SharePoint Online governance decisions

Control, feature, or capability	Details	License	Review frequency
Architecture standards	SharePoint Online supports both Classic and Modern SharePoint architectures. Classic or Modern experiences affect Web Parts' availability, menu and navigation settings, search experiences, and features such as Hub Sites.	SharePoint Online (Any)	Once
Design patterns and practices	Determine what controls will be used and what design or automation practices (such as site scripting) will be used.	SharePoint Online (Any)	Yearly
Site provisioning lifecycle	Determine what events or procedures will govern site creation, administration, and closing.	SharePoint Online (Any)	Yearly
Self-service site provisioning	Choose to allow or block people from creating sites or if your organization will pursue a more curated architecture and design.	SharePoint Online (Any)	Yearly
Sharing policy for SharePoint Online	Determine, globally, how you want to govern SharePoint Online sharing controls. You can allow sharing only within your organization, existing Azure AD guests, new and existing guests, or anyone.	SharePoint Online (Any)	Yearly
Sharing policy for OneDrive for Business	Determine, globally, how you want to govern SharePoint Online sharing controls. You can allow sharing only within your organization, existing Azure AD guests, new and existing guests, or anyone. You cannot configure a more permissive OneDrive for Business sharing policy than what SharePoint Online is configured to use.	SharePoint Online (Any)	Yearly
Allow or block sharing to specific domains	If sharing controls are required, choose how to manage how you allow or block sharing with specified domains.	SharePoint Online (Any)	Yearly
Manage which users or groups are allowed to send sharing invitations	Sharing restriction governing who can send sharing invitations. The ability to share content externally can be configured to allow all users or only users in specific security groups to send external sharing invitations.	SharePoint Online (Any)	Quarterly

Guests must sign in using the same account to which sharing invitations were sent	Choose how to manage the security of external invitations. This control prevents users from forwarding sharing invitations.	SharePoint Online (Any)	Yearly
Allow guests to share items they don't own	Choose how to manage guest security around sharing controls.	SharePoint Online (Any)	Yearly
Automatically expire external sharing links	Evaluate whether or not the permissions granted through a sharing invitation expire after a period of time.	SharePoint Online (Any)	Yearly
Reauthentication period	Configure how often people who use a verification code must reauthenticate.	SharePoint Online (Any)	Yearly
Default sharing access	Review policy to set the default sharing access control (View, Edit).	SharePoint Online (Any)	Yearly
Default sharing scope	Review policy to set the default sharing scope control (specific people only, only people in the organization, or anyone).	SharePoint Online (Any)	Yearly
Unmanaged device access control	Choose what access unmanaged devices will have to SharePoint Online (full access, limited access, block access). There are three ways to control access from unmanaged devices: SharePoint Online controls (native), Microsoft Defender for Cloud Apps, and Conditional Access.	SharePoint Online (Any), Azure AD Premium P1, or Microsoft Defender for Cloud Apps	Yearly
Idle session timeout	Choose how to handle idle sessions. You can configure idle session timeouts via native SharePoint Online controls or through Microsoft Defender for Cloud Apps.	SharePoint Online (Any) or Microsoft Defender for Cloud Apps	Yearly
Network location access	Determine whether to restrict SharePoint access based on network location (IP address ranges). Configuring the native SharePoint control will also impact OneDrive for Business and the Files tab in Microsoft Teams. You can also configure network restrictions via Conditional Access or Microsoft Defender for Cloud Apps.	SharePoint Online (Any), Azure AD Premium P1, or Microsoft Defender for Cloud Apps	Yearly
Require apps to use modern authentication	If your organization is moving to modern authentication protocols, you might want to configure this setting to block legacy and third-party applications from using Basic authentication to connect to SharePoint Online. Blocking Basic authentication will impact PowerShell connections; you'll need to upgrade to a more current version of the SharePoint Online Management Shell to enable modern authentication flows.	SharePoint Online (Any) or Azure AD Premium P1	Yearly

CHAPTER 3

Allow access notifications	Determine if you want to allow users to configure notifications for OneDrive for Business activity.	SharePoint Online (Any)	Once
Days to retain a deleted user's OneDrive	SharePoint Online allows administrators to configure a waiting period between when a user is deactivated and when their OneDrive for Business site is purged. While the governance and control action says retain, it is important to note that this setting is not protecting the data from intentional deletion. This control setting only prevents SharePoint Online from automatically deleting the site. A governance policy should include retaining a departed user's files for a period of time to allow their manager or another person to take over the files and move any pertinent organization data to a new location.	SharePoint Online (Any)	Yearly
OneDrive default storage limit	Depending on the user's assigned license, they might be eligible for several terabytes of storage. The default storage limit is 1TB, but it can be configured up to 5TB with qualifying plans. It may also be reduced to manage user storage consumption.	SharePoint Online (Any)	Once
Allow OneDrive synchronization only for computers joined to a specific domain	Depending on your organization's security requirements, you might consider configuring the SharePoint Online service to only allow computers joined to a specific domain to synchronize files using the OneDrive for Business client.	SharePoint Online (Any)	Yearly
Restrict OneDrive for Business clients to sync only to specified tenants	Depending on your organization's security requirements, you might consider configuring OneDrive for Business clients to only synchronize to tenants belonging to your organization (or partner organizations).	SharePoint Online (Any)	Yearly
Restrict OneDrive for Business clients from synchronizing to specified tenants	Depending on your organization's security requirements, you might consider configuring OneDrive for Business clients to prevent them from synchronizing to a list of specified tenants.	SharePoint Online (Any)	Yearly
Block uploading of specific file types	Your organization might want to implement governance policies restricting what file types or extensions can be synchronized through the OneDrive client.	SharePoint Online (Any)	Yearly
Files on Demand configuration	Your organization might wish to govern the amount of data stored locally on a device by default. Beginning with Windows 10 version 1709, you can configure the OneDrive client to only synchronize a placeholder object to the local filesystem until the file is accessed.	SharePoint Online (Any)	Once

It's important to underscore that configuring security and access controls for SharePoint Online through the native SharePoint Online control plane mechanisms provides the least flexibility. While they can be effective, they also can have unintended consequences that require you to initiate a call with support to roll back configuration changes. Consider using Conditional Access or Microsoft Defender for Cloud Apps for the most granular control.

Microsoft Teams

Microsoft Teams divides content storage between Exchange Online group mailboxes. It also leverages security through Azure AD. In some cases, Teams will inherit governance controls or policies specified in the other control planes. At other times, to achieve the desired outcome, you need to configure controls in more than one place to work effectively together.

Teams has many application features and controls—chat, teams, meetings, voice, and apps. While some are simple options and preferences, many others demand governance consideration. Table 3-4 details some of the more impactful governance decisions that should be considered.

Table 3-4   Microsoft Teams governance decisions

Control, feature, or capability	Details	License	Review Frequency
Allow guest access in Teams	Determine whether or not guests will be allowed to access Microsoft Teams content. To get consistency between workloads, you'll also need to consider guest access settings in SharePoint Online and Azure Active Directory.	Microsoft Teams (Any)	Yearly
Allow users to send emails to a channel email address	This feature enables whether you want to allow a Teams channel to receive submissions via email. This feature is not available in Government Community Clouds.	Microsoft Teams (Any)	Yearly
Allow connecting of third-party storage	Microsoft Teams supports connecting to external file storage providers, such as Citrix, Dropbox, Box, Google Drive, and Egnyte. You can enable or disable each file sharing service individually, but you should review which ones your organization needs.	Microsoft Teams (Any)	Yearly
Native Teams file Upload policy	If your organization relies on third-party storage providers, you can also determine if you will use it in place of native SharePoint storage for files.	Microsoft Teams (Any)	Yearly
Allow creation of private channels	Private channels are restricted channels in a Team and contain their own security controls and SharePoint site. Private channels can only include members and guests of the team. For organizations that experience frequent litigation or discovery, allowing private channels can increase the amount of manual work associated with eDiscovery requests. Private channels can be enabled or disabled globally and per-team basis. You can also use policies to manage which users are authorized to create private channels.	Microsoft Teams (Any)	Yearly

Allow creation of shared channels	Similar to private channels, shared channels allow for a more restrictive membership experience within a Team. Unlike shared channels, however, they can include members of other teams and people external to your organization. Shared channels can be enabled or disabled globally and on a per-team basis. You can also use policies to manage which users are authorized to create shared channels.	Microsoft Teams (Any)	Quarterly
Allow third-party apps	Microsoft Teams, as a platform, allows organizations and vendors to build apps that integrate directly into the Teams experience. Typically, third-party applications store their content outside the boundary of the Microsoft 365 tenant. In commercial environments, access to third-party apps is enabled by default. In sovereign cloud environments such as Government Community Cloud Moderate or Government Community Cloud High, third-party app integration is turned off by default. Apps can be enabled or blocked individually.	Microsoft Teams (Any)	Quarterly
Messaging policies	Determine if message policies are appropriate for your organization. Policies can be applied to users individually, through group assignment, or in batches. A user can only have a single messaging policy applied.	Microsoft Teams (Any)	Yearly
Deleting sent messages	Configure whether users or owners can delete messages.	Microsoft Teams (Any)	Yearly
Editing sent messages	Determine whether people can edit sent messages.	Microsoft Teams (Any)	Yearly
Allow chat	Determine whether 1:1 chat is enabled.	Microsoft Teams (Any)	Yearly
Configure read receipts	Determine whether read receipts are enabled, disabled, or managed by the users.	Microsoft Teams (Any)	Yearly
Allow Giphy in conversations	Determine whether users can include animated GIFs in chat. If enabled, you will also need to set a content rating (no restriction, moderate, strict) to limit access to GIFs with adult content.	Microsoft Teams (Any)	Yearly
Allow memes in conversations	Determine whether users can include memes in conversations.	Microsoft Teams (Any)	Yearly
Allow stickers in conversations	Determine whether users can include stickers in conversations.	Microsoft Teams (Any)	Yearly
Enable URL preview	Determine whether URL preview should be enabled for hyperlinks included in conversations.	Microsoft Teams (Any)	Yearly
Enable sending urgent messages using priority notifications	Enable sending messages using priority notifications. Priority notifications notify users every 2 minutes for 20 minutes or until the marked message is read by the recipient.	Microsoft Teams (Any)	Yearly

Allow sending of voice messages	Determine whether voice messages can be left in a chat, chat or channel, or not at all. Voice messages are not captured in eDiscovery.	Microsoft Teams (Any)	Yearly
Configure supervised chat	Supervised chat is primarily targeted at educational institutions. Supervised chat prohibits peer-initiated chat but allows those with a chat supervision role to initiate chats with others.	Microsoft Teams (Any)	Yearly
Designate presenters in meetings	You can configure defaults for who can present in meetings using the Designated presenter role mode. Available options include Everyone, Authenticated users (including guests), and Organizers only. While organizers can change it on a per-meeting basis, you should choose the most appropriate default option as a governance item.	Microsoft Teams (Any)	Yearly
Meeting registration	The meeting registration policy configures the ability to uses to create webinars. Additionally, with meeting registration enabled, you can specify who can register for and attend webinars (everyone or only members of the organization).	Microsoft Teams (Any)	Yearly
Enable IP audio	Determine if you want IP audio (computer audio) available during meetings. With it disabled, users will have to call in via traditional phone.	Microsoft Teams (Any)	Yearly
Enable IP video	Determine if you want IP video (computer video) available during meetings.	Microsoft Teams (Any)	Yearly
Media bit rate	Govern the amount of bandwidth that media consumes.	Microsoft Teams (Any)	Yearly
Video filters	Set policies determining what background options are available during video meetings (no filters, background blur, default Teams background images, and custom images).	Microsoft Teams (Any)	Yearly
Transcription and recording	You can configure policies to record and transcribe meetings.	Microsoft Teams (Any)	Yearly
Content sharing	Determine if sharing is available during meetings. If sharing is enabled, select what content can be shared (single application or entire screen).	Microsoft Teams (Any)	Yearly
Remote control	Determine if your organization will allow remote control in addition to screen sharing.	Microsoft Teams (Any)	Yearly
PowerPoint Live	Enable or disable the ability to upload a PowerPoint slide deck and present it from Teams (this does not impact the content sharing mode selection where a user can present a desktop or application).	Microsoft Teams (Any)	Yearly
Whiteboard	Determine if the whiteboard application will be allowed in meetings.	Microsoft Teams (Any)	Yearly
Shared notes	Determine if shared notes content can be created during a meeting.	Microsoft Teams (Any)	Yearly

CHAPTER 3

Anonymous meeting join	Determine if anonymous people can join a meeting without an account.	Microsoft Teams (Any)	Yearly
Anonymous meeting start	Determine if leaderless dial-in conference meetings are allowed. With anonymous start disabled, non-authenticated users are placed into a lobby and admitted when an authenticated user admits them.	Microsoft Teams (Any)	Yearly
Automatically admit people	Determine which people are automatically admitted to meetings.	Microsoft Teams (Any)	Yearly
Allow dial-in users to bypass the lobby	Determine if dial-in users are placed in a lobby when joining a meeting or if they need to be admitted.	Microsoft Teams (Any)	Yearly
Live captions	Determine if the option to turn on captions is available during a meeting.	Microsoft Teams (Any)	Yearly
Meeting chat	Determine if chat is allowed in meetings.	Microsoft Teams (Any)	Yearly

While many of the controls shown in Table 3-4 are preferential items, they can also affect other organizational policies, legal regulations, or other requirements that need to be managed.

Retention and data security

While specific retention and data security policies per organization will differ, Table 3-5 lists governance concepts that apply broadly.

Table 3-5   Retention and data security governance decisions

Control, feature, or capability	Details	License	Review frequency
Records management policy parity	Determine if an organization has records management and retention policies that must be adhered to.	N/A	Yearly
Establish functional design of retention policies	Retention policies can be applied per content source or scoped to individual users, groups, or sites. Determine the mechanics of how they should be implemented based on organizational needs.	N/A	Yearly
Review data classification policies	Determine if the organization has records management policies that describe content classification.	N/A	Yearly
Establish functional design of classification policies	Classification is achieved through labeling. Labeling can be applied to content automatically or manually. Labels can be for notification and data classification or can be used to apply security controls such as encryption.	Azure Information Protection P1 or Azure Information Protection P2	Quarterly

Determine if communications barriers or ethical walls are necessary	Some organizations might have regulations that govern communications between groups of people, typically known as ethical walls. Information barriers for Microsoft Teams and transport rules for Microsoft Exchange can help prevent communications between restricted parties. Such regulations include FINRA rules 2241(b)(2)(G); 2242(b)(2)(D); 2242(b)(2)(H)(ii); and 2242(b)(2)(H)(iii).	Advanced Compliance	Yearly
Determine if supervisory control is necessary	Some industries might want (or be required) to implement supervised communications by monitoring a sampling of certain employees' communications. Such examples include FINRA Rule 3310 and FINRA Rule 3120.	Advanced Compliance	Yearly
Determine if insider risk threats need to be managed	Some organizations with sensitive information might want to enable monitoring and governance over certain types of employee activities that could put the organization at risk.	Advanced Compliance	Quarterly

NOTE

It's important to note that each organization will have different requirements and implementations of the Microsoft 365 tools shown in Table 3-5 to achieve their business goals.

eDiscovery

Because of its broad data access, eDiscovery also needs scrutiny to ensure the activities performed meet organizational requirements or other legal responsibilities. See Table 3-6.

Table 3-6   eDiscovery governance decisions

Control, feature, or capability	Details	License	Review frequency
Review and implement default and custom roles eDiscovery and content search	Determine whether the built-in eDiscovery manager role is sufficient or if additional custom discovery roles are necessary to separate duties between discovery, review, and export.	Microsoft 365 E3 or Microsoft 365 E5	Yearly
Review and implement compliance boundaries	Use compliance boundaries to restrict discovery to business units.	Microsoft 365 E3 or Microsoft 365 E5	Yearly
Implement a process to authorize discovery or content search	eDiscovery managers have the unique ability to search and discover data in nearly any part of the organization. Proper governance will include processes to ensure the role is not being misused.	N/A	Yearly

> **TIP**
>
> If your organization has a lot of sensitive data, it might be wise to consider additional auditing and logging around eDiscovery content exports to ensure that data is not being exfiltrated.

What's next?

Governance is an important component of both business and IT operations. In the next chapter, we'll shift from governance as an atomic work item to how it can fit inside a larger organizational goal to maintain regulatory compliance.

Compliance Manager

As organizations transition to the cloud and adopt new services, they need to make sure that doing so enables them to maintain or improve their regulatory and compliance posture. Compliance Manager empowers organizations to review and understand, under a shared responsibility model, what controls are being completed and maintained by Microsoft and what controls or actions must be completed and maintained by the customer.

Compliance Manager provides myriad built-in standard templates that you can use to start tracking your organization's compliance. Also, the Compliance Manager serves as an interface to upload your process or procedural documentation as evidence of supporting compliance.

In this chapter, we'll review the core features of the Microsoft Purview Compliance Manager, including:

- Your organization's compliance score

- Assigning permissions

- Conducting an assessment

- Updating improvement actions

- Working with alerts

Let's get started!

Your organization's compliance score

The compliance score is a metric calculated on your organization's progress toward meeting a given assessment or standard, specifically regarding actions surrounding security, data protection, privacy, and other regulatory standards. Your overall compliance score is visible on the Compliance Manager's Overview tab, located at *https://compliance.microsoft.com/compliancemanager*. See Figure 4-1.

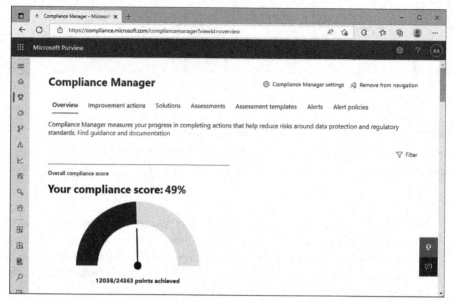

Figure 4-1   Compliance Manager Overview tab

The score is calculated against services enabled on your particular tenant. Compliance Manager, by default, automatically scans your tenant for progress towards completing technical remediation actions and updates your score accordingly.

Your tenant's initial compliance score is calculated against the default Microsoft Data Protection Baseline assessment template, which leverages controls and actions from various standards from industry-recognized organizations, certification bodies, or international regulatory requirements.

An assessment template is a list of controls (sometimes called standards or actions) describing a business process, document, or technical configuration being evaluated. From the Microsoft 365 point of view, assessment templates correlate to industry standards such as NIST 800-53 or ISO 27018:2019 or international regulations such as GDPR.

A group is a logical container that is used is used to organize assessments.

For example, your organization may be required to perform an audit against ISO 27018:2019. As a first step, you may decide to create a group called 2022 – ISO 27108 Audit and then add the ISO 27018:2019 assessment template to that group. Doing so allows you to track the documents and actions in one place, specifically tied to the audit task that you're performing.

Understanding improvement actions

Each activity you undertake can either raise or lower your score. The Compliance Manager's Improvement Actions tab shows various configuration tasks that can be performed and their impact on your score, as shown in Figure 4-2.

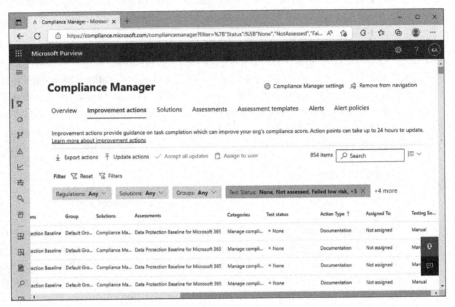

Figure 4-2   Key Improvement Actions

Improvement actions are scored based on their impact. A single action can appear in multiple groups on the Key Improvement Actions page.

Types of improvement actions

Improvement actions are categorized in many ways. Each classification helps determine an action's scoring weight, which can also describe an action's impact on your organization's security or compliance posture.

This section will break down the different categories of actions and evaluate how they impact your overall compliance score.

Action type

The first way to classify an action describes the action type:

- **Documentation**   These actions reflect process or procedural documentation that must be created and maintained by your organization. Documenting the steps of an audit process can fulfill this type of action.

- **Operational**   Operational actions frequently carry out documentation actions. For example, if you have a documented process that requires quarterly auditing members of an administrative group, an operational action would be performing the steps listed in the documented audit process.

- **Technical**   Technical actions are typically related to specific configuration activities, such as enabling multifactor authentication or a privileged identity management solution.

Each type of action affects your score, and each contributes to your score differently. Technical actions, such as changing a configuration, are only scored once, no matter how many groups it appears in. Since you only have to make the technical configuration change once, it is only scored once. Non-technical actions, however, are scored for each instance, regardless of how many groups they appear in. The scoring structure reflects real-world usage and how processes or documentation frequently must be reworked, adapted, or implemented separately for each remediation or improvement action task related to a particular group.

Enforcement type

Actions can be categorized based on their requirement or enforcement type:

- **Mandatory actions**   Compliance with this type of action cannot be bypassed or avoided. Compliance with a password policy is an example of a mandatory action. When prompted, users must update passwords to match the policy (such as complexity, history, or character length) to log in or use a system. Passwords that fail to meet the policy requirement are rejected.

- **Discretionary actions**   This type of action relies on a user following a policy; generally, these actions have no enforcement. For example, you may have a written policy that requires users to fill out a form to check out a mobile projector device before taking it from a resource area. The process or action is discretionary if there is no enforcement.

From a scoring perspective, mandatory actions are worth more than discretionary actions.

Risk type

The third classification for actions is the risk type:

- **Preventative**   These types of actions can be used to address and mitigate specific risk conditions. An example of a preventative action is creating a label policy for detecting personally identifiable information (PII) and applying a sensitivity label that enforces encryption.

- **Detective**   Detective actions are used to monitor a system for irregularities. Using reports to identify privileged access is a form of detective action.

- **Corrective**   These types of actions are used in response to some sort of security incident. Notifying customers of a data breach and restoring systems after a malware attack are two examples of corrective actions.

The combination of enforcement type and risk type drives the final action score, as shown in Table 4-1.

Table 4-1   Compliance Manager action scores

Action type	Action score
Preventative mandatory	27
Preventative discretionary	9
Detective mandatory	3
Detective discretionary	1
Corrective mandatory	3
Corrective discretionary	1

Preventative actions are the most desirable to implement because they can help organizations reduce or avoid risk altogether. Discretionary actions are far less impactful than mandatory actions, as they don't guarantee compliance.

Assigning permissions

You will require the appropriate permissions if you want to work with Microsoft Purview Compliance Manager. Table 4-2 lists the roles and their corresponding capabilities:

Table 4-2   Compliance Manager roles and capabilities

Permission	Compliance Manager role	Azure AD role
Read data	Compliance Manager Readers	Azure AD Global Reader, Security Reader
Edit data	Compliance Manager Contributors	Compliance Administrator
Edit test results	Compliance Manager Assessors	Compliance Administrator
Manage assessments, templates, and tenant data; assign or delegate improvement actions	Compliance Administrator, Compliance Manager Administrators	Compliance Administrator, Compliance Data Administrator, Security Administrator

CHAPTER 4

To assign the appropriate roles, follow these steps:

1. Navigate to the Microsoft Purview Compliance portal (*https://compliance.microsoft.com*) and log in with an account with Global Admin privileges.

2. From the navigation menu, click Permissions.

3. Select Roles under Microsoft Purview Solutions. See Figure 4-3.

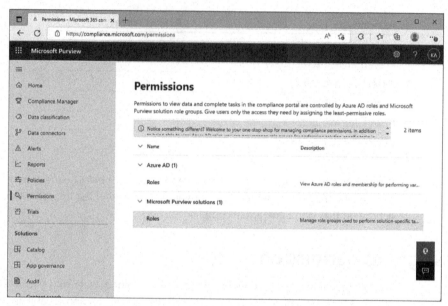

Figure 4-3   Microsoft Purview Compliance portal permissions

4. Select a role, such as Compliance Manager Administrators.

5. Under Members, select Edit, as shown in Figure 4-4.

6. Click Choose Members.

7. Click Add. Locate individuals to add to the role and select the checkbox next to their names. Click Add when finished.

8. Click Done.

9. Click Save.

10. Click Close on the role group flyout window.

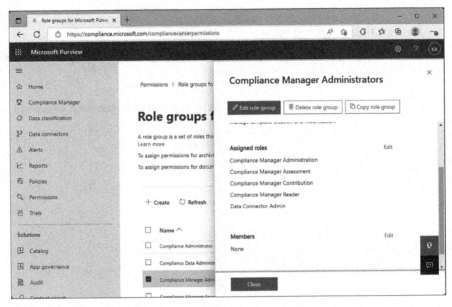

Figure 4-4   Managing role group members

Any user added to a role group will need to log out of all Microsoft 365 services and log back in for their security token to be updated.

Conducting an assessment

Conducting assessments and tracking progress is the heart of the Compliance Manager application. In this section, we'll go through the core steps to create a new group and add an assessment to it.

Creating an assessment

Once you have the appropriate permissions assigned, you'll be able to start creating and conducting assessments. Currently, Microsoft provides 20 built-in assessment templates, as well as 714 premium assessment templates that can be purchased.

To create an assessment based on one of the included templates, follow these steps:

1. Navigate to the Microsoft Purview Compliance portal (*https://compliance.microsoft.com*) and select Compliance Manager from the navigation pane, as shown in Figure 4-5.

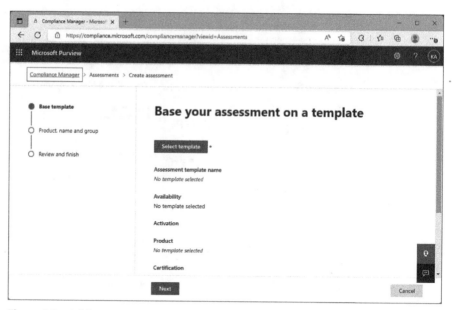

Figure 4-5   Adding an assessment

2.   Select the Assessments tab at the tab list at the top of the page.

3.   Click Add Assessment.

4.   Click Select Template.

5.   Choose a template from the Select A Template flyout menu, such as EU GDPR for Microsoft 365. When creating your own, you can add more assessments if they are all part of the same activity and should be tracked together. Click Save.

6.   Click Next.

7.   Under Assessment Name, add a new name, such as 2022 – GDPR Assessment.

8.   Under Assessment Group, select Create A New Group and enter a new group name, such as 2022 – GDPR Assessment, as shown in Figure 4-6. This will allow you to track tasks and assessments specifically related to this particular assessment activity in one place. Click Next.

9.   Click Create Assessment to save your configuration, create the group, and add the selected assessments.

10.   Click Done to proceed to the assessment.

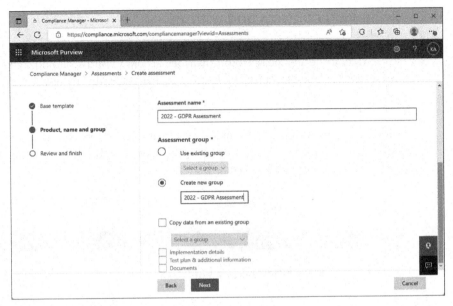

Figure 4-6   Configuring the assessment

Upon completing the group and assessment creation, you'll be presented with a screen showing your progress (points scored) toward completing the assessment and Microsoft's progress. See Figure 4-7.

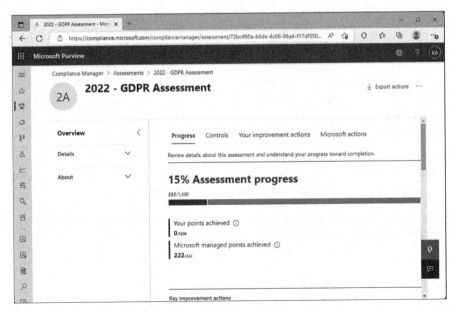

Figure 4-7   A newly added assessment

Scrolling down will reveal the list of improvement actions you can take to increase your score.

Reviewing controls and actions

The assessment dashboard features tabs allowing you to view the controls and actions in your scope to complete and the Microsoft-managed actions toward achieving compliance. This section will look at filtering controls and actions to determine what items you want to focus on.

Controls

The Controls tab lists the various subject areas of the assessment (known as controls). After clicking on the Controls tab, scroll down to the list of controls. You can filter by Family (or category) and Status, as shown in Figure 4-8.

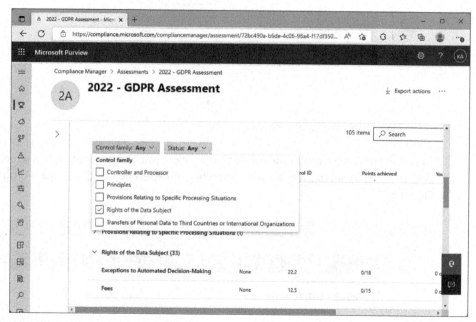

Figure 4-8   Viewing the list of controls

You can expand a family to see the individual control items. Each control item has requirements that need to be met through a combination of documentation, process, and technology configurations. A control contains one or more improvement actions.

By selecting an individual improvement action, you can review the details and suggestions for implementation. See Figure 4-9 for an example.

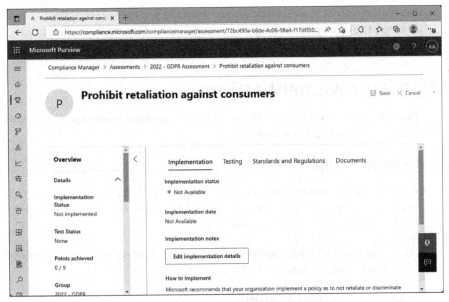

Figure 4-9   Viewing an individual improvement item

The detail view has four main tabs:

- **Implementation**   This tab shows recommendations on how to craft a policy or process to address the item and what types of things you might want to consider depending on your business type. You can also update the implementation status of an item (Not Implemented, Implemented, Alternative Implementation, Planned, or Out Of Scope) and provide notes.

- **Testing**   Many technical controls can be tested manually or automatically within Compliance Manager. The Testing tab shows any historical testing data and notes.

- **Standards and Regulations**   The Standards And Regulations tab shows the mapping between items and Control IDs.

- **Documents**   The Documents tab allows you to manage any evidentiary documentation that supports how you have addressed a control.

You can use these tabs to manage the progress and status of individual controls.

Your improvement actions

Selecting the Improvement Actions tab provides another view of your compliance progress. Instead of being grouped by control family, these items are listed by individual actions you can take and can be filtered by control family, implementation status, and testing source.

Selecting an individual action from this list will route you to the corresponding item details item, showing you actionable tabs (Implementation, Testing, Standards And Regulations, Documents) that you can update.

Updating improvement actions

Now that you understand the basics of creating an assessment and navigating through it, let's dive into working with the actions directly.

Assigning actions

Completing an assessment correctly and thoroughly will most likely involve the input of several individuals from across the organization and might include finance, IT, legal, human resources, executive leadership, or other business units.

With Compliance Manager, you can use assignments to delegate the responsibility for completing an improvement action.

To assign an action, follow these steps:

1.   Navigate to the Microsoft Purview Compliance portal (*https://compliance.microsoft.com*) and select Compliance Manager.

2.   Select the Assessments tab.

3.   Choose an assessment from the list by clicking it.

4.   Select either the Controls or Your Improvement Actions tab.

5.   Select an individual improvement action that you want to assign.

6.   In the Overview pane of the improvement action, scroll down to the Assigned To area and click Assign Action, as shown in Figure 4-10.

7.   Locate a user from the list and select them. Click Assign.

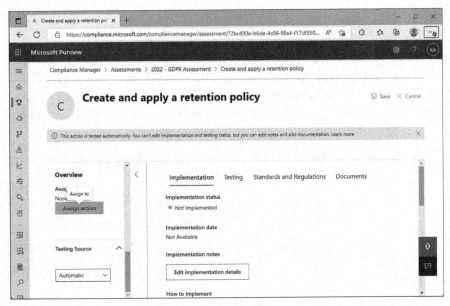

Figure 4-10   Assigning an action

The newly assigned user will receive an email describing the improvement action details and requirements.

In order to view their assigned improvement actions, users will need to be granted permissions to access Compliance Manager.

TIP

We recommend giving users the Compliance Manager Contributors role so they can view and update their assigned tasks.

Depending on the scope of the improvement action, users might need additional permissions in the Microsoft 365 platform to complete their tasks.

Adding supporting documentation

It's recommended that every control has evidentiary documentation supporting how a given policy, process, or technical configuration has been adequately addressed.

Inside Out

Supporting evidence

While many technical actions in the Microsoft 365 system can regularly test for compliance and completion, we recommend that your organization produce documentation describing the technical configuration and review it regularly as part of your configuration management auditing process.

For non-technical actions, we recommend that you produce documentation describing policies, processes, and operational procedures.

In all cases, review the compliance regulations for your governing body and adhere to the stipulations they provide.

Each regulatory compliance body maintains a list of required supporting documentation.

As your team compiles the necessary supporting documentation, Compliance Manager can be used as a repository to hold your supporting documentation. To add supporting evidence to an improvement action, use the following process:

1. Navigate to the Microsoft Purview Compliance portal (*https://compliance.microsoft.com*) and select Compliance Manager.

2. Select the Assessments tab.

3. Choose an assessment from the list by clicking its name.

4. Select either the Controls or Your Improvement Actions tab.

5. Select an individual improvement action to which you want to add documentation.

6. Select the Documents tab.

7. Click Add Evidence, as shown in Figure 4-11.

8. Select either the Document or Link radio buttons on the Add Evidence flyout menu. To upload a static document, use a Document evidence type. The Link option allows you to enter a descriptive name and URL where your supporting evidence is stored. If you choose Document, click Browse and select the supporting evidence file. If you choose Link, add a Name and a URL. After completing either the Document or Link evidence option, click Add when you are done. See Figure 4-12.

9. Repeat steps 7 and 8 to continue adding supporting evidence.

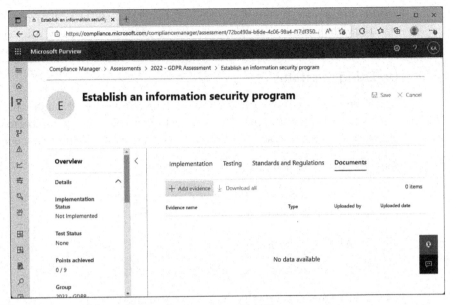

Figure 4-11   Adding evidence to an improvement action

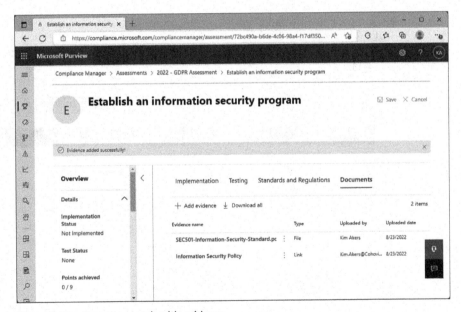

Figure 4-12   Documents tab with evidence

You can add as many supporting evidence documents as you like. Each piece of evidence is stamped with the date it was uploaded and who added it. If necessary, you can also download the documents for an auditing party.

Updating the status

Organizations may need to update an item's status as they work through controls and improvement actions. As previously mentioned, many technical actions may be able to update automatically. Non-technical actions, however, will require human input to configure.

You can update an action's status using this process:

1. Navigate to the Microsoft Purview Compliance portal (*https://compliance.microsoft.com*) and select Compliance Manager.

2. Select the Assessments tab.

3. Choose an assessment from the list by clicking its name.

4. Select either the Controls or Your Improvement Actions tab.

5. Select an individual improvement action to update.

6. On the Implementation tab, select Edit Implementation Details.

7. Update the Implementation Status to reflect the progress toward the action. See Figure 4-13.

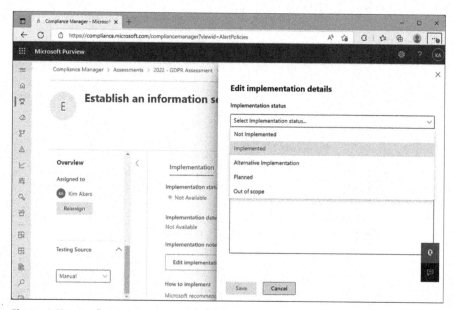

Figure 4-13   Configuring implementation status

8. Configure the Implementation Date and add any notes.

9. Click Save to complete the update.

Compliance Manager updates its scoring daily, so you can check back in 24 hours to see the updated status.

Working with alerts

Working to achieve, maintain, and track compliance can be a daunting task. While organizations do their best to document changes and notify business owners, there are times when changes can adversely affect an organization's compliance posture.

Compliance Manager features an alerting mechanism that allows you to track and generate alerts when items fall out of compliance.

To configure an alert policy, use the following steps:

1. Navigate to the Microsoft Purview Compliance portal (*https://compliance.microsoft.com*) and select Compliance Manager.

2. Select the Alert Policies tab.

3. Click Add to create a new policy.

4. Enter a value for the Name of the policy and click Next.

5. Select the conditions that will trigger an alert and click Add, as shown in Figure 4-14.

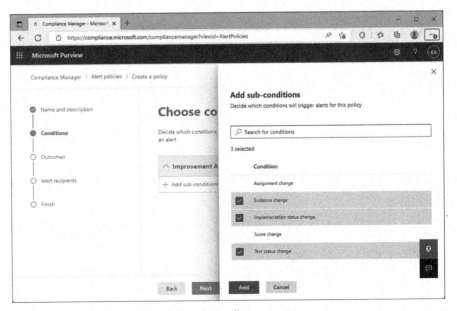

Figure 4-14   Adding conditions to an alert policy

6. Click Next.

7. Set a Severity rating (Low, Medium, or High), and configure the email notification threshold. Click Next when finished.

8. Click Select Recipients to add email notification recipients and click Next.

9. Review the policy settings. Click Create Policy.

Currently, alert policies are not tied to specific groups, assessments, or improvement actions.

What's next?

In this chapter, we reviewed working with Compliance Manager. Compliance Manager can track efforts to attain or maintain compliance with regulatory requirements. In addition to built-in assessment templates covering broad technology or policy domains, organizations can also purchase premium templates to specifically address actions targeted toward their industry or locality.

We'll start working with Microsoft 365 Secure Score in the next chapter. Secure Score is a tool that can help improve the overall security of your organization and fulfill many of the compliance controls found in Compliance Manager.

CHAPTER 4

In this chapter, we will look at how to take advantage of one of the lesser-known but very powerful tools included with Microsoft 365, Secure Score. Like any tool, its utility lies as much in the skill of the craftsman as within the tool itself, so we are going to look at how you can use it to its best advantage and increase your own skills with security assessment across the full set of Microsoft 365 services.

Secure Score is a tool included with Microsoft 365 tenants that helps customers assess and improve their organization's security posture when using Microsoft's cloud services. It is an organic tool that should be used early and often rather than something you run once and consider to be done. As you adopt new services within Microsoft 365 and as Microsoft adds new capabilities, you will find that your score changes.

While a higher score is generally better, you should use Secure Score to ensure that you take full advantage of the features and capabilities within Microsoft 365 and confirm that you have them properly configured. Many actions can influence your score, and not all of them are simple to do. As with any technical matter, your business needs might warrant a choice that decreases your overall score, but you choose to accept that because the benefit outweighs the risk. That is security in a nutshell—making informed decisions on what risks to accept and mitigations you can take to support the business need. Use Secure Score to help you continuously evaluate your posture and understand the potential implications of any configuration or policy settings you make.

Overview

A 2018 study by the Internet Society determined that up to 95 percent of all security breaches could have been prevented if proper hygiene had been in place.

NOTE

You can see the Internet Society report at *http://bit.ly/3F4wtA4*.

Let me translate that for you. That's a polite way of saying, "almost all breaches are self-inflicted wounds." Secure Score is a great way for customers to look at what they have, how it is configured, and what specific actions they can take to improve the security posture. Some of those actions are simple and can be automated, so you just have to click a button. Others might be more complex to deploy, so we will include steps to do them. And some might require you to evaluate the suggestions against how you run your business and choose to accept some risk or pass on some suggestions because that is what you need to do. The point, however, is that rather than spending hours or days just to try to wrap your arms around the state of your organization, Secure Score brings it all into one easy-to-follow-and-use interface. If you are using any of the Microsoft 365 cloud services, then you own this tool. Now, you just need to use it!

Simply put, Secure Score measures your organization's security posture, which considers how you have deployed and configured the products for which you are licensed. Products included are:

- Microsoft 365 (including Exchange Online)
- Azure Active Directory
- Microsoft Defender for Endpoint
- Microsoft Defender for Identity
- Defender for Cloud Apps
- Microsoft Teams

If you have at least one license for a product, the product will be included in the assessment. You will not see information or impact on your score from any product for which you are not licensed.

Secure Score is accessible to several roles in Azure AD. Following are the roles with read/write access:

- Global Administrator
- Security Administrator
- Exchange Administrator
- SharePoint Administrator

Read-only roles include:

- Helpdesk Administrator
- User Administrator

- Service Support Administrator

- Security Reader

- Security Operator

- Global Reader

Assessing your security posture

To start with Secure Score, access it in the portal by logging on to *https://security.microsoft.com/securescore*. You can also get to it through the Security Center by following these steps:

1. Log on to *https://security.microsoft.com*.

2. In the left-hand menu, in the first section, select Secure Score.

3. Once logged in, you will see a screen like the one shown in Figure 5-1.

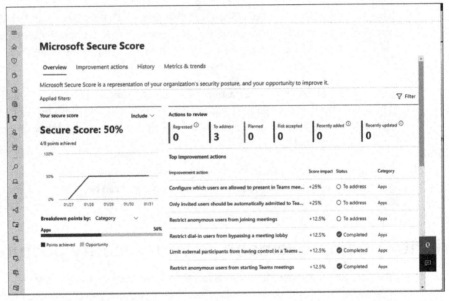

Figure 5-1   The Microsoft Secure Score interface

Start by reviewing your current score and the actions to review that can improve your score. These are grouped by:

- Identity

- Device

- Apps

The Overview tab shows your current score, a chart displaying how your score has changed, a breakdown of your score over categories, and how your score compares to other organizations like yours. Organizations Like Yours shows the average score of other tenants in the same region with a number of licensed users similar to your organization (but otherwise anonymized). Other tabs include Improvement Actions, History, and Metrics & Trends. At the bottom of this page, you will see a history of recent changes, as well as links to related resources and the Microsoft Security blog.

Assessing your security posture is most readily accomplished by reviewing the Secure Score information frequently and taking appropriate actions when new recommendations are shown. Secure Score automatically reviews your tenant's configuration and updates once every 24 hours; you should check it at the very least monthly. Any changes you make will be reflected in your Secure Score the next day, so don't be surprised that your score does not immediately improve when you make a change.

Inside Out

Scores are relative and might change without you doing anything

Your organization's Secure Score will change even if you do nothing. As Microsoft develops new assessments for certain capabilities or introduces new features into the service, you might see your score go up or down based on what defaults are in place and what settings you have previously made.

While that can lead to frustration if you are not using Secure Score regularly—and it might lead to managerial heartburn if your leadership only sees the scores without understanding what goes into them—this should be considered one of the best features of Secure Score.

If you use it regularly, it is very unlikely that you will miss something new, which will help you ensure that your organization is as secure as it can be.

Prioritizing improvements in your security posture

While the top-recommended actions to take are surfaced on the initial screen, selecting the Improvement Actions tab will display the full list of actions you can take to improve your Secure Score based on the services you are licensed for.

TIP

It's important to note that you only need a single license for a feature to appear here as an improvement action. That's true even if that single license is a trial or it's something you would need to obtain more licenses to cover all your users.

From the Microsoft Secure Score screen, you can see all the actions you can take to improve your score, filter actions, get more information about each action, and export the list to a CSV file, as shown in Figure 5-2.

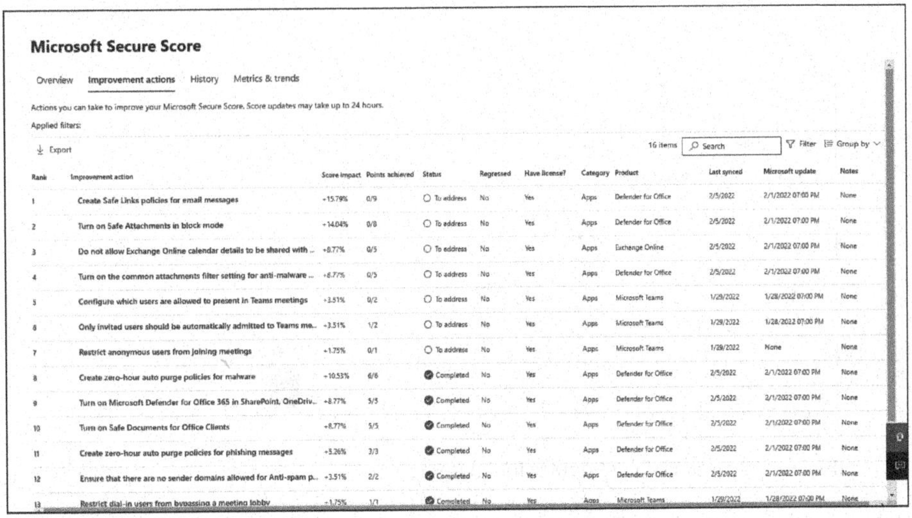

Figure 5-2 Improvement actions

You can also sort on any of the columns, which will help you to prioritize improvements in your security posture. By default, they are displayed by rank, where the lower the rank, the more you should consider doing it first. Rank is calculated based on points increase, difficulty to implement, user impact, and complexity.

The first item should have the biggest improvement for the least effort. Ideally, changes should greatly improve your Secure Score (because they make a corresponding improvement to your security posture), be as simple to deploy as clicking a button, and have no user impact. Some will come close to that, but others, especially those that can provide a big increase to your score, will be more complex to deploy and have a user impact.

Selecting an improvement action will enable you to view more details on the item and take action. As this tenant is licensed for Microsoft Defender for Office 365, we will see that the action with the lowest rank value, hence the one to do first, is to Create Safe Links policies for email messages. That action can improve our score by more than 15 percent! If we click the action, we will see a details screen, as shown in Figure 5-3.

CHAPTER 5

Figure 5-3   Secure Score details for an item

In some cases, this might show more or fewer options. In this instance, we can see the Edit Status & Action Plan action, Manage Tags, Description, Implementation Status, and Manage and Share buttons. Also, Implementation and History tabs are shown.

There are several things we can do here. If we simply click the Manage button, a new tab will open where we can apply a Microsoft Defender for Office Safe Links policy, as shown in Figure 5-4.

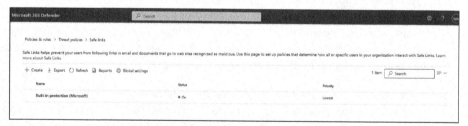

Figure 5-4   Microsoft 365 Defender Safe Links policy

From here, you can create a new policy and apply it to your domains. If you want to share the item, click the Share button. Actions include Copy Link, Email, Microsoft Teams, and Microsoft Planner, as shown in Figure 5-5.

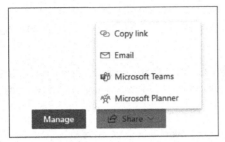

Figure 5-5 Options for sharing an item in Secure Score improvement actions

If you have Microsoft Planner set up and at least one plan created, selecting Microsoft Planner lets you add the item to a project plan and assign it to a user if desired. Once completed, the action will update Secure Score automatically.

You can also click Screen text for a button, which allows you to set the status to the following options: Completed, To Address, Planned, Risk Accepted, Resolved Through Third Party, and Resolved Through Alternate Mitigation. The Action Plan might require you to enter notes when accepting or addressing through third-party or alternate mitigation. The Resolved Through Third Party and Resolved Through Alternate Mitigation options enable you to see improvement in your Secure Score. Also, you can mark complete items that cannot be detected by Microsoft 365 since the solution is external to Microsoft 365. Figure 5-6 shows the Status & Action Plan options.

CHAPTER 5

> ### Status & action plan
>
> **Create Safe Links policies for email messages**
>
> Update the status and action plan for this improvement action. System-generated statuses can't be updated.
>
> **Status**
>
> ○ Completed
> ○ To address
> ○ Planned
> ◉ Risk accepted
> ○ Resolved through third party
> ○ Resolved through alternate mitigation
>
> **Action plan**
>
> Write a note
>
> Notes are required when accepting risk.

Figure 5-6 Status & Action Plan

When an action is marked as Completed, the score is automatically updated when you take actions that Secure Score can detect. It might take 24 hours after completion before you see the status update to Completed.

Prioritizing improvements should look at the rank of all the improvement actions, focusing on the lowest number and working your way through. As you look at each one, consider the following:

- Ensure that you have enough licenses to cover all of your users.

- Whether you have any existing mitigations in place or third-party solutions that address the same issue.

- Whether the recommendation makes sense for your organization.

- Implement the improvements you can; mark as Mitigated those you have addressed through third-party solutions; and mark as Accepted those you choose to accept.

That last one might seem odd but consider items that might not be a good choice for your organization. Having too many Global Administrators is a common item that comes up in larger organizations. However, that recommendation is surfaced when Global Admins contains five or more members. In an organization of 100,000 users, you will probably have many more—and need them all—so you would choose Risk Accepted to accept that risk. You might also need to permit anonymous users to join meetings, but we recommend that you do not. If necessary, mark the item as Accepted, make a quick note that it is a business requirement, and then move on to more important items. Figure 5-7 shows an example of accepting a risk and noting any justifications.

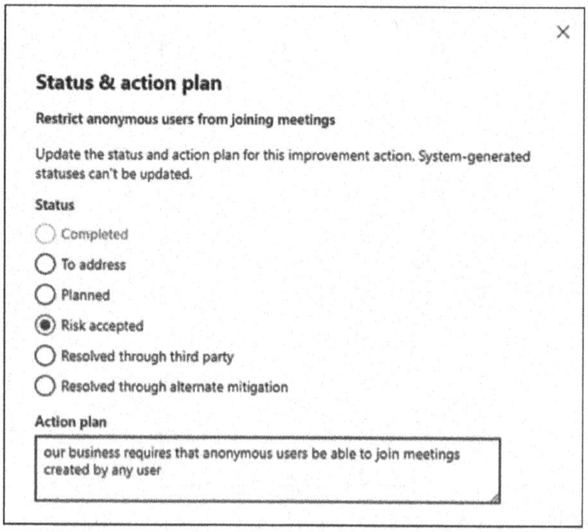

Figure 5-7   Accepting a risk and documenting it

Reporting on your security posture

The Secure Score portal allows you to track your history, see details of activity that has affected your score, and compare your score to other organizations—all from within the portal. The History tab shows a timeline of your score and a line-by-line detail of the activities that have changed it, and whether those activities improved or reduced that score. You can use display filters to see only specific aspects, use screenshots, display in the portal, and export the details to a comma-separated values (CSV) document for further reporting.

Follow these steps to filter the history:

1. Log in to the Secure Score portal at *https://security.microsoft.com/securescore*.

2. Click History; the History tab opens.

3. Below the timeline graph, select the time period you want to view from the dropdown menu, and then click Filter.

4. As shown in Figure 5-8, select whether to show Increases or Regressions; select the Category; click the checkboxes next to the specific Product(s) and Update Type; or filter by Tags, if any.

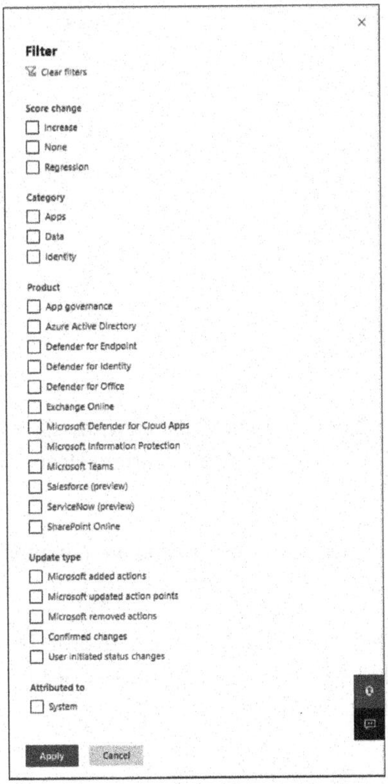

Figure 5-8   Filtering the Secure Score history

5.   When you have the filters set as desired, select Apply.

6.   Select Export to download the history list as a CSV file.

TIP

The ability to filter on Update type can be important when reporting to management. As mentioned early in this chapter, your organization's Secure Score might change as Microsoft adds new detection types, your organization acquires new capabilities that have not been configured by your administrators yet, or other admins take actions. Being able to show just why a score went down can be important when someone is only looking at the score without taking in the bigger picture.

The Metrics & Trends tab displays information about historical changes in your Secure Score. It also provides a comparison of how your score relates to other organizations like your own. There are scenarios you can select to better plan out future actions, so you can work to improve your score. The overall view of Metrics & Trends is shown in Figure 5-9.

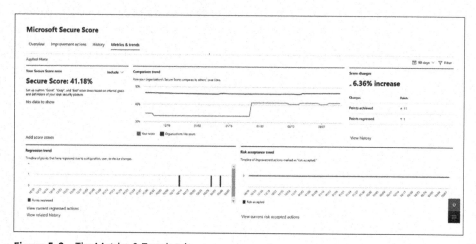

Figure 5-9   The Metrics & Trends tab

By looking at the Secure Score, you can get into more granular views by clicking the Include dropdown and selecting one of three options: Planned Score, Current License Score, and Achievable Score, as shown in Figure 5-10.

Each of the other links on this tab takes you to the corresponding area of one of the other tabs, so you can drill down into the specifics.

Even as security technologies improve, security threats continue to evolve. The *assume-breach* and *Zero Trust* principles are important, but so is situational awareness. Secure Score is a no-cost tool that enables you to maintain that situational awareness.

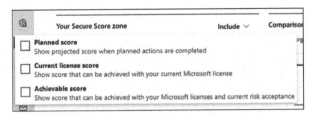

Figure 5-10   Options for displaying your Secure Score

What's next?

Even as security technologies improve, security threats continue to evolve, and if you are not staying on top of your technology space and taking advantage of everything available to you to enhance your security posture, you're asking for trouble. Presume breach and zero trust are important, but so too is situational awareness, and Secure Score is a no-cost tool that enables you to maintain that situational awareness.

Review it at least monthly, if not weekly, and ensure that you are taking the relevant actions that you can take. Remember, continuous improvement is the responsibility of good admins and an ongoing process. Security is a mindset, not a destination, and there will always be things you can do to improve. Staying on top of your Secure Score is as important to your organization as staying on top of your credit score is to you.

In the next chapter, we'll start exploring the concepts around labeling, retention, and eDiscovery.

Labels, retention, and eDiscovery

The Microsoft Purview Compliance portal (formerly the Security & Compliance portal), shown in Figure 6-1, combines multiple aspects of data governance into one portal, including data classification, content search, eDiscovery, and information protection.

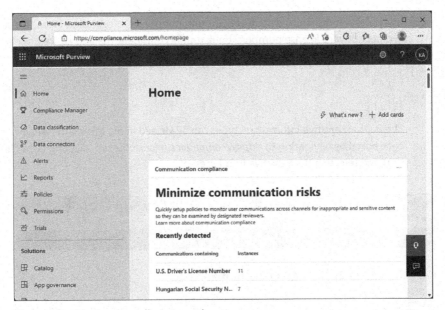

Figure 6-1 Purview Compliance portal

This chapter discusses the data management tools, including data classifications and labels, data loss prevention policies, and the eDiscovery product's core.

Data governance concepts

The classification process allows administrators and users to categorize and manage the life cycle of information. Classification can drive retention, define security rules, and even contribute to the eDiscovery process.

In this section, we'll review some of the terminology and features of the Microsoft Purview product line that can be used as part of your data governance strategy.

Sensitive information types

A sensitive information type (SIT) is a configuration object used to describe the matching requirements for a particular type of content. Sensitive information types can include text or number strings, regular expressions, and other patterns to help identify content.

Microsoft 365 comes with many default sensitive information types. You can also create a custom type based on your organizational requirements (for example, a part number format, a unique identifier format you give customers, or other content you can search for based on regular expressions). Sensitive information types can be used with labels, retention policies, and data loss prevention policies.

Built-in

Currently, Microsoft 365 ships with over 300 built-in sensitive information types. These default SITs can detect driver's license numbers, bank routing numbers, mailing addresses or phone numbers, storage keys and credentials, and a wide variety of personally identifiable information. See Figure 6-2.

NOTE

The built-in sensitive information types can be viewed in the Microsoft Purview Compliance portal by navigating to *https://compliance.microsoft.com*, selecting Data Classification, and selecting the Sensitive Info Types tab.

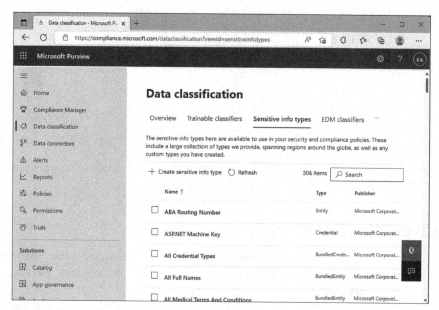

Figure 6-2 Sensitive information types

NOTE

You can also learn more about the built-in sensitive information types by visiting *https://aka.ms/sits.*

Custom

Custom sensitive information types can be defined to identify documents and data based on your own criteria. Custom SITs can be created through the user interface, or PowerShell can leverage pattern-matching techniques, such as keyword lists, dictionaries (large keyword lists), and regular expressions.

While they can be created from scratch, custom sensitive information types can also be created using an existing SIT template. They can even include functions used in the built-in information types.

TIP

If you want to create a custom sensitive information type using PowerShell, you'll need to build a structured XML file containing the pattern elements you wish to match. You can learn more about the XML format here: *https://aka.ms/customsits.*

In addition to using standard and configuration-driven custom sensitive information types, Microsoft Purview supports two additional methods to identify data.

Document fingerprinting

A document fingerprinting sensitive information type is used to identify data inputted onto a form or template. For example, you can upload a tax form or blank patient health record with recognizable fields to use as a template. Document fingerprinting compares email content passing through the data loss prevention engine to the uploaded base document or form.

Exact data match

An exact data match custom sensitive information type is used to find specific data entities, as opposed to using regular expressions or patterns to identify potential content. Exact data match relies on regularly importing a structured dataset containing the specific data elements to be detected.

Classifiers

Trainable classifiers are the newest type of content categorization and identification in the Microsoft 365 platform. Trainable classifiers learn how to identify content by reviewing hundreds of examples of content you're interested in categorizing.

Trainable classifiers are useful for content and data that aren't easily identified through document fingerprints, keywords, and regular expressions. Classifiers can be used to identify items for the application of labels and communication compliance policies.

Pre-trained classifiers

Microsoft has pre-trained about 40 classifiers that can detect various text and image types and categories, including

- Pay stubs

- Tax information

- Source code

- Nudity

- Profanity

- Threatening language

- Sales data

- Merger and acquisitions

- Licensing

- Loan documents

- Healthcare

- Financial statements

NOTE

You can find a current list of pre-trained classifiers at *https://aka.ms/tcdefinition*.

Trainable classifiers

A trainable classifier is trained to identify custom content. In order to create a trainable classifier, you need to provide strong examples of the type of content that you want to be identified. The minimum number of content examples is 50, and the maximum is 500. Microsoft recommends a data set of at least 200 samples to create a well-trained classifier.

NOTE

Creating and training a customer classifier is an involved process requiring dozens of hours. In addition to training the classifier by uploading sample documents, Microsoft 365 needs to perform a baseline evaluation of your environment, which takes 12 days to complete. For more information about creating and training custom classifiers, see *https://aka.ms/trainableclassifiers*.

Labels

Labels are used to categorize or classify information. At its essence, a label is a virtual note—a piece of metadata used to identify content. After a label has been created and published, it's available to users in applications such as Microsoft Outlook, Microsoft OneDrive, and Microsoft SharePoint. When labels are applied to emails or documents (either manually or automatically), the content can be categorized, retained, protected, or deleted based on the settings you specify in policies.

Labels are global features that apply across Microsoft 365 services and features, including user and resource mailboxes in Exchange Online and sites and documents in SharePoint Online, OneDrive for Business, and Microsoft 365 Groups. Because of their global nature, you should start transitioning older per-service data lifecycle management features to labels, including the following:

- **Exchange Online**   Specific features such as retention tags, retention policies, and messaging records management

- **SharePoint Online and OneDrive for Business**   Specific features such as in-place records management, Records Center, and information management policies

The older features will continue to work side by side with labels for the time being, but moving forward, Microsoft recommends using labels created in the Microsoft Purview Compliance portal for your data governance needs.

Label types

There are two main types of labels: sensitivity labels and retention labels.

CHAPTER 6

- **Sensitivity labels**   Sensitivity labels can be used for classification, to apply markings to supported document types, and encrypt contents. Sensitivity labels can be used as conditions in DLP policies. Microsoft also provides software development tools for application vendors to interact with the labeling infrastructure.

- **Retention labels**   Retention labels (along with retention policies) are used to manage the lifecycle of data. Retention, in terms of data governance, includes preserving data for a defined period and destroying data at the end of its useful period.

Content can have both retention and sensitivity labels applied to them at the same time.

Labels can be used as part of policies for automatic application. Labels are reusable classification building block entities that you can use as part of multiple policies. Only one label of each type can be applied per piece of content (such as an email or document), and an explicit label always takes precedence over an auto-apply label. The following are key points regarding label application:

- If a user assigns a label manually, they can change or remove the label.

- If the content has an automatically applied label, a user can replace it manually but might not be able to remove it.

- If a user manually applies a label to content, an auto-apply label cannot replace it.

- If the content is subject to multiple policies that auto-apply labels, the oldest rule's label is assigned.

Labels cannot be applied to Exchange Online public folders, Skype for Business data, or Teams chats. Labels published to users can be applied to Exchange, SharePoint, OneDrive, and Office 365 Groups.

Application methods

Labels can be applied in two ways: manually and automatically.

- **Manual**   Manually applied labels are just that—they need to be selected and assigned by the end user, typically through a supported application's interface (OneDrive for Business or SharePoint site, Outlook, or AIP files scanner).

- **Automatic**   Automatically-applied labels are applied through a policy mechanism. Automatic application of labels is a premium feature and generally requires an E5, G5, or A5 subscription level.

Labels that are auto-applied based on sensitive information types can only be applied to SharePoint and OneDrive, and labels that are auto-applied based on a query can be applied to Exchange, SharePoint, OneDrive, and Office 365 Groups.

Data loss prevention

Data loss prevention (DLP) helps you identify and protect your organization's sensitive data. You can configure policies based on keywords, sensitive information types, or document fingerprints to restrict the content distribution or perform other actions, such as forcing encryption. A DLP policy can identify data across many locations, including Exchange Online, SharePoint Online, and OneDrive for Business. Figure 6-3 shows the DLP Policy Matches page.

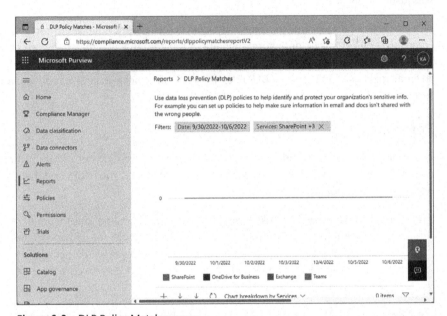

Figure 6-3   DLP Policy Matches page

A DLP policy comprises one or more locations and one or more rules. Locations are the services where sensitive data is stored, such as Exchange Online or OneDrive. Rules contain conditions content must meet and actions to take when content is identified.

Conditions examine content and context. For example, sensitive content might be deemed lower risk if shared internally versus externally.

Depending on where content is being accessed, actions restrict content from being accessed or sent.

When a document meets a policy's conditions for OneDrive or SharePoint content, access is blocked for everyone except the site collection owner and the last user to modify the document. After the document is brought back into compliance, the original permissions are restored. When access to a document is blocked, the document appears with a policy tip icon overlaid on the document's original icon.

For email content, the action blocks the email from being sent. Depending on the DLP transport rule configuration, the sender might receive a non-delivery report (NDR), a policy tip, or an email notification that their message was deemed noncompliant.

There might be instances when users have a business justification to handle sensitive data or transmit it outside the organization. User notifications and user overrides can notify a user that the content violated a policy and present them with an option to override if they have a business justification.

A DLP policy can also include incident notifications. An incident notification can be sent to a compliance officer; it includes information about the item that was matched, the content that matched the rule, and the name of the person who last modified the content. In the case of an email message that triggers a DLP rule, the report also includes information regarding the sender and attaches the message that matches the policy.

Retention

Retention policies are programmatic ways to manage or govern content accumulation, retention, and deletion. Depending on your organization's industry, you might find that you need one or more retention policies configured to:

- Comply proactively with industry regulations and internal policies that require you to retain content for a minimum period of time. For example, the Sarbanes-Oxley Act might require you to retain certain types of content for seven years. In other regulated industries, you might need to retain certain documents pertaining to consumer data for up to 30 years.

- Reduce your exposure in the event of litigation or a security breach by permanently deleting old content that you're no longer required to keep. Your organization's legal team might have policies to reduce the amount of data you store and manage organizationally to reduce the scope of data that could be discovered in a lawsuit.

Retention policies in Office 365 can help you retain content, so it can't be permanently deleted before a specified period or deleting content permanently at the end of a retention period to manage the data life cycle.

Office 365 retention policies enable you to create rules to retain; delete; or retain and delete content based on time frames, locations, or search criteria. You can deploy policies to cover certain data sources (such as Skype, Exchange, or SharePoint) or just certain data types based on keywords or specific sensitive information types.

Some highly regulated industries might require compliance with Securities and Exchange Commission (SEC) Rule 17aa-4, which requires that it cannot be disabled or made less restrictive after a retention policy is enabled. By using the Preservation Lock feature of a retention policy, you can ensure that no one can turn off the policy.

TIP

To apply retention policies to Exchange Online content, mailboxes must be configured with an Exchange Online Plan 2 license or an Exchange Online Plan 1 license with the Exchange Online Archiving add-on license.

Overview of retention policies for content types

When you include a location such as a SharePoint site or mailbox in a retention policy, the content remains in its original location. Users can continue to work with their documents or mail. If the user edits or deletes content covered in the policy, a copy of the content as it existed when you applied the policy is retained.

For sites, a copy of the original content is retained in the Preservation Hold library when users edit or delete it. If the Preservation Hold library doesn't exist for the site when a retention policy is enabled, a new Preservation Hold library is created. The Preservation Hold library is only visible to the site collection administrator.

Suppose the content being protected is modified or deleted during the retention period. In that case, a copy of the original content as it existed when the retention policy was assigned is created in the Preservation Hold library. There, a timer job runs periodically and identifies items whose retention period has expired, and these items are permanently deleted within seven days of the end of the retention period.

If the content is not modified or deleted during the retention period, it's moved to the first-stage Recycle Bin at the end of the retention period. If a user deletes the content from there or purges this Recycle Bin, the document is moved to the second-stage Recycle Bin. A 93-day retention period spans both recycle bins. At the end of 93 days, the document is permanently deleted from wherever it resides, in either the first- or second-stage Recycle Bin.

For a retention policy to maintain copies of versions of documents in a site or library, versioning must be turned on for the site or library. All versions of the deleted document are retained if a document is deleted from a retained site and document versioning is turned on for the library.

If document versioning isn't turned on and an item is subject to several retention policies, the version that's retained is the one that's current when each retention policy takes effect. For example, a document named Doc1.docx dated June 1 exists in a site when the first retention policy is applied to a site. Doc1.docx has been edited several times since the initial retention policy was applied. On July 1, a new retention policy is applied to the same site, and the July 1 version of Doc1.docx is also preserved.

A retention policy can retain content either indefinitely or for a specific period of time. For content to be retained for a specific period, the retention policy can be configured to retain the data based on when it was created or last modified. A retention policy can also delete the content at the end of the retention period. Finally, a retention policy can simply delete old content without having a requirement to retain it for a period of time.

For mailboxes and public folders, the copy is retained in the Recoverable Items folder. These secure locations and the retained content are not visible to users. In the case of a mailbox, the Recoverable Items folder is at the mailbox level. For public folders, the Recoverable Items folder is per folder. Only users who have been granted the eDiscovery role have access to the Recoverable Items folder.

By default, when a user deletes a message in a folder other than the Deleted Items folder, the message is moved to the Deleted Items folder. When a user deletes an item in the Deleted Items folder, the message is moved to the Recoverable Items folder. If the user deletes an item by using Shift+Delete in any other folder, the item is moved directly to the Recoverable Items folder. Content in the Recoverable Items folder is retained for 14 days by default (and can be extended up to 30). At the end of the Recoverable Items retention period, the content is purged permanently unless a retention policy is configured to retain the content for longer.

If a mailbox is deleted or the license is removed while governed by a retention policy or is on Litigation Hold, the mailbox becomes inactive. The contents of an inactive mailbox are still subject to any retention policy placed on it before it was made inactive. The contents are available in an eDiscovery search to users with the eDiscovery role.

Disposition

Broadly speaking, disposition describes the actions taken when governed data reaches the end of its policy cycle. In Microsoft 365, disposition (more specifically, "disposition review") is a prompting that occurs at the end of an item's retention period. Disposition reviews allow content owners and records managers to decide how to handle data permanently. Disposition reviews might result in a variety of actions:

- Permanently deleting content

- Assigning a different retention policy to content

- Moving the content to a new location

Disposition reviews are a premium feature available with Microsoft 365 E5 and other select plans.

Records

In terms of data governance, a record is an item of particular organizational significance. Depending on your organization, you might recognize various types of content as records—major product release milestones, contracts or other legal documents, health data, or human resources information.

Microsoft 365 supports two types of records: standard (or regular) records and regulatory records. Declaring an item as a record limits the actions that can be taken against it (such as restricting editing or moving). In addition, standard records can be either locked or unlocked, providing additional granularity to how marked content can be managed.

Table 6-1 describes the types of actions available for records.

Table 6-1   Record actions

Action	Record (unlocked)	Record (locked)	Regulatory record
Edit Contents	Allowed	Blocked	Blocked
Edit Properties And Metadata, Including Item Rename	Allowed	Allowed	Blocked
Delete	Blocked	Blocked	Blocked
Copy	Allowed	Allowed	Allowed
Move Within Container	Allowed	Allowed	Allowed
Move To New Container	Blocked	Allowed if never unlocked	Blocked
Open/Read	Allowed	Allowed	Allowed
Change Label	Allowed	Allowed (container admin only)	Blocked
Remove Label	Blocked	Allowed (container admin only)	Blocked

Data governance scenarios

Now that you understand some of the basic terminology and concepts regarding data classification and retention, let's look at some usage scenarios.

Sensitivity labels

As mentioned earlier, sensitivity labels are used to tag documents for classification. When combined with a policy, sensitivity labels can drive actions like watermarking and encryption.

Labels are created from the Information protection menu in the Microsoft Purview compliance center. If you've never launched the Microsoft Purview compliance center before or have a new Microsoft 365 E5 subscription, you might be prompted to activate a default set of labels. See Figure 6-4 for an example.

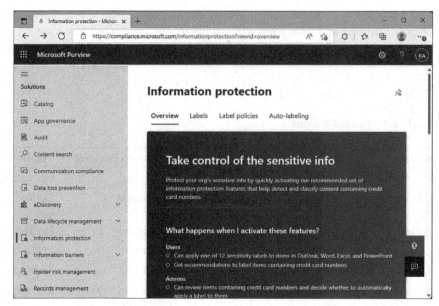

Figure 6-4 Microsoft 365 Information Protection default labeling feature activation

By clicking Activate Features at the bottom of the page, you can deploy a set of 12 sensitivity labels, as well as DLP policies.

NOTE

In order to successfully activate the default labels and DLP policies, you must activate audit logging for your tenant by clicking Start Recording User And Admin Activity on the Microsoft Purview compliance center's Audit page. Select Solutions > Audit.

After activating the default labels and policies, you can review them on the Overview tab of the Information Protection page, as shown in Figure 6-5.

NOTE

Microsoft provides a table describing all the default label settings. The table is available here: *https://aka.ms/defaultlabels*.

However, if you decide not to deploy the default labels and policies (or want to configure additional ones), follow the steps outlined in this chapter to create labels and make them available to your end users.

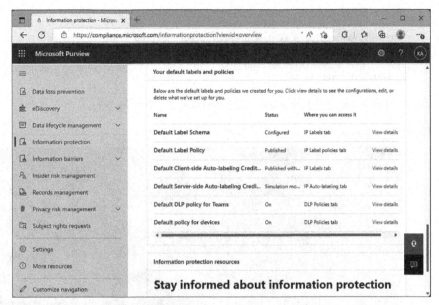

Figure 6-5   Default labels and policies

Preparing teams, groups, and sites for sensitivity labels

Out of the box, sensitivity labels can be used for emails and files stored in SharePoint and One-Drive for business sites. However, with newer products like Microsoft Teams and Microsoft 365 groups occupying an increasing amount of your Microsoft 365-based data estate, you'll want to make sure you can apply protection to those items as well.

In order to get sensitivity labels to work at the team, group, and site container levels, you'll need to do a little extra legwork.

Before you can start preparing your environment, though, you'll need the Azure AD Preview module installed. To install it, launch an elevated PowerShell console session and run the following command:

```
If (!(Get-Module -ListAvailable AzureADPreview)) { Install-Module AzureADPreview}
```

Once you have the Azure AD Preview module ready, you can follow these steps to enable sensitivity labels for containers:

1. From a PowerShell console session, connect to Azure AD using the Azure AD Preview module:

    ```
    AzureADPreview\Connect-AzureAd
    ```

2. Enter your credentials in the authentication window.

3. Retrieve the Azure AD Directory Settings values using this command:

```
$grpUnifiedSetting = (Get-AzureADDirectorySetting | where -Property `
DisplayName -Value "Group.Unified" -EQ)
$Setting = $grpUnifiedSetting
$grpUnifiedSetting.Values
```

Figure 6-6 shows the current Azure AD Directory Settings values.

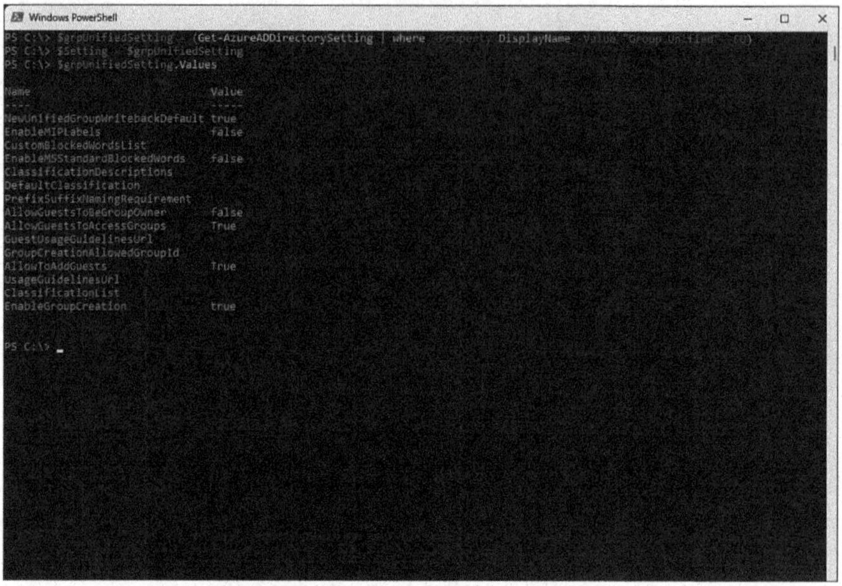

Figure 6-6   Reviewing Azure AD Directory Settings values

TIP

If no group settings have been created, you will only see a blank screen. If Group settings have been configured, review the output for the value of EnableMIPLabels. If the value is set to True, then your environment is already configured to use labels with containers.

4. Enable the feature with the following command:

```
$Setting["EnableMIPLabels"] = "True"
```

5. Save the changes:

```
Set-AzureADDirectorySetting -Id $grpUnifiedSetting.Id -DirectorySetting $Setting
```

6. Import the Exchange Online Management module:

```
Import-Module ExchangeOnlineManagement
```

7. Connect to the Security & Compliance PowerShell using the following command:

```
Connect-IPPSSession
```

8. Synchronize labels to Azure AD:

```
Execute-AzureADLabelSync
```

After the label synchronization process has been completed, you can assign labels to container objects throughout the Microsoft 365 ecosystem.

Inside Out

Microsoft 365 sovereign environments

Depending on your type of subscription, you might need to connect to an endpoint specific to a sovereign cloud. Sovereign cloud endpoints include Microsoft 365, operated by 21Vianet, Microsoft 365 Government Community Cloud (GCC) High, and Microsoft 365 GCC DoD. While Microsoft 365 GCC moderate data storage is sovereign, the Azure AD endpoints are typically the same as the Worldwide Commercial instance.

- **To connect to an environment operated by 21Vianet:**

```
Connect-IPPSSession -UserPrincipalName user@contoso.cn -ConnectionUri `
https://ps.compliance.protection.partner.outlook.cn/powershell-liveid
```

- **To connect to a Microsoft GCC High environment:**

```
Connect-IPPSSession -UserPrincipalName user@govt.us -ConnectionUri `
https://ps.compliance.protection.office365.us/powershell-liveid/ `
-AzureADAuthorizationEndpointUri https://login.microsoftonline.us/common
```

- **To connect to a Microsoft GCC DoD environment:**

```
https://15.ps.compliance.protection.office365.us/powershell-liveid/ `
-AzureADAuthorizationEndpointUri https://login.microsoftonline.us/common
```

Creating a label

In this example, you create two labels—one that will be published for users to apply manually to content they want to retain and one that will be published and automatically applied to email to be retained for a year and then deleted. To create the labels, follow these steps:

1. Navigate to the Microsoft Purview compliance center (*https://compliance.microsoft.com*) and select Information Protection.

2. Select the Labels tab.

3. Click + Create A Label.

4. Enter a name into the Name field and a description in the Description For Users field and click Next, as shown in Figure 6-7.

CHAPTER 6

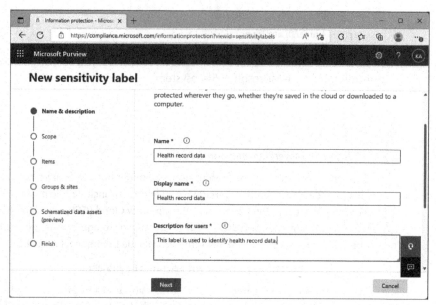

Figure 6-7   Creating a label

5.   On the Define The Scope For This Label page shown in Figure 6-8, choose the areas where you want this label to be available. By default, all options are selected. Click Next to continue.

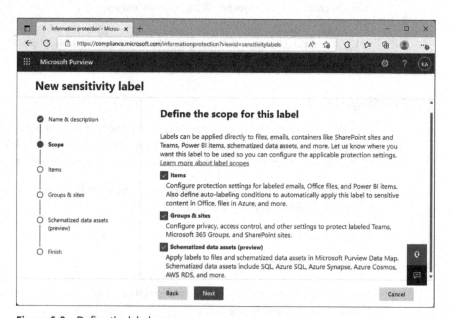

Figure 6-8   Define the label scope

6. Depending on the scope options you have selected, you will need to walk through one or more configuration branches—one for Items, one for Groups & Sites, and one for Schematized Data Assets (Preview).

7. On the Choose Protection Settings For Labeled Items page shown in Figure 6-9, select any options for the label. Click Next to proceed.

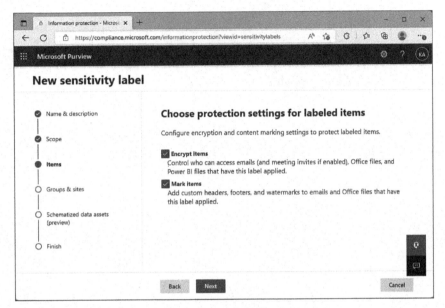

Figure 6-9   Choose protection settings for labeled items

8. If you selected the Encrypt Items checkbox, a configuration branch opens to prompt for additional input:

    ■ Choose Remove Encryption if the file or email item is already encrypted or Configure Encryption settings.

    ■ If Configure Encryption Settings is selected, additional options are available:

        ▼ **Assign Permissions Now Or Let Users Decide**   This option allows the administrator to specify the permissions set on content encrypted with this label or to leave the decision up to the individual applying the label.

        ▼ **User Access To Content Expires**   The available options include Never, On A Specific Date, and A Number Of Days After Label Is Applied.

        ▼ **Allow Offline Access**   The available options include Always, Never, and Only For A Number Of Days. If Never or Only For A Number Of Days are selected, users will need to authenticate before accessing data.

▼ **Assign Permissions**   If you choose to assign permissions as an administrator, you can specify the users, groups, and domains that can access the
data as well as what permissions they have on the Assign Permissions flyout
window.

Figure 6-10 shows the Assign Permissions flyout.

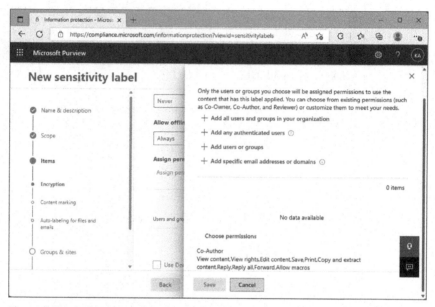

Figure 6-10   Assign Permissions flyout window

▼ **Use Double Key Encryption**   Enable the use of both Azure RMS and
another managed key solution to encrypt data.

9. If you selected Mark Items as a protection settings option, you can enable content
marking on documents and emails. Slide the Content Marking toggle to On, as shown in
Figure 6-11, and then configure settings. Click Next to continue.

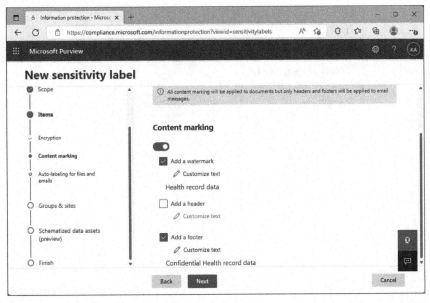

Figure 6-11   Content marking options

10. On the Auto-Labeling For Files And Emails page, slide the toggle On to enable automatic labeling. You can then select conditions under which to apply the label automatically:

   ▪ **Detect Content That Matches These Conditions**   Click Add Condition to create conditions for matching content. You can use sensitive info types or trainable classifiers as content conditions.

   ▪ **When Content Matches These Conditions**   Choose whether to apply a label automatically or simply recommend that the user applies a label.

   ▪ **Display This Message To Users When The Label Is Applied**   Enter a text message (or accept the default message) when the label is applied to content.

   Figure 6-12 shows the New Sensitivity Label wizard with the U.S. Social Security Number (SSN) sensitive information type selected as part of an auto-apply label.

11. Click Next to continue.

12. If the Groups & Sites were selected to be in-scope, you can configure Privacy And External User Access Settings and External Sharing And Conditional Access Settings, as shown in Figure 6-13.

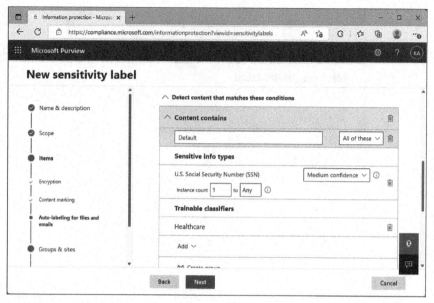

Figure 6-12 Auto-labeling configuration

13. Click Next to continue.

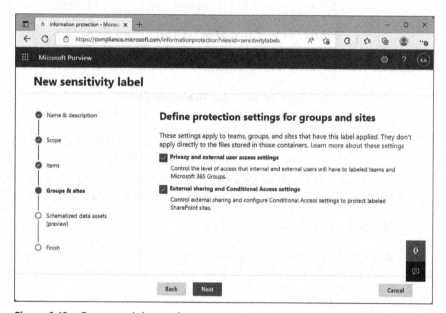

Figure 6-13 Groups and sites settings

14. If you select the Privacy & External User Access protection setting, you will prompt the configuration of a privacy setting if this label is applied to Microsoft 365 groups and teams, as shown in Figure 6-14. Available privacy options include the following:

- **Public** Anyone can access the group and team content and add members.

- **Private** Only team members and owners can access content and add members.

- **None** Team and group members can set the privacy settings themselves.

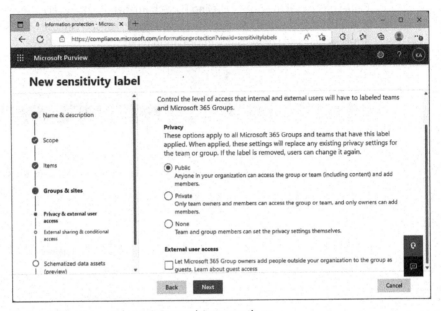

Figure 6-14 Group Privacy & External Access options

15. Under External User Access, you can select the Let Microsoft 365 Groups Owners Add People Outside Your Organization To The Group As Guests checkbox. Clearing the checkbox prevents external users from being added to the group or team.

16. Click Next to continue.

17. On the Define External Sharing And Conditional Access Settings page, you select additional options to manage access to SharePoint data. The options include the following:

- **Control External Sharing From Labeled SharePoint Sites** When selected, this option will replace the existing external sharing permissions configured for a site. The available options mirror those available in the SharePoint admin center: Anyone, New And Existing Guests, Existing Guests, and Only People In Your Organization.

- **Use Azure AD Conditional Access To Protect Labeled SharePoint Sites**   When selected, these options allow you to control access from unmanaged devices. Options include Allow Full Access From Desktop Apps, Mobile Apps, And The Web, Allow Limited, Web-Only Access, and Block Access. You can also choose from an existing authentication context if one has been configured.

18. Click Next to continue.

19. If you selected the Schematized Data Assets (Preview) scope option, as shown in Figure 6-15, you can set the Auto-Labeling For Schematized Data Assets (Preview) slider to On. If you have configured connectivity to other services, you can use Microsoft Purview to apply labels based on sensitive information types.

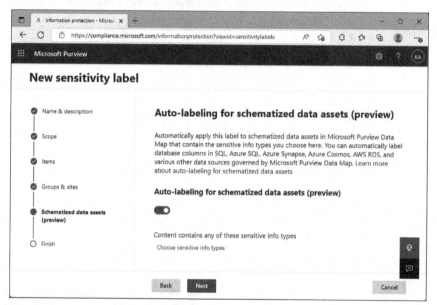

Figure 6-15   Auto-Labeling For Schematized Data Assets page

20. Click Next to continue.

21. On the Review Your Settings And Finish page, confirm the configured settings. Click Create Label.

From this point, you can continue using the wizard to create policies to auto-apply, publish labels, or create them manually. The screenshot shown in Figure 6-16 shows the possible next steps after creating the sensitivity label.

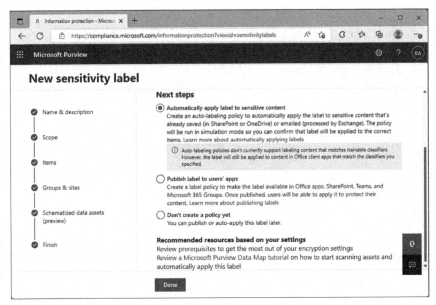

Figure 6-16   Label post-creation options

Selecting one of the action radio buttons initiates the corresponding wizard.

Publishing a label for manual application

After you've created a label, you can choose to publish it for manual application. Users can apply the labels through applications such as Outlook or the SharePoint web interface to protect content.

To publish a label, follow these steps:

1. Navigate to the Microsoft Purview compliance center (*https://compliance.microsoft.com*) and select Information Protection.

2. Select the Label Policies tab.

3. Click Publish Label, as shown in Figure 6-17.

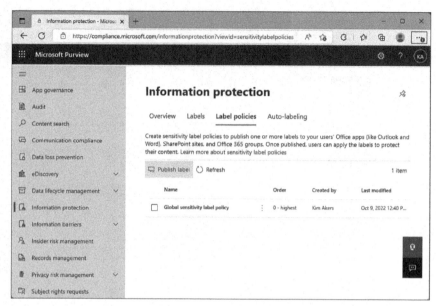

Figure 6-17   Publishing a label

4. On the Choose Sensitivity Labels To Publish page, click Choose Sensitivity Labels To Publish.

5. Search for a label to publish on the Sensitivity Labels To Publish flyout menu. Select the checkbox next to one or more labels and click Add.

6. Click Next.

7. On the Publish To Users And Groups page, you can select individual users or groups to whom you want to make the label available. The default selection includes all users.

8. Click Next to continue.

9. On the Policy Settings page shown in Figure 6-18, configure the appropriate policy settings for the label from the available options:

    - **Users Must Provide A Justification To Remove A Label Or Lower Its Classification**   Users will need to enter a justification note to remove a label or replace it with a lower priority one.

    - **Require Users To Apply A Label To Their Emails And Documents**   Require users to select and apply a label when sending messages or saving files.

    - **Require Users To Apply A Label To Their Power BI Content**   Policy setting requires users to apply a label to content they publish or edit in Power BI.

    - **Provide Users With A Link To A Custom Help Page**   Enter a URL containing instructions or policy guidance to help users make decisions about applying labels.

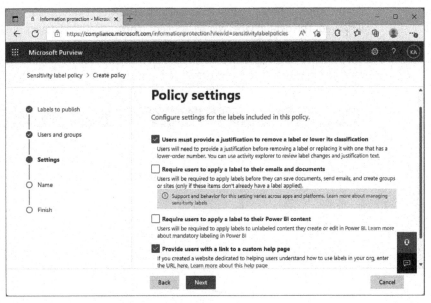

Figure 6-18   Configuring label policy settings

10. Click Next.

11. On the Apply A Default Label To Documents page shown in Figure 6-19, you can choose if you want to apply one of labels being published as a default label for in-scope users.

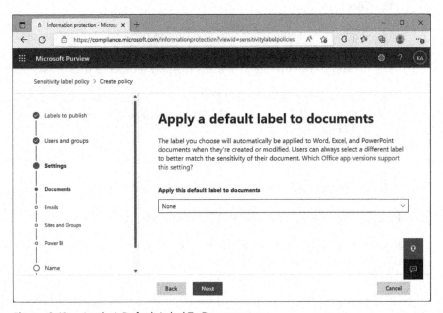

Figure 6-19   Apply A Default Label To Documents

12. On the Apply A Default Label To Emails page shown in Figure 6-20, select a default label if desired. The default label will be applied to new, unlabeled emails but can be changed before sending.

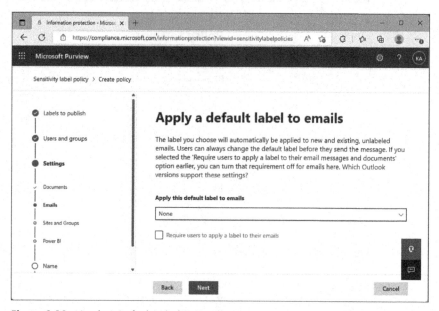

Figure 6-20   Apply A Default Label To Emails

13. Click Next.

14. On the Policy Settings For Sites And Groups page, you can select a default label to apply to sites and groups (Apply This Default Label To Emails) and turn off mandatory labeling for sites and groups (Require Users To Apply A Label To Their Emails). Click Next.

15. On the Apply A Default Label To Power BI Content page, you can select a default label to apply to Power BI reports, dashboards, and datasets. Users can change the default label if it's not the appropriate label. Click Next.

16. On the Name Your Policy page, enter a Name and Description for the policy. Click Next.

17. On the Review And Finish page, review the configured settings. When ready, click Submit.

Publishing a label for automatic application

In addition to making labels available for users to apply manually, you can also use content classification to apply labels automatically.

To configure a policy, follow these steps:

1. Navigate to the Microsoft Purview compliance center (*https://compliance.microsoft.com*) and select Information Protection.

2. Select the Auto-Labeling tab.

3. Click Create An Auto-Labeling Policy.

4. On the Choose Info You Want This Label Applied To page, you can select one of the built-in templates to identify content or create a custom template. In this example, we'll be choosing a built-in template. See Figure 6-21.

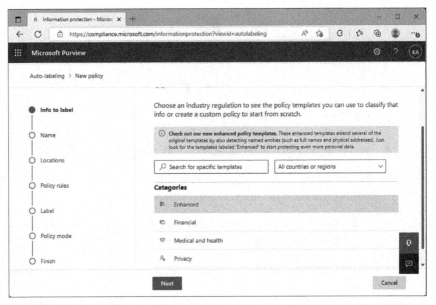

Figure 6-21   Selecting a content template

5. After selecting a template, click Next.

6. On the Name Your Auto-Labeling Policy page, enter a Name and Description and click Next.

7. On the Choose Locations Where You Want To Apply The Label page shown in Figure 6-22, select which locations you want labels automatically applied. By default, all Exchange mailboxes, all SharePoint sites, and all OneDrive accounts are selected, but you can scope it to individuals or groups of users, specific sites, and individual OneDrive accounts.

CHAPTER 6

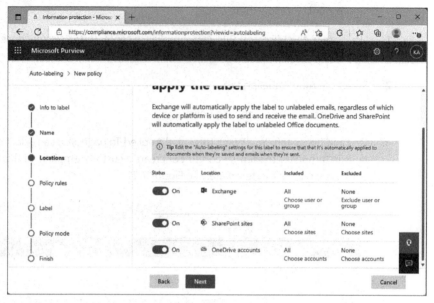

Figure 6-22   Label application locations

8. When you have made the selections, click Next.

9. On the Set Up Common Or Advanced Rules page shown in Figure 6-23, you can create custom rules using a variety of conditions, including:

    - **Email**   Content matches sensitive information types and trainable classifiers, recipients, file extensions, and text patterns.

    - **Files**   Content matches sensitive information types and trainable classifiers or is shared.

10. In this example, we'll select Common Rules.

11. Click Next.

12. On the Define Rules For Content In All Locations page, you can create additional rules for applying the labels by selecting the New Rule button. Rules created here will apply to all content (email and files).

13. When finished creating rules, click Next.

14. On the Choose A Label To Auto-Apply page shown in Figure 6-24, select a label to apply with this rule. Click Next.

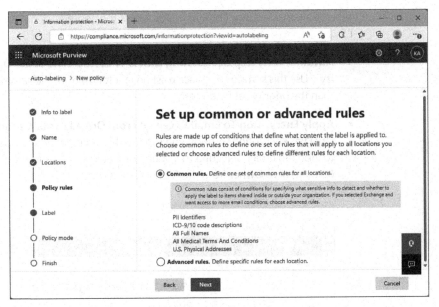

Figure 6-23   Set up common or advanced rules

15. Click Next.

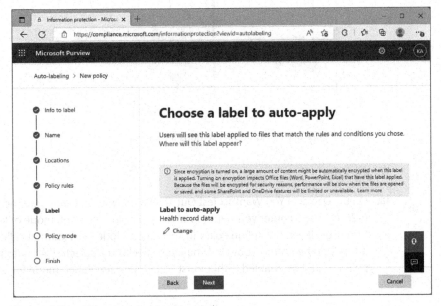

Figure 6-24   Choose a label to auto-apply

16. On the Additional Settings For Email Page, select the desired options, as shown in Figure 6-25:

   - **Automatically Replace Existing Labels That Have The Same Or Lower Priority** Use this setting to replace existing labels that have the same or lower priority than the priority set by this rule.

   - **Apply Encryption To Email Received From Outside Your Organization** If the label has encryption settings, you can use this policy setting to apply encryption to inbound email. Selecting this option will require selecting the designated Rights Management Owner from the Global Address List.

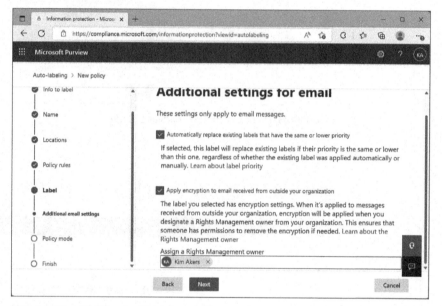

Figure 6-25 Additional settings for email

17. Click Next.

18. On the Decide If You Want To Test Out The Policy Now Or Later page shown in Figure 6-26, choose whether you want to run the policy in simulation mode or leave the policy turned off. If you select Run Policy In Simulation Mode, the Automatically Turn On Policy If Not Modified After 7 Days In Simulation checkbox is selected. An automatically applied policy cannot be enabled without first completing simulation mode for seven days.

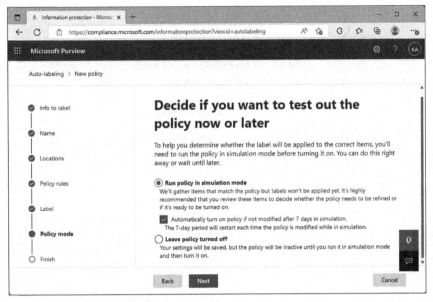

Figure 6-26   Policy mode page

19. Click Next.

20. On the Review And Finish page, examine the policy settings configured and click Create Policy.

21. Click Done after the policy has been created.

After labels have been published and started being used throughout your organization, you can begin tracking their usage through the Data Classification section of the Microsoft Purview compliance manager.

Retention labels

Like sensitivity labels, retention labels can be used to help manage data. Where sensitivity labels are used to manage data classification and protection, retention labels are used to manage the data lifecycle.

The process for creating and publishing retention labels is very similar to that of sensitivity labels.

Creating a label

To create a retention label, follow these steps:

1. Navigate to the Microsoft Purview compliance center (*https://compliance.microsoft.com*), expand Data Lifecycle Management, and then click Microsoft 365.

2. Select the Labels tab and click Create A Label.

3. On the Name Your Retention Label page, enter a Name and a Description for the retention label.

4. Click Next.

5. On the Define Label Settings page, choose an appropriate setting for your usage. The available options are Retain Items Forever Or For A Specific Period, Enforce Actions After A Specific Period, or Just Label Items.

6. Click Next.

If you choose Retain Items Forever Or For A Specific Period, select a value for Retain Items For. The default values are 5 Years, 7 Years, 10 Years, and Forever, or you can set a different value by selecting Custom.

- If you select a time period besides Forever in the Start The Retention Period Based On dropdown, select from the following options:

    - When Items Were Created

    - When Items Were Last Modified

    - When Items Were Labeled

    - Employee Activity (Event Type)

    - Expiration Or Termination Of Contracts And Agreements (Event Types)

    - Product Lifetime (Event Type).

- You can also select Create New Event Type for event-driven retention policies. Click Next.

- On the Choose What Happens After The Retention Period page, the following options are available. (Click Next when you are finished.)

    - **Delete Items Automatically**   Items will be deleted automatically at the end of the retention period with no further notification.

- **Start A Disposition Review**   Select the users to receive the disposition review notice.

- **Change The Label**   You'll need to specify a replacement label.

- **Deactivate Retention Settings**   The label will be removed, and the content will return to an unlabeled and unmanaged state.

- If you choose Enforce Actions After A Specified Period, set the following options:

  - **How Long Is The Period**   The default values are 5 Years, 7 Years, and 10 Years. You can set a different value by selecting Custom.

  - **When Should The Period Begin?**   Select When Items Were Created, When Items Were Last Modified, or When Items Were Created.

- After clicking Next, on the Choose What Happens After The Period page, choose a disposition for the labeled items. The available options are Delete Items Automatically and Change The Label:

  - **Delete Items Automatically**   Items will be deleted automatically.

  - **Change The Label**   You'll need to specify a replacement label. Click Next to continue.

  - If you select Just Label Items, there are no additional settings to configure. The label functions like a sensitivity label with no protection actions. Click Next.

7. On the Review And Finish page, review the configured values and click Create Label.

From this point, you can continue using the wizard to create policies to auto-apply or publish labels or create them manually.

Adaptive scopes

Adaptive scopes present a new way to dynamically select users and content for retention labels and retention policies. You can configure an adaptive scope from the Adaptive scopes tab on the Data lifecycle management page.

To create an adaptive scope, use the following steps:

1. Navigate to the Microsoft Purview compliance portal (*https://compliance.microsoft.com*), select Data Lifecycle Management, and then select Adaptive Scopes.

2. Click Create Scope.

3. On the Name Your Adaptive Policy Scope page, enter a Name and a Description for the scope.

CHAPTER 6

4.   On the What Type Of Scope Do You Want To Create? page shown in Figure 6-27, select
the scope and click Next.

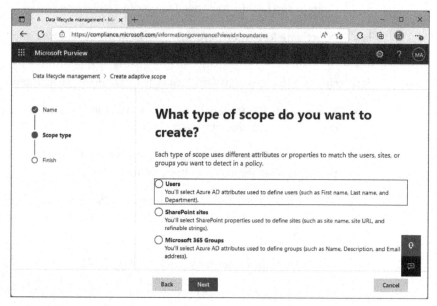

Figure 6-27   Adaptive scope selection

- If you select Users, you can configure a search of users based on attributes, as
  shown in Figure 6-28. Add additional query attributes as desired. Click Next.

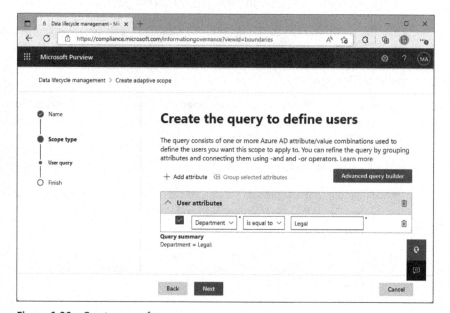

Figure 6-28   Create query for users

- If you select SharePoint Sites, you can add properties such as Site Name and Site URL for searching and selecting sites. Click Next.

- If you select Microsoft 365 Groups, you can add attributes for searching and selecting Microsoft 365 groups (and their members). Click Next.

5. On the Review And Finish page, click Submit.

Configure as many adaptive scopes as necessary to select groups of users or sites. Adaptive scopes are not subject to the per-user and per-site limitations when adding users or sites to retention policies.

Publishing a label for manual application

After you've created a label, you can choose to publish it for manual application. Users can apply the labels through applications such as Outlook or the SharePoint web interface to protect content.

To publish a label, follow these steps:

1. Navigate to the Microsoft Purview compliance center (*https://compliance.microsoft.com*), expand Data Lifecycle Management, and then select Microsoft 365.

2. Select the Label Policies tab.

3. Click Publish Labels.

4. On the Choose Labels To Publish page, click Choose Labels To Publish.

5. On the Choose A Label flyout menu, select the labels to publish and click Add.

6. Click Next.

7. On the Choose The Type Of Retention Policy To Create page, select Adaptive or Static. Adaptive scopes are a new feature that can use attributes to dynamically select Users, SharePoint sites, and Microsoft 365 Groups. Static scopes are explicitly defined users and sites:

   - **Adaptive** If you select Adaptive, click Add Scopes to add a pre-defined adaptive scope. Under Choose Locations To Apply The Policy, select the locations where you want to select data. Click Next.

   - **Static** If you select Static, select the users, groups, sites, and OneDrive accounts where you want to apply the label. Click Next.

8. On the Name Your Policy page, enter a Name and Description. Click Next when finished.

CHAPTER 6

9. On the Finish page, click Submit.

10. Click Done after the label is published.

After the label is published, it can be applied by users to content in the available locations.

Publishing a label for automatic application

Label policies can automatically assign labels and specify actions (such as retain or delete).

On the Label Policies tab of the Data Lifecycle Management page shown in Figure 6-29, you can choose to publish or auto-apply labels you've already created.

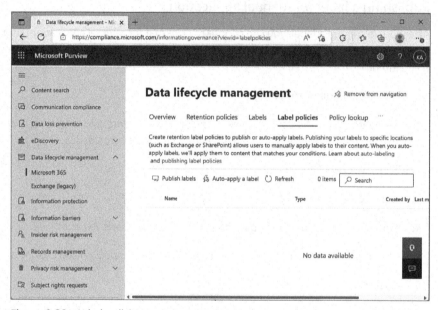

Figure 6-29   Label policies

To auto-apply a label, follow these steps:

1. Navigate to the Microsoft Purview compliance center (*https://compliance.microsoft.com*), expand Data Lifecycle Management, and then select Microsoft 365.

2. Select the Label Policies tab.

3. Click Auto-Apply A Label.

4. On the Let's Get Started tab, enter a Name and a Description. Click Next.

5. On the Choose The Type Of Content You Want To Apply This Label To, select from the following options:

- **Apply Label To Content That Contains Sensitive Info**   If you select this option, choose a sensitive info template and click Next. Configure the template matching requirements and click Next.

- **Apply Label To Content That Contains Specific Words, Phrases, Or Properties**   Enter words or phrases to select content and click Next.

- **Apply Label To Content That Matches A Trainable Classifier**   If you select this option, choose one or more trainable classifiers from the list and click Next.

- **Apply Label To Cloud Attachments Shared In Exchange And Teams**   If you select this option, there are no additional selections to make. Click Next.

6. On the **Choose The Type Of Retention Policy To Create** page, select Adaptive or Static. Adaptive scopes are a new feature that can use attributes to dynamically select Users, SharePoint sites, and Microsoft 365 Groups. Static scopes are explicitly defined users and sites:

- **Adaptive**   If you select Adaptive, click Add Scopes to add a pre-defined adaptive scope. Under Choose Locations To Apply The Policy, select the locations where you want to select data. Click Next.

- **Static**   If you select Static, select the users, groups, sites, and OneDrive accounts where you want to apply the label. Click Next.

7. On the Choose A Label To Auto-Apply page, click Add Label and select a label to apply. Click Next.

8. Click Submit.

Retention labels will be automatically applied based on the settings configured in the auto-apply label policy.

Retention policies

Where retention labels are used to identify specific content to retain (either manually or based on rules configured in a labeling policy), retention policies are used to broadly apply retention across workloads.

CHAPTER 6

To configure a retention policy, follow these steps:

1. Navigate to the Microsoft Purview compliance center (*https://compliance.microsoft.com*), Data Lifecycle Management, and then select Microsoft 365.

2. Select the Retention Policies tab.

3. Click New Retention Policy.

4. On the Name Your Retention Policy page, enter a Name and a Description. Click Next.

5. On the Choose The Type Of Retention Policy To Create page, select Adaptive or Static. Adaptive scopes are a new feature that can use attributes to dynamically select Users, SharePoint sites, and Microsoft 365 Groups. Static scopes are explicity defined users and sites:

   - If you select Adaptive, click Add Scopes to add a pre-defined adaptive scope. Under Choose Locations To Apply The Policy, select the locations where you want to select data. Click Next.

   - If you select Static, select the locations where you retain data: users' mailboxes, groups, sites, and OneDrive accounts; Microsoft 365 groups; Skype for Business users; Exchange public folders; Teams channel messages; Teams chats; Teams private channel messages; Yammer community messages; or Yammer user messages. Click Next.

TIP

Teams private channel messages cannot be included with any other workload or data sources. Teams chats and channel messages might be selected together but cannot be included in retention policies that include other workloads or data sources. If you want to protect all data in a tenant with retention policies, you must create a minimum of three retention policies.

6. On the Decide If You Want To Retain Content, Delete It, Or Both page, select retention options. See Figure 6-30.

7. On the Review And Finish page, review the settings and click Submit.

Retention policies will be enabled for the data and workload sources in-scope.

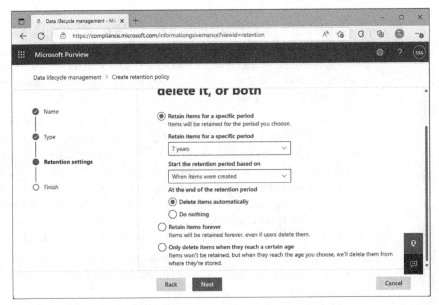

Figure 6-30   Retention settings

Inside Out

Understanding retention precedence

Content can have a number of retention policies or labels applied to it, each with different criteria, actions, and retention periods. In the case of multiple policies, what happens to your data? This figure shows the precedence of policy application.

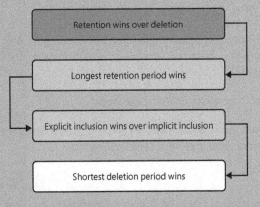

- **Retention wins over deletion**   For example, Retention Policy 1 retains email for 1 year and then deletes it, and Retention Policy 2 retains email for 5 years and then deletes it. After 1 year, the email would be deleted and hidden from the user's view (Retention Policy 1) but retained in the Recoverable Items folder until the content reaches 5 years old (Policy 2).

- **Longest retention period wins**   If content is subject to multiple policies with retention actions, the content is retained for the longest period. In the previous example, Retention Policy 1 deleted email after 1 year, but the Retention Policy 2 action was to retain for 5 years. Policy 2 has the longest retention period, so the content will be retained for 5 years.

- **Explicit inclusion wins over implicit inclusion**   If User 1 applies Label 1 with a retention action of 10 years, but the configuration of Retention Policy 2 is to delete after 5 years, the content will be retained for 10 years as long as the user manually applies Label 1 before the message has been permanently deleted. Labels that are applied by policy are considered implicit. Explicit is also conferred in the concept of specificity, meaning that if Retention Policy 1 retains content in all mailboxes for 1 year, but Retention Policy 2 specifically retains content in User 1's mailbox for 5 years, the content in User 1's mailbox will be retained for 5 years.

- **Shortest deletion period wins**   If content is subject to multiple policies that delete content (with no retention), it will be deleted at the end of the shortest retention period.

Data loss prevention policies

Data loss prevention policies can be used to notify users of potential data leakage as well as protect data as it attempts to be emailed or shared.

In addition to creating DLP policies from scratch, you can also create DLP policies using templates as a technique called *document fingerprinting*.

Template-based content policy

The first step in creating a DLP policy is determining the type of content to protect. Microsoft 365 includes a number of templates (based on sensitive information types) that can be used to give your policy a starting point.

To create a policy from a built-in template, follow these steps:

1. Navigate to the Microsoft Purview compliance center (*https://compliance.microsoft.com*), select Data Loss Prevention, and then select the Policies tab.

2. Click Create Policy.

3. Select a policy category, such as Financial, shown in Figure 6-31, and click Next.

4. Select a policy template and click Next.

5. Confirm your selection and click Next.

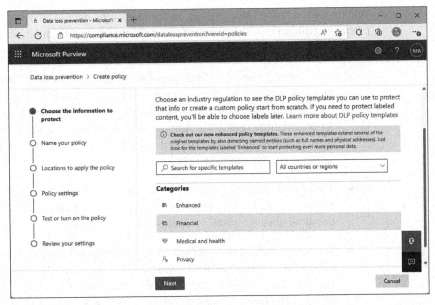

Figure 6-31   DLP policy creation

6. On the Name Your Policy page, enter a name for the policy.

7. Type a name and description for the policy and click Next.

8. Select the locations and workloads you want to protect on the Locations To Apply The Policy page shown in Figure 6-32. Click Next when finished.

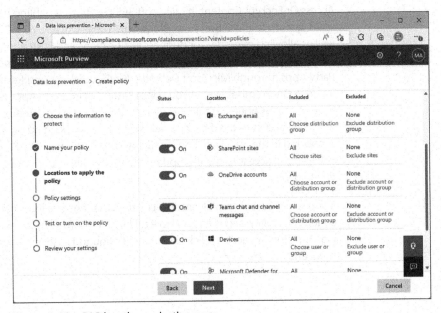

Figure 6-32   DLP locations selection page

9. On the Define Policy Settings page, you can select the default Review And Customize Default Settings From The Template or the Create Or Customize Advanced DLP Rules option:

- If you select Review And Customize Default Settings From The Template, you will be presented with an additional branch of confirmation options. Click Next to proceed through each sub-page. For this exercise, we'll just accept the defaults, but it's important to review the options (there are different options depending on your subscription level, connected third-party applications, protected workloads, and sensitive info type template choices).

- The first sub-page presented is the Info To Protect page, which displays the sensitive information types included with the template. You can click Edit to add additional sensitive information types or Next to continue.

- The second sub-page presented is the Protection Actions page, which displays the options Microsoft 365 will take when content matching the sensitive information types has been detected. Configure the following checkbox options: When Content Matches The Policy Conditions, Show Policy Tips To Users And Send Them An Email Notification, and Detect When A Specific Amount Of Sensitive Info Is Being Shared At One Time. If you choose to detect a specific amount of sensitive info being shared, you can select additional options: Send Incident Reports In Email, Send Alerts If Any Of The DLP Rules Match, and Restrict Access Or Encrypt The Content In Microsoft 365 Locations.

- The third subpage, Customize Access And Override Settings, provides controls for managing access to content that the DLP policy has identified. You can Restrict Access Or Encrypt Content In Microsoft 365 Locations (enabling this selection provides options to Block Everyone, Block Only Those Outside Your Organization, as well as allowing overrides for business justifications and false positives), Audit Or Restrict Activities On Devices Where Sensitive Content Is Discovered, Restrict Third Party Apps (through Microsoft Defender for Cloud apps), and Restrict Access Or Remove On-Premises Files. If you select Restrict Third Party Apps, you can invoke actions such as notifying the file owner that the content is attempting to be shared, removing access to the data, and deleting the file, depending on what features are supported in the app. Selecting Restrict Access Or Remove On-Premises Files allows you to block access to the file, update the file permissions, or move it to a quarantine folder.

- If you select Customize Advanced DLP Rules, the sensitive information types are added to a policy, and then you have to create custom rules for notification, blocking, or restricting access. Click Next after configuring custom conditions, exceptions, and actions.

10. Select how to deploy the policy on the Test Or Turn On The Policy page, as shown in Figure 6-33.

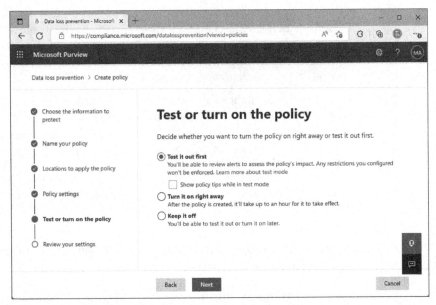

Figure 6-33   Template deployment options

11. Click Next.

12. Click Submit.

Inside Out

Policy application modes

If you're creating DLP policies with a large potential impact, consider rolling out the policy gradually:

- **Configure the policy in test mode, but leave the Show Policy Tips While In Test Mode checkbox clear**   Use the DLP reports to assess the impact. You can use DLP reports to view policy matches' number, location, type, and severity. You can use the reports to tune the queries and policies. In test mode, users will be unaware that DLP policies are scanning their activities. DLP policies will not affect the productivity of people working in your organization. To enable this mode, select the I'd Like To Test It Out First button when configuring the policy.

- **Show Policy Tips While In Test Mode**   After configuring the policy to your lik-
  ing, you can edit the policy and enable Policy Tips. With Policy Tips enabled, users
  are notified while accessing data that matches the policy. At this stage, you can
  also ask users to report false positives so that you can refine the rules further,
  such as by excluding document libraries, users, or recipients of data. To enable
  Policy Tips, edit the policy, click Edit in the Status section, and then select the
  Show Policy Tips While In Test Mode button.

- **Yes, Turn It On Right Away**   After you are confident about the configuration,
  you can begin full enforcement of the policies so that the actions in the rules are
  applied. To enable the policy fully, edit the policy, click Edit in the Status section,
  and then select the Yes, Turn It On Right Away button.

You can turn off a policy at any time. If your policy has multiple rules, you can also disable individual rules if they adversely affect your organization.

DLP activity can then be monitored on the Data Loss Prevention Overview and Activity Explorer
pages in the Microsoft Purview compliance center.

Using document fingerprinting

Document fingerprinting examines a template file and determines if the content being processed matches the document template. It does have limitations, however, such as the inability
to recognize files that are only images, password-protected files, and files that are larger than
10MB.

Document fingerprinting relies on a classification rule package that contains the template document to be matched against. This essentially creates a new sensitive information type that can
be used when creating a custom DLP policy.

To create a document fingerprint, follow these steps:

1. Obtain a copy of the template file and store it in a location on your local PC. The
    document template should have only the form fields that will be matched and should not
    be filled out with sample content.

2. Connect to the PowerShell endpoint for the Microsoft Purview compliance center.

3. Connect-IPPSSession

4. Read the template file from the local disk and store it as a variable:

    ```
    $Template = ([System.IO.File]::ReadAllBytes('C:\Forms\beneficiary.pdf'))
    ```

5. Create a new DLP fingerprint based on the data stored in `$Template`:

```
$TemplateFingerprint = New-DlpFingerprint -FileData $Template -Description `
"Beneficiary Designation Form"
```

6. Finally, create a sensitive information type that contains the data of the fingerprint.

```
New-DlpSensitiveInformationType -Name "Beneficiary Form" -Fingerprints `
$TemplateFingerprint -Description "Message contains a beneficiary `
designation form."
```

After the sensitive information type has been created, you can review it on the Data classification page, as shown in Figure 6-34.

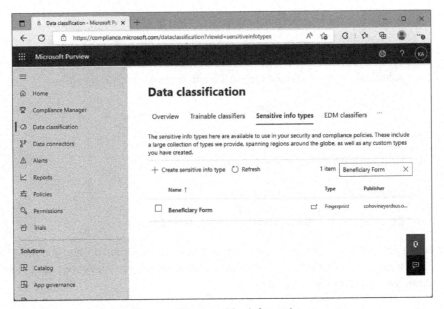

Figure 6-34   Document fingerprinting sensitive information type

The document fingerprint-sensitive information type can be added to either an existing DLP policy or a new custom policy.

Records search

You can perform Content, Audit Log, and eDiscovery searches across all Microsoft 365 services from the Solutions area in the Microsoft Purview compliance portal.

> ## NOTE
>
> Microsoft removed the ability to create in-place eDiscovery searches and holds in the Exchange admin center on July 1, 2017. However, existing cases can still be viewed. Microsoft recommends you recreate searches and holds in the Microsoft Purview compliance center.

In this section, we'll look at conducting searches for audit log data as well as other types of data across Microsoft 365.

Audit log search

The Audit log search enables you to search for user- and administrator-audited events. The Microsoft Purview compliance center presents a unified audit log, so you can search the following types of user and admin activity:

- User activity in SharePoint Online and OneDrive for Business

- User activity in Exchange Online (Exchange mailbox audit logging must be enabled)

- Admin activity in SharePoint Online

- Admin activity in Azure Active Directory

- Admin activity in Exchange Online (Exchange admin audit logging)

- User and admin activity in Sway

- User and admin activity in Power BI for Office 365

- User and admin activity in Microsoft Teams

- User and admin activity in Yammer

- User and admin activity in content search and eDiscovery

Before you can search the audit log, audit logging must be turned on, and you must be a member of a role group that includes either View-Only Audit Logs or Audit Logs roles. Figure 6-35 shows the Audit Log Search page.

Performing a search simply requires selecting the types of activities to view (under the Activities dropdown) and a date range. To refine results further, you can specify users or part of a file name, folder name, or URL. The audit log can be searched for as far back as 90 days (for E3 subscriptions) or 365 days (for E5 subscriptions).

Searches are executed in the background. When the results are ready, you can click on the search to review the data.

After you have performed the search, you can filter and refine the results further by clicking the Filter button, as shown in Figure 6-36.

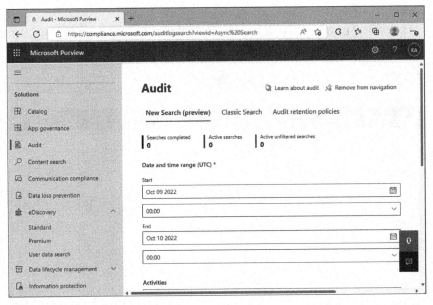

Figure 6-35 Audit Log Search page

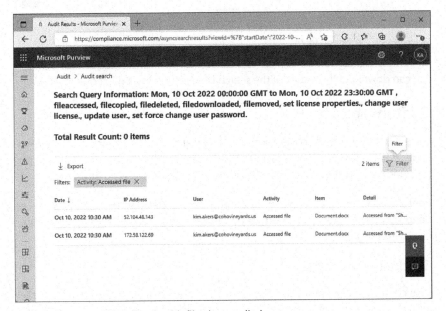

Figure 6-36 Audit log search with filtering applied

After clicking the Filter button, you can add from the IP address, User, Activity, and Detail areas. For example, if you want to filter by activities that accessed files, type Accessed in the activity field, select the appropriate filters, and click Apply, as shown in Figure 6-37.

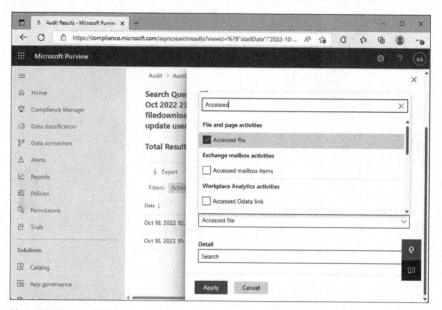

Figure 6-37 Audit log filter

You can download the results of the search by selecting the Export button.

Content search

Use content search to discover content in email and documents stored in SharePoint or One-Drive, Teams conversations, Microsoft 365 groups, and more. Search results can be previewed, exported for download, and delivered as documents, files, and email archives.

Content search and eDiscovery both use the same underlying technology with the same search options available. The terminology and search operators are interchangeable, though the interfaces differ slightly.

Conducting a search

Both content search and eDiscovery share the same goal: finding responsive content (the legal term for content that matches your search criteria). When searching, you can construct a query to help narrow down the scope of the search to return the most responsive results.

The building blocks of a search are condition cards. These are essentially categories of parameters that you can use to scope and refine your search. Condition cards include keywords, message types, date ranges, document authors, and various groupings of senders and recipients.

Access content search by navigating to Content Search in the Microsoft Purview compliance center. Figure 6-38 depicts the Content Search page.

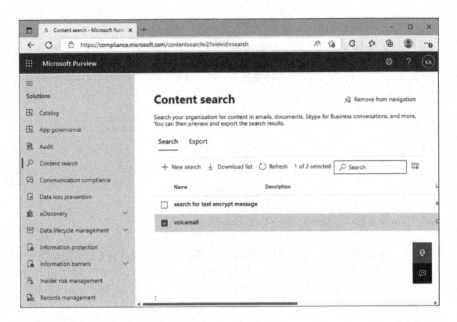

Figure 6-38   Content Search

To perform a search, follow these steps:

1. Navigate to the Microsoft Purview compliance center (*https://compliance.microsoft.com*) and select Content Search.

2. On the Content Search page, click New Search.

3. On the Name And Description page, enter a Name and Description for the search. Click Next.

4. On the Locations page, select locations to search, as shown in Figure 6-39. You can select workload-wide or narrow the search by choosing individual users, groups, teams, and sites.

5. You can search mailboxes, sites, and public folders in the same search. You can choose to search all content locations or specify a custom set based on the requirements of the search.

6. Click Next.

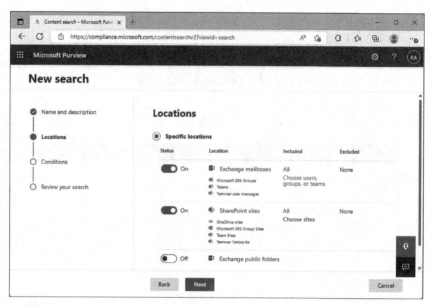

Figure 6-39   Content search locations

7. On the Define Your Search Conditions page, select either the Condition Card Builder or the KQL Editor radio button. By default, the Condition Card Builder radio button is selected, and the Keywords condition card has been added. See Figure 6-40.

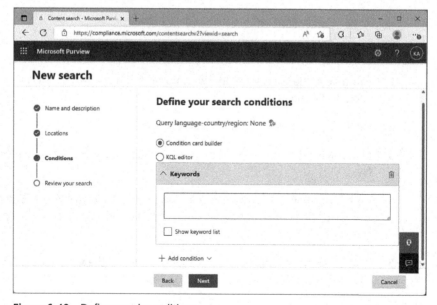

Figure 6-40   Define search conditions

8. Add keywords to the Keywords condition card. You can also select Add Condition button and select additional search criteria, as shown in Figure 6-41.

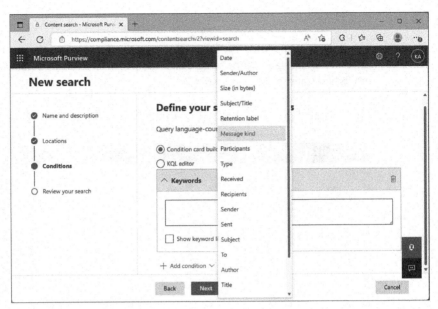

Figure 6-41 Adding conditions

9. After you've added the conditions, click Next.

10. On the Review Your Search page, verify your search settings and click Submit, as shown in Figure 6-42.

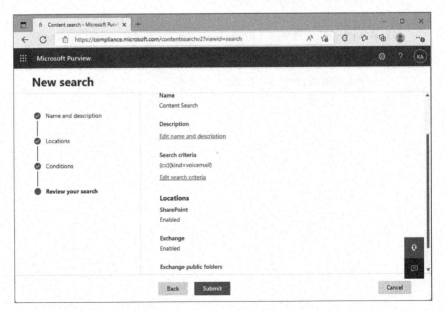

Figure 6-42 Review your search

11. Click Done.

12. After submitting a search, you'll be returned to the Content Search main page, where you can monitor the status of the search. Click the search to reveal its details, including any results and statistics. See Figure 6-43.

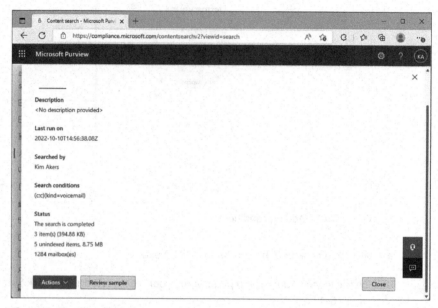

Figure 6-43   Search results

13. You can select Review Sample to review some of the items returned.

14. The Samples page in Figure 6-44 shows a limited list of responsive items. Clicking an item allows you to preview it or download it.

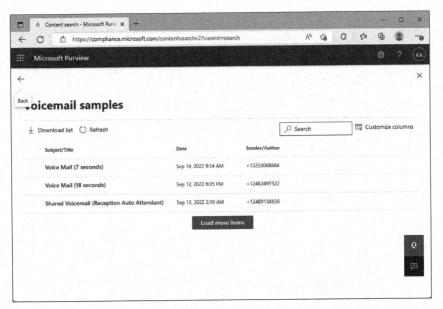

Figure 6-44   Reviewing search samples

Exporting and downloading results

After completing a search and reviewing the results, you can then prepare to download the content. Preparing content for download is a two-step process, requiring you to export the content first. Export is the Microsoft 365 term describing the process of gathering the search results and staging them in an Azure blob for download.

To export and download results, follow these steps:

1. On the Content Search page, select a search.

2. On the Summary tab, click Actions and select Export Results, as shown in Figure 6-45.

3. On the Export Results flyout window, select the options that best meet your needs, as shown in Figure 6-46.

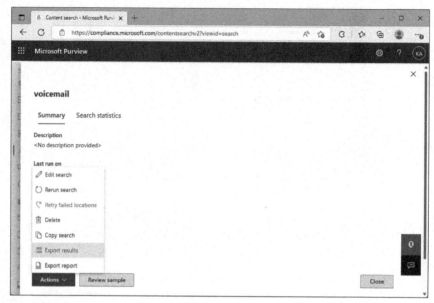

Figure 6-45 Export Results

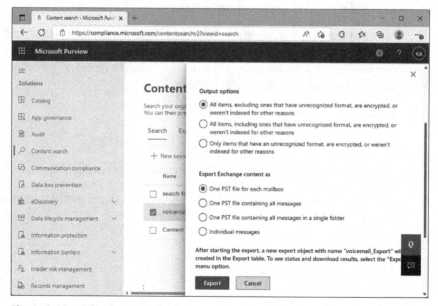

Figure 6-46 Select export options

4. Under Output Options, select an option. Depending on the search results, you might want to run multiple export jobs to group the content accordingly. Encrypted, unindexed, or partially-indexed content might or might not be responsive to your query, so it's generally best to export and download it separately from the known responsive results.

5. If you have Exchange content as part of your responsive data set, under Export Exchange Content As, select how to organize the content. The individuals requesting content might prefer one PST per mailbox, all messages contained in a single PST, or individual responsive email messages. You can also select the Enable De-Duplication For Exchange Content checkbox to reduce the amount of data downloaded if messages are detected in multiple folders in a mailbox.

6. If you have SharePoint content as part of your responsive data set, you can select the Include Versions For SharePoint Files To Include File Versions checkbox.

7. Choose whether to select the Export Files In A Compressed (Zipped) Folder checkbox.

8. Click Export.

NOTE

If you are not a member of a role group that contains the Export role, you won't be able to export results, and an error will appear. If you are a member of the Organization Management role group or Global Admins, you can add yourself as a member of the Export role, sign out of the Microsoft Purview compliance center, sign back in, and retry the export.

9. Click OK to acknowledge the export dialog box.

10. On the Content Search page, select the Export tab.

11. Select the export corresponding to the search you conducted earlier.

12. Scroll the page until you reach the Export Key section. Copy the export key to your clipboard.

13. Scroll back up to the top of the page and click Download Results, as shown in Figure 6-47.

CHAPTER 6

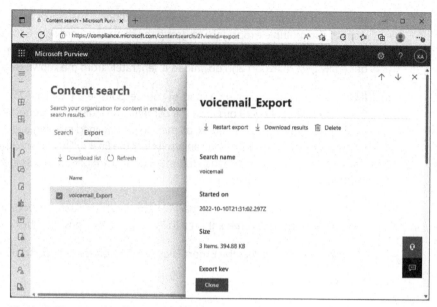

Figure 6-47   Downloading export results

14. A new browser tab will launch, prompting you to open a file if desired. Confirm that the file comes from `complianceclientsdf.bloc.core.windows.net` and click Open, as shown in Figure 6-48.

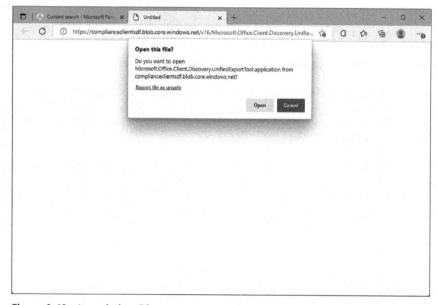

Figure 6-48   Launch the eDiscovery export tool app

15. Click Install to install the eDiscovery Export Tool app.

NOTE

The eDiscovery Export Tool application requires the Microsoft Edge browser to run. It will not run with Firefox or Chrome.

16. Paste the export key from your clipboard into the Paste The Export Key That Will Be Used To Connect To The Source field, as shown in Figure 6-49, and then enter a path where the download will be saved. Click Start.

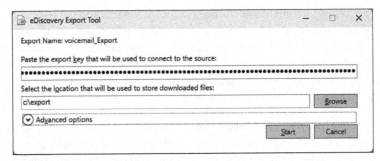

Figure 6-49   eDiscovery Export Tool

17. Wait while the download completes, as shown in Figure 6-50.

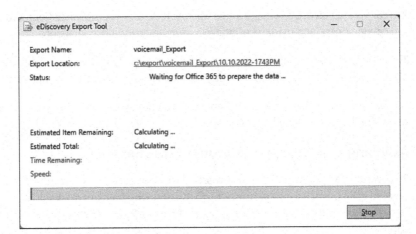

Figure 6-50   eDiscovery Export Tool download

18. After the files have been downloaded, navigate to the path specified in the export location.

The files are saved in a subdirectory named for the search specified. A separate subdirectory is created for exports from each service.

eDiscovery

Content search and eDiscovery share many things, including query structure and user interface components.

There are also some significant differences, including the concept of case management and content holds.

When performing a content search, the details of the search and the results are available to anyone who has been granted the Compliance Search role. This might be trivial for issues like Freedom of Information Act (FOIA) requests or other broad, general information queries. However, some searches (such as those pertaining to legal matters, personally identifiable information, or personnel issues) might require more privacy during the investigative period. That's where an eDiscovery case comes in.

An eDiscovery case is a logical object that acts a container for searches. Only people who have been granted specific access to the case (as well as those with the eDiscovery Administrator role) can see information about the case. This way, you can protect the privacy of the data owners (custodians, in eDiscovery terminology) and limit the organization's exposure.

Case management

You can use the eDiscovery page in the Microsoft Purview Compliance Center to control who can create, access, and manage eDiscovery searches in your organization.

The eDiscovery page enables users with the eDiscovery Manager role to create and manage eDiscovery cases. Users with the Reviewer role can review cases that they are assigned to.

You can also export the results of the content searches associated with a case or prepare search results for analysis in Advanced eDiscovery.

Assigning eDiscovery permissions to case members

Before users can perform eDiscovery searches, review cases, or export results, they must be granted eDiscovery-related permissions. Only users who have membership in an eDiscovery-related role group or a custom role group that has the Reviewer role can be added to an eDiscovery case.

You must be a member of the Organization Management role group (or be assigned the Role Management role) in the Microsoft Purview compliance center to assign eDiscovery permissions.

To grant eDiscovery manager permissions (which, in turn, grants the ability to create and manage cases), follow these steps:

1. Navigate to the Microsoft Purview compliance portal (*https://compliance.microsoft.com*) and select Permissions from the navigation menu.

2. Under Microsoft Purview Solutions, select Roles.

3. Select eDiscovery Manager.

4. On the eDiscovery Manager flyout window, under eDiscovery Manager, click Edit (see Figure 6-51).

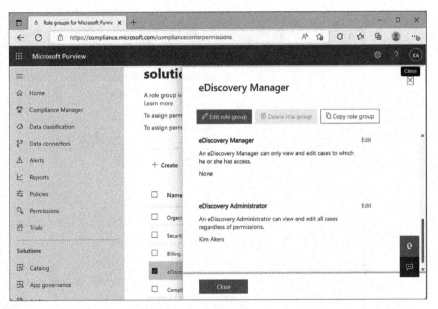

Figure 6-51   eDiscovery Manager flyout window

5. Click Choose eDiscovery Manager.

6. Click Add.

7. On the Choose eDiscovery Manager page, select all the users to whom you wish to grant the eDiscovery Manager role and click Add.

8. Click Done.

9. On the Editing Choose eDiscovery Manager page, click Save.

10. Click Close to close the eDiscovery Manager role group flyout window.

Any users added to the eDiscovery Manager role group (or any other role group) who are currently logged into any Microsoft 365 services must sign out and sign back in for the new permissions to take effect.

Creating a case and adding members

To create a case, you must be a member of the eDiscovery Managers role or role subgroup:

1. From the Microsoft Purview compliance center, expand eDiscovery and select Standard.

2. Click Create A Case, as shown in Figure 6-52.

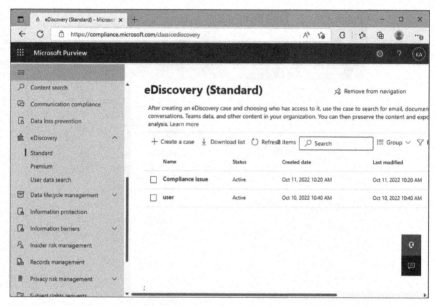

Figure 6-52   eDiscovery case management

3. In the New Case flyout window, give the case a unique name and a description. Click Save.

4. After the case has been created, click the case to open it.

5. Click the Settings tab shown in Figure 6-53 to edit the properties of the case.

6. Under Access & Permissions, click Select to add additional members to the case.

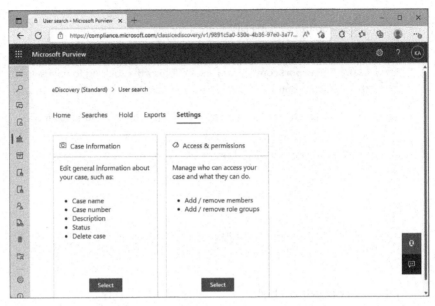

Figure 6-53   eDiscovery case settings

7. Under Manage Members, click Add to add users to the case.

8. On the Add Members flyout window, select the users and click Add.

9. Under Manage Role Groups, click Add to add members of specific role groups to the case.

10. On the Add Role Groups flyout window, select the role groups and click Add.

11. When finished, click Exit to go back to the case settings page.

After users have been added to the case, they can navigate to the Microsoft Purview compliance portal and see the cases to which they are assigned.

Inside Out

Limiting the search scope for eDiscovery managers

There might be instances when you don't want users with the eDiscovery manager role to search organization-wide. For example, suppose your organization has multiple business units. In that case, you might need to restrict the ability of eDiscovery users in each organization to search mailboxes, SharePoint Online, or OneDrive for Business sites in their own business unit.

You can do this with the New-ComplianceSecurityFilter cmdlet.

Suppose you need to restrict the eDiscovery manager Kim Akers so that she can only search and export content for user mailboxes that belong to members of the Marketing distribution group and content located in the Marketing SharePoint site.

You could create a compliance security filter similar to the following:

```
$DG = Get-DistributionGroup "Marketing"
New-ComplianceSecurityFilter -FilterName Marketing -Users `
Kim.Akers@cohovineyards.us -Filters "Site_Site -eq `
'https://cohovineyards.sharepoint.com/sites/Marketing' -and `
Mailbox_MemberOfGroup -eq '$($DG.DistinguishedName)'" `
-Action All
```

For more information, see *https://aka.ms/newcompsecfilter*.

Placing content on hold

You can use an eDiscovery case to create holds to preserve content that might be relevant to proceedings such as a legal inquiry. You can place holds on mailboxes and OneDrive for Business sites for users, Microsoft 365 Group mailboxes, or SharePoint sites (standalone) and sites connected to Yammer networks, teams, and Microsoft 365 Groups. The content is preserved until you remove the hold from the content location or the case is closed.

When creating a hold, you can control the held content's retention within a date range (sent, received, or created), an indefinite hold for all content in a site or mailbox, or a query-based hold that only retains content matching the query terms.

To create a hold, follow these steps:

1. From the Microsoft Purview compliance center, expand eDiscovery and select Standard.

2. Create a new case or select an existing case from the list.

3. Select the Hold tab. See Figure 6-54.

4. On the Hold tab, click Create to launch the New Hold wizard.

5. On the Name Your Hold page, enter a unique name. Click Next.

6. On the Choose Locations page shown in Figure 6-55, use the sliders to toggle on locations where you wish to place a hold. Options include Exchange Mailboxes, SharePoint Sites, and Exchange Public Folders.

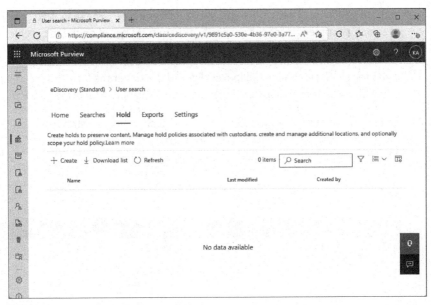

Figure 6-54   eDiscovery case Hold tab

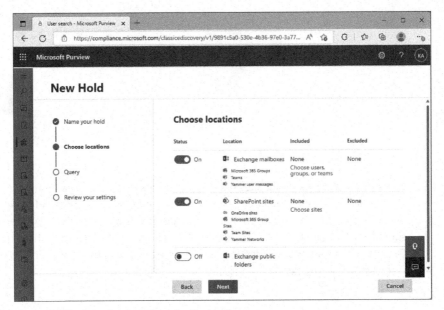

Figure 6-55   Selecting locations for the hold

You can search mailboxes, sites, and public folders in the same search. You can choose to search all content locations or specify a custom set based on the requirements of the search.

7. If you toggle the Exchange Mailboxes slider to On, under the Included column, you can select Choose Users, Groups, Or Teams to restrict the hold to specified custodian sources.

8. Enter a mailbox name or group to search the list. Selecting a distribution group will add the group members to the hold. Scroll to the bottom of the flyout window and click Done when finished, as shown in Figure 6-56.

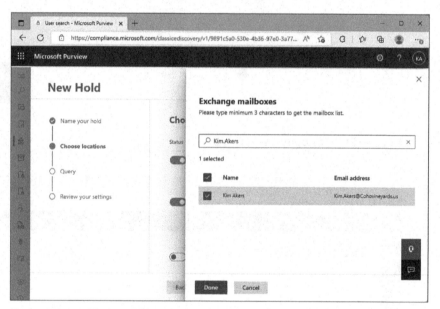

Figure 6-56   Adding a mailbox

9. If you toggle the SharePoint Sites slider to On, under the Included column, you can click Choose Sites to select SharePoint sites to include in the search. Only standalone sites and sites connected to Microsoft 365 groups and teams will be displayed when adding sites. If you want to add a user's OneDrive site, you must enter the full path to the user's OneDrive for Business site collection. Scroll to the bottom of the flyout window and click Done when finished. See Figure 6-57.

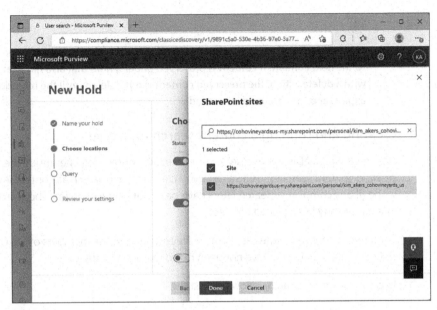

Figure 6-57   Adding a OneDrive for Business site

10. Click Next to continue.

11. On the Query page, enter words and phrases into the Keywords condition card if desired (if no conditions or queries are specified, all content in the selected locations will be put on hold).

Like content search, you can select Add Condition to add condition cards for additional selection and filtering criteria. You can also use the KQL editor to construct exact queries. Click Next when finished.

1. On the Review Your Settings page, review the hold parameters. Click Submit when finished.

2. Click Done to exit the New Hold wizard.

After the hold has been created, you can select the hold from the Hold page to view the statistics, such as the number of mailboxes and sites included and the number of responsive items.

The number of items indicates those from all content sources that are placed on hold. If you've created a query-based hold, this indicates the number of items that match the query.

The number of items on hold also includes unindexed items found in the content locations. If you create a query-based hold, all unindexed items in the content locations are placed on hold, potentially including content that doesn't match the search query.

CHAPTER 6

NOTE

When content is preserved using a case hold, the standard retention principles apply to the held content. If content is preserved under a hold that also has a retention policy with a delete action, the preserved content is not deleted until the retention period expires and the case hold is released.

Creating and running a content search for a case

After creating an eDiscovery case, you can execute content searches inside the case. When creating content searches inside a case, you can choose to search all content inside the search scope (if any compliance search filters have been put in place) or limit the search just to content that has already been placed on hold.

Content searches run in the case context are restricted to the members of the case. They are not visible to individuals who have not been made members of the case.

To create a content search, follow these steps:

1.   From the Microsoft Purview compliance center, expand eDiscovery and select Standard.

2.   Create a new case or select an existing case from the list.

3.   Select the Searches tab.

4.   Click New Search to launch the New Search wizard on the Search page.

5.   On the Name And Description page, enter a unique name for the search. Content searches associated with a case must have unique names across your entire Office 365 organization (including cases you might not have access to).

6.   On the Locations page, select the content locations that you want to search. While the content search locations on this page are very similar to both the normal content search interface as well as the search interface when creating holds, there is also a new radio button for searching Locations On Hold, as shown in Figure 6-58.

7.   You can search mailboxes, sites, and public folders in the same search. You can choose to search all content locations or specify a custom set based on the requirements of the search. If you select the Locations On Hold radio button, only content sources that you've already put on hold, in this case, will be searched (any holds put in place for other cases will *not* be searched).

8.   You can create multiple searches per case, so you might want to perform different sets of keyword queries on the same content to return different results.

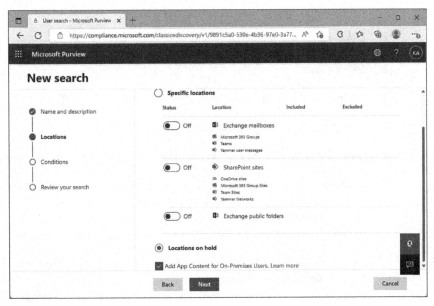

Figure 6-58 eDiscovery case search

9. Click Next when you have finished your content location selection.

10. On the Conditions page, enter words and phrases into the Keywords condition card if desired (if no conditions or queries are specified, all content in the selected locations will be put on hold).

11. Like content search, you can select Add Condition to add condition cards for additional selection and filtering criteria. You can also use the KQL editor to construct exact queries. Click Next when finished.

12. On the Review Your Search page, review the search parameters. Click Submit when finished.

13. Click Done to exit the New Search wizard.

Like content search and eDiscovery case holds, the search will be submitted in the background for execution.

Exporting the case search results

After the search has completed, you can create an export of the results. Exporting from an eDiscovery case is the same as exporting from a content search outside of a case.

To prepare an export for download, follow these steps:

1. From the Microsoft Purview compliance center, expand eDiscovery and select Standard.

2. Select a case.

3. On the Searches page, select one or more searches to export.

4. On the Summary tab, click Actions and select Export Results.

5. Select the options that best meet your needs on the Export Results flyout window.

6. Under Output Options, select an option. Depending on the search results, you might want to run multiple export jobs to group the content accordingly. Encrypted, unindexed, or partially-indexed content might not be responsive to your query, so it's generally best to export and download it separately from the known responsive results.

7. If you have Exchange content as part of your responsive data set, under Export Exchange Content As, select how to organize the content. The individuals requesting content might prefer one PST per mailbox, all messages contained in a single PST, or individual responsive email messages. You can also select the Enable De-Duplication For Exchange Content checkbox to reduce the amount of data downloaded if messages are detected in multiple folders in a mailbox.

8. If you have SharePoint content as part of your responsive data set, you can select the Include Versions For SharePoint Files To Include File Versions checkbox.

9. Choose whether to select the Export Files In A Compressed (Zipped) Folder checkbox.

10. Click Export.

NOTE

If you are not a member of the Export role group, you won't be able to export results, and an error will appear. If you are a member of the Organization Management role group or Global Admins, you can add yourself as a member of the Export role, sign out of the Microsoft Purview compliance center, sign back in, and retry the export. The eDiscovery Manager role group has the Export role included by default.

11. Click OK to acknowledge the export dialog box.

12. On the Content Search page, select the Export tab.

13. Select the export corresponding to the search you conducted earlier.

14. Scroll the page until you reach the Export Key section. Copy the export key to your clipboard.

15. Scroll back up to the top of the page and click Download Results.

16. A new browser tab will launch, prompting if you want to open a file. Confirm that the file comes from *complianceclientsdf.bloc.core.windows.net* and click Open.

17. Click Install to install the eDiscovery Export Tool app.

18. Paste the export key from your clipboard into the Paste The Export Key That Will Be Used To Connect To The Source field, and then enter a path where the download will be saved. Click Start.

19. Wait while the download completes.

20. After the files have been downloaded, navigate to the path specified in the export location.

The files are saved in a subdirectory named for the search specified. A separate subdirectory is created for exports from each service.

Closing a case

When the investigation that an eDiscovery case supported is complete, you can close the eDiscovery case in the Microsoft Purview compliance center.

Closing a case releases any holds that might have been placed as part of the case. Depending on your organization's retention policies, this might result in data being deleted due to not being protected by any other retention labels or policies.

To close a case, follow these steps:

1. From the Microsoft Purview compliance center, expand eDiscovery and select Standard.

2. Select the case you wish to close.

3. On the Home tab of the case, click Close Case, as shown in Figure 6-59.

CHAPTER 6

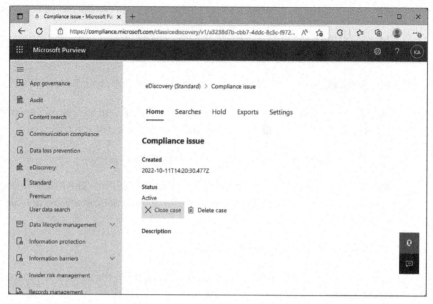

Figure 6-59   Closing a case

4.   Click Yes to acknowledge the case closure warning, as shown in Figure 6-60.

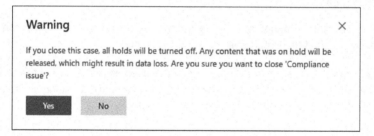

Figure 6-60   Case closure warning

Once the warning has been acknowledged, the case status will be Updated to Closed. You can reopen the case anytime by navigating to the case summary page and selecting Reopen. The searches and holds remain configured even when the case is closed, but you will need to update each to search and hold to reactivate them.

Inside Out

Deep dive into content search and eDiscovery

The detailed information of a search contains the Keyword Query Language (KQL) structure instead of details about the condition cards.

After constructing your query with condition cards, the properties on the cards are converted into KQL to be processed by the system. You can examine the structure of KQL to help you build more complex queries that the condition cards alone won't let you build.

Another new addition to the Microsoft Purview compliance center is the KQL editor, which replaces the KQL condition card. The KQL editor is an IntelliSense-style predictive environment, helping you formulate KQL queries correctly.

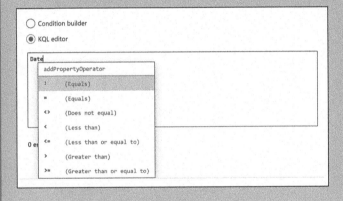

NOTE

For a deeper dive into constructing KQL queries, including detailed usage and examples of using operators such as NEAR, ONEAR, AND, and NOT, see *https://aka.ms/ContentSearchTips*.

What's next?

In the next chapter, we'll begin exploring the available security features in the Enterprise Mobility + Security packages. These features are part of the Microsoft 365 suite and can be used to reduce the attack surface of your Microsoft 365 tenant. Also, they provide automation to further secure workloads.

Enterprise Mobility + Security

The security boundary has moved beyond the organization's four walls and now rests with the identity of the users, wherever they happen to be. Increasingly, users are mobile and want and need to work from anywhere, frequently on any device. To address the challenges of providing the required access while maintaining security, Microsoft has developed Enterprise Mobility + Security (EMS). EMS is a combination of capabilities in Azure Active Directory, Microsoft Intune, Microsoft Endpoint Configuration Manager, Azure Information Protection, Microsoft Defender for Cloud Apps, Microsoft Advanced Threat Analytics, Microsoft Defender for Identity, and Microsoft Secure Score. By leveraging the integrated capabilities of these technologies, customers can address the modern security challenges that come from a connected world across identity and access management, endpoint management, information protection, and identity-driven security.

Overview

Microsoft's Enterprise Mobility + Security (EMS) is a collection of solutions and technologies that provide organizations with robust security capabilities across a broad range of uses. Most of the components of EMS can be purchased separately, but their true strength comes when they are deployed together, and their best value comes when they are purchased as a suite. EMS is available in several licenses, including Microsoft 365 E5. In this chapter and the subsequent one, we will talk about the specific capabilities offered by EMS and only address the difference between the EMS E3 and EMS E5 licenses when there are differences in the capabilities provided or the specific version included. Either SKU offers capabilities across identity and access management (IAM) endpoint management, information protection, and identity-managed security.

In both EMS E3 and E5, customers gain fundamental protections and device management capabilities. E5 provides advanced protections for users and data and adds additional capabilities for cloud services.

EME E3 includes the following products:

- Azure Active Directory Premium P1

- Microsoft Intune

- Azure Information Protection P1

- Microsoft Advanced Threat Analytics (in extended support only)

- Azure Rights Management

- Windows Server CAL rights

EMS E5 includes the following products:

- Azure Active Directory Premium P2

- Microsoft Intune

- Azure Information Protection P2

- Microsoft Cloud App Security

- Azure Active Directory Identity Protection

- Microsoft Defender for Identity

- Azure AD Privileged Identity Management

Because both suites offer enterprises with strong security capabilities, the differences between the P1 and P2 plans might not be so obvious. The information in Table 7-1 should make it easier to understand the difference in capabilities between EMS E3 and EMS E5.

Table 7-1   Feature differences between EMS E3 and E5

EMS feature	EMS E3	EMS E5
Identity and access management (IAM)		
Simplified access management and security	Yes	Yes
Multifactor authentication	Yes	Yes
Conditional access	Yes	Yes
Risk-based access	No	Yes
Advanced security reporting	Yes	Yes
Privileged identity management	No	Yes

Endpoint management		
Mobile application management	Yes	Yes
Advanced Microsoft Office 365 data protection	Yes	Yes
Integrated PC management	Yes	Yes
Integrated on-premises management	Yes	Yes
Information protection		
Persistent data protection	Yes	Yes
Intelligent data classification and labeling	No	Yes
Document tracking and revocation	Yes	Yes
Encryption key management	Yes	Yes
Identity-driven security		
Microsoft Advanced Threat Analytics	Yes	Yes
Microsoft Cloud App Security	No	Yes
Microsoft Defender for Identity	No	Yes

In the following sections, we will look at what each feature offers customers looking to enhance their security.

Identity and access management

Identity and access management (IAM) helps protect organizations with complete integrated security and governance across users, apps, devices, and data. It can use criteria to make decisions about authentication and access, tailoring what an authenticated user can do based on where they are, what device they are using, or if there are risk indicators. It provides a unified identity management approach, which means

- One user can have one identity and leverage it across both Microsoft 365 and third-party needs.

- It ensures identity governance is automated to both provision and deprovision users.

- It ensures least-privilege access is enforced. The solutions discussed in this chapter make up the IAM capabilities within EMS.

Simplified access management and security

The following sections cover topics that help you simplify access management and increase the overall security of your users, your data, and your organization. Admins should consider these actions the bare minimum required actions they should take to help secure their environments and acknowledge that more will be required.

Multifactor authentication

Undoubtedly, the most impactful thing an organization can do to improve security is to enable and enforce multifactor authentication (MFA). If you are not using MFA everywhere, you can—both in business and in personal access—you're doing it wrong. MFA, sometimes called two-factor authentication (2FA), adds another factor besides username and password to the authentication process.

Usernames are easily determined. For many organizations, usernames are the same as a user's email address; if you know one user's email address, you can figure out the rest. When organizations use something else for a username, they simply make it harder for their users to do anything without really improving security on its own. Passwords can be brute-forced or determined through spray attacks, guessed by mining social media, phished through email, or simply purchased on the open market because many users continue using the same password on multiple sites. But with MFA, even if you know my username and my password, you cannot log on as me without having access to a physical thing—such as my cell phone or a token—that contains another factor of authentication. Those physical things can be further secured with a fingerprint, facial recognition, or PIN to unlock, meaning that even if you steal the device, you cannot simply use it to authenticate as another user.

Microsoft freely gives MFA to Office 365 customers via the Microsoft Authenticator App. With EMS, customers can extend the Authenticator App to other applications, whether they're Microsoft or third-party apps, as long as Azure Active Directory is the Identify Provider.

TIP

An Identity Provider (IDP) is a system which serves as the source of authority for the security principal and acts as the authentication service in a federated relationship with the provider of a resource, such as an application. In the case of Azure AD, SaaS, PaaS, and other services can federate with Azure AD, so that user accounts in your tenant can be authenticated and gain access to applications in another system.

Azure Active Directory (AAD) MFA supports the following methods:

- The Microsoft Authenticator App

- Windows Hello for Business

- FIDO2 security keys

- Open Authentication Reference Architecture (OATH) hardware tokens

- OATH software tokens

- SMS (Short Message Service) messages

- Voice calls

When using MFA, users will be prompted to approve a sign-in request, as shown in Figure 7-1.

Figure 7-1   MFA prompting a user to use the Authenticator app to approve a sign-in request

The Authenticator App is a free application that runs on iOS and Android phones and offers a number of authentication options, including the industry-standard Time-Based One-Time Passwords (TOTP). Google, Amazon, Twitter, Facebook, and GitHub support TOTP. Organizations can also use hardware OATH tokens if they prefer. OATH tokens combine the security of an application with the relative ubiquity of the hardware, given how few employees probably do not already own a smartphone.

Hardware tokens include USB and NFC devices and can easily fit on a key ring. Software tokens do require something to run the software upon. SMS messages are perhaps one of the least-secure options, but they are widely used, and users should have experience with them already through their banks or social media. Voice calls are the lowest common denominator because they assume you have a phone available when you need to use them.

Whichever option you choose to deploy, having MFA in place is a major step toward improving user authentication security. You can use MFA alone or combine it with either conditional access, risk-based access, or both.

Conditional access

Azure Active Directory Conditional Access brings signals together about a user—the device they are using and their location—to make decisions and enforce policies about what a user can and cannot do. These policies can be used to enforce granular restrictions on individual users and individual apps to help protect the organization while still enabling users to be productive.

For example, to mitigate the risk of data loss, an organization might want only to permit the Outlook client, which caches mail content on the local drive, to be able to connect to Exchange Online when a user is using their company-issued laptop. Rather than blocking access to company email completely, if the user is on their personal computer, the organization might want to permit Outlook Web Access but block the Outlook client.

Or an organization might want to use MFA, but only when a user is remote. If the user is on the company network, they should not be prompted for MFA because, presumably, the physical security of being "in the office" is sufficient to ensure a user is who they purport to be. So, a conditional access policy could be to prompt for MFA when a user is not on a trusted network segment.

TIP

Yeah, don't be that person. In a zero-trust world, where insider threats are as real as external ones, trusting an authentication request simply because it comes from your corporate network is asking for trouble. It might be a common approach, but it's definitely not a recommended one! One employee might have compromised another, or an attacker might have gained remote access to a machine on your network. Perhaps they are in the parking lot and using your WiFi network. There are just too many ways an attacker would love to see you use network location as a factor to make it worth using.

Risk-based access

While MFA is a critical part of authentication, it is neither the only part nor the only thing you should rely on. Nor is authentication the only component of securing a user's ability to access corporate resources. Access comes after authentication, and what access a user is granted might depend upon the level of risk associated with the user. Risk-based user sign-in protection looks at attributes of an authentication request to decide whether additional scrutiny is required for the authentication request, while risk-based conditional access determines when a user's access should be limited based on attributes, such as the trustworthiness of the connection or the client device state. Risk-based access is a feature of Azure Active Directory Premium Plan 2, which is part of the EMS E5 suite.

You can use risk-based user sign-in protection when considering an authentication request. You might want to require MFA if you have never seen a user trying to authenticate from the source IP address in question, while you might not if the same user has authenticated from the same source IP address before and successfully passed MFA recently. Or you might want to require MFA if you have recently seen several failed authentication attempts for the user. The idea is that all other things equal, if there is one thing that is more suspicious this time, greater scrutiny than normal should be required when evaluating the authentication request. User Risk evaluates whether an account might be compromised and is determined by machine learning within Azure AD. This risk might include indicators of compromise, such as multiple logins from different locations, the discovery of user credentials in lists found elsewhere, logins from known malicious networks, and more. The default User Risk Policy, which is present but not enforced, is shown in Figure 7-2.

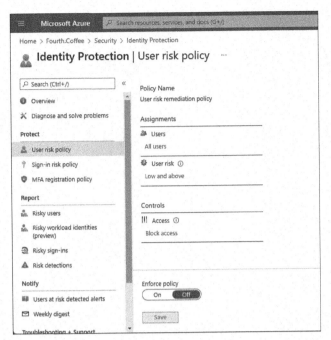

Figure 7-2   The default User Risk Policy

The Sign-In Risk Policy is related to the User Risk Policy and evaluates whether a particular sign-in request is risky. Again, machine learning algorithms evaluate the request to determine if it is risky and can include indicators of compromise, such as a subsequent login attempt from a different network than a previous one, attempts from anonymized IP addresses (such as those provided by TOR networks), and so on. Figure 7-3 shows the default Sign-In Risk Policy, which again, is provided but not enabled.

Risk-based conditional access enables you to provide differing levels of access to the same user based on where they are or what device or client they are using. You might want to grant a user on a company-managed laptop full access, with rich- or web-based clients while limiting that same user to web-based clients only when using a personal device and perhaps to block downloads. It can be applied to any user, including guest users, and against any applications managed through Azure Active Directory. Two default policies are preconfigured by Microsoft—Exchange Online Requires Compliant Device and Office 365 App Control. Neither is enabled, but both give you some insight into what risk-based conditional access can do. You can also create your own policies, either from scratch or using included templates. Figure 7-4 gives you a preview of this, and we will get into more detail in Chapter 8, "Security Features of Enterprise Mobility + Security."

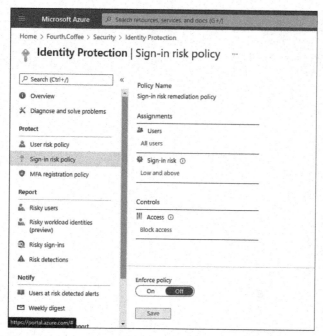

Figure 7-3 The default Sign-In Risk Policy

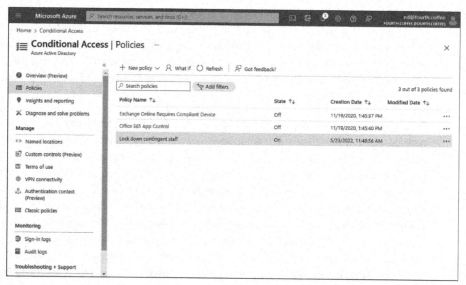

Figure 7-4 Conditional Access Policies

Advanced security reporting

Advanced security reporting is included in both EMS E3 and EMS E5 and covers a range of reporting options within Azure Active Directory. Reports can be run on demand or scheduled, and programmatic access is available through the published APIs so that you can bring the data into a SIEM, such as Azure Sentinel or another third-party tool like Splunk. These reports include the following:

- Audit logs

- Sign-ins

The audit logs in Azure Active Directory give you a view of how your environment is doing and what is going on within the environment. Audit logging is available for all Office 365 customers, regardless of license.

The Sign-Ins report provides information on Azure Active Directory sign-ins, including frequency and pattern. They require an Azure AD Premium Plan 1 license, so they are included with EMS E3 and E5.

Privileged Identity Management

Imagine a world where no one had any administrative rights to anything by default but could be dynamically given those rights only when needed, only for as long as they needed them, and only with appropriate approvals. This is what Privileged Identity Management (PIM) offers customers.

With PIM, no user requires more than a single account, so no more admin accounts, and no user has any standing administrative access. So, if an account is compromised or a user is simply not paying attention, widespread damage resulting from administrative actions cannot take place. But when a user needs to do something as an administrator, the ability to do this can be provisioned through a workflow that can include a level of management confirmation and be time-bound.

- Need to reset a user's password? Become a user admin for ten minutes.

- Need to set up tenant restrictions and test them? Become a Global Administrator for a day.

- Need a manager to confirm the need and provide approval before rights are granted? Set up the workflow, and off you go.

PIM is an extremely powerful and valuable tool that enables organizations to maintain a "zero-standing access" posture for admins, grant the least privilege for the least amount of time needed to accomplish any administrative task, and build in managerial oversite to ensure only valid requests are approved. While larger organizations might consider this a must-have, even smaller organizations can benefit immensely from this approach. PIM is a feature within Azure Active Directory Plan 2, so it comes with EMS E5 but not with E3. PIM includes a tool to manage access using a just-in-time approach, discover existing access, and monitor ongoing access. Figure 7-5 shows the PIM management console. (We will go into more detail about PIM in Chapter 8).

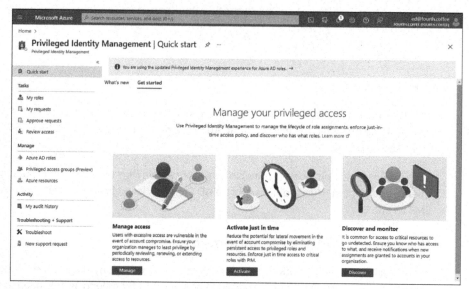

Figure 7-5   Privileged Identity Management admin console

Endpoint management

Microsoft's Enterprise Mobility + Security includes features for endpoint management. Those endpoints can be mobile devices, Windows PCs, or Macs and also includes mobile application management capabilities. Collectively, these features are contained within Microsoft Endpoint Manager and include the following:

- Microsoft Intune, the cloud-based mobile device management (MDM) and Mobile Application Management (MAM) platform

- Microsoft Configuration Manager for management of desktops, servers, and laptops

- Co-management capabilities to provide a unified approach to managing both on-premises and cloud-based endpoints

- Desktop Analytics to provide insights about your endpoints

- Windows Autopilot, which enables you to stage and deploy new devices to users easily

- Azure Active Directory Premium to provide dynamic group membership, auto-enrollment, and conditional access

- Endpoint Manager admin center to provide a single pane of glass for administration

Mobile application management

Mobile Application Management (MAM) is a key part of Microsoft Intune's approach to management endpoints. With MAM, administrators can protect their organization's data within applications using app protection policies (APP) across scores of both first and third-party applications. This can both deliver applications to devices and manage what can and cannot be done within those applications based on a compliance or management status of a device. See Figure 7-6.

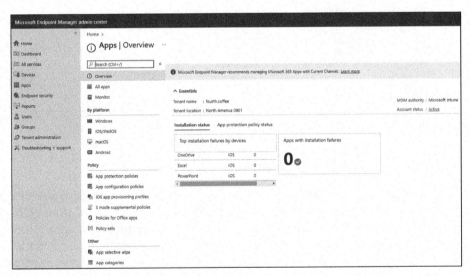

Figure 7-6   The Apps Overview console in Microsoft Endpoint Manager admin center

Advanced Microsoft Office 365 data protection

Advanced Microsoft Office 365 data protection is included in both EMS E3 and E5 and allows you to deliver core line-of-business applications to users' mobile devices, enable them to use BYOD, and even have both corporate and personal email set up in the same Outlook client. Advanced Microsoft Office 365 data protection does all this while blocking the ability to copy company data from a corporate email into a personal email. You can also ensure that if a device contains company data, that company data can be wiped if necessary without wiping a user's personal data. Figure 7-7 shows an example of creating an application policy.

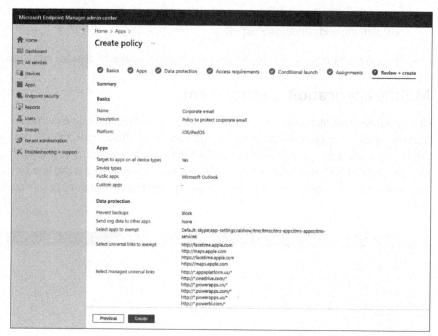

Figure 7-7   Creating an application policy

Integrated PC management

Microsoft Intune and Microsoft Configuration Manager come together to provide integrated PC management, whether the device is a corporate-owned desktop PC in the office or a personally owned tablet that a user wants to use to access company resources and run company applications. This powerful combination of cloud and on-premises management allows companies to fully manage those assets they own while ensuring BYOD devices meet minimum compliance standards and can access data and applications appropriately. Figure 7-8 shows an example of a workstation compliance policy.

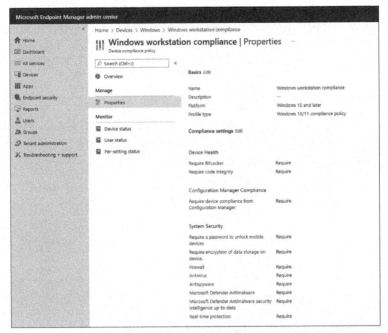

Figure 7-8   A compliance policy in Microsoft Endpoint Manager

Integrated on-premises management

The on-premises management capabilities offered by Microsoft Configuration Manager enable administrators to manage all their corporate IT estate, including servers and clients, with simple to configure and apply policies, robust reporting capabilities, and delegated management.

Information protection

Information protection challenges are legion when it comes to dealing with laptops, thumb drives, access from anywhere, collaboration with anyone, and the need to move data from point A to point B (often across the Internet and onto endpoints beyond your ability to control). That's where the information protection capabilities included with Microsoft EMS come into play. These technologies combine to ensure that organizations have the tools to protect their data, no matter where it is or how it got there—even when it is beyond their control.

Persistent data protection

Azure Information Protection uses encryption to ensure that data control and protection are rooted in the data itself rather than in an endpoint or an application. This protection persists as long as the data does, ensuring that copies or moves from device to device, file system to file system, or network to network do not affect an organization's ability to control who can access their data and what they can do with that access. Figure 7-9 shows an information protection policy.

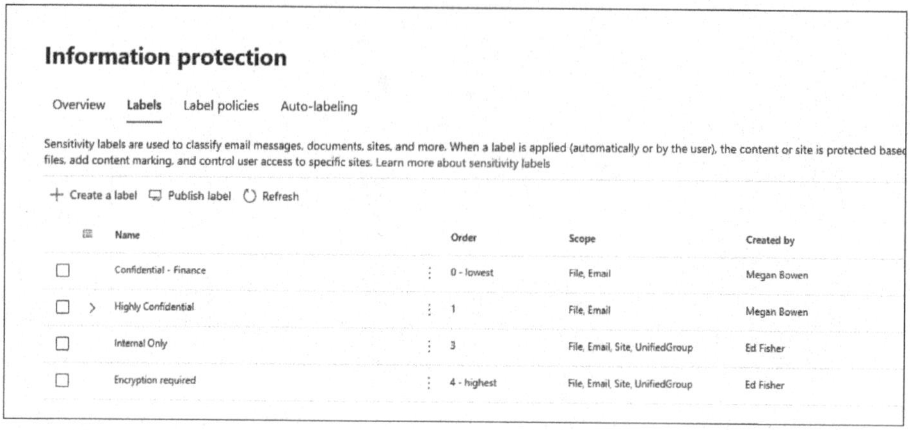

Information protection

Overview   **Labels**   Label policies   Auto-labeling

Sensitivity labels are used to classify email messages, documents, sites, and more. When a label is applied (automatically or by the user), the content or site is protected based files, add content marking, and control user access to specific sites. Learn more about sensitivity labels

+ Create a label   ▢ Publish label   ◯ Refresh

	Name		Order	Scope	Created by
☐	Confidential - Finance	⋮	0 - lowest	File, Email	Megan Bowen
☐ >	Highly Confidential	⋮	1	File, Email	Megan Bowen
☐	Internal Only	⋮	3	File, Email, Site, UnifiedGroup	Ed Fisher
☐	Encryption required	⋮	4 - highest	File, Email, Site, UnifiedGroup	Ed Fisher

Figure 7-9   Information Protection

Intelligent data classification and labeling

The key to a company's ability to protect its data is to identify and categorize that data. While this can be done manually, larger and/or more established companies might have so much data that doing this manually presents a significant challenge. Included with Microsoft EMS E5 is Azure Information Protection Plan 2, which allows customers to create rules that can automatically evaluate data, apply classifications and labels to that data, and use those to apply and enforce information protection policies. It is the only difference between EMS E3 and E5 in the Information Protection category. If a company with thousands of users or millions of files needs persistent data protection, Azure Information Protection Plan 2 can pay for itself by automating most of the process. Figure 7-10 shows how auto-labeling can be configured.

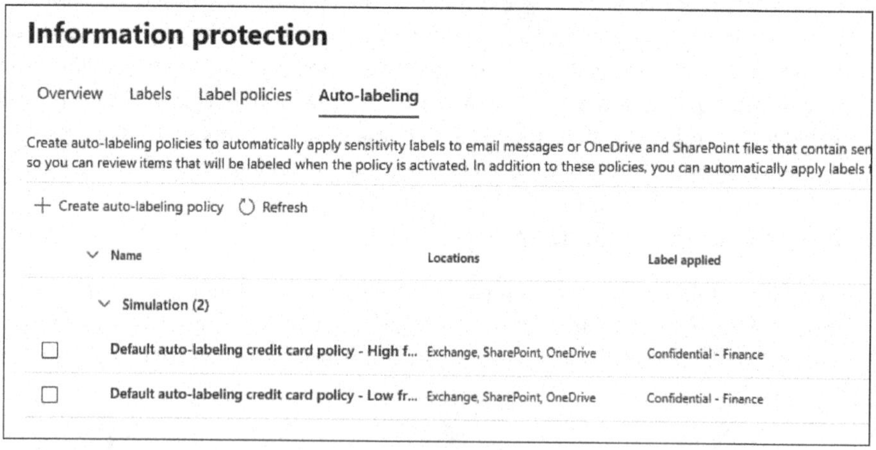

Information protection

Overview   Labels   Label policies   **Auto-labeling**

Create auto-labeling policies to automatically apply sensitivity labels to email messages or OneDrive and SharePoint files that contain ser so you can review items that will be labeled when the policy is activated. In addition to these policies, you can automatically apply labels

+ Create auto-labeling policy   ◯ Refresh

	∨ Name	Locations	Label applied
	∨ Simulation (2)		
☐	Default auto-labeling credit card policy - High f...	Exchange, SharePoint, OneDrive	Confidential - Finance
☐	Default auto-labeling credit card policy - Low fr...	Exchange, SharePoint, OneDrive	Confidential - Finance

Figure 7-10   Information protection auto-labeling

Document tracking and revocation

While your organization is doing all that collaborating and sharing, and all those files are fly-ing across the world, have you ever wondered just who has a copy, where they happen to be, or who wanted to be able to "kill" a file after it's beyond your control? Document tracking and revocation address exactly those needs, leveraging the power of Azure Information Protection to track where a file is by its IP address, identify through authentication who has access to a file. And with a click of a mouse or when a certain date is reached, all access to that file can be revoked. Even if a user had the file and you could open it yesterday, it's a useless encrypted blob today. Figure 7-11 shows how a user can revoke access to a protected document.

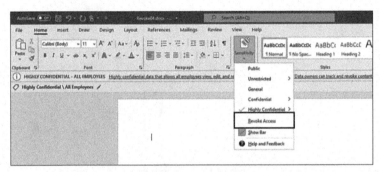

Figure 7-11   Revoking access

Encryption key management

Any solution based on encryption is dependent upon the keys (public and private) used to secure the encryption. Microsoft 365's solutions include key generation and management capa-bilities, but some customers might want to bring their own keys with them when onboarding or even host their own keys in an on-premises infrastructure they control. Bring Your Own Key (BYOK) and Host Your Own Key (HYOK) solutions support these features, so customers can fully control key generation, management, lifecycle, and revocation. These capabilities can be critical when mandated by contractual obligations or corporate policies.

Identity-driven security

In an increasingly mobile world, where more and more work is being done outside of the cor-porate offices, identity is the new security boundary, and identity-driven security is the way to approach security that work. Microsoft EMS includes three solutions that focus on the identity boundary.

Microsoft Advanced Threat Analytics

Microsoft Advanced Threat Analytics (ATA) is an on-premises User and Entity Behavioral Analyt-ics solution that helps organizations to protect against a multitude of cyber and insider threats.

Using a proprietary network parsing engine running on domain controllers or on separate systems using port mirroring, ATA looks at network traffic associated with authentication, authorization, directory services, and name resolution to identify and alert admins regarding reconnaissance, lateral movement, privilege escalation, and more. Companies that remain primarily on-premises might find ATA to be a valuable part of their defense strategy, though it is an on-premises-only solution and is now in extended support. Included with EMS E3, it still has a few years of extended support, and has a ready replacement in Microsoft Defender for Identity, discussed later in this chapter. Figure 7-12 shows a threat map for a user.

Figure 7-12   Microsoft Advanced Threat Analytics

Microsoft Cloud App Security

Microsoft Cloud App Security (MCAS) is a rebranding of Microsoft Defender for Cloud Apps (MDCA), and by the time you read this, that rebranding might be complete. Whether you call it MCAS or MDCA, the product is Microsoft's Cloud Access Security Broker (CASB) and is designed to evaluate network access to applications and enforce company policies and provide visibility into what apps users are using. It can be used to discover apps (especially those considered *shadow IT*), protect information, and even block access to applications not sanctioned for use by the company. It provides even more value when integrated with other security solutions in the Defender family. Figure 7-13 shows some of the built-in Microsoft Defender for Cloud Apps policies.

Figure 7-13   Microsoft Defender for Cloud Apps

INSIDE OUT

What is shadow IT?

While it sounds like the villain in a new comic book movie, shadow IT is even worse. Shadow IT refers to any technology that has been deployed without the involvement of, and oversite by, the IT and/or security teams that normally handle technology projects. Sometimes it is a SaaS app that a department goes out and pays for with a corporate card. Other times, it's an application upon which a business unit builds its processes. Every time, it becomes a headache for IT, who is expected to support it when it falls down and goes boom, and for security, because it usually goes outside of compliance boundaries, has no connection to auditing or provisioning, and seldom meets the corporate security policies. Finding and eliminating shadow IT is of paramount importance. It's not about being in charge; it's about ensuring you can maintain and protect your corporate assets and your customers' data.

Microsoft Defender for Identity

While Microsoft ATA is built for on-premises environments, Microsoft Defender for Identity (MDI) is built for the cloud. This tool is a more advanced UEBA that leverages both your on-premises Active Directory and your Azure Active Directory, and learns as it goes to alert on anomalous behaviors, clear indicators of attack, or potential vulnerabilities in legacy authentication protocols. MDI can help to identify and alert you across a range of activities in the cyber-attack kill-chain, including

- Reconnaissance

- Compromised credentials

- Lateral movements

- Domain dominance

MDI is included in Microsoft EMS E5 and can provide immediate benefits to organizations that deploy it. It also integrates with other security solutions in the Defender family, including MCAS, and provides customers with full visibility into what is happening on and off their networks.

What's next?

This chapter provided a high-level overview of Microsoft Enterprise Mobility + Security and the differences between the E3 and E5 licenses. In Chapter 8, we will look at how to use EMS to solve specific problems, mitigate specific risks, and meet specific security requirements while leveraging capabilities across the entire suite.

Security features of Enterprise Mobility + Security

Now that you understand the technologies that make up Microsoft Enterprise Mobility + Security (EMS), let's look at what you should do with them.

In this chapter, we will go over how to implement some of the security features of Enterprise Mobility + Security to strengthen your corporate security posture and better secure your users and the devices they use—regardless of who owns them or where they are. Instead of following the same order of coverage as Chapter 7, we will address what you should do following a recommended order in which you should do it to get to a minimum-security posture. We will assume that you have EMS E5, so make sure you have access to all of the products and licenses within that suite. If you have E3 instead or opted to obtain product licenses a la carte, feel free to skip around. Also, note that we will not go deeply into every one of the features in EMS, as some of those could fill an entire volume. We will have enough in this chapter to get you started, though.

Before we begin, make sure you consider the following points. First, security is not simply related to how many switches you click and the options you disable. It is negatively impacted by how hard you make things for your end users. There will always be a security trade-off between accepting some risk while maintaining usability. Make the decisions that best support what your organization requires to accomplish its mission, avoiding what risks you can, mitigating those you cannot avoid, and accepting that there is no panacea.

Securing identity

Identity is the security boundary, and attackers no longer break in; they log in. Credentials can be phished from users, pulled from one compromised system, and used to get into another when users reuse passwords, and gigabytes of username/password pairs are for sale on the open market. Securing identity includes making it harder for the bad guys to use someone else's credentials and being able to detect when they do. In this section, we will address both.

Microsoft Defender for Identity

"Assume-breach" might seem to be a very fatalistic point of view, but it's also the right way to approach security today. And if knowledge is power, knowing what is happening within your organization's information technology space is critical to security. Microsoft Defender for Identity (MDI), formerly known as Microsoft Advanced Threat Analytics, is a User and Entity Behavioral Analytics solution that can detect and alert on indicators of compromise (IOCs) and indicators of attack (IOAs). Also, it can learn about the normal operations in your organization so that it can alert on anomalous behaviors, helping you spot compromised accounts and insider threats. MDI is the first tool you will want to deploy when you engage Microsoft's Detection and Response Team to assist with a security incident. This allows Microsoft to get a full view of what's happening, where it's happening, and what security principles are involved.

Outside a security incident, there are several reasons MDI should be the first thing to install:

- First, you only need to deploy an agent on your domain controllers. There is no client software to install, no user training to deliver, or anything else that might take time. It won't impact users or applications at all, as it's a watcher, not a blocker.

- Second, the sooner it is deployed, the sooner it can start to learn what is happening within your organization's IT estate so it can alert on those anomalous behaviors.

- Finally, MDI integrates with other products within the EMS suite and the Microsoft Defender line of products. Starting with it is a good way to get that full, integrated coverage going early.

So, how do you start? Let's look at a high-level overview of the steps. In the following sections, we'll get into the details:

1. Ensure hardware requirements are met.

2. Ensure network requirements are met.

3. Create the service account.

4. Create the instance.

5. Deploy the agents.

6. Start monitoring your environment.

Ensure your hardware is up to the task

MDI relies upon data coming from agents, which typically need to run on ALL your domain controllers and ADFS servers (if present). If you sized your servers appropriately, this should be a non-issue. However, if you are trying to run really lean, especially if they are virtual machines on your platform of choice, you might find your network I/O to be maxed out. This is especially true if they are light in the RAM department or if you have too many apps (or a busy app is pinned to query one domain controller). You might find that network I/O is maxed out. This could lead to missing important events, so ensuring your domain controller hardware is adequate for the task is the first place to start.

RAM is probably the most important resource to consider. Microsoft recommends that the amount of RAM allocated to a domain controller include at least the total required to

- Meet the base operating system requirements, plus

- Cache the entire Active Directory database, plus

- Accommodate all first- and third-party components, including antimalware, backup agents, and, yes, the MDI agent

The MDI agent's needs for RAM are directly related to the number of packets per second of network traffic the domain controller deals with. It also requires a certain number of CPU cores to work efficiently. Table 8-1 documents the minimum RAM and CPU cores recommended to accommodate the MDI agent's needs. Remember that this is on top of what might be required for Active Directory and any other functions the domain controller performs.

Table 8-1   Microsoft Defender for Identity minimum hardware recommendations

Packets per second	Physical CPU cores	RAM
0–1k	0.25	2.5GB
1k–5k	0.75	6GB
5k–10k	1	6.5GB
10k–20k	2	9GB
20k–50k	3.5	9.5GB
50k–75k	5.5	11.5GB
75k–100k	7.5	13.5GB

CAUTION

If you run your domain controllers as virtual machines rather than on physical hardware, make sure you allocate all the RAM required as static. Do not use dynamic memory. The demands of domain controllers, along with the needs of the MDI agent, won't play nicely when dynamic memory is in play. In Hyper-V, you want to ensure that Enable Dynamic Memory is not enabled. In VMware, you want to make sure that Reserve All Guest Memory is enabled. Using dynamic memory not only puts you into an unsupported configuration, it's just asking for problems.

The first thing to do is run the sizing tool to make sure your DCs are up to snuff. Download the sizing tool from GitHub at *https://github.com/microsoft/ATA-AATP-Sizing-Tool/releases*. While MDI requires much less hardware than the Advanced Threat Analytics solution, it still does require both CPU and RAM in direct relation to how much network traffic the domain controller (DC) experiences. When you consider AD, LDAP, DNS, and other traffic, you might find that some DCs are much busier than others, so it's best to run the sizing tool to prevent missing anything. The MDI sensor polls resource consumption on the DC every 10 seconds and dynamically adjusts to ensure there is no impact on DC functions. If a DC is underpowered, MDI will drop traffic (and possibly detections) and log an alert. Review the results of the sizing tool, and make any necessary hardware upgrades. The tool will run against your domain controllers and provide recommendations on upgrades if needed, in a CSV file, as shown in Figure 8-1. You will have to reboot if you need to make any hardware adjustments. Because the MDI sensor requires current patching and .NET Framework 4.7, you might as well make sure that's all in place while you're there.

DC	Sensor Supported	Failed Samples	Max Packets/sec	Avg Packets/sec	Busy
DC1.domain.local	Yes	0	1,256	150	
DC2.domain.local	Yes	0	2,190	194	
DC3.domain.local	Yes	0	3,270	285	
DC4.domain.local	Yes, but additional resources required: +3GB	0	1,960	172	
DC5.domain.local	Yes, but additional resources required: +3GB	0	220	143	
Total			8,896	944	

Figure 8-1   Output of the MDI sizing tool

TIP

If you have DCs (or ADFS) servers that you simply cannot upgrade, there is a standalone sensor deployment option that you can perform using a separate server and port mirroring. However, using this option won't catch everything because the standalone sensor doesn't support the collection of ETW logs; some things might be missed. Therefore, it's not recommended unless there is no other option. For more information, see *https://docs.microsoft.com/en-us/defender-for-identity/prerequisites*.

Make sure the required connectivity is in place

Once your server hardware is set, the next step is ensuring network connectivity. It's recommended that you permit all required connectivity directly, bypassing any proxy servers for access to the service and ensuring all domain controllers have access to all endpoints on the network over the required ports, as shown in Table 8-2.

Table 8-2 MDI network connectivity

Protocol	Transport	Port	Source	Destination
TLS	TCP	443	MDI sensors	MDI cloud service endpoints
DNS	TCP/UDP	53	MDI sensors	All DNS servers
Netlogon	TCP/UDP	445	MDI sensors	All devices on the network
RADIUS	UDP	1813	RADIUS servers	MDI sensors
NTLM	TCP	135	MDI sensors	All devices on the network
NetBIOS	UDP	137	MDI sensors	All devices on the network
RDP	TCP	3389	MDI sensors	All devices on the network
All	All	All	MDI sensors	localhost

Once your connectivity is sorted out, you're ready to proceed to the next step.

Create the service account

As a Global Admin or Security Administrator, you will create the MDI instance. You will need to create an account in your on-premises Active Directory that has read access to all objects in all domains to be monitored. It's recommended to use a group-managed service account (gMSA) rather than a user account.

NOTE

For more about how to assign the rights to a gMSA, see *https://aka.ms/create-gmsa* **for more information on how to create a gMSA and** *https://mdi-gmsa* **for more about creating directory service accounts.**

Create your MDI instance

Once your service account is created and the appropriate rights are assigned, you're ready to create your MDI instance in Azure:

1. Log in to the MDI portal at *https://portal.atp.azure.com/*. You will see a welcome screen, as shown in Figure 8-2.

2. Click Create.

3. If prompted to try a new user experience, close that window.

4. Click the Provide A Username And Password To Connect To Your Active Directory Forest link.

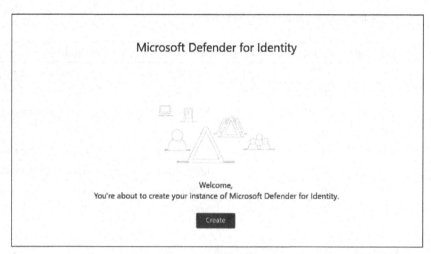

Figure 8-2   The Microsoft Defender for Identity welcome screen

5. Enter the gMSA account name in the Username field and select Group Managed Service Account.

6. In the Domain field, enter the domain name for your on-premises Active Directory, as shown in Figure 8-3.

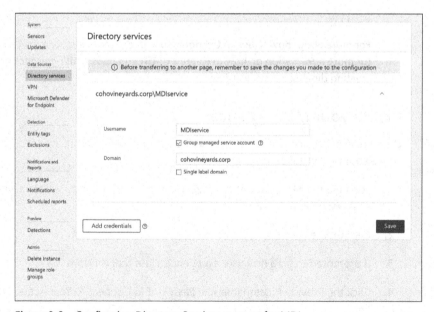

Figure 8-3   Configuring Directory Services account for MDI

7. Click Save.

8. On the left-side menu, click Sensors.

9. Make a note of the Access Key, and then click Download to download the sensor installation package (which will download as a Zip file), as shown in Figure 8-4.

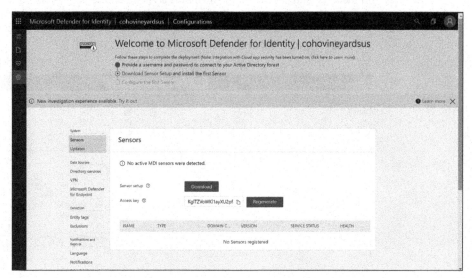

Figure 8-4   Downloading the sensor setup package and the access key

10. Use the zip file created in step 9 to install the sensor on each domain controller in your environment.

CAUTION

Make sure you install the agent on every domain controller in your environment, or you will leave blind spots in your coverage. Upgrade hardware if necessary to ensure you don't miss any activities or overburden a domain controller. You will also want to deploy agents to AD FS servers (and RADIUS servers if you are using them) so you have complete coverage of all authentication events. For more information, see *https://docs.microsoft.com/en-us/defender-for-identity/vpn-integration*.

Monitoring your environment

Once you have MDI set up, you are ready to start using it to monitor your environment. MDI works best when it is fully integrated with the rest of the Microsoft Defender 365 stack and using the investigations in the portal at *https://security.microsoft.com*. MDI works fine on its own, but it is much more powerful when the full stack is deployed because events are automatically correlated across all the Defender platforms, and self-healing behaviors can auto-mate much of the remediation work that traditionally takes SOC personnel hours to perform. You can view alerts from MDI by following these directions:

1. Log in to *https://security.microsoft.com*.

2. In the left-hand menu, expand Incidents & Alerts and select Alerts.

3. On the right side, click the Filter button, and under Service Sources, select only Microsoft Defender For Identity, as shown in Figure 8-5.

Figure 8-5   Filtering for Microsoft Defender for Identity alerts

4. Click Apply.

NOTE

Numerous alerts across all stages of the attack kill-chain are recorded by Microsoft Defender for Identity. For a complete list, see *https://docs.microsoft.com/en-us/defender-for-identity/alerts-overview*.

Multifactor authentication

Multifactor authentication (MFA) should be considered table stakes—the bare minimum—for every organization. MFA blocks 99.9 percent of account attacks. Excuses like "it's too expensive" or "it's too complicated" should be considered unacceptable, as MFA is included with Microsoft 365 for Microsoft apps, the free Authenticator app is available on iOS and Android, and it can be extended to other third-party apps. Also, MFA usage is ubiquitous across social media, consumer shopping, and banking, so almost everyone already knows how to use it. Implementing MFA in Microsoft 365 is very easy to do, and we will go through the process here.

If you created your tenant on or after October 2019, MFA is already enabled for your tenant because it is one of the security defaults. If your tenant is older or someone made the ill-advised decision to disable it, reenabling it should be one of the first things you do. Legacy MFA supported a per-user setting, often used by customers to enable MFA for their admins while leaving their regular users out in the cold. If that describes your tenant, first, you will have to disable this legacy setting. To do that, follow these steps:

1. As a Global Admin, log in to *https://admin.microsoft.com*.

2. In the left-hand navigation, choose Users > Active Users.

3. Choose Multi-Factor Authentication.

4. For any user whose MFA status is set to Enabled, change the status to Disabled. Now, you can set up MFA for the entire organization by enabling Security Defaults.

5. In the left-hand navigation, select Show All and choose Azure Active Directory Admin Center.

6. In the Azure Active Directory admin center, select Active Directory, Properties > Manage Security Defaults.

7. Under Enable Security Defaults, select Yes, and then select Save, as shown in Figure 8-6.

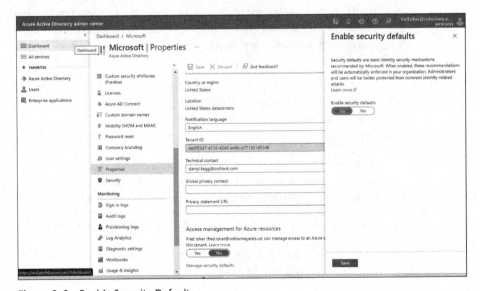

Figure 8-6   Enable Security Defaults

Once security defaults are enabled, MFA will be enabled for all your users, and they will be prompted to register the next time they log in.

Inside Out

Security Defaults

Security defaults help secure your Microsoft 365 tenant (and Azure services) by implementing some minimum settings for basic tenants and are included with the Azure AD free licenses. If your organization is more complex, plans to use Conditional Access, or must allow legacy authentication (for "reasons"), the security defaults are not for you. When you enable security defaults, the following settings are enforced:

1. Requires all users to register for MFA.

2. Requires all admins to use MFA for all activities.

3. Requires users to use MFA when necessary. Azure AD makes this determination based on factors including location, device, role, and task.

4. Blocks legacy authentication.

5. Protects privileged activities.

Enable security defaults now if users are not yet using Microsoft 365, and you're trying to get minimums set now to review later. However, if you have an existing tenant, this might break things without warning. A better choice might be to enable MFA after confirming that all admins have updated their PowerShell modules and no scheduled tasks will fail. Then, review Azure AD logs to ensure legacy authentication is not being used anywhere, and continue working your way through the logs cautiously and quickly. More than 99.9 percent of all identity attacks can be stopped cold simply by using MFA and modern authentication, so you don't want to waste time here.

MFA supports different methods for users to confirm their identity. As an administrator, you can enable some or all of them, depending on your corporate needs. To configure this, do the following:

1. As a Global Admin, log in to *https://portal.azure.com*. If you haven't already configured your own account for MFA, expect to be prompted to enroll now. Complete the enrollment if necessary and then continue to the next step.

2. In the Search box, enter **MFA**, and under Services, click Multifactor Authentication.

3. Under Configure, click Additional Cloud-Based Multifactor Authentication Settings. The defaults are shown in Figure 8-7.

Figure 8-7   Multi-Factor Authentication settings

4. Set the options that you require, and then click Save:

- **App Passwords**   These are useful for legacy applications that do not support MFA. Hopefully, you are not still using any of those in your environment, as they are very old.

- **Trusted IPs**   Trusted IPs enable you to permit users to bypass MFA if they are authenticating from any public IP address you input. The examples are all internal IPs, but if you use Trusted IPs, you will want to enter the public IP address(es) or range(s) to which your users' traffic is NATed. However, this is not recommended because doing so would enable malicious insiders or attackers who have compromised an internal system to authenticate without being prompted for MFA. Verification options are the methods available to users for MFA, once they have completed MFA registration and provided the necessary information.

- **Verification Options**   Call To Phone will make an automated voice call to users, prompting them to confirm by pressing the # key on their phones. It requires a paid Azure AD subscription, and the user's account has their phone number populated in Azure AD, or the user enters the telephone number to which they should be called when they register for MFA. It is not available in trial tenants or tenants that do not have at least Azure AD Plan P1.

NOTE

Only a single phone number can be entered, and the user might incur charges from their mobile carrier if their phone plan charges them for inbound calls. The Text Message To Phone option might also incur mobile carrier phone charges.

- **Text Message To Phone**   This setting uses SMS to send a text message to a user's mobile phone, containing a time-based one-time passcode (TOTP) that they enter when prompted for MFA. Text-based TOTPs have the advantage of being easy for most users to use since they are probably already doing so with their bank or social network accounts. However, text-based TOTPs can also be defeated by a persistent attacker who clones or SIMjacks a target's phone.

- **Notification Through Mobile App**   This setting uses the free Microsoft Authenticator app, available for iOS and Android, to push an authentication verification to the user's app. This uses data rather than voice or text, and the user can confirm or reject an authentication attempt right in the app.

- **Verification Code From Mobile All Or Hardware Token**   This setting lets the user read a TOTP from the app and enter it when prompted. This does not use any data, voice, or text on the phone and does not require the phone to have network connectivity. It's very useful when a user might have Internet access on a laptop but not on their mobile device, such as on a plane or where there is no Wi-Fi or cellular reception.

- **Remember Multi-Factor Authentication On Trusted Device**   This setting lets you determine when a user on a specific device that has passed MFA will be prompted again. This can reduce MFA fatigue if you trust the device's physical security. If you are considering this setting, you should look at Conditional Access, which we will cover in the next section.

NOTE

For more MFA options, see *https://aka.ms/mfa*.

Conditional Access

Azure AD Conditional Access is a feature within Azure Active Directory Plan 1 that allows administrators to enforce access requirements when specific conditions occur. For example:

- You can enforce MFA requirements based on the network location or group membership.

- You can restrict access to compliant devices as determined by Intune or domain membership.

- You can restrict access to specific applications.

- You can set up many other conditions, either starting from scratch or using one of the included templates available in the portal.

Many organizations use Conditional Access to ensure only trusted computers—meaning those that are company assets managed by the company—can have full access to Microsoft 365 applications and data. They might allow untrusted computers to only access Microsoft 365 applications and data through a web browser and block any data downloads.

1. Conditional Access policies are if-then statements, such as this:

   If a user wants to access email, then they must use MFA.

2. They can be joined with AND, so you could create a Conditional Access policy that says:

   If a user wants to access email, then they must use MFA, and they must use Outlook.

3. Also, you could add a second AND statement like this:

   If a user wants to access email, then they must use MFA, and they must use Outlook, and they must be using a compliant computer.

Conditional Access statements evaluate a signal, make a decision, and then enforce the policy, as shown in Figure 8-8.

Figure 8-8   The components of Conditional Access policies

Following are some common signals included in Conditional Access policies:

- Group membership

- Trusted IP addresses

- Device identity

- Application to be used

- Risk detection

- Microsoft Defender for Cloud Apps

CHAPTER 8

Access decisions that can be made by Conditional Access include the following:

- Block access

- Grant access

Applied policies might include the following:

- Require MFA

- Block sign-ins using legacy protocols

- Allow only if coming from a trusted location

- Block risky sign-in behaviors

- Require organization-managed devices

Let's look at setting up a Conditional Access policy. In this example, we will create a conditional access policy from a template to enforce a common requirement only to allow Office 365 when the organization owns the device used. To create this Conditional Access policy, do the following:

1. As a Global Admin, log in to the Azure portal at *https://portal.azure.com*.

2. In the Search box, type **conditional access** and then select Azure AD Conditional Access from the results.

3. Click the +New Policy button to create a new policy.

4. In the Name box, enter a name for your policy, such as **Require Outlook on managed device for email**.

5. Under Assignments, click 0 Users Or Workload Identities Selected, and then under Include, select the All Users radio button to apply this conditional access policy to everyone.

6. Under Cloud Apps Or Actions, click No Cloud Apps, Actions, Or Authentication Contexts Selected, and then click the Select Apps radio button. In the Select flyout, select Office 365, as shown in Figure 8-9.

7. Click Select.

8. Under Conditions, click 0 Conditions Selected, and under Client Apps, click Not Configured.

Figure 8-9   Creating a Conditional Access policy for Office 365

9. In the Client Apps dialog box, select Yes to configure, and then deselect everything except Mobile Apps And Desktop Clients, as shown in Figure 8-10.

Figure 8-10   Configuring Client Apps

10. Click Done.

11. Under Filter For Devices, click Not Configured.

12. Under Configure, click Yes. Under Devices Matching The Rule, select Include Filtered Devices In Policy is selected.

13. In the rule builder, from the Property dropdown, select DeviceOwnership, and from the Operator dropdown, select Equals. From the Value dropdown, select Company. Note the rule syntax that is automatically created for you, as shown below and in Figure 8-11:

```
device.deviceOwnership -eq "Company"
```

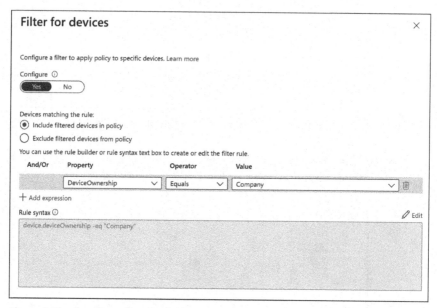

Figure 8-11   Creating a filter for devices condition

14. Click Done.

15. Choose Access Controls > Grant, and click 0 Controls Selected.

16. In the Grant dialog box, make sure the radio button next to Grant Access is selected and select Require Device To Be Marked As Compliant; then click Select.

17. Under Enable Policy, leave the default setting, Report-Only, and then click Create.

TIP

Setting new Conditional Access policies to Report-Only is recommended to ensure you do not lock anyone out, including yourself. Test access and review the logs to ensure your desired results occur before setting the policy to On, addressing any changes required and testing again first.

Risk-based Conditional Access

If you have Azure Active Directory Plan 1 or Plan 2, you can further enhance Conditional Access by using risk-based policies that leverage Identity Protection. Microsoft uses signals from a variety of sources, including Azure Active Directory and law enforcement, to determine if a user's account is at risk. Real-time detections might show up in logs within 10 minutes, while offline detections might not show up for up to 48 hours.

Standard sign-in risk detections—included in both Azure Active Directory Plan 1 and Plan 2—include those shown in Table 8-3.

Table 8-3   Sign-in risk detections

Risk detection	Detection type	Description
Additional Risk Detected	Real-time or Offline	This detection indicates that one of the premium detections was detected. Since the premium detections are visible only to Azure AD Premium P2 customers, they're titled "additional risk detected" for customers without Azure AD Premium P2 licenses.
Anonymous IP Address	Real-time	This risk detection type indicates sign-ins from an anonymous IP address (for example, Tor browser or anonymous VPN). These IP addresses are typically used by actors who want to hide their login telemetry (IP address, location, device, and so on) for potentially malicious intent.
Admin Confirmed User Compromised	Offline	This detection indicates an admin has selected Confirm User Compromised in the Risky Users UI or using the riskyUsers API. To see which admin has confirmed this user is compromised, check the user's risk history (via UI or API).
Azure AD Threat Intelligence	Offline	This risk detection type indicates user activity that is unusual for the given user or is consistent with known attack patterns based on 'Microsoft's internal and external threat intelligence sources.

CHAPTER 8

Leaked Credentials	Offline	This risk detection type indicates that the user's valid credentials have been leaked. When cybercriminals compromise the valid passwords of legitimate users, they often share those credentials. Typically, this sharing is done by posting publicly on the dark web, paste sites, or by trading and selling the credentials on the black market. When the Microsoft leaked credentials service acquires user credentials from the dark web, paste sites, or other sources, 'they're checked against Azure AD 'users' current valid credentials to find valid matches.

Premium sign-in risk detections, which require Azure Active Directory Plan 2, include the ones shown in Table 8-4.

Table 8-4 Premium sign-in risk detections

Risk detection	Detection type	Description
Atypical Travel	Offline	This risk detection type identifies two sign-ins originating from geographically distant locations, where at least one of the locations might also be atypical for the user, given past behavior. Among several other factors, this machine learning algorithm considers the time between the two sign-ins and the time it would have taken for the user to travel from the first location to the second, indicating that a different user is using the same credentials.
		The algorithm ignores obvious false-positives contributing to the impossible travel conditions, such as VPNs and locations regularly used by other users in the organization. The system has an initial learning period of the earliest of 14 days or 10 logins, during which it learns a new user's sign-in behavior.
Anomalous Token	Offline	This detection indicates abnormal token characteristics, such as an unusual token lifetime or a token that is played from an unfamiliar location. This detection covers Session Tokens and Refresh Tokens.
Token Issuer Anomaly	Offline	This risk detection indicates the SAML token issuer for the associated SAML token is potentially compromised. The claims included in the token are unusual or match known attacker patterns.

Malware Linked IP Address	Offline	This risk detection type indicates sign-ins from IP addresses infected with malware that is known to actively communicate with a bot server. This detection is determined by correlating the user's device IP addresses against IP addresses that were in contact with a bot server while the bot server was active.
		This detection has been deprecated. Identity Protection will no longer generate new Malware Linked IP Address detections. Customers with Malware Linked IP Address detections in their tenant will still be able to view, remediate, or dismiss them until the 90-day detection retention time is reached.
Suspicious Browser	Offline	Suspicious browser detection indicates anomalous behavior based on suspicious sign-in activity across multiple tenants from different countries in the same browser.
Unfamiliar Sign-In Properties	Real-time	This risk detection type considers past sign-in history to look for anomalous sign-ins. The system stores information about previous sign-ins and triggers a risk detection when a sign-in occurs with properties that are unfamiliar to the user. These properties can include IP, ASN, Location, Device, Browser, and Tenant IP Subnet. Newly created users will be in the learning mode period where the unfamiliar sign-in properties risk detection will be turned off while our algorithms learn the user's behavior. The learning mode duration is dynamic and depends on how much time the algorithm gathers enough information about the user's sign-in patterns. The minimum duration is five days. A user can return to learning mode after a long inactivity.
		We also run this detection for basic authentication (or legacy protocols). Because these protocols don't have modern properties such as client ID, there's limited telemetry to reduce false-positives. We recommend that our customers move to modern authentication.
		Unfamiliar sign-in properties can be detected on both interactive and non-interactive sign-ins. When this detection is detected on non-interactive sign-ins, it deserves increased scrutiny due to the risk of token replay attacks.
Malicious IP Address	Offline	This detection indicates sign-in from a malicious IP address. An IP address is considered malicious based on high failure rates because of invalid credentials received from the IP address or other IP reputation sources.
Suspicious Inbox Manipulation Rules	Offline	This detection is discovered by Microsoft Defender for Cloud Apps. This detection profiles your environment and triggers alerts when suspicious rules that delete or move messages or folders are set on a user's inbox. This detection might indicate that the user's account is compromised, that messages are being intentionally hidden, and that the mailbox is being used to distribute spam or malware in your organization.

CHAPTER 8

Password Spray	Offline	A password spray attack is where multiple usernames are attacked using common passwords in a unified brute-force manner to gain unauthorized access. This risk detection is triggered when a password spray attack has been performed.
Impossible Travel	Offline	This detection is discovered by Microsoft Defender for Cloud Apps. This detection identifies two user activities (single or multiple sessions) originating from geographically distant locations within a time shorter than the time it would have taken the user to travel from the first location to the second, indicating that a different user is using the same credentials.
New Country	Offline	This detection is discovered by Microsoft Defender for Cloud Apps. This detection considers past activity locations to determine new and infrequent locations. The anomaly-detection engine stores information about previous locations used by users in the organization.
Activity From Anonymous IP Address	Offline	This detection is discovered by Microsoft Defender for Cloud Apps. This detection identifies that users were active from an IP address identified as an anonymous proxy IP address.
Suspicious Inbox Forwarding	Offline	This detection is discovered by Microsoft Defender for Cloud Apps. This detection looks for suspicious email forwarding rules—for example, if a user created an inbox rule that forwards a copy of all emails to an external address.
Mass Access To Sensitive Files	Offline	This detection is discovered by Microsoft Defender for Cloud Apps. This detection profiles your environment and triggers alerts when users access multiple files from Microsoft SharePoint or Microsoft OneDrive. An alert is only triggered if the number of accessed files is uncommon for the user and the files might contain sensitive information.
Possible Attempt To Access Primary Refresh Token (PRT)	Offline	This risk detection type is detected by Microsoft Defender for Endpoint (MDE). A Primary Refresh Token (PRT) is a key artifact of Azure AD authentication on Windows 10, Windows Server 2016, and later versions, iOS, and Android devices. A PRT is a JSON Web Token (JWT) that's specially issued to Microsoft first-party token brokers to enable single sign-on (SSO) across the applications used on those devices. Attackers can attempt to access this resource to move laterally into an organization or perform credential theft. This detection will move users to high risk and will only fire in organizations deploying MDE. This detection is low-volume and will be seen infrequently by most organizations. However, it's high risk when it does occur, and users should be remediated.

NOTE

Anomalous Token is tuned to incur more noise than other detections at the same risk level. This trade-off is chosen to increase the likelihood of detecting replayed tokens that might otherwise go unnoticed. Because this is a high noise detection, there's a higher-than-normal chance that some of the sessions flagged by this detection are false positives. We recommend investigating the sessions flagged by this detection in the context of other sign-ins from the user. If the location, application, IP address, user agent, or other characteristics are unexpected for the user, the tenant admin should consider this as an indicator of potential token replay.

Risk is categorized as one of either no, low, medium, or high, and you can use that to create policies that require different things depending upon that risk, such as requiring MFA when any risk is present even if the user previously completed MFA, forcing a password reset on a medium risk, and blocking access on a high risk.

Securing devices

Microsoft Enterprise Mobility + Security includes Microsoft Intune, a Mobile Device Management (MDM) platform, and a Mobile Application Management (MAM) platform. "Mobile" simply means they are not in a fixed location, so you can use Intune to secure and manage laptops, tablets, and phones.

Microsoft Intune is one feature of the larger Microsoft Endpoint Manager offering. Microsoft Endpoint Manager includes Intune, Configuration Manager for on-premises device management, Desktop Analytics, and Windows Autopilot. In this section, we are focused on Intune. As a cloud-based service, there is no hardware to deploy, though Intune can co-manage with Microsoft Configuration Manager if you have that already deployed on-premises. Intune provides organizations with the following capabilities:

- Configure both corporate-owned and personally-owned devices
- Deploy and authenticate applications on devices
- Control access and sharing of information
- Enforce compliance with corporate security requirements

In addition to the device and application management, Intune can be integrated with Conditional Access, so device management or health can determine what access should be permitted. Companies might choose to use Mobile Device Management, Mobile Application Management, or both to meet their needs.

Mobile Device Management

Mobile Device Management (MDM) can be used to manage various devices, including Windows and Macs and phones and tablets running iOS/iPadOS or Android. This is probably the best choice for managing corporate-owned devices or when you want the highest degree of control of any device that accesses company resources.

Devices you want to manage through Intune's MDM capabilities must first be enrolled into Intune. Enrolling into Intune installs a management profile onto the device along with certificates necessary to support that profile and configures the device to align with your security requirements. End users or IT admins can initiate enrollment and work with corporate-owned and Bring Your Own Device (BYOD) devices.

Mobile Application Management

This might be the better choice for BYOD devices when you need to secure access to the data but minimize the impact on the personally owned device. Management is limited to one or more applications used to access company data, while the rest of the device remains autonomous. Companies can still exert a high degree of control, apply security policies to the applications used to access company data, and ensure that data cannot be moved from a managed application to an unmanaged one without having as much control over the complete device. In some BYOD scenarios, end users might prefer this if they do not want to cede control of their personally-owned hardware to the company.

Getting started with Intune

Assuming you have the necessary licenses and are a Global Admin or an Intune Administrator, you are ready to start with Microsoft Intune. Log in to the Microsoft Endpoint Manager (MEM) portal at *https://endpoint.microsoft.com*. You will see the MEM Home screen, as shown in Figure 8-12.

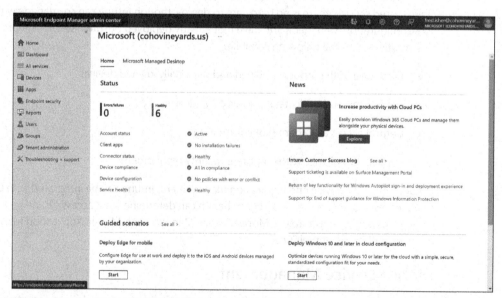

Figure 8-12   The Microsoft Endpoint Manager admin center

Follow these steps to start enrolling devices into Intune:

1. In the left-side navigation column, click Devices. A submenu will appear.

2. Under Device Enrollment, click Enroll Devices.

3. You will see options to enroll Windows, Apple, and Android devices, as well as restrictions, identifiers, and managers, as shown in Figure 8-13.

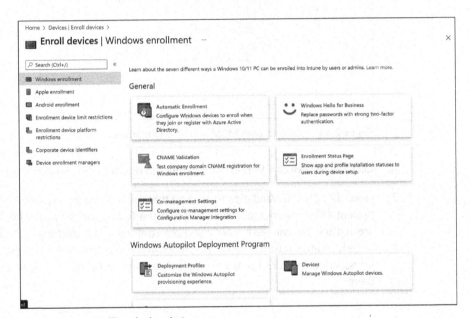

Figure 8-13   Enrolling devices in Intune

4. To set up Intune so that Windows devices automatically enroll when they join your Azure AD tenant, click Automatic Enrollment.

5. You can set up both MDM and MAM here and apply settings to members of groups or all users. You can also customize the URLs if desired. Set both MDM User Scope and MAM User Scope to All, and then click Save. You will see that settings have been updated, as shown in Figure 8-14.

CHAPTER 8

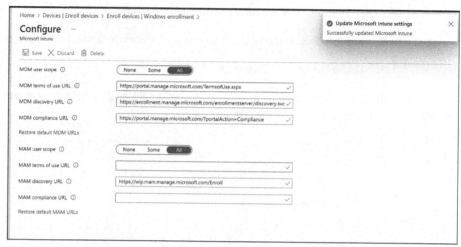

Figure 8-14 Enabling both MDM and MAM for all users

6. Click Enroll Devices > Windows Enrollment to return to the previous menu.

7. Next, click CNAME Validation to confirm that the DNS names required for Intune are present. Enter your domain name and click the Test button. If the CNAME records are in place, you will see a green checkbox confirming this, as shown in Figure 8-15. If there is an error, return to the DNS settings in the Microsoft 365 admin portal at *https://admin.microsoft.com* and create the required CNAME records as documented there.

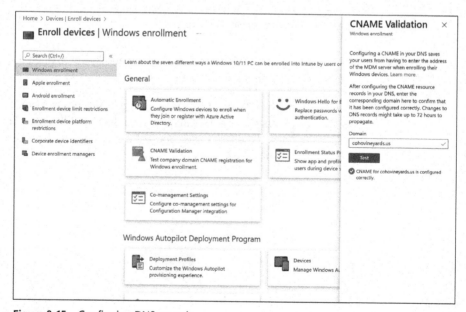

Figure 8-15 Confirming DNS records

Now, when a Windows device is configured to join your Azure AD tenant, it will automatically enroll in Intune. To start securing your Windows devices, you need to establish an Antivirus policy. Follow these steps:

1. In the left-side menu, click Endpoint Security.

2. On the Endpoint Security | Overview page, click Antivirus.

3. On the Summary tab, under AV Policies, click +Create Policy.

4. In the Create A Profile pane, in the Platform dropdown, select Windows 10, Windows 11, and Windows Server. From the Profile dropdown, select Microsoft Defender Antivirus (see Figure 8-16).

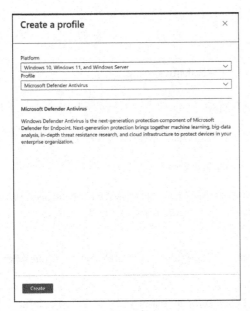

Figure 8-16   Create A Profile

5. Click Create to launch the Create Profile Wizard. Give the profile a name and a description, and then click Next.

6. Scroll through the antivirus settings and configure them to match your corporate policy. A partial view of this is shown in Figure 8-17. When finished, click Next.

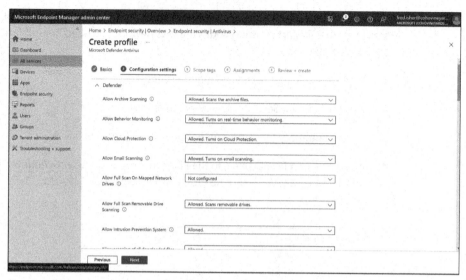

Figure 8-17   A partial view of the antivirus settings

7.   On the Scope Tags tab, click Next.

8.   On the Assignments tab, click +Add All Devices, and then click Next.

9.   Review your settings, and then click Create.

Now, every Windows device joined to the Azure AD tenant will be enrolled in Intune, and Microsoft Defender Antivirus will be configured consistently. You can, of course, configure any of the other settings similarly.

Next, we will use Mobile Application Management to install and configure Microsoft 365 Apps for our Windows devices:

1.   Log in to *https://endpoint.microsoft.com* using a Global Admin or Intune Admin account (if you're not already logged in).

2.   On the left-side menu, click Apps.

3.   On the Apps | Overview menu, under By Platform, click Windows.

4.   On the Windows | Windows Apps menu, click +Add.

5.   In the Select App Type pane, select Windows 10 And Later from the App Type dropdown, as shown in Figure 8-18.

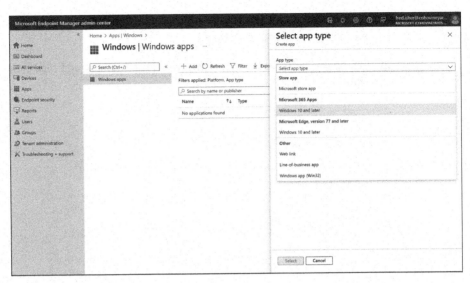

Figure 8-18   Select App Type

6. Click Select.

7. Review the information shown on the App Suite Information tab, make any changes necessary for your organization, and click Next.

8. On the Configure App Suite tab, review the settings and select the Update Channel appropriate for your organization, as shown in Figure 8-19. Click Next.

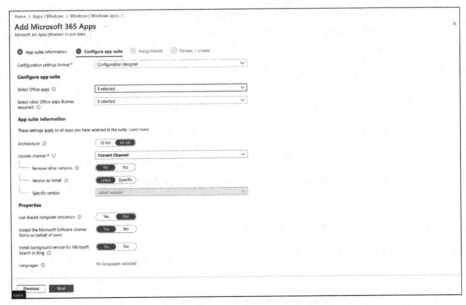

Figure 8-19   Configuring Microsoft 365 apps

CHAPTER 8

9. On the Assignments tab, select the appropriate group to which the applications should be deployed, and then click Next.

10. On the Review +Create tab, review your selected settings and click Create, as shown in Figure 8-20.

Figure 8-20   Deployment of Microsoft 365 apps to enrolled Windows clients

Now, when a Windows client joins the Azure Active Directory tenant, it will receive the 64-bit Current channel installation of Microsoft 365 apps. You can create multiple apps with different options in MAM and assign them to different groups.

You might want to do this in the following instances:

- You have a mix of 32-bit and 64-bit systems.

- You want to have a test group on the Current Channel while the rest of the organization uses the Semi-Annual Channel.

- Depending on the role, you want to have different deployment options for specific Office apps.

Managing mobile phones, tablets, and Mac devices is similar.

What's next?

This chapter will get you well along the path toward securing your environment with Microsoft Enterprise Mobility + Security (EMS), though there is much more you can do.

In the next chapter, you will learn the steps needed to plan your identity and authentication configuration.

NOTE

To learn more about Microsoft Endpoint Manager, see *https://aka.ms/memdocs*. **For a deeper dive into EMS, see** *https://aka.ms/intunedocs*.

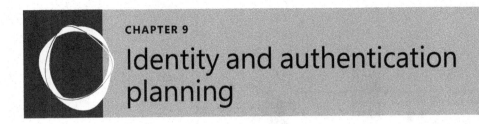

Identity and authentication planning

In a typical Microsoft 365 implementation, your users exist in Azure Active Directory (AAD) primarily because of directory synchronization. (Configuring directory synchronization is discussed in detail in Chapter 10, "Installing AAD Connect.") However, in addition to the available identity types, several options are available for user sign-in and authentication, depending on how your users are created.

Each of these options has a different set of requirements, affecting the implementation of directory synchronization and possibly driving other infrastructure requirements and even Azure AD-licensed features.

This chapter discusses the different types of identities, the sign-in, authentication, and connectivity options available to you, and how they affect your users, environment, implementation, and ongoing Microsoft 365 administration experience.

Identity types

"Identities" refer to security principals—users who can sign in to Microsoft 365 and consume services. Whether it's Exchange Online or Microsoft 365 Office Applications, your users must be able to authenticate with Azure AD before they can use the service. That authentication process varies depending on the type of identity in use.

Synchronized identities

Synchronized users are exactly what that sounds like; they have been synchronized to your Microsoft 365 tenant from your on-premises Active Directory. Your directory synchronization configuration dictates which users are synchronized to Azure AD. Although your users now appear in the Microsoft 365 portal, they are still mastered on-premises and managed using the tools you are already accustomed to using.

Synchronized users are the most common user type in Microsoft 365 and are the easiest to create and maintain. Implementation of the AAD Connect tool automatically populates your Microsoft 365 tenant with synchronized users, essentially replicas of all your existing users, as shown in Figure 9-1. You can start using Office 365 almost immediately.

CHAPTER 9

237

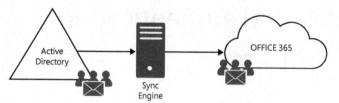

Figure 9-1   Synchronized identities

Several additional configuration options affect the user sign-in process and are discussed later in this chapter. Each carries different requirements and additional tasks that must be performed in Azure AD and your on-premises environment.

Chapters 10 through 12 discuss the synchronization of identities in detail; the following discusses the next identity type, cloud identities.

Cloud identities

Cloud identities are user accounts created manually in the Microsoft 365 tenant. In fact, when you first set up your Microsoft 365 subscription, the account you provided during setup was configured as a cloud user.

These accounts, like synchronized identities, can be used for sign-in to Microsoft 365 and can use Microsoft 365 services just like a synchronized account.

Most often, cloud identities are created by an administrator directly in the portal by entering all the necessary information, such as user principal name, display name, and email address (where applicable), and assigning a password and one or more licenses to the account. When complete, the user can start using Microsoft 365:

1.   To create a cloud identity, simply log in to the Microsoft 365 admin center and select Add A User from the Active Users page, as shown in Figure 9-2.

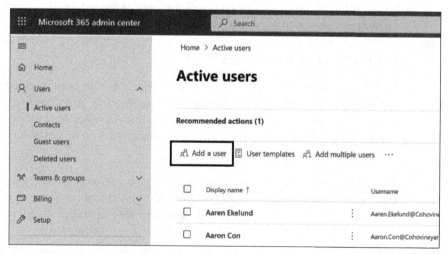

Figure 9-2   Selecting Add A User in the Microsoft 365 admin center

2. After selecting Add A User, the New User dialog box appears, where you can enter the first name, last name, display name, and user name (also known as the UserPrincipalName) for the cloud user account. See Figure 9.3.

    ■   The Domain dropdown displays all the valid domains in use in your Microsoft 365 subscription. If you've just created your subscription, the only domain available in the dropdown is likely the `tenant.onmicrosoft.com` domain. After successfully registering additional domains in your tenant, you can change this value for your cloud users.

    ■   In addition to the name information, you can also enter contact information; attributes such as address, city, state, and zip code; and values such as job title and department.

Figure 9-3   Manually creating a cloud identity

3. You can set a password, role, and one or more product licenses during manual cloud identity creation.

4. If you choose not to set a password, an auto-generated password will be created and sent to the email address set on your admin account.

5. It's important to note that User is the default role for all cloud identities. If this account is meant only to use services in Microsoft 365, you can leave the role selection as is. However, if this account is meant to administer Microsoft 365, you must select the necessary role here.

NOTE

The different role types and their access levels were discussed in Chapter 2, "Preparing your environment for the cloud."

It's possible to create a cloud identity with no product licenses; however, you must select Create User Without Product License before completing the user creation process.

Although it is possible to create cloud identities manually, it becomes rather cumbersome and time-consuming to create more than a few. However, you can perform bulk creation of cloud identities from the Microsoft 365 admin center by using a comma-separated input (CSV) file.

Using a CSV import file, you can quickly create cloud identities when directory synchronization from on-premises is either unavailable or not applicable.

The CSV import file must contain specific header information before importing it into the portal. The CSV header information and even a CSV with sample data can be downloaded from the portal with the Add Multiple Users Wizard. Select Add Multiple Users from the List of Users page and then select either Download A Blank CSV File With The Required Headers or Download A CSV File That Includes Example User Info, as shown in Figure 9-4.

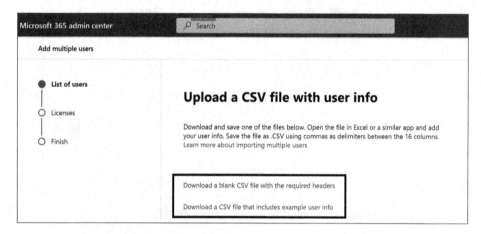

Figure 9-4   Downloading CSV header information or sample CSV file

Each of the fields provided in the CSV has a limit to the number of characters that can be populated, as shown in Table 9-1. Values marked with an asterisk (*) are mandatory values, and you cannot leave them blank; all others are optional.

Table 9-1 User import character limits

Field	Max length
User Name*	79
First Name	64
Last Name	64
Display Name*	256
Job Title	64
Department	64
Office Number	128
Office Phone	64
Mobile Phone	64
Fax	64
Address	1023
City	128
State or Province	128
Zip or Postal Code	40
Country or Region	128

TIP

The user name, or `UserPrincipalName` value, has a limitation of 79 total characters, including the @ symbol. The alias (the left side of the user name before the @ symbol) cannot exceed 30 characters, and the domain name (the user name after the @ symbol) cannot exceed 48 characters.

After you have populated the CSV input file, you can load it by following these directions:

1. Click the Browse button, as Figure 9-5 shows.

2. If you don't yet have domains registered in your tenant, you can use the `@tenant.onmicrosoft.com` suffix for the user name, and the value can be changed later from the portal.

3. After selecting your CSV input file, as shown in Figure 9-5, clicking Next enables you to set the location for your imported users and assign one or more product licenses, as shown in Figure 9-6.

4. Just like the manual creation of a single user, if you don't wish to assign a license to the imported users, you can select Don't Assign Any Licenses and click Next.

5. Clicking Next creates the users automatically.

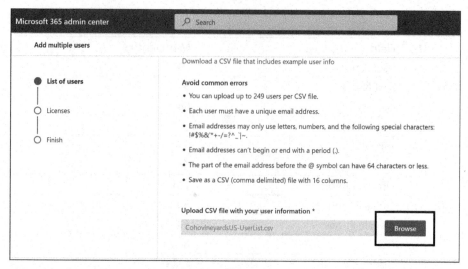

Figure 9-5   Importing a CSV file for bulk user creation

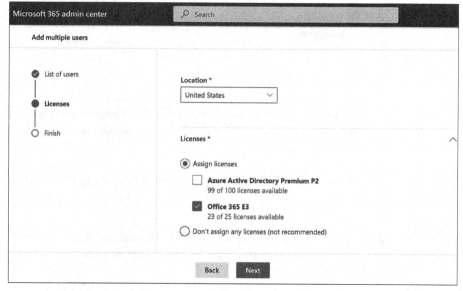

Figure 9-6   Add Multiple Users

CAUTION

There is no Are You Sure? prompt, so you want to be sure that you've selected all the appropriate licenses and sign-in status options for your new users before clicking Next.

Inside Out

Sign-in status

The sign-in status for users indicates whether the user can authenticate to Office 365 and use the services.

For synchronized identities, the sign-in status is set to reflect the `UserAccountControl` status in your on-premises Active Directory. When a user changes from Enabled to Disabled in on-premises Active Directory, the sign-in status in Microsoft Azure is changed to match.

The sign-in status must be set for cloud identities during user creation and changed manually thereafter through the Office 365 admin center or the Microsoft Online PowerShell cmdlets.

It *is* possible to change the sign-in status manually for a synchronized identity from the portal and override the account status synchronized from on-premises.

6. When the cloud user bulk import completes, a message appears, indicating the number of objects created. You are given the option to send passwords to one or more administrators. See Figure 9-7.

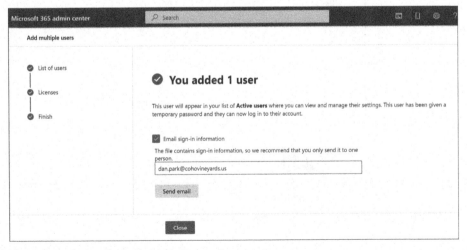

Figure 9-7   Successful bulk cloud user creation message

If you've created a combination of cloud users (possibly for administrator roles) and synchronized identities from your on-premises directory, your Microsoft 365 admin center might be somewhat cluttered.

Unfortunately, identifying cloud users versus synchronized users is not simple because this distinction is not automatically displayed on the Active Users page.

Instead, as shown in Figure 9-8, you will need to follow these steps:

1.   Select Filter > New Filter.

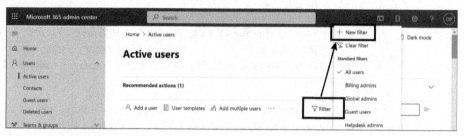

Figure 9-8   Selecting the Filter view option and creating a new filter

2.   On the Custom Filter page, provide a name for your custom filter, scroll to the bottom, click Synchronized Users Only, and then click Add, as shown in Figure 9-9.

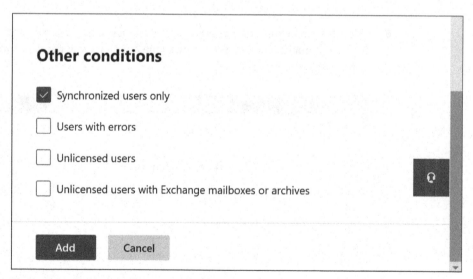

Figure 9-9   Synchronized Users Only

3. This new custom view will be accessible to all Microsoft 365 administrators when using the View dropdown on the Active Users page, as seen in Figure 9-10.

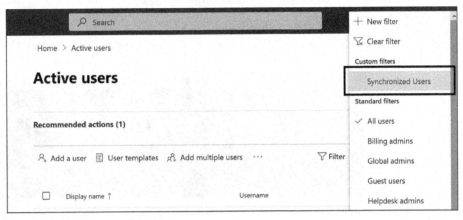

Figure 9-10   Active Users

Inside Out

Filtering your view

The Custom View option in the Microsoft 365 admin center gives you some flexibility in filtering the views of your users; however, it's impossible to create a view of cloud-only users. There is a filter option for synchronized users but not the reverse.

A list of cloud-only users can be retrieved by using the MSOnline PowerShell cmdlets, or you can populate fields such as Job Title or Department with a value that you can use in the Custom View filter.

4. When using PowerShell to identify and categorize users, you can use the MSOnline PowerShell cmdlets to filter these user accounts by using the `LastDirSyncTime` property that is present on all objects in Azure AD. If an object has been synchronized from on-premises through AAD Connect, the `LastDirSyncTime` property contains the date and time of that synchronization. However, for cloud user objects, that value is `null`.

TIP

To connect to MSOnline using Windows PowerShell, you must download and install the Sign-In Assistant from *http://aka.ms/o365-sia* and the MSOnline PowerShell Module at *http://aka.ms/o365-psh*. After the module has been loaded, you use the `Connect-MSOLService` command and provide credentials for an admin account in the tenant.

5. Connecting to MSOnline PowerShell and running the `Get-MsolUser` command with the `-All` switch and a filter of `Where { $_.LastDirSyncTime -eq $null }` provides a list of all cloud user accounts, as shown in Figure 9-11.

6. The complete command would be
   `Get-MsolUser -All | Where { $_.LastDirSyncTime -eq $null}`.

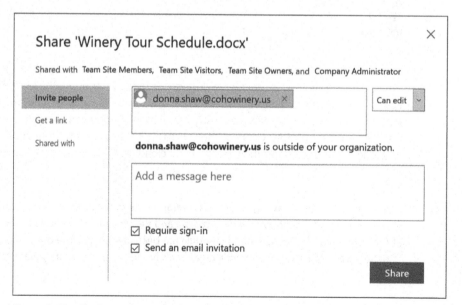

Figure 9-11   Using MSOnline PowerShell to display cloud users

Guest identities

The final identity, although not related to the synchronization process or created manually by an administrator from the portal, is the guest account. Guest accounts are created automatically in Azure AD as the result of an invitation process in SharePoint Online to share individual documents, folders, or OneDrive content or an entire Microsoft SharePoint team site.

When a document, folder, or site is shared in SharePoint Online, your users can invite external identities, as shown in Figure 9-12.

Share 'Winery Tour Schedule.docx'   ✕

Shared with Team Site Members, Team Site Visitors, Team Site Owners, and Company Administrator

| Invite people | 👤 donna.shaw@cohowinery.us ✕ | Can edit ⌄ |

Get a link

Shared with   **donna.shaw@cohowinery.us** is outside of your organization.

Add a message here

☑ Require sign-in
☑ Send an email invitation

Share

Figure 9-12   Sharing a SharePoint Online document with an external user

When the recipient accepts the sharing invite creation and authenticates to Azure AD using their email address, a guest account is automatically created in Azure AD and visible in the Microsoft 365 admin center. This guest account can be seen using the custom Guest Users view on the Active Users page, as shown in Figure 9-13.

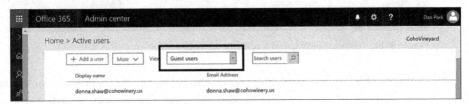

Figure 9-13   Viewing guest user accounts in the Microsoft 365 admin center

When an external or guest account has been created through the sharing process, additional sharing requests are unnecessary when delegating additional permissions to the account. Instead, the guest user account appears in the user list (SharePoint People Picker) when prompting to add members or share additional content.

Typically, guest accounts are not licensed in your Microsoft 365 environment. As a result, these accounts have limited access based on whether they were created through the sharing process or were manually added to other content in your tenant.

Guest accounts have the following capabilities:

- They can access the sites, folders, or documents to which they were granted access through a sharing request in SharePoint Online.

- They can be added to team sites in SharePoint Online as members, enabling them to add, update, and delete lists and documents.

- They can use Office Online to view documents to which they have access in SharePoint Online.

Guest accounts can also be easily identified by using the MSOnline PowerShell cmdlets.

When a guest account is created in Azure AD, the email address used to send the sharing request is converted to the UserPrincipalName of the account; however, some minor changes are applied.

Because the UserPrincipalName can only contain one at sign (@) character, the at sign in the email address of the external account is replaced with an underscore (_), the address is followed by #EXT#, and, finally, the @tenant.onmicrosoft.com suffix is appended to the end.

The result is an easily recognizable UserPrincipalName for guest accounts, as shown in Figure 9-14.

CHAPTER 9

Figure 9-14   Guest user account UserPrincipalName value

Finally, there is one other distinguishing feature of a guest identity in Azure compared to cloud or synchronized accounts. Unlike the other two identity types, guest accounts have different values for the UserType property.

When viewing a guest account by using the MSOnline PowerShell cmdlets, as shown in Figure 9-15, notice that the UserType is Guest versus a cloud or synchronized account, which is set with a UserType of Member.

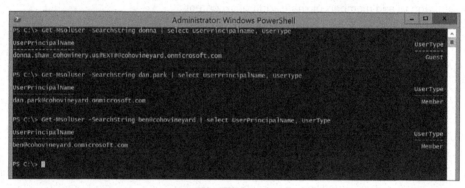

Figure 9-15   Guest user account UserType value

Inside Out

Guest accounts

Whenever a guest account is created in Azure AD, the resulting UserPrincipalName is in the format of <email_address>_domain#EXT#@tenant.onmicrosoft.com.

A sharing request for britta.simon@contoso.com would result in a guest account being created with a UserPrincipalName attribute value of britta.simon_contoso.com#EXT#@yourtenant.onmicrosoft.com.

Now that you are familiar with the different types of identities used with Azure AD, it's important to understand the types of identity federation and user authentication available for each identity type.

User authentication

You must provide a mechanism for authentication for each of the identities present in your tenant, whether they are synchronized or cloud users.

In simplest terms, authentication can be done either by a password, normally referred to as Managed, or using an identity federation tool (for example, ADFS) called Federated. Both options offer several implementation methods, and how you create your identities will affect which options are available.

Password

Using cloud passwords is one of the simplest methods for authentication with Azure AD. Essentially, each identity has a password set on the object itself in Azure AD, and that password is used for authentication purposes when a sign-in to Microsoft 365 is processed.

> ### TIP
>
> **Microsoft 365 and Azure AD are often used interchangeably because Azure Active Directory is the underlying directory when creating objects in Microsoft 365. It is important to note that passwords, federation, and authentication are all features of Azure Active Directory. Microsoft 365 is one of the many services built on Azure Active Directory.**

When signing in to Microsoft 365, as shown in Figure 9-16, you provide the `UserPrincipalName` (UserName) for the identity and the password stored in Azure AD as the identity.

Figure 9-16   The Microsoft 365 Sign In page

CHAPTER 9

Passwords may be set in one of two ways:

- You or the user manually define the password in the Microsoft 365 portal.

- The Azure AD Connect synchronization process synchronizes the password from on-premises Active Directory. Chapter 10 discusses how to do this in more detail.

TIP

Even though the Microsoft 365 admin center enables you to change the password for a synchronized user, this action will not work if the synchronized user account is synchronized with a password from on-premises Active Directory. When you enable Password Hash Sync in Azure AD Connect, only passwords for cloud user accounts can be changed using the Microsoft 365 admin center.

Much like on-premises Active Directory, new user accounts are configured with a default password that must be changed on the first login, and like Active Directory, user passwords in Azure AD have an expiration policy that forces regular password changes.

Remember, the password is automatically generated when the account is created and is provided to the administrator who created the account. This is true whether the account was created individually or in bulk.

If you assign a password manually at the time of account creation, instead of relying on a randomly generated password, you can force the user to change this password on the first login. This is done by using the Reset Password options in the New User dialog box shown in Figure 9-17.

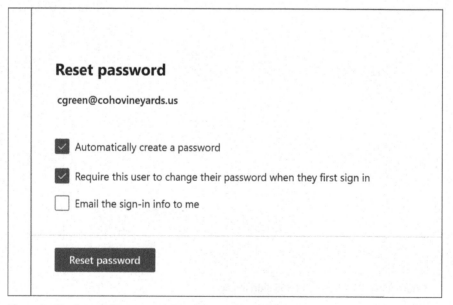

Figure 9-17   Generating or supplying a password and forcing change on sign-in

The user is prompted to change the password in the following situations:

- When logging in for the first time to a new cloud account

- When logging in to an account with an expired password

- When logging in to an account with a password that the administrator has reset

The Update Your Password dialog is shown in Figure 9-18.

Figure 9-18   Password update required

Any passwords created by an administrator or defined while creating a cloud user object are subject to the same password complexity restrictions applied to users when they reset or change their passwords.

Microsoft 365 cloud account passwords have the following requirements:

- 8 characters minimum

- 16 characters maximum

- Cannot contain spaces or Unicode characters

The following requirements apply only to accounts when strong passwords are enforced:

- Cannot contain a period (.) immediately before the at sign (@)

- Must contain a combination of three of the four following conditions:

  - Uppercase characters

  - Lowercase characters

  - Numbers

  - Symbols

Password policy

The password policy options in the Microsoft 365 portal allow you to set the defaults for password expiration and complexity. These settings should be reviewed thoroughly and configured to match your company policy and existing on-premises policies where applicable.

Expiration

The Azure AD password policy that governs password expiration and notification can be configured through the Microsoft 365 admin center by selecting Settings > Org Settings > Security & Privacy > Password Expiration Policy, as shown in Figure 9-19.

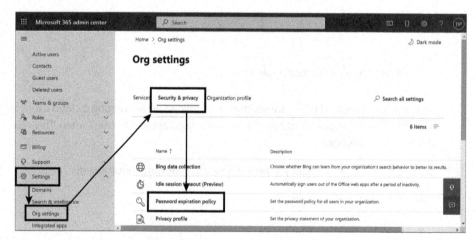

Figure 9-19   Setting the Microsoft 365 password policy

This setting enables you to change the password expiration interval as well as the notification settings for cloud user accounts in Microsoft 365.

TIP

It is always recommended to set the password policies for expiration and notification to match your on-premises Active Directory policies. This way, even cloud identities have the same requirements. If you enable Password Hash Sync with Azure AD Connect, the Azure AD password policies do not apply to synchronized identities.

Complexity

Unlike the settings for password expiration, strong password requirements are enabled on all cloud accounts by default and cannot be changed in the admin center.

To change the strong password enforcement for one or more users, you must use the MSOnline PowerShell cmdlet Set-MsolUser with -StrongPasswordRequired:

```
Set-MsolUser -UserPrincipalName sean.bentley@cohovineyard.onmicrosoft.com
-StrongPasswordRequired $false
```

Changing the complexity requirements for a user does not force them to change their existing password, nor is the user notified that their password complexity policy has changed. They are simply not required to use a complex password on their next password change.

NOTE

Changing the StrongPasswordRequired setting for a cloud user does not change the minimum or maximum password length requirements. These remain at 8 and 16, respectively.

You can view the StrongPasswordRequired setting for a user by using the Get-MsolUser cmdlet, as shown in Figure 9-20.

Figure 9-20 Viewing the StrongPasswordRequired property for a cloud user

Setting password complexity through Windows PowerShell rather than in the admin center means it cannot be done automatically for new users without a custom process. This behavior is by design.

CAUTION

On-premises Active Directory actively enforces password complexity requirements; the same should be true for Azure Active Directory. Change password complexity requirements on a cloud user only if absolutely necessary, and never do it for admin-level accounts because this creates a security risk.

NOTE

If you select Password Hash Sync during Azure AD Connect installation, you cannot set a password on a synced account; you can only set a password on cloud accounts.

Identity federation

So far, you've examined authentication using passwords. Although this authentication method is the simplest, it might not be acceptable due to company policy or other security requirements within your organization. As a result, identity federation can be used to provide an alternate option for user authentication to Microsoft 365.

Identity federation—often referred to as single sign-on—is a process by which the user account in Azure AD uses an on-premises or third-party identity provider to authenticate sign-in attempts, as shown in Figure 9-21. This removes the requirement to maintain separate passwords in Microsoft 365 and secures the authentication process by using the source directory for your users.

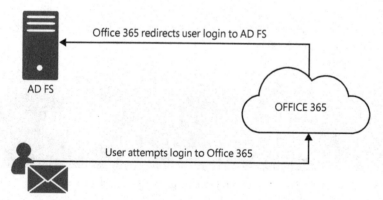

Figure 9-21 Identity federation using Microsoft Active Directory Federation Services (AD FS)

When users sign in to Microsoft 365, they are directed back to on-premises infrastructure to verify their account, and no password data for synchronized accounts is stored in Azure AD.

TIP

Implementation of both identity federation *and* password hash sync is supported. It is simple to configure identity federation for your domain names and select the optional Password Hash Sync feature during the Azure AD Connect installation.

Although using identity federation over passwords is a more secure authentication process, it also introduces more complexity to the sign-in process.

The Password Hash Sync feature is included in the Azure AD Connect tool, and you can easily enable it through the installation wizard existing on the same server. In contrast, identity federation requires additional servers and network changes before you can use it.

Identity federation using Active Directory Federation Services (AD FS) requires a minimum of two additional servers in the environment; however, four or more are typically recommended to allow for failover and high availability.

A minimal AD FS implementation consists of two roles—the Web Application Proxy (WAP) server and the AD FS federation server.

The WAP server is normally deployed in your perimeter network and exposed to the public Internet on port 443. It receives authentication requests when a federated user attempts to sign in to Microsoft 365 and forwards those requests to the federation server for processing.

Unlike a WAP server, which is exposed to the public Internet, a federation server is deployed in your *internal* network and is joined to your Active Directory domain. This server receives requests forwarded by the WAP server and processes them, authenticating the user and returning a response to the WAP. Because the federation server is domain-joined, it can communicate directly with the Active Directory domain controllers to authenticate users. The WAP never communicates directly with your internal network. See Figure 9-22.

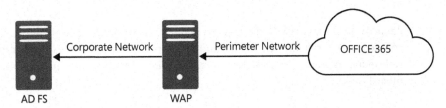

Figure 9-22   Typical AD FS infrastructure

In addition to one or more of each server type (for high availability), additional DNS, firewall, and network configurations are required to implement identity federation.

CHAPTER 9

These configurations could include (but are not limited to) the following:

- A DNS entry in your public DNS that points to the WAP server(s).

- Firewall rules in your perimeter network that allow inbound communication to your WAP servers on port 443 from the public Internet.

- A certificate for your WAP servers provided by a trusted certificate authority.

- Load-balancing configurations for your WAP servers in your network's perimeter network.

- Firewall rules between your perimeter and internal networks, which allow inbound communication between your WAP and federation servers on port 443.

- Load-balancing configurations for your federation servers.

- An internal DNS entry for your federation server farm.

After you have installed and configured this infrastructure, you must then use the MSOnline PowerShell cmdlets to federate each of the domains registered in your tenant with your federation endpoint (the DNS name of your WAP servers on the public Internet). Doing so allows Microsoft 365 to forward authentication requests to your on-premises infrastructure.

You can perform the installation and configuration of AD FS as part of the Azure AD Connect installation wizard; however, Active Directory Federation Services provides additional features that might not be achievable using cloud passwords:

- **On-premises smart-card or multifactor authentication**   If you have an existing on-premises implementation of smart cards or other multifactor authentication (MFA) providers, these are normally integrated with Active Directory or other on-premises infrastructure. Azure AD cannot integrate directly with such providers.

  ### TIP

  Azure AD *does* support MFA directly. You might consider switching from on-premises MFA to cloud-based MFA, enabling cloud passwords and Password Hash Sync and possibly reducing on-premises infrastructure. Cloud-based MFA requires an Azure AD Premium license.

- **Self-service password reset**   If you currently have a self-service password reset tool that is integrated with your existing on-premises Active Directory, you can modify the AD FS sign-in pages to use that service, whereas you cannot modify the forgotten-password link on the standard Office 365 sign-in page. Azure AD supports self-service password reset, though it requires an Azure AD Premium license for each user and additional configuration changes to the Azure AD Connect installation to support password writeback.

- **Sign-in restrictions** Client Access Policy is a feature of AD FS that enables you to define rules limiting where users can authenticate (such as from a VPN only with no public access). You can even specify hours during which users can authenticate and what protocols they're allowed to use (such as ActiveSync).

- **Sign-in auditing** Because the AD FS federation server is domain-joined and uses on-premises domain controllers for authentication, the authentication request is logged in the Windows event logs like any other authentication request when using identity federation with AD FS.

NOTE

Azure AD provides advanced logging for things like sign-in attempts; however, this feature requires an Azure AD Premium license.

What's next?

As you can see, numerous options are available for your authentication approach when using Microsoft 365. However, as discussed previously, a good deal of planning is required to ensure a successful deployment.

In the upcoming chapters, we will dig deeper into directory synchronization with Azure AD Connect and the new Azure Cloud Sync and provide some detail on more advanced synchronization features and scenarios.

CHAPTER 9

Installing AAD Connect

Like other configuration milestones when deploying Microsoft 365, the installation of AAD Connect is non-trivial. The initial installation requires planning for service accounts, directory hierarchy, filtering and permissions, password synchronization, Hybrid Writeback, Azure AD application and attribute filtering, and several authentication features.

Many features selected during the installation can be enabled or disabled later via the AAD Connect Wizard. However, a few key decisions must be made during initial installation, cannot be undone, and will subsequently require a reinstallation of AAD Connect if they need to be changed.

The Custom and Express installation experiences

After the typical license agreement and welcome dialogs, you will first need to decide whether you want to do an Express or Custom installation.

The Express installation is intended for configurations with only one Active Directory forest in your environment (although it can contain multiple child domains). Also, Express installation is intended for configurations on which you intend to enable password synchronization.

Express mode installation is the best method for getting your Microsoft 365 synchronization up and running quickly and provides a limited number of questions regarding your intended configuration. However, if you intend to scope your synchronization to specific organizational units or want to enable features like Group Writeback or attribute filtering, you cannot do those things with an Express mode installation during your initial setup.

However, you can customize the installation after the wizard has completed. Additionally, using Express mode enables the auto-upgrade process, which will allow AAD Connect to automatically upgrade its binaries to the latest version of the software as it is released without any intervention required on your part. Auto-upgrade is not an option when using the Custom installation method. The Express Settings window is shown in Figure 10-1.

NOTE

The Express option is **not** available if your AAD Connect server is not joined to an Active Directory domain.

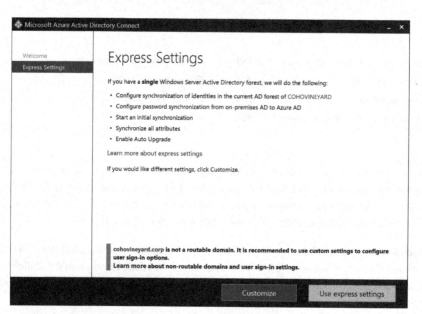

FIGURE 10-1   Express Settings or Customize wizard dialog

As part of the Express Settings setup, the wizard will examine the `UserPrincipalName` suffixes configured for your forest. If your forest is not configured to use any suffixes that represent a routable domain, you will be provided a warning suggesting a customized deployment. This is because AAD Connect uses the default `UserPrincipalName` value when synchronizing users to your Microsoft 365 tenant. A non-routable UPN suffix like `.local` or `.corp` would result in a UPN in the `@yourtenant.onmicrosoft.com` tenant. The `onmicrosoft.com` UPN means your users would be unable to log in to Microsoft 365 using their UPN or email address, and it would be impossible to use an identity provider like Microsoft's AD FS to authenticate logins.

NOTE

Refer to Chapter 1, "Jumping into the cloud," for more details on `UserPrincipalName` considerations and Chapter 9, "Identity and authentication planning" for more information on federated login options.

Inside Out

Express or Custom?

You must use the Custom installation method in the following situations:

- Your environment consists of more than one Active Directory forest.
- Your environment consists of more than 100,000 objects.
- You plan on using AlternateID.
- Your users' UserPrincipalName does not contain an Internet-routable domain suffix.
- You don't want password synchronization.
- You intend to enable things like Group Writeback, AD FS, or pass-through authentication.

Express installation

Once you have selected the Express installation, you will be prompted for credentials for your Microsoft 365 tenant, as shown in Figure 10-2.

FIGURE 10-2   Connect To Azure AD

The credentials provided here will not be used permanently as part of the synchronization process. They are simply used to ensure that you have Global Administrator privilege in your Microsoft 365 tenant so the installation process can proceed.

You must use Global Administrator installation credentials here so the installation wizard can automatically create a directory synchronization account in your Azure AD tenant, as shown in Figure 10-3.

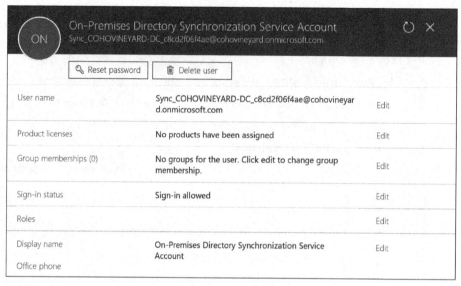

FIGURE 10-3   Automatically created directory synchronization account

The on-premises directory synchronization service account created by the installer will be named Sync_SERVERNAME_randomGUID@yourtenant.onmicrosoft.com and will be a standard User account, not a Global Administrator account, as shown in Figure 10-4.

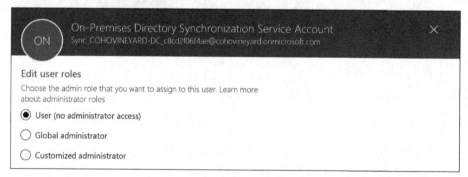

FIGURE 10-4   On-premises Directory Synchronization Service Account tenant permissions

After supplying credentials to connect to Microsoft 365, you will need to supply credentials for your on-premises Active Directory forest, as shown in Figure 10-5.

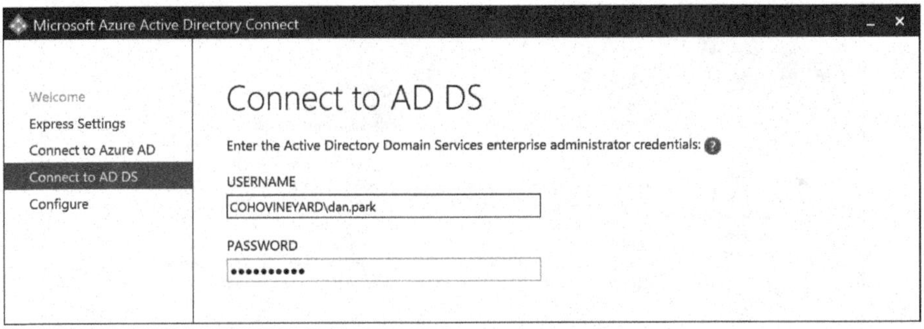

FIGURE 10-5   Connection To AD DS

The on-premises Active Directory account you provide must be a member of the Enterprise Administrators group in Active Directory because the account is not used for the permanent synchronization process. Instead, it's used to create a service account in on-premises Active Directory that will be used for the permanent synchronization process.

If the provided Active Directory account is not a member of the Enterprise Administrators group, a warning will be displayed at the bottom of the dialog, as shown in Figure 10-6, and the installation will not be allowed to continue.

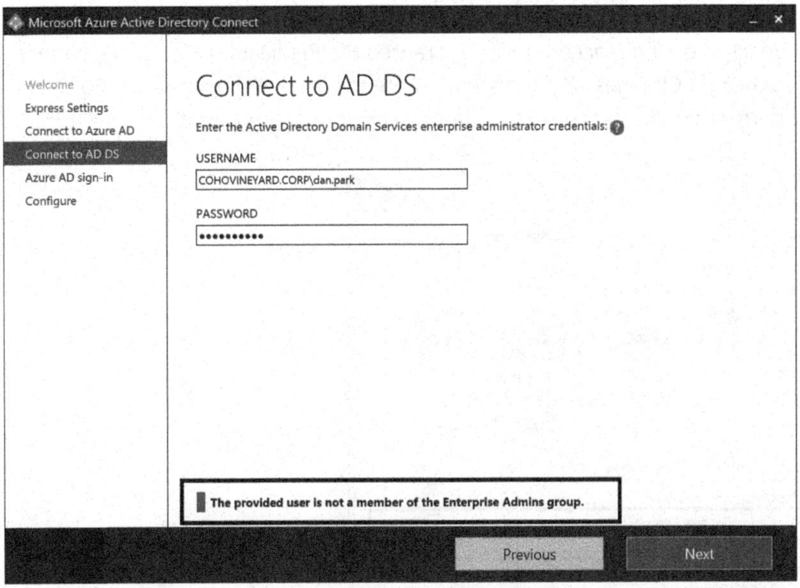

FIGURE 10-6   Account is not a member of the Enterprise Admins group

After the installation wizard has successfully confirmed the account provided is a member of the Enterprise Administrators group in on-premises Active Directory, the installer will automatically create a service account in the default user's organizational unit (OU) in Active Directory, as shown in Figure 10-7.

CHAPTER 10

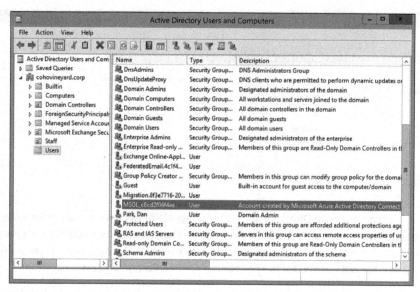

FIGURE 10-7   An automatically created service account in Active Directory

This automatically generated service account will be set with a password that never expires, and the password will not be provided to you.

Additionally, the service account will be granted the Replicating Directory Changes and Replicating Directory Changes All permissions at the top level of the forest, as shown in Figure 10-8. These permissions are necessary to support password synchronization.

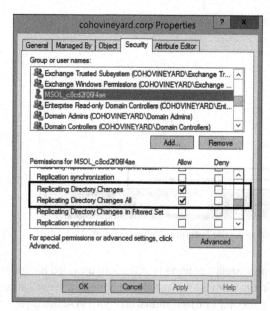

FIGURE 10-8   Permissions required for password synchronization

Once the Express installation has completed, you can move this account out of the Users OU to another OU if desired.

Next, the `UserPrincipalName` suffixes forest will be checked to confirm whether any can be used for authentication with Microsoft 365. Each Active Directory UPN suffix will be displayed, along with confirmation if the suffix is a valid Azure AD domain registered in your tenant. If any of your domains are marked as Not Added, you will receive a warning that your users will not be able to sign in to Azure AD using their on-premises credentials, as shown in Figure 10-9.

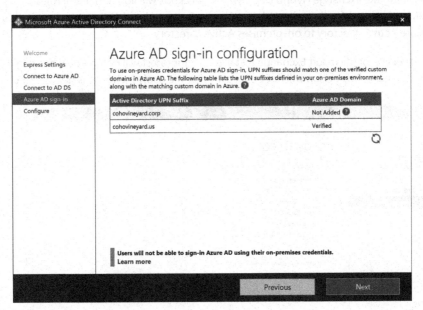

FIGURE 10-9   Active Directory UPN suffix verification

CAUTION

This is only a warning because the wizard cannot confirm if any of your users are using the non-verified UPN suffixes that it found. You can ignore this warning if your users are already using a verified UPN suffix or if you plan to change user UPN suffixes later. No further action regarding UPN suffixes and Azure AD login is required.

NOTE

For more information, refer to Chapter 9 for details on the IDFix tool and user account preparation for synchronization to Microsoft 365.

Finally, the Express installation wizard will summarize the installer's actions to enable directory synchronization with your Microsoft 365 tenant. The final two options available during

CHAPTER 10

the Express installation are the ability to defer synchronization until later and enable Exchange Hybrid deployment.

This is when you might want to deselect the Start The Synchronization Process When Configuration Completes option, so you can make changes to the automatically selected organizational units, add additional UPN suffixes to your forest, update your users' UPN values, or simply wait to synchronize your users until you're ready. See Figure 10-10.

Selecting the Exchange Hybrid Deployment checkbox will add additional rules to the configuration that allow for the writeback of select Exchange-related Active Directory attributes from Azure Active Directory to on-premises Active Directory.

The version of Microsoft Exchange installed in your forest will determine what attributes are written back. This option will not be displayed if Microsoft Exchange is not installed.

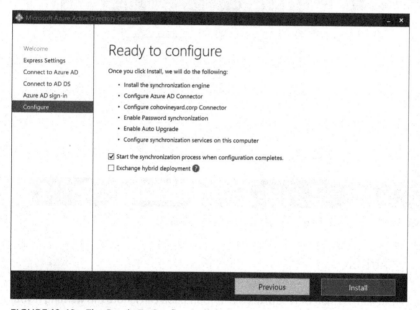

FIGURE 10-10   The Ready To Configure dialog

Once you click Install, the wizard will begin by installing SQL Express and creating the SQL database files in the `C:\Program Files\Microsoft Azure AD Sync\Data` directory. It will then install the synchronization service, the connectors for Azure Active Directory and on-premises Active Directory, create the custom Sync account in the tenant, and install the Azure AD Connect health service.

It is now safe to click Exit, as shown in the Configuration Complete dialog shown in Figure 10-11, and if you left the Start The Synchronization Process When Configuration Completes option selected on the Ready To Configure page, your AAD Connect installation is already busy synchronizing your users to Microsoft 365.

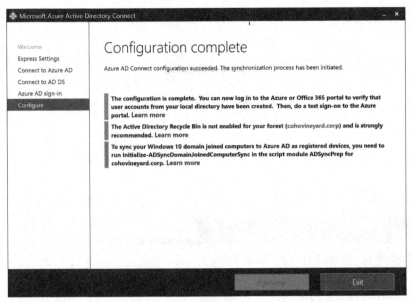

FIGURE 10-11   The Configuration Complete dialog

Custom installation

The custom installation process differs significantly from the Express installation. In the Express installation, you are presented with the minimum of installation choices, quite literally three to four pages, and the installer makes certain assumptions about your preferred configuration options so that you can complete the installation quickly and easily.

On the other hand, the custom installation allows you to customize every aspect of the AAD Connect installation. It is in the custom installation mode where you are presented with a few options that cannot be changed once you complete the installation without a complete reinstallation of the tool.

Selecting Customize during the initial installation dialog, seen in Figure 10-1 earlier in this chapter, will provide you with the first of many configuration pages where you can specify your own custom installation options. Figure 10-12 shows the Install Required Components dialog.

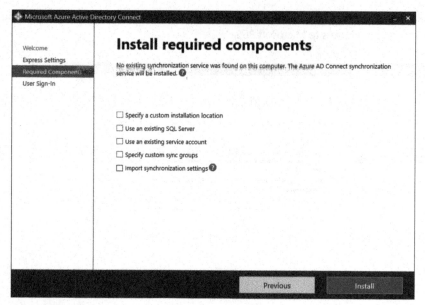

FIGURE 10-12   Install Required Components

Installation location

At this point, you can specify a custom installation for the AAD Connect binaries. The default location is `C:\Program Files\Microsoft Azure AD Sync`, which cannot be changed during Express installations, though in Custom mode, you can specify an alternate drive and/or file path for the installation.

Clicking the Specify A Custom Installation Location checkbox, as shown in Figure 10-13, allows for manual entry of the installation location, or the Browse button can be used to navigate the file system to find a suitable directory.

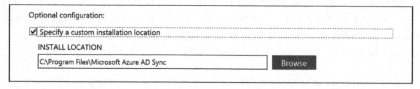

FIGURE 10-13   Specify A Custom Installation Location dialog

It is important to note that while you can select an alternate installation location for the AAD Connect product binaries, there will be a separate directory named `Microsoft Azure Active Directory Connect` in the `C:\Program Files` directory that is installed automatically when the AAD Connect installation is launched. This directory is the result of the downloaded installation MSI file.

CAUTION

This installation option will not allow you to move that directory. It should not be deleted after the installation has concluded, or the AAD Connect customization wizard will not successfully launch if you want to make changes to an existing configuration.

Using Microsoft SQL Server

AAD Connect, in both Express and Custom modes, can support up to 100,000 objects using the included Microsoft SQL Express edition installed as part of the AAD Connect setup process. If your environment has more than 100,000 objects—or if it is within 2,000 objects of the 100,000 limit—the AAD Connect tool must be installed using a full version of Microsoft SQL.

TIP

Note that AAD Connect will not count objects, nor will it tell you if you need to use full SQL versus SQL Express. It will be up to you to review your directory or directories to determine if you can proceed with SQL Express or if you require the full version of Microsoft SQL Server.

When using a full version of Microsoft SQL Server, it is not necessary to implement any of the Microsoft SQL Server high-availability technologies, such as log shipping or clustering. However, those technologies are supported. Typically, it is recommended that instead of high-availability configurations like those mentioned previously, you should install a second AAD Connect server in Staging Mode, to eliminate the need for a more complex back-end Microsoft SQL Server implementation. Staging Mode is discussed in more detail at the end of this chapter.

Inside Out

100,000 objects

The 100,000-object limit advertised when using Microsoft SQL Server Express edition with AAD Connect is a theoretical limit. The actual limit is the size of the SQL database, which is restricted to 10GB. The 100,000-object limit is a recommended limit based on other implementations of the AAD Connect tool and should be carefully considered during installation.

The 100,000-object limit refers to the total number of objects, not the total number of users. When calculating the number of objects, you must consider users, groups, contacts, and organizational units across every domain in the forest.

We recommend that you err on the side of caution and install AAD Connect using a full version of Microsoft SQL Server if any of the following are true:

- If your company is within 10,000–15,000 of the object limit
- If you have any upcoming merger or acquisition activity
- If you are syncing multiple forests to Microsoft 365

An upgrade from the included Microsoft SQL Express edition to a post-installation of the full version of Microsoft SQL Server is not supported. Doing so would require a complete uninstallation and reinstallation of the AAD Connect tool.

Clicking the Use An Existing SQL server checkbox, as shown in Figure 10-14, allows you to provide the name of a Microsoft SQL Server and the instance for the AAD Connect database. The SQL server can be located on a remote server or the AAD Connect server itself; both scenarios are supported. The Instance Name box can remain blank if you are using the default MSSQLSERVER instance on the SQL server. However, if you are using an alternate port for the SQL server, you will need to provide the Instance Name, followed by a comma (,) and the port number.

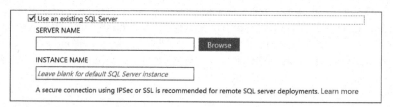

FIGURE 10-14   Use An Existing SQL Server

The installation of SQL will create a database named ADSync on the server, along with the associated stored procedures.

CAUTION

When installing AAD Connect using an existing SQL server, either local or remote, the account you are currently logged in to the server with must have SA permissions on the SQL server, or the installation will fail.

Selecting a service account

Clicking the Use An Existing Service Account checkbox will allow you to select a domain service account that will be used for the *Microsoft Azure AD Sync* windows service when the AAD Connect installation concludes. This service account will also be granted DB Owner and Public rights on the ADSync database as part of the installation process. See Figure 10-15.

A service account does not need to be specified if the SQL server is local to the AAD Connect server. Instead, a local account will be created on the server automatically. This account will be used for the windows service and will be granted DB Owner and Public rights on the ADSync database.

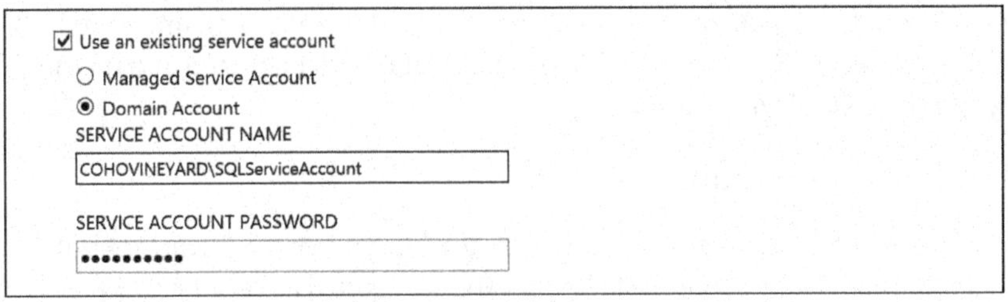

FIGURE 10-15   Selecting a service account

Finally, clicking the Specify Custom Sync Groups checkbox allows you to specify alternate group names for the four groups that delegate rights to the AAD Connect implementation.

These four groups shown above can be domain groups if you are installing AAD Connect on a domain joined server (as pictured in Figure 10-16) or group names that are local to the AAD Connect server. However, in either case, if you specify custom sync groups, they need to be created before the installation. Failure to create the groups before installation causes the installer to fail, and an entry is logged in the Application Event log, indicating the group could not be found.

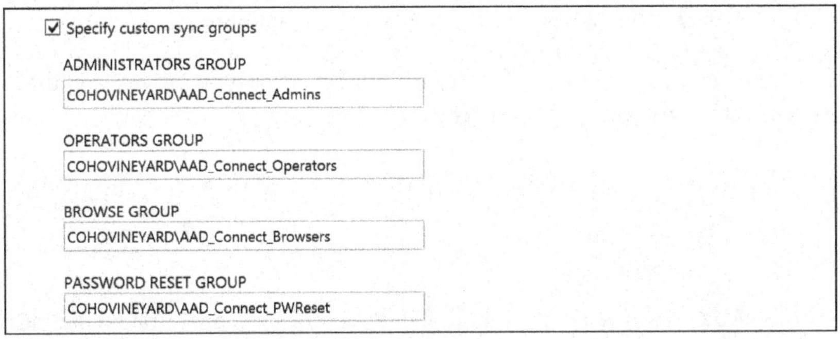

FIGURE 10-16   Specify Custom Sync Groups

If no custom sync groups are provided, the installer will automatically create the following four groups, which are used to secure AAD Connect and are granted the permissions shown in Table 10-1.

Table 10-1   AAD Connect default application groups

GROUP NAME	PERMISSIONS
ADSyncAdmins	Full rights to the AAD Connect tool.
ADSyncOperators	Able to view operations run history; cannot view connectors or objects. Able to view sync rules but unable to edit or delete.
ADSyncBrowse	No access to the Sync service console and cannot view Synchronization rules.
ADSyncPasswordSet	No access to the Sync service console and cannot view Synchronization rules.

The only populated group at the time of installation is the ADSyncAdmins group. The user account used to perform the AAD Connect installation will be placed into this group automatically when the installation completes.

Import synchronization settings

One of the newer features of AAD Connect is the option to import synchronization settings from an existing AAD Connect installation. (This was added in Version 2.0.3.0 in July of 2021.)

This new feature is exceptionally handy when setting up an AAD Connect server in Staging Mode when you have a significant number of rule customizations or organizational unit selections on your existing AAD Connect production server.

In past versions, you were typically forced to use PowerShell to re-create rules; depending on the granularity of the organizational unit selection process, OU selection was an exercise that might take hours. This newer feature will import everything except passwords to the new server, requiring that you enter only the passwords during the installation and nothing else.

Each time a change is made to the AAD Connect configuration using the AAD Connect Wizard, a file named `Applied-SynchronizationPolicy-xxxx.JSON` is automatically exported to `%ProgramData%\AADConnect`. (In this example, xxxx represents a timestamp.)

This file can then be used as part of the AAD Connect installation by checking the box and supplying the path to the appropriate JSON file.

Inside Out

AAD Connect JSON export

The AAD Connect Wizard automatically exports a JSON configuration file each time the installation is changed. However, any changes made via the Synchronization Rules Editor, the Synchronization Service Manager, or by using PowerShell would not be included.

When changes are made without the use of the Wizard, it is necessary to run the AAD Connect Wizard and select the View or Export Current Configuration option to save a new JSON file with the updated configuration.

Selecting your authentication method

Another critical milestone when installing and configuring AAD Connect is selecting the authentication method your users will use to access Microsoft 365. There are several options available during the installation of the AAD Connect tool in Custom mode on the User Sign-In page.

While selecting an authentication method is important to the overall design and deployment of Microsoft 365 and your directory synchronization, you can run the configuration Wizard on the desktop at any time to change these settings. As a result, you might want to simply choose Do Not Configure and bypass the authentication configuration steps during initial installation and return to change them later.

Password synchronization

Selecting Password Synchronization on the User Sign-In dialog shown in Figure 10-17 configures the AAD Connect tool to automatically synchronize user passwords from on-premises Active Directory to Azure Active Directory. This synchronization process occurs independently of the regularly scheduled 30-minute synchronization cycle used by the AAD Connect server to synchronize on-premises Active Directory object properties (such as the name, email address, and so on). That means password changes in on-premises Active Directory are replicated to Microsoft 365 every 1–2 minutes.

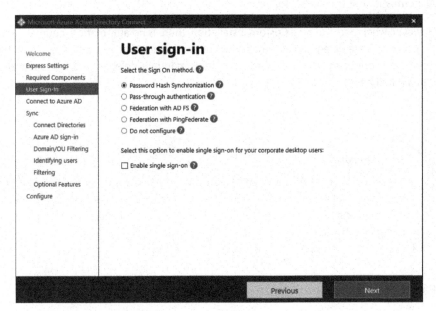

FIGURE 10-17   The User Sign-In dialog

NOTE

Password encryption

Passwords synchronized to Microsoft 365 are not transmitted in cleartext. Instead, the user's password hash is encrypted a second time using an MD5 key and an additional cipher. The result is a hash-of-a-hash or salted-hash and is transmitted via an encrypted HTTPS session between the AAD Connect server and Microsoft 365.

The user authentication, hash expansion, and decryption take place in Azure Active Directory, not the on-premises Active Directory.

Scope

When you enable the password synchronization feature as part of the AAD Connect installation, there is an initial synchronization of all passwords to Microsoft 365 for any users configured within the scope of the solution.

In an Express mode configuration, **all** user objects are automatically within the scope of the solution. However, when performing a Custom installation, the organizational unit selection and any group filtering you enabled defines the users who fall within the configuration scope and which passwords will be initially synchronized.

Permissions

When password synchronization is automatically enabled as part of an Express mode installation, the service account (such as MSOL_xxxxxxx) generated in on-premises Active Directory is automatically delegated the Replicating Directory Changes and Replicating Directory Changes All permissions at the forest's top level.

However, when performing a Custom installation, there is no automatic account creation; therefore, no rights are delegated automatically. The service account you create for the Active Directory Forest connector will need to have the rights manually delegated to the top level of each domain in the forest.

Inside Out

Password policies

It is important to note that when using password synchronization, the cloud account password is set to never expire. This means that an expired password in on-premises Active Directory that remains unchanged is still valid in Microsoft 365 and can be used to log in to the tenant.

Pass-through authentication

Pass-through authentication (see Figure 10-18) is an alternative to password synchronization if your company policies prohibit the transmission of passwords, even in an encrypted format via the public Internet. Instead of syncing user passwords to the cloud and relying on Microsoft 365 to process logins, pass-through authentication allows for authentication requests to be processed by on-premises Active Directory infrastructure without the need to transmit passwords or deploy identity providers like Microsoft's AD FS.

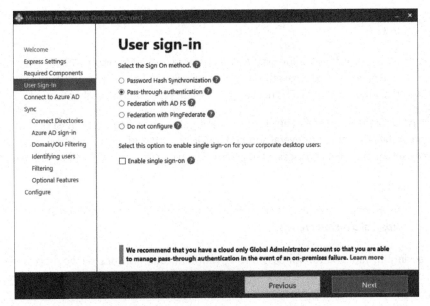

FIGURE 10-18   Selecting Pass-Through Authentication

Overview

The implementation of pass-through authentication requires the deployment of a processing agent added to the AAD Connect server automatically when the option is selected, which operates using outbound-only communication. The agent can be deployed on more than one server for high-availability, provided the server is domain joined to the domain where the users being authenticated reside and the server is running Windows Server 2012R2 or later.

Pass-through authentication behaves similarly to Microsoft's AD FS. However, instead of redirecting authentication requests back to an on-premises server, the request is placed in an Azure queue and picked up via a regularly scheduled process initiated by the processing agent running on-premises. The processing agent sends the request to an Active Directory domain controller, where the domain controller processes it, and the results are returned to the processing agent to be sent back to Azure. Upon receipt, Azure issues a token to the user so they can access Microsoft 365 services.

Requirements

While Azure AD pass-through authentication eliminates the need to synchronize passwords to Microsoft 365 and simplifies the authentication process compared to the implementation of Microsoft AD FS or other identity providers, pass-through authentication has several key requirements that must be met to ensure it will operate properly.

The AAD Connect server and the underlying pass-through processing agent must be installed and domain-joined to the forest where the authentication requests will be directed. All servers running the processing agent must also be Windows Server 2012R2 or later.

Pass-through authentication is supported in a multi-forest configuration, though a forest trust is required.

The UserPrincipalName value used for synchronization to Microsoft 365 must be the value from the UserPrincipalName attribute in on-premises Active Directory and must be a routable UPN suffix. Alternate Login ID is not supported with pass-through authentication.

The AAD Connect server and any servers running the processing agent must be able to reach Azure Active Directory on several additional TCP/IP ports and should not be located behind a proxy server or network devices that perform SSL inspection or URL filtering.

> **NOTE**
>
> **The list of pre-requisites for pass-through authentication can be found at** *https://aka.ms/ptaprereqs.*

Checking the radio button for pass-through authentication will deploy the processing agent as part of the AAD Connect Custom installation. Any additional installations of the processing agent will require the download of the processing agent at *https://aka.ms/ptagent.*

Federation with AD FS and Ping

The AAD Connect Wizard provides a method for installing the AD FS components as part of the normal installation process. Selecting the Federation With AD FS option on the User Sign-In page will add several additional pages to the installation wizard that will allow you to install the AD FS and Web Application Proxy Server roles in your organization. See Figure 10-19.

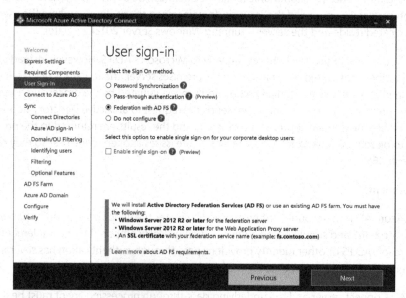

FIGURE 10-19   Federation With AD FS

Follow these steps to complete AD FS installation in conjunction with the AAD Connect Wizard:

1. The AD FS installation is executed by the AAD Connect Wizard, though the installation of AD FS does **NOT** occur on the AAD Connect server. You must have at least two additional servers ready for the AD FS Federation Server and Web Application Proxy Server roles. The AD FS Federation Server should be a domain-joined machine. The Web Application Proxy Server can be either domain-joined or part of a workgroup, based on your company's requirements. Both servers should be Windows Server 2012R2 or later.

2. In addition to the two servers required for AD FS, you will also need an SSL certificate with your federation service name defined (such as adfs.cohovineyard.us) or a wildcard certificate that can be used to secure the Web Application Proxy Server role. On the AD FS Farm dialog shown in Figure 10-20, you can choose to configure a new AD FS farm or select an existing AD FS farm already configured in your environment. When you select Configure A New AD FS Farm, you will need to provide a PFX certificate file that will be used to secure the Web Application Proxy Server.

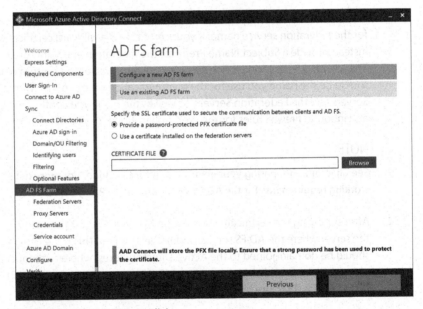

FIGURE 10-20   AD FS Farm dialog

3. Clicking the Browse button will open a File Explorer window where you can navigate to the PFX file you intend to use for the Web Application Proxy Server.

4. Once you have selected the PFX file, you will be prompted to supply the password for the certificate file. See Figure 10-21.

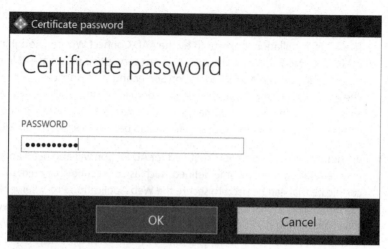

FIGURE 10-21   Certificate Password dialog

5. In the Subject Name dropdown, select the certificate subject name you want to use for the federation service name. If your certificate is a wildcard certificate, you must instead provide a Subject Name Prefix for the federation endpoint (see Figure 10-22). The resulting federation service name will be displayed at the bottom of the dialog. This should be the name you use for the communication between the Web Application Proxy Servers and the Federation Servers, as well as the name you configure in your public DNS and inbound firewall rules for the Web Application Proxy Server.

NOTE

See Chapter 2, "Preparing your environment for the cloud," for more details on the networking requirements for the AD FS Web Application Proxy Server role.

6. After supplying the certificate information, you will be prompted to provide the name of the server where the AD FS service should be installed. This is the Federation Server and should be domain-joined to the Active Directory forest where authentication will take place. You can provide a server name or IP address, or you can use the Browse button to search Active Directory for a server using its name or IP address.

7. Once you have selected the server name and entered the credentials for a Domain Admin, your AD FS Federation Server will appear in the Selected Servers list, as shown in Figure 10-23. Repeat this for each AD FS Federation Server you want the installer to configure for you.

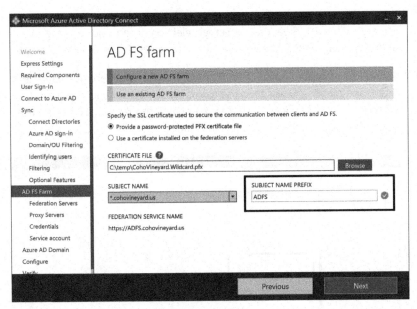

FIGURE 10-22   Selecting a Subject Name Prefix

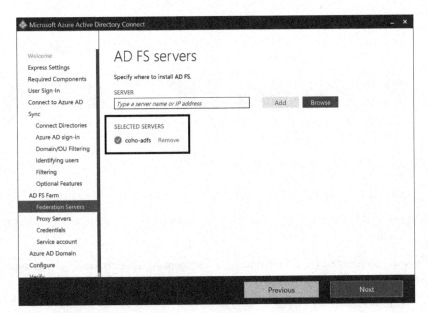

FIGURE 10-23   Selected Servers

8. You will then be prompted to enter the name or IP address of the Web Application proxy server. Like the AD FS Federation Server selection dialog, you can enter the name or IP address directly or click the Browse button to search Active Directory.

9. You will be prompted for credentials, though unless the Web Application Proxy Server is domain-joined, you will need to provide credentials for a local administrator on the server. Your Web Application Proxy Server name should appear in the Selected Servers list once it has been selected, as shown in Figure 10-24.

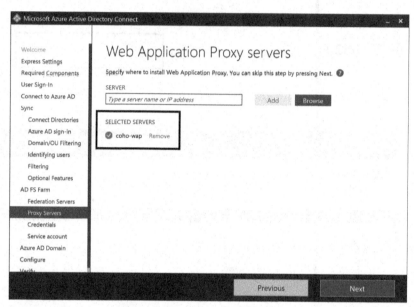

FIGURE 10-24   Selected Web Application Proxy Server

Inside Out

PSRemoting

The installation of the AD FS and Web Application Proxy Server roles depends upon remote PowerShell connectivity to both servers.

First, confirm that the Windows Remote Management service is running on all target servers. Then, enable PSRemoting on each server via the following PowerShell command:

```
Enable-PSRemoting -Force
```

If you are installing the Web Application Proxy Role on a non-domain-joined system, you must also add that server name to the WSMAN trusted hosts list on the AAD Connect server using the following PowerShell command:

```
Set-Item WSMan:\localhost\Client\TrustedHosts -Value <hostname> -Force
-Concatenate
```

10. On the Domain Administrator Credentials dialog, enter the credentials for a Domain Administrator account, which will enable the AAD Connect installation wizard to complete the AD FS configuration on the remote servers. See Figure 10-25.

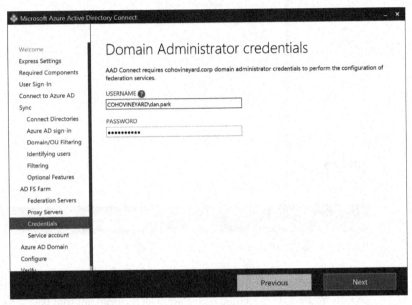

FIGURE 10-25   Domain Administrator Credentials

11. Next, you will need to provide a service account for the AD FS service. This service account can be either a standard domain user account or a Group Managed Service Account. The wizard can be used to create a Group Managed Service Account; you can provide an existing Group Managed Service Account or an existing Domain User Account, as shown in Figure 10-26.

NOTE

It is important to note that if your domain is not a Server 2012 or later domain, the Group Managed Service Account options will not be available to you.

TIP

If you are selecting an existing Domain User Account, the Group Managed Service Account you provide must be a member of the Enterprise Admins group.

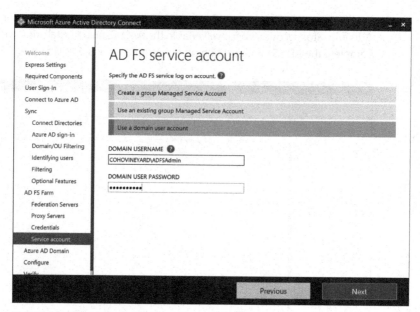

FIGURE 10-26 AD FS Service Account

12. Finally, you will be prompted to select a domain that should be used for the federation process. You will be presented with a list of all the domains that have been registered in your Microsoft 365 tenant. See Figure 10-27.

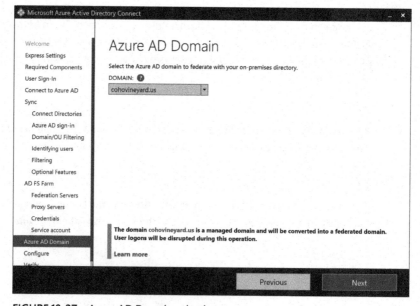

FIGURE 10-27 Azure AD Domain selection

13. Once you have selected a domain, that domain will be converted into a Federated Domain in your tenant. Afterward, any time a user login ending in that UPN suffix is presented while logging in to Microsoft 365, the authentication request will be redirected to the Web Application Proxy Server using the Federation Service Name you selected when you added the certificate.

14. Clicking Next will take you to the final configuration page, where the installation options selected during the wizard can be reviewed, and installation can proceed.

Single sign-on

When enabling either password synchronization or pass-through authentication, you can also enable single sign-on (SSO). Single sign-on forces the authentication process with Azure AD to behave like an integrated Windows authentication, using the on-premises Active Directory domain controllers to create tokens automatically for authenticated users who are accessing Azure resources.

The beauty of single sign-on is that the user is never challenged for credentials. Their authentication request is presented to Azure AD, redirected to an on-premises domain controller, and a token is generated and automatically provided to Azure AD to authorize access—all without any user intervention.

Inside Out

Single sign-on

The single sign-on feature can be used with both password synchronization and pass-through authentication, though when using single sign-on, the user must be on a domain-joined machine and must be running a supported client.

If the client is not supported or the user is not on a domain-joined machine, normal credential prompt activity occurs, and single sign-on is not used.

Supported clients include most current browsers and any applications configured to use modern authentication.

A list of prerequisites for single sign-on and supported clients can be found at *https://aka.ms/ssoclients*.

Once you have selected the appropriate authentication method for your environment, click Next to proceed.

Connecting to your directories

During the AAD Connect custom installation process, after you have selected your authentication method, you will be prompted for credentials for your Azure AD tenant, as shown in Figure 10-28.

These credentials are used to ensure that you are a Global Administrator in your tenant and to retrieve a list of domains registered in your tenant. The installation wizard uses these details in later installation dialogs.

> ### TIP
>
> **The credentials you provide in this step are not stored, nor are they used for the ongoing synchronization process. If necessary, the Global Administrator role can be removed from this account after successfully installing the AAD Connect tool.**

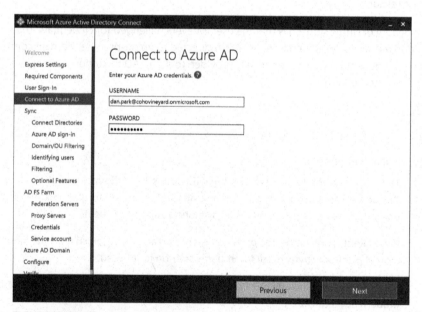

FIGURE 10-28   Connect to Azure AD

The next thing you need to do during the Custom installation process is select all the directories containing objects (users, groups, contacts, devices) that you plan to synchronize to your Microsoft 365 tenant.

NOTE

Currently, the AAD Connect installation wizard offers only one option in the Directory type dropdown—Active Directory. However, the wizard might be updated in future versions to include things like LDAP, AD LDS (ADAM), and other identity sources.

Follow these steps to select the directories containing objects you plan to synchronize to your Microsoft 365 tenant:

1. The forest dropdown will display the name of the forest to which the AAD Connect server is currently joined. You will need to provide credentials to connect to that forest in the form of `DOMAIN\UserName`.

2. If the AAD Connect server is not domain joined, you will need to manually enter the forest name, as it will not be automatically populated.

TIP

The AAD Connect installation wizard requires the forest username credentials in the DOMAIN\UserName format because these credentials are stored in the properties of the on-premises Active Directory connector for ongoing synchronization. Providing the credentials in the UPN format (for example, `dan.park@cohovineyard.corp`) in step 3 will return an error, and the installation wizard will exit, requiring you to restart the entire installation.

3. Once you have entered the username and password for the service account, click the Add Directory button. Using the service account credentials you provided, AAD Connect will examine the forest to ensure the forest can be reached and the provided service account is valid. Additionally, the wizard will examine the forest schema to determine if additional options for features (such as Exchange hybrid) can be added as part of the installation process.

TIP

The credentials entered in this step will be stored in the AAD Connect configuration, and the permanent service account used to connect to the forest for the ongoing synchronization process.

Inside Out

Service account permissions

At a minimum, the service account used for each synchronized directory needs membership in the Domain Users group in Active Directory. If your Domain Users group has been modified in any way, you will need to ensure the account has LDAP read permissions to your forest(s):

- If you intend to use Exchange Hybrid Writeback, the service account requires write permission to the list of Exchange Hybrid Writeback attributes. That list can be found at *https://aka.ms/exchangewriteback*.

- If you intend to use password synchronization, the service account will require Replicating Directory Changes and Replicating Directory Changes All permissions at the top level of each domain in the forest.

- Additionally, features like Group Writeback require additional permissions for the connector service account. Those additional features and requirements can be found at *https://aka.ms/aadcustominstall*. You can also use a tool such as *https://aka.ms/aadpermissions* to configure advanced permissions settings.

4. Additional forests or directories can be added to the configuration by manually typing the name of the forest in the Forest field, providing service account credentials in that forest with the necessary permissions, and clicking Add Directory. See Figure 10-29.

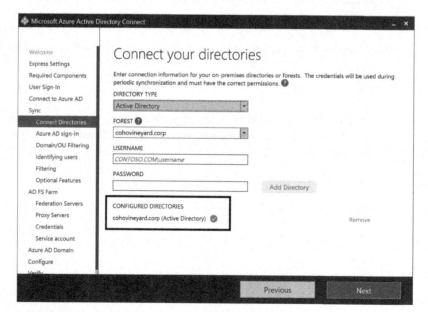

FIGURE 10-29   Connect Your Directories dialog

CAUTION

Adding directories

The order in which you add multiple directories to the AAD Connect configuration is critical and represents another decision that could potentially require reinstallation of the AAD Connect tool.

The synchronization rules created by the wizard are applied in the order in which you added the directories during this step. If you are in a multi-forest scenario where linked mailboxes exist across forests, or you plan on joining user objects between forests, you will want to add the forest that should be precedent for user attributes first.

For example, in a linked mailbox scenario, the resource forest is most commonly added first, so the values visible in the Global Address List are the values used.

Precedence and more detail about synchronization rule ordering are discussed later in this chapter.

5. Once you have successfully added all the directories to your configuration, click the Next button to proceed.

The UserPrincipalName and SourceAnchor attributes

The next page of the Custom installation wizard provides a list of all UPN suffixes that exist across the forest or forests you entered in the Connect Your Directories dialog:

1. Each UPN suffix is compared against the domains that are currently verified in your Microsoft 365 tenant, and if any UPN suffixes do not exist as a verified domain, you will be presented with a warning at the bottom of the screen, indicating users might not be able to log in to Microsoft 365 if they are configured to use a non-verified domain.

TIP

Remember that additional work may be required before authentication will work properly during user login. This work can either be in your tenant, like the registration of additional domains, or in your on-premises Active Directory, like changing your users' UPN values to match those verified domains. It is safe to proceed, even with non-verified domain suffixes, because they can be added later. Proceeding will not affect the installation process nor require the wizard to be run again.

2. However, the other option on this page, the User Principal Name Selection dropdown, represents yet another critical installation milestone that cannot be undone once the installation has concluded. See Figure 10-30.

CHAPTER 10

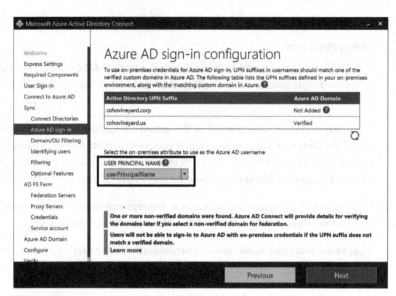

FIGURE 10-30   Azure AD Sign-In Configuration and UserPrincipalName

The UserPrincipalName dropdown allows you to choose the value that will be used as the `UserPrincipalName` value for login and authentication with Azure AD. In most cases, you will accept the default value of `UserPrincipalName` from the on-premises Active Directory schema, though it could be possible an alternate value is used in some environments.

In some environments, the `UserPrincipalName` value might already be used by legacy applications and could prevent you from changing the value for using a UPN domain suffix registered in Microsoft 365. In other environments, company or security policy could prohibit this value's use for authentication purposes.

In those cases, the most common alternate attribute used for `UserPrincipalName` is the `Mail` attribute. This is because both the Mail and UserPrincipalName values use the commonly accepted name@domain format.

CAUTION

When deciding to use an alternate attribute for the UserPrincipalName value, great care should be used. Typically, this process is referred to as *Alternate Login ID*. It requires additional changes to the AD FS implementation and may render other applications incapable of authenticating with Microsoft 365. Those applications expect the `UserPrincipalName` value to be used for things like pass-through authentication.

Additional details regarding alternate login ID and supportability can be found at *https://aka.ms/alternateid*.

Selection of the `UserPrincipalName` value in the AAD Connect Custom Installation wizard is an action that cannot be undone once the installation is complete. If you need to change the `UserPrincipalName` attribute, you will need to uninstall AAD Connect and reinstall it.

3. Once you have confirmed the attribute that should be used for `UserPrincipalName` and have reviewed the list of domain suffixes, click Next to proceed.

Domain and OU filtering

The Domain And OU Filtering dialog allows you to—on a per-directory basis—select or deselect the domain partitions and organizational units that you want in the scope of the solution:

1. Any OU you select will automatically include all objects in that OU and any sub-OU in the synchronization scope. In the case of multiple forests, the Directory dropdown will allow you to choose OUs for each, as shown in Figure 10-31.

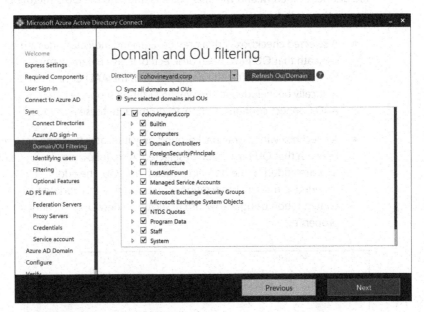

FIGURE 10-31   Domain And OU Filtering

2. The status of each checkbox is important because it provides details about whether the OU and any sub-OUs beneath it will be included or excluded from the synchronization scope, as shown in Figure 10-32.

   ■ An empty checkbox indicates the OU is excluded from the scope of the synchronization, and a selected checkbox indicates the OU is included in the synchronization scope.

   ■ Any selected OU that contains sub-OUs will automatically include those sub-OUs.

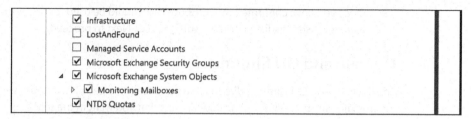

FIGURE 10-32   Checked and unchecked OUs

3.   While the presence or absence of a checkmark may seem obvious, two additional states are distinctly different and will affect how changes to the OU structure post-installation impact the synchronization. See Figure 10-33.

■   A selected checkbox with a gray background indicates one or more sub-OUs beneath that OU have been deselected. It also means if any new OUs are added beneath that OU after the deployment of the AAD Connect tool, they will automatically be included in the synchronization scope. No changes are required to the AAD Connect configuration to accommodate these new OUs.

■   A checkbox with a gray background only indicates that one or more sub-OUs beneath that OU have been deselected. Also, following deployment, if any new OUs are added to the domain beneath that OU, the additional OUs will not be included in the synchronization scope. You need to update the AAD Connect configuration using the wizard to include a new OU or change the connector properties.

FIGURE 10-33   Selected and unselected OUs

4.   Leave this dialog unchanged if you prefer not to make changes to the domain and OU filtering for your directories during the AAD Connect Custom installation. You can re-run the wizard or manually edit the connector properties anytime.

5.   Once you have selected your OU filtering preferences, click Next to proceed.

Uniquely identifying your users

The final set of configuration options that irrevocably affect your AAD Connect installation—requiring reinstallation if you get them wrong—can be found on the Uniquely Identifying Your Users dialog. See Figure 10-34.

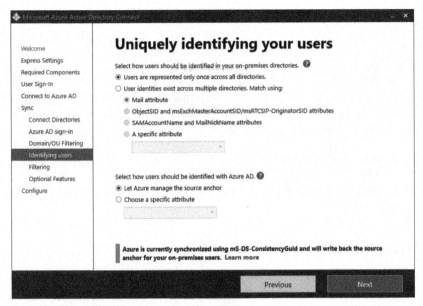

FIGURE 10-34   Uniquely identifying your users

User matching

On this page, you will select the method that AAD Connect will use to join your users. If you have a single directory, you are in luck. Your best option is the Users Are Represented Once Across All Directories radio button shown previously in Figure 10-34. This setting tells AAD Connect that user objects should not be joined in any way, resulting in a one-for-one mapping of users to Azure AD user objects after a successful synchronization with your tenant.

> ### CAUTION
> If you have more than one forest in your enterprise, you will need to give careful consideration to the user-matching options offered here. Failure to choose the correct option will not only require a reinstallation of the AAD Connect tool, but it might also result in objects being synchronized to your tenant that would also need to be deleted. If you discover this error too late—after having already migrated mailboxes to your tenant or started creating SharePoint content—you will not only need to spend time reinstalling AAD Connect, but you might also need to remigrate mailboxes back to on-premises. Also, you might even risk the loss of SharePoint Online and One Drive for Business content.

When reviewing the user-matching options available on this dialog, you must consider how your users appear across your on-premises directories. If user joins are required, you must select the appropriate user-matching configuration.

Inside Out

MailNickname

The presence of the `MailNickname` attribute is critical when configuring AAD Connect to synchronize Exchange mailbox objects to Microsoft 365 because it identifies the account as a mail-enabled object. Make sure all your mail-enabled and mailbox-enabled users in Active Directory have a valid `MailNickname`.

If your users are missing the `MailNickname` value, the AAD Connect synchronization rules related to most Exchange attributes will not apply. Also, the resulting object in Exchange Online will not be correctly populated with Exchange data.

ObjectSID / msExchMasterAccountSID

The `ObjectSID` / `msExchMasterAccountSID` user matching option is designed for use in Exchange resource forest deployments.

Typically, there are two forests in a standard Exchange resource forest scenario. It is possible to have a resource forest linked to more than one account forest, but at a minimum, two forests are required for a linked mailbox scenario.

One forest contains the security principals (`user objects`) and is referred to as the *user forest*, while the other forest contains linked mailboxes and is called the `resource forest`. When linked mailboxes are created, Exchange automatically populates the value of an Active Directory `msExchMasterAccountSID` attribute on the linked `mailbox` object. The `msExchMasterAccountSID` attribute contains the security identifier (also known as the `ObjectSID`) of the user account from the account forest the mailbox is linked to and is populated automatically when the Exchange admin tools create the linked mailbox:

1. The AAD Connect user matching dialog automatically includes an option for Exchange-linked mailbox scenarios via the ObjectSID And msExchMasterAccountSID radio button, as shown in Figure 10-35. This option will configure AAD Connect to join objects based on their `ObjectSID` value in the account forest with the object containing the associated `msExchMasterAccountSID` value in the resource forest.

2. There is no need to identify which forest is which in your configuration because the presence of the `msExchMasterAccountSID` value will identify which forest is the resource forest, and the joins will happen automatically during the synchronization process.

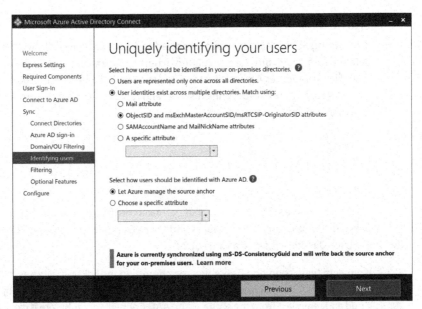

FIGURE 10-35   Joining Linked Exchange Mailboxes

3. It is important to note there are a few assumptions related to the Exchange resource forest, primarily the linked `mailbox` objects' configuration:

    ■ First, in Exchange versions 2007 and later, when a mailbox is created as a linked mailbox, the resulting `user` object associated with that mailbox in the Exchange resource forest is disabled in Active Directory. The `user` object in the Account forest remains enabled and is used for cross-forest login to the mailbox. As a result, AAD Connect assumes any linked `mailbox` objects it synchronizes will consist of two separate `user` objects that it must join. The user account is enabled and used for logging in, while the mailbox account is disabled. This assumption is reflected in the synchronization rules (discussed later in this chapter) created during the installation that apply to enabled and disabled objects. If the Exchange linked mailbox account is enabled in Active Directory, an unsupported—but all-too-common occurrence—synchronization rule behavior might be affected.

    ■ Second, when a linked mailbox is created in Exchange, the `msExchRecipient-TypeDetails` value in Active Directory for that account is set to a value of 2. If this value is changed to a value other than 2, the synchronization rules related to the `SourceAnchor` for the object will behave differently and will likely result in the wrong data being synchronized to Azure AD for the linked mailbox pair.

> **CAUTION**
>
> If the wrong SourceAnchor is synchronized to Azure, not only will the object need to be deleted from Azure, but the msExchRecipientTypeDetails value will need to be corrected in on-premises Active Directory, and the mailbox object will need to be removed from the scope of the AAD Connect server and re-added so that the proper synchronization rules will apply to that object.

Inside Out

Linked mailboxes

If your environment consists of Exchange-linked mailboxes, you must ensure that the linked mailbox accounts are disabled and the msExchRecipientTypeDetails attribute in Active Directory is set to a value of 2.

If either of these conditions is not met, synchronizing the linked mailboxes to Azure will most likely include data from the wrong forest. You will need to delete the object from the cloud and remove it from the scope of the AAD Connect server before it can be corrected.

Mail

When there is no traditional Exchange resource forest/account forest model in use, but the Mail attribute is populated with the same information in both forests, the Mail radio button can be used to configure AAD Connect to perform joins between objects using the Mail attribute. See Figure 10-36.

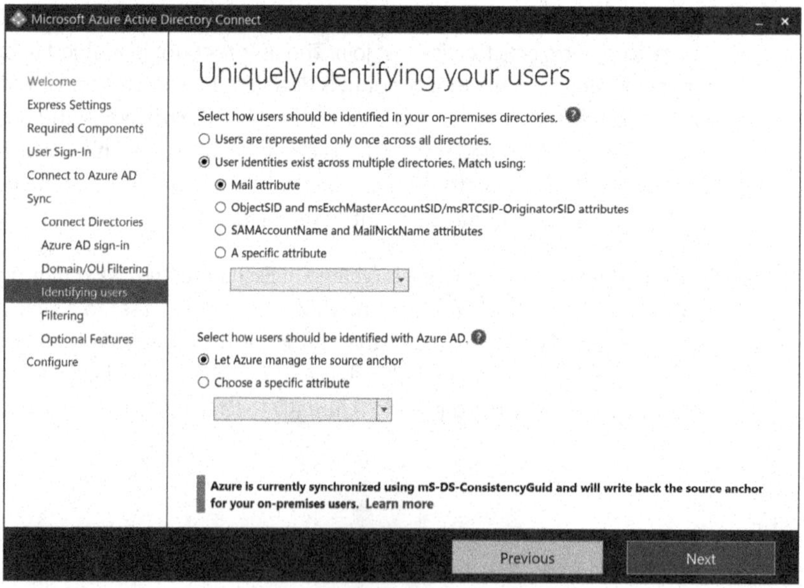

FIGURE 10-36   Joining using the Mail attribute

The Mail attribute user join configuration is most commonly used when two or more directories containing Exchange Mailboxes are configured to use the Microsoft Identity Manager or Forefront Identity Manager product to perform Global Address List synchronization (such as GalSync) between those forests.

GalSync is a process where mail-enabled or mailbox-enabled users, mail-enabled groups (distribution or security), and traditional contact objects in one Exchange-enabled forest are synchronized to another Exchange-enabled forest as contact objects. Typically this is done to allow for full fidelity of the Exchange global address list between the two directories, allowing users with mailboxes in one forest to see the mailboxes, groups, and contacts from the other forest in their Global Address List. Figure 10-37 shows how GalSync works.

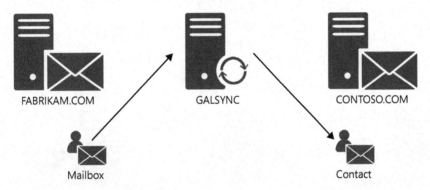

FABRIKAM.COM   GALSYNC   CONTOSO.COM

Mailbox   Contact

FIGURE 10-37   GalSync configured between two forests

GalSync represents a particularly interesting challenge when these mail-enabled objects are synchronized to Microsoft 365. This is especially true when performing a multi-forest AAD Connect synchronization of all objects to the same Microsoft 365 tenant because mailboxes in one forest are represented as contacts in the other forest(s) and vice versa. Because Azure AD does not allow you to synchronize two mail-enabled objects with the same email address to the same tenant, if no special configuration changes were made, one of the objects would fail to synchronize properly to Microsoft 365. See Figure 10-38.

CHAPTER 10

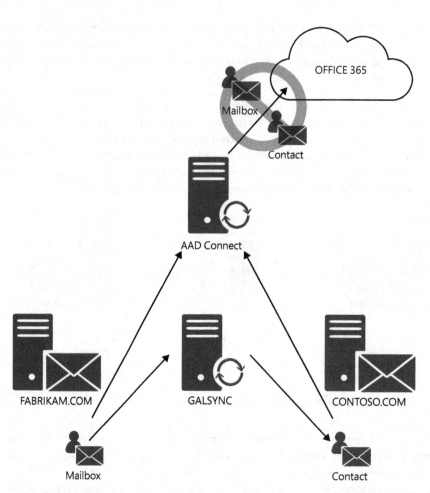

FIGURE 10-38 GalSync with AAD Connect configured without a join on the Mail attribute

The Mail attribute join option can be used to overcome any potential problems in multi-Exchange forest scenarios using GalSync. When using the Mail attribute join option, any mail-enabled or mailbox-enabled user objects in one forest are joined automatically with the contact object that represents them from the second forest, resulting in a single user object synchronized to Microsoft 365. This prevents email address duplication issues in the synchronization process and allows the proper object type—a user—to be synchronized to Azure AD for authentication once the mailbox has been migrated to Exchange Online. See Figure 10-39.

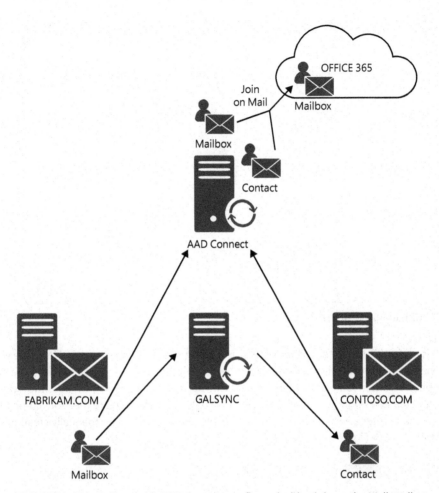

FIGURE 10-39 GalSync with AAD Connect configured with a join on the Mail attribute

It is important to note that you can only select one option on the user-matching dialog in some multi-forest configurations with a combination of linked mailboxes, standard mailboxes, AND GalSync. In those cases, you should select the `ObjectSID / msExchMasterAccountSID` join option. The additional join on `Mail` can be added after the configuration has been completed by cloning the `In from AD–User Join` rule for each forest and adding a new scoping group with a single clause joining `Mail` with `Mail`. See Figure 10-40.

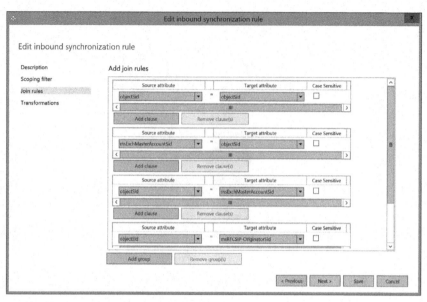

FIGURE 10-40   In from AD—User Join rule

It is preferable to use the `ObjectSID / msExchMasterAccountSID` option from the wizard and add `Mail` manually after installation because the `ObjectSID / msExchMasterAccountSID` option results in four `join` criteria (previously shown in Figure 10-40), whereas the `Mail` option only creates a single `join` criterion. It is easier to let the wizard create the more complex set of four `join` criteria and simply add the single join rule yourself versus manually creating the four join rules. See Figure 10-41.

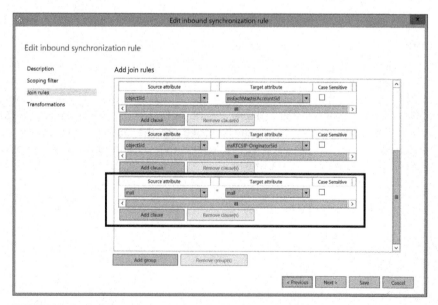

FIGURE 10-41   In from AD—User Join rule modified with join on Mail

Inside Out

Users and contacts

When joining a user object with a contact object, the default behavior of AAD Connect, regardless of the attribute used for the join, is to create the cloud object as a user. A user is created because the assumption is the user object will be used for signing in to Microsoft 365.

If the contact object was synchronized first and the user was added later, the contact object will automatically be deleted from Azure AD and replaced with a user object.

It is important to point out that adding the Mail join rule is only required on user objects. A join on Mail is already configured for contact objects by the installation wizard and is the default configuration for contacts, regardless of what join condition is selected for user objects during this part of the installation.

Important notes about GalSync and AAD Connect

So far, we've only discussed joining mailboxes with the contact object that represents them cross-forest. However, the GalSync solution also synchronizes group objects from one forest as contact objects into all other forests. This represents a particularly interesting problem, primarily because of how AAD Connect stores the different object types in its database.

AAD Connect can successfully join user objects with contact objects because despite being two different object types in the on-premises Active Directory, they are stored as a single object type (for example, a person object) in the AAD Connect database. However, group objects are not stored as person objects; instead, group objects are stored as groups. This is primarily because of the attributes specific to the object type. Groups have attributes like ManagedBy and Member, whereas user and contact objects do not.

We can add a join rule on Mail for user objects, so they successfully join with the contacts representing them. However, there is no easy way to create a join between a contact and a group. For that reason, even though you can add a join rule for Mail on group objects, it would never allow a join with a contact because the join rule is only applied to objects of the same type in the AAD Connect database.

If no action is taken to deal with this situation, and if GalSync is configured to synchronize groups as contacts, you are left with two options, as described in the upcoming sections.

Modifying the GalSync configuration

One option is to modify the GalSync configuration so that group objects are synchronized as contact objects but are placed into a different target OU in each forest. This way, the OU used for contacts representing group objects could be excluded from the AAD Connect synchronization scope via OU filtering in the installation wizard, and contacts representing groups would never be synced to Azure. See Figure 10-42.

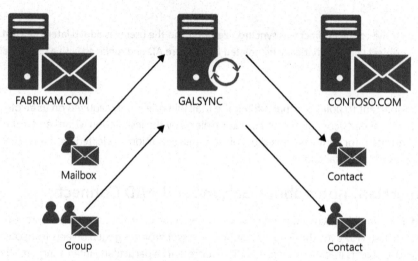

FABRIKAM.COM   GALSYNC   CONTOSO.COM

Mailbox   Contact

Group   Contact

FIGURE 10-42   GalSync configured to write group contacts to an alternate location

The challenge with this option is that although GalSync is a pre-canned solution, which is relatively easy to implement, the default configuration is designed to place all contacts into a single OU in the target forest. This configuration cannot be changed without updating the GalSync source code to support multiple OUs. While the GalSync source code is freely available as part of the GalSync deployment, it requires someone knowledgeable in Visual Basic and Microsoft Visual Studio to make the necessary changes.

Modifying the contact objects

The other option is to modify the contact objects representing groups populated in the target directory so that they can be easily identified as having come from a group. Then, you can filter those contacts using customizations to the AAD Connect implementation. See Figure 10-43.

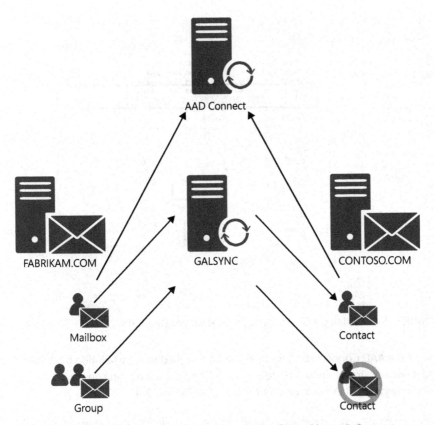

FIGURE 10-43 GalSync contacts representing groups filtered by AAD Connect

This option involves editing the outbound synchronization of contacts representing groups on the GalSync server and adding a keyword or description in the properties of the contact object as they are written to the target directory. You use any string attribute value in Active Directory (such as ExtensionAttribute15 or Description) that is not in use and add a pre-defined constant (such as group) to every object created by GalSync. See Figure 10-44.

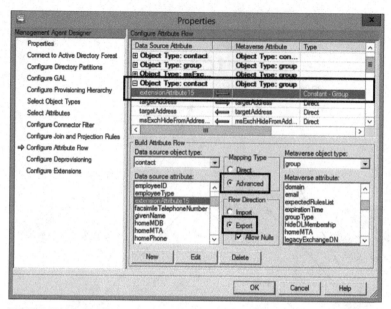

FIGURE 10-44   Adding a Group constant to ExtensionAttribute15

Then, the AAD Connect configuration can be modified post-installation by cloning the `In from AD-Contact Join` rule to include a scoping filter that will exclude any `contact` object with the group keyword in `ExtensionAttribute15`. See Figure 10-45.

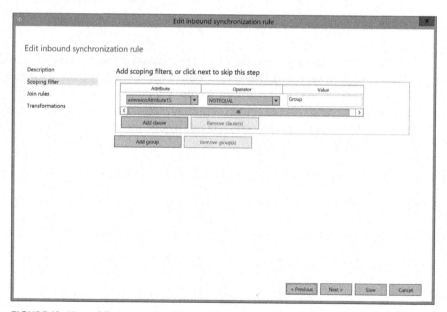

FIGURE 10-45   Adding a scoping filter on ExtensionAttribute15

This will effectively filter out any `contact` object created by GalSync representing a group object while allowing all other contacts to be read by the sync engine, join with their associated user object, and flow to Microsoft 365.

When dealing with multi-forest Exchange configurations that include GalSync, the last consideration is related to the Exchange Hybrid Writeback option available later in the AAD Connect installation wizard.

Enabling Exchange Hybrid Writeback during the installation inserts several rules into the AAD Connect synchronization process. These rules allow for the Writeback of key Exchange attributes to the on-premises Active Directory for a rich coexistence between the migrated mailbox in Exchange Online and the on-premises remote user mailbox that represents that cloud mailbox.

The attribute used in the Exchange Hybrid Writeback process that causes this problem is the `ProxyAddresses` attribute. If no changes are made to the default GalSync or AAD Connect configurations, both synchronization engines will attempt to make changes to the `ProxyAddresses` attribute values that the other server will detect and try to remove.

When GalSync creates a `contact` object in the target forest, it populates the `ProxyAddresses` attribute with all the values from the `source` object it represents. GalSync then manages the `contact` object, updating the `ProxyAddresses` values whenever the `source` object changes (such as when addresses are added or removed). This process is uni-directional. See Figure 10-46.

Source User Object   GALSYNC   Target Contact Object

FIGURE 10-46   Updates to ProxyAddresses flow from User to Contact

As a result, GalSync is considered authoritative for each `contact` object in the target forest, maintaining updates to the object on a regularly scheduled cycle. The problem begins when AAD Connect is introduced into the environment, is scoped to include the OU where the GalSync solution places its `contact` objects, and Exchange Hybrid Writeback is enabled as part of the AAD Connect configuration.

Once AAD Connect synchronizes the `contact` object to Microsoft 365—either as-is or joined with a user object—the cloud `object` is stamped with a `LegacyExchangeDN` value. Then, that value is written back as an x500 address into the `ProxyAddresses` array of the `source` object. This means AAD Connect will update every contact with one new x500 address in the `ProxyAddresses` array. See Figure 10-47.

CHAPTER 10

1) New mail-enabled object is created.   2) ProxyAddresses flow to Exchange Online.

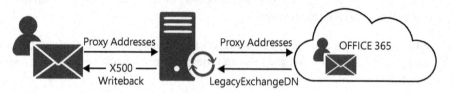

5) cloudLegacyExchangeDN value is   4) cloudLegacyExchangeDN value is   3) Unique LegacyExchangeDN value
written back to ProxyAddresses.   returned from Exchange Online.   is generated in Exchange Online.

FIGURE 10-47   x500 writeback attribute flow

The next time the GalSync server scheduled synchronization process runs, it detects a change to the ProxyAddresses array (in the form of a new x500 proxy address). Because it did not write that value, it immediately removes the value from the object.

On its next scheduled synchronization cycle, AAD Connect will detect that the value is gone from the contact object and write it again.

With two servers battling over the values in the ProxyAddresses array of each contact object, a sort of ping-pong effect occurs, constantly adding, deleting, and re-adding the value as frequently as every 30 minutes, as shown in Figure 10-48.

1) GalSync creates new contact object.   2) AAD Connect writes object to Office 365
                                                             and writes back x500 address to contact.

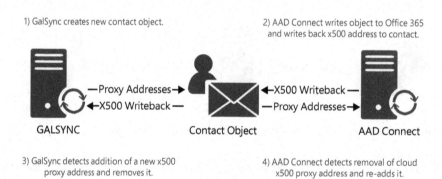

3) GalSync detects addition of a new x500   4) AAD Connect detects removal of cloud
proxy address and removes it.   x500 proxy address and re-adds it.

FIGURE 10-48   GalSync and AAD Connect x500 ping-pong condition

There are essentially five options for dealing with this scenario, which are explained in the following sections.

Option One: Ignoring the problem

The issue can be ignored, resulting in constant updates to the objects. While this does not harm the objects in any way, it does result in an abnormally large number of object updates that must be replicated to every domain controller in your environment.

Depending on the size of the environment, the number of contacts, and the replication cycle frequency on the two servers, this would result in a large amount of unnecessary replication traffic and an increase in the size of the DIT (directory information tree) file on your Active Directory domain controllers. As shown in Figure 10-49, the `Repadmin` command with the `/ShowObjMeta` switch is used on an Active Directory domain controller for a contact object exhibiting this condition.

FIGURE 10-49   Repadmin ShowObjMeta output

Notice the version history (Ver Attribute column) for the `ProxyAddresses` attribute as compared to other mail-related attributes like `Mail`, `TargetAddress`, and so on. This is indicative of the race condition occurring between the AAD Connect and GalSync servers, which causes an abnormally high number of attribute updates.

> **NOTE**
>
> A race condition refers to an instance where two separate systems continue to make changes to the same data, over and over, each change overwriting the previous in an endless loop. Race conditions are a sign of a bad configuration and are detrimental to the systems that rely on that data because the data is always changing.

Option Two: Avoiding the Exchange Hybrid Writeback feature

The second option is to simply avoid the Exchange Hybrid Writeback feature. Enabling the feature instructs AAD Connect to update the `ProxyAddresses` array. Without it, the addresses are left unchanged, and this ping-pong effect does not occur.

CHAPTER 10

The downside to not using Exchange Hybrid Writeback is that the Writeback feature was designed to provide a rich coexistence between on-premises Exchange and Exchange Online. If a migrated mailbox needs to be migrated from the cloud back to on-premises Exchange (off-boarded), any changes related to voicemail settings, litigation hold, or safe or blocked senders will not be updated in the on-premises Exchange object. Therefore, they will not be present after migrating back to on-premises.

If you are not planning to migrate mailboxes back to on-premises after they have been migrated to Microsoft 365, avoiding the Exchange Hybrid Writeback might be an option.

Option Three: Modifying the sync rule configuration

Alternatively, instead of completely disabling the Exchange Hybrid Writeback feature, you could modify the sync rule configuration so that the standard writeback process only applies to user and group objects.

By default, the Exchange Hybrid Writeback feature creates three outbound synchronization rules for Writeback to on-premises Active Directory—one rule for each object type (for example, user, group, or contact). See Figure 10-50.

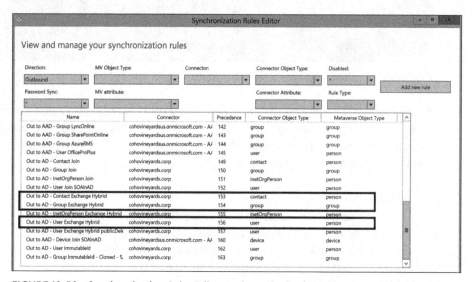

FIGURE 10-50   Synchronization Rules Editor outbound rules for Exchange Hybrid Writeback

Disabling writeback for contact objects would be done post-installation via the Synchronization Rules Editor and would require modification to the Out to AD—Contact Exchange Hybrid rule to disable it.

Inside Out

Disabling sync rules

Disabling the default synchronization rules in AAD Connect is the only condition where it's recommended that you edit an out-of-the-box rule without cloning.

When the AAD Connect server is upgraded to a newer version, the installer will review all the default rules, and depending on changes to the AAD Connect tool, they might be deleted and replaced with newer rules that support added features. Any customizations made to the out-of-the-box rules will be lost when this occurs. The only exception is the enabled \ disabled status.

If you want to disable a default rule, edit it, choose No when prompted to clone the rule, and select the Disabled option. This change will not be overwritten, even if the rule is deleted and replaced with a newer version. The newer version of the rule will remain disabled.

CHAPTER 10

Option Four: Modifying the GalSync DLL

The fourth alternative to dealing with the x500 writeback issue when using GalSync contact objects and Exchange Hybrid Writeback is to modify the GalSync DLL. The default GalSync source code was developed many years ago before the existence of Exchange Online and Microsoft 365. As a result, this race condition exists because the GalSync code does not accommodate the Hybrid Writeback values contributed by AAD Connect.

It is possible to modify the GalSync source code to allow for a peaceful co-existence between the GalSync and AAD Connect servers when dealing with the ProxyAddresses attribute. It consists of a minor update to the GalSync source code to evaluate the contact object Proxy-Addresses during synchronization. If an x500 writeback contributed by AAD Connect is found—for example, any x500 proxy address containing /o=ExchangeLabs—it is maintained and added to the GalSync server's list of ProxyAddresses expected on the contact object.

Like the other GalSync DLL code modification mentioned previously, even though the Gal-Sync source code is freely available as part of the GalSync deployment, making the necessary changes requires someone knowledgeable in Visual Basic and Microsoft Visual Studio.

Option Five: Modifying the AAD Connect default writeback rule

The final alternative to dealing with the race condition caused by deploying AAD Connect and Exchange Hybrid Writeback into an Exchange organization already using GalSync is to modify the AAD Connect default writeback rule for ProxyAddresses, so it only applies to contact objects not located in the OU used by the GalSync solution to create contact objects.

This option five is similar to the third option—modifying the sync rule configuration. However, instead of completely stopping the writeback for `contact` objects (there might be `contact` objects in on-premises Exchange to which you want to writeback the ExchangeLabs x500), we're only preventing the writeback to the GalSync `contact` objects.

This is accomplished by creating a new value in the AAD Connect database (called the Metaverse) to store the Distinguished Name of the contact object. We will use this Distinguished Name value as part of a filter applied to each contact as it is processed. If the contact's DN value contains the GalSync target OU, the contact is ignored.

This option requires three modifications to the AAD Connect implementation following completion of the installation wizard:

1. First, open the Synchronization Service Manager, select the Metaverse Designer button, choose the person from the Object Types column, and select Add Attribute from the Actions pane, as shown in Figure 10-51.

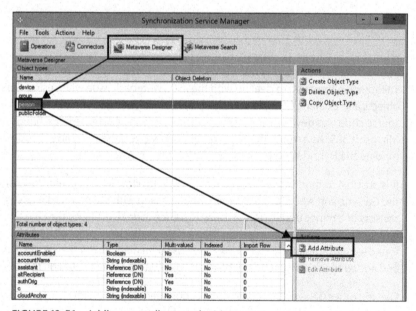

FIGURE 10-51   Adding an attribute to the Metaverse

2. Next, click the New Attribute button, and the New Attribute dialog will appear; in the Attribute Name field, enter the name of the new Attribute (**DN**). Choose String (Indexable) from the Attribute Type dropdown, and click OK. See Figure 10-52.

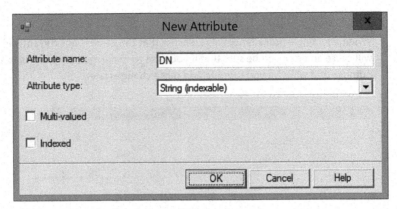

FIGURE 10-52   Naming the new attribute

3. Once you have created the new attribute in the Metaverse, you will then need to create a new inbound synchronization rule for `contact` objects that will flow the Distinguished Name value created in step 2, DN, into the Metaverse Designer.

4. Open the Synchronization Rules Editor, and from the Direction dropdown, choose Inbound rules, and click Add New Rule. See Figure 10-53.

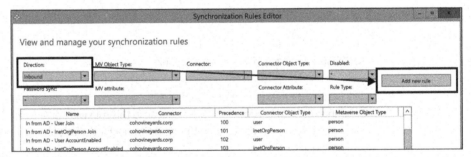

FIGURE 10-53   Add a new inbound synchronization rule

5. In the Name field, enter a descriptive name for the rule, and in the Description field, add an optional description if desired.

6. Select your Active Directory forest from the Connected System dropdown and Contact from the Connected System Object Type dropdown. This will ensure the rule only applies to `contact` objects in your Active Directory forest.

7. Select Person from the Metaverse Object Type dropdown. (Remember, `contact` and `user` objects both appear as `person` objects in the AAD Connect database.)

8. Select Join from the Link Type menu (more about this later in the chapter), and enter a Precedence value less than 100, as shown in Figure 10-54.

TIP

When selecting a precedence value, ensure that the value is not currently in use, as this will cause an error, and be sure that if you plan to make multiple new rules, you choose a number that will give you room to add more changes later.

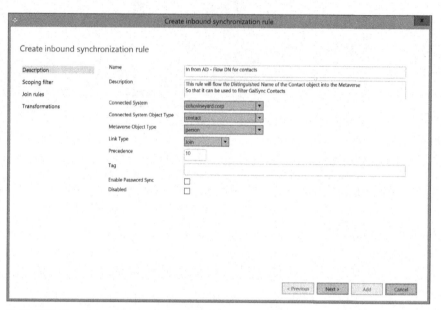

FIGURE 10-54   Create the new Inbound Rule

9. Click Next twice to skip past the Scoping Filter and Join Rules dialogs. We aren't going to scope this rule to any subset of objects because this rule will apply to all `contact` objects residing in the OUs you defined in the AAD Connect installation. You're not going to use this rule to join any objects.

10. In the Transformations dialog, click the Add Transformation button, select the value DN you created in the first step as the Target Attribute, and select dn from the Source dropdown. See Figure 10-55.

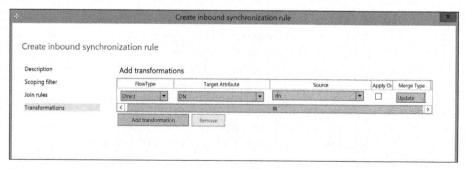

FIGURE 10-55   Adding the DN to DN transformation

11. This will remain a Direct transformation (meaning AAD Connect will flow the value, as-is, from Active Directory to the Metaverse). There is no need to change the Merge Type. Click Add to finish the rule creation.

12. Lastly, we need to modify the Out to AD—Contact Exchange Hybrid rule to only apply to contact objects **not** found in the GalSync OU. You will do this by cloning the rule as a new rule and changing the Scoping Filter to only apply to objects with distinguished names that do not contain the GalSync OU distinguished name (or part of it).

13. From the Direction dropdown in the top-left part of the Synchronization Rules Editor, select Outbound, locate the Out to AD—Contact Exchange Hybrid rule, and click Edit.

14. When you click Edit on a default rule installed as part of the installation, the Edit Reserved Rule Confirmation dialog will prompt you to clone the rule. In this case, click Yes to create an editable copy and disable the original rule, as shown in Figure 10-56.

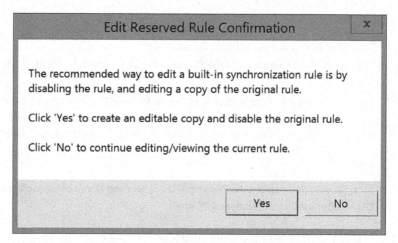

FIGURE 10-56   Prompt to clone a default AAD Connect rule

15. The rule will be opened for editing, and the Precedence value will be set to -1. This change ensures the precedence value is changed before you save the new cloned rule.

16. Enter a value of 50 in the Precedence field, clear the Description field, enter a new description indicating the reason for the rule edit, and then click Next. See Figure 10-57.

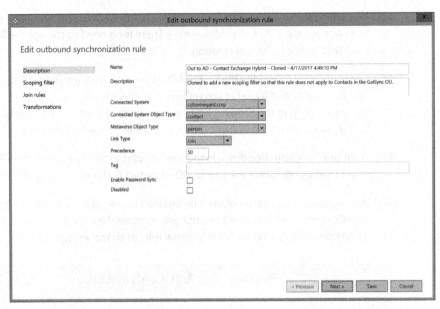

FIGURE 10-57   Cloned copy of the Out to AD—Contact Exchange Hybrid rule

17. On the Scoping Filter page, click Add Group followed by Add Clause to add a single scoping filter to your newly cloned rule. In the Attribute dropdown, select DN. Select NOTCONTAINS from the Operator dropdown. In the Value field, type **GalSync**.

TIP

Alternatively, you could enter the entire Distinguished Name of the GalSync OU (such as OU=GalSync,DC=cohovineyard,DC=us).

18. Finally, click Save to save your newly cloned rule. See Figure 10-58.

Once the preceding steps have been completed, a full synchronization of the AAD Connect solution will successfully solve the GalSync contact writeback issue.

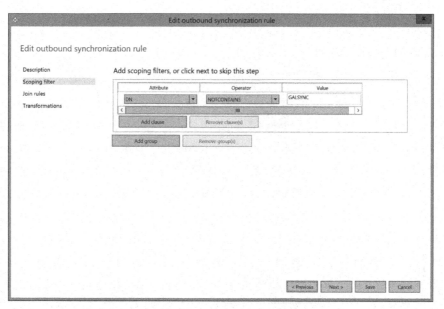

FIGURE 10-58   Adding a scoping filter for the DN value

Inside Out

Sync rule scoping

Scoping filters for sync rules in AAD Connect vary between inbound and outbound rules:

- When creating a scoping filter for an inbound synchronization rule, the values that can be used for filtering must come from the source connector (typically Active Directory).

- When creating a scoping filter for an outbound synchronization rule, the values that can be used for filtering must come from the Metaverse.

- If you want to use an Active Directory value as a scoping filter for an outbound rule, you must add that value to the Metaverse (if it's not already present) and flow the Active Directory value into the Metaverse using an inbound rule first.

SamAccountName and MailNickname

An alternate method for joining user objects is to use the SamAccountName and MailNickName attributes. When using this option, AAD Connect will attempt to join user accounts cross-forest using the SamAccountName first, followed by the MailNickName, as shown in Figure 10-59 in the In from AD–User Join rule's join criteria.

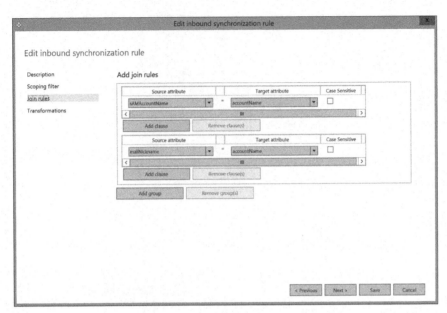

FIGURE 10-59   User join rules when selecting SamAccountName or MailNickName

The purpose of this configuration is to accommodate those organizations where the `mail` value is not unique or not populated cross-forest, though the customer has created objects that share a `SamAccountName`, a `MailNickName`, or both. See Figure 10-60.

> **CAUTION**
>
> It's important to note that the `SamAccountName` and `MailNickName` values are expected to be unique in their own forests. If they are not, you will need to work with your administrators and potentially Microsoft premier support to resolve conflict scenarios.

Inside Out

User joins

User joins are only allowed across directories. If you attempt to join two users from the same domain within the same forest, AAD Connect will return an ambiguous join error. User objects between domains in the same forest may be joined.

It is important that when using joins for attributes like `Mail`, `SamAccountName`, `Mail-NickName`, and so on, the values within each directory are unique to that directory.

Running the IDFix tool before implementing AAD Connect can help identify these common issues so they can be corrected before starting synchronization.

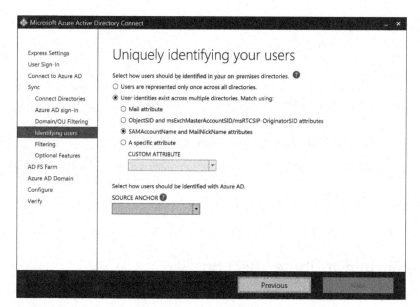

FIGURE 10-60   SamAccountName and MailNickName join selection

If necessary, the SamAccountName and MailNickName join conditions can be updated post-installation to include Mail as an additional join criterion for those multi-forest environments where GalSync has been deployed. Like the `ObjectSID \ msExchMasterAccountSID` option, it is easier to add a single condition to a more complex set of conditions. Like `ObjectSID \ msExchMasterAccountSID`, it would require that the `In from AD-User Join` rule be cloned versus modifying the out-of-the-box rule created by the installation wizard. See Figure 10-61.

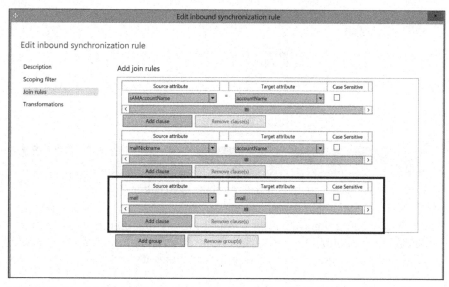

FIGURE 10-61   Adding Mail to the SamAccountName and MailNickName join resulting from the SamAccountname and MailNickName join option

CHAPTER 10

Inside Out

Groups and Clauses

When adding join rules in AAD Connect, it is important to pay close attention to groups and clauses because they affect how the joins are evaluated:

- When you have two clauses inside a single group, the clauses are an AND condition, meaning both must be true for the join to work.

- When you have two groups with a single clause in each, the clauses are an OR condition, meaning either condition can be true for the join to work.

This same approach applies to scoping filters.

Custom join attribute selection

The final option available during the user-matching configuration is the selection of a custom attribute for user joins (see Figure 10-62).

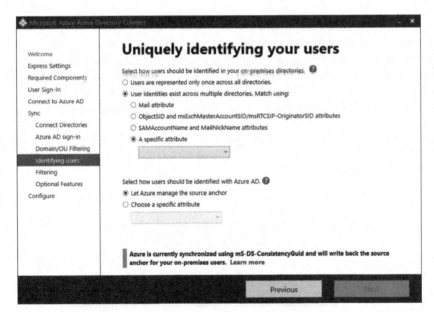

FIGURE 10-62   Selecting the A Specific Attribute radio button

On the Identifying Users tab on the Uniquely Identify Your Users dialog, select the A Specific Attribute radio button. From the A Specific Attribute dropdown, you may choose from a list of all available on-premises Active Directory attributes. It's important to note that most Active

Directory attributes represented in this list—which were taken directly from the Active Directory schema when adding your directories—are also available in the Metaverse.

There are several restrictions that are important to note when manually selecting an attribute to use for joins between objects:

- First, if you want to use the SamAccountName attribute, be sure to use the SamAccount-Name And MailNickName Attributes radio button instead of selecting SamAccountName from the dropdown.

  The pre-built selection for the *SamAccountName And MailNickName Attributes* option will ensure that the joins use the AccountName attribute in the database, where the AAD Connect configuration synchronizes the SamAccountName value. If you choose SamAc-countName manually, you will receive an error because there is no SamAccountName attribute in the AAD Connect Metaverse, as shown in Figure 10-63.

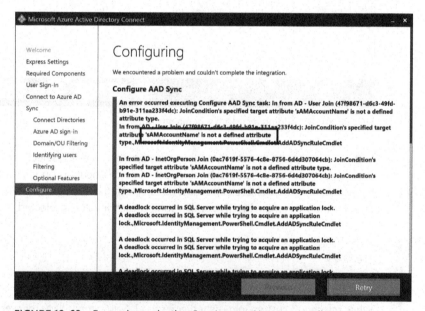

FIGURE 10-63   Error when selecting SamAccountName manually

- Next, note that the dropdown does not allow the use of any Multi-Valued attributes in Active Directory, such as ProxyAddresses, because the join condition only works for sin-gle-valued attributes. It is not capable of performing joins using a multi-valued attribute because it cannot enumerate the individual values.

- Additionally, if you have extended your Active Directory schema with custom attributes, you should not select any of these custom attributes because they will behave similarly as selecting SamAccountName, and return an error indicating the attribute is not a defined attribute. (See Figure 10-64.) Consequently, the installation will fail.

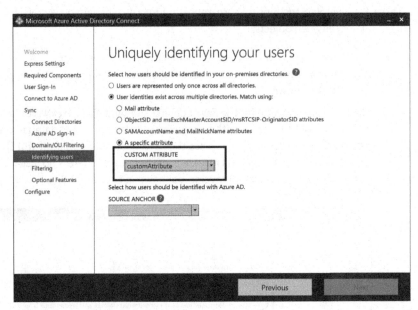

FIGURE 10-64   Adding a custom schema attribute

- Lastly, it is important to note that when a custom join criteria is selected on the Uniquely Identifying Your Users dialog, the value in the Source Anchor dropdown—typically ObjectGUID—will be cleared and must be re-selected before you can proceed. In fact, the Next button will remain inactive until a Source Anchor value is selected.

Inside Out

Selecting a custom join

When selecting a custom join—whether it's Mail, SamAccountName, or even a custom attribute—the AAD Connect tool will not synchronize that user if the selected value is null.

Typically, this is not an issue in multi-forest configurations, though if you select Mail as the join criteria, only users with the Mail attribute populated will be allowed to synchronize to Azure AD.

Keep this in mind when selecting a join condition.

Source Anchor

This brings us to the Source Anchor attribute selection and the last setting you will be prompted for as part of the installation that cannot be changed once you have completed the setup process. Like the other critical decision milestones mentioned previously, if you select the wrong value during this step, AAD Connect will need to be uninstalled and reinstalled to correct the error.

More importantly, if you have already synchronized objects to Azure AD using the wrong Source Anchor, you will most likely need to delete those objects from Azure as well.

The selection of the Source Anchor value is extremely important because it represents a key component of each object's lifecycle and its synchronization to Azure AD.

Key values like UserPrincipalName and eMail address, which are used for critical services like authentication or mail routing, can be changed during a user's life; AAD Connect will flow those updated values to Azure.

Source Anchor, however, is permanent because it uniquely identifies the object and "anchors" it to the source object that it represents in the on-premises directories.

Inside Out

Changing Source Anchor

Changing the Source Anchor value for an object in Azure AD causes the object to be deleted and re-created as a net-new object, even if every other attribute of the object is identical.

In fact, changing the Source Anchor value for an object is so impactful that if AAD Connect detects the Source Anchor for an object is changing, it will display an error and prevent the change.

By default, the Source Anchor attribute in AAD Connect is derived from the ObjectGUID value in on-premises Active Directory. This is because the ObjectGUID value for an object in Active Directory is unique for the lifetime of that object. It cannot be changed, either programmatically or from the GUI, and if the object is deleted and subsequently recovered from the Active Directory recycle bin, the ObjectGUID is preserved.

The ObjectGUID value is a binary value, and like the security identifier or ObjectSID, it is generated at the time of creation. The GUID, or Globally Unique Identifier, is generated on an Active Directory domain controller, is unique within the forest, and never changes for the lifetime of that object.

In fact, because of the way the GUID is generated using the object's creation date, time, MAC address of the network card on the domain controller that created the object, and a 12-digit random hexadecimal value, some will argue that the ObjectGUID value created for an object is universally unique across time and space, and not just unique across the Active Directory forest where it exists.

As part of the synchronization process, AAD Connect will use an object's ObjectGUID, converted from a binary object to a Base64-encoded string, to populate the SourceAnchor value in the Metaverse, as seen in the logic flow in Figure 10-65. The SourceAnchor value will then be synchronized to Azure AD and represented as the ImmutableID value of the object.

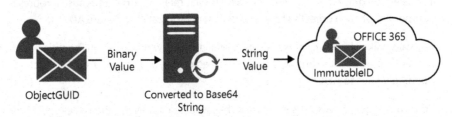

FIGURE 10-65   ObjectGUID to SourceAnchor to ImmutableID transition

Selecting the ObjectGUID as the origin of the SourceAnchor value in AAD Connect is done to ensure that objects will remain unique; while you have the option to select an alternate Active Directory attribute to represent the SourceAnchor for your objects, great care should be given to the selection process.

When selecting an alternate attribute, you should consider the following:

- **Select an attribute that will never change**—Changing the value in Active Directory, either purposely or accidentally, will break the synchronization of the object. Some examples of possible attributes are EmployeeID or Badge Number. Provided you have a mature identity management system that prevents any duplication and prohibits reuse, employee ID numbers or other unique company identifiers are good candidates for SourceAnchor.

CAUTION

Social Security Number

A Social Security Number, while intentionally unique, represents PII (Personally Identifiable Information), is used in U.S. privacy law, and its use carries with it very specific laws and requirements. If you do not store PII today, you should work with your legal and corporate security teams before using this data when synchronizing with Microsoft 365.

Because the SourceAnchor value is converted to Base64 from its source and then written to Azure AD, it is very easy to reverse engineer the value. Anyone with rights to your tenant (such as Global Administrators, User Administrators. and even Microsoft Premier Support) would have access to that PII.

- **Select an attribute that will be unique for every object everywhere**—Duplicating the value on two or more objects will break the synchronization of all but the first object synchronized to Azure with that value.

Most organizations select an alternate SourceAnchor because they are multi-forest in nature (or are involved in frequent merger, acquisition, or divestiture activities) and expect to move objects across forests regularly (or at least once during an object's lifecycle). Consideration must be given to values like EmployeeID (or other *potentially* unique alphanumeric or numeric values that are sequential in nature) because while they are unique within *your* organization, it's possible that an acquisition or merger with another Microsoft 365 customer could result in duplication of values that were thought to be unique.

CAUTION

As you can see, using an attribute other than ObjectGUID for the SourceAnchor carries with it some design considerations that will likely involve several groups within your organization and might not result in a quick decision. Waiting to decide IF you should use an alternate attribute and WHAT attribute to use is something that should be done well in advance of the AAD Connect implementation.

Let Azure manage the SourceAnchor (mS-DS-ConsistencyGuid)

The selection of ObjectGUID as the SourceAnchor attribute was not a trivial decision during the design of the default Azure synchronization process.In fact, the goal of identifying an attribute that will never change for the lifetime of an object left very few options. Given that every organization is different and uses its Active Directory attributes differently, it was impossible to identify many attributes that would fulfill this criterion and be future-proof. As a result, ObjectGUID was the best option available and is the cornerstone of the synchronization process.

The good news is that even though ObjectGUID cannot be changed, it provides a globally unique value that can be used for the lifetime of an object, even when it moves between forests.

Inside Out

Moving users in AD

When moving users between domains in the **same** Active Directory forest, the ADMT tool should be used because it is designed to maintain the ObjectGUID value of the object and will not create a new ObjectGUID.

This allows you to move users between domains and not affect the Azure AD object.

CHAPTER 10

In later versions of AAD Connect, a feature was added that includes support for `ObjectGUID` writeback of an object (namely users) to an alternate binary-type attribute in Active Directory called `mS-DS-ConsistencyGUID`. By writing back to this attribute, the `ObjectGUID` of the object can be automatically stamped on an alternate attribute; that value can be copied cross-forest in merger, acquisition, and divestiture scenarios. This allows the original user `ObjectGUID` to follow the account when it migrates to other forests but still sync the same anchor value to Azure AD.

Inside Out

Use of ConsistencyGuid

The `mS-DS-ConsistencyGUID` writeback is automatically added to `User` objects when the feature is selected in the wizard, though there is no writeback for `Group` or `Contact` objects.

Out of the box, `Group` objects will support the same `ConsistencyGUID` logic as users, but they do NOT have rules to writeback to AD. This behavior would need to be added via custom sync rules.

TIP

It is strongly suggested that you use the Let Azure Manage The Source Anchor feature during the AAD Connect installation process. Alternatively, if you are upgrading from an older version of AAD Connect that did not support the `mS-DS-ConsistencyGUID`, you can use the wizard in newer versions to enable the support of this attribute.

Filter users and devices

During the installation of the AAD Connect tool, you will be able to select one group from each forest that can be used to filter users, groups, contacts, or devices for synchronization to Azure AD.

By default, all users present in the organizational units you selected earlier in the installation process will be synchronized to Azure AD, as shown in Figure 10-66.

This optional group selection method is meant to serve as a way for piloting your deployment to Microsoft 365, and as a result, only the objects in the group will be synchronized to your tenant. It further limits the number of objects that are synchronized to Microsoft 365.

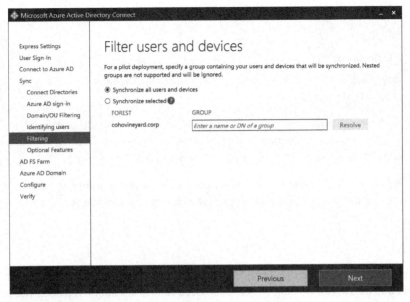

FIGURE 10-66   Filter users and devices

Selecting the Synchronize Selected radio button, as shown in Figure 1-66, will allow you to enter the name of an on-premises Active Directory group in the GROUP box.

If the group name is located in Active Directory, clicking the Resolve button will display the complete distinguished name of the group and a green check mark to indicate success, as shown in Figure 10-67.

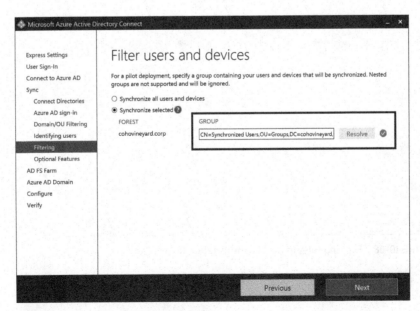

FIGURE 10-67   Successfully resolving a group

Inside Out

Filtering groups

Any group used for filtering must reside in an organizational unit that is within the scope of the solution.

If you enter a group name, and that group is not located in an OU that you included (checked) during installation, it will create the rules for group filtering, but the group will not work, and no objects will synchronize to Azure AD.

No error is displayed during group selection in the wizard or during synchronization afterward—group filtering will simply fail to function, and no objects will be synchronized to Azure.

It is important to note that the group filtering option does not support nested groups, and it is intended to be used for piloting only and removed when the solution is placed into production use.

Additionally, the associated rules created by selecting this option cannot be removed by re-running the AAD Connect Wizard after initial installation, so it will be necessary to either delete or manually disable the rules in the Synchronization Rules Editor in order to go live with the solution. See Figure 10-68.

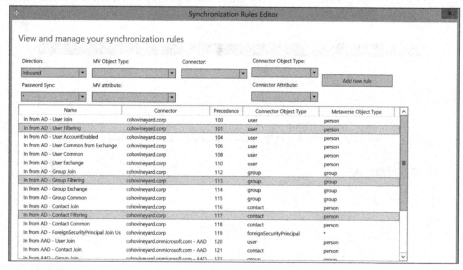

FIGURE 10-68 Filtering rules in the Synchronization Rules Editor

Optional features

The next batch of settings, called Optional Features, allow you to enable enhanced functionality as part of the AAD Connect installation process. These features range from Exchange Hybrid Writeback, discussed earlier, to password synchronization and attribute filtering.

The options presented on the Optional Features dialog can be changed anytime using the AAD Connect Wizard located on the desktop after the installation has been completed. The list of enhanced features grows with each release of the AAD Connect tool, so they are not discussed in detail in this book.

> ## NOTE
>
> Any features flagged as (Preview) indicate they are not finalized and might change between versions. It's also important to note that some features require additional subscriptions (such as Azure AD Premium licensing) to be used. As each version of AAD Connect is released, further information about the optional features can be found at *http://go.microsoft.com/fwlink/?LinkId=532861*.

Exchange Hybrid deployment

Exchange Hybrid (discussed earlier in this chapter because it directly affects user-matching and subsequent GAL synchronization in multi-forest scenarios) is a feature that allows the AAD Connect tool to writeback into on-premises Active Directory a select number of attributes. These attributes are determined by the version of Exchange installed in the target forest, and include (but are not limited to) the following:

- **Proxy Addresses** The `cloudLegacyExchangeDN` value from Exchange Online is written back into the Proxy Addresses array of `User`, `Group`, and `Contact` objects as x500 addresses. If mailboxes are migrated from Microsoft 365 back to on-premises, any messages sent internally while in Microsoft 365 can be replied to without risking delivery errors after migration.

- **Safe Senders, Blocked Senders, Safe Recipients** These values are hash values stored in Active Directory and updated whenever a user makes changes to these settings in their Outlook client. Once a user's mailbox has migrated to Microsoft 365, these values are then managed in Azure AD and written back to on-premises Active Directory so that if the mailbox is ever migrated out of Microsoft 365, those on-premises values will be up-to-date.

- **VoiceMail settings** Like the safe and blocked senders lists, these values are updated in Azure AD when a user enabled for Skype for Business Online or Microsoft Teams makes changes to their settings, and then their account is migrated back to on-premises.

- **Archive status**   Although a mailbox resides in Exchange Online, it is possible that the mailbox may not have had an archive before migration, and it has only been activated afterward. This attribute will tell on-premises Exchange if an archive exists.

The proxy addresses writeback is automatically configured for groups, users, and contacts, while the remainder of the attributes only applies to user objects.

As discussed earlier in the chapter, these rules are created as part of the installation process but can be modified or disabled manually afterward. However, subsequent upgrades of the AAD Connect tool may modify or restore the rules to their original state, so it is important to review all rule modifications before the upgrade. Also, we recommended that you clone existing rules instead of modifying them directly so that their settings will be maintained during the upgrade.

Azure AD app and attribute filtering

Selecting the Azure AD app and attribute filtering feature provides an additional set of wizard dialog pages, allowing you to tailor your installation to either a specific Microsoft 365 workload (Exchange Online only) or set of workloads or to specifically exclude one or more attributes from the synchronization to Azure AD.

The first of these additional pages is the Azure AD Apps filtering dialog shown in Figure 10-69.

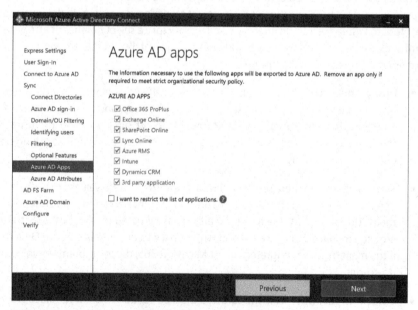

FIGURE 10-69   Azure AD apps filtering

Azure AD app filtering allows you to identify the relevant attributes for Azure AD applications that you want to synchronize to Microsoft 365. Deselecting an application will remove all the outbound rules from the configuration related to that Azure AD application, preventing the attributes from on-premises Active Directory from reaching Microsoft 365. See Figure 10-70.

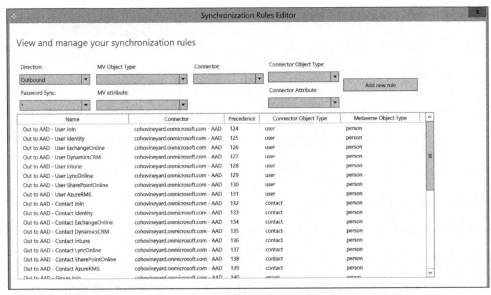

FIGURE 10-70   Default outbound synchronization rules with no Azure AD app filtering

Figure 10-70 shows that a default AAD Connect installation with no Azure app filtering enables outbound synchronization rules for Exchange Online, Dynamics, Lync Online, SharePoint Online, Intune, AzureRMS, and the common attribute sets.

However, as you can see in Figure 10-71, Azure App filtering is only enabled to allow Exchange Online; all other applications are now absent from the synchronization to Azure AD.

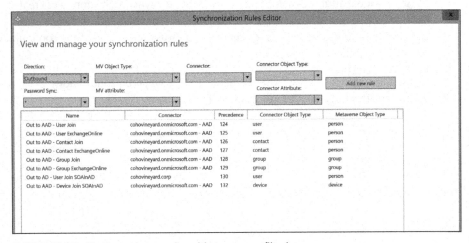

FIGURE 10-71   Outbound sync rules with Azure app filtering

Alternatively, if you want to prevent the synchronization of one or more attributes instead of eliminating a particular Azure App from being synchronized with Microsoft 365, you can select the Azure AD Attributes filtering dialog. See Figure 10-72.

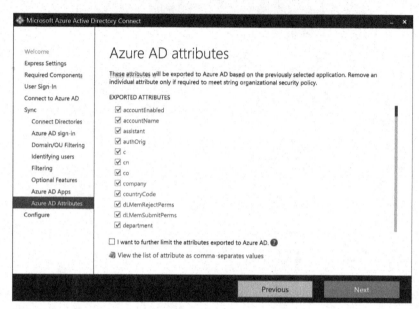

FIGURE 10-72 Azure AD Attributes

Azure AD attribute filtering is provided because it might be necessary to filter some attributes used by your organization that are included in the default set of attributes for a particular work-load (such as Exchange Online) but contain data that you might not want to be synchronized to Azure AD.

Those individual attributes can be deselected, and any synchronization rules created by the installation that normally contain those attributes will be modified, so they are not included. Note in Figure 10-73, the ExtensionAttribute15 was excluded from the configuration via the Azure AD attribute filtering dialog.

As a result, in the Out to AAD–User Exchange Online synchronization shown in Figure 10-74, there is no attribute flow for ExtensionAttribute15.

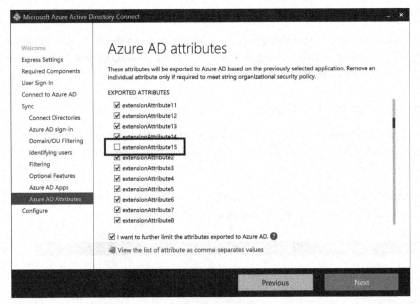

FIGURE 10-73   Deselecting ExtensionAttribute15

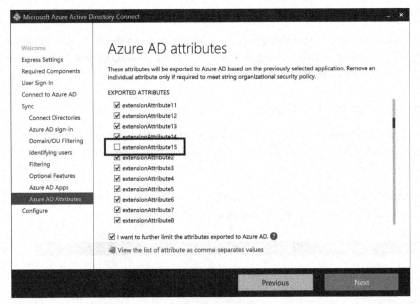

FIGURE 10-74   Out to AAD—User Exchange Online rule missing ExtensionAttribute15

TIP

It is important to note that any customizations made on the Azure AD app and attribute filtering dialogs can be changed at any time using the AAD Connect Wizard found on the desktop after the installation has been completed.

Password synchronization

Even though the password synchronization option is displayed earlier in the configuration process on the User Sign-In dialog, it is also displayed on the Optional Features dialog shown in Figure 10-75.

If you selected the Password Synchronization option previously, it will be selected for you automatically on the Optional Features dialog and cannot be deselected.

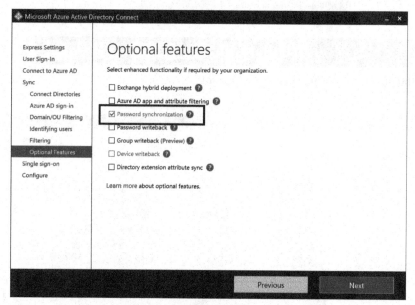

FIGURE 10-75   Password Synchronization is selected automatically on the Optional Features dialog.

However, if you chose another option on the User Sign-In dialog, such as pass-through authentication or AD FS, it is possible to select Password Synchronization here as an additional option.

Password synchronization, in conjunction with alternate user sign-on options, is a supported scenario and provides for a fail-safe configuration if your primary user sign-in option is not working.

NOTE

Additional information about using password synchronization as a backup for AD FS can be found at *https://aka.ms/phsbackup*.

As discussed earlier in this chapter, to implement password synchronization using the customize AAD Connect Implementation, the service account must be selected on the Connect Your Directories dialog. Also, you must delegate the Replicating Directory Permissions and Replicating Directory Permissions All to the service account at the forest's top level.

TIP

Unlike the regularly scheduled 30-minute sync cycle for AD attributes, the AAD Connect password synchronization process happens automatically in the background, independently of the scheduler. You should expect password changes in Active Directory to replicate to Azure AD within 1–2 minutes.

Password Writeback

Another feature related to passwords that can be enabled in the optional features dialog is Password Writeback. Password Writeback allows your users to change their passwords in Azure Active Directory using the portal and automatically update that password in on-premises Active Directory.

Requirements

The Password Writeback feature has several limitations and requirements for being deployed in an enterprise:

- First, using the Password Writeback feature requires the user to be licensed for Azure AD Premium. An Azure AD Premium P1, P2, or Enterprise Mobility Suite (EMS) license qualifies for this feature and will allow your users to use the Password Writeback feature.

- Second, Password Writeback is supported for synchronized users, without or without Password Synchronization enabled, and for federated users using AD FS and users configured to use pass-through authentication. Cloud-only accounts do not qualify for Password Writeback.

- Finally, any user who wants to utilize Password Writeback and reset their user passwords from Azure must have the Password Writeback feature enabled for their account. They must also have the challenge data required for the organization populated on their account.

Enabling Password Writeback

Enabling Password Writeback consists of the following steps:

1. Enabling password reset for the Azure AD tenant.

2. Configuring the Azure AD tenant's password reset policy.

3. Entering the registration data for each user.

Group Writeback

The Group Writeback option, available on the Optional Features dialog, allows you to configure AAD Connect to writeback Microsoft 365 (also known as *unified*) groups created in the portal into on-premises Active Directory.

Selecting the Group Writeback option enables Microsoft 365 groups to be written back to on-premises Active Directory as Exchange Distribution groups so that on-premises mailboxes can send and receive emails from the group. Group Writeback has the following requirements and limitations:

- The Group Writeback feature requires Azure AD Premium licenses to be available in your Azure AD subscription.

- Group Writeback requires the on-premises Exchange organization to be a minimum of Exchange 2013 CU8 or later.

- Groups written back into on-premises Active Directory will not be visible in the on-premises Exchange Global Address List (GAL) unless the objects are manually updated using the Update-Recipient Exchange PowerShell cmdlet.

- Group Writeback is only supported for single Exchange forest deployments.

- The Group Writeback feature is for Microsoft 365 groups only. Security and distribution groups are not supported.

It is important to also note that if none of your on-premises Active Directory forests contain the Exchange schema, this option will not be available in the AAD Connect Optional Features dialog.

Selecting the Group Writeback option, as shown previously in Figure 10-75, will open the Writeback dialog shown in Figure 10-76, which allows you to select the on-premises Active Directory organizational unit that should be used for any Microsoft 365 groups that are written back.

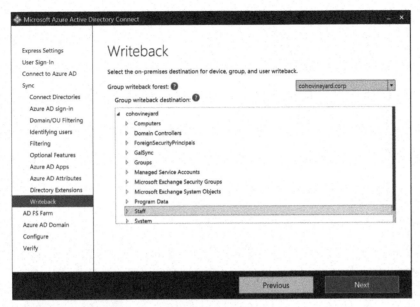

FIGURE 10-76   Selecting the Group Writeback location

It is important to note that only one OU can be selected for the writeback of groups, and if that OU was not selected in the Domain / OU Filtering dialog earlier in the installation process, you will receive an error indicating the selected OU is currently excluded.

An alternate OU can be selected, or the Previous button can be used to return to the Domain / OU Filtering dialog to include the OU in the synchronization scope.

Device Writeback

Device Writeback, located on the Optional Features dialog page, allows you to configure AAD Connect to perform a writeback of devices that have been joined to your Azure AD tenant.

This writeback is provided so that conditional access with AD FS can be configured to secure applications by only allowing access from those trusted devices that have been successfully registered in Azure AD. However, these devices must exist in on-premises Active Directory so that the AD FS on-premises infrastructure can use them for conditional access.

Selecting the Device Writeback option, as shown previously in Figure 10-75, will open an additional Writeback dialog, where you select the on-premises forest that should be used for any devices written back. See Figure 10-77.

CAUTION
It is important to note that in a multi-forest configuration, only one forest can be selected as a target for Device Writeback. Using Device Writeback for more than one Active Directory forest is not supported.

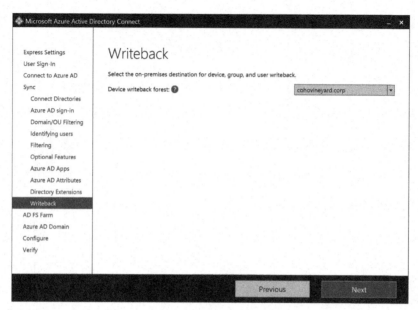

FIGURE 10-77   Selecting the forest for Device Writeback

Device Writeback has the following requirements and limitations:

- The Device Writeback feature requires Azure AD Premium licenses to be available in your Azure AD subscription.

- Device Writeback does not support a multi-forest implementation of AAD Connect.

- The devices written back to on-premises Active Directory must be in the same Active Directory forest as the users.

- Conditional access with AD FS requires AD FS 2012R2 or later.

- Device Writeback can take up to three hours to successfully writeback newly registered devices to on-premises AD.

- There must be at least one Windows Server 2012 R2 joined to Active Directory.

- It is necessary to use the MSOnline PowerShell module to enable Device Writeback in Active Directory.

- Enabling Device Writeback in Active Directory will create an OU named RegisteredDe-vices at the top level of the forest.

Once you have enabled Device Writeback, it is necessary to configure additional conditional access policies in your AD FS infrastructure before the devices can be used to secure applications. Also, issuance rules for your applications will need to be modified to support the IsRegisteredUser claim type.

NOTE

See a step-by-step guide to enabling conditional access in AD FS 2.0 with Device Writeback at *https://bit.ly/3P99c3m*.

Inside Out

Device Writeback

Before Device Writeback can be used, you must first enable it using a series of Power-Shell commands that are part of the `MSOnline` PowerShell module.

If you attempt to install AAD Connect before enabling Device Writeback, the option will be unavailable on the Optional Features page in the installer.

You can complete the installation, execute the necessary commands, and use the AAD Connect Wizard on the desktop to change the configuration to include Device Writeback later.

Directory Extension Attribute Sync

The Directory Extension Attribute Sync option on the Optional Features dialog allows you to synchronize additional attributes to Azure AD that are not part of the default attributes synchronized by the AAD Connect installation.

Selecting the Directory Extension Attribute Sync option will enable an additional wizard dialog used to allow the selection of attributes from the on-premises forest that should be included in the sync. See Figure 10-78.

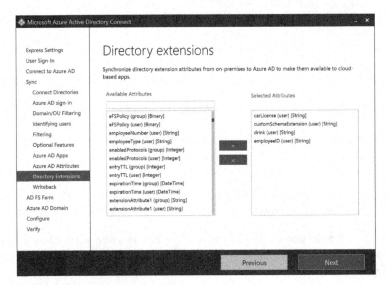

FIGURE 10-78   Directory Extensions

Directory Extension Attribute Sync has the following requirements and limitations:

- Directory Extension Attribute Sync is limited to a total of 100 additional attributes.

- Attributes can only be 250 characters or less in length. Characters beyond 250 are truncated during the synchronization.

- Attributes synchronized in this manner are not visible in Exchange, SharePoint, and so on; they are only visible using Microsoft Graph or GraphAPI.

- Any attribute synchronized using AAD Connect's Directory Extension Attribute Sync is considered to be mastered on-premises and cannot be modified in Azure AD.

Once the Directory Extension Attribute Sync has been configured, the AAD Connect installation will add to the configuration a new outbound synchronization rule containing the selected attributes, as shown in Figure 10-79.

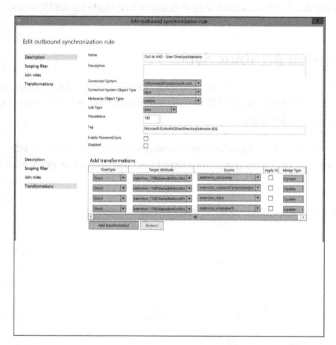

FIGURE 10-79   Additional outbound rule for directory extension attributes

If additional attributes are required, these rules cannot be edited. You must use the AAD Connect Wizard located on the desktop to add additional attributes to the configuration.

Finally, the Directory Extension Attribute Sync will also register a new application in Azure AD that can be found by selecting Azure Active Directory in the portal and selecting App Registrations. See Figure 10-80.

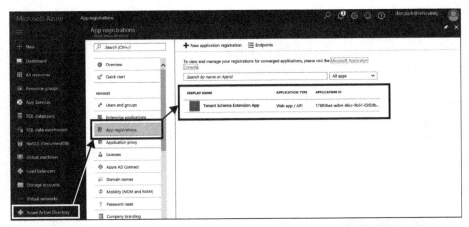

FIGURE 10-80   Tenant Schema Extension App

It's important to mention the application ID for the new Tenant Schema Extension App shown in Figure 10-80. This application ID will be used when naming for all custom schema attributes created in Azure AD. A GraphAPI view of the new attributes synchronized for the user can be seen in Figure 10-81. Note that the attributes are in the `Extension_ApplicationID_On-Prem-AttributeName` format.

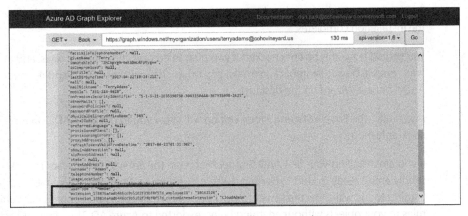

FIGURE 10-81   GraphExplorer view of custom attribute sync values

Finalizing the installation

Once you have completed the Optional Features selections, clicking Next opens the Ready To Configure dialog shown in Figure 10-82, which provides a summary of the selections you made during the installation wizard and provides you with two final options before proceeding with the installation.

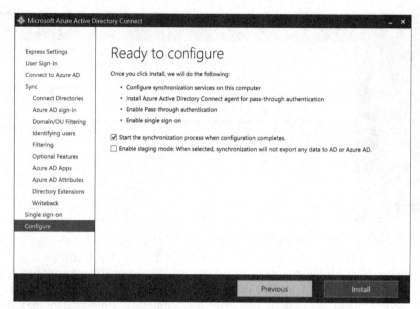

FIGURE 10-82   Ready To Configure dialog

Selecting the Start The Synchronization Process When Configuration Completes option tells the AAD Connect installation wizard to start the synchronization process automatically as soon as the installation completes.

You should leave this box unchecked if you plan to edit synchronization rules, add additional rules, enable Device Writeback, or make any other changes that might require you to run the AAD Connect Wizard on the desktop.

And finally, the Enable Staging Mode option will allow you to put the AAD Connect server in read-only mode.

If you are installing your first AAD Connect server in the enterprise but want to make changes or simply aren't ready to start exporting users and groups to Azure, you can enable Staging Mode. Staging Mode will allow the server to read from Active Directory and apply synchronization rules to your objects without anything being exported to Azure AD. This allows you to review the results of your configuration and make changes without ever exporting to Microsoft 365.

> **NOTE**
>
> Find more information about staging later in this chapter in the "Staging Mode—your ace in the hole" section.

Configuration complete

Once the AAD Connect installation has been completed, the installation wizard will present a Configuration Complete screen (see Figure 10-83) that summarizes the status of the installation, any warnings about the environment, and the synchronization status.

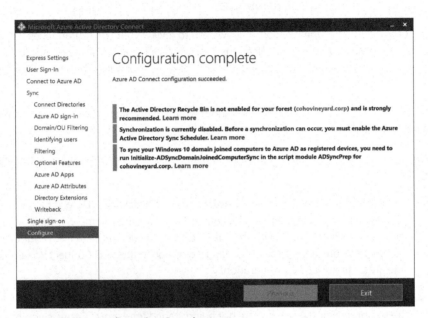

FIGURE 10-83   Configuration Complete

1. You should review all notifications and warnings the installer displays and take any additional action if required.

2. If synchronization was disabled (deselected) on the final installation screen, you will be reminded to re-enable the scheduler before synchronization occurs.

3. It is now safe to click Exit.

TIP

Once you have successfully completed the AAD Connect tool installation, we recommend you create a backup of the configuration. This backup can then be used with the AAD Connect Documenter tool to generate an HTML report of your configuration. The documenter will also allow you to report on differences between configuration backups.

See *https://github.com/Microsoft/AADConnectConfigDocumenter*.

When should you start synchronizing?

If you enabled Staging Mode at the end of the installation wizard, you can safely start the AAD Connect Scheduler. The tool will begin reading objects from your directories, applying synchronization rules, and staging exports to Azure AD. This process will continue every 30 minutes, but nothing will be exported until you are ready.

This is the beauty of Staging Mode. It allows you to review your configuration, especially if you are not 100 percent sure all your selections are correct or if you are aware of unique configurations in your environment, but you are not sure what the tool will do with your data and how those objects will sync to Azure.

Staging Mode allows you to do all this without writing any data to the cloud or making any changes to your environment!

Now, you should take your time to review as many objects as possible and consider the following scenarios:

- **Data that shouldn't leave on-premises Active Directory.**   Do you have data that should NOT leave your on-premises Active Directory? For example, is the EmployeeID your users' Social Security Number? If so, either remove that data from your environment or use the Azure app and attribute filtering option in the AAD Connect Wizard to remove the attribute from the configuration.

- **Data that should be synced but isn't being staged.**   Do you have objects that should be synchronized to Azure but are not being staged for export? Confirm you have selected the correct OUs, and if necessary, run the AAD Connect Wizard and use Domain / OU filtering to include the missing OUs.

- **Too many objects staged for export to Azure.**   Confirm you have selected the correct OUs, or use group membership filtering to reduce the object count. Depending on your directory hierarchy, it might be necessary to create additional synchronization rules to filter these objects in other ways.

- **User objects being properly joined across forests.**   Take careful note of the attributes flowing to Azure when joining object types between your forests. It might be necessary to use the Synchronization Rules Editor to change the precedence for one or more synchronization rules, or you might need to create your own.

It's often said that nothing shines a light on bad identity data like synchronizing it to Azure. Conditions that are possible in on-premises Active Directory, such as duplicate values for Mail, are not allowed in Azure AD, and the AAD Connect tool will flag these conditions as errors during the export process.

Remember, once you start synchronizing objects to Azure AD, it becomes increasingly more difficult to make changes to the configuration, especially if there are changes to the SourceAnchor value. Also, data cleanup will be critical in order to get your data to the cloud.

Starting synchronization

Now that you've reviewed your configuration thoroughly and tested as many of your objects as possible, you're ready to start exporting your data to the cloud:

1. First, if you enabled Staging Mode, you will need to disable it. To do this, you need to use the AAD Connect Wizard on the desktop.

2. Launch the AAD Connect Wizard, and on the welcome screen, select Configure. You will be presented with several options on the Additional Tasks dialog (see Figure 10-84).

3. Select Configure Staging Mode and click Next.

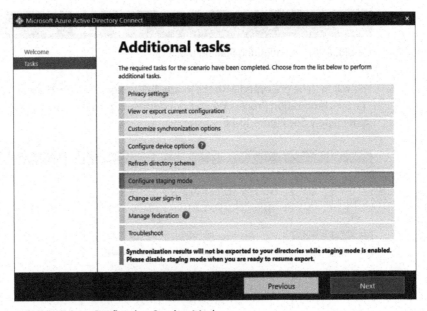

FIGURE 10-84   Configuring Staging Mode

4. Enter credentials for a Global Administrator in the tenant and click Next.

NOTE
It's important to note that these credentials are not stored in the configuration. They are used to ensure that you have the proper privileges to enable the synchronization of objects to your Azure AD tenant.

5. Deselect Enable Staging Mode and click Next. See Figure 10-85.

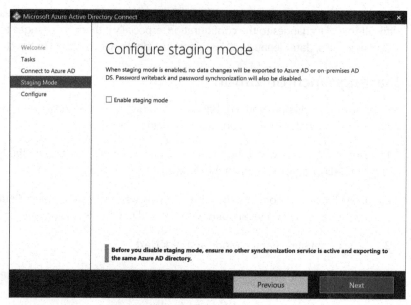

FIGURE 10-85   Configuring Staging Mode

6. You will then be presented with the Ready To Configure dialog. Here, selecting Start The Synchronization Process When Configuration Completes starts the synchronization immediately. See Figure 10-86.

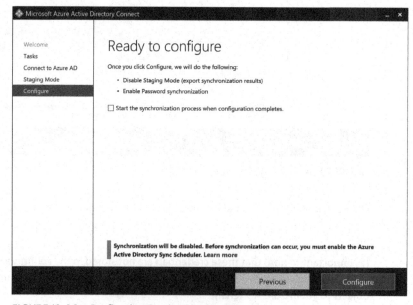

FIGURE 10-86   Configuring Staging Mode

7. Click Configure to complete the change.

8. If you selected the Start The Synchronization Process When Configuration Completes, the synchronization will start immediately, and objects will begin exporting to your Microsoft 365 tenant. No further action is required. However, if you did not enable immediate synchronization, you can start the synchronization process later using PowerShell.

9. Simply open an Administrative PowerShell prompt and issue the command:

```
Start-ADSyncSyncCycle
```

10. This command will start the synchronization process immediately, though it will only execute once, leaving the scheduled sync cycle disabled.

11. During the initial population of the Azure AD tenant, this single export to Azure will help identify any issues with data—in the form of export errors—while giving you time to review and correct the data before a second synchronization cycle occurs.

12. When you are ready to enable the regular 30-minute sync cycle, enter the PowerShell command to enable the scheduler for a regular 30-minute synchronization interval:

```
Set-ADSyncScheduler -SyncCycleEnabled $True
```

13. If you want to view the status of the scheduler later, use the following command:

```
Get-ADSyncScheduler
```

14. And finally, if you want to disable the scheduler again, enter the command:

```
Set-ADSyncScheduler -SyncCycleEnabled $False
```

Staging Mode—your ace in the hole

Previously, we discussed Staging Mode as an option for reviewing the synchronization of objects and testing the configuration of the AAD Connect installation before the first export of data to Azure AD.

However, the Staging Mode server has another equally important purpose in a typical Azure AD synchronization strategy. It is designed to provide a warm-standby server that can be used for failover purposes in the event the primary synchronization server is down.

The added benefit of a Staging Mode server is that instead of relying on SQL high-availability features like log shipping, or clustering, AAD Connect can be installed on a separate stand-alone server, with its own SQL database, without any need to interact with the primary synchro-nization server. Because both databases are independent of one another, if any SQL database corruption were to occur on the primary server, it would not be replicated to the staging server.

CHAPTER 10

Migrating from the primary synchronization server to the staging server is simply a matter of running the AAD Connect Wizard on the desktop and disabling Staging Mode. When this action is performed, it is assumed that the primary server is down or unavailable, and you must ensure the secondary server is returned to Staging Mode before bringing the primary server back online.

NOTE
Synchronizing two AAD Connect servers to the same tenant is not supported.

What's next?

Now that you have successfully completed the installation of AAD Connect and are synchronizing at least a few users, groups, and contacts to your Microsoft 365 tenant, we will review the Azure AD Cloud Sync tool and how it can be used in lieu of—or along with—the AAD Connect tool to manage your directory synchronization.

Azure AD Cloud Sync

Until now, we've been discussing the flagship Azure AD Synchronization tool, AAD Connect. Over the past 11 years, AAD Connect has had a long and distinguished career in the Microsoft 365 directory synchronization space and, as a result, has been called by several different names as the product evolved:

- **DirSync**   Originally known as DirSync, it was a purpose-built tool for Azure synchronization, but compared to today's Azure AD Connect, it had a significant number of limitations. In addition to lacking any ability to customize attribute flows, DirSync could only sync to Azure from a single on-premises Active Directory forest, could not support Exchange resource forest scenarios, and had no support whatsoever for synchronizing passwords.

- **FIM + WAAD**   To help provide multi-forest support and Exchange resource forest sync, a custom management agent (also known as a *connector*) was developed for the Forefront Identity Manager 2010 platform. This Windows Azure Active Directory (WAAD) management agent enabled customers to deploy a synchronization solution that not only allowed for the synchronization of multiple on-premises Active Directory forests to Azure but also supported multi-forest Exchange configurations, custom attribute flows, filtering, and minimal writeback. FIM + WAAD was only provided for complex customer scenarios, typically required a Microsoft Consulting Services engagement to deploy, and would never support password synchronization of any kind. While the FIM+WAAD solution allowed multi-forest and multi-Exchange customers to move to Azure and eliminated a roadblock in the Azure sync story, it also bought the Microsoft product group time to work on the next evolution of directory synchronization—AADSync.

- **AADSync**   When comparing past versions of the Azure AD Connect tool to AADSync, AADSync is the most similar. This is primarily because Azure AD Connect actually refers to a "toolset" and not just a synchronization engine, while AADSync remains the engine. AADSync was rebranded as Azure AD Connect when it became clear that the Azure synchronization strategy would include other on-premises and cloud-based features. Early in its development cycle, AADSync was improved to include features not found in prior versions of the synchronization engine, such as password synchronization; multi-forest and multi-Exchange support; advanced filtering; custom synchronization rules; and password writeback of passwords, groups, and devices.

Inside Out

AdminDescription

For a very short time, AADSync included a feature called User Writeback that would create Active Directory users on-premises from cloud-only users. Any user created by this writeback process would have the AdminDescription attribute stamped with User_xxxxxx, where xxxxxx was the source cloud user's Azure ObjectID.

The AdminDescription StartsWith User_ user filter was implemented to ensure that Cloud Writeback users were not synced back to Azure.

Though User Writeback is no longer enabled or supported, the filter remains in place due to the feature's adoption by many customers.

- **AAD Connect**   Ultimately, it became clear that while AADSync was continually evolving to support advanced synchronization requirements, more and more features were being added to the solution and Microsoft 365, so AADSync was rebranded as AAD Connect. In fact, if you were to compare DirSync, FIM+WAAD, AADSync, and AAD Connect based purely on the interface, most people would be unable to distinguish AADSync from AAD Connect without using the Help \ About menu.

The Azure AD Connect story doesn't stop there. Microsoft 365 is constantly evolving—as are customer and security requirements—and because of the administrative overhead of maintaining the server infrastructure, network, and firewall configurations, it became evident it was time to provide Azure AD Synchronization as a cloud-based service. As a result, Azure AD Cloud Sync was born.

Azure AD Cloud Sync

Azure AD Cloud Sync is a cloud-based Azure synchronization solution that eliminates the need for costly on-premises infrastructure like Windows Servers, Microsoft SQL servers and licensing, security updates, patching, group policy management, and firewall rules. It allows customers to configure user, group, and contact synchronization from the Azure portal and eliminate any complex setup and configuration tasks.

For Azure AD Cloud Sync to work in your environment, you will need to install at least one provisioning agent and create a Group Managed Service Account (gMSA) for the agent to connect to Active Directory. Also, you will need to create an Azure AD hybrid identity admin account in your tenant. The creation of the gMSA will require a Domain Administrator or Enterprise Administrator account, and the provisioning agent requires a Windows Server 2016 or later operating system.

Although Azure AD Cloud Sync will work with just a single agent install, Microsoft recommends a minimum of three provisioning agent installations for high availability. The Azure AD Cloud Sync configurations are performed and maintained in your Azure tenant, so no additional configuration is required on the server once the provisioning agent installation has been successfully completed.

Azure AD Cloud Sync removes the need for an on-premises server (and possibly SQL infrastructure) and allows you to configure and maintain the solution from your tenant. Another great thing about Azure AD Cloud Sync is that it does not require line-of-sight between forests in your environment to sync because Azure AD Cloud Sync is an agent-based solution.

With Azure AD Connect, it is necessary for all your on-premises Active Directory forests to be resolvable and reachable by the AAD Connect server if you want to synchronize objects from a directory. In merger, acquisition, and divestiture scenarios, where connectivity is either impossible or not allowed, the synchronization process is more complex, sometimes requiring alternative identity management solutions, third-party software implementations, and possibly even manual data exports and imports.

Because Azure AD Cloud Sync is agent-based, no network connectivity between Active Directory forests is required. You only need to install the Azure AD Cloud Sync provisioning agent in each forest, regardless of whether a connection is available to the other forests, and it will synchronize users, groups, and contacts from that forest.

While Azure AD Cloud Sync sounds like an easy win, there are still many features that are not yet available that might not make it a good fit for your organization. As of June 2022, the primary features of AAD Connect that Azure AD Cloud Sync does NOT support include the following:

- Device synchronization and hybrid Azure AD Join

- Writeback

- Pass-through authentication

- Directory extensions

- Custom attribute flows and rule editing

- SourceAnchor

See the following sections for more about these unsupported AAD Connect features.

Device synchronization and hybrid Azure AD Join

Azure AD Cloud Sync currently does not support device synchronization. If you have devices you intend to synchronize to Azure AD, you will need to either continue to use Azure AD Connect or reconfigure your existing Azure AD Connect instance to only synchronize Devices and convert your user, group, and contact synchronization to Azure AD Cloud Sync.

CHAPTER 11

> **NOTE**
> This configuration is supported by the Microsoft product group. More information can be found at *https://aka.ms/plancloudsync*.

If you intend to deploy both Azure AD Connect and Azure AD Cloud Sync in the same environment, it's strongly recommended that you pilot this configuration first to ensure there are no interoperability issues.

> **NOTE**
> More information on piloting this configuration can be found at *https://aka.ms/pilotcloudsync*.

Later in this chapter, we will review the changes needed to pilot a configuration change from Azure AD Connect to the Azure AD Cloud Sync tool.

Writeback

Azure AD Cloud Sync does not currently support writeback of any attributes to on-premises Active Directory. If you are currently using Group Writeback, Device Writeback, or Exchange Hybrid Writeback, you are likely not a good candidate for Azure AD Cloud Sync. Also, you would need to either review the features and remove them from your business requirements or continue using Azure AD Connect until they are added to the Azure AD Cloud Sync tool.

Password writeback is the only exception to this limitation. Currently, password writeback is supported when using Azure AD Cloud Sync. Additionally, like Azure AD Connect, Azure AD Cloud Sync also supports Password Hash Sync (PHS), so both PHS and password writeback can be configured to support password sync and self-service password writeback.

Pass-through authentication

Azure AD Cloud Sync does not support pass-through authentication (PTA). The PTA feature of Azure AD Connect requires an authentication agent on one or more servers. (Microsoft recommends a minimum of 3 and a maximum of 40.) However, the PTA feature requires the Azure AD Connect server for communication with the authentication agents. Because Azure AD Cloud Sync does not include any on-premises infrastructure, PTA will not work.

Directory extensions

Azure AD Cloud Sync does not support directory extension attribute synchronization. You won't be able to use Azure AD Cloud Sync if your current AAD Connect installation is configured to sync extended directory attributes, or you must sync directory extension attributes not included in the default Azure AD Cloud Sync installation.

Custom attribute flows and rule editing

Unlike Azure AD Connect, the Azure AD Cloud Sync tool does not support complex attribute flows or customized sync rules. If your current implementation of Azure AD Connect utilizes customized sync rules or you have implemented complex attribute flows, you will need to review those against the Azure AD Cloud Sync tool options to see if they are still possible.

Later in this chapter, we will review the types of filtering and custom attribute flows available in Azure AD Cloud Sync.

SourceAnchor

Azure AD Cloud Sync contains support for both `ObjectGUID` and `mS-DS-ConsistencyGuid` as the `SourceAnchor`. If `mS-DS-ConsistencyGuid` contains a value, it will be used by default; otherwise, it will default to the `ObjectGUID`. If your current Azure AD Connect implementation uses a value other than `mS-DS-ConsistencyGuid` or `ObjectGUID`, it is not supported by Azure AD Cloud Sync and will not be a good option for you until you can change your `SourceAnchor` attribute.

> ## Inside Out
>
> *Writeback*
>
> If you perform frequent inter-forest migrations, be aware that because Azure AD Cloud Sync does not support writeback, your user objects will not have their `mS-DS-ConsistencyGuid` attributes set like Azure AD Connect does by default. You will need to manually stamp the `mS-DS-ConsistencyGuid` on the target user account using the `ObjectGUID` value.

Installing Azure AD Cloud Sync

To install the Azure AD Cloud Sync tool, you will need to log in as an Enterprise Administrator to a Windows 2016 or later server where you intend to host the agent:

1. Open a browser and navigate to *https://portal.azure.com*.

2. Log in as a user with the Global Administrator privilege and select the Azure Active Directory pane. Click Azure AD Connect on the left and select the Manage Azure AD Cloud Sync link, as shown in Figure 11-1.

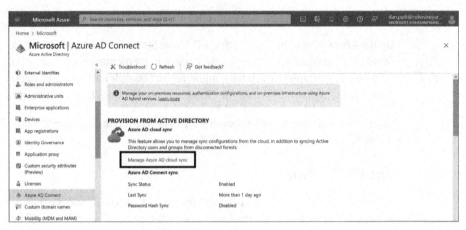

FIGURE 11-1   Manage Azure AD Cloud Sync selection

3. On the Azure AD Cloud Sync screen, in the Configuration section, you should be instructed to install an agent to get started. Click the Download Agent option at the top of the screen, as shown in Figure 11-2.

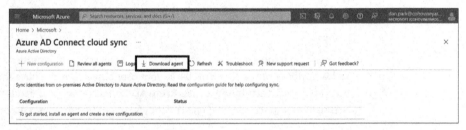

FIGURE 11-2   Downloading the agent

4. On the Azure AD Provisioning Agent dialog, you will be prompted to accept the license terms by clicking the Accept Terms & Download button before you can download the agent, as shown in Figure 11-3.

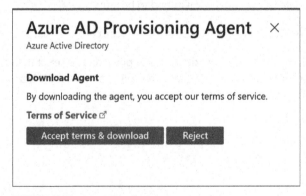

FIGURE 11-3   Accepting license terms

5. Once you have successfully downloaded the installation agent MSI file, click the file to open it, and as shown in Figure 11-4, check the I Agree To The License Terms And Conditions and click Install.

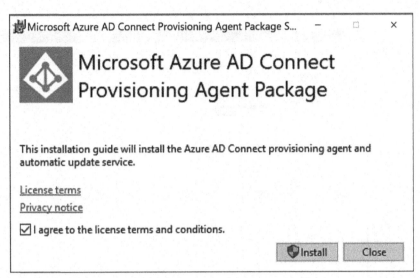

FIGURE 11-4   Installing the Provisioning Agent Package

6. Once the installation wizard has started, as shown in Figure 11-5, you will notice that it looks very similar to the Azure AD Connect installation wizard; click Next to continue the installation process.

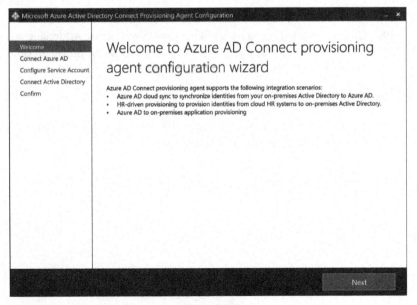

FIGURE 11-5   The Provisioning Agent Configuration

7. The installation will proceed to the Connect Azure AD dialog, and you should be automatically prompted to authenticate to Azure AD, as shown in Figure 11-6. If you are not prompted automatically, click the Authenticate button to be prompted for sign-in credentials.

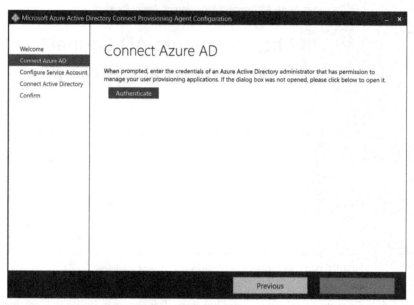

FIGURE 11-6   Connect Azure AD

8. Enter credentials for a Global Administrator account and fulfill any multifactor prompts for text messages.

9. Once you have successfully authenticated to your Azure AD tenant, you will be prompted to create a Group Managed Service Account (gMSA) by providing Domain Administrator credentials, as shown in Figure 11-7.

10. Enter your credentials and click Next to create the account.

11. The installer will validate your credentials and display the domain in the Configured Domains column, as shown in Figure 11-8.

FIGURE 11-7 Creating a Group Managed Service Account

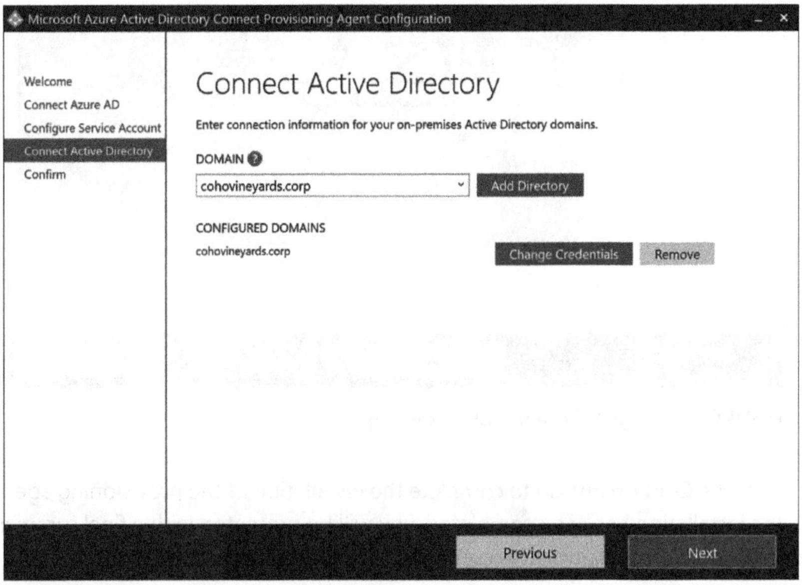

FIGURE 11-8 Connected Directories

12. If you have additional directories that should be added to the configuration (and those directories are resolvable and reachable from this system), enter the name of that domain in the Domain box and click Add Directory. You will be asked for Domain Administrator credentials for that domain so an additional Group Managed Service Account can also be created in that domain.

13. Once all the preferred domains are listed in the Configured Domains column, click Next to continue the installation.

14. The Agent Configuration dialog will display a summary of all domains selected during the provisioning agent stage of the wizard. This summary will list each domain, the name of the Group Managed Service Account created in the domain for use by the provisioning agent, and the account logged into the portal when the configuration was created. See Figure 11-9.

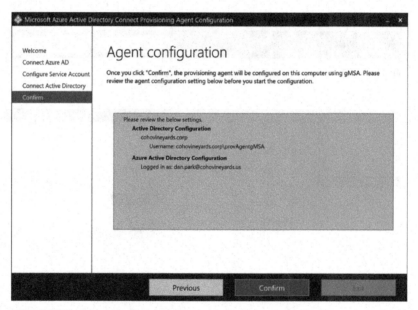

FIGURE 11-9   Agent Configuration summary

15. Click the Confirm button to complete the installation of the provisioning agent. Once the installation has been completed, you will be presented with a final summary screen verifying the installation was complete, as shown in Figure 11-10.

16. Click Exit to close the installation wizard.

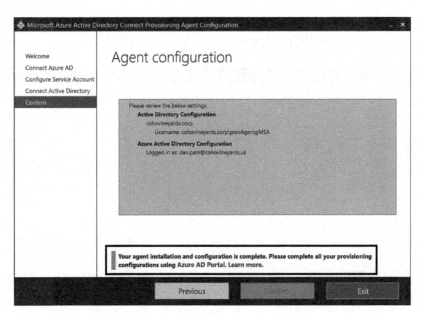

FIGURE 11-10   Agent Configuration completed

Configuring Azure AD Cloud Sync

Once the Azure AD Cloud Sync provisioning agent has been installed on at least one server in your enterprise, follow these steps:

1. Return to the Azure AD portal and navigate to Azure Active Directory as before, selecting Azure AD Connect on the left and managing Azure AD Cloud Sync as before.

2. As shown in Figure 11-11, the page will not display any new information in the Configuration and Status columns. However, unlike last time, the New Configuration option will be available.

FIGURE 11-11   Creating a New Configuration

3. Select New Configuration to begin the configuration of your Azure AD Connect Cloud Sync service.

4.   As shown in Figure 11-12, the New Provisioning configuration screen will be displayed, and you will be prompted for which Active Directory domain you'd like to sync.

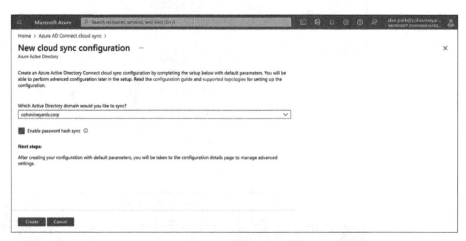

FIGURE 11-12   Selecting the Active Directory domain for your new configuration

5.   You must select the correct Active Directory domain from the dropdown menu, confirm whether you'd like password hash sync enabled, and click Create.

6.   If you've only installed agents in one Active Directory forest, you will only have one option in the dropdown menu. It's okay if you're not sure about password hash sync; you can always return to this screen later and enable it.

7.   Once you've clicked Create, you will see a notification pop-up in the upper-right corner that your configuration was successfully saved, and you will be presented with a number of configuration options, as shown in Figure 11-13.

8.   It's important to note that the configuration has been saved, though until you complete the configuration options provided, the actual synchronization of objects will not begin.

FIGURE 11-13   Editing the Cloud Sync configuration

9. Under Step 1, Scope, the Click To Edit Scoping Filters hyperlink allows you to edit scoping filters. This option allows you to choose between automatically syncing all users, syncing users who are members of security groups, or syncing users in specific organizational units (OUs) in the domain.

10. As shown in Figure 11-14, you can select from one the following three user-selection options:

   - **All Users**—This option, as the name implies, automatically includes all users in the scope of the synchronization. If there are users in your directory you do not want to include, you can add additional attribute filtering in a later step.

   - **Selected Security Groups**—Using this option, you can limit the scope of synced users to only members of the security groups that you define. To enter a group, you will need to provide the full distinguished name of the group (such as CN=Synced Users, OU=Security Groups, DC=cohovineyards, or DC=corp). The setup will not check entries you supply on this page, so if you enter an incorrect distinguished name, you will receive an error later during the synchronization phase.

   TIP

   It's important to note that this option does not support nested groups, so only direct members of a group will be included in the sync; also, subgroups are not included. Just like with Azure AD Connect, Microsoft support recommends that you only use the security group option for pilot scenarios because of the overhead required to check each user's membership when evaluating a synchronization.

   - **Selected Organizational Units**—This option will allow you to enter the Distinguished Name of Organizational Units in your directory. Like the Selected Security Groups option, it will not check for the validity of the provided OU.

11. In our example, we will select two Organizational Units to be synchronized to Azure using Cloud Sync. These users will be out of the scope of the Azure AD Connect client that is currently installed and synchronizing users to Azure.

   TIP

   Synchronizing objects from an Active Directory forest using both Azure AD Connect and Azure AD Cloud Sync is fully supported. You simply need to make sure the users are not in the scope of both sync engines.

12. As shown in Figure 11-14, check the Selected Organizational Units radio button; in the Distinguished Name Of Object field, enter the distinguished name of the OU or OUs you want to include in the sync scope. After you enter each OU name, click Add.

CHAPTER 11

FIGURE 11-14   Scoping Users

13. The best way to ensure you have entered a distinguished name correctly when configuring the scope of object sync in Azure AD Cloud Sync is to select the Organizational Unit in Active Directory Users And Computers, right-click the preferred Organizational Unit, and select Properties. Once you've displayed the default properties, click the Attribute Editor tab and double-click the `distinguishedName` attribute. You can then copy the value directly, as shown in Figure 11-15.

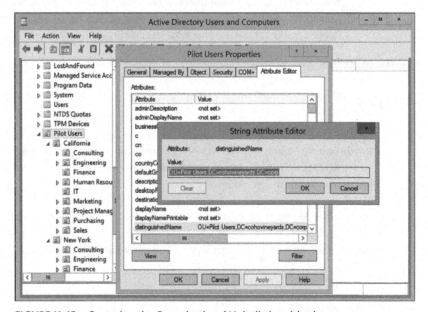

FIGURE 11-15   Capturing the Organizational Unit distinguished name

14. Click Add for each of the name or names of the OUs you want to include in the sync; make sure they appear under the heading Distinguished Name heading at the bottom of the page, as shown in Figure 11-16, and then click Done.

FIGURE 11-16   Entering distinguished names on the Scope Users dialog

15. Once you have selected one or more OUs for the synchronization scope, you can either proceed to configuring attribute mappings and testing a pilot user. Or, you can proceed directly to the bottom of the page to enable the sync. For our purposes, we will configure some attribute mappings.

16. As shown in Figure 11-17, select the Click To Edit Mappings link. You should also note that if you did not enable password hash sync in your earlier installation of the provisioning agent, the Enable setting will not be selected. Selecting it here will enable it.

FIGURE 11-17   Managing synchronization attributes

17. Click the Add Attribute Mapping link to edit mappings, as shown in Figure 11-18. You will then be presented with a list of each object type supported by Azure AD Cloud Sync (such as User, Group, or Contact) at the top of the page, along with all the attribute mappings automatically populated when the configuration is enabled.

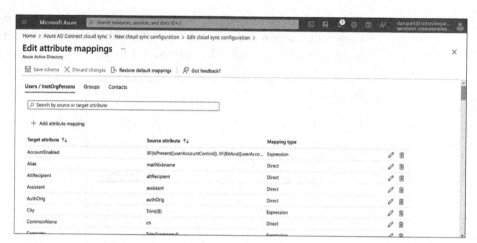

FIGURE 11-18   Edit Attribute Mappings

The attribute mappings provided for each object type match those supported by the Inbound Attribute Flows available in the sync rule editor in Azure AD Connect. These attribute mappings can be modified or deleted.

Deleting attribute mappings

As shown in Figure 11-19, it is possible to remove an attribute mapping by selecting the attribute you do not want to flow to Azure AD and selecting the trashcan icon to the right of the mapping name:

1. In this example, we will remove the attribute flow for `ExtensionAttribute15` by selecting the trashcan icon to the right of the mapping expression for the attribute. See Figure 11-19.

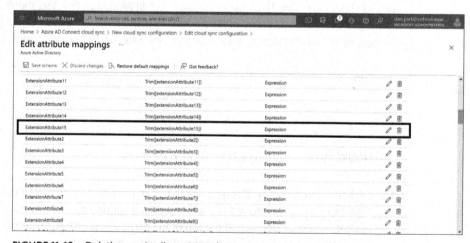

FIGURE 11-19   Deleting an Attribute Mapping

NOTE

It is important to remember that Azure AD Cloud Sync does not currently support writeback attributes, so the attribute mappings displayed are Inbound only. The user interface doesn't make this distinction. The first column is the on-premises Active Directory attribute name, whereas the second column references the corresponding Azure AD attribute.

2. Once you have clicked the trash can icon next to a mapping, you will be prompted to confirm the deletion of the attribute mapping, as shown in Figure 11-20.

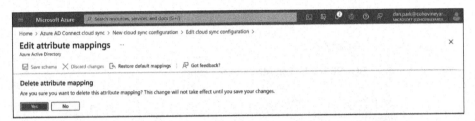

FIGURE 11-20   Delete Attribute Mapping confirmation

3. It's also important to note that this mapping deletion will not take effect until all changes to this cloud sync configuration are saved by clicking the Save Schema button at the top of the screen. Deleting the mapping for an existing enabled cloud sync configuration will not apply until you save the complete configuration.

Editing attribute mappings

In addition to deleting attribute mappings, you can modify any existing mapping by selecting the pencil icon next to the trashcan icon to the right of each mapping:

1. In the example shown in Figure 11-21, we are changing the attribute mapping for ExtensionAttribute1 from the default expression Trim([extensionAttribute1]), which removes, or "trims," any leading or trailing spaces from the attribute value, to Left(Trim([extensionAttribute1]),448), which will continue to trim the value but also only flow the first 448 characters of the attribute's value.

TIP

This is especially useful for scenarios where the attribute contains a very long value that would otherwise cause issues with attribute flow.

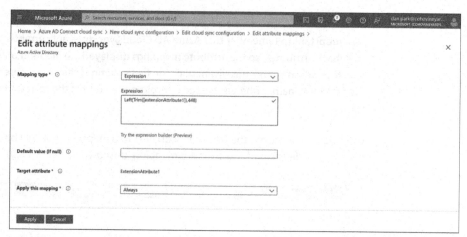

FIGURE 11-21   Edit Attribute Mappings

Inside Out

448 Characters

The 448-character limit is a limitation in SQL server for the maximum size of an indexed string value. This is why Azure AD Connect uses the 448-character limit in most `Left()` functions; that limitation has been maintained in Azure AD Cloud Sync to remain consistent with the Azure AD Connect attribute mappings.

2. Clicking Apply will save any changes to your attribute mapping; like deleting mappings, the changes will not go into effect until you save the schema.

TIP

It's also important to note that any attribute mappings added or modified in the configuration will be moved out of alphabetical order and appear at the top of the list of attribute mappings.

Adding attribute mappings

Finally, Azure AD Cloud Sync allows you to add new inbound attribute mappings so you can reconfigure any attribute mapping you might have deleted or create a new mapping for any of the remaining available Azure attributes.

There are two important things to note:

- You cannot configure mappings for custom Azure extension attributes or custom on-premises Active Directory schema extensions. Neither will appear in the list of target attributes.

- If you need to sync non-standard or custom attributes from the on-premises Active Directory schema, you will need to install the full version of Azure AD Connect and enable the Directory Extension Attribute Sync feature.

Follow these steps to add attribute mappings:

1. As shown in Figure 11-22, after clicking the Add Attribute Mapping button at the top of the screen, you will be prompted to select the Mapping Type, Default Value, Target Attribute, and the initial flow option.

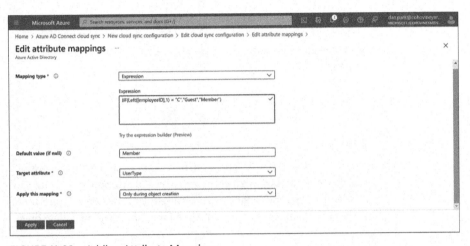

FIGURE 11-22   Adding Attribute Mappings

2. In Figure 11-22, Expression has been chosen from the Mapping Type dropdown, and the Target Attribute has been set to UserType.

3. The expression, located in the Expression field, consists of VBA functions that can be used to control the evaluation of the Source attribute and define specific behavior based on those rules.

NOTE

More information about writing expressions can be found at *https://aka.ms/cloudsyncref*.

TIP

Note that there is no Source Attribute dropdown because the Expression Builder will be used to specify the source or sources. The Source dropdown will only appear for Direct Mapping types, where no change or transformation is made to the value.

4. In this example, we are using a combination of the inline IF statement (IIF), along with the ToUpper and Left functions.

5. The inline IF function consists of three parts—a condition, followed by the action taken if True, and the action taken if False. Commas separate the three parts, and each of the True and False parts can also consist of other VBA functions, resulting in a very long and complex expression under certain conditions.

6. The Left function returns a specific number of characters starting at the left side of a string or attribute. Strings are specified by surrounding them with a quote (") character, and attributes are specified by surrounding them with brackets—[]. The ToUpper function simply converts a string to all uppercase text.

7. In this example, we used the Left([employeeID],1) function to return the left-most character from the attribute employeeID, and then we applied the ToUpper function to set the results to all uppercase. Finally, we use the equals sign (=) check to determine if it equals the letter C.

Inside Out

Case sensitivity

Despite the use of the ToUpper function in our example, the expression would evaluate to True regardless of whether the employeeID attribute starts with c or C because the operator = does not honor case. To ensure the expression is future-proof if case sensitivity is added later, we used the ToUpper function as a good coding practice.

8. Based on the result of our equals (=) operator, if true, the UserType will either be set to Guest, if True; if false, the UserType will be set to Member.

TIP

Additionally, the Expression Builder allows you to define a default value used if the expression's output returns Null. This is especially helpful in eliminating additional functions like IsNullOrEmpty and IsPresent from your expressions because it will allow you to set a value without needing to test.

9. Finally, the Apply This Mapping dropdown allows you to configure an expression that will either apply every time the object is synced or only when the object type is created. This is typically referred to as a one-time-only (OTO) or on-provision mapping.

10. Once you have completed the custom expression, click the Apply button to add the expression to the configuration. The expression will now appear at the top of the list, as shown in Figure 11-23.

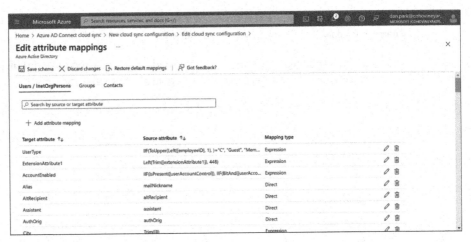

FIGURE 11-23   Reviewing Attribute Mappings

11. Once you have completed the customizations you need, you will need to click the Save Schema button in the top-left corner.

NOTE

Note that if this is a not-yet-enabled new configuration, this change will not start the synchronization. You will need to return to the main configuration page to enable it.

Additional complex mapping examples

Before we move on, following are a few more complex examples of attribute mappings that are commonly used in Azure AD Connect, along with the comparable Azure AD Cloud Sync mapping expressions.

Let's say you want to transform the `Display Name` from `First Last` to `Last, First John Smith -> Smith, John`).

When performing migrations or sanitizing data synchronized to Azure, customers frequently change the format of certain attributes in Azure AD while leaving the on-premises Active Directory attribute unchanged. One reason they do this might be to identify users who have migrated their mailboxes to Exchange Online. Because the Azure attribute values are displayed in the Microsoft 365 Outlook address book, any on-premises user mailboxes will still display the legacy values, so the difference will be obvious.

`Display Name` is one of the most common examples of this practice. Users who migrated their mailboxes to Exchange Online will see the new Display Name format, while those who retain on-premises mailboxes will see the older format.

In this example (see Figure 11-24), we are transforming the `Display Name value` from "First-name Lastname" to "Lastname, Firstname".

1. Begin by editing the cloud sync configuration and entering the word **display** in the search bar to display all mappings using an attribute that contains the word "display."

2. Click the pencil icon to the right of the `DisplayName` mapping to edit the value.

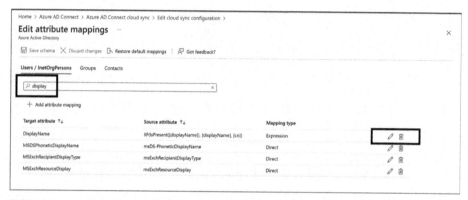

FIGURE 11-24   Searching for Attribute Mappings

3. Once you have opened the editor, leave the Mapping Type set to Expression, but replace the existing value with the following new expression, as shown in Figure 11-25:

```
IIF(IsPresent([sn]),IIF(IsPresent([givenName]),PCase(Join("",[sn],", ",
[givenName])),[displayName]),[displayName])
```

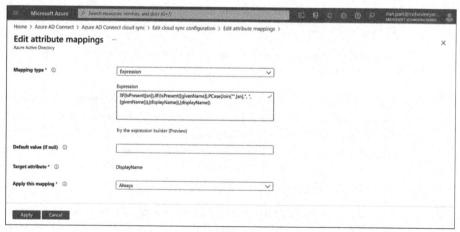

FIGURE 11-25   Modifying the DisplayName Attribute Mapping

4. Click Apply to save this new expression.

Inside Out

Breaking down the expression

Now, we'll break down this expression, which is comprised of two inline IF (IIF) expressions that are used to check whether the First Name (GivenName) and Last Name (Surname) values are present. As we mentioned previously, the inline IF expression consists of an evaluation statement, followed by the True and False actions.

In this example, the first inline IF expression looks like this:

```
IIF(IsPresent([sn]), True, False)
```

If the [sn], or Surname attribute, is present, it will apply the True action, as shown above. The True part of the expression is another IIF expression that looks like this:

```
IIF(IsPresent([givenName]), True, False)
```

This expression checks to see whether the givenName, also commonly called First Name, is present. So far, the combined expression would look like this:

```
IIF(IsPresent([sn]), IIF(IsPresent([givenName]), True, False), False)
```

The logic in this expression reads, "If Surname is present AND givenName is present, the result is True, though if either of those attributes is not present, the result is False."

It's important to note that when using nested inline IF statements, the expression in the True part is treated as an AND condition, while the expression in the False part is treated as an OR condition. You can use this approach to create complex expressions with multiple AND and/or OR conditions by nesting the IIF statements accordingly.

We can then apply our desired formatting for the DisplayName when the result is True. That expression looks like this:

```
PCase( Join("",[sn], ", ", [givenName]) )
```

This expression is performing two actions. We start with the inner-most expression, a Join, shown here in bold:

```
PCase( Join("", [sn], ", ", [givenName]) )
```

This Join expression combines three values: the Surname (sn) attribute, followed by a comma and a space, and finally, the givenName attribute.

When using VBA expressions in AAD Connect and Azure AD Cloud Sync, you need to surround attributes with brackets [ ] and strings with quotes "". A bracketed name (such as [displayName]) means you want the value of the displayName attribute, whereas a quoted name (such as `"displayName"`) means you want the actual text inside the quotes. Also, remember that when using attributes, the names are case-sensitive.

The `Join` expression takes a series of arguments and joins them, with the first argument defining the separator value. In this example, the separator value is `null` `""`, so nothing is added between the three other arguments provided.

In this example, the other three arguments are:

```
Surname
", "
GivenName
```

The result of a `Join` expression with a `null` separator would be `"LastName, FirstName"`.

Alternatively, you could replace the `null` `""` with another value, such as a period (`"."`) if you wanted to construct a `DisplayName` that looked like `"FirstName.LastName"` or `"LastName.FirstName"`.

Finally, we are wrapping the `Left` function in a `PCase` function. PCase is designed to convert a string to proper case. This ensures each word in the string is case-proper. The PCase function can also handle names containing hyphens, apostrophes, and other dia-critics, so it is a great option when working with usernames.

Lastly, if neither or either of the `Surname` or `GivenName` values is missing, then our result is `False`, and we must rely on the existing `Display Name`. Remember, attributes are wrapped in brackets, so our `False` part would simply be

```
[displayName]
```

Our final expression is:

```
IIF( IsPresent( [sn] ),IIF( IsPresent( [givenName] ),PCase( Join("", [sn], ", "
, [givenName] )), [displayName]), [displayName])
```

5. Using the same example, let's add a bit of complexity by adding a requirement to include the user's department in parentheses after their name. Here, we are transforming the `Display Name` and adding `Department` in parentheses—for example, `Smith, John (Finance)`.

6. Like before, open the editor for `Display Name` and leave the Mapping Type as Expression, but replace the existing value with this new expression, as shown in Figure 11-26:

```
IIF(IsPresent([sn]),IIF(IsPresent([givenName]),IIF(IsPresent([department]),
PCase(Join("",[sn],", ",[givenName]," (",[department],")")),PCase(Join("",
[sn],", ",[givenName]))),[displayName]),[displayName])
```

CHAPTER 11

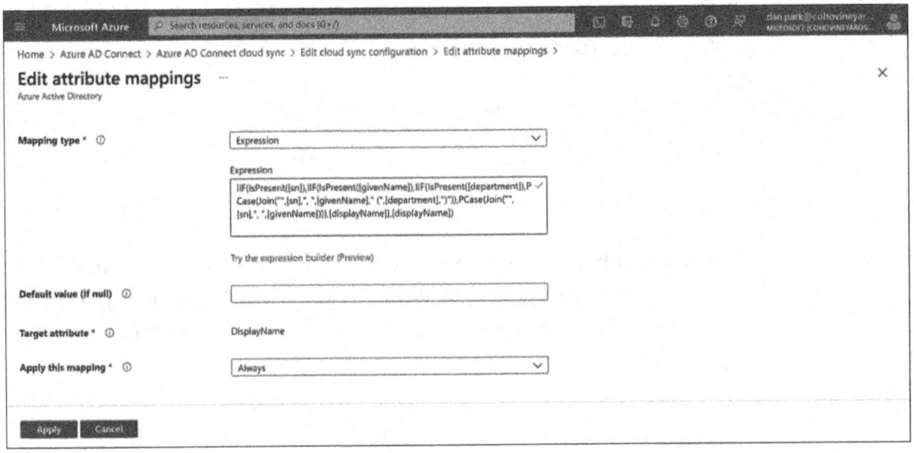

FIGURE 11-26   Modifying the DisplayName Attribute Mapping

7. Like before, we use a series of nested inline IF statements to determine if givenName or Surname are present:

```
IIF(IsPresent([sn]), IIF(IsPresent([givenName]), True, False), False)
```

8. However, in place of the True statement above, add a third inline IF that will evaluate if the Department attribute is present:

```
IIF(IsPresent([department]), True, False)
```

9. As a result, the body of the expression now includes three IF statements, each evaluating a different attribute:

```
IIF(IsPresent([sn]), IIF(IsPresent([givenName]), IIF(IsPresent([department]),
True, False)

, False), False)
```

10. Like before, we now replace the True part above with our PCase and Join expression:

```
PCase(Join("",[sn],", ",[givenName]," (",[department],")"))
```

11. However, instead of three separate strings preceded by the separator (which is still null) for our Join expression, there are now six separate strings:

```
Surname
", "
GivenName
" ("
Department
")"
```

12. The result of this `Join` expression with a `null` separator would be `"LastName, FirstName (Department)"`.

13. And finally, we wrap that in `PCase` like before:

    `PCase ( Join( "", [sn], ", ", [givenName], " (", [department], ")" ))`

    ## NOTE

    One final thing to note is that this new expression has added a third AND condition for Department, so instead of all three `False` statements resulting in just `[displayName]`, our first `False` statement—which occurs if `First Name` and `Last Name` are present, but Department is not—would be

    `PCase( Join( "", [sn], ", ", [givenName] ))`

    This is because `First Name` and `Last Name` are present, so we can use the original expression from our first example.

14. Our final `False` statement, like the first example, defaults to `Display Name` because either the `First Name` or `Last Name` is missing, as shown here:

    ```
    IIF(IsPresent([sn]),IIF(IsPresent([givenName]),IIF(IsPresent([department]),
    PCase(Join("",[sn],", ",[givenName]," (",[department],")")),
    PCase(Join("",[sn],", ",[givenName]))),[displayName]),[displayName])
    ```

Decompressing

If you're not familiar with VBA expressions, these two examples, while relatively simple, can still be confusing. Feel free to read the explanations again a few more times, and hopefully, it will become clearer.

NOTE

To help you understand the functions available when writing your own expressions, refer to *https://docs.microsoft.com/en-us/azure/active-directory/cloud-sync/reference-expressions*.

TIP

If things still aren't quite clicking, don't despair. The Azure team has created a tool called the Expression Builder that can help you construct your own expressions. You will still need an understanding of the functions and structure, but the Expression Builder allows you to test your expressions with sample data before you commit the expression to your configuration.

Using the Expression Builder

Follow these steps to use the Expression Builder:

1. Click the Try The Expression Builder link, as shown in Figure 11-27.

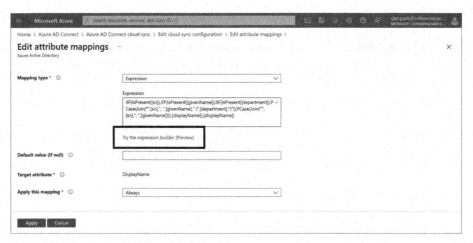

FIGURE 11-27   Try The Expression Builder

2. You will be presented with the Expression Builder screen, and the current expression in use will be displayed on the right side.

3. Under Test Expression on the left, you can select the necessary attributes and enter a sample value that can be used for testing.

4. As shown in Figure 11-28, to test our Display Name expression, we are providing test values for Given Name, Surname, Department, and Display Name. Entering these values and clicking the Test Expression button will output the result.

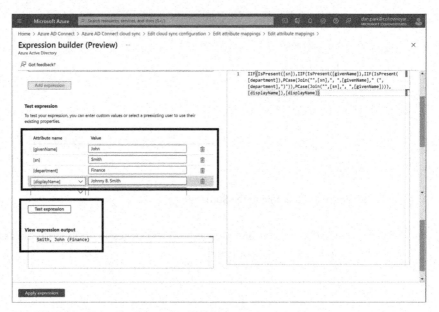

FIGURE 11-28   Using the Expression Builder

5. You can then remove values to review the results when the source attributes change.

6. Removing `Given Name` and pressing the Test Expression button should result in the existing `Display Name` being used, as shown in Figure 11-29.

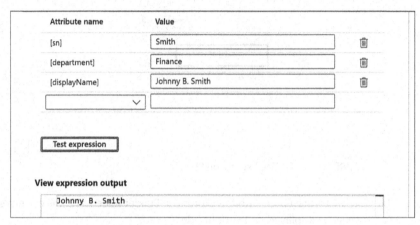

FIGURE 11-29   Removing the Given Name

7. Removing `Surname` and pressing the Test Expression button should result in the existing `Display Name` being used, as shown in Figure 11-30.

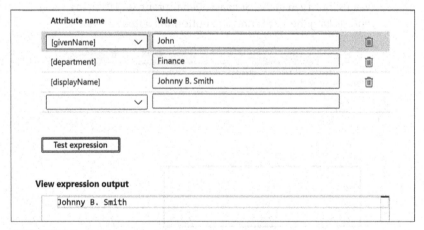

FIGURE 11-30   Removing the Surname

8. Removing `Department` and pressing the Test Expression button should result in `Last, First`, as shown in Figure 11-31.

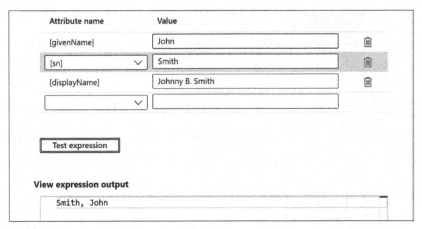

FIGURE 11-31   Removing Department

9. Using the Expression builder will allow you to check the syntax and completeness of your expression and supply test data to ensure your expression returns the correct data under each condition.

10. Once you are satisfied with your expression, you can click Apply Expression to save the data and return to the Edit Attribute Mapping page, where you can choose Apply to save the mapping.

11. And finally, if you are happy with all the changes to your attribute mappings, you can click the Save Schema button in the top-left corner of the screen.

Provisioning a user (the validate step)

Now that you've successfully configured your cloud sync configuration, the only remaining step is to enable the configuration. However, the Cloud Sync tool allows you to actually test a pilot user without enabling the configuration. This is especially helpful when you've made customizations to attribute mappings because you can see the results of the changes applied to a live user. It allows you to see real data, confirm that your customizations are returning the right information, and ensure that no other changes might be needed before going live:

1. As shown in Figure 11-32, you can test the provisioning of a single user by clicking the Provision A User button on the Edit Cloud Sync Configuration page.

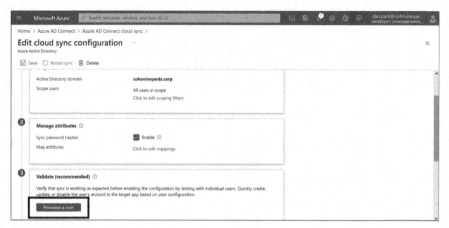

FIGURE 11-32   Provision A User

2.   Clicking the Provision A User button will open the Provision On Demand page and prompt you for the distinguished name of a user. See Figure 11-33.

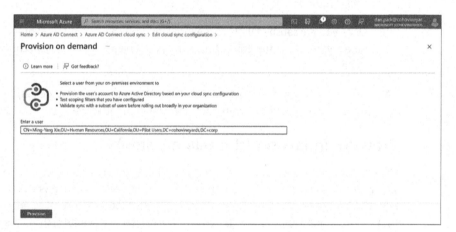

FIGURE 11-33   Providing the distinguished name

3.   Once you have entered the distinguished name of a user, click the Provision button to start the provisioning process.

Inside Out

Piloting a user

When piloting (aka testing) a user, it does not matter if the user is in an in-scoped OU. The user will still be provisioned in Azure. If the user already exists, it will be updated by the Azure AD Cloud Sync Configuration, and then any changes made will be reverted by the Azure AD Connect server if the user is already synchronized using that tool.

4. As shown in Figure 11-34, once you have selected the Provision option, you will be presented with output from the provisioning process, which includes import statistics that include all the attribute values of the user object in your on-premises Active Directory.

5. In this example, you will note that our `sn`, `givenName`, `Department`, and `displayName` attributes are present and that the current `Display Name` value is in the `"First Last"` format.

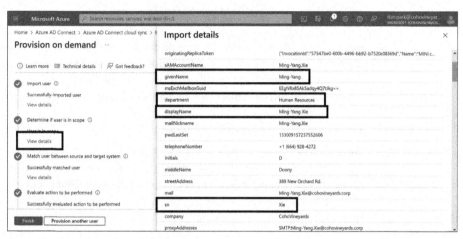

FIGURE 11-34   Viewing the Import Details

6. Next, you need to evaluate your scope. We specified a single OU (pilot users) at the top level of the forest when we originally configured our scoping. As you can see in Figure 11-35, this object is considered "in scope" of the provisioning process because it is located in an OU below the one you provided in the configuration.

FIGURE 11-35   Viewing the scoping details

7. Next, clicking Matching Details, as shown in Figure 11-36, will display the matching status of the user. If this user is already in Azure AD—either because the user was previously piloted or is in scope of another synchronization process—you will be notified that the user will be updated in Azure Active Directory.

CHAPTER 11

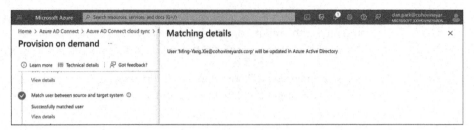

FIGURE 11-36   Viewing the Matching Details

8.   Next, you can view any errors that could occur as part of the user provisioning action by using the Processing Details view. In Figure 11-37, the user account is being provisioned in Azure, though the Manager attribute is being skipped because the manager has not yet been synchronized (and therefore, that attribute cannot be used).

TIP

When piloting users, this error is to be expected because, in this example, Manager is a reference to another user that does not yet exist. A similar error will occur when testing group provisioning if some or all the group members have not yet been synchronized to Azure Active Directory. However, you cannot currently test provisioning of any object type other than User.

FIGURE 11-37   Processing Details

9.   Finally, clicking View Details under the Perform Action option on the left will display all the attributes for the user being exported to Azure Active Directory. You will notice in Figure 11-38 that we've highlighted the DisplayName attribute, the custom expression we defined for DisplayName earlier in this chapter is applied here, and the DisplayName is now in the format of Last, First (Department).

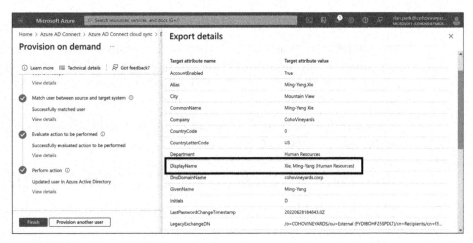

FIGURE 11-38   Export Details

10. Once you have reviewed the output, click Finish to close the Provision On Demand dialog or select Provision Another User to return to the page where you can enter another distinguished name.

Notification and deletion protection

From the Settings section of the Edit Cloud Sync Configuration page, you can enable a threshold that will prevent accidental deletions from occurring if there are more than the specified number queued at any given time. This is particularly useful when setting up a new configuration or moving OUs; accidental changes could result in deleting user objects in your Azure Active Directory.

Figure 11-39 shows that you can enable or disable Prevent Accidental Deletion by clicking its checkbox. The Accidental Delete Threshold can be set to a value larger (or smaller) than the default 500. Also, you can enter a single email or comma-separated list of email addresses into the Notification Email field. Those users will receive notifications from the Azure AD Cloud Sync service.

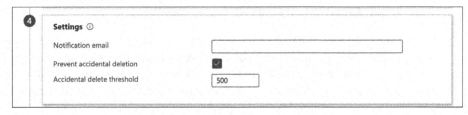

FIGURE 11-39   Viewing the Notification and Deletion settings

CHAPTER 11

Enabling the configuration

The final step in the Azure AD Cloud Sync setup is to enable (deploy) the sync configuration. Until you make this change, none of the settings you have configured so far will apply to your environment, and the only users who will be present in Azure Active Directory will be those you have provisioned on-demand with the aforementioned pilot option.

To enable the configuration, navigate back to the Edit Cloud Sync Configuration page and toggle the Deploy slider to Enable, as shown in Figure 11-40.

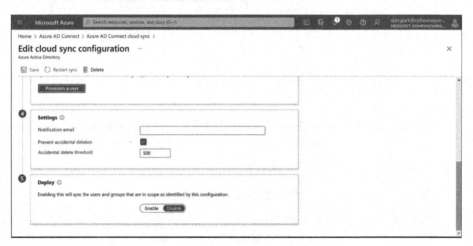

FIGURE 11-40   Deploy the configuration

Moving the slider to Enable and clicking Save in the upper-left corner of the page will automatically start the synchronization process. Updates will be processed every two minutes. You will be prompted to confirm this action.

Moving from Azure AD Connect to Azure AD Cloud Sync

Congratulations, you have successfully installed, configured, tested, and enabled Azure AD Cloud Sync in your enterprise. Your users, groups, and contacts are now being synchronized to Azure Active Directory on a regular two-minute schedule.

If you already have Azure AD Connect in place in your enterprise, you probably only configured a single OU for testing. This means you now need to convert your existing synchronization process from Azure AD Connect to Azure AD Cloud Sync, update the scope of your Azure AD Cloud Sync configuration to include all objects, and decommission your Azure AD Connect servers.

NOTE

This process is very straightforward, and a detailed walk-through can be found at
https://aka.ms/pilotcloudsync.

What's next?

In the past two chapters, we reviewed the Azure AD Connect installation and configuration and the Azure AD Cloud Sync tools. You should now understand the differences and limitations when using these two tools to synchronize your users to Azure. In the next chapter, we will discuss advanced synchronization scenarios you might encounter in your organization that will help you decide which synchronization tool(s) you should use.

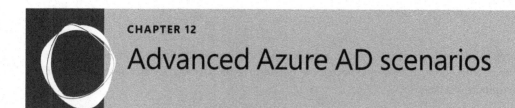

Advanced Azure AD scenarios

It goes without saying that the standard deployment of a Microsoft 365 tenant and the supporting technologies is a complex undertaking and fraught with difficult decisions. Add additional complexities in the form of merger, acquisition, and divestiture (MAD) activities, and the challenges increase exponentially.

To help lessen the pain involved in these types of scenarios, there are several options available, ranging from advanced, fully supported Azure AD Connect configurations to Microsoft service offerings that carry a one-time, monthly, or per-user fee. Deciding which one is right for you can be an equally daunting task.

CAUTION

In a typical customer deployment, the types of custom rules discussed here and at the end of Chapter 10 are probably outside the scope of most configurations. However, it is important to understand the power of the Azure AD Connect tool. You might need to leverage it to support complex sync scenarios, mergers, acquisitions, or divestitures. Or, you might need to make informed decisions about the types of options available when complex scenarios are discussed. When in doubt, it is recommended that you contact Microsoft Premier Support or your Microsoft account team to discuss your needs and ensure that any changes you plan to make are both appropriate and supported.

Migrations and the SourceAnchor

As discussed in Chapter 10, the selection of the SourceAnchor is extremely important because the attribute represents a key aspect of an object's lifecycle while it's synchronized to Azure AD, and we've already discussed how the SourceAnchor is permanent because it uniquely identifies the object and "anchors" it to the source object that it represents in the on-premises directories.

As you might remember, by default, the SourceAnchor attribute in AAD Connect is derived from the ObjectGUID value in on-premises Active Directory. This ensures that objects will remain unique. While you have the option to select an alternate Active Directory attribute to represent the SourceAnchor for your objects, it's best to leave the SourceAnchor attribute value as-is during installation to avoid the Herculean effort required to change to a different attribute at a later date.

That said, what happens when a week, month, or even years after your AAD Connect installation is complete, you suddenly find yourself involved in a merger, acquisition, or divestiture?

Changing your SourceAnchor isn't an option, regardless of the number of objects in your tenant, because it involves several complex and potentially dangerous steps. The least of which is disabling directory synchronization in your tenant so that you can rewrite the Immutable ID value on every user, a task that requires 72 hours, both up-front and when you re-enable synchronization.

But what happens if your company is in the business of frequent mergers, acquisitions, and divestitures? You need a way to future-proof your Microsoft 365 tenant synchronization strategy.

To solve this dilemma, Microsoft introduced support for the mS-DS-ConsistencyGuid.

Beginning in May 2017, with AAD Connect version 1.1.524, support was introduced to include the mS-DS-ConsistencyGuid attribute in the SourceAnchor process.

Despite this feature being added in 2017, a few AAD Connect customers are either unaware of it, unsure of its use, or simply terrified of using it.

The good news is that this feature is non-destructive, it will not impact your existing installation of Azure AD Connect, and even if you don't plan to do any migrations in the future, it can be a worthwhile change to make.

More importantly, the change to support mS-DS-ConsistencyGuid can be made using the Azure AD Connect wizard and does not require any reinstallation of the tool or changes to your current SourceAnchor. The only required manual change is the delegation of writeback permissions to the mS-DS-ConsistencyGuid attribute to user objects for all on-premises Active Directory service accounts.

NOTE

Setting permissions

Inside Out series author Aaron Guilmette (and one of the authors of this book) maintains a PowerShell module that can be used with a variety of switches to enable the service account permissions required. See *http://aka.ms/aadpermissions*.

Alternatively, if you prefer to delegate permissions manually, the list of accounts and the required permissions can be found at *http://bit.ly/3F4fM7I*.

Enabling the support of mS-DS-ConsistencyGuid in the SourceAnchor process is a simple matter of launching the AAD Connect installation wizard from the desktop and selecting the Configure Source Anchor option. See Figure 12-1.

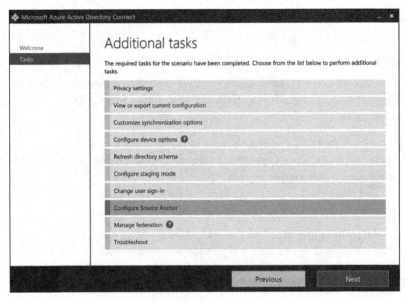

FIGURE 12-1   Additional Tasks dialog and the Configure Source Anchor option

Once you select Configure Source Anchor and click Next, you will be prompted to enter the credentials for a Global Administrator in your tenant (see Figure 12-2).

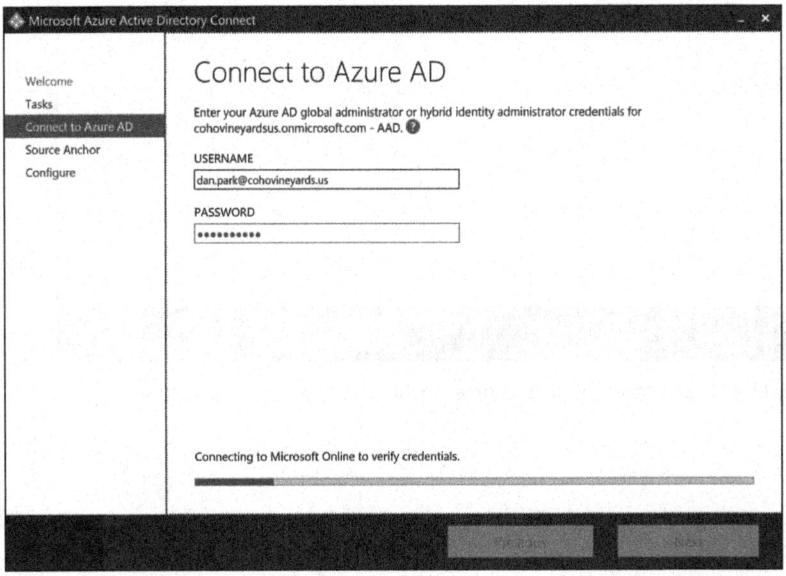

Microsoft Azure Active Directory Connect

Welcome
Tasks
Connect to Azure AD
Source Anchor
Configure

Connect to Azure AD

Enter your Azure AD global administrator or hybrid identity administrator credentials for cohovineyardsus.onmicrosoft.com - AAD.

USERNAME

dan.park@cohovineyards.us

PASSWORD

••••••••••

Connecting to Microsoft Online to verify credentials.

FIGURE 12-2   Connect To Azure AD with Global Administrator credentials

It is important to note that the Azure AD Connect installation wizard will perform a check against on-premises AD to ensure that no user objects are already using the mS-DS-ConsistencyGuid attribute.

> ## Inside Out
>
> ### LDAP Query
>
> The Azure AD Connect installation wizard will query Active Directory to find any objects where mS-DS-ConsistencyGuid is in use, though that query is limited to a maximum of two minutes.
>
> If your on-premises directory is large and an LDAP query to search every domain and user for the mS-DS-ConsistencyGUID attribute would take longer than two minutes, make sure you do your own queries.

If any use of the attribute is detected, the Azure AD Connect installation wizard will display the error shown in Figure 12-3, and the configuration will not proceed.

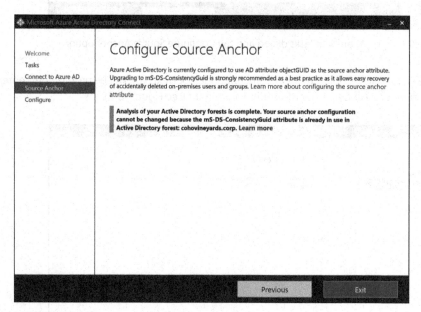

FIGURE 12-3 Failure to configure Source Anchor

If the attribute is in use and you still want to enable the feature in AAD Connect, you have three options available:

- You can remove the attribute by using the Active Directory Users and Computers tool. This option assumes you know what objects are currently using the attribute.

- You can use PowerShell to query Active Directory for all users where the attribute is in use and then remove the mS-DS-ConsistencyGuid attribute. Figure 12-4 shows a sample of the PowerShell command—Get-ADUser—required to query for the mS-DS-ConsistencyGuid value.

```
Administrator: Windows PowerShell
PS C:\>
PS C:\> $users = Get-ADUser -filter {mS-DS-ConsistencyGuid -like "*"}
PS C:\>
PS C:\> $users.count
1184
PS C:\> _
```

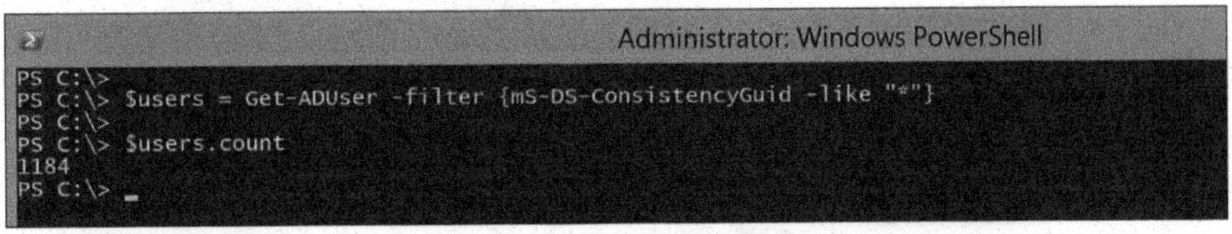

FIGURE 12-4   Get-ADUser PowerShell command to get all users with the mS-DS-ConsistencyGuid set

Once you've retrieved all users with the mS-DS-ConsistencyGuid value set, you can then use the Set-ADUser command, as shown in Figure 12-5, to clear that attribute value for those accounts.

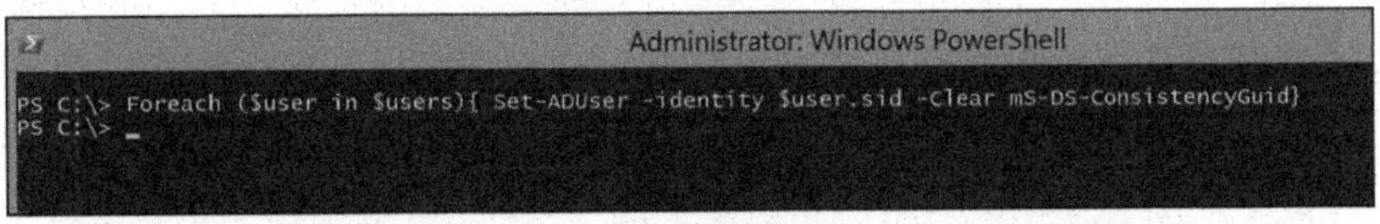

```
Administrator: Windows PowerShell
PS C:\> Foreach ($user in $users){ Set-ADUser -identity $user.sid -Clear mS-DS-ConsistencyGuid}
PS C:\> _
```

FIGURE 12-5   Get-ADUser command PowerShell command to clear the mS-DS-ConsistencyGuid attribute

- The third option is to launch the Azure AD Connect wizard from the command prompt with the /SkipLdapSearch switch, as shown in Figure 12-6.

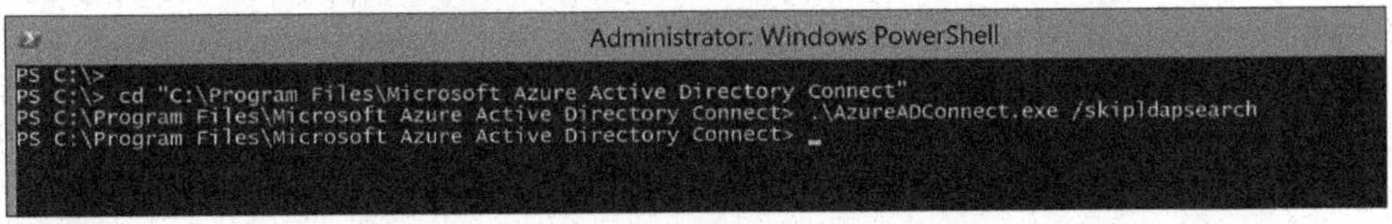

```
Administrator: Windows PowerShell
PS C:\>
PS C:\> cd "C:\Program Files\Microsoft Azure Active Directory Connect"
PS C:\Program Files\Microsoft Azure Active Directory Connect> .\AzureADConnect.exe /skipldapsearch
PS C:\Program Files\Microsoft Azure Active Directory Connect> _
```

FIGURE 12-6   Launching the Azure AD Connect Wizard

When you launch the wizard with the SkipLdapSearch option, the Azure AD Connect wizard will not attempt to find users in the directory using the mS-DS-ConsistencyGuid attribute and will instead proceed, allowing you to change it.

CHAPTER 12

CAUTION

It is important to note that launching the installer in this fashion will allow you to over-write the value currently present on all user accounts in the directory, so it should not be done unless you are certain that the attribute can be overwritten or is already the expected value (as would be the case when reinstalling Azure AD Connect).

Once it is safe to use the mS-DS-ConsistencyGuid, you will be prompted by the Azure AD Connect Installation Wizard to confirm the change to the SourceAnchor attribute, as shown in Figure 12-7.

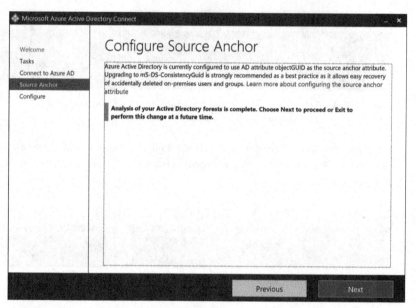

FIGURE 12-7 Configure Source Anchor

Clicking Next will display the Ready To Configure page, as shown in Figure 12-8. Choose Config-ure on this screen to add mS-DS-ConsistencyGuid support to Azure AD Connect.

Once the change has been made to the Azure AD Connect installation, you will be presented with the Configuration Complete dialog, as shown in Figure 12-9 . Click Exit to close the wizard.

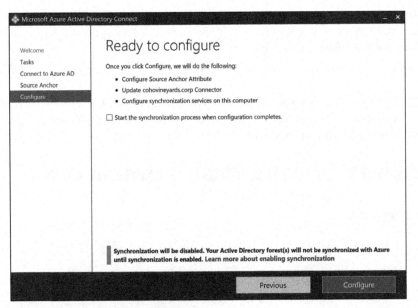

FIGURE 12-8   Ready To Configure dialog

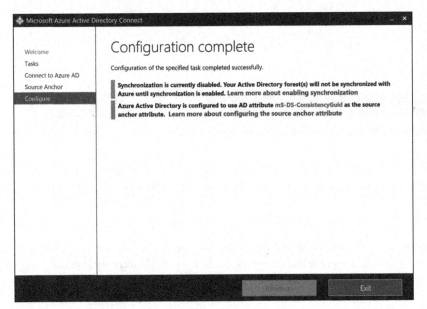

FIGURE 12-9   Configuration Complete

It's important to note that if the Azure AD Connect configuration has already been modified to support mS-DS-ConsistencyGUID, the Configure Source Anchor option will not appear on the Additional Tasks dialog, as shown in Figure 12-10.

CAUTION

Once the Source Anchor has been configured, it is not possible to revert the configuration without reinstalling Azure AD Connect because the Configure Source Option is no longer presented in the wizard.

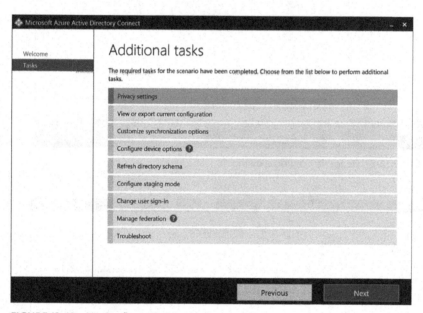

FIGURE 12-10   No Configure Source Anchor option

Once you have configured support for mS-DS-ConsistencyGuid as the Source Anchor, you can view the status of the Source Anchor by launching the Azure AD Connect Wizard on the desktop, selecting View Or Export Current Configuration, and locating the Source Anchor setting under Synchronization Settings, as shown in Figure 12-11.

When the Azure AD Connect configuration is updated to support mS-DS-ConsistencyGuid, a number of changes are made to the synchronization rule logic for user and group objects, as explained in the next section.

FIGURE 12-11   Review Your Solution dialog with the Synchronization Settings for Source Anchor

What does mS-DS-ConsistencyGuid support add to the configuration?

The default SourceAnchor logic flow, present in the In from AD - User Account Enabled and In from AD - User Common rules, will use the ObjectGUID value as-is for the sourceAnchorBinary Metaverse attribute and will use a Base64-encoded string version of the ObjectGUID for the SourceAnchor Metaverse attribute. As shown in Figure 12-12, the rules are a type of VBA expression. The expressions are displayed by hovering over them in the Source box.

TIP

If you have no experience with VBA, a learning curve will be involved in reading and creating your own expressions. Because of its age and extensive usage, numerous resources are online for learning VBA.

However, once the support for mS-DS-ConsistencyGuid has been added via the wizard, the attribute flow logic in those rules is updated automatically and becomes more complex. Figure 12-13 shows that the sourceAnchorBinary attribute flow changes to include additional IIF, inline IF, and statements to evaluate whether the mS-DS-ConsistencyGuid attribute is populated. The VBA Expression for the SourceAnchorBinary attribute flow has been updated to support additional VBA expression logic.

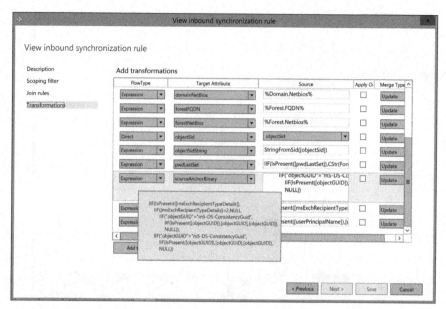

FIGURE 12-12   The default SourceAnchor and sourceAnchorBinary VBA expressions

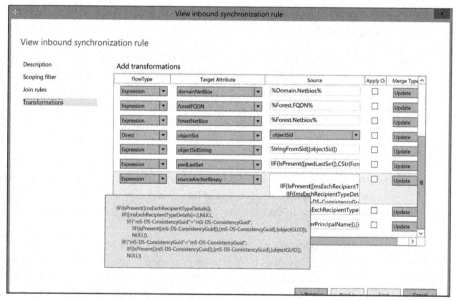

FIGURE 12-13   The updated SourceAnchor and sourceAnchorBinary VBA expressions for mS-DS-ConsistencyGuid

This updated attribute flow now includes an `IsPresent` condition for the `mS-DS-Consisten-cyGuid` attribute that will ensure that `mS-DS-ConsistencyGuid` is used first, if it exists. Otherwise, the flow will default to the `ObjectGUID`.

In addition to the logic flows for `SourceAnchor` and `sourceAnchorBinary`, the `In from AD -User Join` rule changes from the default configuration shown in Figure 12-14.

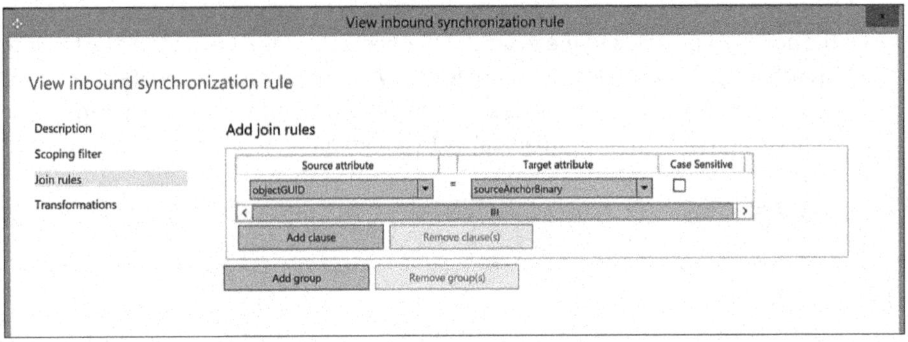

FIGURE 12-14   Default In from AD – User Join rules

The updated `In from AD - User Join` rule now adds `mS-DS-ConsistencyGuid` as an additional join criteria, as shown in Figure 12-15.

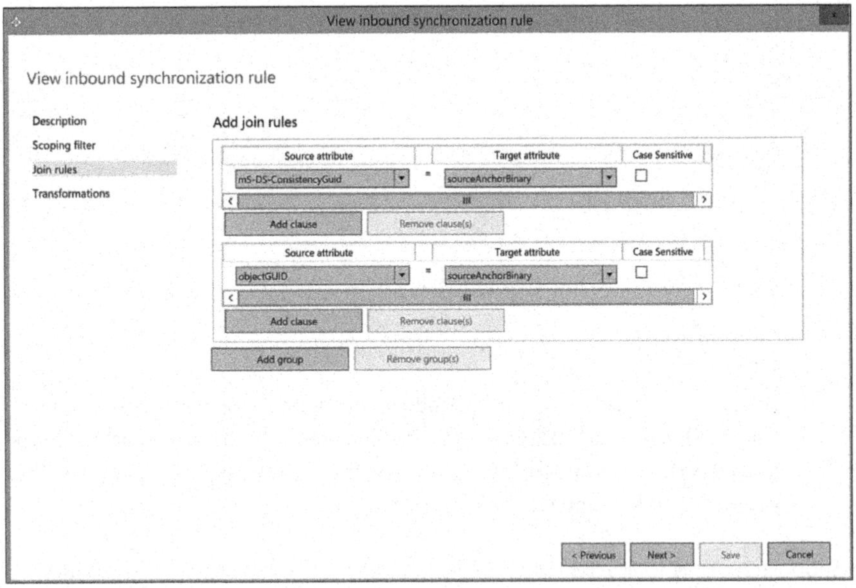

FIGURE 12-15   Updated In from AD – User Join rules

TIP

The Azure AD Connect Wizard will update In from AD – User Join rules when the default ObjectGUID join rule is in place, though if any other join types were selected during the Azure AD Connect installation (such as msExchMasterAccountSID or SamAccountName), those will not be updated. You will need to clone those rules manually and add the join on mS-DS-ConsistencyGuid.

The next change made to the Azure AD Connect sync rules is the addition of a writeback rule to each on-premises Active Directory forest, which will populate the mS-DS-ConsistencyGuid value for each user account in the scope of the synchronization. As shown in Figure 12-16, a rule named Out to AD – User ImmutableId is added to the list of outbound sync rules.

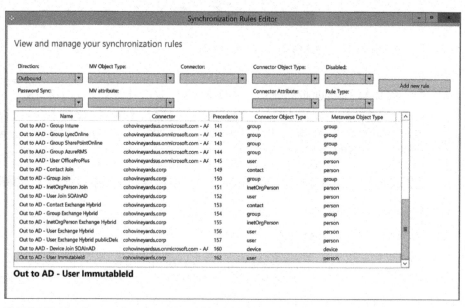

FIGURE 12-16   Out to AD – User ImmutableId rule

TIP

The Azure AD Connect Wizard will add an outbound sync rule for User objects, which will writeback the mS-DS-ConsistencyGuid, though no rule will be added for Group objects. In order to support the writeback of the mS-DS-ConsistencyGuid for groups, you will need to manually create a custom rule.

Suppose support for mS-DS-ConsistencyGuid writeback is required for Group objects. In that case, you can simply clone the newly created Out to AD – User ImmutableId rule and change the object type and precedence, as described in the following steps:

1. Begin by launching the Azure AD Connect Synchronization Rules Editor and selecting Outbound from the Direction dropdown in the top-left corner of the tool, as shown in Figure 12-17.

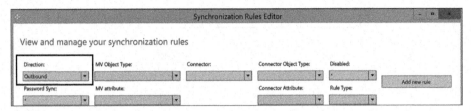

FIGURE 12-17   The Synchronization Rules Editor Direction dropdown

2. In the list of outbound rules that appears, scroll to the bottom, select the the `Out to AD - User ImmutableId` rule, and click the Edit button. Take note of the rule's Precedence value in the Precedence column. See Figure 12-18.

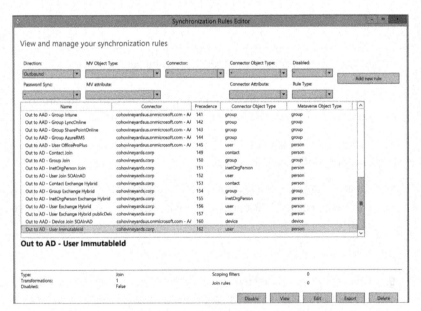

FIGURE 12-18   Selecting the Out to AD – User ImmutableId rule

3. You will be prompted with a warning that the rule will need to be cloned and disabled; click Yes to continue.

4. A copy of the rule will be displayed, as shown in Figure 12-19.

CHAPTER 12

Change the word "User" to "Group"

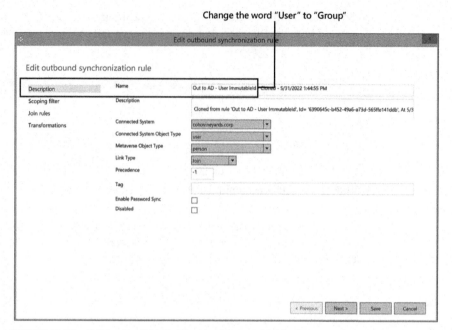

FIGURE 12-19   Editing the Out to AD – User ImmutableId rule

5. Change the name of the rule, replacing the word "User" with "Group". Doing so will help other administrators understand this rule is for groups and is a clone of another rule.

6. Update the Connected System Object Type and Metaverse Object Type dropdowns, changing both values to Group.

7. Finally, change the Precedence value from -1 to a value larger than the previous rule number. In Figure 12-19, our User rule was 162, so we will enter 163, as shown in Figure 12-20.

8. Click Save.

9. Now that you've added the outbound writeback rule for Group objects, you will need to ensure that your Active Directory service account has the necessary permissions to update the attribute mS-DS-ConsistencyGuid. Also, you will need to perform a full synchronization on the Azure AD Connect tool before the values are written back to Active Directory.

10. Finally, make sure to enable the User Writeback rule, which was automatically disabled when you edited and copied it. Select the rule and click Enable at the bottom of the screen.

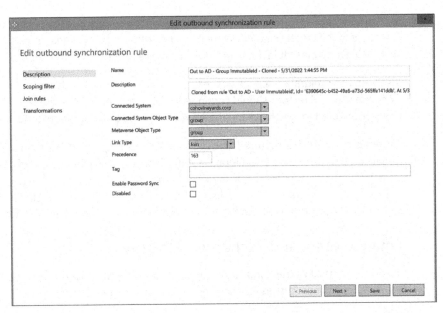

FIGURE 12-20   The new Out to AD – Group ImmutableId rule

Performing migrations

So far, we've talked about the role of the mS-DS-ConsistencyGuid in merger, acquisition, and divestiture scenarios, though this is only part of the solution. The writeback of the mS-DS-ConsistencyGuid to user (and possibly group) objects in a single on-premises directory enables cross-forest migrations from a SourceAnchor perspective, so the associated identity can move without the risk of deleting or orphaning the Azure AD object. However, there some considerations for other Active Directory attributes that are synchronized to Azure AD and control other Microsoft 365 services like Exchange Online.

As you plan and evaluate cross-forest migration activities and the effect those changes will have on your synchronization to Azure, you will want to consider the things in the coming sections.

UserPrincipalName

The UserPrincipalName value, unlike the SamAccountName value in on-premises Active Directory, defines how users will log in to Azure AD. This means the UserPrincipalName should ideally remain the same during a migration event. However, utilizing the same UserPrincipalName value cross-premises can be a tricky proposition. This is primarily because the same value cannot be used in the name suffix routing configuration for a trust between two forests.

While it's true the UserPrincipalName value can be copied from source to target forest, the source forest UserPrincipalName suffix (@contoso.com) cannot be added to the name suffix routing configuration in the target if it is present in the source. The `UserPrincipalName` value can be set in the target using PowerShell or some other identity management solution, but the suffix will not be present in the `UserPrincipalName` dropdown in the target.

Ideally, in most migration scenarios, the `UserPrincipalName`, which can only flow to Azure from one source directory, should continue to flow from the on-premises directory that is currently configured to sync to Azure (the source) until the user migration occurs.

Once the migration has occurred, one or more Active Directory attributes in the source and target could then be used as a migration status indicator. Through the use of custom Azure AD Connect rules, the `UserPrincipalName` could then flow to Azure from the target forest. This is normally done through a process called Source of Authority (SOA) and relies heavily on several key Azure AD Connect rules and the use of precedence, which is discussed later in this chapter.

Email address and Exchange attributes

In addition to the key user login attributes like `UserPrincipalName`, `ObjectSID`, and `SourceAnchor`, most customers also emphasize email-related attributes.

Of course, when we refer to the attributes related to email, the Active Directory attribute `mail` (the email address) is important. However, attributes that will appear in the Global Address List (GAL) when viewing a user in Outlook are equally important. This includes attributes such as Display Name, Title, Manager, Department, Location, and Street Address, to name a few.

As a result, it is critical these attributes are maintained when synchronizing objects between forests, and the synchronization of these attributes to Azure should not be changed unless there is a business reason to do so.

As discussed previously, an SOA project (in which the primary attribute sync process is transitioned from one Azure AD Connect server to another to ensure the synchronization to a single tenant is uninterrupted) is critical to nearly all merger, acquisition, and divestiture projects. The SOA process ensures users are unaware of changes in the infrastructure until it's necessary to migrate their logins. Even then, the number of disruptions should be kept to a minimum and well communicated.

The key to a successful SOA transition is a clear understanding of business requirements, the current Azure AD Connect sync methodology, and how to properly customize Azure AD Connect to support these changes

Group and user SIDs

The Security Identifier (SID) for user and group objects in Active Directory is synchronized to Azure Active Directory automatically as part of the standard Azure AD Connect configuration. The SID is used by Azure when using Azure AD–joined devices so that seamless access to on-premises resources is maintained.

For this reason, it is critical that cross-forest migration activities also include the migration of the source user and group SID in the form of the sIDHistory value for each corresponding target object. Failure to do so will result in issues with Azure AD–joined devices and could break on-premises application access altogether.

Microsoft options for cross-forest migrations

While the attributes listed previously are a good foundation for a successful migration cross-forest where Azure AD and Azure AD Connect are involved, they are in no way a complete list. Each organization involved in these activities should review all attributes in their directories in-depth and identify any long-term effects of moving or failing to move any attribute values to the new forest.

To help address the complexity of these topics, Microsoft offers a number of options, ranging from free tools in the form of ADMT and community-maintained custom PowerShell scripts to pay services like the Active Directory Migration Service (ADMS) and custom engagements using Microsoft Consulting Services (MCS). Depending on your skill level and appetite, you may want to consider one, or a combination of, the following options:

- **ADMT**   ADMT is a long-standing migration tool with years of documented use cases and support forums. It is provided free of charge by Microsoft and can be found at *https://www.microsoft.com/en-us/download/details.aspx?id=56570*.

- **PowerShell**   The strength and flexibility of PowerShell is coupled with an in-depth knowledge of Active Directory and migration strategies, making it a viable option for more advanced administrators. There are plenty of sample scripts, forums, and blogs on using PowerShell.

- **Active Directory Migrations Service (ADMS)**   ADMS is a paid Microsoft subscription that allows for a turnkey migration solution. This solution includes structured and targeted consulting based on the type and size of the migration, SOA planning and management, and a user self-service portal for individual and bulk migrations. A demo of the ADMS tool and more resources can be found at *http://aka.ms/adms-demo*.

Additional Azure AD Connect considerations

Like other configuration milestones when deploying Microsoft 365, the installation of AAD Connect is not a trivial event. The initial installation requires planning for service accounts, directory hierarchy, object filtering and permissions, password synchronization, hybrid writeback, Azure AD application and attribute filtering, and several features related to authentication.

What follows is a list of some additional advanced topics related to the installation, configuration, and use of AAD Connect.

Password Writeback

Password Writeback allows your users to change their passwords in Azure Active Directory using the portal; their passwords are automatically updated in on-premises Active Directory. However, this writeback feature has several limitations and requirements for enterprise deployment, which are covered in the following sections.

Requirements

Password Writeback has the following requirements:

- First, using the Password Writeback feature requires the user to be licensed for Azure AD Premium. An Azure AD Premium P1 or P2 license or Enterprise Mobility Suite (EMS) license qualifies.

- Second, Password Writeback is supported for synchronized users, without or without Password Sync enabled, as well as for federated users using AD FS and users configured to use pass-through authentication. Cloud-only accounts do not qualify for Password Writeback.

- Finally, any user wanting to utilize Password Writeback and the Password Reset portal must have the Password Writeback feature enabled for their account, and they must have the challenge data required for the organization populated on their account.

Enabling Password Writeback

Enabling Password Writeback consists of the following steps:

1. Enabling password reset for the Azure AD tenant

2. Configuration of the password reset policy for the Azure AD tenant

3. Entry of registration data for each user

Enabling password reset for the Azure AD tenant

Follow these steps to enable password reset:

1. Log in to the Office 365 portal by navigating to *https://portal.microsoftonline.com* and selecting the Admin icon at the left, as shown in Figure 12-21.

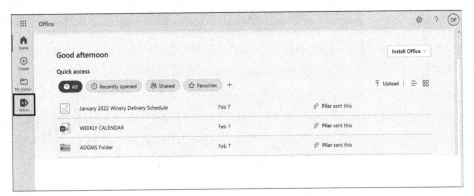

FIGURE 12-21   Microsoft 365 Admin icon

2. On the lower-left side of the Admin page, click Admin Centers and select the Azure Active Directory admin center icon, as shown in Figure 12-22.

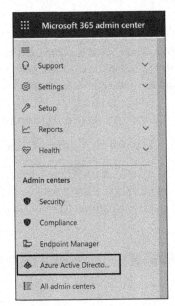

FIGURE 12-22   Azure Active Directory admin center icon

3. Choose Azure Active Directory on the left side of the admin center console. At the right, under Self Service Password Reset Enabled, you can choose All, Selected, or None, as shown in Figure 12-23. If you choose the Selected option, you will be prompted to select a group that has been synchronized to your tenant. If you have not yet synchronized any groups from your on-premises Active Directory, you can select All and return to the portal later to change to a specific synchronized group.

CHAPTER 12

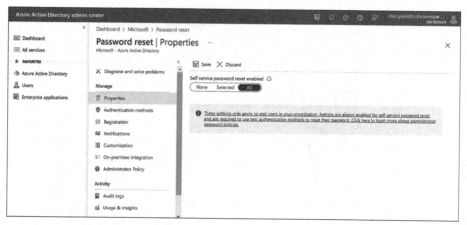

FIGURE 12-23   Azure AD Admin portal dashboard

4. Click the Save button at the top of the screen to save your changes.

TIP

Password policies selected in the Azure AD admin portal apply to users only. Administrators are secured differently, and their settings cannot be changed. Administrator accounts require both a mobile phone number and an email address for the challenge questions.

Configuring the password reset policy for the Azure AD tenant

Follow these steps to configure the password reset policy for the Azure AD tenant:

1. Selecting Authentication Methods on the left side of the Azure Active Directory admin center page will allow you to select the number of methods required to reset a password. In the Methods Available To Users list, select each method type you want to allow, as shown in Figure 12-24.

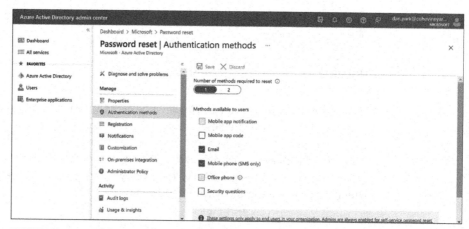

FIGURE 12-24   Configuration of password reset

2. If you select the Security Questions option, additional options will be presented (see Figure 12-25), which allow you to identify the number of questions required to register versus the number required to reset a password. Also, the current list of security questions configured will be displayed.

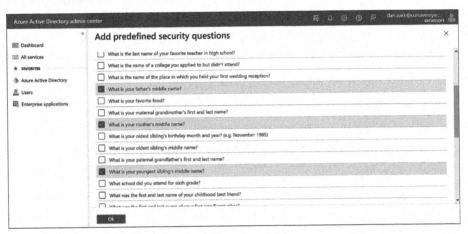

FIGURE 12-25   Add Predefined Security Questions

3. If you are enabling password reset for the first time, you will be prompted to configure the security questions.

4. At the top of the page, you will be prompted to select from a list of predefined questions or to enable your own custom questions.

5. Clicking either option will display additional options on the right side of the screen, and you can select from the predefined list of questions or enter your own custom questions.

6. Once you have completed the selection, click OK. You will be returned to the authentication methods screen, and the number of security questions selected will be displayed at the bottom of the screen.

7. Click Save.

Entry of registration data for each user

Once the password reset options have been enabled in the tenant, you must ensure that the data selected for registration (such as email, mobile phone, and office phone) has been populated in your on-premises Active Directory so that it will synchronize to Azure AD. This is done via the AAD Connect tool using the on-premises Active Directory as the data source. Therefore, the Active Directory-populated data must be accurate, or the password reset process will not work properly.

Alternatively, you can direct your users to *https://aka.ms/ssprsetup* to register their authentication methods manually:

1. Navigating to that URL will prompt the user to verify their phone, set up an authentication email, and set up security questions by clicking the hyperlink to the right of each item. See Figure 12-26.

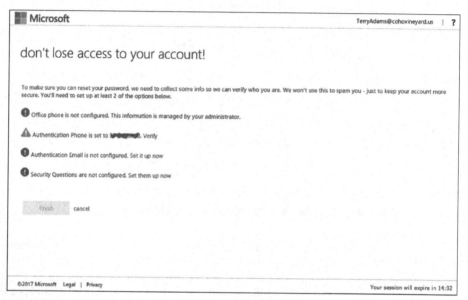

FIGURE 12-26   Entry of authentication detail for password reset

CAUTION

It's important to note that any authentication methods registered manually via the Self Service Password Reset portal are maintained in Azure AD only. They are not written back to on-premises Active Directory.

2. Once all the appropriate authentication methods have been successfully configured, the user can reset their password via the Office 365 portal by selecting Can't Access Your Account? on the sign-in page, as shown in Figure 12-27.

FIGURE 12-27   Can't Access Your Account?

3. The user will then be redirected to the Password Reset portal, where they will be prompted for their User ID and asked to provide Captcha information.

4. Once that has been successfully confirmed, the user will be prompted for their challenge information, as shown in Figure 12-28.

FIGURE 12-28   Get Back Into Your Account

5. Successful entry of your challenge information will allow you to reset your password in the portal, and that password change will be written back to on-premises AD.

Precedence

Precedence is defined as "priority in importance, order, or rank." When used to refer to directories or synchronization rules in AAD Connect, this definition could not be more relevant.

When performing a multi-forest installation of AAD Connect, ordering the Active Directory forests is critical to the precedence of values as they are synchronized. However, even in a single-forest configuration, precedence could be a concern if there are planned configuration changes after deployment. While it might not be obvious during the installation of the tool, the resulting synchronization rules will dictate the value synchronized to Azure AD for each object, so it's important to understand precedence and its impact on the configuration.

Each object falling within the scope of the AAD Connect implementation via OU membership (or even group filtering) is subject to the precedence order of the synchronization rules that were created by the AAD Connect installer based on selections you made during the setup wizard:

1. First, synchronization rules, as seen in Figure 12-29, are ordered by direction (inbound versus outbound), followed by object type, and then by order of importance—or precedence.

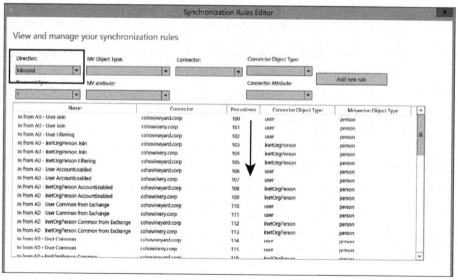

FIGURE 12-29   Precedence of synchronization rules

2. Each rule is assigned a precedence value, typically starting from 100 and increasing in value as the order of importance decreases. As a result, the lower the numerical value of a rule, the higher its precedence.

3. When a new object enters the scope of the AAD Connect sync, each rule is applied to the object based on its object type. This is visible in the Connector Object Type column shown previously in Figure 12-29, starting at the top of the precedence list and working downward.

4. Depending on their purpose, some rules might not apply to an object. For example, an Exchange synchronization rule will not apply to an object that is not mail-enabled.

5. The rules that are applied to an object can be found at the bottom of the preview pane for a user (discussed in Chapter 10), and the rule that contributed to each attribute is visible in the Synchronization rule column.

6. In Figure 12-30, you can see the value for AccountEnabled, which is visible in the Metaverse Attribute column, is set to True via the In from AD - User AccountEnabled rule.

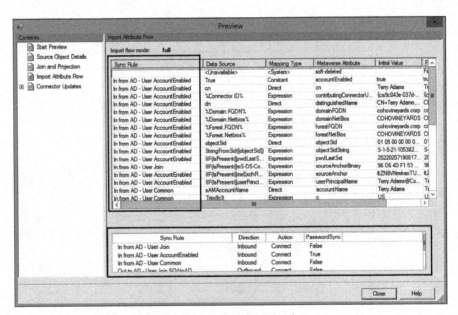

FIGURE 12-30   Preview pane showing synchronization rules

7. The In from AD - User AccountEnabled rule has a precedence value of 106. If you wanted to create a new rule that forced the value of AccountEnabled to False, your new rule would need a precedence that is higher than (meaning a lower numerical value) rule number 106, as shown in Figure 12-31.

8. This new synchronization rule is an inbound rule, which you know because of the Edit Inbound Synchronization Rule header in the upper-left portion of the dialog. This rule is configured to apply to User objects from the CohoVineyard.Corp forest with a precedence value of 90.

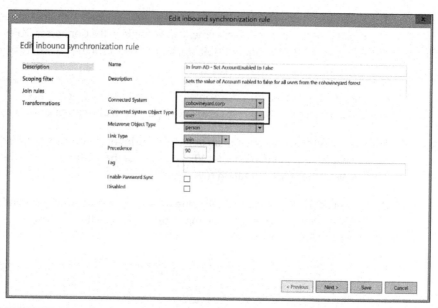

FIGURE 12-31   Edit Inbound Synchronization Rule with a higher Precedence setting

9. This means that the `AccountEnabled` value (not shown here but configured on the Transformations page) will be set to `False` when the user account is re-synchronized. See Figure 12-32.

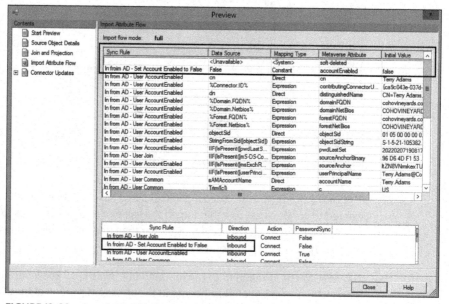

FIGURE 12-32   AccountEnabled value changed to False

As you can see, synchronization rule precedence can be used to change one or more attribute values for objects by creating new synchronization rules or customizing the rules created by the AAD Connect installation wizard. However, it is even more important to understand the ordering of synchronization rules in a multi-forest configuration where objects are configured to join attributes like `Mail`. The order the forests were added to the AAD Connect wizard will affect the resulting objects synchronized to Azure AD.

In the following example, two Active Directory forests are configured to synchronize to Azure. Each forest is enabled for Exchange, contains a combination of mail users and mailboxes, and a `Mail` attribute `join` was selected in the AAD Connect installation wizard:

1. If you compare the precedence value of the `In from AD - User Join` rules, you can see that the `cohovineyard.corp` forest was added first in the installation wizard because it has a precedence value that is higher than (lower numerical value) the `cohowinery.corp` forest's precedence value, as shown in Figure 12-33.

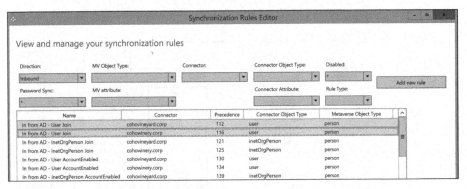

FIGURE 12-33   The In from AD – User Join rules for two forests

TIP

Identifying precedence

The order in which forests were added to the AAD Connect configuration can be easily identified by reviewing the `In from AD - User Join` **rules.**

As each forest is added, the `In from AD - User Join` **rule—the provisioning rule which is responsible for determining if an object should be synchronized—is inserted into the configuration after the previous forest's** `In from AD - User Join` **rule.**

As more forests are added, all the rules are renumbered, but the `In from AD - User Join` **rules, which start at 100, remain at the top of the rules list and will show the precedence order for each forest.**

2.   Once you can recognize the precedence order used by the synchronization engine to process objects, you can quickly identify where problems could occur. It is best to understand this rule-ordering process before installation. However, in some cases, you could inherit an existing installation of AAD Connect and won't have the luxury of reinstallation.

3.   Under those circumstances, it might be necessary to clone existing rules to change the behavior of the synchronization rules or create new rules to force an alternate precedence configuration.

4.   In Figure 12-34, two objects are joined on the `Mail` value to create a single object that will be synchronized to Office 365—a mailbox from the `cohowinery.corp` forest with a `mail` user from the `cohovineyard.corp` forest.

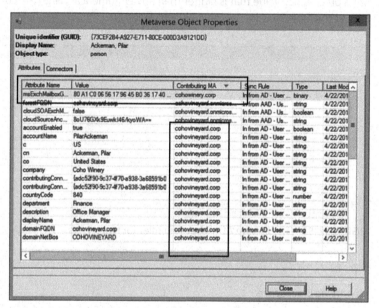

FIGURE 12-34   Metaverse object properties for a joined user object

5.   Also, in Figure 12-34, notice in the Contributing MA column that all the user attributes are coming from the `cohovineyard.corp` forest, except for the `msExchMailboxGUID` value, which comes from the `cohowinery.corp` forest. Because the `cohovineyard.corp` forest is the precedent forest, it's `In from AD - User Join` rule has a value of 100 and, therefore, has a higher precedence than `cohowinery.corp` for ALL values.

6.   The only reason `msExchMailboxGUID` is coming from the `cohowinery.corp` forest is because the `cohovineyard.corp` object is a mail user and has no `msExchMailboxGUID` in `cohovineyard.corp`.

7. In this example, if the properties for the values from cohovineyard.corp were the values expected in Azure AD, nothing further would be needed. The synchronization process would flow the object to Office 365 as a mail user, which is the object type in the precedent forest. The msExchMailboxGUID attribute would be ignored.

8. However, if there were values from cohowinery.corp forest that should take precedence, it would be necessary to make changes to the synchronization rules so those values *were* precedent. There are two methods available for achieving this goal:

   - Clone the synchronization rule(s) that flow those attributes as a higher precedence (lower numeric value).

   - Create a new inbound synchronization rule with a higher precedence for the attributes in question.

In this example, we will select the second option because we are only concerned with the Title and Department values.

1. First, we will create a new inbound synchronization rule with a precedence higher than 100 for user objects from the cohowinery.corp forest, as shown in Figure 12-35.

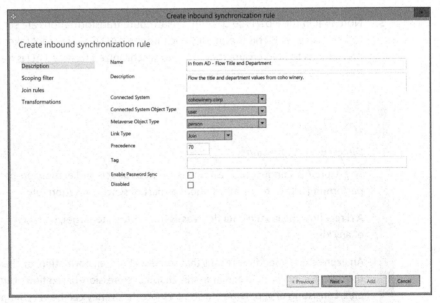

FIGURE 12-35   Creation of a new synchronization rule for title and department

2. Then, we will add the attribute transformations for the title and department values, as shown in Figure 12-36.

CHAPTER 12

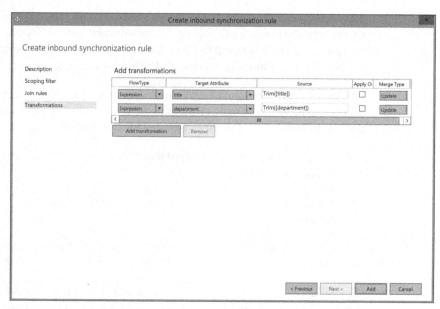

FIGURE 12-36   Transformations for the title and department attributes

3. Note that in the FlowType column, the attribute transformations are set to Expression rather than Direct. This is primarily because the AAD Connect tool takes certain precautions to help ensure that the data synchronized to Azure AD is free from formatting errors.

Inside Out

Direct versus Expression

The Azure AD Connect tool uses the concept of direct- and expression-based flows when performing attribute transformations as part of synchronization rules.

A direct flow means the data flows as-is from source to target, with no change or update of any kind.

An expression-based flow means that some sort of transformation, or change, is made to the data. As you learned earlier in this chapter, expression-based flows can be very complex, consisting of very large blocks of VBA code, or they can be very simple, performing tasks like Trim() which removes any whitespace (empty space) at the beginning and end of an attribute.

4. In the Source column, the `title` and `department` values use the `Trim()` function to eliminate any leading or trailing whitespace.

5. Additionally, we did not need to create the expressions used in this rule. Instead, we searched the synchronization rules for the rule that would ordinarily flow those two values (`In from AD - User Common`) and copied the existing transformation expression to our new rule. Searching the synchronization rules is simply a matter of using the dropdowns at the top of the Synchronization Rules Editor, as shown in Figure 12-37. Selecting the Connector, Connector Object Type (such as User), and Connector Attribute (such as Title) will cause the Synchronization Rules Editor to filter all rules that do not meet that criteria. You can then edit these rules, review the transformation for the attribute in question, and duplicate that transformation in your new rule.

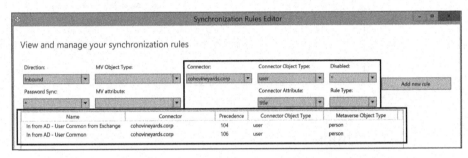

FIGURE 12-37   Filtering in the Sync Rule Editor

6. Once the new synchronization rule has been saved, re-synchronization of the `user` object shows the values being synchronized to Azure AD for `title` and `department` are now coming from the `cohowinery.corp` forest via the newly created synchronization rule. See Figure 12-38.

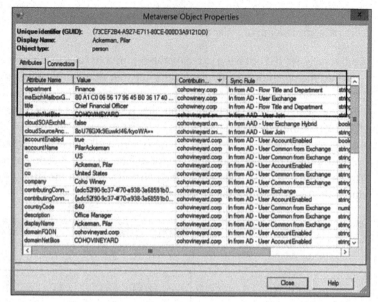

FIGURE 12-38   Attribute values flowing from the cohowinery forest

CAUTION

Although it is possible to make precedence changes by cloning rules, or creating new rules, depending on the number of customizations, it might ultimately make more sense to uninstall and reinstall the AAD Connect tool. Doing so will keep the number of customizations to a minimum and simplify the configuration, especially if Azure AD Connect was deployed incorrectly or is in a state that is no longer necessary to support your organization and its goals.

What's next?

In the next chapter, we will focus on Azure Automation, which allows you to leverage features built directly into your Azure tenant to automate scripts, provisioning, monitoring, and other workloads that you would otherwise have to do using third-party software or custom scripts and code.

Azure Automation

As organizations move more workloads and infrastructure to the cloud, batch jobs and other automation scripts that used to be run against on-premises applications must be re-tooled. For many organizations, these types of recurring routines help achieve a certain level of consistency, security, and standardization.

While many cloud service providers include automation technologies for common tasks, some other customizations and settings can't be done with out-of-the-box tooling. This level of routine customization and configuration is perfect for a service such as Azure Automation.

In this chapter, you'll learn how Azure Automation can continuously apply settings or updates to Azure AD objects.

Azure Automation concepts

Azure Automation is a service that allows you to publish scripted procedures (commonly referred to as *runbooks*) to accomplish tasks.

Runbooks

Runbooks, as mentioned earlier, are collections of procedures (scripts, commands, web service calls, or other logic components) used to accomplish various automation tasks.

Azure Automation currently supports five types of runbooks:

- **PowerShell**   Text-based runbook that uses Windows PowerShell. Code can be edited directly in the Azure portal or any offline text editor and imported.

- **PowerShell workflow**   Text-based runbook that uses Windows PowerShell workflows (scripts that use Windows Workflow Foundation). A workflow is a sequence of connected steps or functions used to perform long-running tasks or tasks requiring the coordination of multiple nodes. One benefit of workflows is that they can survive interruptions, such as network disconnects and computer restarts.

- **Graphical**   Runbook based on Windows PowerShell but built with the graphical editor in the Azure portal. Graphical runbooks create their own scripting, abstracted from the user.

- **Graphical PowerShell workflow**   Runbook based on PowerShell workflow but built with the graphical editor in the Azure portal. Like graphical runbooks, graphical Power-Shell workflow runbooks create their own scripting, abstracted from the user.

- **Python**   Text runbooks that are compiled under Python 2 and Python 3. As with other text-based runbooks, Python runbooks can be edited in the Azure portal or with an offline text editor and imported.

The type of runbook you use will depend on the components you're trying to manage or update.

Hybrid Runbook Worker

The Hybrid Runbook Worker is an agent-based design that allows you to run Azure Automation runbooks on Windows and Linux machines (virtual or physical).

Authentication

Like most scripting or service solutions, Azure Automation requires some sort of authentication to ensure that the runbook has the correct rights and permissions to execute.

Webhooks

Webhooks are like a notification service for applications. Instead of creating a service or a script to continuously or periodically communicate with another application to check for new data, a webhook works by sending a notification that an event has happened (such as adding or updating a record in a database).

Configuring authentication

Using Azure Automation for Microsoft 365 will require two types of credentials:

- Azure AD Service Account

- Azure Automation Account

In this next section, we'll configure both accounts. While Azure, Azure AD, Microsoft Graph, and Exchange Online support certificate-based authentication, the Microsoft Teams and SharePoint Online modules currently do not. As such, we'll be configuring a traditional credential-based authentication.

Microsoft 365 service account

First, you must create a service account and grant it the appropriate permissions.

> **NOTE**
>
> For the purposes of this example, we'll create a single account and grant it Global Admin privileges so you can understand the process. However, when configuring service accounts for your organization, it's recommended to use a least-privilege model and only grant the account the minimum amount of rights and permissions necessary to perform its function. Implementing a single administrative service account per product, service, or workload may be a good starting point when working with cloud-based service accounts. There's no charge or license required for service accounts.

To configure a service account with the Global Admin role, follow these steps:

1. Connect to Azure AD with an account with the Global Admin role:

   ```
   Connect-AzureAD
   ```

2. Run the following commands to create a new Azure AD user with a strong password stored in the variable $PasswordProfile.Password, as shown in Figure 13-1. Add the user to the Global Admins role group, where UserPrincipalName is a value appropriate for your tenant, as shown in Listing 13-1.

   Listing 13-1   Add user to the Global Admins group

   ```
   $PasswordProfile = New-Object -TypeName Microsoft.Open.AzureAD.Model.
   PasswordProfile
   $PasswordProfile.Password = ((([char[]]([char]33..[char]95) + ([char[]]([char]97..`
   [char]126)) + 0..9 | sort {Get-Random})[0..25] -join '')
   $PasswordProfile.ForceChangePasswordNextLogin = $False
   $PasswordProfile.EnforceChangePasswordPolicy = $False
   $params = @{
     AccountEnabled     = $true;
     DisplayName        = "Microsoft 365 Service Automation Account";
     mailNickname       = "M365Service";
     PasswordProfile    = $PasswordProfile;
     PasswordPolicies   = "DisablePasswordExpiration";
     UserPrincipalName  = "Microsoft365-Automation@cohovineyardsus.onmicrosoft.com"
     }
   $AzureADUser = New-AzureADUser @params
   Add-AzureADDirectoryRoleMember -ObjectId (Get-AzureADDirectoryRole -Filter`
   "DisplayName eq 'Global Administrator'").ObjectId -RefObjectId $AzureADUser.ObjectId
   ```

3. Copy the password value to your clipboard using the following command:

   ```
   $PasswordProfile.Password | Clip
   ```

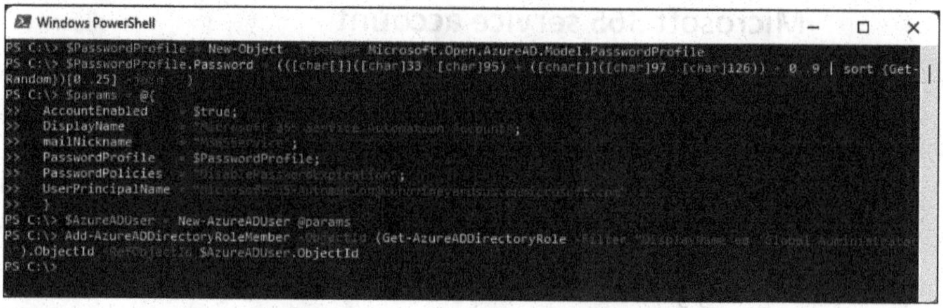

Figure 13-1   Creating a Microsoft 365 Automation service account

Optionally, you can paste the contents of the password to a note location where you can use it when setting up the automation account profile.

Azure Automation account

Before you can script tasks, you need to create an automation account. The automation account will have associated modules, credentials, and runbooks.

TIP

Working with Azure Automation requires an Azure Subscription. You can activate a free Azure Trial Subscription from the Azure portal under Subscriptions. To start a free subscription, navigate to the Azure portal (*https://portal.azure.com*), search for Subscriptions, and click + to add a new trial subscription.

Creating an Azure Automation account

The Azure Automation account configuration will be used to store the Microsoft 365 credential you created in the previous steps.

To create an automation account, follow these steps:

1. Navigate to the Azure portal (*https://portal.azure.com*) and type `automation accounts` in the search bar. See Figure 13-2.

2. Click Create.

3. Select an Azure subscription from the Subscription dropdown.

4. Select a resource group from the Resource Group dropdown or click Create New to create a new resource group. A resource group is simply a configuration container to store resources related to each other.

CHAPTER 13

Figure 13-2   Azure Automation Accounts page

5. Under Instance Details, enter an Automation Account Name and select a Region where this resource account will primarily be used. When finished, click Review + Create, as shown in Figure 13-3.

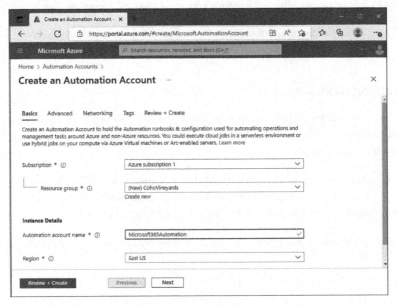

Figure 13-3   Create an Automation Account

CHAPTER 13

6. Click Create.

Wait while the Azure Automation Account is created. Next, we'll begin adding modules to the account.

Inside Out

Azure Automation accounts and credentials

There are a number of different types of methods to access Microsoft 365 resources and services. The automation account method presented here works for all workloads in the Microsoft 365 platform, including Exchange Online, Azure AD, SharePoint Online, and Microsoft Teams.

Other methods, such as Run As accounts, require registering an Azure AD application, generating a certificate, and delegating rights. You can use Run As accounts when working with the Exchange Online and SharePoint PnP cmdlets, but they are not compatible with Microsoft Teams and the classic SharePoint Online Management Shell.

Managed identities present another authentication avenue. Managed identities are used to access Azure-based resources without the application needing to be configured with credentials. Microsoft does not fully support using managed identities for administering Microsoft 365 resources at this time.

To learn more about RunAs accounts, see
https://learn.microsoft.com/en-us/azure/automation/manage-run-as-account.

To learn more about managed identities, see *http://bit.ly/3ODvp9v.*

Adding modules

Like installing PowerShell modules on a workstation or server, importing modules to an automation account allows you to access cmdlets for managing applications, services, devices, and other infrastructure:

7. After the automation account has been created, click Go To Resource. If the Go To Resource button does not appear, you can navigate to the Azure portal, choose Automation Accounts, and select your automation account.

8. In the navigation pane, scroll to Shared Resources and select Modules, as shown in Figure 13-4.

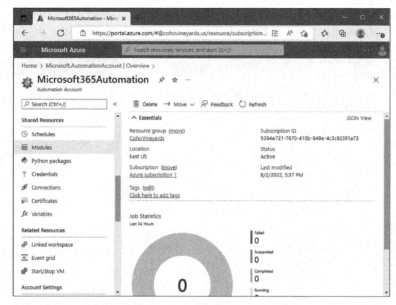

Figure 13-4   Azure Automation Account management page

9.   On the Modules page, click Browse Gallery, as shown in Figure 13-5.

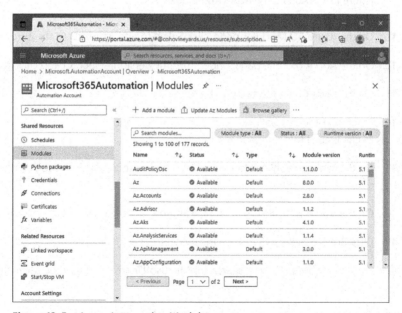

Figure 13-5   Azure Automation Modules page

CHAPTER 13

10. From the Modules Gallery, search for AzureAD, and select it from the list of items that appears, as shown in Figure 13-6.

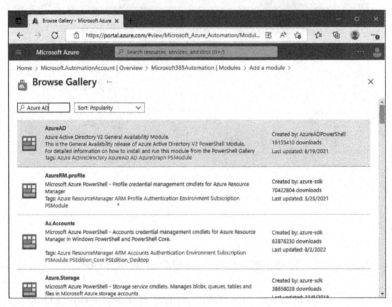

Figure 13-6   Adding the Azure AD module

11. On the Azure AD Modules page, click Select to add AzureAD to the automation account.

12. On the Add A Module page, under Runtime Version, select 5.1 and click Import.

13. Click Browse Gallery to browse the Module Gallery.

14. From the Modules Gallery, search for Exchange, and add the ExchangeOnlineManagement module.

15. On the ExchangeOnlineManagement module page, click Select to add it to the automation account.

16. On the Add A Module page, under Runtime Version, select 5.1 and click Import.

17. Click Browse Gallery to browse the module gallery.

18. From the Module Gallery, search for MicrosoftTeams, and add the MicrosoftTeams module.

19. On the MicrosoftTeams module page, click Select to add it to the automation account.

20. On the Add A Module page, under Runtime Version, select 5.1 and click Import.

You've added PowerShell modules to the automation account. Next, we'll add the Microsoft 365 credential created earlier under the Microsoft 365 Service Account section.

Adding a credential

Earlier, you created a service account and added it to the Global Admins directory role. In this section, you'll store that credential object in the automation account. Once the credential object is stored, it can be retrieved and used by the runbooks connected to the automation account:

1. From the automation account, scroll down to the Shared Resources section in the navigation pane and click Credentials.

2. Click Add A Credential, as shown in Figure 13-7.

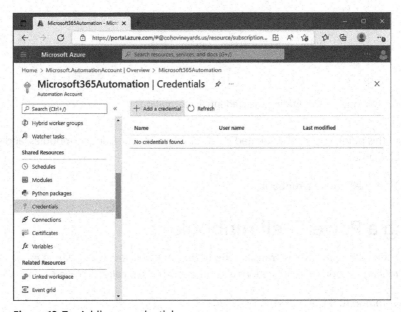

Figure 13-7   Adding a credential

3. In the New Credential flyout menu, enter a Name and Description. In the User Name text box, enter the value used for the UserPrincipalName when you created the automation account. In the Password and Confirm Password text fields, paste the password stored in your clipboard, as shown in Figure 13-8. Click Create.

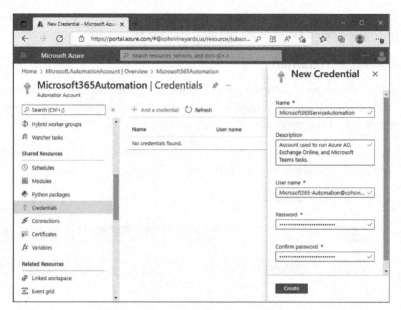

Figure 13-8   Adding the credential information

At this point, you've now created an automation account, added modules, and stored a credential.

Next, we'll create a runbook.

Creating a PowerShell runbook

For most organizations, transitioning to runbooks will involve updating existing scripts and tooling to suppress notifications and other output typically displayed on a screen.

Common runbook tasks might include:

- Checking the expiration of a legal hold and notifying the legal department

- Configuring regional settings on a new mailbox

- Adding a label to a Microsoft team

- Configuring guest permissions in a team

Any frequent administration task is a potential task for a runbook.

Prepare an Exchange Online script

Management scripts used by your organization can likely be converted to PowerShell runbooks.

The sample script shown in Listing 13-2 is designed to identify mailboxes that have a litigation hold date set. One of the most important features to note is the retrieval of the automation account's stored credential using the `Get-AutomationPSCredential` cmdlet. It works very similarly to the `Get-Credential` cmdlet, only instead of using interactive input, `Get-AutomationPSCredential` imports the credential referenced through the -Name parameter.

Listing 13-2   Identifying mailbox with litigation hold dates

```
$Credential = Get-AutomationPSCredential -Name "Microsoft365ServiceAutomation"
Connect-ExchangeOnline -Credential $Credential
$SmtpServer = "cohovineyards-us.mail.protection.outlook.com";
$To = @("legalholdreview@cohovineyards.us");
$From = "no-reply@cohovineyards.us";
$NotificationWarningWindow = 7;
[System.Collections.ArrayList]$obj = @();
$Today = Get-Date;
[array]$mailboxes = Get-Mailbox -ResultSize Unlimited -Filter { LitigationHoldEnabled`
-eq $true } | Select DisplayName, PrimarySmtpAddress, Litigation*
If ($mailboxes) {
foreach ($mailbox in $mailboxes)
{
    $ExpirationDate = $mailbox.LitigationHoldDate + $mailbox.LitigationHoldDuration;
    If (($ExpirationDate - $Today).Days -lt $NotificationWarningWindow)
    {
        $hashtemp = @{
        DisplayName = $mailbox.DisplayName;
        PrimarySmtpAddress = $mailbox.PrimarySmtpAddress;
        ExpirationDate = $ExpirationDate
        };
    $objtemp = New-Object PSObject -Property $hashtemp;
    $obj += $objtemp;
    Remove-Variable hashtemp,objtemp
    }
}
[String]$Body = $obj.GetEnumerator() | %{ "'n$($_.ExpirationDate)," +`
"$($_.PrimarySmtpAddress)," + "$($_.DisplayName)" }
If ($Body) { Send-MailMessage -Port 25 -SmtpServer $SmtpServer -To $To -From $From`
-Subject "Litigation Hold expiring in the next 7 days" -Body $Body }
Else
{ Send-MailMessage -Port 25 -SmtpServer $SmtpServer -To $To -From $From -Subject "No
Litigation Holds expiring in the next 7 days" -Body "No mailboxes with Litigation Holds
are expiring in the next 7 days." }
}
Get-PSSession | ? { $_.ConfigurationName -eq "Microsoft.Exchange" } | Remove-PSSession
```

With that script sample, we can now create a runbook.

CHAPTER 13

Creating a runbook with a script

Follow these steps to create a runbook:

1. Navigate to the automation account in the Azure portal.

2. Under Process Automation, select Runbooks.

3. Click Create A Runbook, as shown in Figure 13-9.

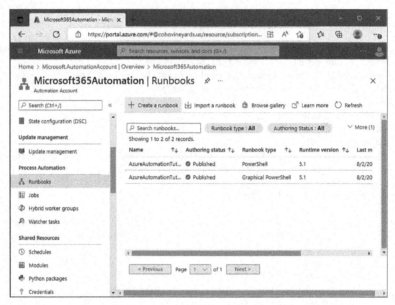

Figure 13-9   Creating a runbook

4. On the Create A Runbook page, enter a Name, set the Runbook Type to PowerShell, and set the Runtime Version to 5.1 (to match the version selected for the modules), as shown in Figure 13-10. When finished, click Create.

5. Expand the Runbooks node and locate the name of the runbook that you just created.

6. Type or paste the contents of the runbook in the code window, as shown in Figure 13-11.

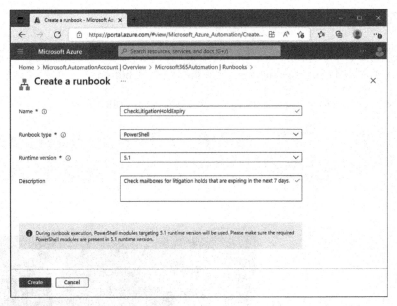

Figure 13-10   Configuring a runbook

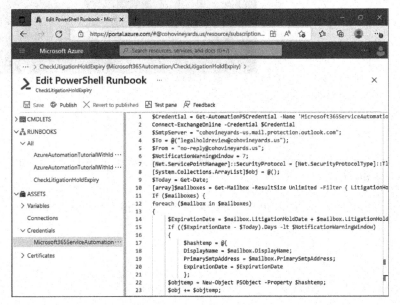

Figure 13-11   Pasting the code for the runbook to the code window

7. Click Save.

You've now created a runbook.

Testing a PowerShell runbook

Now that the runbook is saved, you can test it to see if any modifications need to be made:

1.   With the runbook still open, click the Test Pane button.

2.   Click Start to execute the runbook, as shown in Figure 13-12.

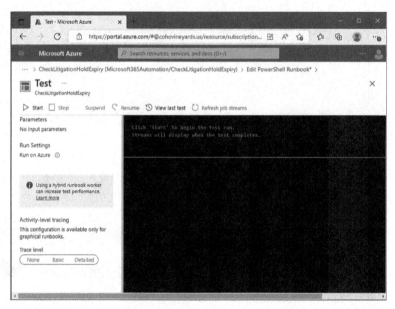

Figure 13-12   Testing a runbook

3.   Wait while the runbook executes.

4.   Check the output screen for errors, as shown in Figure 13-13. If errors are present, resolve them.

5.   Continue updating and testing the runbook script until it returns successfully, as shown in Figure 13-14.

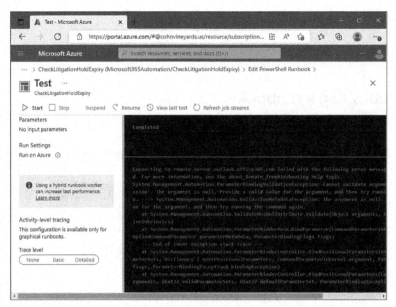

Figure 13-13   Reviewing errors in the test pane

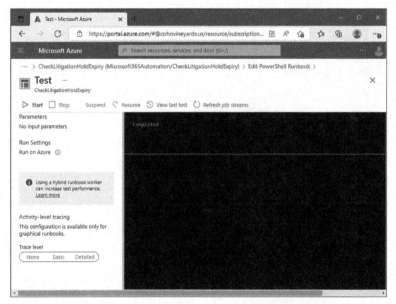

Figure 13-14   PowerShell runbook test completed successfully

6. Click the X to close the Test pane.

7. Figure 13-14 shows that the runbook was successfully completed with no output errors or abnormal terminations.

Publishing a runbook

Now that you have a working runbook, it's time to publish it and schedule it to run regularly:

8. From the Edit PowerShell Runbook page, click Publish Runbook, as shown in Figure 13-15.

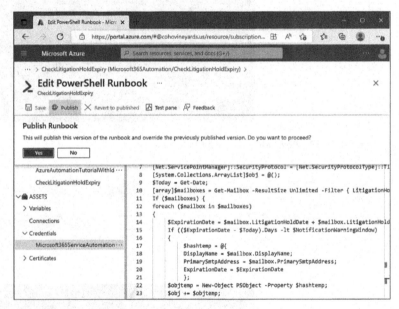

Figure 13-15   Publish a runbook

9. Click Yes to publish the runbook.

10. On the runbook page, select Schedules in the navigation pane under Resources, as shown in Figure 13-16.

11. Click Add A Schedule.

12. Expand Schedules.

13. Click Add A Schedule.

14. On the New Schedule flyout menu, configure a schedule to execute the runbook and click Create, as shown in Figure 13-17.

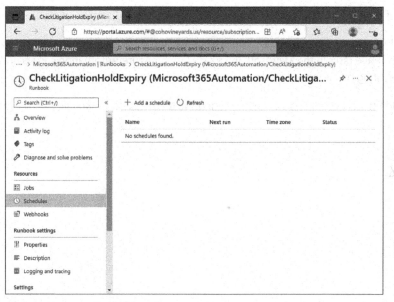

Figure 13-16   Runbook schedule

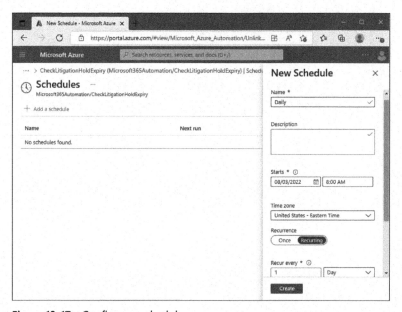

Figure 13-17   Configure a schedule

15. On the Schedule Runbook page, click OK.

Congratulations! You've now successfully configured a runbook for your Exchange Online environment using a stored credential.

What's next?

This chapter focused on learning how to use runbooks to perform common or repetitive administrative tasks in the Microsoft 365 environment. Azure Automation can securely extend your existing management scripts to run against the Microsoft 365 environment.

In the next chapter, we'll start exploring the features and capabilities of Exchange Online.

Exchange Online overview

The Exchange Online component of Microsoft 365 supports cloud-only deployments, hybrid coexistence, and staged, cutover, and hybrid migration paths. Before configuring your existing Exchange on-premises environment to connect to Microsoft 365, plan to take a step back to evaluate the current state of your Exchange organization. Ensuring you meet all the prerequisites before undergoing coexistence or migration steps will help save time and reduce the risk of failure.

Exchange Online deployment concepts

If you are familiar with Exchange on-premises, you might already have a good basis for understanding how Exchange Online works. Just as Exchange on-premises uses an Active Directory environment to store attributes and properties for configuration and recipient objects, Exchange Online also stores its configuration information in Active Directory. In the case of Exchange Online, the Active Directory component is Azure Active Directory, a multitenant directory service designed to scale to billions of objects.

For those not familiar with Exchange Server on-premises, don't worry! We'll cover everything necessary to successfully deploy a cloud-only or hybrid environment.

Recipients

Exchange Online has many types of recipients, and all of them have some relationship to an underlying Active Directory object. Mailboxes, contacts, and distribution groups build on a corresponding Active Directory object by adding Exchange-specific attributes (`mail`, `proxyAddress`, and `mailNickname` are a few examples) and exposing them to the Exchange interfaces.

Mail routing

Similar to Exchange on-premises, Exchange Online uses the concept of connectors to manage mail flow. You can scope (or restrict) connectors to send traffic for one or more domains on a specific route or receive from one or more hosts by using a specific configuration. In Exchange on-premises, you designate connectors as either Send Connectors (which control outgoing mail flow from a server) or Receive Connectors (which control incoming mail to a server). In Exchange Online, the analogous connectors are Outbound (Send) and Inbound (Receive) and are labeled from the perspective of the Exchange Online service.

In addition to connectors, Exchange Online also enables you to define connection filters to allow or block connections from specific IP addresses or ranges and transport rules to filter or further modify inbound and outbound traffic.

When establishing mail flow with a foreign system (Exchange Online or an external messaging environment), you might configure one or more connectors and filters to control the mail flow. You can also configure Exchange Online to act as an extension of your on-premises Exchange infrastructure through the hybrid configuration process. Configuring Exchange Hybrid is covered in Chapter 15, "Exchange Online Hybrid planning and deployment."

NOTE

For more advanced mail flow configurations and scenarios, see "Mail flow best practices for Exchange Online and Microsoft 365 (overview)" at *https://docs.microsoft.com/en-us/exchange/mail-flow-best-practices/mail-flow-best-practices*.

Autodiscover

Autodiscover is the process that Microsoft Outlook uses to determine the location of a user's mailbox. Autodiscover can be configured to use one or more methods, including looking for specific DNS records or service connection points (SCPs) in Active Directory.

Autodiscover is also used as part of the free/busy lookup process whereby a user's calendar is queried to check availability for meeting requests. In previous versions of Exchange, it was unnecessary to configure Autodiscover to configure Outlook. However, Microsoft 365 requires using Autodiscover to configure mailboxes correctly.

Depending on your configuration and business requirements, you can configure Autodiscover differently than the recommended records in the Microsoft 365 portal. In hybrid configurations, you should configure Autodiscover DNS records to point to the on-premises mail system because Exchange on-premises can redirect requests to Microsoft 365 but not vice versa. When all mailboxes are migrated, you can choose to update your Autodiscover records to point to Microsoft 365 to remove the local Exchange server dependency.

Each Outlook client goes through a predefined Autodiscover lookup order, which can be modified through either Group Policy or by creating and updating registry values in `HKCU\ Software\Microsoft\Office\x.0\Outlook\Autodiscover`. The Autodiscover process has undergone several updates since its first release in 2007.

> ### NOTE
>
> **In November 2021, Outlook 2010 was blocked from connecting to Exchange Online. If you are planning a migration to the Exchange Online service, you will need to include upgrading client endpoints as part of the process.**

The updated Autodiscover process includes a new high-priority step that queries Microsoft 365 to see if a mailbox exists. Autodiscover for Outlook 2016 and later uses the following order:

1. **Check for restart scenarios**   In some scenarios, configuring Outlook inserts pre-boot information to the local registry, which Outlook uses to complete its launch. If this registry data is located, but Outlook fails to retrieve the cached data the registry references, the Autodiscover process is aborted, and no further steps are taken.

2. **Local XML**   Outlook can also be configured to use a local XML file, which requires manually creating an `autodiscover.xml` file and modifying the local computer's registry to point to the XML file's path. This is controlled by two registry or policy settings:

   - **PreferLocalXML** (REG_DWORD type)

   - **<domain.FQDN>** (REG_SZ type) This entry is used to specify the domain and path to the XML file. For example, if you are configuring this setting for the `contoso.com` domain to use an XML file stored at `C:\ProfileData\contoso.xml`, the value name would be `contoso.com`, and the value data would be `"C:\ProfileData\contoso.xml"`.

3. **Cached URL (Last Known Good)**   Upon successful retrieval of the Autodiscover payload, the data is stored locally, sometimes called the "last known good" configuration. This step can be controlled through the REG_DWORD policy value `ExcludeLastKnownGoodURL`.

4. **Microsoft 365 as priority**   Outlook attempts to determine if the user is located in Microsoft 365. This step was introduced to help alleviate problems caused by misconfigured Autodiscover records. This step can be controlled through the REG_DWORD policy value `ExcludeExplicitOffice365Endpoint`.

5. **Service connection point**   The class service connection point is defined in the Active Directory schema. SCP objects published in Active Directory contain information that clients can use to bind to a particular service or host offering a service. Exchange Service Connection Point objects are created under the `CN=Autodiscover,CN=Pr otocols,CN=<Exchange Server>,CN=Servers,CN=Exchange Administrative Group,CN=Administrative Groups,CN=<Exchange Organization>,CN=Microsfot`

Exchange,CN=Services container. The value in the serviceBindingInformation attribute is configured as https://<exchange server FQDN>/autodiscover/ autodiscover.xml. This step can be controlled through the REG_DWORD policy value ExcludeScpLookup.

6. **HTTPS root domain query**   When Outlook is running on a machine that is not joined to an Active Directory domain, the client constructs a URL based on the domain portion of the user's email address. For example, if your email address is danjump@cohovineys.us and you are attempting to configure Outlook on a computer that is not domain-joined, it attempts to query the Autodiscover service at *https://cohovineyards.us/autodiscover/autodiscover.xml*. This step can be controlled through the REG_DWORD policy value ExcludeHttpsRootDomain.

7. **HTTPS Autodiscover domain query**   If the previous queries don't return the location of an Autodiscover service, Outlook uses the domain portion of the user's email address to try a new URL. Using the previous domain as an example, Outlook tries *https://autodiscover.cohovineyards.us/autodiscover/autodiscover.xml*. This is the default Autodiscover record format that appears on the Microsoft 365 Domains configuration page. This step can be controlled through the REG_DWORD policy value ExcludeHttpsAutoDiscoverDomain.

8. **Local data check**   Outlook checks to see if a local XML file containing an Autodiscover payload exists. There is no way to manage this step.

9. **HTTP redirect method**   If an HTTPS Autodiscover domain query fails, Outlook retries the same URL, using HTTP instead of HTTPS. If a valid URL is returned, Outlook will follow the redirect to retrieve the payload. This step can be controlled through the REG_DWORD policy value ExcludeHttpRedirect.

10. **SRV record query**   The next method Outlook uses to locate a user's mailbox is by querying DNS for a service locator (SRV) record, using a predefined format. The record is configured as _autodiscover._tcp.domain.com, with the hostname pointing to the Exchange server hosting the Autodiscover service and the port value configured as 443. This step can be controlled through the REG_DWORD policy value ExcludeSrvRecord.

11. **Microsoft 365 Failsafe**   The final step in Autodiscover is using a more loose set of heuristics to determine if the mailbox is in Microsoft 365. If Outlook determines that it's possible, it attempts to retrieve the Autodiscover payload from the known Microsoft 365 endpoints (*https://autodiscover-s.outlook.com/autodiscover/autodiscover.xml* and *https://autodiscover-s.partner.outlook.cn/autodiscover/autodiscover.xml*). Like step 4, this step can be controlled through the REG_DWORD value ExcludeExplicitOffice365Endpoint. Configuring this with a value of 1 will disable both steps 4 and 11.

As a reference, Outlook versions prior to 2016 used the following lookup order:

CHAPTER 14

1. Service connection point

2. HTTPS root domain query

3. HTTPS Autodiscover domain query

4. HTTP redirect method

5. SRV record query

6. Local XML

7. Cached URL (Last Known Good)

> ### TIP
> You can use Group Policy or modify the registry to disable specific Autodiscover methods. There are also additional policy controls for managing things such as HTTP timeouts and authentication negation. For more information, see *http://bit.ly/3AOXftN* and *http://bit.ly/3EA2zSM*.

Migration and coexistence methodologies

When planning a coexistence with or migration to Exchange Online, you will want to consider both your long-term and short-term goals in addition to your current Active Directory, Exchange, desktop configuration, and network topologies. Depending on your business requirements and environment, you might be able to choose one or more of these migration coexistence strategies:

- **Cutover migration**   If your on-premises environment is running Exchange 2003, Exchange 2007, Exchange 2010, or Exchange 2013, and you have fewer than 2,000 mailboxes, you can use a cutover migration. Because of the nature of a cutover, you have to migrate everyone together. Although the maximum number of users that can be migrated with this method is 2,000, limiting it to environments with 150 or fewer mailboxes is more realistic.

- **Staged migration**   If your on-premises environment is running Exchange 2003 or Exchange 2007 and you have more than 150 mailboxes, you can run a staged migration. Staged migrations require using Azure Active Directory Connect (AAD Connect).

- **Express migration**   You can use an express migration if your on-premises environment is running Exchange 2010 or later, you don't plan to use any directory synchronization technologies long-term to manage your users, and don't need to maintain the ability to look up free/busy status between Microsoft 365 and on-premises users. Express migrations can also be referred to as minimal hybrid migrations.

- **Hybrid migration**   If your on-premises environment is running Exchange 2010, Exchange 2013, or Exchange 2016, you can use a hybrid migration. You can also use hybrid migrations in Exchange 2003 or Exchange 2007 environments if you deploy an Exchange 2010 or Exchange 2013 server. Hybrid migrations support the idea of online mailbox migrations if mailboxes are hosted on Exchange 2007 or later servers. This means the user's mailbox stays mounted and online until the moment of cutover, and then the user's Outlook profile can be redirected to Microsoft 365. If mailboxes are hosted on Exchange 2003, the mailbox is locked and unavailable until the migration for that mailbox is completed. Public folders hosted on Exchange 2003 must be migrated to Exchange 2007 before hybrid coexistence or migration can be performed.

- **IMAP migration**   If your source environment is running a version of Exchange before 2003 or a foreign email system, you can use an IMAP migration. Typically, IMAP migrations cannot migrate calendars and contacts. Most organizations that need to perform migrations from non-Microsoft or hosted platforms work with a partner specializing in migrations or using third-party tools.

NOTE

This book focuses on hybrid migrations. For more information on planning and configuring Exchange hybrid scenarios, see Chapter 15, "Exchange Online Hybrid planning and deployment."

From the planning perspective, you'll need to analyze each type of recipient you want to migrate, the transport rules, business requirements, and your existing environment—all of which are covered in the following sections.

Exchange and Active Directory on-premises environment

Your existing Exchange and Active Directory environments will be at the core of your migration planning. To ensure a smooth coexistence or deployment, make sure you spend time reviewing your current environments.

Active Directory versions and configuration

The minimum requirement for configuring Azure AD Connect is that your Active Directory is upgraded to at least a Windows Server 2003 forest functional level. If you plan to use the password writeback feature of Azure AD Connect, your domain controllers must run an updated version of Windows Server 2008 or later.

Inside Out

Read-only domain controllers

The read-only domain controller (RODC) was introduced with Windows Server 2008 to provide authentication services in environments that needed an extra layer of security, such as extranets or facilities without good physical security.

If you have deployed read-only domain controllers (RODCs) in your environment, you'll want to avoid using them for directory synchronization to Microsoft 365 because they can create difficult troubleshooting scenarios. You might even consider creating a new Active Directory site that does not have RODCs or specifying a custom list of domain controllers to ensure that you don't contact them.

You must take special consideration to ensure that AAD Connect is not using RODCs for password writeback. If you will be configuring password hash synchronization, you must also make sure that the passwords are cached on read-only domain controllers if an RODC is queried. Finally, if Azure AD Connect uses read-only domain controllers, make sure the filtered attribute set contains all the attributes you will be synchronizing to Microsoft 365.

You can use the Azure AD Connect Network Communications Test tool to verify server and networking requirements (including the presence of RODCs) before configuring Azure AD Connect. To obtain the tool, visit *https://aka.ms/aadnetwork* or run `Install-Script -Name AADConnect-CommunicationsTest` from an elevated PowerShell console session.

CHAPTER 14

Autodiscover

A properly configured Autodiscover service is necessary for access to Microsoft 365. In addition, if you are going to configure hybrid coexistence for public folders, on-premises Autodiscover is necessary so that the Public Folder proxy mailboxes can locate the on-premises Exchange Public Folder tree.

In topologies with mixed versions of Exchange, the Autodiscover service should be configured to point to the latest version of Exchange.

Inside Out

Autodiscover advanced configurations

Although the best-practices recommendation is to configure external Autodiscover to point to the latest version of Exchange, there might be situations when that's not possible due to existing network configurations, custom integrated software deployments, or shared infrastructure resources. In these cases, it is possible to configure parameters in Microsoft 365 through the `Set-OrganizationRelationship` cmdlet to control how services that require those features will respond.

You can use the `TargetAutodiscoverEpr` parameter to set the specific Autodiscover URL of Exchange Web Services for the external organization (in this case, the on-premises Exchange organization).

The `TargetSharingEpr` parameter can be used to control the exact endpoint for Exchange Web Services requests. If both `TargetAutodiscoverEpr` and `TargetSharingEpr` are configured, `TargetSharingEpr` takes priority and `TargetAutodiscoverEpr` is ignored. More information about the `TargetSharingEpr` and `TargetAutodiscoverEpr` parameters is located in Chapter 18, "Managing Exchange Online."

Certificates

Confirm that a third-party certificate has been installed and configured correctly and is used in publishing Exchange services, including Exchange Control Panel (ECP), Exchange Web Services (EWS), Offline Address Book (OAB), and Outlook Web App (OWA). Occasionally, the certificate file that has been installed might seem to be fine but causes problems with the hybrid configuration setup.

To check your certificate, run the following cmdlet in the on-premises Exchange Management Shell against the thumbprint of the certificate you use for hybrid configuration, as shown in Figure 14-1.

```
Get-ExchangeCertificate -ThumbPrint <thumbprint> | Format-List
HasPrivateKey,IsSelfSigned,RootCAType,Status
```

In order to work correctly for hybrid deployments, you must have a valid third-party certificate with a private key.

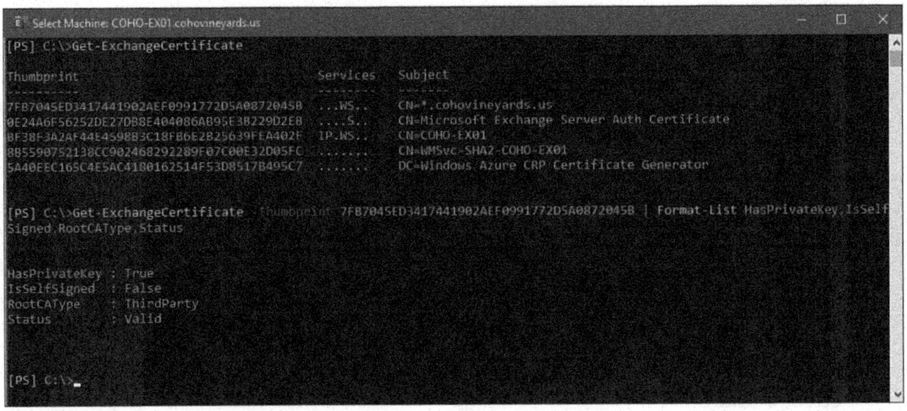

Figure 14-1   Exchange certificate details

Exchange versions, service packs, cumulative updates, and rollups

Before starting a migration or hybrid configuration, verify that the most recent Exchange service packs, cumulative updates, and rollups are applied. This is especially important for Exchange hybrid deployments because the Hybrid Configuration Wizard implements features and connectors in the Exchange environment and performs compatibility tests. For every version of Exchange Server supported in a hybrid topology, the servers must be at N-2 current (current version and up to two previous versions of cumulative updates or rollups) to be successfully configured.

Your organization's long-term management strategy should dictate which version of Exchange you deploy for Exchange Online coexistence or migration. For example, if you decide to transition to a purely cloud-based environment or have an existing Exchange 2003 deployment, you might choose to do the bare minimum to transition to Microsoft 365. You can use the information in Table 14-1 to help determine which versions of Exchange are supported for your environment.

Table 14-1   Exchange support matrix

On-premises environment	Exchange Server used for hybrid endpoint			
	Exchange 2019	Exchange 2016	Exchange 2013	Exchange 2010
Exchange 2019	Supported	Supported	Not supported	Not supported
Exchange 2016	Supported	Supported	Not supported	Not supported
Exchange 2013	Supported	Supported	Supported	Not supported
Exchange 2010	Not supported	Supported	Supported	Supported
Exchange 2007	Not supported	Not supported	Supported	Supported
Exchange 2003	Not supported	Not supported	Not supported	Supported

CHAPTER 14

> **NOTE**
>
> You can find information about Exchange updates at *https://docs.microsoft.com/en-us/Exchange/new-features/build-numbers-and-release-dates*.

Exchange Best Practices Analyzer

Depending on your version of Exchange, the Best Practices Analyzer might be included or available as a separate download. Run the Exchange Best Practices Analyzer to identify potential configuration issues. The Exchange Best Practices Analyzer can make recommendations for memory or logging configurations, identify databases that haven't been backed up in a long time, identify outdated network or storage drivers, or point out other less favorable configurations.

For Exchange 2003, the most current Best Practices Analyzer is available at *https://www.microsoft.com/en-us/download/details.aspx?id=22485*. Starting with Exchange 2007, the Best Practices Analyzer is included in the product.

IDFix

Microsoft provides the IDFix tool to help identify and resolve common directory attribute errors in your on-premises Active Directory and Exchange environments. Common issues might include invalid characters in the UserPrincipalName (UPN) or mailNickname attributes or instances when two or more users have been configured with the same SMTP proxy address.

There are certain error conditions that it can't detect yet, such as identifying when a user and a group might share the same SMTP address. These errors are frequently discovered when you synchronize your environment to Microsoft 365 with Azure AD Connect. IDFix can identify when user objects have UPNs that have non-public, top-level domains (TLDs) but cannot identify whether you have UPNs or proxy addresses that have not been configured in your Microsoft 365 tenant.

> **NOTE**
>
> You can download and run the IDFix tool from *https://aka.ms/idfix*. IDFix supports fixing some types of errors in the tool itself.

If you begin receiving errors such as duplicate proxy addresses during synchronization by Azure AD Connect, you can use the script at *https://aka.ms/finddupes* to identify the conflicting objects. The script identifies all instances of the conflicting address across all object types.

SSL offloading

Some organizations might configure Secure Sockets Layer (SSL) offloading, using one or more network devices to terminate the SSL connections. This is frequently configured in large organizations that have deployed server farms so that administrative teams don't have to manage certificates across many servers. Although SSL offloading is supported for Outlook Web App traffic and other Exchange Web Services calls, it is not supported for Mailbox Replication Service (MRS) traffic. MRS is used for mailbox migrations to and from Microsoft 365 and expects end-to-end SSL encryption of the traffic. If your organization uses SSL offloading, you will most likely need to configure a separate virtual IP (VIP) interface for the servers used for hybrid mailbox moves.

Windows updates

An often-overlooked basic environment check is ensuring servers are up to date with Windows and Exchange updates. Updates can include performance, security, or feature enhancements that your migration or coexistence environment needs to function optimally.

Recipients

From a coexistence or migration perspective, some objects might be fully migrated, whereas others might be only synchronized. Depending on your long-term business and technology objectives, you might have a deployment that has objects directly managed in Microsoft 365, objects that are managed on-premises, or both.

For example, after your migration is done, you might decide you just want to manage objects in the cloud, so you disable directory synchronization and decommission Exchange from your on-premises environment. You might continue to manage your Active Directory objects on-premises, synchronize them to Microsoft 365, and manage Exchange features through either the Microsoft 365 and Exchange admin centers or Windows PowerShell. You might even choose to migrate some objects to Microsoft 365 for full cloud management but keep other objects on-premises.

Contacts

A contact is a mail-enabled object that provides visibility in the global address list for an external recipient. Contacts can represent external users, resources, or distribution groups. Contacts can be synchronized from your on-premises directory to Microsoft 365 and managed on-premises, or they can be created in Microsoft 365 as stand-alone objects.

Mailboxes

The mailbox object, whether user, shared, or resource, is a data storage object that will exist in either the on-premises environment or Microsoft 365. In deployments with synchronized identity, the Exchange properties for a mailbox might be configured in the on-premises environment and synchronized through AAD Connect to Microsoft 365 or managed directly in Microsoft 365.

Relationship between mail-enabled users and mailboxes

Suppose you are new to Exchange or have never migrated objects between Exchange organizations. In that case, you might have noticed that objects in synchronized environments can appear differently, depending on which interface you're using.

When you synchronize on-premises users to Microsoft 365, it's important to understand the relationship between the on-premises and cloud objects. From the Active Directory perspective, the on-premises user's objectGuid value is converted to a Base64 string value and stored as the ImmutableID on the object's corresponding Azure Active Directory object.

The relationship between the on-premises objectGuid and the cloud ImmutableID values can be expressed this way, as shown in Figure 14-2.

```
[system.convert]::ToBase64String(objectGuid).ToByteArray()
```

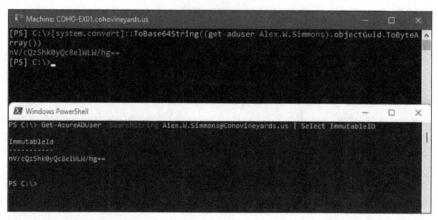

Figure 14-2   Active Directory objectGuid and Microsoft 365 ImmutableID

The primary differences between a mailbox user and a mail-enabled user are

- In addition to a primary SMTP address in the local Exchange environment, mail-enabled users have a targetAddress (a type of forwarding address) in an external environment.

- The values for msExchRecipientTypeDetails (128) and msExchRecipientDisplayType (6) that tell Exchange it's only a mail-enabled object.

- Mailbox users do not have a targetAddress value and instead have a value for homeMDB, which specifies where their on-premises mailbox is located. Mailbox users have values in msExchRecipientTypeDetails (1) and msExchRecipientDisplayType (0), indicating they are mailboxes.

Before migration, when you look at a mailbox user from Exchange on-premises, they are seen as a local mailbox user. When viewed from the perspective of Exchange Online, that same user is displayed as MailUser.

After you migrate that same user account, when you view their details from Exchange on-premises, their Recipient Display Type indicates they are now a MailUser, while their Recipient Type Details indicate they are a Remote Mailbox User (a subtype of MailUser). When looking at that migrated user from Exchange Online, they appear as Mailbox User.

Message sizes and attachments

If you are migrating from an Exchange on-premises environment to Microsoft 365, using either a cutover or hybrid migration, you can migrate messages that are up to 150 MB each. However, if you are migrating using IMAP or Exchange Web Services (third-party tools typically use Exchange Web Services), the maximum message size that can be migrated is 35 MB. Depending on your migration strategy and how your users communicate, you might want to evaluate your mailboxes for large attachments so you can notify users that those objects will not migrate successfully.

Accepted domains and addressing

Accepted domains are the domains over which your organization claims ownership. Although you can add any domains you like to your on-premises Exchange organization, you may only add and confirm domains in your Microsoft 365 environment for which you can prove ownership through DNS record registration. You can synchronize users and contacts with any email addresses to Microsoft 365, but you can only migrate mailboxes for users that have verified domains in your tenant.

If you have a mailbox with proxy addresses for domains not confirmed in your tenant, the migration will fail. As part of a migration process, make sure your Microsoft 365 tenant has all the domains used by your environment added to it.

Any domains not matching must be removed from mailboxes before migration. The script located at *https://aka.ms/RemoveExchangeProxies* can help you remove addresses from objects.

One of the tasks performed by the Hybrid Configuration Wizard is adding the tenant mail routing domain to all the email address templates containing domains selected in the hybrid setup.

In Exchange 2010, this email address policy update generates a very large address book update. In some cases, very large updates may have an unexpected network or client impact and could reconfigure users' primary email addresses if they were modified via Active Directory Users and Computers and do not have the EmailAddressPolicyEnabled property set to False. To avoid the automatic address book rebuild when using the Hybrid Configuration Wizard, you might want to update your email address templates beforehand.

If you have many templates, this can be a daunting task. You can use the script at *https://aka.ms/UpdateEAPs* to help bulk update your email address templates and then update the address books on your own schedule.

When migrating mailboxes to Microsoft 365 and enabling successful Autodiscover and cross-premises mail routing, mailboxes need to have a proxy address matching *<tenant>.mail.onmicrosoft.com.* Mailboxes without a matching tenant proxy address will fail migration.

Users with `EmailAddressPolicyEnabled` set to `False` will not get the tenant proxy address stamped on them during the email address policy update and thus fail the mailbox migration. You can use the script at *https://aka.ms/AddTenantProxy* to stamp mailboxes with the necessary tenant proxy address or add an Out-To-AD rule to Azure AD Connect to update the on-premises Active Directory users automatically. You can use the script at *https://aka.ms/NewAADConnectRuleAddProxy* to modify AAD Connect to perform this function.

Mail-enabled users

Your organization might have on-premises security principals configured as mail-enabled users. Mail-enabled users are not the same as mailbox users because they do not have local mailbox storage in your organization. You can think about a mail-enabled user as a combination of a security principal (user) and a contact, resulting in a user who might have login privileges to your network and a display entry in the global address list.

By default, mail-enabled users are synchronized to Microsoft 365. If you have a mail-enabled user with a value in `msExchMailboxGuid` that is synchronized to Microsoft 365, the object will be flagged as a mailbox awaiting migration in Microsoft 365.

Groups

Groups, quite simply, are collections of mail-enabled objects, regardless of whether they are mailboxes, mail-enabled users, contacts, or other distribution groups.

When synchronized from an on-premises environment, most group properties can only be managed from the on-premises environment. Some organizations are accustomed to managing distribution groups through the Outlook interface, allowing users to add or remove group members as they need to without assistance from the service desk.

As far as considerations go, this is an important decision. If groups are mastered on-premises and synchronized to Microsoft 365, then Microsoft 365 users cannot use Outlook to manage group membership. Groups must be re-created in Microsoft 365 to continue enabling users to manage distribution groups through Outlook. However, this can pose problems for mail-enabled security groups that are used as both distribution lists for mail recipients and as a mechanism for granting permissions to on-premises network resources.

In these instances, you might need to make a break between the security and distribution list functions, create a script to copy members from one group to another regularly (so that the group membership is the same between both cloud and on-premises), or manage two groups separately. If you choose to maintain separate groups, you can filter those particular groups, so they are not synchronized.

Inside Out

Active Directory Group Modernization Service

One option for managing groups, post-Exchange Online migration, is to convert all on-premises synchronized distribution groups to cloud-only groups. This allows users to continue managing their groups using the Outlook client and eliminates the need to manage groups in two places.

Microsoft offers a SaaS (Subscription as a Service) platform that allows customers to self-service migrate on-premises synchronized distribution groups into cloud-only groups. This monthly subscription service, called the Active Directory Group Modernization Service (ADGMS), can be enabled for a tenant, and customers can convert groups at their leisure.

A quick overview video with information about ADGMS can be found at *https://www.youtube.com/watch?v=ideXFP20pd8.*

You can learn more about the service by emailing *admsinfo@microsoft.com.*

Dynamic distribution groups

Although dynamic distribution groups are supported in Microsoft 365, they are only supported when created directly in the cloud. On-premises dynamic distribution groups cannot be synchronized to Microsoft 365.

If you have dynamic distribution groups on-premises that you want to show up in Microsoft 365, you can create a mail-enabled contact in Microsoft 365 to provide global address list visibility for the group. Or, you can convert the dynamic group to a static group and manage it as a normal group.

Microsoft 365 groups

Microsoft 365 groups (also known as Office 365, modern, or unified groups) are a new type of group object in Microsoft 365 and do not exist in the on-premises versions of Exchange. If your organization decides to use Microsoft 365 groups, they will exist only in-cloud.

The Group Writeback feature in Azure AD Connect enables you to write a mail-enabled distribution group back on-premises Active Directory to provide global address list visibility to on-premises users for these groups. Group writeback is discussed in detail in Chapter 10, "Installing AAD Connect."

Inside Out

Microsoft 365 Group Writeback Sender Authentication

Azure AD Connect enables you to configure a mail-enabled object to be written on-premises for Microsoft 365 groups. However, the value for msExchRequireAuth-ToSendTo, which controls whether external users may send to an Exchange recipient, supplies the constant TRUE value in the Azure AD Connect attribute transformation. If you have configured Microsoft 365 groups to allow external mail, have enabled group writeback, and have configured your MX record to point to your on-premises environment, external senders attempting to deliver mail to an Microsoft 365 will receive a non-delivery receipt (NDR). To work around this issue, either manually modify the msExchRequireAuthToSendTo attribute for the on-premises object representing the Microsoft 365 group or create an Azure AD Connect rule to populate that attribute manually with FALSE.

Permissions and delegation

Part of the email migration planning exercise is determining the migration schedule. Although it's important to map out the schedule from the perspective of end-user communication, it's also important for another reason: permissions and delegation. It's critical to make an effort to move delegators and delegates together because not all the permissions work cross-premises. Although full mailbox access permissions should work, on-premises users won't be able to exercise certain rights (such as Send-As) against cloud mailboxes and vice versa.

Typically, users are delegated rights to other mailboxes or resources in their own work group or department, so that might be one way to attempt to organize and map out migration groups to preserve permissions and mailbox access.

Public folders

Depending on how long your on-premises Exchange organization has existed, you might have public folders (either older or modern). You can migrate both types of public folders to Microsoft 365. However, just like mailbox migrations, there are several things to check before migration, such as folder uniqueness and proper attribute validation.

The standard IDFix tool does not detect mail-enabled public folders. If you are planning to migrate a significant number of mail-enabled public folders, you might find it helpful to ensure they don't have any invalid characters or improperly formatted SMTP addresses. You can use the script at *https://aka.ms/PFIDFix* to help identify potential problems with your mail-enabled public folders.

NOTE

To properly support the migration of public folders to Exchange Online, you will need the latest version of the Azure AD Connect tool and enable the Exchange Public Folder support feature from the Azure AD Connect Installation Wizard.

Mail routing

Mail routing between on-premises and cloud environments is a crucial component of a migration or coexistence. It is important to ensure that the servers designated for hybrid transport can send to and receive from Exchange Online.

Data loss prevention

Microsoft 365 offers data loss protection features integrated with Exchange Online protection. Data loss prevention templates can be implemented to scan for sensitive data types such as Social Security numbers or credit cards and perform block, notify, redirect, or encrypt actions on those messages.

In addition, your organization might have an existing investment in data loss prevention technologies that meets specific requirements, and you might need to configure Microsoft 365 to route outbound mail through that environment. If that is a requirement, you will most likely use a centralized mail transport configuration, criteria-based routing transport rules, or a combination. For more information about centralized mail transport, see Chapter 13.

Message encryption

Your organization might require you to encrypt messages sent to particular recipients or that contain certain types of data. In these instances, you might need to configure forced-TLS connectors or enable Microsoft 365 message encryption settings. For more information about centralized mail transport, see Chapter 15, "Exchange Online Hybrid Planning and Deployment."

Message hygiene

Most organizations have some sort of message hygiene (anti-spam, anti-malware, or heuristic analysis) products or services configured, either on-premises or hosted by a service provider. Depending on your organization's configuration and investment in those technologies, you might wish to continue using them or transition fully to Exchange Online Protection (EOP).

Although it is possible to configure multiple products for message hygiene in succession, it is not recommended. Exchange Online Protection uses IP reputation (among other technologies and algorithms) to determine whether a sending system is safe. Chaining multiple filtering products can adversely affect the EOP's ability to provide the highest level of service.

Instead, you might consider cataloging rules and filters in your existing system and prepare to configure similar rules and filters in Exchange Online Protection.

Networking

When planning a migration of a core service, such as messaging to an external system, consider how you will connect to that system both during the migration process and as you transition to operational management.

Bandwidth

One of the core questions surrounding network requirements is discovering how much bandwidth your users will consume post-migration. You can use a tool such as the Exchange Client Network Bandwidth Calculator to help estimate your bandwidth based on client profile and location or time zone data.

NOTE
You can download the calculator from *http://bit.ly/3GVKSQx*.

Firewall

For mailbox migrations, free/busy lookups, Autodiscover, and mail transport to work correctly between on-premises and cloud environments, you must work with network administrators to enable the necessary communications.

From the perspective of the Exchange servers configured with hybrid connectivity, you need to set the following:

- Port 25 for inbound communication and outbound for mail transport

- Port 443 inbound for Autodiscover, the Mailbox Replication Service, and free/busy

- Ports 80 and 443 outbound for Exchange Federation and Certificate Revocation List checking

NOTE

For a complete list of hybrid endpoints, see "Microsoft 365 URLs and IP address ranges" at *https://aka.ms/O365Endpoints*.

Load balancing

Many large organizations use either software or hardware load balancers as part of a solution to provide highly available access to services. Load balancers can be configured to work with Microsoft 365. However, there are several things to consider, depending on the version of Exchange used for hybrid transport and mailbox migration.

SSL offloading, termination, or bridging is not supported for Mailbox Replication Service traffic. In addition, for configuring hybrid migration endpoints, it is recommended that you create one-to-one Network Address Translation (NAT) addresses for each server used for mailbox migrations. This provides the most granular method to manage mailbox migration endpoints. If you plan to use load balancers in your Exchange hybrid deployment, review any provided vendor documentation for configuring them with Exchange Server.

Proxy

Microsoft recommends that you bypass proxy environments for Microsoft 365. If your outbound traffic uses proxies, you might experience performance problems or service connection problems when attempting to use Microsoft 365 services.

Typically, proxy services are used either to perform web-filtering requests (to ensure users' traffic conforms to the organization's acceptable usage policy) or to provide caching and accelerate performance for frequently accessed resources. All traffic between on-premises and Microsoft 365 endpoints is encrypted by SSL, so most proxy implementations cannot view or cache the traffic (without sophisticated man-in-the-middle or SSL bridging capabilities).

DNS

Many tasks performed in Microsoft 365 require you to configure specific DNS records to enable or complete service enablement.

Autodiscover

Autodiscover is the service whereby clients (whether they are desktop, web, or mobile clients or remote Exchange systems) locate Exchange resources. For most Microsoft 365 deployments, Autodiscover is configured through a DNS CNAME record that points to either the on-premises Exchange organization (before migration) or Microsoft 365 (post-migration).

Domain verification records

To make a domain available to use in Microsoft 365, you must add it and then confirm ownership with a DNS TXT record. You can find more information about how to configure DNS TXT verification records in Chapter 2, "Deployment milestones."

Microsoft Federation Gateway

When configuring Exchange on-premises to share free/busy information with Exchange Online or other Exchange on-premises organizations or as part of the Hybrid Configuration Wizard, you must confirm ownership of your Exchange organization for the Microsoft Federation Gateway. To streamline the process, you can generate the DNS verification record before running the Hybrid Configuration Wizard.

> **NOTE**
>
> **For more information about configuring DNS records for the Microsoft Federation Gateway, see Chapter 15, "Exchange Online Hybrid Planning and Deployment."**

MX record

The Mail eXchanger (MX) record tells mail transport agents where to route mail. Before migration, your MX record points to either your on-premises mail gateway or, perhaps, a hosted mail gateway service that provides antivirus and antispam services.

Post-migration, it's recommended that you update your MX record to point to Exchange Online Protection.

SPF, DKIM, and DMARC records

These records help prove the authenticity and authority of sending email systems. Although they are not required, it is recommended that you configure them to improve the deliverability of messages to external recipients.

In addition, if you are already using them in your environment, plan to include Microsoft 365 services to ensure that recipients can continue to receive your mail.

For more information about configuring DKIM, see Chapter 18, "Managing Exchange Online."

Network security appliances

In addition to firewalls and proxies, many organizations deploy network security appliances that inspect traffic, looking for suspicious activity. You can deploy intrusion detection systems (IDSs) and intrusion protection systems (IPSs) to monitor, alert, and take action on network traffic based on rules and activity profiles.

In some instances, these can slow or stop the flow of migration activities. Flood mitigation and exfiltration protection are two security appliance features that can cause considerable delays or troubleshooting activities. Depending on the vendor, the exact terminology might vary. However, the features restrict or deny the continued outbound data flow from your on-premises servers to Microsoft 365, detecting the continuous stream of traffic to an off-premises destination as an anomalous activity that might indicate data compromise or theft.

If your organization has deployed these types of devices, you will want to exclude traffic between the hybrid migration endpoints and Microsoft 365 from any policies interrupting the flow of the data migration.

Things that don't migrate

Although the directory synchronization and hybrid migration processes have become increasingly complete, there are still things that don't translate between environments. For example, if you are using third-party tools to migrate from hosted or older systems, you'll need to capture parameters and attributes in the source environment that did not make it to the target system.

Access protocol configuration

Certain mailbox parameters, such as what access protocols are allowed, are not migrated in hybrid or third-party migrations. If you are using CASMailbox settings to control access to ActiveSync, POP3, IMAP, or Exchange Web Services, you will find that those settings do not persist between on-premises and cloud environments.

Calendar processing information

Calendar processing is the set of rules typically applied to shared and resource mailboxes, such as automatic booking, delegates, and scheduling horizons. These settings are not migrated in either hybrid migrations or third-party migrations.

> TIP
>
> **You can build your own method to export and import these properties or use a script such as at *https://aka.ms/CalendarProcessing* to capture and reapply those configurations.**

Forwarding addresses

If you have mailboxes configured with forwarding addresses (ForwardingAddress or ForwardingSmtpAddress), those values are not maintained in either hybrid or third-party migrations.

> TIP
>
> **You can use the script at *https://aka.ms/ForwardingAddress* to export the data from your on-premises environment and reapply it to cloud objects post-migration.**

CHAPTER 14

Retention tags and policies

Retention policy tags and retention policies are not synchronized or transferred between environments automatically. If you are using Exchange retention policy tags on-premises and want to continue using them in Microsoft 365, you must export them from your on-premises environment and import them to Microsoft 365 before migrating mailboxes.

The `Export-RetentionTags.ps1` and `Import-RetentionTags.ps1` scripts are available in `%EXCHANGEINSTALLDIR%\Scripts`.

> ## Inside Out
>
> ### Journaling retention tags
>
> Although journaling as a feature is supported in Microsoft 365 and Exchange Online, retention policies and retention policy tags with journaling cannot be imported. Depending on your version of Exchange, you might need to modify the `Import-RetentionPolicyTags.ps1` script.
>
> To make the necessary changes to the Import-RetentionPolicyTags.ps1 script, locate the lines that contain the following text and comment them out:
>
> - `tagExists.LabelForJournaling`
> - `tagExists.MessageFormatForJournaling`
> - `LabelForJournaling`
> - `MessageFormatForJournaling`

> **NOTE**
>
> You can find more information about exporting and importing retention policy tags at *https://docs.microsoft.com/en-us/exchange/export-and-import-retention-tags-exchange-2013-help*.

Transport rules and configurations

Transport rules and configurations are not migrated between environments. Depending on your organization, these might or might not be necessary. When migrating to Microsoft 365, many organizations take the opportunity to create new rules. However, if your organization has a high degree of customization, you might find it helpful to transfer those settings and then remove what is unnecessary.

In addition, if you are in a position to need to migrate to a new Microsoft 365 tenant, you might need to export and import transport rules as well.

> **TIP**
>
> You can use a script such as those you can find at *https://aka.ms/MigrateEOP* to help with this task—either from on-premises to cloud or between cloud organizations.

Additional tools

In addition to the tools and scripts mentioned in this chapter, Microsoft provides planning, deployment, and troubleshooting tools to help you plan and complete your migration.

Remote Connectivity Analyzer

The Exchange Remote Connectivity Analyzer is a web-based tool that can troubleshoot Autodiscover, free/busy, and mail flow issues and works with both Microsoft 365 and Exchange on-premises deployments.

You can access the tool at *https://testconnectivity.microsoft.com*.

Exchange Deployment Assistant

The Exchange Deployment Assistant is a web-based tool you can use to determine which components you need to install and the steps you need to follow to complete a hybrid migration. The Exchange Deployment Assistant is available at *https://docs.microsoft.com/en-us/exchange/exchange-deployment-assistant*.

What's next?

As you've seen in this chapter, Exchange Online has many similarities to—as well as many differences from—Exchange Server. It's important to understand how the two platforms interact as well as what features are available in both.

In the next chapter, we'll start exploring how to connect an existing on-premises environment with Exchange Online through the configuration of Exchange Hybrid.

CHAPTER 14

Exchange Online hybrid planning and deployment

Most organizations that have been managing on-premises infrastructure and want to move to software-as-a-service offerings (such as Exchange Online) won't be able to pivot and begin using online services immediately. They need to understand the features and capabilities, test the resiliency and features, and plan for coexistence, migration, and user experiences.

Deploying Exchange Online in a hybrid configuration enables you to test the features of Office 365 as well as provide a path to migrate your data and configurations online at a pace that meets your organization's requirements.

This chapter covers architecture and planning for Exchange Online hybrid configurations, enabling the on-premises and cloud infrastructures, migrating mailboxes between the platforms, public folder coexistence and migration, and management.

This chapter is broken down into five topics:

- Overview of Exchange Online hybrid features

- Planning

- Office 365 Hybrid Configuration Wizard

- Mailbox provisioning

- Decommissioning the hybrid environment

Overview of Exchange Online hybrid features

Although the overall architecture of an organization's Exchange on-premises and Exchange Online deployment varies based on technical, security, or business constraints, each organization must identify the components and features it will be using.

Configuring a hybrid environment enables your organization to take advantage of several features, such as the following:

- Secure mail flow between on-premises and cloud environments with a shared namespace

- A unified global address list (GAL) for both on-premises and cloud users

- Free/busy and calendar sharing

- A single Outlook Web Access URL

- Ability to move mailboxes between on-premises and online environments

- Centralized mailbox management and provisioning from the on-premises environment

- Cross-premises mailbox search, MailTips, and message tracking

- Cloud-based archiving for both on-premises and cloud mailboxes

From an architectural perspective, implementing an Exchange Online hybrid configuration is similar to a multi-forest Exchange organization with identity synchronization, permissions delegation, and mail routing concerns. For services to work across environments, you must allow network connectivity between Exchange Online and your organization, manage identity, and provide a way for users to resolve resources in either environment.

The Office 365 Hybrid Configuration Wizard, formerly known as the Exchange Hybrid Configuration Wizard, is an organization-wide Exchange configuration toolset.

INSIDE OUT

Introducing the Hybrid Agent

In addition to the traditional Hybrid Configuration Wizard, there is also a hybrid connectivity option based on Azure App Proxy called Hybrid Agent.

The Hybrid Agent doesn't support all of the features and scalability options as the traditional hybrid route. Some of the Hybrid Agent limitations include:

- Does not support Hybrid Modern Authentication
- Does not support multiple on-premises Exchange organizations
- Does not support multiple migration endpoints
- Does not support cross-premises message tracking and multi-mailbox search
- Does not support SMTP mail flow

If your organization requires these features, the Hybrid Agent is likely unsuitable for your deployment.

The Hybrid Configuration Wizard runs a series of Windows PowerShell commands against both the on-premises Exchange Server configuration and the Office 365 Exchange Online tenant. The Hybrid Configuration Wizard configures organization-level and server-level parameters to support the rich coexistence topology with two key protocols, HTTPS and SMTP, to build the bridge between one or more on-premises Exchange organizations and Exchange Online.

Although many people refer to the server(s) that the Hybrid Configuration Wizard has been run against as "the hybrid servers," there isn't a role for a hybrid server during the Exchange installation process. You can run the Hybrid Configuration Wizard on any server with the appropriate connectivity in the organization, and it can enable or disable the participation of other servers in the hybrid configuration. Only servers with an enabled transport role appear selectable in the Hybrid Configuration Wizard. This role name differs by version: Hub Transport role in Exchange 2010, Client Access Server (CAS) and Mailbox role in Exchange 2013, and Mailbox role in Exchange 2016 and later.

CHAPTER 15

INSIDE OUT

Client access server roles and the Hybrid Configuration Wizard

In previous versions of the Hybrid Configuration Wizard, it was possible to choose which servers participated in the hybrid configuration for transport and mailbox migration functions. When a server was selected for a client access role, the MRSProxy service was enabled on the selected servers for performing mailbox migrations. In very large organizations, the enumeration of client access servers could take hours and lead to timeouts and failures during configuration.

Now the Hybrid Configuration Wizard automatically enables MRSProxy for all eligible client access servers in the organization. The ExternalUrl property on eligible client access servers is populated (Get-WebServicesVirtualDirectory). The Hybrid Configuration Wizard returns a warning if an organization has only a single CAS and the ExternalUrl property is null. If an organization has more than one CAS and the ExternalUrl property on at least one of them is defined, MRSProxy is silently enabled on that server.

Outbound traffic (HTTPS for connections to Exchange Online and HTTP for certificate revocation list checking) must be allowed for every server with the Client Access Server role in Exchange 2010, the Client Access Server and Mailbox roles in Exchange 2013, and the Mailbox role in Exchange 2016. Inbound HTTPS routing for Autodiscover and mailbox migration requests can be directed to specific servers as a function of the DNS and load-balancing configuration.

The most critical planning topics are Autodiscover, free/busy, mail flow and transport, public folders, and cross-premises access.

Planning

Before implementing a hybrid configuration, ensure that your environment meets all the basic requirements and notify your network team of any changes that might need to be made. In addition, some organizations have strict requirements around configuring endpoints for access to the Internet, so you might also need to work with your organization's security team to ensure that your deployment meets both the operational and security requirements of the business.

General

One of the most often overlooked planning steps in an Exchange Online hybrid configuration is ensuring your environment meets the prerequisites. Please refer to Chapter 14, "Exchange Online overview," for details on minimum software versions and other important server and networking prerequisites.

Autodiscover

Clients use the Autodiscover service to locate mailboxes. Clients can be users or servers querying on their behalf. The best practice for Exchange deployments is to update the Autodiscover configuration to point to the newest version of Exchange to enable the newest feature set and ensure the widest compatibility. When designing a hybrid solution, the best-practice recommendation is no different. If you are deploying a newer version of Exchange into your environment than currently exists, it is recommended to update Autodiscover to use the newer version of Exchange.

For more information about Autodiscover, see Chapter 10.

Azure Active Directory Connect

To synchronize mailboxes as mail-enabled users to Office 365 as well as perform the necessary writeback of Exchange hybrid permissions, you must install and configure Azure Active Directory Connect (Azure AD Connect or AAD Connect).

For information about how to deploy and configure AAD Connect, please review Chapter 9, "Identity and authentication planning," and Chapter 10, "Installing AAD Connect." For additional information about configuring permissions delegation for Azure AD Connect scenarios, see *https://aka.ms/aadpermissions*.

Cross-premises access and delegation

Cross-premises access is the ability to continue to access a mailbox as an additional resource after it has been moved to Exchange Online. Currently, only the Full Access mailbox permission is supported for a migrated mailbox when an on-premises mailbox accesses it.

Other permissions, such as Send As, Receive As, or Send on Behalf Of, are not supported in a cross-premises scenario. Delegation using the Microsoft Outlook client is also not supported cross-premises. Office 365 Dedicated and International Traffic in Arms (ITAR) (vNext) environments are the exception because they support additional functionality more closely aligned with an Exchange resource forest model.

When mailboxes are moved to Exchange Online, most permissions and delegation of those mailboxes are also moved. Careful analysis of who to move with whom is required so certain things don't break, such as cross-premises access or delegation. For instance, if you move an executive to Office 365 Exchange Online and do not move the executive's assistant, and the executive's assistant has delegated calendar rights to the executive's calendar, that breaks their connection temporarily. For that reason, they should be in the same migration batch and migrated together.

TIP

Mailbox permissions are typically translated to Office 365 during properly batched hybrid MRS moves. However, there are still scenarios in which permissions must be audited on-premises and reapplied after migration. Permission auditing and reapplication require third-party migration tools or non-inherited permissions, such as when granting Send As to a distribution group. In these instances, it's best to back up permissions before migrations start and then reapply them if necessary post-migration.

DNS

Successful Exchange Online hybrid environment configuration requires adding records to your organization's external DNS. All domains to be shared between Exchange Online and Exchange on-premises must be verified in the Office 365 tenant, which is accomplished by a DNS TXT record. Federation also requires external DNS records to prove domain ownership.

Email address policies and proxy addresses

The Exchange hybrid configuration process updates the email address policies of domains selected to be shared between the on-premises and online environments. After the email address policy update, users configured to inherit email address policies are updated.

Because updating proxy addresses can greatly impact your address book (and, subsequently, offline address book downloads), you might want to manually perform the email address policy and proxy address templates. If the Hybrid Configuration Wizard detects that the policies have been updated, that step will be skipped.

TIP

Email address policies and proxy addresses can be updated manually:

- The default email address policy format is `<alias>@<tenant>.mail.onmicrosoft.com` or by using a script (see *https://aka.ms/UpdateEAPs*).

- The proxy address can also be updated using a script (see *https://aka.ms/AddTenantProxy*) or by adding a rule to AAD Connect (see *https://aka.ms/NewAADConnectRuleAddProxy*).

Exchange Server Deployment Assistant

The Microsoft Exchange Server Deployment Assistant is a web-based tool that you can use to build a roadmap or checklist of tasks to complete for a number of Exchange server configurations, including hybrid, based on your organization's existing topology and business requirements. It asks several questions about your current infrastructure and then prescribes a set of general steps to follow to complete the configuration. You can find the Microsoft Exchange Server Deployment Assistant at *http://aka.ms/exdeploy*.

Exchange server versions

A hybrid configuration can be performed with on-premises Exchange servers from 2003 and later. However, there are certain coexistence requirements based on your deployed version of Exchange. See Table 15-1 for a version support matrix.

Table 15-1   Supported Exchange server versions

Minimum Exchange version	Minimum hybrid configuration version based on Exchange coexistence
Exchange 2003	Exchange 2010 coexistence required. Exchange 2013 or Exchange 2016 are not options because they cannot be installed in a forest with Exchange 2003 present.
Exchange 2007	Exchange 2010 coexistence or Exchange 2013 if OAuth is required. Exchange 2016 is not an option.
Exchange 2003 and Exchange 2007	Exchange 2010 coexistence required. Exchange 2013 and Exchange 2016 are not options because they cannot be installed in a forest with Exchange 2003 or earlier present in the forest.
Exchange 2007 with Exchange 2010	No additional version requirements unless OAuth is required. If OAuth is necessary, deployment with Exchange 2013 is required. Exchange 2016 is not an option because it cannot be installed in a forest with Exchange 2007 or earlier present in the forest.
Exchange 2010	No additional version requirements unless OAuth is required. If OAuth is necessary, deployment with Exchange 2013 or Exchange 2016 is required.
Exchange 2013	No version requirement. Use existing topology.
Exchange 2016	No version requirement. Use existing topology.
Exchange 2019	No version requirement. Use existing topology.

Free/busy and hybrid authentication

Free/busy is the ability to check calendar availability for one or more users or resources. Free/busy endpoints are located through the availability service, looking by default for the Autodiscover endpoint. For more information about the Autodiscover service, refer to Chapter 10.

Depending on the versions of Exchange in the environment, the Hybrid Configuration Wizard might allow the configuration of two free/busy lookup methods: OAuth (Open Authorization) and DAuth (Delegated Authentication).

Delegated authentication occurs when a network service accepts a request from a user, obtains a token to act on behalf of that user, and then initiates a new connection to a second network service on behalf of the user. OAuth is an authorization mechanism whereby a third-party application or service accesses a user's data without the user providing credentials.

Exchange 2010 uses DAuth to facilitate the server-to-server communication required for free/busy lookups. Environments that include only Exchange 2013 or later can use OAuth in addition to DAuth to provide authentication for additional features. Table 15-2 explains which authentication configurations are available, configured as part of the Hybrid Configuration Wizard, and require additional configuration.

Table 15-2   Hybrid configuration DAuth and OAuth options

Versions	DAuth	OAuth
Exchange Server 2003/2007/2010	Part of Hybrid Configuration Wizard Configuration	Not available
Exchange Server 2007/2010/2013	Part of Hybrid Configuration Wizard Configuration	Manual configuration
Exchange Server 2010/2013/2016	Part of Hybrid Configuration Wizard Configuration	Manual configuration
Exchange Server 2013/2016	Part of Hybrid Configuration Wizard Configuration	Part of Hybrid Configuration Wizard Configuration
Exchange Server 2013	Part of Hybrid Configuration Wizard Configuration	Part of Hybrid Configuration Wizard Configuration
Exchange Server 2016	Part of Hybrid Configuration Wizard Configuration	Part of Hybrid Configuration Wizard Configuration

CHAPTER 15

Inside Out

Manual OAuth configuration

OAuth configuration is required if advanced features such as Messaging Records Management (MRM), In-Place eDiscovery, and cross-premises archiving are required. You can learn about the process to enable OAuth by following the steps located in this article:

"Configure OAuth Authentication Between Exchange and Exchange Online Organizations" at *https://technet.microsoft.com/en-us/library/dn594521(v=exchg.150).aspx*

This configuration process requires Windows PowerShell and the ability to connect to Exchange on-premises, Exchange Online, and Azure Active Directory.

If you have already configured OAuth and are experiencing issues or want to learn about potential problems you might encounter, you can review the information at *https://aka.ms/oauthtroubleshooting.*

For an in-depth look at the hybrid authentication flow, see *https://aka.ms/hybridauth.*

As Table 15-2 shows, DAuth is always configured. This means the administrator must configure at least one federated domain proof prior to running the Hybrid Configuration Wizard or during the Hybrid Configuration Wizard process. If you do not create a federated trust prior and add a domain proof, it will be done as part of the Hybrid Configuration Wizard process. Configuring a domain proof (either before or during the Hybrid Configuration Wizard) requires the ability to add an external DNS text record.

The Azure Active Directory Authentication Service is a trust broker between two federated Exchange organizations. Configuration of the federation trust is required to enable sharing free/busy information. Because each organization's federation trust is configured with the Azure Active Directory Authentication Service, it can be used to enable federated sharing with other organizations using Exchange on-premises or Exchange Online.

Organization relationships contain the parameters for free/busy in Exchange on-premises and Exchange Online; specify which domains are part of the configuration and the target endpoint to resolve the free/busy query.

When planning free/busy for your organization, you must enable network access to the endpoints for free/busy lookup. Your organization might require exchanging availability information with other organizations, which can be managed with additional organization relationships. If you attempt to federate with an organization already in Exchange Online, you must configure additional organization relationships to create a mesh topology.

NOTE

The architecture of a hybrid mesh can be found on the Exchange Team Blog at *https://aka.ms/hybridmesh.*

Message sizes

The Mailbox Replication Service migration method enables you to migrate individual messages up to 150 MB. If you will be migrating mail with third-party tools or have items larger than 150 MB, review the number of messages exceeding the threshold. You can use the following PowerShell cmdlet to retrieve large items:

```
Get-Mailbox -Resultsize Unlimited | Get-MailboxFolderStatistics -IncludeAnalysis `
-FolderScope All | Where-Object {(($_.TopSubjectSize -Match "MB") -and `
(($_.TopSubjectSize).ToString().Split(" ")[0] -GE 150.0)) -or `
($_.TopSubjectSize -Match "GB")} | Select-Object Identity, TopSubject, TopSubjectSize
```

Some third-party tools may use Exchange Web Services to migrate content. If EWS is used, then the threshold for migrations is 35MB. To capture items larger than 35MB, modify the cmdlet to run with these parameters:

```
Get-Mailbox -Resultsize Unlimited | Get-MailboxFolderStatistics -IncludeAnalysis `
-FolderScope All | Where-Object {(($_.TopSubjectSize -Match "MB") -and `
(($_.TopSubjectSize).ToString().Split(" ")[0] -GE 35.0)) -or ($_.TopSubjectSize `
-Match "GB")} | Select-Object Identity, TopSubject, TopSubjectSize
```

Mail transport

Planning for mail transport is essential to the overall hybrid deployment process. By default, the hybrid configuration enables secure mail between on-premises and cloud environments by creating inbound and outbound connectors in Exchange Online and either creating new or modifying existing connectors in your Exchange on-premises environment. Mail originating from the Internet is delivered to the host listed in your organization's MX record (whether the record points to your on-premises environment or Exchange Online). Then, Exchange continues to route the mail to its final destination, relaying over the hybrid mail flow connectors to reach recipients in the connected environments.

Mail originating in Office 365 and Exchange Online is routed, by default, out to the MX hosts for recipient organizations. Mail originating on-premises continues to egress through the existing configuration. This configuration is suitable for most organizations, but you might have other requirements, depending on your business or security posture.

If your organizations have Exchange Server 2013 or later Edge Transport servers, they can be configured during the hybrid configuration, if desired, although they add complexity to the overall solution. They will require manual configuration if you plan to use Exchange Server 2010 Edge Transport servers.

CHAPTER 15

NOTE

You can find specific instructions for Exchange Server 2010 Edge Transport servers in the Exchange Deployment Assistant at *http://aka.ms/exdeploy.*

Centralized mail transport (CMT) is a mail routing architecture that routes all outbound mail from Office 365 through the on-premises environment. Centralized mail transport (also referred to as central mail flow or centralized mail) is frequently used when organizations must apply additional processing to outbound mail. Such requirements might include the following:

- On-premises data loss prevention (DLP) systems

- On-premises encryption gateways

The physical and logical network requirements for either standard or centralized mail transport are the same (both requiring inbound and outbound port 25 between your transport servers and Exchange Online Protection). A criteria-based routing rule must be configured separately if centralized mail transport is enabled, but a specific domain needs a different path.

Interruption of the SMTP/TLS mail flow between Exchange Online and the Exchange onpremises systems with a third-party appliance is not supported. Breaking the TLS handshake results in the messages being seen as "out of organization" and might prevent name resolution of user email addresses when displayed in Outlook or cause automatic resource booking requests to fail.

Suppose your organization will be configuring a hybrid environment by using Exchange Server 2010 hub transport servers behind a network address translation (NAT) device. In that case, you might need to plan to modify the Office 365 receive connector on each hub/transport server to include the IP address of the device performing the translation.

Networking

Configuring a hybrid Exchange Online environment has the following network requirements:

- Exchange on-premises servers that will be configured for mail transport must have inbound and outbound access on port 25 to Exchange Online Protection (see *http://aka.ms/o365endpoints*) with no pre-authentication, Secure Sockets Layer (SSL) offloading, or packet inspection.

- Exchange on-premises servers with the Client Access Server role must be accessible (at a minimum) from Exchange Online over port 443 to resolve Autodiscover requests for free/busy and to perform mailbox moves.

Public folders

Many organizations have deployed public folders on-premises. If your organization has deployed them on-premises and needs to maintain them, plan for hybrid connectivity to public folders and, potentially, a migration to Exchange Online modern public folders. Both hybrid coexistence and migration are covered later in this chapter.

Public folders can be enabled in a hybrid fashion (so that cloud users can access on-premises public folders). This can be configured immediately to provide continued access to the public folder data throughout a migration. It is recommended to migrate public folders last.

Hybrid public folder configuration is relatively straightforward and requires a working organization relationship. Hybrid public folders rely on the organization relationship created during the Hybrid Configuration Wizard.

Office 365 Hybrid Configuration Wizard

The Office 365 Hybrid Configuration Wizard is a tool that configures one or more on-premises organizations to connect to Office 365. It simplifies configuring federation and secure mail flow and enabling your on-premises environment for mailbox migrations.

Starting in September 2015, the product group released the third version of the Hybrid Configuration Wizard, rebranding it the Office 365 Hybrid Configuration Wizard. The new Office 365 Hybrid Configuration Wizard is now hosted in the Office 365 service, and the most recent configuration updates are downloaded and used each time the wizard is run.

Overview

The Office 365 Hybrid Configuration Wizard itself has been improved in many ways:

- **Version-agnostic hybrid experience**   Before this release, the hybrid configuration experience depended on the specific Exchange Server version, service pack, cumulative update, or roll-up. Hosting the engine in the service automatically applies the latest version and features to the configuration. The new wizard is no longer tied to the Exchange update release cycle, so updates based on best practices and user feedback can be integrated with the process more quickly.

  ### TIP

  You can open the Hybrid Configuration Wizard from the Exchange admin center or by going directly to *http://aka.ms/hybridwizard*.

- **Early access for First Release customers**   Another benefit of a stand-alone, web-based distribution method is the ability to pilot specific versions as needed. The First Release version is available at *http://aka.ms/taphcw*.

CHAPTER 15

- **Enhanced error handling and logging**   Logging detail has been updated and is easier to understand. The wizard now has more information per phase and task, error codes that map to specific errors, a specific error-handling option code (HCW8****), and access to log files in %appdata%\Microsoft\ExchangeHybridConfiguration by using a shortcut. Diagnostic information can be accessed by pressing F12 during the wizard. This F12 function also enables launching dedicated Windows PowerShell consoles connected to both Exchange on-premises and Exchange Online, each with a different color background to make it easier to differentiate between the two environments.

- **Telemetry**   By default, every execution of the Hybrid Configuration Wizard uploads the logs for analysis. Uploading logs provides the team invaluable insight into the running of the configuration wizard and helps the team diagnose and fix issues faster than ever before. Uploading logs can be disabled using a registry key if required.

- **Multiple hybrid scenarios**   The Hybrid Configuration Wizard can be used to configure any of the supported hybrid scenarios, including Full, Minimal, and Hybrid Agent configurations.

The Hybrid Configuration Wizard enables the following features over HTTPS for coexistence:

- Free/busy between the two (or more) Exchange organizations by using OAuth and Intra-Organization connectors or the Azure Active Directory authentication service.

- Mailbox migrations using the Mailbox Replication Service Proxy (MRSProxy). In conjunction with the synchronization of the Exchange Mailbox GUID by AAD Connect, MRS-based mailbox moves preserve the user's Outlook Offline Storage (OST) file and allows for automatic post-migration profile configuration. This feature also provides offboarding from Office 365 if needed.

- MailTips to display important informative messages (such as data loss prevention-related tips or out-of-office messages) during message composition.

- Cross-premises E-discovery search, Exchange Online Archiving, and Messaging Records Management policy cross-premises, using OAuth configuration.

- Outlook Web Access redirection to Office 365 from on-premises Outlook Web Access using organization relationship settings.

The Hybrid Configuration Wizard enables secure SMTP mail flow using one of the following methods (depending on the versions of the Exchange servers involved in hybrid transport):

- TLS-secured transport using certificates between Exchange Server 2013 or Exchange Server 2016 and Exchange Online

- TLS-secured transport between Exchange Server 2010 and Exchange Online, using remote domains and remote IP address ranges and certificates

The Hybrid Configuration Wizard also enables these features regardless of the Exchange version:

- Message tracking records messages to and from the on-premises and online Exchange organizations.

- Accepted domains/remote domains and email address policies configured to support hybrid mail flow by using *tenant.mail.onmicrosoft.com*.

TIP

The Hybrid Configuration engine is the component that runs the actual configuration. A number of server-, domain-, and organization-level changes are performed in both the Exchange on-premises and Exchange Online environments.

The components modified by the Hybrid Configuration engine are detailed in Table 15-3.

Table 15-3   Hybrid Configuration engine architecture

On-premises Exchange organization			Exchange Online organization	
Exchange server	**Domain**	**Organization**	**Domain**	**Organization**
Mailbox Replication Service Proxy	Accepted domains	Exchange federation trust	Accepted domains	Exchange federation trust
Certificates	Remote domains	Organization relationship	Remote domains	Organization relationship
Exchange Web Services virtual directories	Email address policies	Availability address space		Inbound and outbound connector
Receive connector		Send connector		Migration endpoint
		OAuth configuration		OAuth configuration

The engine runs through the following task sequence when you run the Hybrid Configuration Wizard:

1. The wizard runs `Get-HybridConfiguration` cmdlet, starting the process.

2. The hybrid configuration engine examines the stored desired state from the hybrid configuration object stored in Active Directory. The values are null if the Hybrid Configuration Wizard has not been run previously. If the wizard has been run before, values retrieved from the hybrid configuration object are populated.

3. Changes made during the navigation of the wizard are stored in memory as the new desired state configuration.

4. The hybrid configuration engine runs a discovery process against the on-premises Exchange organization, checking the current topology and configuration.

5. The hybrid configuration engine runs a discovery process against the Exchange Online organization, checking the current topology and configuration.

6. The current state and new desired state are compared, and any differences are applied using `Set-HybridConfiguration`. The engine runs the specific tasks to establish the new desired state.

As you work through the wizard, no changes are made to the system. If you cancel the wizard before clicking Update, no changes will be made. After the updates have been set in the configuration object and you have clicked the Update button, the desired state configuration is applied. If the desired state matches the existing state, no changes occur.

Prerequisites

The minimum architecture required to use the Office 365 Hybrid Configuration Wizard varies by Exchange version:

- Exchange 2016 and later requires a mailbox server role because the roles have been combined in the most recent Exchange version.

- Exchange 2013 requires the Client Access and Mailbox Server roles; although they can be split between separate servers, deploying them on the same server is recommended.

- Exchange 2010 requires the Client Access Server role and the Hub Transport role. The mailbox server role is required if the Exchange 2010 environment coexists with an Exchange 2003 environment.

The Hybrid Configuration Wizard also requires an Office 365 Global Admin account as well as an account that has been granted the Exchange Organization Management role.

There is no sizing guide for Office 365 Hybrid Configuration Wizard because it is simply a tool to configure features already present in Exchange Server. It updates your organization's configuration parameters and extends them to the cloud. Use the Microsoft Exchange Server Role Requirements calculator located at *http://aka.ms/exchangecalc*. Calculate using the existing or projected maximum number of users in the organization and follow the published calculator guidance.

NOTE

You can find more information about the release announcement of the updated Office 365 Hybrid Configuration Wizard at *https://aka.ms/hcwstandalone.*

Inside Out

Exchange management servers

When migrating from a third-party mail platform, most organizations don't have an on-premises Exchange server. Some organizations haven't even deployed Active Directory but might deploy it so they can synchronize with Azure Active Directory and provision Exchange Online mailboxes. If you have a greenfield environment or an environment that has never had Exchange, you can use the tool at *https://aka.ms/ConfigExMgmtNode* to configure the default attributes for deploying Exchange in your environment before running the Hybrid Configuration Wizard.

The only supported method to manage the Active Directory attributes for users synchronized through AAD Connect is to use the Exchange admin center or Exchange Management Shell with an on-premises Exchange Server. Remote mailbox provisioning and MRS mailbox moves between cloud and on-premises use the `targetAddress` attribute to determine mailbox location. Outlook for on-premises mailbox users uses the `targetAddress` attribute data to redirect the client to Office 365. The Hybrid Configuration Wizard configures email address policies for all domains included in the hybrid domain selection and updates the proxy addresses for all users with `EmailAddressPolicyEnabled` set to `True` with a proxy address of `<alias@tenant.mail.onmicrosoft.com>`.

Many organizations migrating from third-party mail systems might not require a full hybrid configuration and can use the express hybrid migration option. Express hybrid configures the addressing components for the Exchange organization, such as email address policy and accepted domains, and enables the MRS proxy. Regardless of the type of hybrid configuration being deployed, the on-premises environment still requires a supported version of Exchange Server.

Installing the Office 365 Hybrid Configuration Wizard

As previously mentioned, the Office 365 Hybrid Configuration Wizard is a stand-alone tool with components downloaded on the server from where it is run. Because the tool checks for updates each time it is launched, the server requires Internet access to complete the configuration.

TIP

You can disable sending Microsoft telemetry for the Hybrid Configuration wizard by creating a new REG_DWORD value named `DisableUploadLogs` **with a value of** `1` **under** `HKEY_LOCAL_MACHINE\SOFTWARE\Microsoft\ExchangeServer\v15\Update-HybridConfiguration` **(for Exchange 2013) or** `HKEY_LOCAL_MACHINE\SOFTWARE\Microsoft\ExchangeServer\v16\Update-HybridConfiguration` **(for Exchange 2016 or later).**

Follow these steps:

1. Log in to an Exchange server in your organization. It does not have to be one that will be included in the hybrid configuration.

2. Launch the Hybrid Configuration Wizard through one of the three methods.

3. For any version of Exchange, open a browser and navigate to *http://aka.ms/hybridwizard*.

4. For Exchange Server 2013 or later, launch the Exchange admin center, navigate to the hybrid node, and click Configure.

5. For any version of Exchange, log on to the Office 365 admin center, navigate to the Classic Exchange admin center, select the Hybrid node, and then click the Configure button located under the Exchange Hybrid Deployment text, as shown in Figure 15-1.

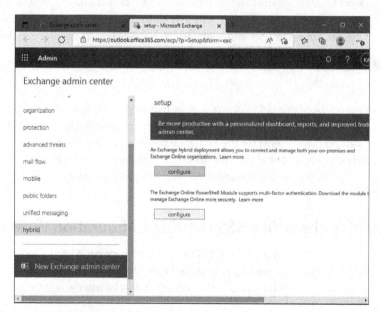

Figure 15-1   Exchange hybrid setup page

6. After clicking Configure, click Open to download and run the `Microsoft.Online.CSE.Hybrid.Client.application` file.

7. After the process launches, click the Install button. If you've already installed the Hybrid Configuration Wizard before, you can launch it by clicking the desktop shortcut. If a newer version is available, you are prompted to update. Click Yes if prompted. After the installation is complete, the configuration wizard launches automatically.

8. Click Cancel to close the configuration portion of the wizard.

Running the Office 365 Hybrid Configuration Wizard

Before starting the configuration, review the configuration settings described in Table 15-4 to understand which configuration option (Minimal, Express, Full) configures the features necessary for your environment.

Table 15-4   Office 365 Hybrid Configuration Wizard selection options

Hybrid features	Minimal	Express	Full
Email Address Policy and Domain Configuration	Yes	Yes	Yes
Send and Receive Connector Configuration	No	No	Yes
OAuth Configuration	No	No	Yes (Exchange version-dependent)
Federation Trust and Organization Relationship	No	No	Yes
MRS Endpoint Configuration	Yes	Yes	Yes
AAD Connect in Express Configuration	No	Yes	No

Inside Out

Exchange Federation Trust

In previous versions of the Hybrid Configuration Wizard, a Federation Trust was configured between the on-premises environment and the Microsoft Federation Gateway.

As of the March 2020 update, the federation trust is no longer configured unless there are Exchange 2010 servers present in the environment.

If you still have Exchange 2010 servers, you can pre-create the trust to optimize the configuration time. During the Hybrid Configuration Wizard, you are asked to configure DNS records to prove ownership of your domains for the federation trust. Depending on your organization's change control process or access to external DNS, you might choose to configure those records before the actual Hybrid Configuration Wizard. Otherwise, you must wait to complete the Hybrid Configuration Wizard until those records (proofs) have been added to DNS.

If the federation trust has already been completed, the Enable Federation Trust page is suppressed in the Hybrid Configuration Wizard. Also, a Hybrid Domains selection page appears, displaying the list of accepted on-premises domains verified in the Office 365 tenant.

Follow these steps to enable the federation trust before running the Hybrid Configuration Wizard:

1. Launch the Exchange Management Shell and then run the following commands to create a self-signed certificate, create the federation trust, and generate domain proof values for all of the organization's accepted domains:

```
$ski = [System.Guid]::NewGuid().ToString("N")
New-ExchangeCertificate -FriendlyName "Exchange Federated `
Delegation" -DomainName $env:USERDNSDOMAIN -Services Federation `
-KeySize 2048 -PrivateKeyExportable $true -SubjectKeyIdentifier $ski
Get-ExchangeCertificate | ?{$_.friendlyname -eq "Exchange Federated `
Delegation"} | New-FederationTrust -Name "Microsoft Federation Gateway"
Get-AcceptedDomain | % { Get-FederatedDomainProof -DomainName `
$_.DomainName.ToString() | Select DomainName,Proof } | FL
```

2. For each domain entry, create a TXT record containing the value of the associated proof.

3. After DNS proofs have been created, you can run the wizard again to complete the federation configuration or use Set-FederatedOrganizationIdentifier.

   To use Set-FederatedOrganizationIdentifier, select the primary domain for your organization for the AccountNameSpace parameter or use the command as displayed to select the first domain that appears in Get-AcceptedDomain:

```
Set-FederatedOrganizationIdentifier -DelegationFederationTrust `
"Microsoft Federation Gateway" -AccountNamespace `
(Get-AcceptedDomain)[0].DomainName.ToString() -Enabled $True
```

4. Use Add-FederatedDomain to add the domains to the federation trust. You can specify your domains individually with the -DomainName parameter or use the following command example to add all your accepted domains:

```
Get-AcceptedDomain | % { Add-FederatedDomain -DomainName `
$_.DomainName.ToString() }
```

After deciding which options to select for the Hybrid Configuration Wizard, double-click Microsoft Office 365 Configuration Wizard on the Exchange Server desktop to begin the configuration process. Follow these steps to complete the wizard:

1. On the Office 365 Hybrid Configuration Wizard launch page, click Next.

2. On the On-Premises Exchange Server Organization configuration page, shown in Figure 15-2, the wizard determines the optimal Exchange server to use for the configuration process.

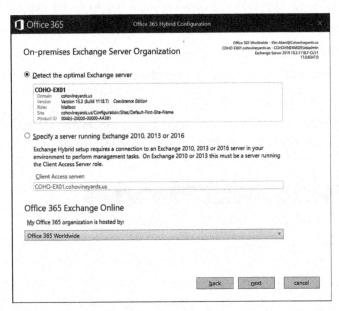

Figure 15-2   Selecting the on-premises Exchange server

3. If you prefer to use a specific server, select the Specify A Server Running Exchange 2010, 2013, Or 2016 button and then enter the fully qualified Client Access Server domain name.

4. From the Office 365 Exchange Online dropdown, select the appropriate Office 365 hosting organization. For most organizations, this is Office 365 Worldwide. Other options include

   - Office 365 (Legacy Login)

   - Office 365 China (formerly listed as 21ViaNet)

- Office 365 Germany

- Office 365 Germany (Legacy Login)

- Office 365 U.S. Government GCC High

- Office 365 U.S. Government DoD

- Office 365 Airgap

5. If you're unsure which Office 365 instance you're hosted in, check with your reseller or look at your license information.

6. Click Next to continue.

   For the Hybrid Configuration Wizard to complete successfully, credentials for both the Exchange on-premises and Exchange Online environments must be supplied, as shown in Figure 15-3. If the Use Current Windows check box is selected, the currently logged-on account will be used to connect to Exchange on-premises. The account must be an organization administrator to complete the on-premises configuration and must be a local administrator on each server that will be configured.

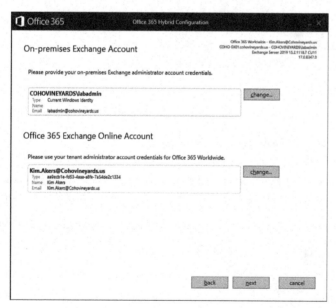

Figure 15-3   Office 365 Hybrid Configuration Wizard account selection

7. If necessary, click the Sign In button under Office 365 Exchange Online Account and enter an Office 365 Global Admin account credential.

8. After both sets of credentials have been entered, as shown in Figure 15-3, click Next.

9. The Office 365 Hybrid Configuration Wizard tests connectivity using the provided credentials on the Gathering Configuration Information page. If successful, information for both the on-premises and online environment is collected, as shown in Figure 15-4.

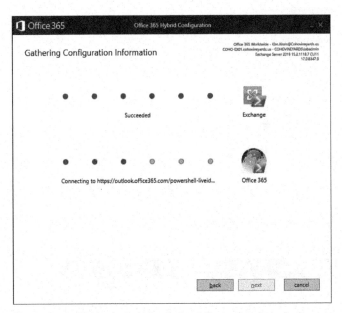

Figure 15-4   Gathering configuration information from Exchange environments

10. Click Next.

11. On the Hybrid Features page, select the appropriate hybrid features set. Full Hybrid configuration is recommended for most installations. Select the Full Hybrid Configuration button (shown in Figure 15-5) and click Next.

12. On the Hybrid Topology page, select the appropriate topology configuration. It is recommended to use the Exchange Classic Hybrid Topology. See Figure 15-6.

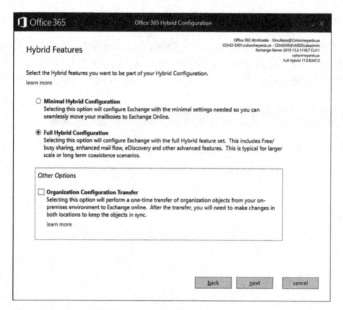

Figure 15-5   Hybrid features selection

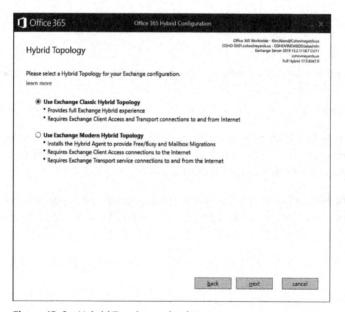

Figure 15-6   Hybrid Topology selection page

13. If prompted, configure the Web Services Virtual Directory. If you need to change the external web services directory URL, update it, click the Update Virtual Directory button, shown in Figure 15-7, and then click Next.

Figure 15-7   Updating the Web Services Virtual Directory

14. On the On-premises Account For Migration page, click Enter to add an on-premises credential that will be used to create the migration endpoint. You can use the same account you used earlier in the wizard to connect to the on-premises organization.

15. On the Hybrid Configuration page, you can select what type of mail transport options you will use. The default option, Configure My Client Access And Mailbox Servers For Secure Mail Transport (Typical), is recommended. If you need to enable Centralized Mail Transport, click Advanced to show the option and then select the Enable Centralized Mail Transport box, as shown in Figure 15-8. Click Next when ready.

Figure 15-8   Configuring mail transport options

INSIDE OUT

Edge transport server and Centralized Mail Flow

If your configuration requires using edge transport servers, keep these important things in mind:

- Although you can select edge transport servers in the Hybrid Configuration Wizard, one additional step must still be performed on each edge transport server after completing the wizard. From the Exchange Management Shell on each edge transport server, run the appropriate command, depending if you are connecting to Office 365 Worldwide or U.S. Government deployments:

```
Set-ReceiveConnector -Identity "Edge\Default Internal Receive Connector"
-TlsDomainCapabilities mail.protection.outlook.com:AcceptOOrgProtocol
-FQDN <Edge Server FQDN>

Set-ReceiveConnector -Identity "Edge\Default Internal Receive Connector"
-TlsDomainCapabilities mail.protection.office365.us:AcceptOOrgProtocol
-FQDN <Edge Server FQDN>
```

- Hybrid configurations with edge transport servers require Edge Transport Server Sync to be configured. For more information about Edge Transport Server Sync, see *https://aka.ms/edgesubscriptions*.

- The Edge Transport server certificate must be exported from the edge servers and imported into the machine certificate store of a reference Exchange server. When importing the certificate and configuring SMTP, make sure to select No when prompted to overwrite the default self-signed certificate. After selecting Edge Transport Configuration in the Hybrid Configuration Wizard, you are prompted to select the reference server where the Edge certificate has been imported.

If your organization configuration requires Centralized Transport, all mail flow (between cloud mailboxes or cloud and on-premises mailboxes) will be sent across the hybrid mail flow connector, which will significantly increase the amount of traffic across your hybrid environment.

16. On the Receive Connector Configuration page, select which servers will be configured to receive mail from Exchange Online. If you select servers running Exchange Server 2013 or later, the Hybrid Configuration Wizard modifies the default receive connector to support hybrid mail transport. If you select servers running Exchange Server 2010, the Hybrid Configuration Wizard creates a new receive connector.

17. After selecting servers, click Next.

TIP

The servers selected must be able to receive mail from the Exchange Online Protection IP address ranges. For more information about the Exchange Online Protection endpoints, see *http://aka.ms/o365endpoints*.

18. On the Send Connector Configuration page, select one or more servers to be used to host the send connector to Exchange Online. If you are configuring Exchange Server 2013 or later, the server must be configured with the Mailbox role. If you are configuring Exchange Server 2010, the server must have the Hub Transport role.

TIP

The servers selected must be able to connect on port 25 to the Exchange Online Protection IP address ranges and will be responsible for relaying mail to the *tenant.mail.onmicrosoft.com* address space. For more information about the Exchange Online Protection endpoints, see *http://aka.ms/o365endpoints*.

19. On the Transport Certificate page, select the third-party certificate that will secure mail (see Figure 15-9) and click Next.

TIP

This certificate must be installed on all servers involved in mail transport to or from Exchange Online.

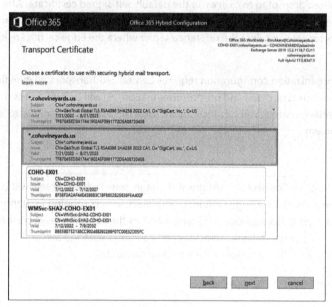

Figure 15-9   Office 365 Hybrid Configuration, Transport Certificate page

20. On the Organization FQDN page, enter the fully qualified name for the on-premises mail hosts that will be sending to Exchange Online. The name entered must match a name in either the Subject or Subject Alternative Name field on the transport certificate. If you selected a wildcard certificate, enter a name valid for the certificate domain. The name entered must be resolvable on the Internet. Click Next when finished.

21. On the Ready For Update page, click Update.

22. The Office 365 Hybrid Configuration Wizard runs the necessary configuration steps. During the configuration process, a progress meter and information about the current task appear (see Figure 15-10). If you click the Stop button, the wizard stops the configuration process, but no changes will be rolled back.

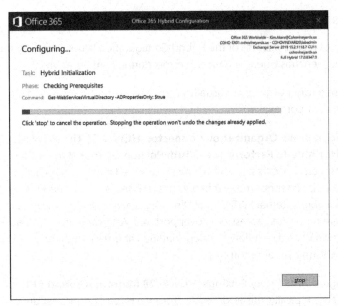

Figure 15-10   Hybrid Configuration Wizard processing changes

23. After the Office 365 Hybrid Configuration has been completed, a final screen appears so you can rate the experience and provide feedback if desired. Click Close to complete the wizard.

When the Hybrid Configuration Wizard has been completed successfully, you are ready to route mail between your on-premises and cloud environments, migrate mailboxes, and configure public folders.

Rerunning the Hybrid Configuration Wizard

After the initial hybrid configuration, there are four instances when the Hybrid Configuration Wizard needs to be run again:

- Adding or removing transport servers

- Adding or removing hybrid domains

- Changing between standard and centralized mail flow

- Updating the transport certificate

The Hybrid Configuration Wizard does not need to be run after updates, roll-ups, or cumulative updates are applied unless otherwise specified in the update.

Once you complete the Hybrid Configuration Wizard with the Full Hybrid Configuration option, you can no longer select Minimal Hybrid Configuration on subsequent runs of the application.

CHAPTER 15

Troubleshooting

While the most recent versions of the Hybrid Configuration Wizard are very robust and reliable, there may be scenarios where you receive errors during configuration.

Most of these errors, however, are usually pretty easy to troubleshoot and are usually linked to DNS resolution or port availability:

- **Configure Intra-Organization Connector–HCW8064 The HCW Has Completed, But Was Not Able To Perform The OAuth Portion Of Your Hybrid Configuration**   Typically, this error occurs because the name specified in the public-facing URL EWS Virtual Directory is either not resolvable or is not responding. You'll need to verify that the public DNS for your external EWS Virtual Directory is externally resolvable and that no firewall rules are preventing accessing it over port 443. Afterward, you can rerun the Hybrid Configuration Wizard or follow the steps outlined at *https://aka.ms/configoauth* to manually setup OAuth configuration.

- **Configure MRS Proxy Settings–HCW8078 Migration Endpoint Could Not Be Created**   Typically, this error results from the Hybrid Configuration Wizard app's inability to connect to the /EWS/mrsproxy.svc path on the listed EWS Virtual Directory.

- **The Legacy Email Address Policy Cannot Be Automatically Updated And Must Be Manually Upgraded**   If your organization has been through upgrades (for example, from Exchange 2003 to Exchange 2010), then email address policies might not have been updated as part of the upgrade process. To resolve these issues, you should verify that your filters are no longer using the legacy LDAP filtering syntax (see *https://aka.ms/convertfilters* for a script that can convert LDAP filters to the modern OPATH syntax). Afterward, run Get-EmailAddressPolicy | Update-EmailAddressPolicy to verify email address policies have been updated.

Mailbox provisioning

When the hybrid configuration is complete, new mailboxes can be provisioned directly in Exchange Online from the Exchange Management Shell. These new mailboxes are provisioned as *remote mailboxes*. The remote mailbox is a special type of mail-enabled user:

- In Exchange Server 2010, the objects are referred to as *remote mailboxes*.

- In Exchange Server 2013 and Exchange Server 2016, the display name has changed to Office 365 Mailbox.

The following steps illustrate how to create a new user and remote mailbox in one step or enable an existing user as a remote mailbox with Exchange Management Shell. In either case, after the next AAD Sync cycle is run, a mailbox is instantiated in Exchange Online. If it is a user mailbox, then it must be licensed in Office 365 to make it a fully functional mailbox (shared, room, and equipment mailboxes don't require licenses for core operations):

1. Launch a browser and connect to the Exchange admin center for the on-premises Exchange organization.

2. Navigate to Recipients > Mailboxes.

3. Click the plus sign (+) and select Office 365 mailbox, as shown in Figure 15-11.

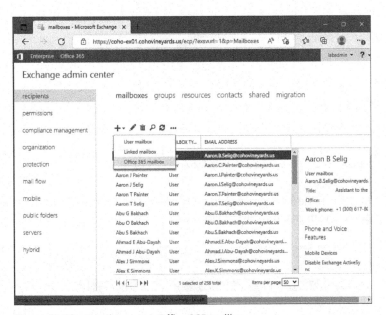

Figure 15-11   Creating a new Office 365 mailbox

4. Fill out the new Office 365 Mailbox page with the required attributes, as shown in Figure 15-12.

NOTE

The email address policy that the Hybrid Configuration Wizard updated creates the proper proxy address for the remote mailbox and sets its remote routing address to the Exchange Online organization.

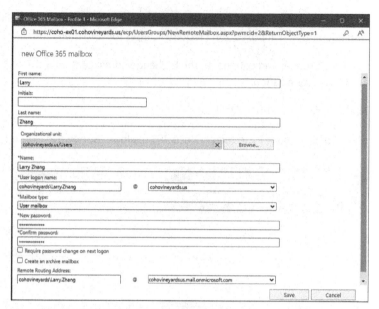

Figure 15-12   New Office 365 Mailbox dialog box

5.   Click Save. The Exchange admin center shows the newly created Active Directory user account with an Office 365 mailbox. See Figure 15-13.

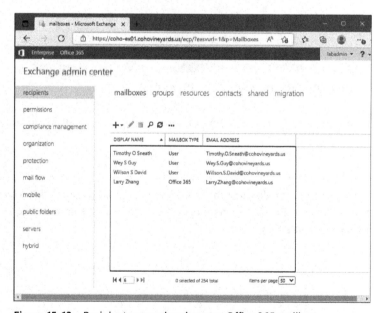

Figure 15-13   Recipients page showing new Office 365 mailbox

6. Double-click the newly created user and select the Email Address tab, as shown in Figure 15-14. View the email address details, including the remote routing address. Click Cancel.

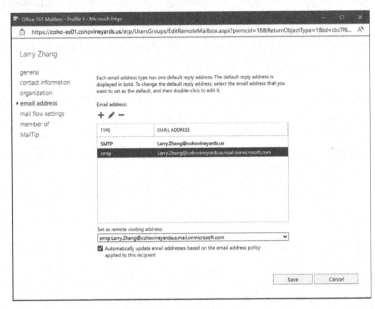

Figure 15-14 User email address properties

Decommissioning the hybrid environment

Depending on the mail flow configuration, many existing Exchange servers can be decommissioned after all migrations have been completed.

Unless your organization is completely removing AAD Connect and moving to a cloud-only identity management scenario, keeping a minimum of one Exchange server on-premises for attribute management and mailbox provisioning is strongly recommended.

Inside Out

Managing recipients in Exchange Hybrid environments using Management Tools

Starting in June 2022, a new management option was released to allow organizations to manage recipients without having Exchange servers running. With Exchange Server 2019 Cumulative Update 12, an updated Management Tools option was made available that allows for PowerShell-only management of Exchange Online recipients. All of the servers in the Exchange organization can be decommissioned except one, though the last server

> may be powered down. Uninstalling the last server removes critical components neces-
> sary for the management tools to function. This option targets organizations that only
> use Exchange for recipient management (with no other routing or public folder depen-
> dencies) and are comfortable administering objects from PowerShell only.
>
> For more information on this updated option, see *https://aka.ms/exmgmttools*.

If you are still hosting Exchange Public Folders on-premises, you will need to either migrate
them to Exchange Online or fully decommission them before decommissioning the Exchange
on-premises infrastructure. Additionally, if you use a vendor's disaster recovery tools, centralized mail transport, or still utilize Exchange as part of your mail flow topology, you'll need to
evaluate if you can perform these steps.

If you decide you want to remove your entire Exchange environment, including the hybrid components, you must remove or disable the following items:

- Inbound and outbound hybrid connectors in Exchange Online

- The O365 to On-Premises Organization Relationship in Office 365

- Intra-Organization connectors if OAuth has been configured

- Hybrid configuration object

- Service Connection Endpoints

You can run the following cmdlets when connected to Exchange Online to remove the hybrid
components:

```
Get-OutboundConnector | ? {$_.ConnectorType -eq "OnPremises" -and $_.ConnectorSource `
-eq "HybridWizard"} | Remove-OutboundConnector
Get-InBound | ? {$_.ConnectorType -eq "OnPremises" -and $_.ConnectorSource -eq `
"HybridWizard"} | Remove-InboundConnector
Get-IntraOrganizationConnector | ? { $_.Name -like "HybridIOC*"} | `
Set-IntraOrganizationConnector -Enabled $False
Get-OrganizationRelationship | ? { $_.Name -like "O365 to On-premises*" } | `
Remove-OrganizationRelationship
```

You can run the following cmdlets when connected to the on-premises Exchange Management
Shell to remove the hybrid components:

```
If (Get-Command Get-ClientAccessServer) { Get-ClientAccessServer | `
Set-ClientAccessServer -AutoDiscoverServiceInternalUri $Null }
If (Get-Command Get-ClientAccessService) { Get-ClientAccessService | `
Set-ClientAccessService -AutoDiscoverServiceInternalUri $Null }
Remove-HybridConfiguration
```

For more information about decommissioning scenarios, please see
https://docs.microsoft.com/en-us/exchange/decommission-on-premises-exchange, "How and
when to decommission your on-premises Exchange servers in a hybrid deployment."

What's next?

This chapter discussed the planning and configuration aspects of an Exchange hybrid environment, including Autodiscover, free/busy setup, name resolution, networking, transport, and public folders.

The configuration of an Exchange Online hybrid environment enables your organization to transition seamlessly from a current or older on-premises environment to Office 365 while maintaining mail flow and operational management capabilities. In the next chapter, we'll put this hybrid configuration to use to migrate mailboxes to the cloud.

After the Hybrid Configuration Wizard has completed, your environment should be configured to enable you to move mailboxes between on-premises and cloud environments.

Mailbox migrations can be performed using either the Exchange admin center or Windows PowerShell. When a mailbox migration is run, the Mailbox Replication Service Proxy (MRSProxy) queues and manages the requests.

For a mailbox to be migrated to Exchange Online, the following criteria must be met:

1. The mailbox must be synchronized to Exchange Online as a mail-enabled user.

2. The synchronized mail-enabled user must have a value for ExchangeGuid that matches the value of the on-premises mailbox being migrated.

3. The synchronized mail-enabled user must have a proxy address with a domain suffix that matches <tenant>.mail.onmicrosoft.com.

4. The synchronized mail-enabled user must not have any proxy email addresses containing domains not verified in Office 365.

5. The mailbox must have Active Directory inheritance enabled.

6. The migration endpoint must be accessible by HTTPS from Exchange Online. SSL Offloading is not supported.

Migration endpoints

The Hybrid Configuration Wizard attempts to create a migration endpoint in Exchange Online, named Hybrid Migration Endpoint - <FQDN>, where <FQDN> is the external Exchange Web Services (EWS) URL of your on-premises environment. If that was unsuccessful, you can create the endpoint manually by using the following steps:

1. Log in to the Office 365 portal, navigate to the Classic Exchange admin center, and click Recipients.

2. On the Recipients page, select Migration. To view existing migration endpoints, click the ellipsis and select Migration Endpoints. See Figure 16-1.

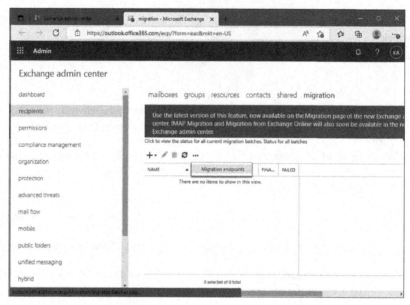

Figure 16-1   Viewing migration endpoints

3. Click the plus sign (+) to add a new migration endpoint, as shown in Figure 16-2.

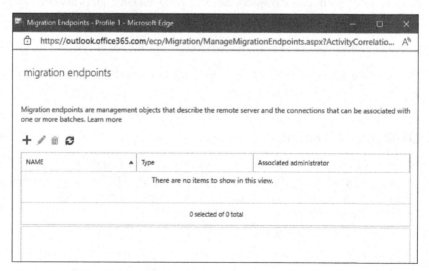

Figure 16-2   Migration Endpoints page

4. On the Select The Migration Endpoint Type page, select the Exchange Remote button (see Figure 16-3) and click Next.

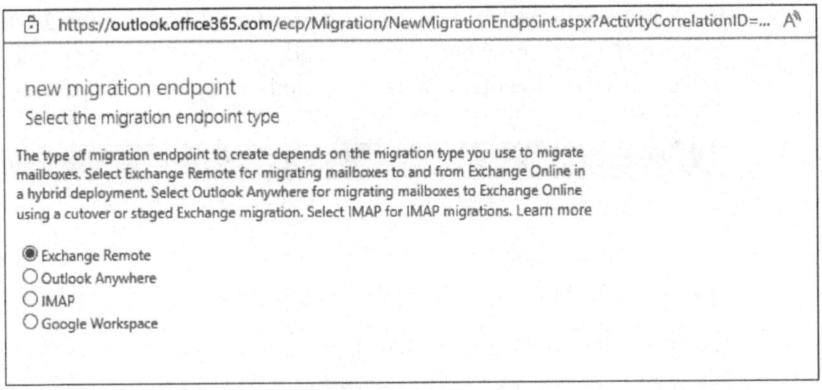

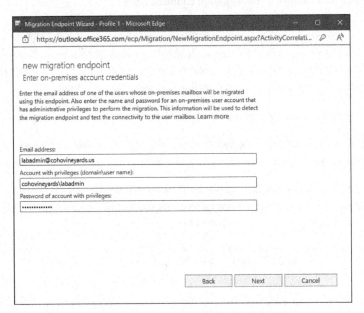

Figure 16-3   Select The Migration Endpoint Type page

5. Enter the email address of an on-premises mailbox that Autodiscover can discover and credentials for the account to be used to run the migration. The user account used for mailbox migrations must be a member of the on-premises Organization Management or Recipient Management Role Based Access Control Group. See Figure 16-4. Click Next.

Figure 16-4   Enter On-Premises Account Credentials page

6. Enter the Fully Qualified Domain Name (FQDN) of the remote MRS proxy server. Normally, this is the same hostname as the external EWS URL or the external-facing Client Access Server with the MRSProxy service enabled. When using the Hybrid Configuration Wizard, you enter and confirm this hostname for the Web Services Virtual Directory. If Exchange Online cannot determine the endpoint, you'll see the error listed in Figure 16-5 and be prompted to enter a value to proceed. When finished, click Next.

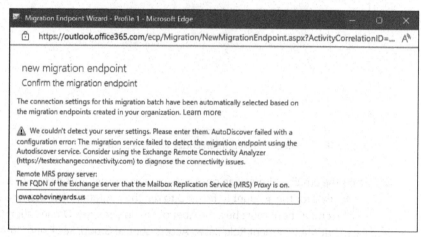

Figure 16-5 Confirm The Migration Endpoint page

7. Enter a migration endpoint name. This example mirrors what the Hybrid Configuration Wizard would call the *migration endpoint*. The value for Maximum Concurrent Migrations is set to 100 (raised from 20) by default and can be increased up to 300. The value for Maximum Concurrent Incremental Syncs is set to 20 by default.

8. Click New to create the migration endpoint.

After the migration endpoint has been created, the Migration Endpoints page is updated with the newly created endpoint, as shown in Figure 16-6.

If you need to pre-stage migration endpoints or encounter transient problems during the creation of a migration endpoint, you can also configure endpoints through the Exchange Online PowerShell interface using the -SkipVerification parameter:

```
New-MigrationEndpoint -Name "<Endpoint Name>" -ExchangeRemoteMove -RemoteServer <Server
FQDN> -Credentials (Get-Credential DOMAIN\<Username>) -MaxConcurrentMigrations 100
-SkipVerification
```

At this point, migration batches can be created to move mailboxes to or from the on-premises environment.

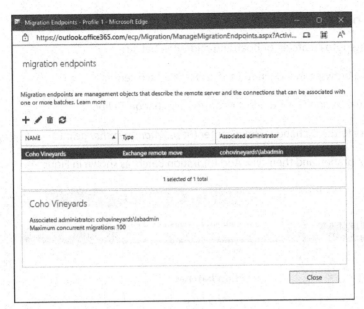

Figure 16-6 New migration endpoint created

Migration batches

Migration batches are configuration objects containing mailboxes to be moved between organizations. A migration batch can contain one or more mailboxes, and settings configured for the batch apply to all mailboxes in the batch.

After a batch is created, a validation process checks the availability of the endpoint and credentials and that the included mailboxes meet the prerequisites. Migration batches configured for manual completion are set for automatic incremental synchronizations to keep batches up to date and minimize the time to finalize a migration. Migration batches also include notification and reporting.

After a migration batch has been validated, Exchange Online generates a move request for each mailbox being migrated. Migration batches are the recommended method for migrating mailboxes.

Onboarding

Onboarding is the process of migrating a mailbox to Exchange Online. After the batch is completed, the on-premises mailbox is migrated to Exchange Online, the on-premises mailbox is disconnected from the user account, and the on-premises mailbox account is converted to a remote mailbox user. The target address for the on-premises account is updated to point to *<tenant>.mail.onmicrosoft.com*.

Creating a batch

Follow these steps to create an onboarding migration batch:

1.   Launch a browser and log in to the Exchange admin center.

2.   Click the plus sign (+) and select Migrate To Exchange Online.

3.   Navigate to the Exchange admin center (*https://admin.exchange.microsoft.com*).

4.   Select Migration and then click Add Migration Batch, as shown in Figure 16-7.

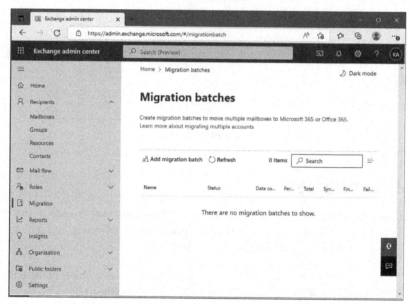

Figure 16-7   Exchange admin center Migration Batches page

5.   Enter a name and select the migration path Migration to Exchange Online.

6.   Select the Remote Move Migration option from the Select The Migration Type dropdown, as shown in Figure 16-8, and click Next.

7.   On the Prerequisites For Remote Migration page, review the prerequisites and then click Next.

8.   On the Set A Migration Endpoint page, select a migration endpoint from the Select A Migration Endpoint dropdown and click Next.

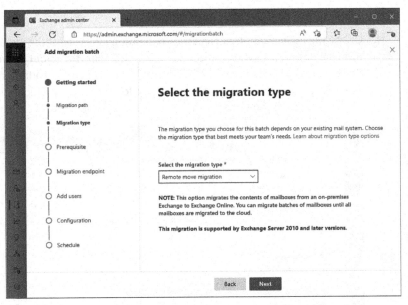

Figure 16-8   Select The Migration Type page

9. On the Add User Mailboxes page, start typing to add mail-enabled users from the Global Address List, as shown in Figure 16-9. Alternatively, you can upload a comma-separated value (CSV) populated with email addresses. The CSV must have the EmailAddress header.

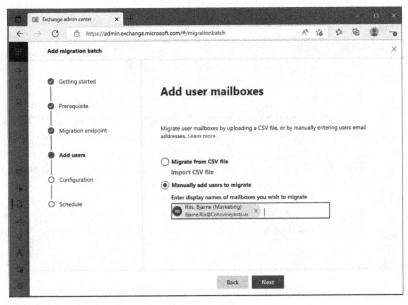

Figure 16-9   Select The Users page

10. Verify the users to migrate and click Next.

11. On the Move Configuration page shown in Figure 16-10, select the target delivery domain from the dropdown. When moving to Exchange Online, the target delivery domain is the domain ending in `<tenant>.mail.onmicrosoft.com`. A proxy address with this domain suffix will be configured as the target address for the mail user account in the Exchange on-premises environment after the mailbox move is complete. Click Next.

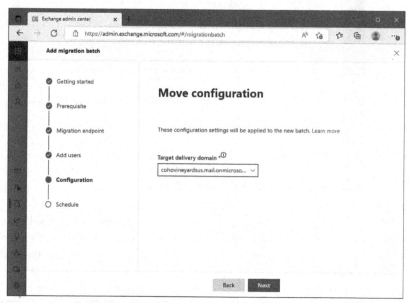

Figure 16-10 Move Configuration page

Inside Out

Alternate mailbox migration interface

Microsoft has begun migrating the Exchange admin center tools to a new interface. However, the new wizards don't have the same options as previous editions. For example, migrations from Exchange Online back on-premises are not yet supported in the new interface, so to see those options, you'll have to use the Classic Exchange admin center.

If you need to specify settings beyond those displayed in the new interface, you'll need to navigate to the Classic Exchange admin center and run the migration from that interface.

In the classic interface, you have these additional configurable options:

- You can choose to move either the primary and archive mailbox or just the archive mailbox to Exchange Online.

- You can manage the settings for Bad Item Limit. The Bad Item Limit indicates the number of items the migration skips before failing the migration. The default is 10 and can be increased to Unlimited.

- You can also manage the settings for the Large Item Limit. The maximum size for an individual message migrating to Office 365, including all attachments, is 150MB. If the limit is set to zero, any large message exceeding 150MB causes the migration to fail. If the Large Item Limit is set to a non-zero number, that number of large messages are skipped before the migration fails. Choosing a non-zero limit results in data loss for the messages exceeding the 150MB limit.

12. Select a user or distribution list on the Schedule Batch Migration page to receive email notifications about the batch.

13. Select a batch start method (manually, automatically, or at a scheduled time). The Automatically Start The Batch button is selected by default. The batch starts synchronizing immediately.

14. Select an End The Migration By option, which sets the batch completion method (manually, automatically, or at a scheduled time), as shown in Figure 16-11. By default, the Manually Completing The Batch Later (By Clicking The "Complete This Migration Batch" Link On The Right Pane, After The Link Becomes Active) button is selected. With this option selected, the batch synchronizes all selected mailboxes and leaves the migration process at 95 percent complete. The migration batch automatically performs an incremental synchronization every 24 hours.

15. Click Save to create the batch and start the synchronization process.

CHAPTER 16

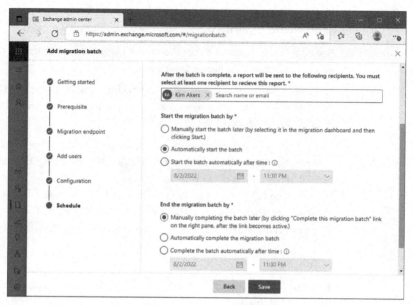

Figure 16-11 Starting the batch

INSIDE OUT

One batch a time

It is important to note that a mailbox can be part of only a single batch. If a mailbox is present in a batch and then added to a second batch, the mailbox in the second batch will fail with the `UserDuplicateInOtherBatchException` error.

Similar to how a move request must be cleared in an Exchange on-premises environment when moving a mailbox between servers, a mailbox must be removed from one batch (even if it is completed) before it can be added to another batch.

Monitoring a batch

The migration status page shows the status of each batch. The newly created batch is shown in Figure 16-12.

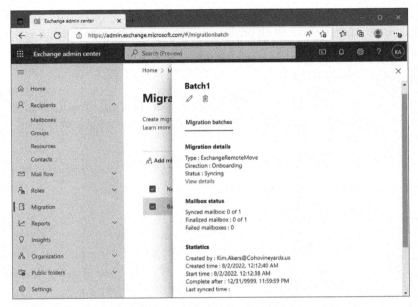

Figure 16-12   Exchange admin center migration batch status

If the batch is selected, statistics appear on the right side in a column. Two links on the status page are actionable:

1. **Complete The Migration Batch**   For synchronized batches, selecting Complete The Migration Batch starts the finalization process.

2. **View Details**   Select View Details to see more details on the migration process, including completed mailboxes, synchronization statistics, and errors. Review Figure 16-13 to see a detailed example.

Figure 16-13   Migration details

CHAPTER 16

You can view the details of an individual mailbox in the batch by clicking the mailbox in the details list. The per-mailbox details provides information on the amount of data migrated, rate of migration transfer, and errors.

Retrying a user with errors

Occasionally, you may encounter transient problems during a migration, such as network communications failures, that could stall the process. You can see the status of migration batches in the Exchange admin center in Figure 16-14.

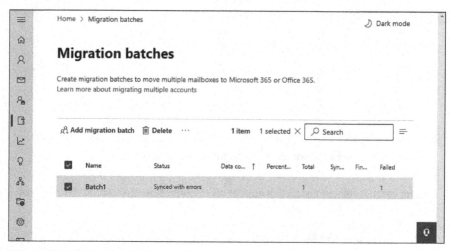

Figure 16-14   Migration batches

Follow these steps to investigate these errors:

1. Click the batch name to see the details, and then click View Details in the fly-out menu to begin reviewing failed mailboxes, as shown in Figure 16-15. If the View Details button is not available, select the ellipses to expand the menu bar first.

2. Select the mailbox name and then click Resume Migration. See Figure 16-16.

3. Click Confirm on the flyout menu to resume the migration.

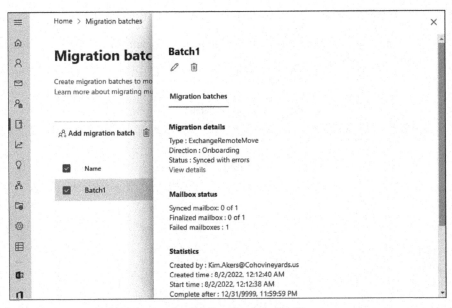

Figure 16-15   Overview of migration batch with a failed mailbox

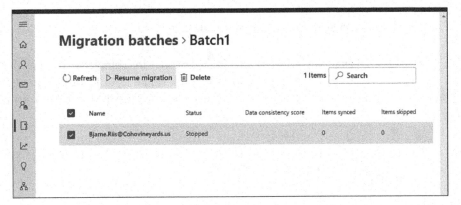

Figure 16-16   Resuming a migration batch

Completing a batch

Batches configured for manual completion automatically perform an incremental update every 24 hours after the initial synchronization has been completed.

Follow these steps to complete the migration to Exchange Online:

1. Select a batch and click the Complete Migration Batch link, as shown in Figure 16-17.

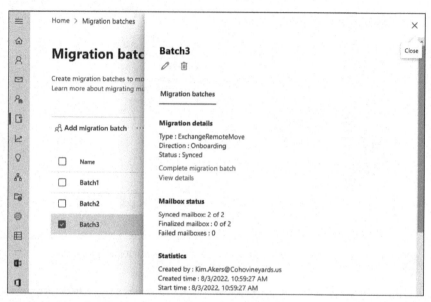

Figure 16-17   Migration batch ready to complete

2. When prompted, select Confirm to continue the completion process. The status changes from Synced to Completing, as shown in Figure 16-18. In the background, the mailbox move process synchronizes the mailbox delta since the last incremental sync.

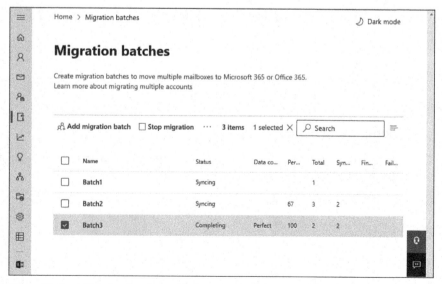

Figure 16-18   Migration batch completing

3. During the last stage of the completion process, the target Exchange Online mail user is converted to a mailbox, the on-premises mailbox is converted to a Remote User Mailbox (a special type of mail-enabled user) with the target or external email address set to `alias@<tenant>.mail.onmicrosoft.com`, and the local mailbox is disconnected.

4. After all mailboxes in the batch have completed the migration process, the batch status is updated to Completed, as shown in Figure 16-19.

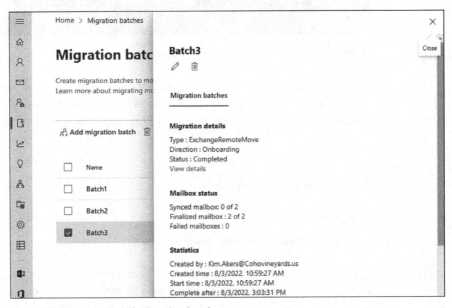

Figure 16-19   Completed migration batch

Completing a user within a batch

If you have configured a migration batch, you might want to complete just a single user to ensure everything works correctly. You can accomplish this task, though not through the Exchange admin center. To complete an individual user in a migration batch, follow these steps:

1. Connect to Exchange Online PowerShell.

2. Identify the migration batch with the following command. (The data returned should look like the data shown in Figure 16-20.)

```
Get-MigrationBatch | FL Identity,CompleteAfter
```

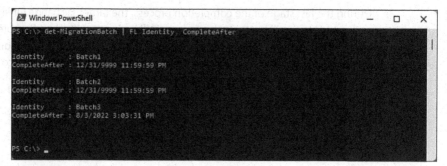

Figure 16-20   Reviewing migration batches

3. The `CompleteAfter` date indicates the earliest time the batch can be completed. Tenants that have been configured for Protocol Agnostic Workflow (PAW) have the `CompleteAfter` date set for the year 9999. PAW can be confirmed with the following command:

```
Get-MigrationConfig | FL Identity,Features
Identity : cohovineyardsus.onmicrosoft.com
Features : MultiBatch, PAW
```

NOTE

If PAW is in the Features list, the tenant is enabled.

4. Locate a user to complete using the `Get-MigrationUser` cmdlet, as shown below. Users who can be individually completed will have a Synced status, as shown in Figure 16-21.

```
Get-MigrationUser | FT -Autosize
```

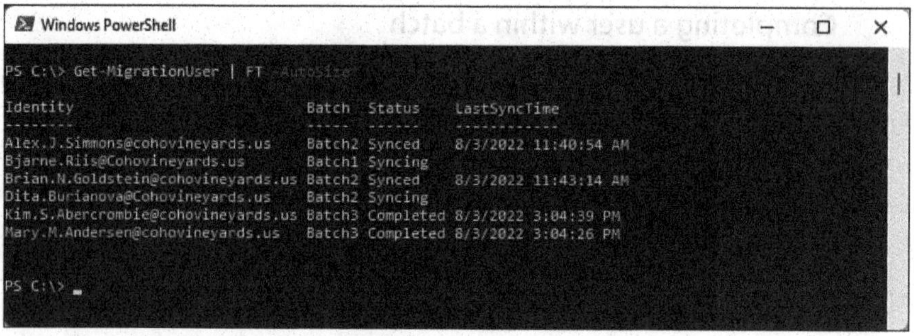

Figure 16-21   Identifying users that can be manually completed.

5. Update the user's move request, which changes the `CompleteAfter` date for the individual user within the batch to the day before the current date and completes the migration for the user without completing the entire batch. Use the following code to update the user's move request:

```
Get-MoveRequest -Identity user@contoso.com | Set-MoveRequest -CompleteAfter
(Get-Date).AddDays(-1)
Resume-MoveRequest -Identity user@contoso.com
```

6. Now that the migration process is complete, the user should be redirected to Exchange Online. When Outlook is launched, it reconfigures the profile to connect to Exchange Online. Mail sent to the user is also redirected to the Exchange Online mailbox.

Protocol Agnostic Workflow (PAW) is a new feature in Office 365 tenants designed to better manage migration batches. Tenants with PAW enabled can use the additional benefits for migration batches listed in Table 16-1.

Table 16-1   Protocol Agnostic Workflow

Feature	Pre-PAW (Legacy)	PAW
Start/Stop/Remove	Allowed at only certain times, making it difficult for admins to start, stop, and remove batches.	Allows start, stop, and remove operations at any time for the batch.
Failure retry behavior	Restarts whole batch and all items from the beginning.	Restarts each failed item from the beginning of the step where it left off.
Failure retry management	Must use `Start-MigrationBatch` to retry failures unless batch has completed, in which case must use `Complete-MigrationBatch`.	Always use `Start-MigrationBatch` to retry failures.
Completion options	Automatic or manual.	Automatic, manual, or scheduled.
Completion semantics	Must choose between "AutoComplete" and "Manual Completion" at the beginning.	Can convert between any completion option at any time before completion has occurred.
User management	Can only remove users with status Synced or Stopped.	Can remove a user from a batch at any time, regardless of status, as well as start, stop, or modify individual users.
Duplicate users	Results in validation warnings and zero-sized batches.	Results in two `MigrationUser` objects (one per batch), only one of which can be active at a time. If the first one was Completed, it processes the second one. Otherwise, it fails the second one with a message indicating the first one is being processed. That failed user can later be resumed and completed successfully or removed from the batch.

CHAPTER 16

Throttling	Handled by `MigrationService`, leading to inefficient resource usage. Throttling limit is rarely (if ever) reached, resulting in less than optimal performance.	Handled by MRS, which is already used to handling resource usage (maximized throughput resulting in throttle limit being reached).
Reports	Only initial sync and completion reports.	Initial sync reports, completion reports, and periodic status reports.
Counts	15-minute delay in generating accurate reports.	Real-time reports.

All new tenants are PAW-enabled. To convert a tenant to PAW, all existing migration batches (new, synced, failed, or completed) must be removed. The PAW enablement process happens automatically as long as there are no existing batches in the tenant.

Removing a user from the batch

Sometimes during the migration process, a mailbox that should not be part of a migration batch is identified. You can remove mailboxes from a batch by selecting the mailbox in the batch and then choosing Delete, as shown in Figure 16-22.

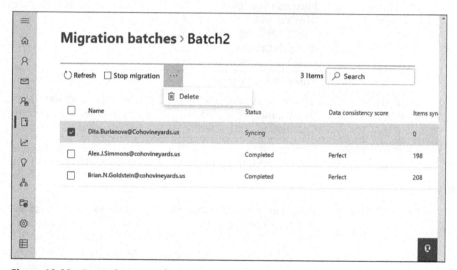

Figure 16-22   Removing a user from a batch

After selecting Delete, click Confirm to delete the migration user from the batch.

Offboarding

At some point, it might be necessary to migrate users from Exchange Online to an on-premises Exchange environment. You can complete this migration process, referred to as *offboarding*, through the Exchange admin center or with Exchange Online PowerShell.

The overall process is nearly identical to onboarding. It requires you to select a migration endpoint, users to migrate, and target delivery domain (which is generally the primary SMTP address domain). The only additional piece of information required is the on-premises target database name.

When offboarding a mailbox, the same requirements must be met for onboarding (such as valid proxy addresses and an ExchangeGuid). There is also the additional consideration of archive mailboxes. If you are offboarding to an Exchange Server 2007 or Exchange Server 2010 environment, you must first migrate the content to the primary mailbox, disable the archive, and then migrate.

Depending on how a cloud mailbox was enabled, the on-premises remote mailbox might also be missing the ExchangeGuid. For mailboxes that were moved to Exchange Online from an on-premises environment, the ExchangeGuid property will be populated. However, for mailboxes created online, using the New-RemoteMailbox or Enable-RemoteMailbox commands, the on-premises account will not have a valid ExchangeGuid. To check a remote mailbox for the presence of the ExchangeGuid, follow these steps:

1. Connect to the Exchange Management Shell.

2. Run Get-RemoteMailbox user@domain.com | FL Name,ExchangeGuid to view the user's ExchangeGuid property:

```
Get-RemoteMailbox lzhang | FL Name,ExchangeGuid
Name        : Larry Zhang
ExchangeGuid : 00000000-0000-0000-0000-000000000000
```

TIP

The ExchangeGuid **property has all zeros for the value. This is normal for mailboxes provisioned using** New-RemoteMailbox **or** Enable-RemoteMailbox **commands.**

To update the ExchangeGuid for a user, follow these steps:

1. Connect to Exchange Online PowerShell.

2. Run Get-Mailbox user@contoso.com | FL Name,ExchangeGuid to display the mailbox's ExchangeGuid.

3. Copy the ExchangeGuid.

4. Launch the Exchange Management Shell on-premises and run the following command:

    ```
    Set-RemoteMailbox -identity user@contoso.com -ExchangeGuid <ExchangeGuid value
    copied in step 3>
    ```

5. After the `ExchangeGuid` is synchronized, you can offboard the mailbox.

To complete the offboarding, specify an Exchange mailbox database in the on-premises environment where the offboarded mailbox will be migrated. Depending on the version of the target Exchange environment, you might need to specify the databases based on the destinations as follows:

- **Exchange Server 2010 or later destinations**   A single name (such as `MBXDB01`)

- **Exchange Server 2003 or Exchange Server 2007 destinations**   `SERVER\DATABASE` format (`CONTOSOSERVER\MBXDB02`)

You can also use the mailbox database GUID to identify the target database. To obtain a list of database GUIDs, run `Get-MailboxDatabase -IncludePre | FT Name,Guid`.

To create the migration batch for offboarding, you can use the Classic Exchange admin center (selecting Migrate From Exchange Online on the Recipients | Migration page) and select the users and endpoint details or use Windows PowerShell, as shown in the following steps:

1. Create a CSV with the header `EmailAddress` and enter the email addresses of the users to offboard, one per line, and save to a temp folder (such as `C:\Temp\Offboard.csv`).

2. Connect to Exchange Online PowerShell.

3. Run the following command, which is also shown in Figure 16-23:

    ```
    New-MigrationBatch -Name Offboard -CSVData ([System.IO.File]::ReadAllBytes("C:\
    Temp\Offboard.csv")) -TargetEndpoint ((Get-MigrationEndPoint)[0]).Identity
    -TargetDeliveryDomain <PrimarySMTPDomain> -TargetDatabases MBX1 -AutoStart
    -AutoComplete -NotificationEmails adminuser@contoso.com
    ```

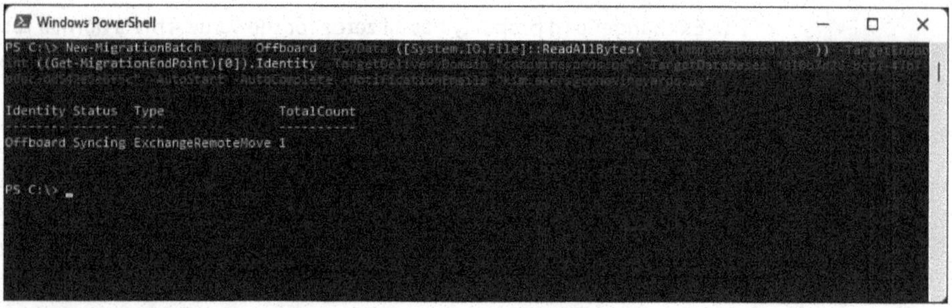

Figure 16-23   Offboarding mailboxes through PowerShell

The mailbox user will be offboarded to the on-premises target database matching GUID `010b7d26-bcc2-47b7-b8bc-d8542e5e6f5c`.

Troubleshooting

Before you begin in-depth troubleshooting, it may be helpful to review the list of prerequisites for a successful mailbox migration:

1. There must be at least one migration endpoint configured in Exchange Online.

2. There must be network connectivity between the on-premises server responsible for the Mailbox Replication Service (MRS) and Exchange Online.

3. The source mailbox must have at least one proxy address that matches a domain in the target environment. If onboarding to Exchange Online, that means that the source mailbox must have a proxy address matching @<tenant>.mail.onmicrosoft.com. If offboarding to Exchange on-premises, the on-premises user must have a proxy address matching a validated domain in Exchange Online.

4. The target mail user object must have a value for the ExchangeGuid attribute that matches the source mailbox:

   - If you are onboarding to Exchange Online, the value stored in the mail user's ExchangeGuid attribute must match that of the on-premises mailbox's msExch-MailboxGuid attribute.

   - If you are offboarding to Exchange on-premises, the value stored in the on-premises Active Directory user's msExchMailboxGuid attribute must match that of the Exchange Online user's ExchangeGuid attribute.

5. The user to be migrated cannot be a part of any other migration batches.

Once all those requirements are met, you should be able to successfully move mailboxes in either direction between an Exchange on-premises environment and Exchange Online.

If you've met all of those prerequisites, it may be time to dig deeper. Mailbox moves might fail for a number of reasons, including network timeouts, inaccessible databases, insufficient permissions, invalid proxy addresses, or missing Exchange GUIDs. For any migrations that fail, you can export the underlying move request and use the MRS Explorer tool (at *https://github.com/zarkatech/MRS-Explorer/blob/master/MRS_Explorer.ps1*) to examine the error. Some of the more common errors (and resolutions) follow:

1. **You Can't Use The Domain Because It's Not An Accepted Domain For Your Organization**

   This error occurs because a proxy address on the source mailbox doesn't match an accepted domain in the target environment. This frequently happens if you have removed accepted domains in your on-premises environment without updating the proxy address for the users, or if you have not added and verified all on-premises accepted domains in the Exchange Online environment.

You can use the following script to identify proxy addresses that are causing this error:

```
$Users = (Get-MigrationUser -Status Failed | ? { $_.ErrorSummary -match "not an
accepted domain" }).Identity
[regex]$AcceptedDomainsRegex = '(?i)(' + (($Domains |foreach
{[regex]::escape($_)}) -join "|@") + ')$'
Foreach ($user in $users)
  {
  Write-host processing $user
  $obj = Get-MailUser $user
  for ($i=($obj.EmailAddresses.count)-1; $i -ge 0; $i--)
    {
    $address = $obj.EmailAddresses[$i]
    if ($address -notlike "*@*")
      {
      Continue
      }
    if ($address -inotlike "*x500:*" -and $address -like "*@*" -and $address
-notmatch $AcceptedDomainsRegex)
        { Write-Host -ForegroundColor Red "   Address $($address) doesn't match" }
      else { }
    }
  Write-host "-----------"
    }
```

Review the output and then add the necessary domains to the Office 365 tenant or remove the offending proxy addresses from the on-premises users and retry the migration.

Inside Out

Unverified domains in Exchange Online

There are some exceptions to having to remove unverified domains from the source objects:

- If you apply an Exchange Online license to a user before migration, the incompatible proxy addresses will be dropped during the migration process.

- You can also choose to remove proxy addresses on an outbound synchronization flow to Azure AD Connect while leaving the on-premises object intact. This may be necessary for some internal applications or cross-organization operations with another on-premises Exchange organization or directory synchronization product. You can use a script such as the one found at *https://aka.ms/NewAADConnectRuleRemoveProxy* to create an Azure AD Connect outbound rule that will strip specified outbound proxy domain addresses.

2. **Target Mailbox Doesn't Have An SMTP Proxy Matching** `<tenant>.mail.`
`onmicrosoft.com`

During an Exchange mailbox migration, the source mailbox's `targetAddress` attribute is configured to point to an email address in the new Exchange environment. The Hybrid Configuration Wizard configures an email address template for all email address policies that contain domains selected on the Hybrid Domains page of the wizard. The email addresses are applied during the next email address policy update cycle.

However, if you have mailboxes with the `EmailAddressPolicyEnabled` attribute set to False, those mailboxes will never receive the updated proxy address from the email address template. Without a valid proxy address matching the Exchange Online routing domain, MRS cannot configure the `targetAddress` value for the source account.

To resolve this error, add a proxy address for the mailbox in the format of `<alias>@<tenant>.mail.onmicrosoft.com`. You can use a script, such as the one at *https://aka.ms/AddTenantProxy*, to help automate this task.

3. **Insufficient Access Rights To Perform The Operation (INSUFF_ACCESS_RIGHTS)**

This error frequently occurs when Active Directory inheritance has been disabled for the mailbox account being migrated.

The two primary sources of permissions inheritance problems are the following:

- A security policy for least-privilege access to sensitive accounts

- `adminSDHolder` and `SDProp`

Exchange depends on the presence of a certain set of permissions for the migration account to update the attributes of the migrated user. If permissions inheritance has been disabled, the permissions for the Exchange Server groups will not be applied to the mailbox.

To resolve this error, verify that Active Directory object security inheritance is enabled on all mailboxes being migrated. You can use a script, such as the one at *https://aka.ms/FixBrokenInheritance*, to identify and resolve accounts with disabled inheritance.

4. **The User Object Does Not Have A Valid** `ExchangeGUID` **Property And Cannot Be Migrated**

As previously mentioned, for a mailbox migration to be successful, the `ExchangeGuid` (`msExchMailboxGuid` when viewed from Active Directory) property of the source user mailbox and target mail-enabled user must be populated with the same value.

If the ExchangeGuid property of the target mail-enabled user in Exchange Online is not synchronized, remove the user from Azure AD and re-synchronize the user account with the following steps:

1. Connect to Azure AD PowerShell by using the Connect-MsolService cmdlet.

2. Remove the user object from Azure AD and the Azure AD recycle bin:

   ```
   Remove-MsolUser -UserPrincipalName <user@domain.com> -Force
   Remove-MsolUser -UserPrincipalName <user@domain.com>
   -RemoveFromRecycleBin -Force
   ```

3. Wait for AAD Connect to run a delta synchronization (or run a manual delta synchronization task).

   If this error occurs during an offboarding scenario, follow the steps under *Offboarding* to ensure that the msExchMailboxGuid value in the user's on-premises Active Directory account matches the user's ExchangeGuid value in Exchange Online.

5. **A Recipient Wasn't Found For** user@domain.com **On The Target**

   No mail-enabled user in Exchange Online matches a mailbox in the migration batch. This usually happens because an address specified in a CSV file was typed incorrectly. Verify that all mailboxes in the CSV file for migration have a matching recipient object in the Office 365 tenant.

6. **This Mailbox Exceeded The Maximum Number Of Corrupted Items That Were Specified For This Move Request**

   If the mailbox being migrated has more bad items or large items than either the BadItemLimit or LargeItemLimit thresholds, the migration generates this error. There are two ways to resolve the error:

   - Remove the corrupt or large items from the source mailbox.

   - Increase the BadItemLimit and LargeItemLimit parameters for the move request by using Set-MoveRequest -BadItemLimit <number> -LargeItemLimit <number> -AcceptLargeDataLoss

7. **Target User Already Has A Primary Mailbox**

   This error occurs when a user is included in a migration batch that has already been migrated. Remove the user from the migration batch.

8. **Mailbox Is Already Being Moved To** <databasename>

   This error can happen if a move request is created manually using the New-MoveRequest cmdlet before the mailbox's inclusion in a batch. Either remove the existing move request or remove the user from the migration batch.

9. **The Request Channel Timed Out While Waiting For A Reply**

This error is frequently caused by an incorrect load-balancer configuration or another device interrupting the MRSProxy traffic (such as an intrusion detection/intrusion prevention appliance or an SSL offloading configuration). Make sure Exchange Online can reach the on-premises Exchange server environment without any packet-inspecting devices acting as intermediaries.

10. **EndpointNotFoundTransientException: The call to 'https://server.domain.com/ EWS/mrsproxy.svc' failed because no service was listening on the specified endpoint.**

This can occur if the inbound firewall to the migration endpoint listed in the error does not have port 443 open. Additionally, if you manually create an endpoint and specify an invalid server or a server that has not had MRSProxy enabled on it, you might also receive this message. Ensure that the endpoint listed has successfully been configured by the Hybrid Configuration Wizard. Make sure the listed endpoint resolves correctly over the Internet and has inbound port 443 accessible from the Exchange Online service.

What's next?

In this chapter, we reviewed migrating mailboxes to and from Exchange Online. In the next chapter, we'll explore working with hybrid public folders and the process for migrating public folders to Exchange Online.

Migrating public folders to Exchange Online

Public folders are a storage concept that allows multiple users to post and read data in a folder-like structure from within Outlook. Public folders were originally introduced in Exchange 4.0 in 1996 and included their own database and multi-master replication structure. With the release of Exchange Server 5.5, public folders were updated to allow them to receive email.

With Exchange 2013, the architecture was updated to use the database availability group (DAG) storage and replication engine. The public folder contents are now stored inside a special mailbox object.

In a hybrid Exchange deployment, public folders can exist either on-premises or in-cloud. They can only exist in one place at a time, so it's important to plan where they will be, based on your user mailbox locations and Exchange versions.

Typically, the recommended migration plan is to move public folders to Office 365 after all the mailboxes have been moved to Exchange Online. However, public folders can be migrated at any point during a larger Exchange Online migration project.

Exchange Online prerequisites

Starting in June 2021, Microsoft began disabling Basic Authentication in tenants where telemetry shows it is not being used. While it is important for the overall posture of Microsoft's customers, there are instances where this can pose challenges. One such challenge is with Exchange Public Folder migrations, as the synchronization and migration scripts still rely upon Basic Authentication.

To enable Basic Authentication in your tenant, follow these steps:

1. To do this, log into the Exchange Admin Center and click the Need Help? icon, as shown in Figure 17-1.

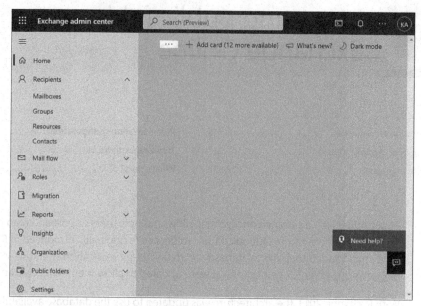

Figure 17-1 Accessing the Help menu from the Exchange admin center

2. In the Search box, type Diag:Enable Basic Auth for EXO and click the Search arrow, as shown in Figure 17-2.

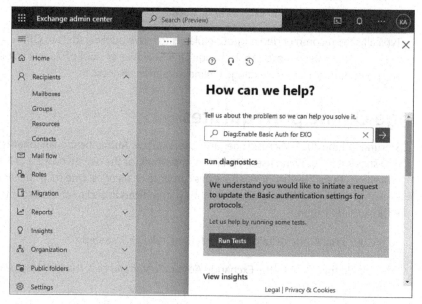

Figure 17-2 Searching for the diagnostic process

3. Click **Run Tests**.

4. If protocols have been disabled in your tenant, the diagnostic will show you which ones have been disabled. Under Protocol To Enable, select Exchange Online Remote PowerShell. Next, select the I Acknowledge Clicking 'Update Settings' Will Make The Changes Described Above To The Tenant Configuration checkbox, and then click Update, as shown in Figure 17-3.

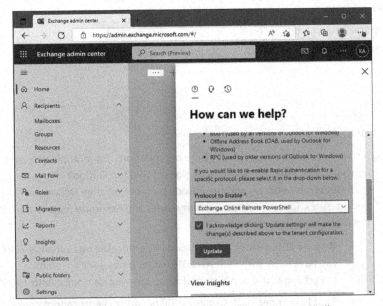

Figure 17-3   Enabling basic auth for Exchange Online PowerShell

5. After it has completed, you should receive a message that Basic Authentication has been re-enabled.

Ensuring Basic Authentication is enabled is necessary for all public folder migrations, regardless of the source Exchange Server version.

Configuring hybrid public folders

There are two types of hybrid public folder implementations—those in which the public folders exist on-premises and those in which the public folders exist online. Use the information in Table 17-1 to determine what options are available based on your public folder and user mailbox locations.

Table 17-1   Hybrid public folder topologies

Public folder location	On-premises Exchange 2007 or Exchange 2010 mailbox	On-premises Exchange 2013 or later mailbox	Exchange Online mailbox
Exchange 2003	Not supported	Not supported	Not supported
Exchange 2007 or Exchange 2010	N/A	N/A	Supported
Exchange 2013 or later	N/A	N/A	Supported
Exchange Online	Not supported	Supported	N/A

Inside Out

Outlook versions and feature availability

It's not uncommon, especially in large organizations, for multiple versions of desktop software to be installed. Multiple versions of desktop Outlook clients, Exchange on-premises server versions, and the introduction of Exchange Online can lead to unexpected issues. To minimize connectivity issues and maximize feature availability, keep the following points in mind:

- Outlook 2016 cannot access public folders hosted on Exchange 2007 or earlier. If you have users with Outlook 2016, either move your on-premises public folders to Exchange 2010 or newer or downgrade your Outlook clients to 2013 or earlier.

- As of November 2021, Outlook 2010 or earlier clients cannot connect to Exchange Online.

- Outlook for Mac and Outlook for Mac for Office 365 are not supported for cross-premises public folder access. Outlook for Mac clients can only access public folders hosted in the same location as the user mailbox.

On-premises public folders

The most common coexistence or migration strategy is hybrid public folder deployments in which the public folders are on-premises. In this case, you might be migrating your users and data to Office 365 and need to provide access to on-premises public folders for users whose mailboxes have already been moved.

This is the simplest deployment because the requirements are the easiest to meet, and the configuration steps can be minimal, depending on your on-premises environment. The prerequisites are as follows:

- Your on-premises Exchange environment is accessible through the Internet.

- Autodiscover is configured properly and points to an on-premises endpoint. Hybrid public folders in Exchange Online use Autodiscover to locate on-premises public folders.

- Outlook Anywhere has been configured on your Exchange servers.

- You have the correct permissions or role group memberships:

    - For Exchange Online, you are a member of the Organization Management role group.

    - For Exchange 2010, you are a member of the Organization Management or Server Management role-based access control (RBAC) groups.

    - For Exchange 2007, you have been assigned the Exchange Organization Administrator or Exchange Server Administrator roles as well as the Public Folder Administrator role. You are also a member of the local Administrators group on the Exchange server hosting the public folder database.

- For Exchange 2007, if your server is running Windows Server 2008 x64 or Windows Server 2003 x64, you have upgraded to Windows PowerShell 2.0 and WinRM 2.0.

- All Exchange Online users attempting to access on-premises public folders are represented by an on-premises mail-enabled user object.

- You have downloaded the public folder sync scripts from *https://www.microsoft.com/en-us/download/details.aspx?id=46381* and saved them to a folder on one of the public folder servers, such as `C:\PFScripts`.

Exchange 2007

When configuring prerequisites for hybrid public folders or public folder migrations for Exchange 2007, you only need to create a mailbox database and a mailbox and then update the organization configuration in Exchange Online to point to the new mailbox. Follow these steps:

1. Create an empty mailbox database on each public folder server. This mailbox database will be used for the public folder proxy mailbox you create. No other mailboxes should be placed on this database:

    ```
    New-MailboxDatabase -StorageGroup "<PFServerName\StorageGroup>" -Name`
    <NewPFDatabaseName>
    ```

2. On each public folder server, add a mailbox in the database created in the previous step:

    ```
    New-Mailbox -Name <PFMailbox1> -Database <NewPFDatabaseName>
    Set-Mailbox -Identity <PFMailbox1> -HiddenFromAddressListsEnabled $true
    ```

CHAPTER 17

3. Launch a Windows PowerShell session and change to the folder containing the public folder sync scripts.

4. Run the following command daily to synchronize the mail-enabled public folders to Exchange Online, using your Office 365 credentials when prompted:

```
Sync-MailPublicFolders.ps1 -Credential (Get-Credential) -CsvSummaryFile:`
sync_summary.csv
```

5. Connect to Exchange Online PowerShell and run the following command, specifying all the public folder mailboxes created in step 1 for the RemotePublicFolderMailboxes parameter:

```
Set-OrganizationConfig -PublicFoldersEnabled Remote -RemotePublicFolderMailboxes`
PFMailbox1,PFMailbox2,PFMailbox3
```

Exchange 2010

The prerequisites for configuring hybrid public folders or public folder migrations for Exchange 2010 are a little more involved, requiring everything that Exchange 2007 does and the configuration of the Client Access Server role on public folder servers. Follow these steps:

1. Install and configure the Client Access Server role on all mailbox servers with a public folder database. The public folder servers do not have to be part of a client access load balancing, but they need the Microsoft Exchange RpcClientAccess service to be running.

2. Create an empty mailbox database on each public folder server and exclude it from the mailbox provisioning load balancer. This mailbox database will be used for the public folder proxy mailbox you create. No other mailboxes should be placed on this database:

```
New-MailboxDatabase -Server <PFServerName> -Name <NewPFDatabaseName>`
-IsExcludedFromProvisioning $true
```

3. On each public folder server, add a mailbox in the database created in the previous step:

```
New-Mailbox -Name <PFMailbox1> -Database <NewPFDatabasename>
Set-Mailbox -Identity <PFMailbox1> -HiddenFromAddressListsEnabled $true
```

4. On each public folder server, enable Autodiscover to return the public folder mailboxes:

```
Set-MailboxDatabase <NewPFDatabaseName> -RPCClientAccessServer <PFServerName>
```

5. Launch a Windows PowerShell session and change to the folder containing the public folder sync scripts.

6. Run the following command daily to synchronize the mail-enabled public folders to Exchange Online, using your Office 365 credentials when prompted:

```
Sync-MailPublicFolders.ps1 -Credential (Get-Credential) -CsvSummaryFile:`
sync_summary.csv
```

7. Connect to Exchange Online PowerShell and run the following command, specifying all the public folder mailboxes created in step 1 for the `RemotePublicFolderMailboxes` parameter:

```
Set-OrganizationConfig -PublicFoldersEnabled Remote -RemotePublicFolderMailboxes`
PFMailbox1,PFMailbox2,PFMailbox3
```

Exchange 2013 and later

Because of the consolidation of server roles for Exchange 2013 and later, the Client Access Server role is already present on any servers on which mailboxes or public folders are deployed. Exchange 2013 and later use modern public folders (where the public folder data is stored in public folder mailboxes), so the steps to create separate public folder mailboxes are unnecessary. You only need to configure Exchange Online with the on-premises public folder mailbox names:

1. Get a list of all on-premises public folder mailboxes from Exchange Management Shell:

```
Get-Mailbox -PublicFolder | Select Alias
```

2. Launch a Windows PowerShell session and change to the folder containing the public folder sync scripts.

3. Run the following command daily to synchronize the mail-enabled public folders to Exchange Online, using your Office 365 credentials when prompted:

```
Sync-MailPublicFolders.ps1 -Credential (Get-Credential) -CsvSummaryFile:`
sync_summary.csv
```

4. Connect to Exchange Online PowerShell and run the following command, specifying all the public folder mailboxes obtained in step 1 for the `RemotePublicFolderMailboxes` parameter:

```
Set-OrganizationConfig -PublicFoldersEnabled Remote -RemotePublicFolderMailboxes
PFMailbox1,PFMailbox2,PFMailbox3
```

Online public folders

In this type of hybrid configuration, your mailbox users are on-premises, and your public folders are online. You might have already migrated your public folders to Exchange Online or created and begun using new public folders in Exchange Online. In either case, you need to synchronize contacts for the mail-enabled public folders to your on-premises environment, so they are available as mail recipients. The prerequisites are as follows:

- All user mailboxes are hosted on Exchange 2013.

- Autodiscover is configured properly and points to an on-premises endpoint.

- Outlook Anywhere has been configured on your Exchange servers.

- You have downloaded the public folder sync scripts from *https://www.microsoft.com/en-us/download/details.aspx?id=52037* and saved them to a folder on one of the Exchange servers, such as `C:\PFScripts`.

To configure Exchange Online public folders, follow these steps:

1. Launch a Windows PowerShell session and change to the folder containing the public folder sync scripts.

2. Run the following command daily to sync mail-enabled public folders from Exchange Online to your on-premises Active Directory:

   ```
   Sync-MailPublicFoldersCloudToOnprem.ps1 -Credential (Get-Credential)
   ```

3. Run the following command daily to sync public folder mailboxes from Exchange Online to your on-premises Active Directory:

   ```
   Import-PublicFolderMailboxes.ps1 -Credential (Get-Credential)
   ```

4. From the on-premises Exchange Management Shell, run the following command to enable access to Exchange Online public folders:

   ```
   Set-OrganizationConfig -PublicFoldersEnabled Remote
   ```

Public folder migration

Public folders can be migrated from Exchange 2007, Exchange 2010, and Exchange 2013 or later to Exchange Online. The following are the general prerequisites to do this:

- Your on-premises Exchange environment is accessible through the Internet.

- Autodiscover is configured properly and points to an on-premises endpoint. Hybrid public folders in Exchange Online use Autodiscover to locate on-premises public folders.

- Outlook Anywhere has been configured on your Exchange servers.

- You have the correct permissions or role group memberships:

  - For Exchange Online, you are a member of the Organization Management role group.

  - For Exchange 2007, you have been assigned the Exchange Organization Administrator role or Exchange Server Administrator role as well as the Public Folder Administrator role. You are also a member of the local Administrators group on the Exchange server hosting the public folder database.

- For Exchange 2010 and later, you are a member of the Organization Management or Server Management role-based access control (RBAC) role groups.

- You have checked your public folders for invalid names by using IDFix for Public Folders, available at https://aka.ms/PFIDFix.

- SMTP addresses and aliases for mail-enabled public folders are unique across your organization.

- There are no orphaned public folder mail objects in the Microsoft Exchange System Objects container in Active Directory.

- You have checked your public folders for size. If you have any individual folders greater than 2GB, consider deleting some content, migrating some content to another folder, or increasing the public folder quota size.

- You don't have more than 10,000 subfolders in any particular folder, which can cause the migration to fail. Typically, this is only an issue in the DUMPSTER_ROOT folder. To see whether this could affect you, run the following command from the on-premises Exchange Management Shell:

```
(Get-PublicFolder -GetChildren "\NON_IPM_SUBTREE\DUMPSTER_ROOT").Count
```

- You have verified that your servers meet the minimum software requirements:

    - For Exchange 2007, your servers are running Service Pack 3 with RollUp 15 or later.

    - For Exchange 2007, if your server is running Windows Server 2008 x64 or Windows Server 2003 x64, you have upgraded to Windows PowerShell 2.0 and WinRM 2.0.

    - For Exchange 2010, your servers are running Service Pack 3 with RollUp 8 or later.

    - For Exchange 2013, you have deployed Cumulative Update 15 or later.

Exchange 2007 or Exchange 2010

Before you begin migrating, you must ensure your environment meets the prerequisites and you have completed the planning exercises necessary.

In addition to the general prerequisites, there are some version-specific prerequisites:

- You have downloaded the Public Folders Migration Scripts and supporting files from *https://www.microsoft.com/en-us/download/details.aspx?id=38407* and saved them to a folder on one of your Exchange servers in a directory such as C:\PFScripts.

- You have downloaded the Mail-Enabled Public Folder Directory Sync script and supporting files from *https://www.microsoft.com/en-us/download/details.aspx?id=46381* and saved them to a folder on one of the public folder servers, such as C:\PFScripts.

If you are using Azure AD Connect to synchronize your directories, ensure that you are not synchronizing Exchange mail public folders because it conflicts with the public folder sync and migration scripts. If you are not using AAD Connect, you can skip to step 12.

To migrate public folders, follow these steps:

1. Launch the Azure AD Connect Setup Wizard on the server running AAD Connect.

2. Click Configure.

3. Click Customize Synchronization Options and then click Next.

4. On the Connect To Azure AD page, enter your Office 365 credentials and click Next.

5. On the Connect Your Directories page, click Next.

6. On the Domain And OU Filtering page, click Next.

7. On the Optional Features page, ensure that the Exchange Mail Public Folders checkbox is not selected, as shown in Figure 17-4. If it is selected, deselect it, and click Next. Otherwise, you can cancel the wizard and exit it.

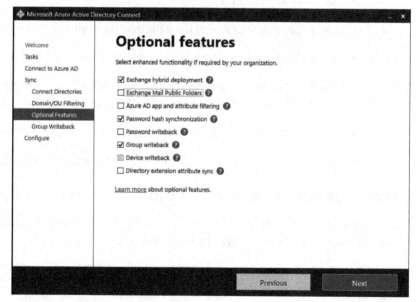

Figure 17-4   Azure AD Connect Optional Features configuration page

8. If Group Writeback was selected on the Optional Features page, click Next on the Group Writeback page.

9. On the Ready To Configure page, click Configure.

10. Click Exit.

11. If you had to deselect the Exchange Mail Public Folders checkbox on the Optional Features page, you must run a full import and synchronization. This is because the wizard removes six synchronization rules and clears the public folder object type in the connector properties.

12. On the public folder server where you have downloaded the public folder scripts, launch a Windows PowerShell session, change to the directory containing the downloaded public folder scripts, and connect to Exchange Online:

```
$Session = New-PSSession -ConfigurationName Microsoft.Exchange -ConnectionUri
https://outlook.office365.com/powershell-liveid -Authentication Basic
-AllowRedirection -Credential (Get-Credential)
Import-PSSession $Session
```

13. On the public folder server to which you have downloaded the public folder scripts, launch an Exchange Management Shell session and change to the directory containing the downloaded public folder scripts.

14. Check for existing public folder migrations in both Exchange Online and Exchange on-premises management shells and ensure all entries are returned as False:

```
Get-OrganizationConfig | FL Public*Migration*
```

15. The screen output should look similar to the following:

```
PublicFoldersLockedForMigration     : False
PublicFolderMigrationComplete       : False
PublicFolderMailboxesMigrationComplete : False
```

16. If any of the preceding conditions are True, a public folder migration has been started, completed, or is underway.

17. If you are certain that no public folder migrations have occurred or are in progress, you can set the values to False with the following command:

```
Set-OrganizationConfig -PublicFoldersLockedforMigration:$false `
-PublicFolderMigrationComplete:$false
```

CHAPTER 17

18. Check to ensure that no public folder mailboxes have been created in Exchange Online. If they have, remove them with the following commands from your Exchange Online PowerShell session:

```
Get-PublicFolderMigrationRequest | Remove-PublicFolderMigrationRequest`
-Confirm:$False
$PFMigrationBatch = Get-MigrationBatch | ? { $_.MigrationType.ToString() -eq`
"Public Folder" }
$PFMigrationBatch | Remove-MigrationBatch -Confirm:$False
Get-MailPublicFolder | where {$_.EntryId -ne $null}| Disable-MailPublicFolder`
-Confirm:$false
Get-PublicFolder -GetChildren \ | Remove-PublicFolder -Recurse -Confirm:$false
$hierarchyMailboxGuid = $(Get-OrganizationConfig).RootPublicFolderMailbox.`
HierarchyMailboxGuid
Get-Mailbox -PublicFolder:$true | Where-Object {$_.ExchangeGuid -ne`
$hierarchyMailboxGuid} | Remove-Mailbox -PublicFolder -Confirm:$false
Get-Mailbox -PublicFolder:$true | Where-Object {$_.ExchangeGuid -eq`
$hierarchyMailboxGuid} | Remove-Mailbox -PublicFolder -Confirm:$false
```

19. Check the public folder quota sizes by using the following command from your Exchange Online PowerShell session:

```
Get-OrganizationConfig | fl *quot*
```

20. The default output will show this:

```
DefaultPublicFolderIssueWarningQuota : 1.7 GB (1,825,361,920 bytes)
DefaultPublicFolderProhibitPostQuota : 2 GB (2,147,483,648 bytes)
```

21. If you have any public folders larger than 2GB, adjust this to a larger value to account for public folder growth. It's typical to estimate for 20–30 percent growth, but your organization may need more or less. For example, this command can be run in the Exchange Online PowerShell session to set the public folder warning quota to 9.5GB and the hard quota to 10GB.

```
Set-OrganizationConfig -DefaultPublicFolderIssueWarningQuota 9.5GB
-DefaultPublicFolderProhibitPostQuota 10GB:
```

22. Capture the public folder statistics and permissions by using the following commands from the on-premises Exchange Management Shell:

```
Get-PublicFolder -Recurse -ResultSize Unlimited | Export-Clixml`
.\LegacyPFStructure.xml

Get-PublicFolder -Recurse -ResultSize Unlimited | Get-PublicFolderStatistics |
Export-Clixml .\LegacyPFStatisticsRecurse.xml

Get-PublicFolder -Recurse -ResultSize Unlimited | Get-PublicFolderClientPermission
| Select-Object Identity,User -ExpandProperty AccessRights | Export-Clixml`
.\LegacyPFPerms.xml
```

23. From your on-premises Exchange Management Shell, create an accepted domain to be used to route mail for mail-enabled public folders. The `DomainName` parameter is a well-known ID, so be sure to create it as specified, replacing `<tenant>.onmicrosoft.com` with your Office 365 tenant ID:

```
New-AcceptedDomain -Name "PublicFolderDestination_78c0b207_5ad2_4fee_8cb9_`
f373175b3f99" -DomainName <tenant>.onmicrosoft.com -DomainType InternalRelay
```

24. Run a final check to ensure that you don't have any public folders with forward slashes or backslashes:

- For Exchange 2007, run this command from the Exchange Management Shell:

```
Get-PublicFolderDatabase | % { Get-PublicFolderStatistics -Server $_.Server`
| ? { ($_.Name -like "*\*") -or ($_.Name -like "*/*")} | FL Name,Identity
```

- For Exchange 2010, run this command from the Exchange Management Shell:

```
Get-PublicFolderStatistics -ResultSize Unlimited | ? { ($_.Name -like "*\*")`
-or ($_.Name -like "*/*")} | FL Name,Identity
```

25. Back up the Send-As permissions. From the Exchange Management Shell, run the following command:

```
Get-MailPublicFolder -ResultSize Unlimited | Get-ADPermission | ? {($_.Extended-
Rights -Like "Send-As") -and ($_.IsInherited -eq $False) -and -not ($_.User -like`
"*S-1-5-21-*")} | Select Identity,User | Export-Csv Send_As.csv -NoTypeInformation
```

26. Back up the Send-On-Behalf permission. From the Exchange Management Shell, run the following script:

```
Get-MailPublicFolder | Select Alias,PrimarySmtpAddress,@
{N="GrantSendOnBehalfTo";E={$_.GrantSendOnBehalfTo -join "|"}} | Export-Csv Grant-
SendOnBehalfTo.csv -NoTypeInformation
$File = Import-Csv .\GrantSendOnBehalfTo.csv
$Data = @()
Foreach ($line in $File)
  {
  If ($line.GrantSendOnBehalfTo)
    {
    Write-Host -ForegroundColor Green "Processing Public Folder $($line.Alias)"
    [array]$LineRecipients = $line.GrantSendOnBehalfTo.Split("|")
    Foreach ($Recipient in $LineRecipients)
      {
      Write-Host -ForegroundColor DarkGreen "   $($Recipient)"
      $GrantSendOnBehalfTo = (Get-Recipient $Recipient).PrimarySmtpAddress
      $LineData = New-Object PSCustomObject
      $LineData | Add-Member -Type NoteProperty -Name Alias -Value $line.Alias
      $LineData | Add-Member -Type NoteProperty -Name PrimarySmtpAddress -Value`
$line.PrimarySmtpAddress
      $LineData | Add-Member -Type NoteProperty -Name GrantSendOnBehalfTo -Value`
$GrantSendOnBehalfTo
```

```
            $Data += $LineData
        }
    }
}
$Data | Export-Csv .\GrantSendOnBehalfTo-Resolved.csv -NoTypeInformation
```

27. Run the `Export-PublicFolderStatistics.ps1` script from the Exchange Management Shell:

    ```
    .\Export-PublicFolderStatistics.ps1 C:\PFScripts\PFStatistics.csv <PFServerName>
    ```

28. If you have more than 10,000 public folders and you are running the `Export-PublicFolderStatistics.ps1` script on Exchange Server 2007, you might need to modify the script because of the way the shell handles the modulus operator. Look for the `$index%10000` string and update it to `$index%100000` (or a number higher than your existing public folder count), as shown in Figure 17-5.

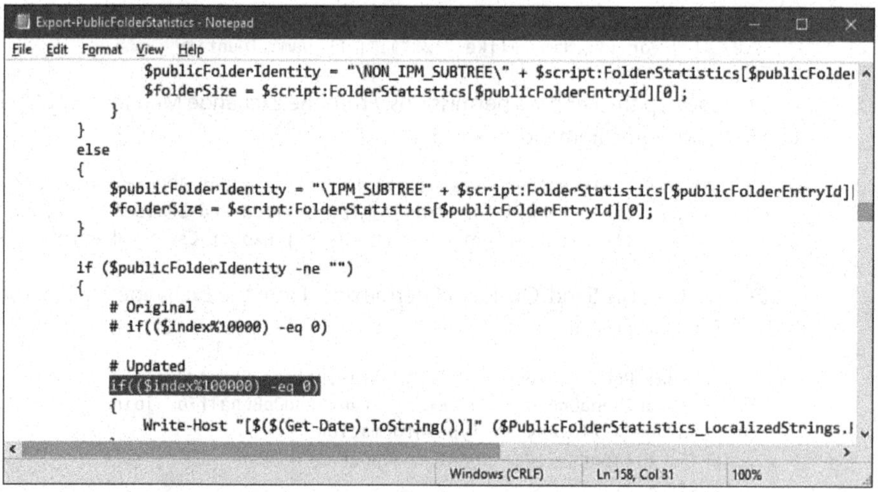

Figure 17-5   Updating code for public folder count

29. Run the public folder mapping generator (`PublicFolderToMailboxMapGenerator.ps1`). This process creates an output CSV that assigns public folders to public folder mailboxes.

30. The mapping generator reads the CSV created in the previous step and assigns branches of the public folder tree to individual public folder mailboxes based on the size of the public argument you give it. The syntax is as follows:

    ```
    .\PublicFolderToMailboxMapGenerator.ps1 <size> <Name of CSV from previous step>`
    <output map file>
    ```

31. For example, if you want to divide the public folder content into 10GB mailboxes, use the previously generated `PFStatistics.csv` file and set the output to `PFMapFile.csv`:

```
.\PublicFolderToMailboxMapGenerator.ps1 10000000000 PFStatistics.csv PFMapFile.csv
```

32. You should receive output that looks similar to the following:

```
[4/8/2017 4:02:22 AM] Reading public folder list...
[4/8/2017 4:02:22 AM] Loading folder hierarchy...
[4/8/2017 4:02:24 AM] Allocating folders to mailboxes...
[4/8/2017 4:02:24 AM] Trying to accommodate folders with their parent...
[4/8/2017 4:02:24 AM] Exporting folder mapping...
```

33. The public folder map file output is a list of target public folder mailboxes and which branch of the public folder tree is first in the public folder mailbox. The public folder mapping generator processes the public folder statistics output and distributes the public folder branches among the public folder mailboxes by using the specified target public folder mailbox size. Because the output is readable, you can edit it and make adjustments based on your working knowledge of the public folder hierarchy, how you might expect data to grow, or how active a particular folder or branch might be. See Figure 17-6.

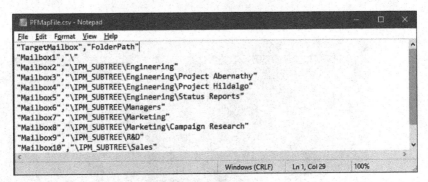

Figure 17-6   Public folder mapping generator output

34. After completing the mapping file, you can update the name of the mailboxes in the `TargetMailbox` column to something else, such as `PFMailbox`. The next step will create public folder mailboxes in Exchange Online based on the mapping file.

35. Switch to the Windows PowerShell window connected to Exchange Online and then use the `Create-PublicFolderMailboxesForMigration.ps1` script to complete this task:

```
.\Create-PublicFolderMailboxesForMigration.ps1 -FolderMappingCsv C;\PFScripts\`
PFMapFile.csv -EstimatedNumberOfConcurrentUsers 40000
```

Inside Out

Estimating the number of users

Public folder design is as much art as it is science. In addition to the public folder limits (1,000,000 public folders, 1,000 public folder mailboxes, and 100GB per public folder mailbox), you also have to plan for the number of active users in your organization who will be using public folders. To keep contention low, you want no more than 2,000 users per public folder mailbox.

Depending on how many users you have, the `Create-PublicFolderMailboxesFor-Migration.ps1` script might generate more public folder mailboxes than the mapping generator tool said you needed. The `Create-PublicFolderMailboxesForMigration.ps1` script creates one mailbox for every 2,000 users. If there are more mailboxes than the mapping generator recommended, you are prompted to acknowledge the update. After it has completed, you see an output similar to the figure shown here. If you were prompted to create more mailboxes, you see them named `AutoSplit_GUID`, and the `IsMigrationTarget` property is set to `False` for those mailboxes.

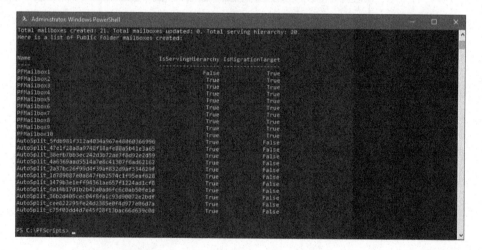

36. Launch a new Windows PowerShell prompt and run `.\Sync-MailPublicFolders.ps1` to sync the mail objects to Exchange Online. Don't run this from the Exchange Management Shell *or* the existing Windows PowerShell prompt connected to Exchange Online. After the sync has run, you can close this Windows PowerShell window:

```
.\Sync-MailPublicFolders.ps1 -Credential (Get-Credential) `
-CsvSummaryFile:SyncOutput.csv
```

37. Review the output in the CSV Summary File for errors. These errors must be resolved before migration.

38. In your Exchange Management Console window, ensure that you are in the directory containing the extracted public folder migration scripts, and then run the following commands:

```
(Get-Mailbox <admin user>).legacyExchangeDN | Out-File .\MailboxLegacyExchangeDN.`
txt
(Get-ExchangeServer <public folder server>).ExchangeLegacyDN | Out-File`
.\ServerExchangeLegacyDN.txt
$OAEndpoint = ((Get-ExchangeServer | ? { $_.ServerRole -match "ClientAccess"})`
[0]|Get-OutlookAnywhere).ExternalHostName
$OAEndpoint | Out-File .\OAEndpoint.txt
```

Inside Out

Outlook Anywhere endpoint selection

If your organization has more than one Outlook Anywhere endpoint or you have configured the `TargetAutoDiscoverEpr` in your Office 365 tenant, use that value instead. This value is used for creating the migration endpoint, so your public folder migrations might fail if it is not the endpoint you are using for mailbox migrations.

For example, in your Office 365 tenant, you can run this command:

```
Get-OrganizationRelationship | FL TargetAutoDiscoverEpr
```

By default, the output is null, but if you have configured it, it will look something like this:

```
TargetAutodiscoverEpr : https://hybrid.domain.com/autodiscover/autodiscover.`
svc/WSSecurity
```

Use the endpoint hostname (`hybrid.domain.com`, in this example) instead in the Exchange Management Shell window:

```
$OAEndPoint = "hybrid.domain.com"
$OAEndPoint | Out-File .\OAEndPoint.txt
```

39. Switch to the Windows PowerShell window connected to Exchange Online and ensure that you are in the `C:\PFScripts` directory because that is where the output of the previous step's commands was saved. Run these commands in the Exchange Online PowerShell window:

```
cd \PFScripts
$OAEndopint = gc .\OAEndpoint.txt
$MailboxLegacyExchangeDN = gc .\MailboxLegacyExchangeDN.txt
$ServerExchangeLegacyDN = gc .\ServerExchangeLegacyDN.txt
$Credential = Get-Credential <domain\admin user>
```

40. The credential specified in the `$Credential` variable must be an on-premises administrator account in `DOMAIN\Username` format. If it is not in that format, the endpoint creation will fail with an authentication negotiation error.

41. Create the public folder migration endpoint in Exchange Online. From the Exchange Online PowerShell window, run the following command:

```
$PFEndpoint = New-MigrationEndpoint -PublicFolder -Name PublicFolderEndPoint`
-RpcProxyServer $OAEndPoint -Credentials $Credential -SourceMailboxLegacyDN`
$MailboxLegacyExchangeDN -PublicFolderDatabaseServerLegacyDN`
$ServerExchangeLegacyDN -Authentication Basic
```

42. Create the public folder migration batch:

```
New-MigrationBatch -Name PublicFolderMigration -CSVData (Get-Content .\PFMapFile.`
csv -Encoding Byte) -SourceEndpoint $PFEndpoint.Identity -NotificationEmails`
<emailaddress>
```

43. To begin the migration, run the following command:

```
Start-MigrationBatch -Identity PublicFolderMigration
```

44. To check on the status of the migration, you can run:

```
Get-Migrationuser -BatchID PublicFolderMigration | Get-MigrationUserStatistics |`
Select Identity,Status,SyncedItemCount,SkippedItemCount,BytesTransferred,`
PercentageComplete
```

45. After all mailboxes show the Synced status, you can complete the migration batch. To do this, lock the public folders on the source side first. From the on-premises Exchange Management Shell, run the following command:

```
Set-OrganizationConfig -PublicFoldersLockedForMigration $True
```

46. Run the `Complete-MigrationBatch` command from the Exchange Online PowerShell session to complete the migration:

```
Complete-MigrationBatch -Identity PublicFolderMigration
```

Exchange 2013 or later

Before you begin migrating, you must ensure your environment meets the prerequisites and that you have completed the planning exercises necessary.

In addition to the general prerequisites, make sure you have downloaded the scripts and supporting files from *https://www.microsoft.com/en-us/download/details.aspx?id=54855*; save them to a folder on one of your Exchange servers in a directory, such as `C:\PFScripts`.

To migrate public folders, follow these steps:

1. If you are using Azure AD Connect to synchronize your directories, ensure that you are not synchronizing Exchange mail public folders because doing so causes the migration to fail. If you are not using AAD Connect, you can skip this step.

2. Launch the Azure AD Connect Setup Wizard on the server running AAD Connect.

3. Click Configure.

4. Click Customize Synchronization Options and then click Next.

5. On the Connect To Azure AD page, enter your Office 365 credentials and click Next.

6. On the Connect Your Directories page, click Next.

7. On the Domain And OU Filtering page, click Next.

8. On the Optional Features page, make sure the Exchange Mail Public Folders checkbox is not selected. If it is selected, clear it and click Next. Otherwise, you can exit the wizard.

9. If Group Writeback was selected on the Optional Features page, click Next on the Group Writeback page.

10. On the Ready To Configure page, click Configure.

11. Click Exit.

CAUTION

If you had deselected the Exchange Mail Public Folders checkbox on the Optional Features page, you must run a full import and synchronization because the wizard removes six synchronization rules and clears the public folder object type in the connector properties.

12. On the Exchange server where you have downloaded the public folder scripts, launch a Windows PowerShell session, change to the directory containing the downloaded public folder scripts, and connect to Exchange Online:

```
$Session = New-PSSession -ConfigurationName Microsoft.Exchange -ConnectionUri
https://outlook.office365.com/powershell-liveid -Authentication Basic
-AllowRedirection -Credential (Get-Credential)

Import-PSSession $Session
```

13. On the Exchange server to which you have downloaded the public folder scripts, launch an Exchange Management Shell session and change to the directory containing the downloaded public folder scripts.

14. Check for existing public folder migrations in the Exchange Online PowerShell window and make sure all entries are returned as `False`. From the Exchange Online PowerShell, run the following commands to clear any existing migration requests:

```
Get-PublicFolderMigrationRequest | Remove-PublicFolderMigrationRequest
Get-MigrationBatch | ?{$_.MigrationType.ToString() -eq "PublicFolder"} |`
Remove-MigrationBatch
```

15. Remove any existing public folder mailboxes or public folders created in Exchange Online. If any public folders or public folder mailboxes exist, you should confirm that others are not using them and that the data is no longer needed. Existing public folder mailboxes or public folders will cause the migration to fail if not removed. From the Exchange Online PowerShell window, run the following commands:

```
Get-MailPublicFolder -ResultSize Unlimited | where {$_.EntryId -ne $null}|`
Disable-MailPublicFolder -Confirm:$false
Get-PublicFolder -GetChildren \ -ResultSize Unlimited | Remove-PublicFolder`
-Recurse -Confirm:$false
$hierarchyMailboxGuid = $(Get-OrganizationConfig).RootPublicFolderMailbox.`
HierarchyMailboxGuid
Get-Mailbox -PublicFolder | Where-Object {$_.ExchangeGuid -ne`
$hierarchyMailboxGuid} | Remove-Mailbox -PublicFolder -Confirm:$false -Force
Get-Mailbox -PublicFolder | Where-Object {$_.ExchangeGuid -eq`
$hierarchyMailboxGuid} | Remove-Mailbox -PublicFolder -Confirm:$false -Force
Get-Mailbox -PublicFolder -SoftDeletedMailbox | Remove-Mailbox -PublicFolder`
-PermanentlyDelete:$true
```

16. Check for any existing public folder migrations in your on-premises environment. You might have previously migrated to Exchange 2013 or 2016, so you must remove those migration requests and artifacts to migrate to Office 365. From the on-premises Exchange Management Shell, run the following command:

```
Get-OrganizationConfig | Format-List PublicFoldersLockedforMigration,`
PublicFolderMigrationComplete, PublicFolderMailboxesLockedForNewConnections,`
PublicFolderMailboxesMigrationComplete
```

17. If either the `PublicFoldersLockedforMigration` or `PublicFolderMigrationComplete` parameters are `$true`, it means you have migrated older public folders at some point. Make sure any older public folder databases have been decommissioned before you continue.

18. If any of the properties from the preceding command are listed as `$true`, set them to `$false` by running the following command in the on-premises Exchange Management Shell:

```
Set-OrganizationConfig -PublicFoldersLockedforMigration:$false`
-PublicFolderMigrationComplete:$false -PublicFolderMailboxesLockedForNewConnection
s:$false -PublicFolderMailboxesMigrationComplete:$false
```

19. Run the following commands from the on-premises Exchange Management Shell to capture information about the current public folder structure:

```
Get-PublicFolder -Recurse -ResultSize Unlimited | Export-CliXML`
OnPrem_PFStructure.xml
Get-PublicFolderStatistics -ResultSize Unlimited | Export-CliXML`
OnPrem_PFStatistics.xml
Get-PublicFolder -Recurse -ResultSize Unlimited | Get-PublicFolderClientPermission
| Select-Object Identity,User -ExpandProperty AccessRights | Export-CliXML`
OnPrem_PFPerms.xml
Get-MailPublicFolder -ResultSize Unlimited | Export-CliXML OnPrem_MEPF.xml
```

20. Run the following command from the on-premises Exchange Management Shell to capture Send-As permissions:

```
Get-MailPublicFolder -ResultSize Unlimited | Get-ADPermission | ? {($_.`
ExtendedRights -Like "Send-As") -and ($_.IsInherited -eq $False) -and -not ($_.
User -like "*S-1-5-21-*")} | Select Identity,User | Export-Csv Send_As.csv
-NoTypeInformation
```

21. Run the following script from the on-premises Exchange Management Shell to capture Send-On-Behalf permissions:

```
Get-MailPublicFolder | Select Alias,PrimarySmtpAddress,@
{N="GrantSendOnBehalfTo";E={$_.GrantSendOnBehalfTo -join "|"}} | Export-Csv
GrantSendOnBehalfTo.csv -NoTypeInformation
$File = Import-Csv .\GrantSendOnBehalfTo.csv
$Data = @()
Foreach ($line in $File)
  {
  If ($line.GrantSendOnBehalfTo)
    {
    Write-Host -ForegroundColor Green "Processing Public Folder $($line.Alias)"
    [array]$LineRecipients = $line.GrantSendOnBehalfTo.Split("|")
    Foreach ($Recipient in $LineRecipients)
      {
      Write-Host -ForegroundColor DarkGreen "    $($Recipient)"
      $GrantSendOnBehalfTo = (Get-Recipient $Recipient).PrimarySmtpAddress
      $LineData = New-Object PSCustomObject
      $LineData | Add-Member -Type NoteProperty -Name Alias -Value $line.Alias
      $LineData | Add-Member -Type NoteProperty -Name PrimarySmtpAddress -Value`
$line.PrimarySmtpAddress
      $LineData | Add-Member -Type NoteProperty -Name GrantSendOnBehalfTo -Value`
$GrantSendOnBehalfTo
      $Data += $LineData
      }
    }
  }
$Data | Export-Csv .\GrantSendOnBehalfTo-Resolved.csv -NoTypeInformation
```

22. From the on-premises Exchange Management Shell, run the `Export-ModernPublicFolderStatistics.ps1` script to create the initial statistics data you will use for the public folder mapping generator:

```
.\Export-ModernPublicFolderStatistics.pf1 PFStatistics.csv
```

CHAPTER 17

23. From the on-premises Exchange Management Shell, run the `ModernPublicFolderToMailboxMapGenerator.ps1` script to create the CSV file that maps public folder branches into individual public folder mailboxes. The script is broken down as follows:

   ▪ The `MailboxSize` parameter specifies the maximum size each public folder mailbox should be.

   ▪ The `MailboxRecoverableItemsSize` parameter is the recoverable items quota for Exchange Online mailboxes.

   ▪ The `ImportFile` parameter specifies the public folder statistics file created in the previous step.

   ▪ The `ExportFile` parameter specifies the output file containing the public folder's destination mailbox mapping.

   This is the complete script:

   ```
   .\ModernPublicFolderToMailboxMapGenerator.ps1 -MailboxSize 25GB -MailboxRecover-
   ableItemsSize 1GB -ImportFile .\PFStatistics.csv -ExportFile PFmap.csv
   ```

24. From the Exchange Online PowerShell window, run the following commands to create the public folder mailboxes:

   ```
   $mappings = Import-Csv PFMap.csv
   $primaryMailboxName = ($mappings | Where-Object FolderPath -eq "\" ).TargetMailbox
   New-Mailbox -HoldForMigration:$true -PublicFolder -IsExcludedFromServingHierarchy:`
   $false $primaryMailboxName
   ($mappings | Where-Object TargetMailbox -ne $primaryMailboxName).TargetMailbox |`
   Sort-Object -unique | ForEach-Object { New-Mailbox -PublicFolder`
   -IsExcludedFromServingHierarchy:$false $_ }
   ```

25. From the on-premises Exchange Management Shell, run the following script and enter your Office 365 credential when prompted:

   ```
   .\Sync-ModernMailPublicFolders.ps1 -Credential (Get-Credential)`
   -CsvSummaryFile:sync_summary.csv
   ```

26. From the on-premises Exchange Management Shell, run the following commands:

   ```
   (Get-Mailbox <admin user>).legacyExchangeDN | Out-File .\MailboxLegacyExchangeDN.`
   txt
   (Get-ExchangeServer <public folder server>).ExchangeLegacyDN | Out-File`
   .\ServerExchangeLegacyDN.txt
   $OAEndpoint = (Get-ExchangeServer).[0].ExternalHostNameHostnameString
   $OAEndpoint | Out-File .\OAEndpoint.txt
   ```

27. Switch to the Windows PowerShell window connected to Exchange Online and ensure that you are in the directory containing the downloaded public folder migration scripts

because that is where the output of the previous step's commands was saved. Run these commands in the Exchange Online PowerShell window:

```
cd \PFScripts
$OAEndopint = gc .\OAEndpoint.txt
$MailboxLegacyExchangeDN = gc .\MailboxLegacyExchangeDN.txt
$ServerExchangeLegacyDN = gc .\ServerExchangeLegacyDN.txt
$Credential = Get-Credential <domain\admin user>
```

CAUTION

The credential specified in the `$Credential` **variable must be an on-premises administrator account in** `DOMAIN\Username` **format. If it is not in that format, the endpoint creation will fail with an authentication error.**

28. Create the public folder migration endpoint in Exchange Online. From the Exchange Online PowerShell window, run the following command:

```
$PFEndpoint = New-MigrationEndpoint -PublicFolder -Name PublicFolderEndPoint`
-RpcProxyServer $OAEndPoint -Credentials $Credential -SourceMailboxLegacyDN`
$MailboxLegacyExchangeDN -PublicFolderDatabaseServerLegacyDN`
$ServerExchangeLegacyDN -Authentication Basic
```

29. Create the public folder migration batch using this command:

```
New-MigrationBatch -Name PublicFolderMigration -CSVData (Get-Content`
.\PFMapFile.csv -Encoding Byte) -SourceEndpoint $PFEndpoint.Identity`
-NotificationEmails <emailaddress>
```

30. To begin the migration, run the following command:

```
Start-MigrationBatch -Identity PublicFolderMigration
```

31. To check on the status of the migration, run this command:

```
Get-Migrationuser -BatchID PublicFolderMigration | Get-MigrationUserStatistics |`
Select Identity,Status,SyncedItemCount,SkippedItemCount,BytesTransferred,`
PercentageComplete
```

32. After all mailboxes show the Synced status, you can complete the migration batch. To do this, lock the public folders on the source side first. From the on-premises Exchange Management Shell, run the following command:

```
Set-OrganizationConfig -PublicFoldersLockedForNewConnections $True
```

33. After the `PublicFoldersLockedForNewConnections` parameter has replicated, run the following command from the Exchange Online PowerShell window:

```
Compete-MigrationBatch -Identity PublicFolderMigration
```

CHAPTER 17

> ## Inside Out
>
> ### Cannot Access the `PublicFoldersLockedForNewConnections` *parameter*
>
> If you cannot access the PublicFoldersLockedForNewConnections parameter, it could be that you did not prepare Active Directory during the Cumulative Update installation. From the Exchange Cumulative Update download, launch an elevated command prompt and run the following command:
>
> ```
> Setup.exe /PrepareSchema /IAcceptExchangeServerLicenseTerms
> ```

Post-migration configuration

After the migrations have been completed, you might need to reapply permissions, configure the location of public folders in both the Exchange cloud and on-premises organizations, and update the mail routing configuration.

Exchange Online public folder location

Update the organization settings to use Exchange Online as the public folder source. From an Exchange Online PowerShell session, run the following commands:

```
Set-OrganizationConfig -PublicFoldersEnabled Local -RemotePublicFolderMailboxes`
$null
Get-Mailbox -PublicFolder | Set-Mailbox -PublicFolder`
-IsExcludedFromServingHierarchy $false
Set-Mailbox -Identity <test user> -DefaultPublicFolderMailbox <public folder`
mailbox1>
```

After waiting for a few minutes, log in to Outlook as the user specified in the `-Identity` parameter and access the public folders.

Exchange Online mail-enabled public folder routing

Depending on how the on-premises organization is configured and where the organization's MX record is configured, you might need to perform one or more mail routing configurations.

If your MX record is pointed to Office 365, disable Directory-Based Edge Blocking (DBEB), so mail-enabled public folders can receive Internet mail. From the Exchange Online PowerShell window, run the following command to disable DBEB:

```
Set-AcceptedDomain -Identity <domain.com> -DomainType InternalRelay
```

Exchange Online mail-enabled public folder external email address

If your on-premises public folders were migrated from Exchange 2013 or later, run the following script to update the on-premises mail-enabled public folder objects with the appropriate Exchange Online object. From the on-premises Exchange Management Shell, run the following script from the `C:\PFScripts` directory:

```
.\SetMailPublicFolderExternalAddress.ps1 -ExecutionSummaryFile:mepf_summary.csv
```

Exchange on-premises mail routing domain

If your MX record points to an on-premises gateway or on-premises systems send mail to mail-enabled public folders in Exchange Online, you might need to configure the on-premises Office 365 connector to route messages for mail-enabled public folders over the Office 365 hybrid transport connector. This step might not be necessary if you have disabled DBEB in Exchange Online.

Modify the properties for the on-premises Outbound To Office 365 connector and add the `<tenant>.onmicrosoft.com` domain that was created as part of the public folder migration process.

Exchange on-premises public folder migration complete

Set the `PublicFolderMigration` property to `true`. From the on-premises Exchange Management Shell, run the following command:

```
Set-OrganizationConfig -PublicFolderMigrationComplete $True
```

Apply Send-As permissions

From the Exchange Online PowerShell session, change to the `C:\PFScripts` directory containing the exported Send-As permissions file (`SendAs.csv`) created during the migration process and run the following script:

```
$SendAs = Import-Csv .\SendAs.csv
$i=1
foreach ($obj in $SendAs)
  {
  write-host "$($i)/$($SendAs.Count) adding $($obj.User) to $($obj.Identity)"
  Add-RecipientPermission -Identity $obj.Identity.Split("/")[2] -Trustee $obj.User.`
Split("\")[1] -AccessRights SendAs -confirm:$false; $i++
  }
```

Apply Grant-Send-On-Behalf-To permissions

From the Exchange Online PowerShell session, change to the `C:\PFScripts` directory containing the exported Send-On-Behalf permissions file (`GrantSendOnBehalfTo-Resolved.csv`) created during the migration process and run the following script:

```
$GrantSendOnBehalfTo = Import-Csv .\GrantSendOnBehalfTo-Resolved.csv
$i=1
Foreach ($obj in $GrantSendOnBehalfTo)
  {
  Write-host "$($i)/$($grantsendonbehalfto.count) Granting $($obj.GrantSendOnBehalfTo)`
Send-On-Behalf to folder $($obj.PrimarySmtpAddress)"
  Set-MailPublicFolder -Identity $obj.PrimarySmtpAddress -GrantSendOnBehalfTo $obj.`
GrantSendOnBehalfTo
  $i++
  }
```

Troubleshooting

While migrating public folders, you might run into a number of errors, especially if your organization has a long history of public folder usage and upgrades. Here are common errors you might encounter during migrations and how to resolve them.

Active Directory Operation Failed. The Object Already Exists.

Error text:

```
7/14/2022 6:11:16 PM,1a3a8d9e-0eb6-4b8a-bf00-a305f5229c2e,Update,"Active Direc-
tory operation failed on CY1PR13A001DC04.NAMPR13A001.PROD.OUTLOOK.COM. The object
'CN=FolderName,OU=tenant.onmicrosoft.com,OU=Microsoft Exchange Hosted Organizations,
DC=NAMPR13A001,DC=PROD,DC=OUTLOOK,DC=COM' already exists.","Set-EXOMailPublicFolder
-OnPremisesObjectId:""ae9563f4-1056-44c1-846a-c948c771720b"" -HiddenFromAddressListsEn
abled:""False"" -ExternalEmailAddress:""FolderName@domain.com"" -Alias:""FolderName""
-EmailAddresses:@(""X400:C=US;A= ;P=ORG;O=Exchange;S=FolderName;"",""SMTP: FolderName@
domain.com"",""x500:/O=ORG/OU=EXCHANGE/CN=RECIPIENTS/CN=FOLDERNAMEC89080BC4725C2AEEDFB7
4A5292C16AE6F7CEE"",""smtp: FolderName@tenant.onmicrosoft.com"") -Name:""Folder Name""
-Identity:""CN=Folder Name,OU=tenant.onmicrosoft.com,OU=Microsoft Exchange Hosted Organi
zations,DC=NAMPR14A001,DC=PROD,DC=OUTLOOK,DC=COM"" -ErrorAction:""Stop"" -WindowsEmailAd
dress:""FolderName@domain.com"" -DisplayName:""Folder Name"""
```

Cause:

This error appears in the `CSVSummaryFile` generated by the `Sync-MailPublicFolders.ps1` file. It means there is a mail-enabled public folder and another mail-enabled public folder, mail-enabled group, contact, or user with one or more of the same values.

Resolution:

You can use the following command in the on-premises Exchange Management Shell to locate it, replacing "`Folder Name`" with the value referenced in the error message:

```
    Get-Recipient -anr "Folder Name"
```

Exceeded Maximum Number Of Corrupted Items

Error text:

```
Error: This mailbox exceeded the maximum number of corrupted items that were specified
for this move request.
```

Cause:

The number of corrupt or unreadable source items exceeded the `BadItemLimit` threshold.

Resolution:

Remove corrupt items in the source public folder(s) or increase the error threshold. Increasing the error threshold is the simpler solution (and the result is the same):

```
Set-MigrationBatch -BadItemLimit 10000
```

Subscription Couldn't Be Loaded

Error text:

```
WARNING: The subscription for the migration user <Mailbox> couldn't be loaded. The fol-
lowing error was encountered: A subscription wasn't found for this user.
```

Cause:

Transient error retrieving mailbox information from Office 365.

Resolution:

Non-fatal. This error usually resolves itself.

Make Sure Public Folder Access Is Locked

Error text:

Before finalizing the migration, it is necessary to lock down public folders on the legacy Exchange server (downtime required). Make sure public folder access is locked on the legacy Exchange server, and then try to complete the batch again.

Cause:

When running `Complete-MigrationBatch`, you might receive this error if you haven't updated the organization configuration to lock the public folders or have not waited long enough for the change to replicate.

Resolution:

Wait for the `Set-OrganizationConfig` command to replicate. If you have not run it, run the following command in the on-premises Exchange Management Shell and wait 15 minutes before attempting to complete the migration:

```
Set-OrganizationConfig -PublicFoldersLockedForMigration $True
```

No Such Request Exists

Error text:

```
Couldn't find a request that matches the information provided. Reason: No such request
exists.
```

Cause:

Transient error when running `Get-MigrationUser <mailbox>` on a failed public folder mailbox. This error can happen during a database failover or while the mailbox request is being restarted.

Resolution:

This error will resolve itself.

Public Folder "/Path" Could Not Be Mail-Enabled

Error text:

```
Public folder "/Path/To/Public Folder" could not be mail-enabled. This error message is
displayed when reviewing the Get-MigrationUserStatistics report for a failed mailbox.
```

Cause:

The mail-enabled public folder is missing required attributes.

Resolution:

1.   Launch the public folder administration tool and navigate to the public folder path specified in the error. Mail-disable the folder.

2.   Mail-enable the folder again.

3.   Run `Sync-MailPublicFolders.ps1` again.

4.   Restart the migration batch.

Public Folders Could Not Be Mail-Enabled

Error text:

```
Error: There are {n} Public Folders that could not be mail-enabled. Please, check the
migration report starting at [date] [time] for additional details. This may indicate
that mail public folder objects in Exchange Online are out of sync with your Exchange
deployment. You may need to rerun the script Sync-MailPublicFolders.ps1 on your source
Exchange server to update mail-enabled public folder objects in Exchange Online Active
Directory.
```

Cause:

The Microsoft Exchange System Objects container in Active Directory contains orphaned objects (objects without a parent path).

Solution:

1. From the on-premises Exchange Management Shell, run the following script:

```
$resultsarray = @()
$mailpub = Get-MailPublicFolder -ResultSize unlimited
foreach ($folder in $mailpub) {
 $email    = $folder.primarysmtpaddress.local + "@" + $folder.primarysmtpaddress.`
domain
 $pubfolder = Get-PublicFolder -Identity $folder.identity
 $folderpath = $pubfolder.parentpath + "\" + $pubfolder.name
 # Create a new object for the purpose of exporting as a CSV
 $pubObject = new-object PSObject
 $pubObject | add-member -membertype NoteProperty -name "Email" -Value $email
 $pubObject | add-member -membertype NoteProperty -name "FolderPath" -Value`
$folderpath
 # Append this iteration of our for loop to our results array.
 $resultsarray += $pubObject
}
$resultsarray | export-csv -Path .\mail-enabled-public-folders.csv -NoType
$NoPublicFolderPath = Import-Csv C:\Temp\mail-enabled-public-folders.csv | ? {`
$_.Parentpath -eq "" } | Export-Csv .\NoFolderPath.csv -NoType
```

2. Launch Active Directory Users And Computers, select View Advanced Features from the menu bar, and navigate to the Microsoft Exchange System Objects container.

3. Review the NoFolderPath.csv and remove the corresponding items in the Microsoft Exchange System Objects container.

4. Run Sync-MailPublicFolders.ps1 again.

5. Restart the migration batch.

What's next?

In the next chapter, we'll learn about managing Exchange Online environments. The management techniques will apply to both native Exchange Online deployments and hybrid environments with supported versions of Exchange Server.

Managing Exchange Online

Whether you have performed a greenfield deployment to Exchange Online or started or completed a migration (or you are somewhere in between), you'll need to administer the environment at some point.

This chapter is divided into sections based on the areas you typically need to manage:

- Recipients

- Transport services

- Organization settings

- Auditing

- Hybrid configuration

Although many settings can be configured inside the Exchange admin center, some tasks are quicker to perform or can only be achieved through Windows PowerShell.

Exchange admin center

If you are familiar with managing Exchange Server 2013 or later on-premises, the Exchange admin center in Office 365 will look familiar, though some things have been updated to reflect the new admin center interface styling. Figure 18-1 shows the updated Exchange admin center.

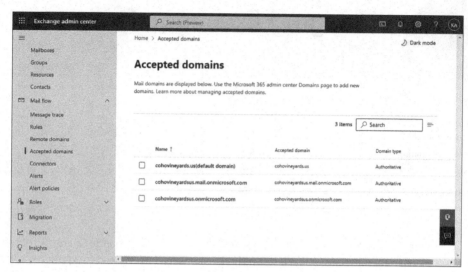

Figure 18-1   Exchange admin center in Office 365

The layout of the Exchange admin center for Exchange Online is very similar to the Exchange admin center for Exchange Server, with just a few feature changes.

They both are styled similarly, with the Office 365 or Exchange Online version of the admin center displaying a dashboard, additional reporting capabilities, and an Other Features navigation node that helps you locate familiar features. The on-premises Exchange Server version has fewer menu items but does include one for servers to allow you to manage individual server and database components. Because you are not responsible for the underlying server health in Office 365, there is no need to expose the server options in Office 365.

The Exchange Server admin center also has two tabs at the top—Enterprise and Office 365—that enable you to enter credentials and switch back and forth between the two environments inside a single browser window.

Recipient management

Most of the things you will be administering in Office 365 are recipients of some sort—whether they are mailboxes, mail-enabled users, contacts, or one of the distribution groups.

This next section gives you some ideas about tasks you can perform against the various recipient types in Office 365.

Mailboxes

User mailboxes are one of the most common recipient types used in Exchange Online. A mailbox is a storage unit that can contain mail, folders, calendars, contacts, tasks, and rules. A mailbox's management rights can be delegated to others (both users and groups).

Permissions and rights

One of the most common tasks you will perform is managing permissions or rights for a mailbox. From the Exchange admin center, mailbox permissions can be managed through the Delegation tab on a mailbox's property sheet.

To access the property sheet in the Exchange admin center, expand Recipients, select Mailboxes, and then click the name of the user whose properties you want to modify. See Figure 18-2.

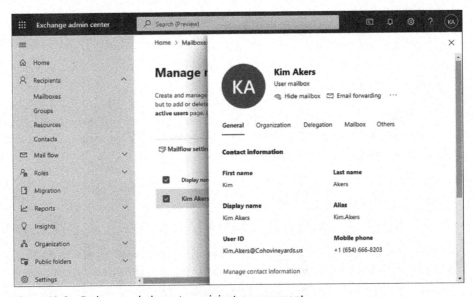

Figure 18-2   Exchange admin center recipient management

The following sections cover some common scenarios.

Grant full mailbox access

With full mailbox access, the delegate can perform any mailbox management task that the original owner can perform, such as creating or deleting folders or moving messages.

To grant full mailbox access for a mailbox to another user, you can add the permission through the admin center by navigating to Recipients > Mailboxes, selecting a recipient, and clicking the user's name to bring up the property sheet. Select the Delegation tab, and then under Read And Manage (Full Access), click Edit. See Figure 18-3.

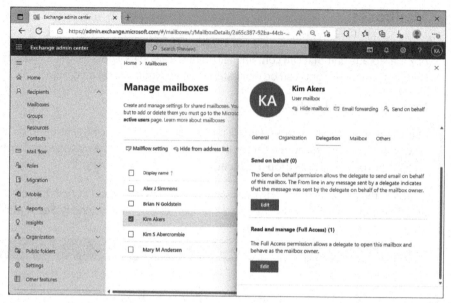

Figure 18-3   Mailbox delegation

From there, you can add names from the address list, meaning these users will be able to manage the mailbox. Click Add Members, select the user to whom you want to grant access, and then click Save.

Inside Out

AutoMapping and that extra mailbox

If you have configured full mailbox access permission for a mailbox in the Exchange admin center, your users might say the mailbox is automatically appearing in their Outlook profiles and that they have no way to close or disconnect it.

This happens because the Exchange admin center enables AutoMapping when it is used to grant full mailbox access. AutoMapping is an Exchange feature that automatically mounts mailboxes to which a user has full access. When a mailbox is automatically added, the user has no way to remove it. This can be a useful feature, but many people find it undesirable—especially if they only administer a secondary mailbox occasionally.

To remove an automatically mounted mailbox from an Outlook profile, remove the Full Access permissions entry and re-add it through Windows PowerShell, using this syntax:

```
Remove-MailboxPermission -Identity <mailbox> -User <delegate> -AccessRights `
FullAccess
Add-MailboxPermission -Identity <mailbox> -User <delegate> -AccessRights `
FullAccess -InheritanceType None
```

NOTE

For more information about adding mailbox permissions, see the "Add-MailboxPermission" section at *https://aka.ms/addmailboxpermission*.

Grant Send-On-Behalf or Send-As permissions

If your users need to perform activities (such as sending mail) as another mailbox, then you must grant them Send-On-Behalf or Send-As permissions. A common scenario is to include sending as a shared mailbox (such as Sales) to mask the sender.

Users access the Send-As and Send-On-Behalf feature in the same way—by exposing the From field in Outlook and then entering the mailbox address they're acting as. The difference is in how the recipient sees it. Messages sent on behalf of someone else include both the sender and the original mailbox owner's name in the From line (such as "From Kim on behalf of Dan"), whereas messages sent using the Send-As permission show the mailbox owner as the sender.

Both Send-On-Behalf and Send-As can be granted from the Mailbox Delegation page in the Exchange admin center, as shown previously in Figure 18-3, or through Windows PowerShell:

```
Add-RecipientPermission -Identity <mailbox> -GrantSendOnBehalfTo <delegate>
Add-RecipientPermission -Identity <mailbox> -AccessRight SendAs -Trustee <delegate>
```

NOTE

For more information on managing recipient permissions, see the "Add-RecipientPermission" section at *https://aka.ms/addrecipientpermission*.

Folder permissions

If you configure shared mailboxes to be used as calendars or want to update calendar permissions for your users, you can use the Add-MailboxFolderPermission, Set-MailboxFolderPermission, or Remove-MailboxFolderPermission cmdlets. Although you can use those cmdlets to manage the permissions on any folder in the mailbox, the most common usage for it is to manage the calendar. You can specify the folder by using the <mailbox>:\Folder syntax.

Table 18-1 lists the individual permissions you can assign.

Table 18-1 Folder permissions

Permission	Description
CreateItems	The user can create items in the specified folder.
CreateSubfolders	The user can create subfolders in the specified folder.
DeleteAllItems	The user can delete all items in the specified folder.

DeleteOwnedItems	The user can only delete items that they created from the specified folder.
EditAllItems	The user can edit all items in the specified folder.
EditOwnedItems	The user can only edit items they created in the specified folder.
FolderContact	The user is the contact for the specified public folder.
FolderOwner	The user is the owner of the specified folder. The user can view the folder, move the folder, and create subfolders. The user can't read, edit, delete, or create items.
FolderVisible	The user can view the specified folder but can't read or edit items in the specified public folder.
ReadItems	The user can read items in the specified folder.

The permissions are grouped into roles, which can also be assigned using the Add-MailboxFolderPermission or Set-MailboxFolderPermission cmdlet. Table 18-2 lists the roles and their associated permissions.

Table 18-2   Roles and permissions

Role	Permissions
Author	CreateItems, DeleteOwnedItems, EditOwnedItems, FolderVisible, ReadItems
Contributor	CreateItems, FolderVisible
Editor	CreateItems, DeleteAllItems, DeleteOwnedItems, EditAllItems, EditOwnedItems, FolderVisible, ReadItems
None	FolderVisible
NonEditingAuthor	CreateItems, FolderVisible, ReadItems
Owner	CreateItems, CreateSubfolders, DeleteAllItems, DeleteOwnedItems, EditAllItems, EditOwnedItems, FolderContact, FolderOwner, FolderVisible, ReadItems
PublishingEditor	CreateItems, CreateSubfolders, DeleteAllItems, DeleteOwnedItems, EditAllItems, EditOwnedItems, FolderVisible, ReadItems
PublishingAuthor	CreateItems, CreateSubfolders, DeleteOwnedItems, EditOwnedItems, FolderVisible, ReadItems
Reviewer	FolderVisible, ReadItems
AvailabilityOnly	View only availability data (only applicable to Calendar folder)
LimitedDetails	View availability data with subject and location (only applicable to Calendar folder)

The following examples illustrate how to manage the permissions:

- Grant the user Ayla Kol the ability to create items on Dan Jump's calendar, using permissions granted in the Author role:

  ```
  Add-MailboxFolderPermission -Identity DanJump:\Calendar -AccessRights Author `
  -User AylaKol
  ```

- Change the default permission for all calendars from `AvailabilityOnly` to `LimitedDetails`:

```
Get-Mailbox -ResultSize Unlimited | % { Set-MailboxFolderPermission `
-Identity "$($_.Alias):\Calendar" -User Default -AccessRights LimitedDetails }
```

NOTE

For more information on folder permissions cmdlets, see the Add-MailboxFolderPermission section at *https://aka.ms/addmailboxfolderpermission*.

Email addresses

All the addresses a mailbox can receive mail as are listed in the `EmailAddresses` attribute. The name of the underlying attribute in Active Directory (and Azure Active Directory) is `proxyAddresses`.

If your objects are authored in the cloud, you can modify the `EmailAddresses` attribute in the Microsoft 365 or Exchange Online admin centers. If they are synchronized from an on-premises environment, you must modify the mail-enabled user object or remote mailbox object from that environment. In either scenario, the syntax is the same—simply replace `mailbox` in the cmdlet with `remotemailbox`.

To add a proxy address to a user mailbox, use:

```
Set-Mailbox TerryAdams -EmailAddresses @{add="newaddress@contoso.com"}
```

You can also replace all the proxy addresses by using a different syntax for the `-EmailAddresses` parameter:

```
Set-Mailbox TerryAdams -EmailAddresses @("SMTP:terryadams@cohovineyards.us", `
"tadams@cohovineyards.us", "terrya@cohovineyards.us")
```

Inside OUT

Using SMTP and smtp

When working with the `EmailAddresses` parameter in the second example, you have the opportunity to specify the primary SMTP address using the `SMTP:` prefix. The uppercase `SMTP:` prefix in the `EmailAddresses` array designates which address will be primary in the array. If you do not pick one, `Set-Mailbox` uses the first value in the array as the primary SMTP address. Entries prefixed with lowercase `smtp:` are used as secondary addresses that can be used as alias or alternate email addresses.

CHAPTER 18

Automatic calendar processing

When you create shared mailboxes for equipment or conference rooms, you might not be able to enter all the configuration parameters that accurately describe how the resource is to be used. One of those areas might be calendar processing.

Calendar processing controls how the Calendar Attendant or Resource Booking Attendant manages meetings for a given mailbox. For example, you can control who is allowed to book a conference room, whether recurring meetings will be accepted, or whether meetings need to be approved by a delegate.

By default, user mailboxes have calendar processing set to AutoUpdate, and resource mailboxes have calendar processing set to AutoAccept.

With calendar automation, requests fall into two classes:

- **In-policy requests**   In-policy requests don't violate any of the resource scheduling options, such as conflicts or duration.

- **Out-of-policy requests**   Out-of-policy requests violate one or more resource scheduling options.

Seven settings work together to form the foundation of booking policies:

AllBookInPolicy   Everyone can automatically reserve a resource with a valid, in-policy meeting request. The default setting is $True.

BookInPolicy   Use this setting to specify a list of users who can automatically book a resource with a valid, in-policy meeting request if AllBookInPolicy is set to $False.

AllRequestInPolicy   Everyone can request to reserve the resource with a valid, in-policy meeting request. The request is routed to the value stored in the mailbox's ResourceDelegates property. The default setting is $false.

RequestInPolicy   Use this setting to specify a list of users who can request to reserve a resource with a valid, in-policy meeting request. The request is routed to the value stored in the mailbox's ResourceDelegates property.

AllRequestOutOfPolicy   Everyone can reserve a resource with a valid, in-policy meeting request. If the meeting request violates the policy defined in the scheduling options, the request can be approved by one of the mailbox's resource delegates stored in the mailbox's Resource-Delegates property. The default value is $false.

RequestOutOfPolicy   Use this setting to specify a list of users who can automatically reserve a resource with a valid, in-policy meeting request. If the request violates the policy defined in the scheduling options, the request can be approved by one of the mailbox's resource delegates, stored in the ResourceDelegates property.

ResourceDelegates   This setting is for users who can approve or decline meeting requests on behalf of a resource mailbox.

Here are some examples of how you might configure the Room1 conference room:

- Enable Room1 to accept meeting requests from people outside the organization. This might be useful if you have a facility with public meeting rooms, such as a library, that you want to allow people outside the organization to schedule:

```
Set-CalendarProcessing -Identity Room1 -ProcessExternalMeetingMessages $True
```

- Specify the additional text to be sent back to a meeting organizer when the resource is booked:

```
Set-CalendarProcessing -Identity Room1 -AddAditionalResponse $True `
-AdditionalResponse "Your room has been successfully booked. Please `
arrive at least 5 minutes prior to your scheduled meeting."
```

- Choose to retain attachments on resource mailboxes. By default, attachments to meeting requests are deleted:

```
Set-CalendarProcessing -Identity Room1 -DeleteAttachments $False
```

- Allow only members of the mail-enabled Marketing security group to be able to schedule meetings in Room1:

```
Set-CalendarProcessing -Identity Room1 -BookInPolicy Marketing -AllBookInPolicy `
$False
```

- Allow only members of the mail-enabled Marketing security group to schedule meetings in Room1 but allow members of the mail-enabled security group Sales to schedule a meeting with the delegate's approval. Finally, set Lori Penor as the delegate:

```
Set-CalendarProcessing -Identity Room1 -BookInPolicy Marketing `
-AllBookInPolicy $False -RequestInPolicy Sales -ResourceDelegates LoriPenor
```

NOTE

For more information about the Calendar Attendant and Resource Booking Attendant, see "Set scheduling permissions for an equipment mailbox" at *https://aka.ms/resourcescheduling*.

Mail-enabled users

A mail-enabled user is a security principal (an object that has an account and can log on to a system) that has the mail properties of a contact attached to it. It allows for a number of unique business and technical scenarios, such as assigning a vendor a local account but using their external email address while allowing them to show up in a GAL, hybrid mailbox users, or user objects linked to mailboxes in other forests.

Mail-enabled users can have many of the same properties of mailbox user, but it is only a routing entity from the global address list's point of view. Following are the core properties of a mail-enabled user:

- **msExchRecipientDisplayType** This property is set to 6.

- **msExchRecipientTypeDetails** This property is set to 128.

- **Mail** This property is set to an email address, either inside or outside of your environment's authoritative domain name space.

- **targetAddress** This property is set to an email address, typically outside of your environment's authoritative name space.

For example, you can create a mail-enabled user with the following syntax:

```
New-MailUser -Name "Jeff Hay" -FirstName Jeff -LastName Hay -ExternalEmailAddress `
jeffhay@cohovineyard.com -MicrosoftOnlineServicesID `
jeffhay@cohovineyardsus.onmicrosoft.com
```

The user account would have a primary SMTP address matching the value for ExternalEmailAddress, and you would be able to sign in to the Office 365 service with the password you assigned to it. Because mail-enabled users are security principals and mail recipients, they can be granted management permissions on objects and become members of distribution lists.

Contacts

Contacts are designed to give representation only to mail objects inside the global address list. They are recipients and can be made members of distribution groups but cannot be granted management rights or permissions, nor can a contact object be used to log in to Office 365.

Contacts can be created from the Exchange admin center or with Windows PowerShell:

```
New-MailContact -FirstName Tanja -LastName Plate -Name "Tanya Plate" `
-ExternalEmailAddress tanya@tailspintoys.com
```

Distribution groups

Distribution groups are collections of objects designed to make addressing simpler. Office 365 has several kinds of groups, including distribution (mail-enabled groups), security groups, mail-enabled security groups, and Microsoft 365 groups:

- **Distribution groups** In on-premises environments, distribution groups are not added to a user's security token and are generally not used to grant access to resources.

- **Security groups** Both mail-enabled and non-mail-enabled security groups contain a security identifier and may be used to grant access to resources. Mail-enabled security groups include mail properties and can also be used like distribution groups.

- **Microsoft 365 groups**   These are a special type of object with both persistent storage like a mailbox and distribution group functionality.

Restricting delivery

You might need to restrict sending to users or groups at some point. You can set different restrictions, including allowing or prohibiting sending to users and groups or ensuring that content goes through review (perhaps by a manager) before being delivered to recipients.

Restrict delivery from outside senders

You can configure both users and distribution groups to accept mail only from internal users. To do this, you can set the RequireSenderAuthenticationEnabled property to $True, as shown in the following examples:

```
Set-Mailbox TerryAdams -RequireSenderAuthentication $True
Set-DistributionGroup "Quality Control" -RequireSenderAuthentication $True
```

Inside OUT

Microsoft 365 groups and anonymous senders

Although configuring delivery from anonymous senders can be easily managed using the RequireSenderAuthenticationEnabled property, there is a set of conditions under which it will not work correctly:

- Office 365 Group Writeback is enabled.
- RequireSenderAuthenticationEnabled is set to False for an Office 365 group.
- The organization's MX record is configured to point on-premises.

In this scenario, external emails sent to Office 365 groups are returned to the sender with the error, "You do not have permission to send to this recipient." This happens because the RequireSenderAuthenticationEnabled property is set to the constant value True in AAD Connect rule 168, Out to AD - Group SOAInAAD - Exchange. To enable sending to Office 365 groups in this scenario, you must modify the constant value specified in the rule or manually update the msExchRequireAuthToSendTo property for the on-premises object to False.

Restrict delivery to allowed senders

You can also restrict delivery to users or distribution lists to usage by named individuals by using the AcceptMessagesOnlyFrom parameter. The following example configures the All Employees distribution group to allow only Lori Penor to send to it:

```
Set-DistributionGroup "All Employees" -AcceptMessagesOnlyFrom LoriPenor@cohovineyards.us
```

CHAPTER 18

If you want to grant a group send-to permissions (instead of a user), you can use the `AcceptMessagesOnlyFromDLMembers` parameter. If you want to restrict sending to a user or group by using a combination of named users and group memberships, you can use the `AcceptMessagesOnlyFromSendersOrMembers` parameter.

NOTE

The `AcceptMessagesOnlyFromSendersOrMembers` **overwrites the values in** `Accept-MessagesOnlyFromDLMembers` **and** `AcceptMessagesOnlyFrom`.

Moderate messages sent to a group

You can also configure moderation for a distribution group. Messages sent to a distribution group are first routed to the listed moderator for approval. You can configure moderation by using the `ModerationEnabled` and `ModeratedBy` parameters, as shown in the following example:

```
Set-DistributionGroup "Ask the CEO" -ModerationEnabled $True -ModeratedBy DanJump
```

Require approval for messages sent to a user

Before delivery, you can configure a transport rule to redirect messages to another user (such as a manager).

Follow these steps to configure a rule redirecting all messages using the Exchange admin center:

1. In the Exchange admin center, select Mail Flow > Rules.

2. Click the plus sign (+) and then select Create A New Rule.

3. In the Name box, enter a name for the rule.

4. In the Apply This Rule If dropdown, select The Recipient Is and then choose a name from the Select Members dialog box.

5. In the Do The Following dropdown, select Forward The Message For Approval To and then choose a name from the Select Members dialog box.

6. Click Save.

7. Using Windows PowerShell, use the following command to configure a transport rule to redirect all messages intended for Ayla Kol to Dan Jump for approval:

```
New-TransportRule -SentTo AylaKol -ModerateMessageByUser DanJump -Name 'Moderate `
Messages Sent to Ayla Kol' -StopRuleProcessing:$false -Mode 'Enforce' `
-RuleErrorAction 'Ignore' -SenderAddressLocation 'Header'
```

8. As with any transport rule, you can add additional conditions and exceptions to meet your requirements.

Transport

The default mail routing configuration is sufficient for many organizations that move to Office 365. In the default Office 365 mail flow, all outbound mail goes directly to the Internet from Office 365. Inbound mail is received directly from the Internet (if your MX record is pointed to Office 365), from your on-premises environment (if you have on-premises applications or mailboxes delivering through a hybrid environment), or both.

Connectors

Connectors are configuration objects that direct mail flow. In Office 365, connectors go in two directions: inbound (into Office 365) and outbound (out from Office 365). These map to the on-premises receive (into the Exchange environment) and send (out to other servers or systems) connectors. If you have a hybrid environment, you have inbound and outbound connectors in Office 365 and send and receive connectors in your Exchange on-premises environments.

To manage connectors, you can navigate to the Exchange admin center and select Mail Flow > Connectors. By default, Exchange Online has no connectors and routes mail directly to the Internet.

You can control the path taken by a connector or restrict it to handle traffic only for certain domains. Exchange automatically uses the connector with the most specific match:

```
PS C:\> Get-OutboundConnector
Name        RecipientDomains          SmartHosts Enabled
----        ----------------          ---------- -------
Coho Vineyard {cohovineyard.com}        {[1.2.3.4]} True
Marketing   {marketing.cohovineyard.com} {[5.6.7.8]} True
```

If you sent a message to TerryAdams@marketing.cohovineyard.com, the message would use the connector marketing.cohovineyard.com with the smart host 5.6.7.8 because the email address domain marketing.cohovineyard.com is an exact match for the Marketing connector.

Transport rules

Transport rules are a set of logic that can be applied to messages as they pass through the system to influence which route a message might take or other actions that can happen to a message based on sender, recipient, or contents in the header or message body.

Transport rules are made up of three parts:

- **Conditions**   Conditions are settings or properties under which a particular rule is applied. Conditions might specify senders or recipients; sensitive information types; contents in the subject, body, or header; attachments; or other message properties. Conditions are also referred to as predicates in some documentation.

- **Actions**   Actions specify which functions are performed on a message. Actions might include forwarding a copy of a message to another recipient, redirecting the message to a new recipient, applying encryption, redirecting the message to a designated connector, or rejecting the message.

- **Exceptions**   Exceptions are conditions or properties under which a particular rule is blocked or skipped. For example, you might configure a rule to add recipients to the Cc line if the subject is Sales Order but make an exception if the subject contains the text RE: at the beginning.

You configure transport rules on the Mail Flow page (see Figure 18-4) in the Exchange admin center or through Windows PowerShell.

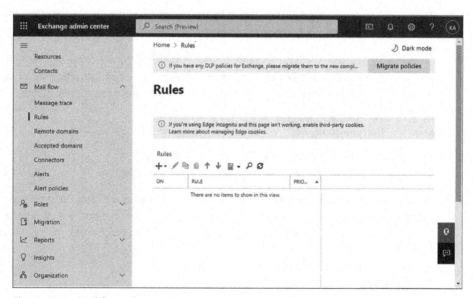

Figure 18-4   Mail flow rules

Follow these steps to create a rule:

1. Click the plus sign (+) and select from the available options. The dropdown has a number of available rule templates, or you can select Create A New Rule to start with a blank rule.

2. When you create a new rule, it might seem like there aren't a lot of choices for actions (see Figure 18-5).

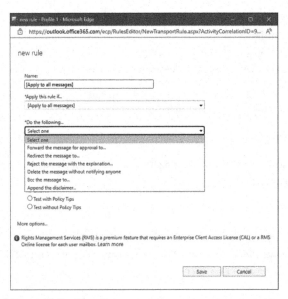

Figure 18-5   New Rule page

3. Click the More Options link near the bottom of the page. The page refreshes to show the Except If button to specify rule exceptions, and the list of available actions under the Do The Following dropdown is updated.

4. You can then create the rule, using all the available predicates and actions. The rule shown in Figure 18-6 redirects all mail intended for Lori to Ayla's mailbox, except if the messages are of the type Read Receipt or are more than 2 MB in size.

Figure 18-6   Mail redirect rule

5. You can also create the same rule with Windows PowerShell by using the New-TransportRule cmdlet:

```
New-TransportRule -SentTo LoriPenor@cohovineyards.us -RedirectMessageTo `
AylaKol@cohovineyards.us -ExceptIfMessageTypeMatches 'ReadReceipt' `
-ExceptIfMessageSizeOver 2MB -Name 'Redirect Lori''s mail to Ayla' `
-StopRuleProcessing:$false -SetAuditSeverity 'DoNotAudit' -Mode 'Enforce' `
-RuleErrorAction 'Ignore' -SenderAddressLocation 'Header'
```

Attachment blocking

Attachment blocking occurs when your organization might want to block all attachments or all attachments of a certain type.

NOTE

Many of the security features, such as the Malware Filter, Spam Filter, Connection Filter, and Quarantine, have moved from the Exchange admin center to the new Microsoft 365 Defender portal.

In this example, you can block a message with attachments based on type using a malware filter rule.

NOTE

The first time you customize security settings or other default parameters in your organization, you might be required to run Enable-OrganizationCustomization **from the Exchange Online management shell.**

1. Navigate to the new Microsoft 365 Defender portal at *https://security.microsoft.com*.

2. Expand Email & Collaboration and select Policies & Rules.

3. Select Threat Policies.

4. On the Threat Policies page, select Anti-Malware.

5. On the Anti-Malware page, click the plus sign (+) to add a new filter, as shown in Figure 18-7.

6. On the Name Your Policy page, add a Name such as Block File Types (and optionally, a Description) to the policy and click Next.

7. On the Users And Domains page, add individual users, groups, or domains to which the policy will apply. You must add at least one name, group, or domain. Click Next when finished.

8. Under Protection Settings, click Select File Types to specify file types. Note that there are already 13 selected file types (.aci, .ani, .app, .cab, .docm, .exe, .iso, .jar, .jnlp, .reg, .scr, .vbe, .vbs).

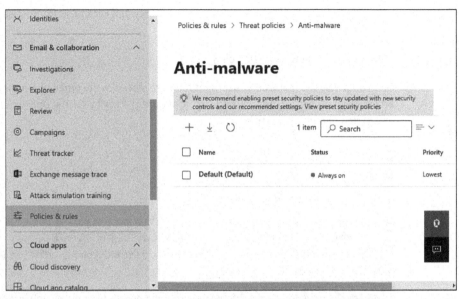

Figure 18-7   Anti-Malware Policy page in Microsoft 365 Defender portal

9.   On the Select File Types page, you can add additional file types to automatically treat as malware or remove any of the existing file types. To add a new extension, type the extension name (without the leading ".") in the input box and click Add (see Figure 18-8). Click Done when finished.

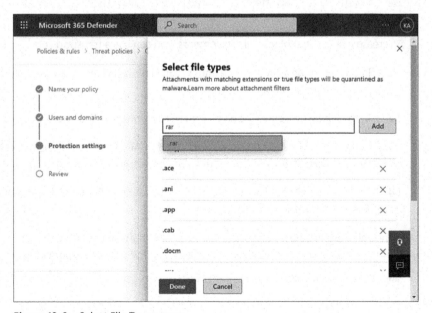

Figure 18-8   Select File Types page

10. Update any notification settings for the policy and click Next to proceed to the Review page.

11. Click Submit to save the policy.

Files caught by the malware attachment filter are stored in the email quarantine. All users can access them by default, but you can also configure the policy so that only administrators can manipulate files in quarantine.

Inside Out

Managing blocked file types

Previously, if you wanted to add a file type that was not present in the file types list, you were required to either create the rule in PowerShell using the `New-MalwareFilter-Policy` cmdlet or edit an existing rule to add the file type using the `Set-MalwareFilterPolicy` cmdlet.

For example, to add the ZIP file type to the malware filter policy you just created, you can run this command:

```
[array]$FileTypes = (Get-MalwareFilterPolicy "Block File Types").FileTypes
$FileTypes += "zip"
Set-MalwareFilterPolicy "Block File Types" -FileTypes $FileTypes
```

You can then view the malware filter policy to make sure your file type has been added.

To create a policy that blocks all attachments, you can use a transport rule:

1. In the Exchange admin center, under Mail Flow, select Rules, click the plus sign (+), and select Create New Rule.

2. In the Name box, specify a name for the rule and then click More Options.

3. In the Apply This Rule If... dropdown, point to Any Attachment and select The Size Is Greater Than Or Equal To Condition. Enter a size of 1KB.

4. Under Do The Following, configure an action such as Redirect The Message To or Block The Message and click Save.

Although 1KB will detect most attachments, there might still be some that get through. You can modify the policy in Windows PowerShell by using the `Set-TransportRule` cmdlet:

```
Set-TransportRule <Rule> -AttachmentSizeOver 1B
```

However, many senders have images in their email signatures that, depending on the formatting of the message, might be inserted as attachments. This setting renders those undeliverable, so make sure you understand your organization's requirements before configuring this.

Encryption

You can configure Office 365 Message Encryption to enable users to send encrypted messages to users inside or outside the organization. Common scenarios for message encryption might be to enable encryption if certain keywords are detected in the message or subject or certain sensitive information types are present.

To use encryption, Azure Rights Management Services (RMS) licenses must be applied to users, the Rights Management service must be enabled in your tenant, and you must have created transport rules to apply encryption.

Office 365 users—inside or outside the organization—can now read encrypted messages in their client or browser.

Encrypted message recipients on other platforms (such as Yahoo, Outlook.com, or Gmail) receive a notification that they must log in to the Office 365 encryption portal to view the message content. From there, users can read and reply to the secure messages.

Activate Azure Rights Management

Previously, organizations were required to activate Azure Rights Management services separately. However, Azure Rights Information Management Services are now automatically activated on any qualifying subscription purchased after February 2018.

If you want to perform a phased deployment for onboarding or only allow Azure Information Protection and Rights Management services to be used by a subset of users, follow these steps:

1. Connect to your Azure AD tenant with the Azure AD PowerShell module.

2. Create a security group:

    ```
    $RMSGroup = New-AzureADGroup -DisplayName "Azure AD RMS Group" -Description `
    "Azure AD RMS Uses" -SecurityEnabled $True -MailEnabled $False -MailNickname `
    AzureADRMS
    ```

3. Use the newly created group objectId to restrict access to the feature:

    ```
    Set-AipServiceOnboardingControlPolicy -UseRmsUserLicense $False `
    -SecurityGroupObjectId $RMSGroup.ObjectId
    ```

4. Add members to the security group. When you are ready to expand the scope to all users, you can run the following command:

    ```
    Set-AipServiceOnboardingControlPolicy -UseRmsUserLicense $True
    ```

Create rule to encrypt messages

After Information Rights Management has been enabled and configured in your tenant, you can configure transport rules to apply encryption to messages. You can configure DLP rules to automatically detect content that meets your organization's requirements for encryption. In addition, you can also create transport rules that can be triggered by keywords in the subject or message body.

To create an Office 365 Message Encryption rule in the Exchange admin center that will encrypt messages sent to recipients outside the organization if the subject contains the keyword #encrypt, follow these steps:

1. In the Exchange admin center, select Mail Flow > Rules.

2. Click the plus sign (+) and then select Apply Office 365 Message Encryption And Rights To Messages.

3. In the Name box, enter a name for the rule.

4. In the Apply This Rule If dropdown, point to The Subject Or Body Matches, and then select The Subject Matches These Text Patterns.

5. Enter the value **#encrypt**. Click the plus sign (+) and then click OK.

6. Next to the Do The Following dropdown, click Select One, and then choose the Encrypt template from the provided list.

7. Click OK.

8. Click Save to configure the rule.

Create rule to decrypt messages

When a user receives an encrypted message in the Office 365 encryption portal, the message will be automatically rendered if they are using the native Outlook or Outlook on the Web experience. However, if they are using a client that is not enlightened and cannot decrypt the messages natively, you can create a rule to decrypt messages in transit and store them in the recipient's mailbox as plain text.

> ## NOTE
>
> You can only decrypt messages that are sent within your organization or are replies to messages sent from your organization. You cannot automatically decrypt messages that originate outside your organization.

To create a rule to remove Office 365 Message Encryption, follow these steps:

1. In the Exchange admin center, navigate to Mail Flow > **Rules**.

2. Click the plus sign (+) and then select Create A New Rule.

3. In the Apply This Rule If dropdown, point to The Recipient Is Located, and select Inside This Organization.

4. Under Do the Following, point to Modify The Message Security, and select Remove Office 365 Message Encryption Applied By The Organization.

5. Click Save.

Inspecting message attachments

Exchange Online transport rules can both look at the message properties when determining how to handle them and inspect the message content—even if it's buried inside another attachment (such as a Microsoft Excel workbook inserted in a Word document or inside a ZIP file).

To use these features, you can use the following predicates:

- `AttachmentContainsWords` This predicate matches messages with supported file type attachments containing a specified string or group of characters.

- `AttachmentMatchesPatterns` This predicate matches messages with supported file type attachments containing a text pattern matching the specified regular expression.

- `AttachmentNameMatchesPatterns` This predicate matches messages with attachments whose file names contain specified characters.

- `AttachmentExtensionMatchesWords` This predicate matches messages with attachments with the specified file name extension.

- `AttachmentSizeOver` This predicate matches messages with attachments greater than or equal to the specified size.

- `AttachmentProcessingLimitExceeded` This predicate matches messages when an attachment is not inspected by the transport rules agent.

- `AttachmentHasExecutableContent` This predicate matches messages that contain executable files as attachments.

- `AttachmentIsPasswordProtected` This predicate matches messages with password-protected attachments.

- `AttachmentPropertyContainsWords` This predicate matches messages when the specified property of the attached Office document contains specified words.

The Any Attachment menu option accesses the predicates under Apply This Rule If, as shown in Figure 18-9.

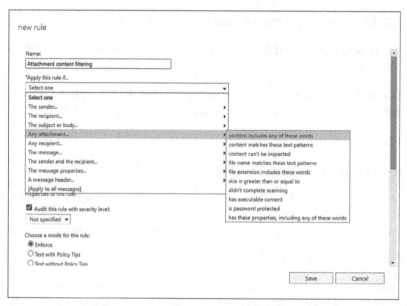

Figure 18-9   Attachment content filtering

> # NOTE
>
> For more information about transport rule predicates, see "Mail flow rule conditions and exceptions (predicates) in Exchange Online" at *https://aka.ms/etrconditions*.
>
> For more information on transport rule actions, see "Mail flow rule actions in Exchange Online" at *https://aka.ms/etractions*.

Central mail transport

If your organization has more complex requirements, such as an on-premises data loss prevention (DLP) infrastructure or an on-premises encryption gateway, you might find that you need to configure your outbound mail from Exchange Online to route through your on-premises environment. Central Mail Transport (also referred to as *Central Mail Flow* in some documentation) routes all outbound mail to the on-premises environment through the hybrid mail connector for further processing.

CAUTION

If you want to use Central Mail Transport but still route mail back out to Exchange Online for egress through Exchange Online Protection, you must create a transport rule to insert an X-header in your message when you leave your on-premises environment. You can then create an additional transport rule in Exchange Online to check for that header and process the message differently. This is important because otherwise, you'll end up in a loop with Exchange Online following Central Mail Transport to deliver mail on-premises and then Exchange On-Premises forwarding mail to Exchange Online.

You can enable Central Mail Transport by running the Hybrid Configuration Wizard on your on-premises Exchange Server and selecting the options as described in Chapter 15, "Exchange Online Hybrid planning and deployment."

Manage IP filtering lists

If you want to ensure messages from a trusted source aren't blocked, you can use the connection filter policy to create an Allow list. Conversely, if there are sources that you know you don't trust or want to block from delivering mail to your organization, you can modify the connection filter policy to create a block list.

NOTE

Connection filtering has moved from the Exchange Online admin center to the Microsoft 365 Defender portal.

To configure settings for the default connection filter policy, navigate to Email & Collaboration > Policies & Rules > Anti-Spam Policies inside the Microsoft 365 Defender portal (*https://security.microsoft.com/antispam*), as shown in Figure 18-10, and click Connection Filter Policy (Default).

You can add IP addresses and classless interdomain routing (CIDR) blocks to either of the following fields, as shown in Figure 18-11:

- Always Allow Messages From The Following IP Addressees or Address Range

- Always Block Messages From The Following IP Addressees or Address Range

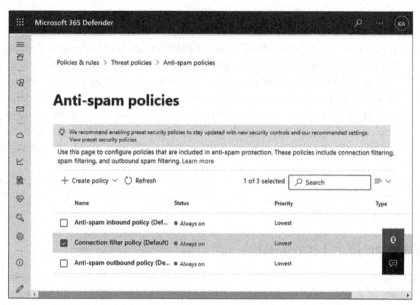

Figure 18-10 Connection Filter Policy

Figure 18-11 Allow and block list management

Selecting the Turn On Safe List check box also adds connections from a trusted sender list that Microsoft maintains.

Enhanced filtering for connectors

If you have configured IP filtering to always allow certain organizations to deliver mail to your Exchange Online tenant, you might find that the filtering doesn't work as expected if the external organization introduces additional mail hops in their outbound mail flow.

Consider a scenario where you have configured a connector for an external organization that hosts their own mail on-premises. After implementation, the external organization then introduces a third-party-hosted mail gateway solution. If you add the hosted mail gateway's IP address ranges, you could inadvertently be allowing any organization utilizing that gateway to bypass some of your security measures to deliver mail.

Enhanced filtering (also known as skip listing) is configured per connector and allows you to specify how to handle these situations:

- **Disable Enhanced Filtering For Connectors**   This option is default and disables enhanced filtering.

- **Automatically Detect And Skip The Last IP Address**   With this option, Exchange Online Protection looks at messages received over the specified connector and uses the second to last hop for connector IP filtering restrictions.

- **Skip These IP Addresses That Are Associated With The Connector: (If Your Messages Pass Through Multiple Gateways, You Should Include Each Gateway IP Address)**   This option is useful if the remote environment has multiple gateways (either parallel or serial) that are responsible for handling mail on the remote environment's behalf.

Message trace

As part of administration duties, you might need to find out what happened to an email message. You can do this by performing a message trace. To access the message trace interface, navigate to Mail Flow > Message Trace.

The updated Message Trace interface now includes the ability to use common standard message trace settings and create custom queries. Default queries are prepopulated with standard parameters and are ready for further customization to narrow the scope of the search.

The default queries are:

- Messages sent from my primary domain in the last day

- Messages received by my primary domain in the last day

- Messages pending delivery to users in my organization

CHAPTER 18

- All quarantined messages for the last seven days

- All failed messages for the last seven days

You can create or edit message trace parameters using date ranges, senders, recipients, delivery status, message IDs, and directionality. See Figure 18-12 for an example of configuring a message trace.

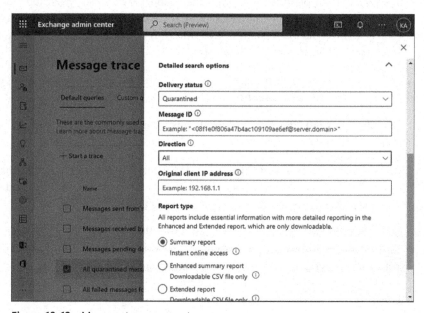

Figure 18-12   Message trace parameters

Message tracing is also available from Exchange Online PowerShell, using the Get-MessageTrace cmdlet. You can filter your search based on starting and ending dates (using the starting date as the earlier of the two dates), sender, recipient, subject, and status.

For example, to search for all messages sent between Dan Jump and Ayla Kol in the past seven days, you can use this command:

```
$Users = @('DanJump@cohovineyards.us','AylaKol@cohovineyards.us')
Get-MessageTrace -SenderAddress $Users -RecipientAddress $Users -StartDate `
(Get-Date).AddDays(-7) -EndDate (Get-Date)
```

Migration of transport settings between Office 365 tenants

At some point, your organization might need to divest a business unit to a new Office 365 tenant. Fortunately, you can export and copy your existing transport settings between organizations.

You can use the script at *https://aka.ms/migrateeop* to help you migrate all mail routing configuration parameters between tenants, including malware filter policies, connection filter policies, transport rules, and connectors.

Migration of transport rules collections

If you are migrating to Office 365 from an Exchange 2007 or later on-premises environment, you can export your transport rules and import them into Office 365 using the Export-TransportRuleCollection and Import-TransportRuleCollection cmdlets. Transport rules can also be migrated between Office 365 tenants by using the same procedure.

Export transport rules

Exporting transport rules is a straightforward task. From the Exchange Management Shell, run the following script:

```
$file = Export-TransportRuleCollection
Set-Content -Path "C:\temp\Rules.xml" -Value $file.FileData -Encoding Byte
```

The transport rules are exported to the Rules.xml file.

Import transport rules

Importing transport rules is also a straightforward task. After connecting to Exchange Online through remote PowerShell, you can run the following script to import the rules exported in the previous section:

```
[Byte[]]$Data = Get-Content -Path "C:\temp\Rules.xml" -Encoding Byte -ReadCount 0
Import-TransportRuleCollection -FileData $Data
```

Inside OUT

Transport rules collections

The format for the exported rules has changed a few times between Exchange Server versions. Rules collections from 2007 and 2010 are in a structured XML format with nodes for each parameter and value:

```
<rule name="Transport Rule">
   <fork>
        <ConditionParameter1 value="value"/>
   </fork>
   <Condition>
        <and>
            <true />
            <ConditionParameter2 property="">
               <value>Value</value>
            </ConditionParamete2r>
```

```
        </and>
     </Condition>
     <Action name="Action">
        <argument value="Value" />
     </Action>
  </rule>
```

However, rules for on-premises Exchange Server versions 2013 and later (as well as Exchange Online) are formatted differently, with the entire rule and all of its parameters exported as a `New-TransportRule` command:

```
<rule name="Transport Rule" id="224623e8-1a02-4c09-aa6f-83937c84dd4a"
format="cmdlet">
<version requiredMinVersion="15.0.3.0">
<commandBlock><![CDATA[New-TransportRule -Name 'Transport Rule -Comments ''
-Mode Enforce -ConditionParameter1 'Value' -ConditionParameter2 'Value' -Action
'value']]></commandBlock>
     </version>
  </rule>
```

You cannot import rules from Exchange 2007 or Exchange 2010 directly into Exchange Online. You must import them to an Exchange Server 2013 server first and then run `Export-TransportRuleCollection` against that server.

One advantage of running `Export-TransportRuleCollection` from an Exchange Server or later environment is that if you view the XML file. You can extract the command in the `<commandBlock>` tag and use it to import rules selectively or see what is created if you import the entire collection.

Importing a transport rule collection overwrites any rules in the destination environment, so you should back up your destination environment before running `Import-TransportRuleCollection` in case you need to back out your changes.

DKIM

DomainKeys Identified Mail, or DKIM, is an authentication process that relies on DNS records and message signing to indicate that messages originated from users inside your organization.

DKIM allows recipient organizations to validate that a message originated from systems managed by your organization and that they weren't modified in transit.

DKIM is based on public key cryptography. Message content has a calculated hash based on the private key stored in the service. When a recipient organization processes a message, they use the published DNS records (called *selectors*) to locate the public key data and use that to validate the hashed data. Public key cryptography ensures that only services holding the private key can generate the hash value.

You can view or configure DKIM settings for your organization by navigating to Email & Collaboration > Policies & Rules > Threat Policies > Email Authentication Settings inside the Microsoft 365 Defender portal or by browsing directly to *https://security.microsoft.com/dkimv2*.

By default, DKIM is not configured. You should configure DKIM signing to help assure external recipients that your mail is authentic.

To configure DKIM signing for your custom domains, follow these steps:

1. Navigate to the DomainKeys Identified Mail (DKIM) page inside the Microsoft 365 Defender portal at *https://security.microsoft.com/dkimv2*.

2. Select a domain to configure by clicking it.

3. Click Create DKIM Keys.

4. Add the DNS CNAME values provided by the wizard, as shown on the Publish CNAMEs dialog box in Figure 18-13, to your external DNS environment.

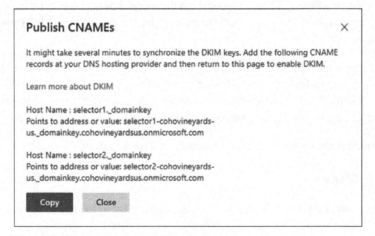

Figure 18-13   DKIM selector DNS values

5. Once the DNS settings have propagated, toggle the Sign Messages For This Domain With DKIM Signatures slider to Enabled and click Close.

Once DKIM signing has been configured, messages will have a hash value applied to them as they leave the organization. Recipient systems will be able to use the public key stored in the selector DNS data to verify that the Exchange Online service generated the email.

Spam, phish, and malware filtering

Aside from recipient management tasks, managing your organization's malware, phish, and spam settings will most likely be the next most common administrative task. In Exchange Online, malware, phish, and spam are separate items:

- **Malware**   Malware is reserved to describe content that performs adverse actions in your environment, such as a virus or trojan downloader.

- **Phish**   Phish is message content designed to trick users into giving away privileged information, such as credentials or financial data.

- **Spam**   Spam is generally recognized as unwanted email, such as unsolicited bulk email.

Malware filter

The malware filter is normally configured to manage the flow of messages with attached executable content. However, as we mentioned earlier in the chapter when discussing attachment blocking, the malware filter was configured to block attachments based on file extension.

You can create multiple malware filters for your organization, applying different settings and parameters to different types of content or different groups of users. To configure the malware filter, navigate to the Anti-malware settings page in the Microsoft 365 Defender portal at *https://security.microsoft.com/antimalwarev2.*

You can customize a malware filter policy to respond with custom text, block certain attachment types, and notify internal or external senders about email disposition as well as notify an administrator. You must configure a malware filtering policy to apply to a group of users. You can configure the scope based on user, domain, or distribution group.

The default malware filter applies to all users in the organization.

Phish filter

Microsoft has updated the Exchange Online Protection plans to include built-in anti-phishing features. A default policy is automatically enabled to protect all users.

Common protection settings include checking common email usage patterns as well as checking for spoofed domains:

- **Impersonation**   *Impersonation* is a collection of techniques that attempts to trick recipients into thinking that a source is legitimate by using familiar sounding names or nicknames (Rob instead of Robert, for example) or by using lookalike characters (such as lowercase "L" and uppercase "i," which can appear similar depending on the display fonts used).

- **Spoofing** *Spoofing* refers to attempts by malicious senders to mask their sending domain with a well-known, reputable, or trusted source to trick recipients. Such attacks may include trying to forge the sender's address to appear to come from a different messaging system.

Impersonation protection requires the identification and configuration of protected users and domains. Typically, you would want to configure impersonation protection for common business partner domains as well as important users or services that may handle sensitive information. For example, if your organization utilizes an external third-party payroll service, you might want to add that domain to the protected domains list.

To manage the Anti-phishing settings, navigate to Policies & Rules > Anti-Phishing in the Microsoft 365 Defender security portal *(https://security.microsoft.com)*. See Figure 18-14.

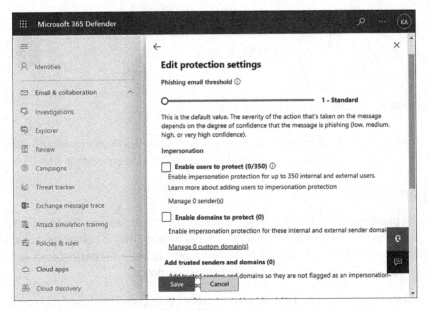

Figure 18-14   Phishing protection settings

You can also choose to configure certain domains to spoof on purpose and to not have their messages flagged. For example, your organization might use an external human resources service that sends mail using your domain name from a certain network infrastructure. To ensure the messages originating from that network are not flagged as spoofed mail, you can configure a name/IP address pair to indicate which IP address ranges are allowed to use which domain names. See Figure 18-15.

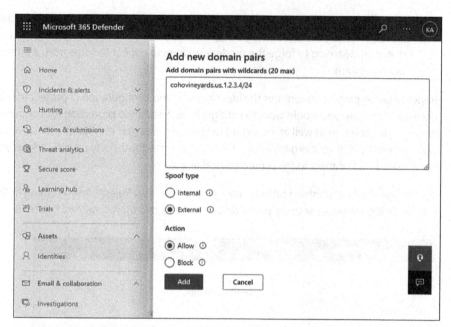

Figure 18-15   Configure tenant spoofing pairs

You can only configure one spoof type per rule, so if you need to configure both Allow and Block rules for internal and external spoofing, you will need to create four rules.

Spam filter

Similar to the malware filter policies, you can configure multiple spam filter policies for your organization. To configure a spam filter policy, navigate to Email & Collaboration > Policies & Rules > Threat Policies > Anti-Spam in the Microsoft 365 Defender portal. Select Anti-Spam Inbound Policy (Default) to edit the default anti-spam policy.

To edit the aggressiveness of the spam policy, select Edit Spam Threshold And Properties.

Under Bulk Email Threshold, you can set the aggressiveness of the filter. A higher spam confidence level (SCL) value means more messages will be delivered. There are a number of properties that you can use to increase a message's individual spam score. By lowering the bulk mail threshold and increasing the spam score for messages that meet your organization's criteria, you can shape how much mail gets delivered to your end users.

Following are the properties used to increase the spam score:

- Image links
- Numeric IP addresses

- URL-based redirect to another port (for example, `http://server.domain.com:81` or `https://server.domain.com:444`)

- Links containing `.biz` or `.info` domains

In addition, you can also use the following characteristics to immediately mark a message as spam:

- Empty messages

- Embedded HTML tags

- JavaScript or VBScript in HTML

- HTML form tags

- HTML frame or iframe tags

- Other `<object>` tags

- Words matching a Microsoft-maintained sensitive word list

- Messages that failed `SenderID` filtering

- Messages that fail Sender Policy Framework (SPF) checks

- Backscatter (a type of spoof-based spam where the sender spoofs the sending address, delivers messages to a legitimate SMTP server, which then rejects the message back to the spoofed sending address and delivers the spam through a bounce message)

- Language filtering (reject messages with specified foreign languages)

- Region filtering (reject messages originating from specified countries or regions)

By default, spam messages are sent to the user's Junk Email folder. Under the Actions section, you can configure where junk message are sent. You can configure the action instead to either the Delete Message or Quarantine Message options. If you select Quarantine Message, you can configure Retain Spam For (Days), after which it will be automatically deleted. If you select the Quarantine Message action, messages will show up in quarantine in the Exchange admin center and can be released by an administrator or by the user.

When specifying the quarantine settings, you can also assign users to a quarantine policy (either one of the built-in quarantine policies or custom policies). Policies determine what types of actions the users can take inside of the quarantine management interface.

On the Block List and Allow List pages of the spam filter, you can configure allow and block lists for domains and senders. The default spam filter applies to all users in the organization.

Inside Out

Processing allow and block lists

There are a number of places you can specify allow and block lists for senders and domains. Depending on what kinds of actions you want to take or how granular you want to be will determine where you want to make your configuration changes.

The mail flow diagram featured in Figure 18-16 depicts how mail travels through Exchange Online Protection. When evaluating mail control techniques, you can use the diagram as a reference to understand what part of the mail flow your configuration will impact.

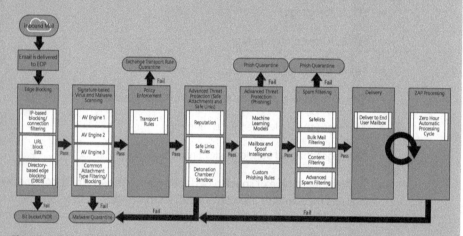

Figure 18-16   Mail flow operational view

A more detailed view of Figure 18-16 is available at *https://aka.ms/MailFlowView*.

You can be the most granular with transport rules, including filtering for DMARC, recipient and attachment filtering, and more. You can also use transport rules to bypass the spam filtering engine. All messages, regardless of transport rule settings, will get scanned for malware.

NOTE

For more information about the spam filter settings, see "Recommended settings for configuring EOP and Defender for Office 365 Security," at *https://aka.ms/eoprecommendedsettings*.

Quarantine

The spam quarantine holds messages deemed to be spam by the service. By default, messages flagged as spam are delivered to the user's Junk Email folder. To quarantine messages, you have to configure spam filter or content filter policies to deliver messages to quarantine instead of the user's Junk Email folder.

With the most recent update of spam and quarantine settings, you can no longer enable user spam notifications on the default policies. If you want to enable user spam notifications, you will have to create a new policy and assign that policy as a target when configuring a spam policy.

To configure a new quarantine policy, open the Quarantine Policy configuration page by navigating to the Microsoft 365 Defender portal and selecting Email & Collaboration > Policies & Rules > Threat Policies > Quarantine Policy. Click the plus sign (+) to create a new policy.

When configuring a policy, you use the default Limited Access option (read-only view of their quarantine), or you can use the Set Specific Access (Advanced) option to configure a custom permissions set, as shown in Figure 18-17.

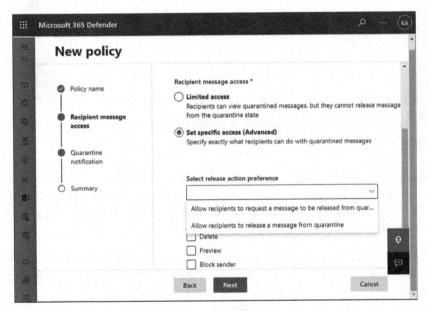

Figure 18-17   Configuring a new quarantine policy

CHAPTER 18

You can create multiple custom quarantine policies, granting different access controls so you can allow different groups of users to perform various actions on quarantined messages, such as releasing them (or requesting them to be released), previewing or deleting them, and blocking the sender.

After configuring the policy settings, the Summary page is shown to confirm settings, as shown in Figure 18-18.

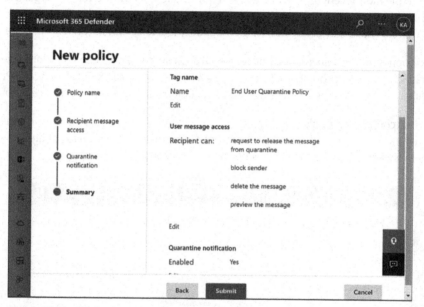

Figure 18-18   Reviewing new quarantine policy settings

Users can access their quarantined messages by following the link in the spam notification email or by navigating to *https://admin.protection.outlook.com/quarantine*. The user quarantine is simple to use and includes the ability to search, view the details of a message, and release messages to the mailbox. See Figure 18-19.

The interface for the user quarantine still uses the classic Exchange admin center styling, while the administrator quarantine view has been relocated to the Microsoft 36 Defender portal, which you can access by choosing Email & Collaboration > Review or visiting *https://security.microsoft.com/quarantine*.

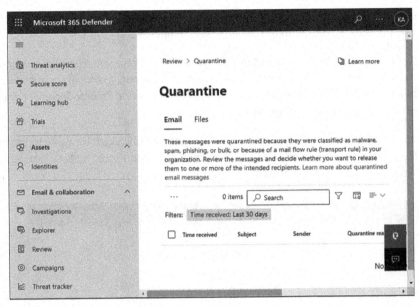

Figure 18-19   Quarantine interface

Outbound spam

Outbound spam filtering is enabled automatically for all Office 365 and Exchange Online sub-scribers. Senders are flagged as possible spam senders by usage patterns.

On the Outbound Spam Protection Settings page, you can configure internal, external, and total daily message limits. Also, you can configure notification settings to inform administrators or senders when messages are suspicious or blocked.

To configure outbound spam filtering notifications, navigate to Email & Collaboration > Policies & Rules > Threat Policies > Anti-Spam in the Microsoft 365 Defender portal. Select the Anti-Spam Outbound Policy (Default) to edit the default outbound spam policy.

Blocked accounts

If a user repeatedly sends messages that are classified as spam or meets the limits specified in the outbound spam policy, they will be blocked from sending any more messages. You can con-figure the Outbound Spam settings to notify an administrator when an account is blocked.

Users who have been blocked from sending by the outbound spam policy will receive the following non-delivery report (NDRs) when they attempt to send:

"Your message couldn't be delivered because you weren't recognized as a valid sender. The most common reason for this is that your email address is suspected of sending spam and it's no longer allowed to send email. Contact your email admin for assistance. Remote Server returned 550 5.1.8 Access denied, bad outbound sender."

To allow them to continue sending, they will need to be unblocked. Navigate to the Restricted Entities page in the Microsoft 365 Defender portal by expanding Email & Collaboration > Review > Restricted Entities. See Figure 18-20.

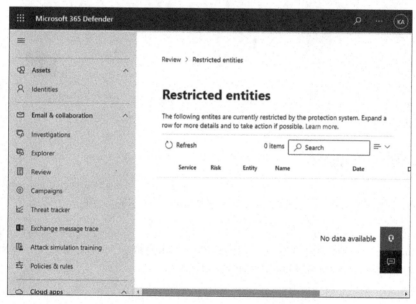

Figure 18-20   Restricted Entities page

Organization management

At some point, you might need to configure calendar sharing with another organization. This other organization might use Office 365, Exchange on-premises, or a hybrid scenario in which users might exist in either location.

Organization relationships, sharing policies, and available address spaces all play a part in how Exchange Online locates resources in your own or other Exchange organizations.

Organization relationships

An organization relationship is the container object used to configure a sharing relationship with an external organization. The organization relationship object describes the other organization's domains with which you'll be sharing, what level of calendar and free/busy information sharing you'll grant, and what remote endpoints the relationship will use to connect to the other organization.

To manage organization relationships, navigate to Organization in the Exchange admin center, as shown in Figure 18-21, and select Sharing.

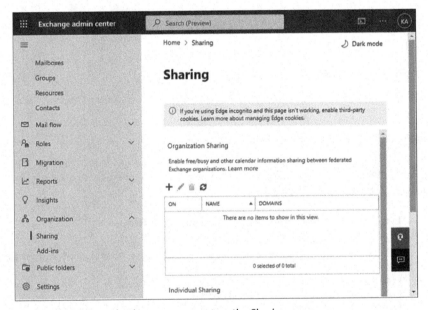

Figure 18-21   Organization management on the Sharing page

Click the plus sign (+) in the Organization Sharing area to create a new organization relationship. See Figure 18-22 for an example of creating a new organization relationship.

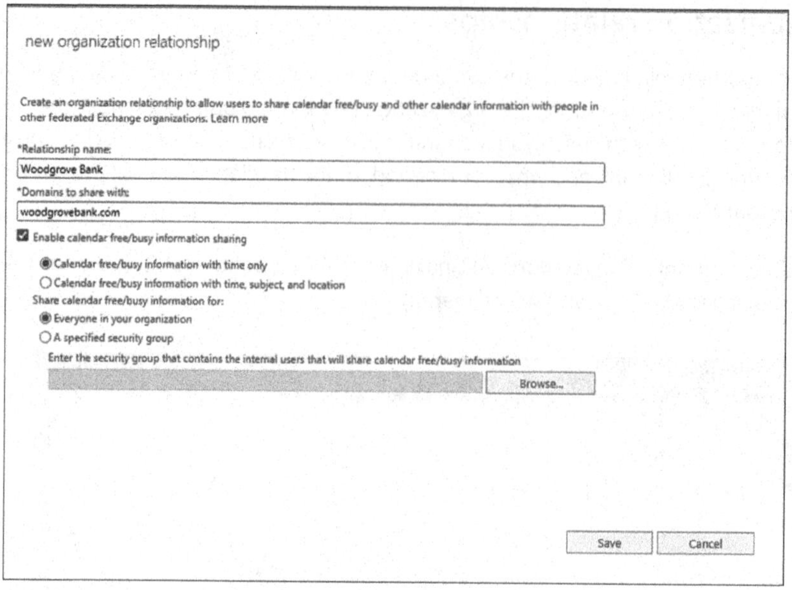

Figure 18-22 New Organization Relationship page

To verify the organization relationship settings, you can use the `Get-OrganizationRelation-ship` cmdlet, as shown in Listing 18-1:

Listing 18-1 Get-OrganizationRelationship settings

```
PS C:\> Get-OrganizationRelationship | FL
DomainNames        : {woodgrovebank.com, woodgrovebank.mail.onmicrosoft.com, wood-
grovebank.onmicrosoft.com}
FreeBusyAccessEnabled : True
FreeBusyAccessLevel  : AvailabilityOnly
FreeBusyAccessScope  :
MailboxMoveEnabled   : False
MailboxMoveDirection : None
DeliveryReportEnabled : False
MailTipsAccessEnabled : False
MailTipsAccessLevel  : None
MailTipsAccessScope  :
PhotosEnabled        : False
TargetApplicationUri : outlook.com
TargetSharingEpr     :
TargetOwaURL         :
TargetAutodiscoverEpr : https://autodiscover-s.outlook.com/autodiscover/autodis-
cover.svc/WSSecurity
OrganizationContact  :
Enabled              : True
ArchiveAccessEnabled : False
AdminDisplayName     :
ExchangeVersion      : 0.10 (14.0.100.0)
```

```
Name            : Woodgrove Bank
DistinguishedName    : CN=Cohovineyard,CN=Federation,CN=Configuration,CN=cohoviney
ardsus.onmicrosoft.com,CN=ConfigurationUnits,DC=NAMPR14A003,DC=PROD,DC=OUTLOOK,DC
=COM
Identity        : Woodgrove Bank
Guid            : 29065b56-cf6a-4da7-aabc-fb1a3a6a08c7
ObjectCategory    : NAMPR14A003.PROD.OUTLOOK.COM/Configuration/Schema/
ms-Exch-Fed-Sharing-Relationship
ObjectClass        : {top, msExchFedSharingRelationship}
Id            : WoodgroveBank
IsValid        : True
ObjectState        : Changed
```

The output shows the settings that were automatically configured per the New Organization Relationship wizard.

Inside Out

When you need settings other than default

There are times when the remote organization has other settings configured than the defaults the New-OrganizationRelationship cmdlet is designed to locate automatically. The remote organization could also have restricted external access to its environment or have another endpoint that it wants to use for federated sharing requests. When any of those is the case, you can create the organization relationship manually in Windows PowerShell by using the TargetApplicationUri, TargetAutodiscoverEpr, and TargetSharingEpr parameters.

TargetApplicationUri

The TargetApplicationUri parameter specifies the target Uniform Resource Identifier (URI) of the external organization. The parameter is specified by Exchange when requesting a delegated token for the external organization. This is typically the top-level Outlook Web App URL of the organization. For retrieving free/busy information from an Office 365 organization, this setting uses *outlook.com* as the target. If the organization's Outlook Web App server URL is *https://mail.woodgrovebank.com*, then the TargetApplicationUri would be mail.woodgrovebank.com.

To update the TargetApplicationUri to use the Outlook Web App server at *https://mail.woodgrovebank.com*, you would use the following command:

```
Set-OrganizationRelationship -Identity <Identity> -TargetApplicationUri `
mail.woodgrovebank.com
```

TargetAutodiscoverEpr

The `TargetAutodiscoverEpr` parameter specifies the Autodiscover URL of Exchange Web Services for the external organization. For example, if the external organization's external Autodiscover service points to *autodiscover.woodgrovebank.com*, the URL would most likely be *https://autodiscover.woodgrovebank.com/autodiscover/autodiscover.svc/wssecurity*.

Exchange uses the Autodiscover service to detect the correct client access server endpoint automatically for external requests. To update the `TargetAutodiscoverEpr` to point to the Autodiscover service located at *https://exchangeserver.woodgrovebank.com*, you would run this command:

```
Set-OrganizationRelationship -Identity <Identity> -TargetAutodiscoverEpr `
https://exchangeserver.woodgrove.com/autodiscover/autodiscover.svc/wssecurity
```

TargetOwaURL

The `TargetOwaURL` parameter specifies the Office Outlook Web App URL of the external organization. It is used for Outlook Web App redirection in a cross-premises Exchange scenario. Configuring this attribute enables users in the organization to use their current Outlook Web App URL to access Outlook Web App in the external organization.

TargetSharingEpr

The `TargetSharingEpr` parameter specifies the URL of the target Exchange Web Services for the external organization. If the `TargetSharingEpr` parameter is used, it takes precedence over the `TargetAutodiscoverEpr` parameter information to locate the client access server. In Exchange Hybrid scenarios, this might need to be updated if the URL specified in `TargetAutoDiscoverEpr` points to a version of Exchange Server prior to Exchange Server 2010 SP3.

To update `TargetSharingEpr` to use the server located at *https://hybrid.woodgrovebank.com*, use the following command:

```
Set-OrganizationRelationship -Identity <Identity> -TargetSharingEpr `
https://hybrid.woodgrovebank.com/EWS/Exchange.asmx
```

Sharing policies

Although organization relationships govern the sharing between federated Exchange organizations, sharing policies can be used to provide sharing capabilities on a mailbox-level basis to external users in external Office 365 or Exchange on-premises environments. If the external users aren't in an Exchange-based organization, sharing policies allow the sharing of calendar information through the use of Internet Calendar Publishing.

To create a sharing policy from the Exchange admin center, navigate to Organization > Sharing and click the plus sign (+) in the Individual Sharing area.

After naming the policy, click the plus sign (+) to define the sharing rules. See Figure 18-23 for an example of available options.

Figure 18-23   Sharing Rule configuration

You can add multiple domains to a single sharing policy and configure the scope of sharing information per domain.

Hybrid management

In hybrid coexistence environments, you must perform several administrative tasks—such as creating new users and adding or removing domains your organization uses for email routing.

Provisioning remote mailboxes

As you enter the daily routine of Office 365 and Exchange Online administration, you will undoubtedly need to create mailboxes. Using the Exchange admin center from your on-premises Exchange Server, you can create a new Active Directory account and enable it as an Exchange Online mailbox or add a mailbox to an existing Active Directory user.

You can also use either the `Enable-RemoteMailbox` cmdlet to provision the Exchange attributes on an existing Active Directory user account or the `New-RemoteMailbox` cmdlet to create a new local Active Directory user and enable it as a mailbox in Office 365.

After the object has been provisioned and the mailbox attributes set, AAD Connect synchronizes the attributes to Office 365, triggering mailbox creation in Exchange Online.

Updating domains in a hybrid configuration

If you need to add or remove domains in your hybrid configuration, you can re-run the Hybrid Configuration Wizard and use it to update the hybrid configuration:

1. Add the domain to your Office 365 tenant.

2. Configure the domain as an accepted domain in your on-premises Exchange Server environment. To do this, you can run the New-AcceptedDomain cmdlet from the on-premises Exchange management shell:

    ```
    New-AcceptedDomain -DomainName newdomain.com -DomainType Authoritative
    ```

3. Run the Hybrid Configuration Wizard and select the new domain to add. This generates a DNS TXT record you must add to your external DNS. To create the record ahead of time, you can use the Get-FederatedDomainProof cmdlet:

    ```
    Get-FederatedDomainProof -DomainName newdomain.com
    ```

4. Add the DNS record to the external DNS.

5. Continue the Hybrid Configuration Wizard and select I Have Created A TXT Record For Each Token In DNS and click Verify Domain Ownership.

6. Complete the Hybrid Configuration Wizard.

NOTE

For more information about completing the Hybrid Configuration Wizard, see Chapter 15, "Exchange Online Hybrid planning and deployment."

What's next?

Next, we'll start exploring the architecture of newest workplace collaboration product in the Microsoft 365 suite—Teams. Microsoft Teams replaces the instant messaging and voice capabilities of Skype for Business and brings an entirely new perspective on what productivity means in today's world of hybrid work.

Microsoft Teams overview

Microsoft Teams is the next evolution of communication and collaboration in the Microsoft 365 ecosystem. In addition to collaboration, Microsoft Teams is a development platform.

As a collaboration tool, it gives users an interface for familiar features like calendaring and Microsoft 365 group-based document management. From a communications perspective, it replaces both the instant messaging and telephony capabilities of Skype for Business. From a tooling perspective, its integration with other Power Platform components lets developers build applications with Power Apps, Power Automate, and other native Microsoft 365 application programming interfaces (APIs) that can seamlessly be connected to the Teams interface.

This chapter reviews the foundational concepts of Microsoft Teams, including the architecture and user interface, which are key to understanding advanced Teams concepts.

Architecture

Microsoft Teams is built using components of several existing cloud services. While it might have a simple user interface (UI), Teams unites a lot of services under the hood to present a cohesive experience.

The foundational object in Microsoft Teams is a *team* and is based on a Microsoft 365 group. A Microsoft 365 group is a special Azure object with an Exchange group mailbox, a SharePoint site collection, and a OneNote notebook. Microsoft Teams builds on a group with an extensible interface.

Any exiting Microsoft 365 group or group-connected SharePoint site can be converted into a Microsoft Teams team object. Some refer to this upgrade or conversion as *Teamifying* a group. See Figure 19-1 for an example of adding Teams to a SharePoint site.

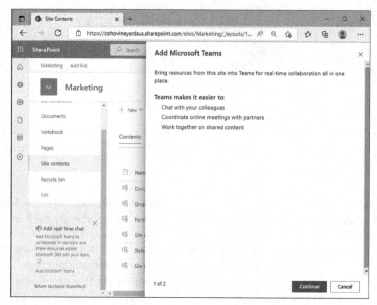

Figure 19-1   Adding Teams to an existing SharePoint site

A team also can be viewed as a sort of container object, holding structural elements that can be used to group related conversations and resources. Inside the team, channels and tabs can be used to further organize content around topics, departments, categories, projects, or functions. Figure 19-2 shows the Microsoft Teams user interface and how these concepts of teams and channels are presented.

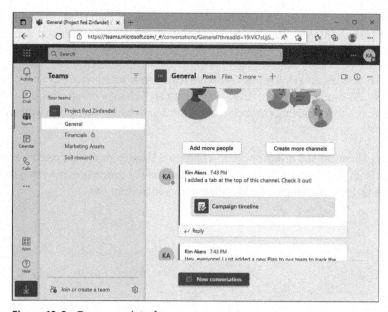

Figure 19-2   Teams user interface

Different content types, such as files and messages, are stored and managed inside the team. While a Microsoft 365 group is somewhat of a flat object, extending a group into a team object creates structures and links to other endpoints and containers inside the team and other Microsoft 365 services. Figure 19-2 shows the expanded team channels, which appear like subfolders under the main team object. Each channel maps to a unique subfolder inside the Microsoft 365 group's corresponding SharePoint Online site, as shown in Figure 19-3.

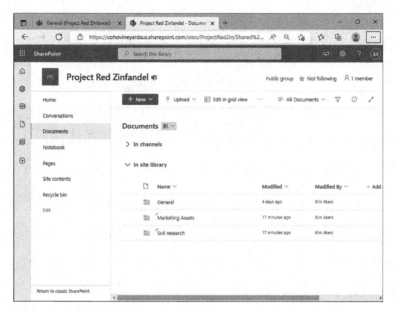

Figure 19-3   SharePoint Site structure

The exception is a private channel (depicted in Figure 19-2 as the channel with a lock icon next to it). Private channels can restrict information to a subset of users inside the team. As opposed to sharing the same permissions and membership list as normal channels in a team, private channels maintain their own discrete membership list. While private channels are displayed in the team's navigation hierarchy, each private channel's content storage is located in a separate SharePoint site with a different set of permissions. This security structure prevents members of the broader team (but not the private channel) from gaining access to the data stored in that channel.

Figure 19-4 looks deeper at the connections between services, applications, and storage inside the Microsoft Teams ecosystem.

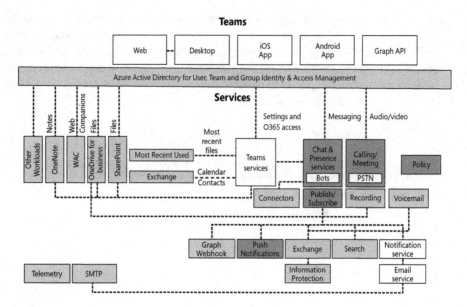

Figure 19-4   Teams architecture overview

Following are some of the core features and integrated components:

- Identity

- Files

- Messaging and chat services

- Connectors

- Voicemail

- Recording

- Calendars and meetings

- Contacts

Let's expand further on some of these.

Identity

Identity is the foundation of everything in the Microsoft 365 ecosystem. Microsoft has emphasized the phrase "identity is the new security boundary" as part of its Zero Trust design strategy. Azure AD provides identity management (authentication, access control, and auditing) for all Microsoft 365-based workloads, including Microsoft Teams and its constituent services.

As the identity storage and provider, Azure AD hosts a Microsoft 365 group—the directory object on which a team is built. Azure AD also hosts the other security principals (such as user and external guest accounts), which can be added to Microsoft 365 group (and, ultimately, team) memberships. These identity components work in concert to provide the infrastructure and security for all Microsoft 365 workloads.

Files

As shown earlier, each team is connected to a SharePoint site. Files can be added directly to the team's SharePoint site through either the SharePoint Online or OneDrive for Business interfaces, to a particular channel's Files tab through the Teams user interface, or uploaded to a channel's Posts tab.

TIP

Any file posted to a team channel's Posts tab will automatically be uploaded to the team's SharePoint site, and a link to the actual file will be placed in the conversation. If posting a file to a 1:1 or group chat (as opposed to a Microsoft Teams team conversation), the file will be linked from the sharer's OneDrive (or the source location if it is referencing an existing file stored in SharePoint). A 1:1 or group chat does not have its own file storage.

Messaging and chat services

Earlier in this chapter, we referenced the Microsoft 365 group, including a special Exchange mailbox component. Since Microsoft 365 groups are a cloud-only component, there is no corresponding Exchange Server on-premises object.

Each Microsoft Team has a default channel named General, which can neither be deleted nor renamed. For reference, Figure 19-2 depicts a team and how channels are displayed.

From an organizational or categorization perspective, channels are typically used to group related subtopics or content inside a team. Each channel contains default tabs, including Posts, Files, and Wiki. The Posts tab on any channel contains threaded text posts called Conversations. Chat content posted in a team's conversation is ingested through the Azure chat service and then stored in the team's corresponding Exchange Online group mailbox. This mailbox storage serves multiple purposes, including providing chat history and context to individuals who are added to a team in the future and enabling compliance capabilities like retention and eDiscovery.

Chat or instant messaging content (as opposed to channel conversations) is ingested into the participating users' mailboxes. The exception is chat on a private channel, which is also ingested into the participating users' personal mailboxes.

Connectors

Connectors are webhook interfaces designed to receive updates from services. Connectors allow services to post data into Teams and allow Teams users to subscribe to those updates and receive notifications.

Voicemail

If a Teams user is configured for telephony features (such as Phone System), any voicemails received are stored as audio files in the user's mailbox.

Recording

When Microsoft Teams was launched, meeting and call recordings were processed by Azure Media services and then encoded for long-term storage in Microsoft Stream. Microsoft has recently updated the storage architecture—individual user or non-channel meeting call recordings are now stored in the user's OneDrive. In contrast, recordings of channel meetings are stored with the Team in SharePoint Online.

Calendars and meetings

Teams does not have its own calendar storage; instead, it relies on users' Microsoft Exchange mailboxes. Teams can access either Exchange Online mailboxes or Exchange Server on-premises through an Exchange Hybrid configuration.

Contacts

Like calendars and meeting objects, contacts are stored in an individual user's Exchange mailbox (online or on-premises). Connecting to an on-premises mailbox requires Exchange Hybrid, as detailed in Chapter 16, "Migrating mailboxes to Exchange Online."

Other components

There are a lot of familiar components used in Teams. Generally, you can expect to find communications-related content stored in a mailbox (either in the team's Exchange Online group mailbox or the user's mailbox). Conversely, the file content is stored in either a team's SharePoint site or in a user's OneDrive site.

Other Microsoft 365 services might interact with and process data, but they will typically store their data in one of those locations. It's important to note that the primary Teams data and artifact storage locations are Exchange and SharePoint Online—both of which can be governed by Microsoft 365 data retention policies.

Other Microsoft 365 ecosystem applications (such as Approvals, Power BI, Power Automate, or Tasks by Planner and To Do) might have additional data storage locations, such as Dataverse or other dedicated storage containers. While these applications and services store data elsewhere in the Microsoft 365 ecosystem, they have very tight API integration with Microsoft Teams.

CAUTION

If your organization uses any third-party applications with Microsoft Teams, it's important to read their terms of service to understand their security controls and data storage locations. Many third-party services will store data outside of the Microsoft 365 ecosystem. Their data will likely not be captured, indexed, or preserved by any Microsoft 365 retention policies and might be subject to additional privacy or data-sharing agreements.

Architecture deep dive

Now that you have a basic understanding of the components at a high level, let's go a little bit deeper into both the Microsoft 365 and Microsoft Teams architectures. First, we'll look at the Microsoft 365 group architecture.

Microsoft 365 groups

As we mentioned earlier in the chapter, the foundation of a team is a Microsoft 365 group. A Microsoft 365 group is an Azure AD object with an Exchange group mailbox, a SharePoint site collection, and a OneNote Notebook.

A Microsoft 365 group can be provisioned in many ways, including:

- Microsoft 365 Admin center
- Azure AD Admin center
- Microsoft Planner
- Yammer (as a Connected Group)
- Exchange Online (as a Microsoft 365 group or a Unified Group)
- Outlook (as a Microsoft 365 group)
- PowerShell
- Dynamics CRM
- Graph API
- SharePoint Online (as a Group-Connected SharePoint Site Collection)
- Client-Side Object Model for SharePoint Online

All Microsoft 365 groups provisioned through any of these interfaces will have the same underlying components (a group mailbox, a site, and a notebook). The provisioning service or application will use the Microsoft 365 group membership for its administration and security controls.

From a membership and role perspective, a Microsoft 365 group has the following concepts:

- **Owners**   Owners can administer the membership or other aspects of the group.

- **Members**   Members can participate in group messages but cannot control the membership or features of the group.

- **Guests**   Guests function much like members but might have their permissions further tightened by the group owners so that they might only view or contribute. When a group is converted to a Microsoft Team, guests might also be restricted from additional features, such as the ability to use messages or GIFs.

Microsoft 365 group owners are mapped to the SharePoint Site Collection Administrators and Site Owners groups. The members are mapped to the SharePoint Site Members group, while guests are mapped to the SharePoint Site Visitors group.

The OneNote Notebook is stored inside the Site Assets document library. Files sent to the group are stored in the default Documents library.

Microsoft 365 groups have a number of properties exposed through various interfaces, including Exchange Online, Azure AD, and Microsoft Graph. Table 19-1 lists the major properties and how they are used.

Table 19-1   Microsoft 365 group properties

Property	Type	Description
allowExternalSenders	Boolean	Determines if entities external to the organization can send messages to the group.
assignedLabels	Collection	List of sensitivity label pairs (label ID, label name) associated with the group.
assignedLicenses	Collection	List of licenses assigned to the group.
autoSubscribeNewMembers	Boolean	Indicates if members added to the group will be configured to receive emails (as a distribution list). Users can unsubscribe.
Classification	String	Describes the classification of the group.
createdByAppId	String	Application ID (guid) of the application or method used to create the group. Might be null.

createdDateTime	DateTimeOffset	Timestamp of when the group object was created.
deletedDateTime	DateTimeOffset	Timestamp of when the group was deleted.
Description	String	Option description value for the group.
displayName	String	The display name value of the group.
expirationDateTime	DateTimeOffset	A timestamp indicating when the group will expire.
groupTypes	String collection	Specifies the group type. Potential values include Unified and DynamicMembership. If the groupTypes value is null, it is a Security group.
hasMembersWithLicenseErrors	Boolean	Indicates group has members with errors from group-based licensing operation.
hideFromAddressLists	Boolean	Group is hidden from Outlook address book.
hideFromOutlookClients	Boolean	Group is hidden from Outlook client operations. Also referred to as HiddenFromExchangeClientsEnabled.
Id	String	Unique identifier of the group. Guid value represented as string.
InformationBarrierMode	String	Specifies the mode in which InformationBarriers is implemented. Possible values include Open, Implicit, Explicit, Owner Moderated.
isAssignableToRole	Boolean	Group can be assigned to an Azure AD role.
isSubscribedByMail	Boolean	Indicates if the signed-in user is subscribed to receive email conversations.
licenseProcessingState	String	Indicates the status of group-based license processing.
Mail	String	SMTP email address for the group.
mailEnabled	Boolean	Specifies if the group is mail-enabled.
mailNickname	String	Email alias.
membershipRule	String	If the group is dynamic, it indicates logic was used to calculate membership.
membershipRuleProcessingState	String	Dynamic group membership rule status. Possible values include Evaluating, Processing, Update complete, Processing error, and Update paused.

CHAPTER 19

onPremisesDomainName	String	Contains on-premises Domain name. Null for Microsoft 365 groups, as they are not synchronized from on-premises AD.
onPremisesLastSyncDateTime	DateTimeOffset	Contains date value for the last time synchronized from on-premises environment. Null for Microsoft 365 groups because they are not synchronized from on-premises AD.
onPremisesSecurityIdentifier	String	Contains on-premises security identifier (SID). Null for Microsoft 365 groups, as they are not synchronized from on-premises AD.
onPremisesSyncEnabled	Boolean	Indicates if sync is enabled. False for Microsoft 365 groups, as they are not synchronized from on-premises AD.
preferredDataLocation	String	Preferred geographic data location for the group.
proxyAddresses	Collection	Multivalued attribute containing all proxyAddresses associated with the object, including SMTP, X400, and X500 addresses.
renewedDateTime	DateTimeOffset	Datestamp for most recent group renewal.
resourceBehaviorOptions	String collection	Specifies group behaviors that can be set for a Microsoft 365 group during creation. Possible values include AllowOnlyMembersToPost, HideGroupInOutlook, SubscribeNewGroupMembers, and WelcomeEmailDisabled.
SecurityEnabled	Boolean	Indicates if the group is security-enabled. False for Microsoft 365 groups.
SecurityIdentifier	String	Security Identifier of group, SID format.
Theme	String	Specifies Microsoft 365 Group color theme.
unseenConversationsCount	Int32	Count of new conversations or posts since the signed-in user's last visit to the group. Same value as unseenCount.
UnseenCount	Int32	Count of new conversations or posts since the signed-in user's last visit to the group. Same value as unseenConversationsCount.
Visibility	String	Visibility of group. Possible values include Public, Private. Also referred to as AccessType.

The Microsoft 365 group properties can be used to configure a number of aspects of the group's interactions, capabilities, restrictions, and visibility.

Teams

Building on the structure of a Microsoft 365 group, Figure 19-5 depicts how the Microsoft Teams components integrate with the core Microsoft 365 group object.

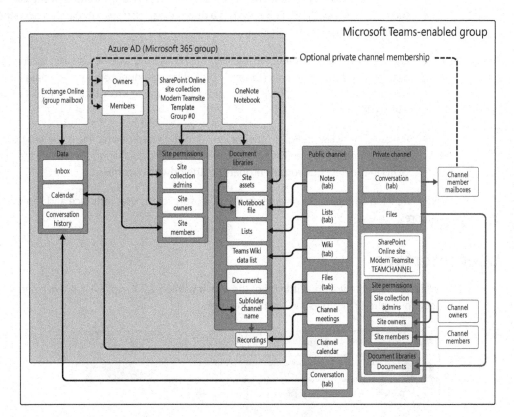

Figure 19-5   Microsoft Team components and storage locations

Layering on the additional Microsoft Teams components, you can see how the channel data (files, meetings, conversations, and more) are mapped to various endpoints and locations inside the Microsoft 365 group. Some notable links between the objects include:

- The data for the Wiki tab is stored in a new SharePoint list called Teams Wiki Data.

- Channel meeting recordings are stored in a Recordings subfolder of the channel's folder in the default Documents library.

- Conversation data from the Posts tab is stored in the group mailbox's Conversation History folder.

- Each channel's calendar data is stored in the group mailbox calendar.

You'll also notice that data and permissions for a private channel are handled differently:

- The files are stored in a new SharePoint site, not the existing SharePoint site connected to the team. The new SharePoint site has a discrete permissions list mapped from the private channel owners and membership.

- Each private channel member's mailbox becomes a storage destination for the related data on the Posts tab (conversations). The private channel conversation data is stored in the member's Conversation History folder, not in the team's group mailbox Conversation History folder.

- Private channel SharePoint sites are linked to their parent site. The linkage is not visible from the user interface. The relationship is managed by storing the parent site's object GUID in the RelatedGroupID property of the private channel site.

Next, we'll look deeper into navigating the Microsoft Teams user interface and some of its features.

User interface

While we've already seen a little bit of the user interface, we'll explore it in more detail in this section. Figure 19-6 shows the Teams interface.

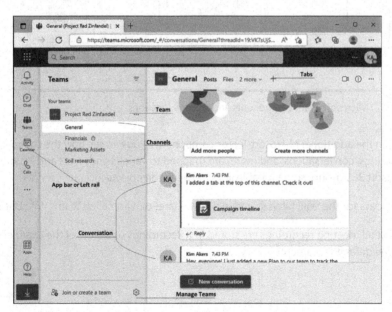

Figure 19-6   Microsoft Teams

There are many icons and areas in the Teams interface. Here's a quick run-down of the pieces.

Menu bar

Several functions are shown at the top of the user interface. The Menu bar displays Forward and Back navigation buttons (if you're using the Teams client), as well as a Search bar, which can be used to search across all Teams areas. The Menu bar also displays the logged-in user's personal avatar or a personalized initial icon (either the user's initials or an image if they choose to upload one), along with a colored bubble indicating their presence (sometimes referred to as "status") information.

App bar

Sometimes also called the "left rail" or "Navigation bar," this is the vertical area on the left side of the screen where icons such as Activity, Chat, Teams, Calendar, Calls, and Files appear. Administrators can manage the apps that appear here, and users can edit their displayed order.

List pane

This is the middle area of the user interface and displays the things that correspond to the view selected on the App bar. For example, in Figure 19-6, the Teams view is selected, so the List pane shows the teams the user has joined. The list pane also has a Filter button at the top, which allows you to search and filter items in the List pane. The Join Or Create A Team button is at the bottom of the list pane, and the gear icon next to it is the Manage Teams button, which allows you to manage settings across the teams you own.

Main content area

Also called the "body pane," this is the large focus area in the user interface. The content in this area updates to display the selected item in either the List pane or the App bar (depending on the context). For example, in Figure 19-6, the Project Red Zinfandel team is selected, and the main content area displays the Posts tab data from the General channel.

Now that you're familiar with the overall structure and layout of the Teams user interface, let's expand on each item in the left rail.

Exploring the App bar

In this section, we'll cover the core apps on the App bar.

Activity

If you're familiar with mobile phone applications, you're probably familiar with the concepts of seeing others' activities and notifications. Microsoft Teams also uses notification bubbles to highlight new items.

The Activity Feed view shown in Figure 19-7 is used to draw your attention to things specifically targeted to you or a team or channel you're participating in, displayed from oldest (at the bottom) to newest (at the top):

- The user Dan has added the logged-in user to a new team.

- The user Dan has assigned a task to the logged-in user.

- The user Dan mentioned the logged-in user in a team channel conversation.

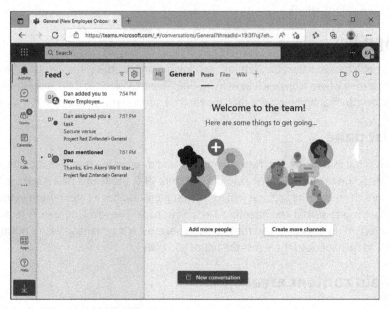

Figure 19-7   Teams Activity view

Like social media platforms, you can use the @ symbol to alert, mention, or tag an individual, channel, or team. These notifications (called mentions) will show up in the Activity view for the individual user mentioned (or for each member of a channel or team mentioned). In addition to other users mentioning you or your teammates, apps can also generate notifications that will show up in your activity feed.

Chat and presence

By selecting the Chat app, you can initiate 1:1 or group conversations. Chat is an essential part of the Microsoft Teams experience. You can search for users from the address book and add them to conversations.

User icons or avatars have a presence indicator in the form of a bubble, which lets others know the individual's status. Status options include:

- Available

- Busy

- Do Not Disturb

- Away (Be Right Back)

- Away (Appear Away)

- Appear Offline

Each status has a corresponding color. Some statuses might include additional detail (such as Focusing, Presenting, In A Meeting, or In A Call).

If you select Do Not Disturb as your status, you do not get audio or visual notifications (unless the person is on your Priority Access list).

Teams

You should already be familiar with the Teams view shown previously in Figure 19-6. The Teams view shows all the teams to which you're currently joined and gives you a way to navigate the various teams and channels.

Calendar

The Calendar view displays the Outlook calendar (whether Exchange Online or on-premises) and allows you to create both impromptu and scheduled meetings. See Figure 19-8.

Creating a meeting through the Teams Calendar app automatically adds a Teams meeting link if the meeting has attendees and a conferencing number if the organizer is licensed for audio conferencing. See Figure 19-9.

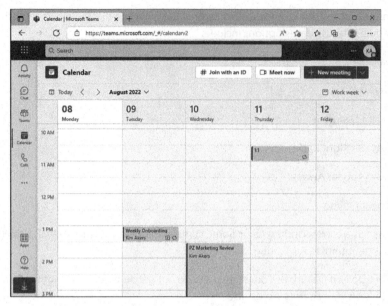

Figure 19-8   Calendar app

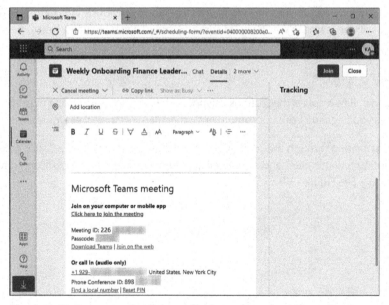

Figure 19-9   Teams meeting link and dial-in conferencing information

Calls

The Calls app shows different information depending on what features are enabled. As shown in Figure 19-10, the app will show calling-related items, such as a call log and voice mail history, as well as the option to view contacts stored in the user's Exchange mailbox. If the user has a voice plan (either via Calling Plans or has been activated for Direct Routing or Operator Connect), then the List pane will display a dial pad to allow dialing out to the Public Switched Telephone Network (PSTN).

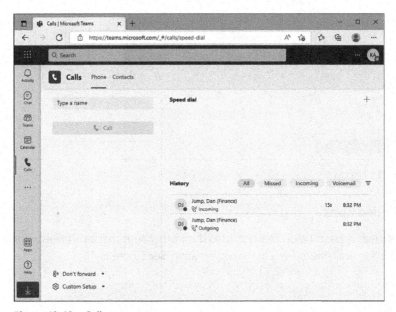

Figure 19-10   Calls app

The History log shows directionality (whether a call was incoming or outbound). There is also a status icon indicating if a caller left a voicemail.

Files

The Files view displays files that the user has stored in their OneDrive for Business site and files that have been shared with them through Teams, OneDrive, or SharePoint. Users will see recently accessed files and can connect to external storage providers (such as Box, DropBox, Egnyte, and Google Drive/Workspace). See Figure 19-11.

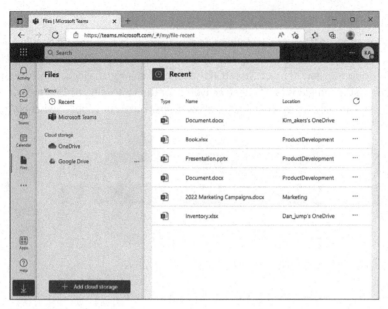

Figure 19-11   Files app

More added apps

The ellipsis that appears below files is used to show other apps that an administrator has config-ured and made available to users in the organization. See Figure 19-12.

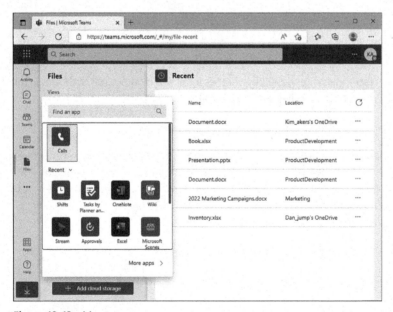

Figure 19-12   More apps

Administrators can add and remove apps, making them available to the organization as a whole or scoped to individuals and groups of users.

App store

The App store is a marketplace with apps available in the Microsoft Teams environment. Administrators can block or allow apps, bots, and connectors from being added to the channels or the interface. Additionally, administrators can deploy apps to individuals or groups through policies. Finally, organizations can develop and upload their own apps to be distributed to their users.

Help

The Help link provides access to training, information about updated features, and feedback options.

Download mobile app

Clicking Download Mobile App at the bottom of the App bar displays a QR code that can be scanned with a mobile phone. The QR code links to the Microsoft Teams application in the appropriate platform's mobile app store.

The Microsoft Teams user interface has a lot of apps, options, and features and can connect users to everything in the Microsoft 365 ecosystem.

What's next?

Microsoft Teams is the newest platform tool in Microsoft's growing productivity software space. By incorporating existing cloud services such as Exchange Online and SharePoint Online, Microsoft can make use of organizations' existing Microsoft platform investments.

In the next chapter, we'll start configuring Teams communication features, such as meetings, webinars, and live events.

CHAPTER 19

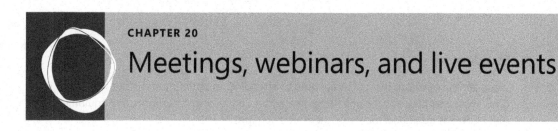

CHAPTER 20

Meetings, webinars, and live events

Hosting and attending meetings comprise a large part of the business work culture. Microsoft Teams provides a variety of ad-hoc and scheduled meeting options, as well as webinar and live event capabilities to help further expand your organization's reach.

In this chapter, we'll cover a variety of collaborative group scenarios, including how to configure and administer:

- Meetings

- Webinars

- Live events

By the end of the chapter, you'll understand the differences between the different types of meetings and be able to configure the settings to manage the organizer and participant experiences.

Meetings

Meetings are one of the core functions of the Microsoft Teams experience. Whether participants are located across the hall or around the world, Teams makes it easy to connect and collaborate.

Types

Microsoft Teams features three basic types of meetings:

- Standard

- Channel

- Webinar

Standard

These are the meetings most of us are used to attending. In both physical office and virtual settings, these meetings can include things like invitees or participants, rooms, and equipment. Also known as *traditional meetings*, there are two types:

- **Scheduled meetings**   An organizer invites participants to meet at a particular time in the future.

- **Ad hoc**   Individuals collectively decide to meet immediately.

Individuals can schedule traditional meetings using the familiar Outlook calendaring tool or by clicking the New Meeting button in the Microsoft Teams Calendar app, as shown in Figure 20-1.

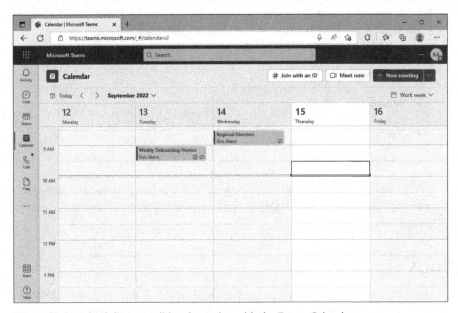

Figure 20-1   Scheduling a traditional meeting with the Teams Calendar app

An ad-hoc meeting (also called an "instant meeting") can be initiated using the Meet Now button in the Teams Calendar app. When the Meet Now button is clicked, the organizer is prompted to enter a name for the meeting and can get a link to distribute the invite via instant message or email. See Figure 20-2.

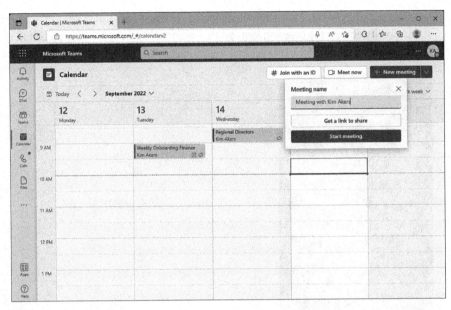

Figure 20-2   Meet Now

With both scheduled and instant meetings, the organizer can configure a number of controls to manage meeting features, as shown in Figure 20-3.

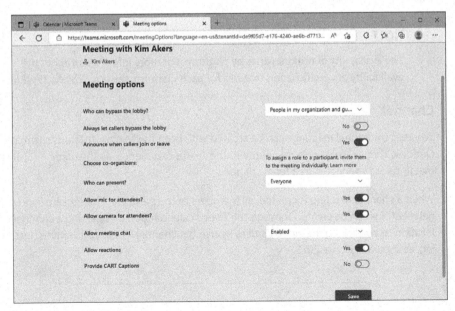

Figure 20-3   Meeting options

Meeting options can be accessed for instant and scheduled meetings after they have been scheduled by editing the meeting item on the calendar. Options can also be edited while in the meeting. See Figure 20-4.

Figure 20-4   Meeting options

NOTE

The availability of options varies by platform. For more information about the availability of specific Teams features for each platform, see *http://bit.ly/3Vy1EJu*.

Channel

Whereas traditional meetings can be created with both the Microsoft Teams client as well as Outlook, channel meetings are unique to the Teams experience. As the name indicates, channel meetings are connected to a team channel.

When a channel meeting is created, all members of the particular channel are invited. Channel meetings can be created through the Teams calendar app by selecting a channel under the location or by clicking the video camera icon in the channel where you want to host the meeting, as shown in Figure 20-5.

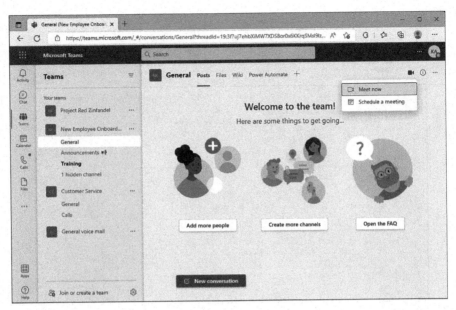

Figure 20-5   Channel meeting creation

Like a standard or traditional meeting, channel meetings can be created ad hoc or scheduled in advance. The channel meeting content is stored in the channel where it was created. This information is available after the meeting has ended for anyone with access to the channel.

Webinars

Webinars are essentially the same as standard meetings with an added registration component.

Like channel meetings, webinars can only be created from the Teams Calendar app. You can create a webinar in two ways (see Figure 20-6):

- Select New > Webinar from the Teams Calendar app.

- From a standard meeting's Require Registration dropdown, select

  - For People In Your Org

  - For Everyone

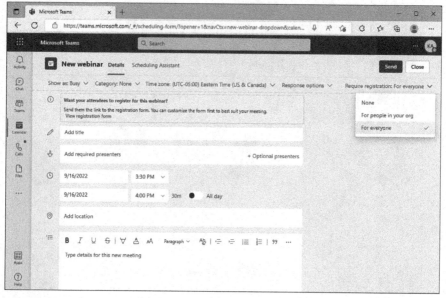

Figure 20-6 Create a webinar

If you select View Registration Form from the meeting invitation, you can design the form that attendees will fill out, as shown in Figure 20-7.

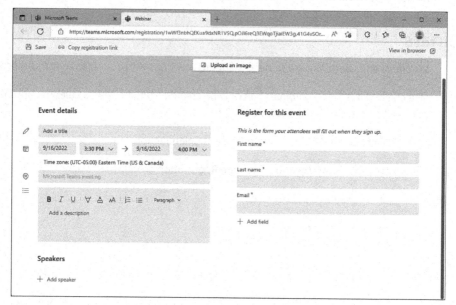

Figure 20-7 Webinar registration form

You can preview the form in the browser to ensure it looks appropriate.

Inside Out

Differences between standard meetings and webinars

Webinars and standard meetings are almost identical in nature. Following are the primary differences:

- Webinars require registration.
- Webinars have designated speakers.
- Webinars cannot be held in channels.

When editing the registration options for a meeting, if you select any options other than None, some subtle changes happen to the invitation:

- A link to a registration form is provided. You can customize the registration form with images as well as add additional registration fields.
- The Attendees field is changed to Presenters.
- The ability to schedule the meeting in a channel is removed because webinars are not limited to the scope of members in a channel.
- Meeting options are updated to include webinar-specific options and defaults.

In addition to a registration form, webinars have slightly different wording and options with different defaults, as shown in Figure 20-8.

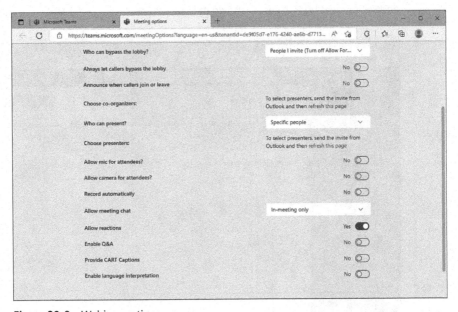

Figure 20-8 Webinar options

While many options are similar, note the differences, such as selecting presenters and enabling a Q&A.

Administration

Now that you understand some of the features of Teams meetings and webinars, let's look at the features that can be controlled or administered.

Because webinars are a subset of meetings, the options and policies you configure will apply to both scenarios. Configurable options for meetings fall into two categories, both of which are managed in the Teams admin center:

- Meeting policies

- Meeting settings

Meeting policies

Meeting policies control particular features available to organizers, presenters, and attendees of meetings and webinars.

Policies can be applied organization-wide as well as scoped to individuals and groups. The policies that apply during a meeting are inherited from the settings assigned to the meeting organizer.

Configure general settings

To configure the general settings, follow these steps:

1. Navigate to the Teams admin center at *https://admin.teams.microsoft.com*. Expand Meetings and select Meeting Policies, as shown in Figure 20-9.

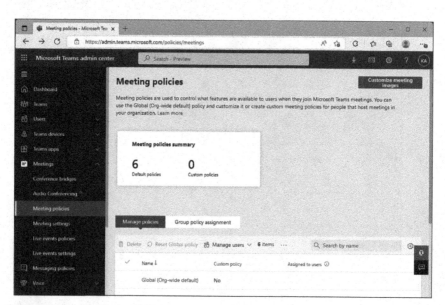

Figure 20-9   Meeting policies

2. Click Add to add a new policy or select an existing policy to edit it. (If Add is not displayed, expand the ellipsis and select Add.)

3. If you are creating a new policy, enter a Name and Description.

4. Configure the settings using the descriptions in the following sections.

5. Click Save to configure the policy.

6. The policy can now be assigned.

Under General, configure these settings:

- **Meet Now In Channels**   This setting controls whether a user to whom the policy applies can start an ad-hoc meeting in a Teams channel.

- **Outlook Add-In**   This setting controls whether a user to whom the policy applies can use Outlook to schedule a Teams meeting. If this setting is disabled, the New Teams Meeting button won't show up in the Outlook ribbon.

- **Channel Meeting Scheduling**   This setting controls whether a user to whom the policy applies can schedule channel meetings. If this policy is turned off, users will not be able to create new scheduled meetings, but organizers will be able to edit existing channel meetings.

- **Private Meeting Scheduling**   This setting controls whether a user to whom the policy applies can schedule private (non-channel) meetings.

- **Engagement Report**   This setting controls whether a user to whom the policy applies can download a meeting attendance report (a report that shows who registered and attended meetings and webinars).

- **Meeting Registration**   This setting controls whether a user to whom the policy applies can require registration for meetings (turning them into webinars).

- **Who Can Register**   This setting controls who can register for meetings. The available options are Everyone and Everyone In The Organization. If the Meeting Registration setting is disabled, this option is disabled.

Configure audio and video settings

Under Audio And Video, configure these settings:

- **Mode For IP Audio**   This setting controls whether a user to whom the policy applies can use audio for meetings and group calls. The available options are Outgoing And Incoming Audio Enabled (audio is allowed in the meeting) and Not Enabled (outgoing and incoming audio is turned off). If this option is set to Not Enabled for a user, they must dial

CHAPTER 20

in to the meeting using the PSTN or have the meeting call them if they want to participate with audio. This only applies to meetings and group calls, not to 1:1 calls (also known
as private calls). Configuring this setting to Not Enabled also disables IP video.

- **Mode For IP Video**   This setting controls whether a user to whom the policy applies can
  use video for meetings and group calls. The available options are Outgoing And Incoming Video Enabled (video is allowed in the meeting) and Not Enabled (outgoing and
  incoming video is turned off). If this policy is set to Not Enabled for a user, they cannot
  turn on their own video or see the video displayed by others. This setting only applies to
  users and does not apply to Teams Room and Surface Hub devices.

- **IP Video**   This setting controls outgoing video only and is applied at both the organizer
  and participant level. If multiple policies are applied to the organizer and users, the most
  restrictive setting applies to a particular user in a meeting.

Inside Out

Audio and video settings

When configuring the media options, it's important to understand what features need
to be configured carefully. To obtain the desired result, consult the following table.

Desired result	Meeting policy options
Disable audio and video for participants in meetings; participants must use PSTN for audio.	Mode For IP Audio: Not enabled Mode For IP Video: Not enabled IP Video: N/A
Enable incoming audio and video for meeting participants.	Mode For IP Audio: Outgoing and incoming audio enabled Mode For IP Video: Outgoing and incoming video enabled IP Video: Off
Disable meeting participant video; enable meeting participant audio.	Mode For IP Audio: Outgoing and incoming audio enabled Mode For IP Video: Not enabled IP Video: N/A
Enable audio and video for meeting participants. (Default setting if no policies have been configured or applied.)	Mode For IP Audio: Outgoing and incoming audio enabled Mode For IP Video: Outgoing and incoming video enabled IP Video: On

Remember, the most restrictive setting between the meeting organizer's and user's policies applies.

- **Local Broadcasting**   This setting controls whether the user to whom this policy applies can use a network device interface (NDI) or serial digital interface (SDI) for broadcasting. If this policy is enabled, users can enable broadcasting from the Teams client's meeting controls. For more information on setting up a client for NDI, see *https://learn.microsoft.com/en-US/microsoftteams/use-ndi-in-meetings*.

- **Media Bitrate**   This setting sets the media bitrate for a user to whom the policy applies. The minimum bitrate is 30Kbps, while the maximum bitrate value is 50Mbps (50,000Kbps).

NOTE

Microsoft documentation indicates that the minimum bitrate is 30Kbps, but the lowest value that the Teams admin center will allow you to configure is 50Kbps. The highest acceptable value is 2,147,483,647 (the maximum 32-bit floating-point integer value).

- **Network configuration lookup**   This setting controls whether an in-scope user's Teams client will attempt to use network configuration lookup for feature availability.

Inside Out

Network-based configurations

Network configuration lookup allows the Teams client to use local network settings configured to override the users' assigned Teams meeting policy.

Network sites are typically used in conjunction with Location-Based Routing (LBR), Local Media Optimization (LMO), and Direct Routing configurations.

For Teams to use a network configuration lookup, the following supporting objects must be created:

- Network regions
- Network sites
- Network subnets
- Trusted IP addresses

For example, let's assume you need to create a region for the United States with sites in Chicago and New York:

- **Subnet**   The Chicago site will have subnet 10.0.0.0/24 associated with it, while the New York site will have subnet 10.0.1.0/24 associated with it.
- **External NAT**   The Chicago site will have an external NAT of 172.16.0.1, while the New York site will have an external NAT of 172.16.1.1.

To configure these with the Microsoft Teams PowerShell module, use the following commands:

```
New-CsTenantNetworkRegion -NetworkRegionID "United States"
New-CsTenantNetworkSite -NetworkSiteID "Chicago" -NetworkRegionID "United `
States"
New-CsTenantNetworkSite -NetworkSiteID "New York" -NetworkRegionID "United `
States"
New-CsTenantNetworkSubnet -SubnetID 10.0.0.0 -MaskBits 24 -NetworkSiteID `
"Chicago"
New-CsTenantNetworkSubnet -SubnetID 10.0.1.0 -MaskBits 24 -NetworkSiteID "New `
York"
New-CsTenantTrustedIPAddress -IPAddress 172.16.0.1 -MaskBits 32 -Description `
"Chicago Trusted IP"
New-CsTenantTrustedIPAddress -IPAddress 172.16.1.0 -MaskBits 32 -Description `
"New York Trusted IP"
```

As a Teams client comes online, their external IP address will be matched against the Trusted IP Address values to determine if that client is inside the corporate network. If they match, then further processing will occur to match the Teams client to a particular subnet and site ID. If a match is found, that Teams client can use network-based policies.

Configure recording and transcription settings

Under Recording & Transcription, modify these settings:

- **Transcription**   This setting affects both the organizer and participants in a meeting. The organizer must have the Transcription feature enabled to turn transcription on or off for their meetings. If the organizer turns off the transcription feature, meeting attendees cannot enable transcription for a meeting. Participants cannot start recording a meeting if the organizer has this setting disabled.

- **Cloud Recording**   This setting controls whether meetings can be recorded. If enabled, the organizer can start a meeting recording. A participant for whom Cloud Recording is enabled can also start recording if they are an authenticated user in the same tenant as the organizer. External users cannot start recording.

- **Meetings Automatically Expire**   This setting controls whether the platform can expire the recorded meeting content. If enabled, you can configure an expiration time (measured in days). The maximum integer value supported is 99999. However, if configuring the meeting policy via the `Set-CsTeamsMeetingPolicy` PowerShell cmdlet, you can also use the `-NewMeetingRecordingExpirationDays` parameter to -1, which will set the expiration of meeting content to forever. The default expiration policy is 120 days.

- **Store Recordings Outside Of Your Country Or Region**   This setting controls whether saved meeting content can be stored outside your organization's regional datacenters.

Configure content-sharing settings

Under **Content Sharing**, configure the settings:

- **Screen Sharing Mode**   The effective setting combines the organizer and participant settings. Participants that do not have a specific policy assigned inherit the organizer's policy setting. If both the participant and the organizer have policies configured, the most restrictive policy applies to the participant. The available options are Entire Screen (allows the entire screen or a single application to be shared), Single Application (allows a single application or window to be shared), and Disabled.

- **Participants Can Give Or Request Control**   This per-user setting manages the ability to give and request control of a shared content window. If this policy is set to Off, the user to whom it applies cannot give control or request control in a meeting.

- **PowerPoint Live**   This per-user policy setting manages the ability for a participant to upload a PowerPoint deck and run the presentation from Teams. This only affects the PowerPoint Live service. If a meeting participant has this setting disabled and the screen-sharing setting configured to one of the enabled options, they can still share a Power-Point deck through the normal content-sharing mechanism.

- **Whiteboard**   This per-user policy setting manages the ability for a participant to share the whiteboard in a meeting. External users inherit the policy setting of the meeting organizer.

- **Shared Notes**   This per-user policy setting manages the ability for a participant to create and share meeting notes (which appear on the Meeting Notes tab of a meeting). External users inherit the policy setting of the meeting organizer.

- **Select Video Filters**   This per-user policy manages the ability for participants to enable filters during meetings with filters. The available options include All Filters, Background Blur And Default Images, Background Blur Only, and No Filters. Setting the No Filters option will prevent users from customizing their backgrounds.

Configure participant and guest settings

Under Participants & Guests, configure these settings:

- **Let Anonymous People Join A Meeting**   This per-organizer setting manages the ability for users to join meetings anonymously using the link in the meeting invitation.

- **Let Anonymous People Start A Meeting**   This per-organizer setting controls leaderless meeting joins—meaning that an anonymous dial-in user can start a scheduled meeting without an authenticated user from the organizer's tenant in attendance. If this setting is turned off, dial-in users will wait in the lobby to be admitted. If anonymous users join the call and are placed into the lobby before an organization user joins the call, the organization user can only admit them from the Teams client.

- **Who Can Present In Meetings** This per-organizer setting manages the default for new meetings for users to whom the policy applies. The available options are Everyone, But User Can Override; Everyone In The Organization, But User Can Override; and Everyone, But User Can Override. In this case, User Can Override means the meeting organizer can change the presenter in the meeting options.

- **Automatically Admit People** This per-organizer policy manages who can join the meeting directly and who must wait in the lobby until admitted by an authenticated user. This setting *does not* affect dial-in users; their automatic join settings are managed by the Dial-In Users Can Bypass The Lobby setting. Following are the available options:

  - **Everyone, People In My Organization And Guests** Authenticated organization users and authenticated guests.

  - **People In My Organization, Trusted Organizations, And Guests** Authenticated users, authenticated guests, and organizations permitted in the Users > External Access > Teams And Skype For Business Users In External Organizations setting).

  - **People In My Organization** Only individuals in the organizer's tenant.

  - **Organizer Only** Only the organizer will join automatically. Additional users can be admitted after the meeting has started.

  - **Invited Users Only** Only individuals specifically indicated in the meeting invitation. Users included as part of a distribution list must wait in the lobby.

- **Dial-In Users Can Bypass The Lobby** This per-organizer policy manages whether dial-in phone users will be automatically admitted to meetings, regardless of the Automatically Admit People setting.

- **Meet Now In Private Meetings** This per-user setting manages whether a user can start an ad-hoc meeting.

- **Live Captions** This per-user setting manages whether a user can turn on live captions through the Teams client during a meeting. The available settings are Not Enabled But The User Can Override and Not Enabled. If the setting is configured as Not Enabled, the user to whom this policy applies is unable to turn on captions during a meeting.

- **Chat In Meetings** This per-user and per-organizer setting controls how chat functions in a standard meeting (not a channel meeting). The most restrictive setting applies if the organizer and participants have different policies set. The availability options are: Turn It On For Everyone, Turn It Off For Everyone, and Turn It On For Everyone But Anonymous

Users. If Turn It On For Everyone But Anonymous Users is configured for the organizer, anonymous users can read messages in chat but not compose any.

- **Teams Q&A**   This per-organizer policy manages the availability of the Questions & Answers experience. If Q&A is enabled in the meeting policy, Yammer must be enabled for sign-in through Azure AD admin center > All services > Enterprise Applications > Office 365 Yammer > Properties, and the Teams Q&A app must not be blocked.

- **Meeting Reactions**   This per-organizer and per-user policy manages the availability of reaction icons during a meeting.

Assign a meeting policy to a user

Meeting policies can easily be assigned to users through the Teams admin center. To assign a meeting policy to individual users, follow these steps:

1. Navigate to the Teams admin center at *https://admin.teams.microsoft.com*.

2. Expand Meetings and select Meeting Policies.

3. Select the Manage Policies tab.

4. Select a policy to assign.

5. Select Manage Users.

6. From the Manage Users dropdown, select Assign Users.

7. On the Manage Users flyout, search for and add users to the policy.

8. Click Apply to save changes.

The users will now receive the new meeting policy settings.

Assign a meeting policy to a group

If you create policies that need to be applied to many users at once, you can also apply policies via a group membership. Policies assigned via group can be ranked.

To assign a meeting policy to a group, follow these steps:

1. Navigate to the Teams admin center at *https://admin.teams.microsoft.com*.

2. Expand Meetings and select Meeting Policies.

3. Select the Group Policy Assignment tab.

4. Click Add.

5. In the Assign Policy To Group flyout menu, select a group that will be assigned the policy.

6. In the Select Rank box, enter a ranking value for the policy. If a user is a member of more than one group with a policy assigned, the policy with the lowest-ranking value will be the winning policy.

7. In the Select A Policy dropdown, choose a policy.

8. Click Apply to save changes.

When setting the rank of a policy assignment, if you select a value that is already in use, the new policy assignment will take its place. The previously existing policy at that particular ranking (and all lower-ranking policies) will shift down by one.

Meeting settings

Meeting settings can be used to manage features available to anonymous users, information about meeting invitations, and network settings. These settings apply to all users in the organization.

To manage the meeting settings, follow these steps:

1. Navigate to the Teams admin center at *https://admin.teams.microsoft.com*.

2. Expand Meetings and select Meeting Settings, as shown in Figure 20-10.

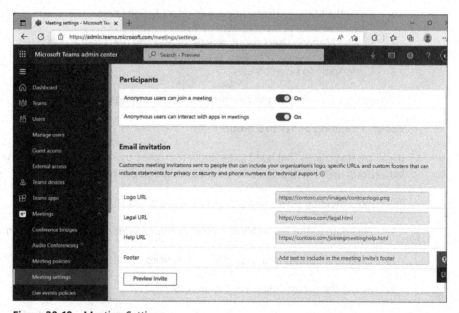

Figure 20-10   Meeting Settings

3. Under Participants, configure these settings:

    ■ **Anonymous Users Can Join A Meeting**   This organization-wide setting controls whether anonymous users can join meetings by clicking the link in the meeting invitation. Configuring this setting to Off overrides the Let Anonymous People Join A Meeting meeting policy setting.

    ■ **Anonymous Users Can Interact With Apps In Meetings**   This organization-wide setting controls whether anonymous users are allowed to interact with apps used in meetings. If this setting is turned off, anonymous users cannot use meeting apps. If this setting is turned on, anonymous users inherit the global default permission policy.

4. Under Email Invitation, update the Logo URL, Legal URL, and Help URL values to point to public-facing web pages containing appropriate content for your organization.

5. Under Email Invitation, update the Footer value to include any additional text you want to attach to the meeting invitation.

6. Under Network, configure the Quality Of Service (QoS) settings.

    ## NOTE

    For information on properly configuring QoS for Microsoft Teams endpoints and networking devices, see "Enabling QoS for Teams devices and mobile devices" in Chapter 21, "Phone system planning."

7. Click Save.

After a brief policy refresh, the meeting settings will be applied.

Live events

Unlike other meetings, live events are broadcast-style events designed to stream content to audiences of up to 10,000 attendees (or up to 100,000) through the Microsoft 365 Live Events Assistance Program. (See *https://aka.ms/LiveEventAssist.*)

Live events leverage many of the same features and technology of meetings and then layer on top of that the ability to use things like Stream and Yammer with external encoders for production and content delivery networks (CDNs) to make your event available more broadly.

Live events policies

By default, all users with a Teams license can schedule and conduct live events. However, there might be limits your organization wants to place on those capabilities.

Configure a live events policy

To manage live events policies, follow these steps:

1. Navigate to the Teams admin center at *https://admin.teams.microsoft.com*.

2. Expand Meetings and select Live Events Policies.

3. On the Manage Policies tab, click Add to create a new policy, or select an existing policy to edit. See Figure 20-11.

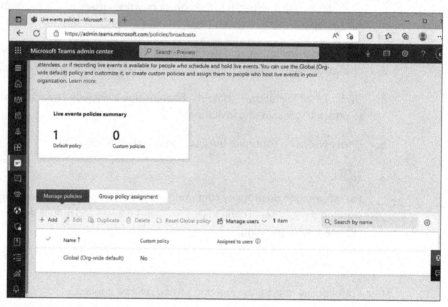

Figure 20-11   Live events policies page

4. Configure the settings, as shown in Figure 20-12:

    - **Live Events Scheduling**   This setting controls whether the users affected by this policy have the ability to schedule live events. The default is On. The organizer will also need a Microsoft Stream license and third-party equipment and services for live events produced with external apps or devices.

    - **Transcription For Attendees**   This setting controls whether the users affected by this policy can see live captions or subtitles during the event. The event must be produced in Teams.

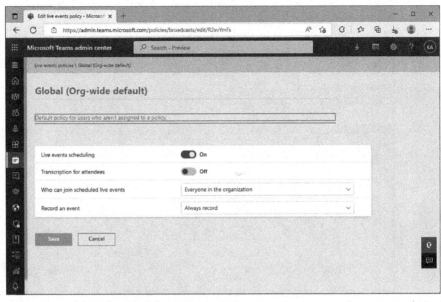

Figure 20-12   Live events policy settings

- **Who Can Join Scheduled Events**   This setting controls who is allowed to join events. The available options include

  - ▼ **Everyone**   Allows external users to join.

  - ▼ **Everyone In The Organization**   Limited to authenticated members of the tenant.

  - ▼ **Specific Users And Groups**   Limited to authenticated members of the tenant.

- **Record An Event**   This setting controls the recording of the event. The available options are Always Record, Never Record, and Organizer Can Record.

Recordings from live events produced in Microsoft Teams are not currently stored in SharePoint, OneDrive, or Microsoft Stream. Instead, they are stored in Azure Media Services. After a meeting, they can be downloaded from the event's calendar item and uploaded to a location such as Stream or a Teams channel. Review the example meeting details page shown in Figure 20-13.

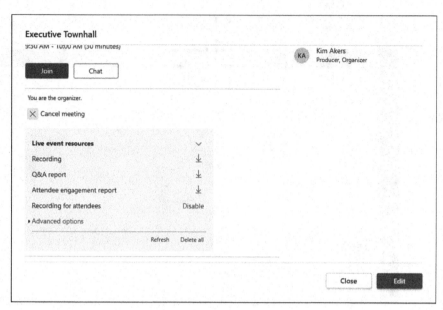

Figure 20-13   Details for a completed meeting

5.   Click Save to configure the policy.

If you have edited the Global policy, those edits will apply to all users for which a specific policy is not enabled.

Live events can be created through the Teams interface by navigating to the calendar and selecting New > Live Event. Live event scheduling is very similar to webinar scheduling, including how to specify presenters, attendees, and options.

Assign a live events policy to a user

Live events policies can easily be assigned to users through the Teams admin center. To assign a live events policy to individual users, follow these steps:

1.   Navigate to the Teams admin center at *https://admin.teams.microsoft.com*.

2.   Expand Meetings and select Live Events Policies.

3.   Select the Manage Policies tab.

4.   Highlight and select a policy to assign. Select Manage Users.

5.   From the Manage Users dropdown, select Assign Users.

6.   On the **Manage Users** flyout menu, search for and add users to the policy.

7.   Click Apply to save changes.

8.   The users will now receive the new live events policy settings.

Assign a live events policy to a group

If you create policies that need to be applied to many users at once, you can also apply policies via a group membership. Policies assigned via group can be ranked.

To assign a meeting policy to a group, follow these steps:

1.   Navigate to the Teams admin center at *https://admin.teams.microsoft.com*.

2.   Expand Meetings and select Live Events.

3.   Select the Group Policy Assignment tab.

4.   Click Add.

5.   In the Assign Policy To Group flyout, select a group that will be assigned the policy.

6.   In the Select Rank box, enter a ranking value for the policy. If a user is a member of more than one group with a policy assigned, the policy with the lowest-ranking value will be the winning policy.

7.   In the Select A Policy dropdown, choose a policy.

8.   Click Apply to save changes.

When setting the rank of a policy assignment, if you select a value that is already in use, the new policy assignment will take its place. The previous policy at that particular ranking (and all lower-ranked policies) will shift down by one.

Live events settings

The Live Events Settings page shown in Figure 20-14 allows you to manage organization-wide settings for your live streaming events.

CHAPTER 20

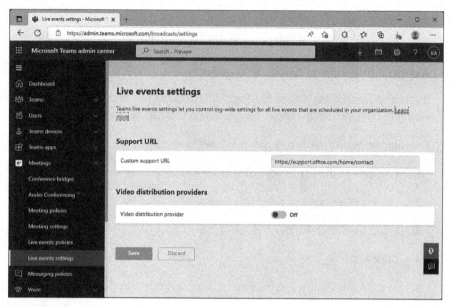

Figure 20-14   Live events settings

There are only two configurable settings on this page:

- Support URL

- Video Distribution Providers

Support URL

Under Support URL, the Custom Support URL setting is very straightforward. Simply specify a public web page containing support information that will be available to your meeting attendees. This information might include a frequently asked questions (FAQ) page, a support email address, a phone number, or a link to a support ticket system to request assistance.

Video distribution providers

The Video Distribution Provider setting shown in Figure 20-15 is set to Off by default. This setting allows you to specify the content distribution network settings for live events.

Depending on the size and locations of your audience, you might want to consider using a content delivery network (CDN) to relieve congestion and optimize distribution to meeting participants.

Typically, using a CDN provider requires a license or subscription. Typical options include a software delivery network (SDN) API key, license key, or template URL.

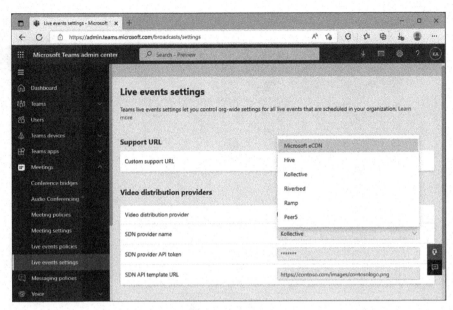

Figure 20-15   Video Distribution Providers setting

Integrated services

In addition to producing and managing live events through Microsoft Teams, you can also initiate them through Stream and Yammer.

Stream

Anyone with a Microsoft Stream license can create and produce live events in the service. To manage the Stream settings for live events, follow these steps:

1. Navigate to the Microsoft Stream portal at *https://web.microsoftstream.com* and log in with your Microsoft 365 credentials.

2. On the navigation bar, click the gear icon to expand the settings, and then select Admin Settings.

3. In the left-side navigation panel, expand Manage Stream and select Live Events, as shown in Figure 20-16.

CHAPTER 20

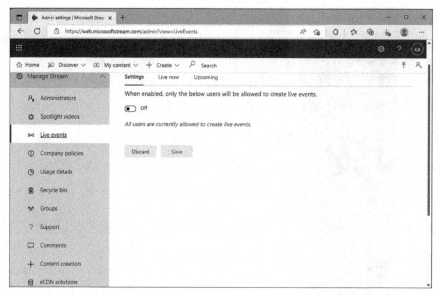

Figure 20-16   Live Events settings

4. On the Settings tab, move the slider to On to specify users that will be able to create Live events from the Stream interface.

5. From the navigation pane, select eCDN Solutions.

6. Move the Enable A Third Party eCDN Solution slider to On if you need to configure a third-party content delivery network. See Figure 20-17.

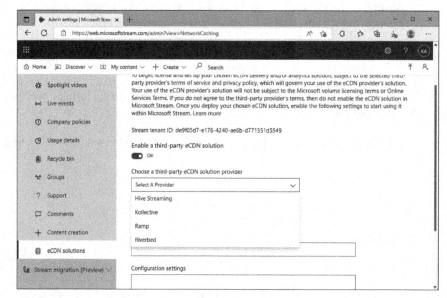

Figure 20-17   Stream eCDN configuration

7. Under Choose A Third Party eCDN Solution Provider, select the eCDN provider you will use.

8. Populate the values for Customer ID, Analytics Report URL and Configuration Settings per your CDN's configuration information.

9. Click Save.

10. Optionally, select Verify Setup and select a video that will be used to test your eCDN configuration parameters.

In addition to configuring Stream, your third-party production solution might also have places to enter configuration parameters pertaining to the CDN service.

Inside Out

What's an eCDN?

A Content Delivery Network (CDN) is a network of strategically placed servers world-wide used to help deliver static or streaming content to geographically dispersed endpoints. CDNs act as amplification devices to reduce latency by redistributing the download traffic away from the original content source.

An Enterprise Content Delivery Network (eCDN) functions much the same way, typically moving the client distribution infrastructure inside the boundary of a corporate net-work. Rather than thousands of individual endpoints traversing an Internet link to the same content source, an eCDN manages one or two data streams to the outside content source and can scale internally to provide lower latency and better delivery to devices.

When the configuration is complete, users can create a live event from Stream by selecting Create > Live Event, as shown in Figure 20-18.

The live event producer can enter the appropriate settings (Event Name and Description, Video Language, and Event Schedule). Also, you can configure the encoder settings that will be used for the event.

CHAPTER 20

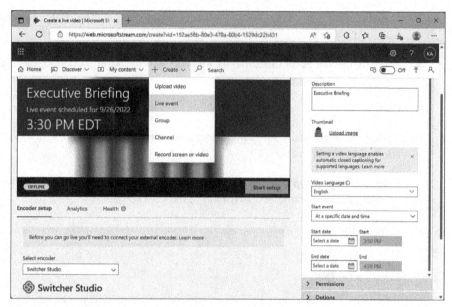

Figure 20-18   Create a live event in Stream

Yammer

Yammer can also be used to host and produce live events. There are two prerequisites for creating live events in Yammer:

● The event creator must have a Stream or Teams license assigned.

● The event creator must not have a Teams policy preventing them from creating live events.

Live events can be created by selecting the Create Live Event button on the community's Events page, as shown in Figure 20-19.

As with creating a live event in the Teams or Stream interface, Yammer presents organizers with configuration values for adding an Event Name, Presenters, and Start and End Dates, as shown in Figure 20-20.

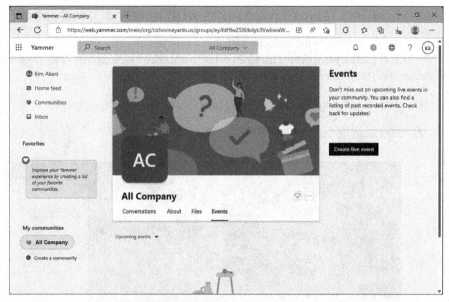

Figure 20-19   Yammer Events page

Create a new event   ×

Event name

Add a short, engaging event name

Presenters

Producers

Start date	End date	From	To
Thu, Sep 22, 2022	Thu, Sep 22, 2022	16:00	16:30

Description

Tell people what the event is about

Additional settings Learn more

This is a test event (don't show this event information to my organization when it's live)   ○ Yes   ○ No

Enable Q&A and comments for attendees.   ⬤

Figure 20-20   Yammer Create A New Event wizard

Configuring Teams Live events with external production

You'll need to configure the encoder with a server ingestion URL if your organization has decided to produce live events using an external encoder that supports Real-Time Messaging Protocol (RTMP). Follow these steps:

1. After scheduling a Teams live event for external production, click Join.

2. Click Start Setup, as shown in Figure 20-21.

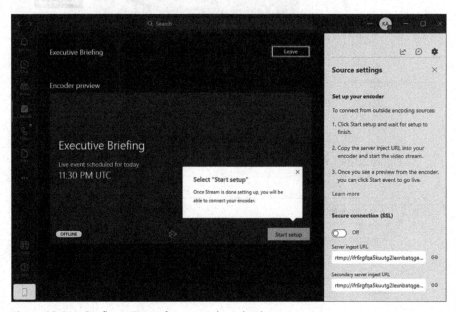

Figure 20-21   Configure Teams for external production

3. If your encoder supports it, enable SSL by moving the Secure Connection (SSL) slider to On.

4. Copy the Server Ingest URL value and enter it into the appropriate configuration area in your encoder.

5. If your encoder supports a backup or secondary stream, copy the Secondary Server Ingest URL value and enter it into the appropriate configuration area in your encoder.

6. Once connected to the encoder, you can start the live event by clicking Start Event.

7. When you are ready to finish, click End Event, as shown in Figure 20-22.

Figure 20-22   Live event produced with external encoder

After the event has been produced, you can download it from Stream by navigating to the Stream portal at *https://web.microsoftstream.com* and searching for the video. Once you've located the event, you can click the Download link to save the video locally.

Also, you can download the event by opening it on the Microsoft Teams calendar and clicking the Stream link, which will direct you to the video with a download option.

What's next?

In this chapter, you learned about the configurable options for managing meetings, webinars, and live events. These policies can be scoped to individual users, groups, and even the entire organization.

In the next chapter, we'll start exploring phone system planning, which will help you design a comprehensive calling solution.

CHAPTER 20

Phone system planning

Microsoft Teams, in addition to its broad collaboration and application development platform capabilities, also boasts a full spectrum of phone system capabilities. As the successor to Skype for Business Online (retired in July 2021) and its capabilities, Teams Phone System allows organizations to deploy full-featured telephony solutions.

In this chapter, we'll introduce the Teams Phone System concepts and guide you through selecting the architecture that best meets your organization's goals.

Overview of Teams Phone concepts

Selecting a telephony architecture to suit your organization's physical, regulatory, and business needs is a key decision in your planning process. While there are several ways to connect to the public switched telephone network (PSTN), choosing the best option will be key to limiting disruptions during deployment.

There are three major architectures you can select from, each with its own set of distinct advantages and features:

- Calling Plans for Microsoft 365

- Operator Connect

- Direct Routing

Before we dive into selecting an architecture, it's important to understand the terminology and concepts related to the platform.

Teams Phone concepts and terminology

The Microsoft Teams telephony platform has undergone several branding changes (such as Cloud PBX and Phone System), finally landing with Teams Phone. The Phone System term persists, now referring to the licensing assignment that enables various telephony features.

Teams Phone is the Microsoft-hosted public branch exchange (PBX) system, providing both internal (PC-to-PC) and external calling capabilities.

Audio conferencing

Many organizations host telephone conferences. With hybrid work scenarios, most participants join from their computers. However, there still exists a need for meeting participants to be able to dial in to attend a phone conference. This feature is commonly known as a conference line, conference bridge, or simply a bridge number.

While most Microsoft Teams users will join via the Teams client (either on their computer or through a mobile device), there may be scenarios where that isn't possible. Joining a call via the Teams client requires high-speed Internet connectivity to maintain call and video quality. If call participants find themselves without high-speed Internet, the audio-conferencing feature allows them to dial a traditional phone number and join meetings.

In addition to dial-in to meetings, audio conferencing allows you to dial out from a meeting and add additional people to the call. You can also add toll-free dial-ins to your audio conferencing by purchasing communications credits.

Auto attendants

If you've ever called a business and navigated through a menu of options (such as "Press 1 to create a case"), then you've used an interactive voice response (IVR) system. In Teams Phone, this feature is called an auto attendant.

Auto attendants can be used to route to several destinations, including

- The operator

- An internal subscriber

- Another auto attendant or a call queue

- Voicemail

- An external phone number

- An announcement message (either pre-recorded audio or a text message that the system can read to the caller)

Auto attendants can also be scheduled, allowing you to configure different routing and navigation options for working hours, after-hours, and holidays.

Call queues

A call queue is a method of routing inbound calls to a pool or group of related agents or individuals. Callers can be added to a queue by calling a service number directly; they may also be added to the queue by an auto attendant.

Agents are the individuals responsible for answering the calls in the queue.

A call queue typically provides a greeting message or other audio during the hold time. Calls are typically handled on a first-in, first-out (FIFO) basis. A queue can specify how to handle overflow and timeout scenarios.

Contact centers

A contact center is a third-party platform that integrates line-of-business applications (frequently customer relationship management tools) and the Microsoft Teams Phone System. Contact centers may be integrated through Direct Routing, the Graph Communications API, or custom Power Platform connectors.

Dial plans

A dial plan is a set of rules that defines how Teams will respond to dialed numbers. This includes external dialing prefixes as well as internal objects.

Teams Phone has two types of dial plans: service-scoped and tenant-scoped:

- **Service-scoped**   Service-scoped dial plans are non-configurable and are built-in. There is a service-scoped dial plan configured for every region where service is available. The service-scoped dial plan is assigned to every user automatically, based on their location.

- **Tenant-scoped**   A tenant-scoped dial plan is configured at the tenant level. Tenant dial plans fall into two categories: tenant-scoped and user-scoped. A user plan is specifically applied to individual users, while a tenant plan covers everyone in the tenant.

Inside Out

Effective dial plans

A user's *effective* dial plan is the result of the combination and evaluation of the service-scoped plan for their region and the user or tenant dial plan.

There are three possible effective dial plans, depending on the tenant's configuration:

- **Service Country**   This is the default dial plan applied to all users. If there is no tenant plan or user plan configured and assigned, the user's effective dial plan will be set to the service-scoped plan for their assigned region.

- **Tenant Global–Service Country**   For organizations that have a tenant dial plan defined, the effective dial plan is an evaluation of the service-scoped dial plan that applies to the user's assigned location and the tenant dial plan (for users who don't have a user dial plan assigned).

- **Tenant User–Service Country**   Finally, if an organization has defined a user dial plan and assigned it to a user, the user will receive an effective dial plan that is the evaluation of their service country dial plan and assigned user dial plan.

A tenant can contain up to 1,000 dial plans.

Phone numbers

The phone number is one of the most visible parts of a telephony solution. When planning a phone system, two of the earliest questions in the process will typically be: "Where will I obtain phone numbers?" and "How will I manage phone numbers?"

To determine the answer to those questions, you'll need first to answer design questions such as:

- Do you want all-new phone numbers, or must you maintain existing numbers?

- Do you want a simplified number assignment process through a user interface, or is your organization comfortable with a command-line interface?

- If you are bringing your own numbers, what business organization currently owns the phone numbers? Will a service agreement be necessary to transfer ownership?

- Are there any interoperability concerns with legacy or analog equipment?

- Do you have existing service provider contracts that need to be maintained?

These questions will invariably lead you to select one of the three available options:

- **Calling Plans**   Calling Plan is a subscription that includes a phone number and a bundle of minutes. For the simplest experience, you can use Microsoft-provided phone numbers.

- **Direct Routing**   Direct Routing uses custom appliances called Session Border Controllers (SBC) to connect your on-premises phone system with the Microsoft cloud. With Direct Routing, you can use your service provider's numbers and calling plans.

- **Operator Connect**   Operator Connect is essentially a carrier-managed Direct Routing implementation. With Operator Connect, the carrier manages session border controllers for your organization.

Each Teams Phone solution has its advantages, depending on your organization's telephony needs, such as simplicity, integration, or management.

Porting

Porting is the process of transferring or migrating numbers from one service provider to another. If you want to use Microsoft Teams Calling Plans with your existing phone numbers, you will need to port your numbers from your existing service provider to Microsoft.

Resource accounts

A resource account is a type of service account that utilizes service and device features, such as Teams Rooms, auto attendants, and call queues.

When used for auto attendants or call queues, resource accounts require a license: either a Phone System–Virtual User (free) license or a Phone System (paid) user license.

Service numbers

In addition to phone numbers for end users, many organizations need general phone numbers that connect to automated features such as call queues or auto attendants. Service numbers can be either toll-based or toll-free and allow for a high concurrency of inbound callers. Service phone numbers can be ported from your existing carrier or operator to Microsoft.

Session border controller

A Session Border Controller (SBC) is a network edge appliance (either software or hardware) used to connect and manage communications traffic between disparate systems. SBCs are used in Direct Routing infrastructures to coordinate the negotiation between user agents and SIP systems. SBCs manage traffic that traverses trunks—the logical unit of circuits or channels between endpoints.

Session Initiation Protocol

Session Initiation Protocol (SIP) is a communications protocol used for initiating, maintaining, and terminating sessions for voice and video. SIP is primarily used by Internet protocol-based telephony systems that utilize the Voice over Internet Protocol (VoIP).

Calling features

The Teams Phone system has myriad calling features designed to provide parity with traditional on-premises PBX systems.

Caller ID

Microsoft Teams Phone supports caller ID features for both inbound and outbound calling scenarios. Caller ID displays two pieces of information: the calling line ID (CLID) or public switched telephone network (PSTN) number and the calling party name (CNAM).

The Phone System will show the incoming PSTN number as the caller ID for inbound calls. If the number is associated with a contact, Teams will resolve it and display the CNAM based on that information. If the incoming number is not associated with a contact, the CNAM provided by the carrier will be displayed if it is available.

CHAPTER 21

For outbound calls, Teams Phone can be configured to show the following information:

- Anonymous (displayed when a policy blocking outbound caller ID is configured)

- Calling party name

- Actual telephone number assigned to a user

- A service number to mask the calling line identity

- Caller ID settings are managed in the Teams admin center

Call parking

Call parking describes a feature set that allows a user to place a call on hold and then transfer or resume the call.

Emergency calling

With traditional telephony solutions, a phone number is directly linked to a physical or street address in the carrier or service provider's database. When the phone number is moved to a new service location, the provider updates the physical location in their records, which allows emergency services to be routed accurately.

The portability of phone numbers to both mobile devices and Internet-based telephony services means that the actual usage location for a particular phone number might not match the address stored in the provider's records.

Inside Out

Kari's Law and Ray Baum's Act

In 2019, the United States Federal Communications Commission (FCC) adopted rules under Section 506 of Ray Baum's Act. The rules addressed two core requirements for emergency dialing in the United States—elimination of a prefix (such as "dial 9 for an outside line") to access an emergency number and requiring specific location information to be provided with a 911 call. To comply with the rule, dispatchable location information (including a civic address and details like a building, floor, suite, or room number) must be provided for emergency calls after January 6, 2022. For more information on dispatchable locations, see *https://www.fcc.gov/911-dispatchable-location*.

When working with emergency calling, the following terms are used:

- **Public safety answering point**   The public safety answering point (PSAP) is a call center responsible for routing emergency (911) calls.

- **Emergency address**   An emergency address is a physical location, also known as a civic address or a street address. This address may be different than a mailing address; the emergency address is where emergency personnel must be sent. This address routes calls to the appropriate local dispatch service for notifying emergency services.

- **Place**   A place is a more specific data element used to refine an emergency address. A place can be descriptive information such as a floor, building number, office or suite number, or wing.

- **Emergency location**   The emergency location, like the emergency address, is a civic or street address. So, if you have an emergency address of 123 Any Street and a place of Suite 201, the emergency location represents both values. If you add one or more places to an emergency address, a unique location ID is created for each emergency address and place combination.

- **Registered address**   A registered address is a specific address assigned to each user. A registered address may also be referred to as a static emergency address or an address of record.

- **Dynamic emergency calling**   Utilizing the geolocating features of the Microsoft Teams client, emergency location information is automatically routed to the appropriate PSAP.

In addition to the civic address, emergency locations may have geographic coordinates attached to ensure that emergency responders are directed to the correct location.

Correctly configuring emergency calling is extremely important to ensure the most efficient routing of emergency personnel.

NOTE

When configuring a Teams Phone System, the emergency location information must be configured before numbers can be fully assigned to users.

Inbound call blocking

Some organizations may desire to block inbound calls from the PSTN. Teams Phone supports using regular expressions (RegEx) to define number patterns to block. This advanced feature is currently only configurable via PowerShell.

Shared line appearance

Shared line appearance allows individuals (managers or delegators) to assign access to another user (delegate) to make and receive calls on their behalf. Delegates can make and receive PSTN and Teams calls on behalf of the delegator and park and resume calls on their behalf.

Voicemail

Cloud voicemail is automatically enabled for licensed Teams Phone System users. Voicemail messages are deposited in the user's associated Exchange mailbox (either in Exchange Online or Exchange on-premises for hybrid configurations). In addition to customized greetings and visual voicemail features, mail flow or transport rules can be configured to encrypt voicemail messages. Voicemail messages can be managed in the Teams Phone app on the left rail.

Choosing an architecture

Now that you understand the basic calling features and terminology as applied to Teams Phone, we can explore architectures at a deeper level.

When choosing a Teams Phone architecture, you can choose from more simple, hosted deployments to more complex scenarios that allow integration with existing VoIP infrastructure, devices, and service providers. Table 21-1 shows feature availability across architectures, which can be used to help guide design decisions.

Table 21-1   Architecture features

	Calling plans	Operator connect	Direct routing
Existing PSTN infrastructure (session border controllers or voice trunks) will continue to be operated		✓	✓
Microsoft-provided numbers	✓		
Customer-provided telephone numbers	✓	✓	✓
Fully managed infrastructure solution		✓	
Fully hosted or cloud-native solution with no new on-premises voice infrastructure or hardware	✓	✓	
No previous or existing on-premises voice infrastructure hardware	✓		
Quick pilot or proof-of-concept	✓		
Centralized billing through Microsoft or CSP	✓		
Sites located in calling plan markets	✓		
Supports coexistence with existing telephony infrastructure			✓
Supports coexistence or migration from a legacy phone system			✓
Mix and match infrastructures	✓	✓	✓

	Calling plans	Operator connect	Direct routing
Maintain existing telephony service provider agreements		✓	✓
Telephone number assignment Integrated in Teams Admin Center	✓	✓	
Telephone number assignment from PowerShell	✓	✓	✓
Supports third-party interoperability scenarios		✓	✓
Supports local PSTN calling via survivable branch appliances			✓
Ability to maintain local or regional regulatory requirements			✓
Supports localities outside of Microsoft Calling Plans regions		✓	✓
Supports integration of analog devices			✓

With the features from Table 21-1 in mind, review the details of each architecture in the following sections.

Calling Plans for Microsoft 365

Calling Plans are Microsoft's native solution and will provide the fastest route to using Teams Phone System. A Calling Plans deployment only requires software licensing from Microsoft and making the appropriate cloud-based configuration choices to get started.

While dedicated client hardware devices (such as headsets and handsets) can be used, they are not required. The Microsoft Teams client is designed to be able to make and receive calls directly from the user interface. Modern desktop and notebook devices with integrated microphones, cameras, and speakers provide enough capability to get started.

For the quickest and simplest deployments, you can use Microsoft-provided phone numbers. If you want to maintain your existing numbers, you can initiate the porting process to transfer your numbers from your current provider to Microsoft.

Calling plan minutes are pooled across all users in the organization. Once you've exceeded the number of minutes in the pool, you can purchase communications credits to cover the additional minutes you'll need.

Communications credits are also required when configuring toll-free dial-in conferencing numbers.

NOTE

Communications credits are pooled pre-paid minutes that are drawn down as your users make phone calls to the public switched telephone network (PSTN). Internal Teams calling (sometimes referred to as *PC-to-PC calling*), inbound local or long-distance calls, and inbound calls to service numbers do not consume calling plan or communications credits minutes.

Each calling plan license is measured in minutes per licensed or assigned per user, per month. It's important to note that unassigned licenses will not contribute to the pool. Minutes are pooled within the tenant according to the calling plan's country and tier.

For example, if an organization had 1,000 users in one country, all licensed with 120-minute calling plans, the tenant/country would own a pool of 120,000 minutes. If an organization had 1,000 users with 500 users each in two counties, and each was licensed with 120-minute calling plans, each group of 500 users would have a shared pool of 60,000 minutes.

While calling plans don't require the purchase of additional telephony routing hardware, they may not be available in all worldwide regions.

NOTE

For the most up-to-date regional availability, see *https://aka.ms/callingplans*.

Direct Routing

Direct Routing is an architecture that allows Teams Phone integration through a Session Border Controller (SBC) to a third-party analog gateway, SIP-based public branch exchange (PBX), or SIP trunking service. This allows for the integration of on-premises, hosted, and non-VoIP-based technologies (like analog devices and gateways) into the Teams cloud-based architecture.

Many larger organizations with enterprise telephony services evaluate Direct Routing due to their existing infrastructure and devices. The core advantage of Direct Routing is that it works with any existing carrier and can be configured in regions where Microsoft does not offer calling plans.

Direct Routing enables an organization to configure a certain level of interoperability between the platforms. While phone numbers are typically provided through the existing service operator or carrier agreement, you can also use calling plans if they're available in your region.

Unlike a Calling Plans solution (where Microsoft hosts all infrastructure), Direct Routing requires compatible network infrastructure to complete the configuration. Three types of devices can be integrated in Direct Routing scenarios:

- Session border controllers

- Survivable branch appliances

- Analog telephone adapters

Direct Routing can be configured with customer-premises equipment, as shown in Figure 21-1.

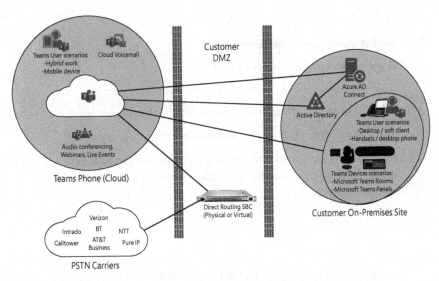

Figure 21-1   Direct Routing with customer premises equipment

As depicted in Figure 21-1, a physical or virtual SBC is placed on the customer premises. Peering is configured between the on-premises SBC appliance and Teams Phone system in Microsoft 365. The SBC will also be peered to the PSTN carrier.

Inside Out

Peering relationships

Peering is a business agreement between organizations to connect their networks without using additional interconnected parties. Peering arrangements are configured at an *Internet exchange point (IXP)*—a common location where both organizations have networking equipment.

Organizations entering a peering arrangement must generally meet the following requirements: a publicly routed autonomous system number (ASN), a block of public IP addresses, and a network edge router capable of running Border Gateway Protocol (BGP) with enough capacity to advertise the necessary routes.

If you don't want to provide an on-premises SBC, you can also select a session border controller hosted by an on-premises or cloud provider. Many such virtual appliances can be acquired through the Azure Marketplace. In this case, the SBC is collocated on virtual infrastructure, and the peering relationships are configured at the collocation or cloud hosting service provider instead of your own managed datacenter.

Inside Out

Hosted session border controller options

Some vendors provide preconfigured SBCs:

- AudioCodes Live   https://liveteams.audiocodes.com
- TeamMate   https://www.teammatetechnology.com
- Call2Teams   https://www.call2teams.com

Many carriers provide SBC-as-a-service offerings that can be bundled with their SIP trunk offerings, giving you the advantages of both a session border controller and a managed service.

NOTE

The current list of Microsoft-certified session border controllers can be found at https://docs.microsoft.com/en-us/MicrosoftTeams/direct-routing-border-controllers.

Media Bypass

Media Bypass is a feature that allows you to route Teams media traffic between a Teams client and session border controller directly instead of routing it through the service. This shortens the path the data must travel, keeping media local to the corporate network instead of routing to the Microsoft 365 service and back again.

Figure 21-2 depicts how the local media bypass allows Teams media data to route between the on-premises users via the SBC while the signaling path travels the Teams Cloud Voice service.

Without Media Bypass in place, both the media and the signaling would go via the Teams Cloud Voice service and get routed back on-premises.

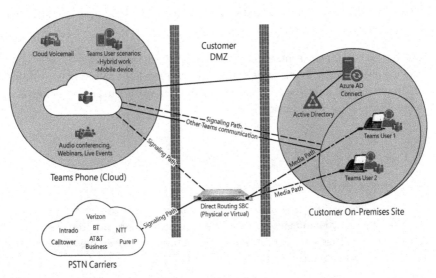

Figure 21-2   Teams Direct Routing Media Bypass

Inside Out

Media Bypass Deep Dive

Media Bypass is a complex networking concept that requires careful network planning, focusing largely on the number of internal users, types of conversations, and endpoints that will be parts of conversations.

Additional information on Media Bypass for Direct Routing can be found at *https://docs.microsoft.com/en-us/microsoftteams/direct-routing-plan-media-bypass*.

Local Media Optimization

Local Media Optimization (LMO) lets you manage voice quality on your network by controlling how media traffic flows between the Teams client and SBCs in the on-premises environment. It allows media to remain local within the boundaries of a corporate network's subnets. It allows media streams between the Teams client and the SBC, even if the SBCs are behind corporate firewalls with private IPs that the Microsoft cloud cannot see.

Whereas media bypass relies on the external IP address of the SBC for communication, local media optimizations allow clients to communicate with both the internal and external addresses of the SBC. LMO allows clients to detect whether the endpoint they're communicating with is on the local intranet or external to the site.

LMO is designed for environments with multiple SBC-enabled sites that use a centralized SIP trunking environment. In this environment, downstream SBCs can communicate via an edge SBC to the Teams Cloud Voice service, even if those downstream SBC IP addresses are not visible to the Teams Cloud Voice service.

Inside Out

Local Media Optimization deep dive

Much like media bypass, Local Media Optimization is a complex networking topic that depends on your individual site architecture, networking, and hardware capabilities. The number of sites, endpoints in a site, and bandwidth between sites determine the best LMO configuration.

Additional information on Local Media Optimization for Direct Routing can be found at *https://docs.microsoft.com/en-us/microsoftteams/direct-routing-media-optimization.*

While we won't go into configuration detail for Local Media Optimization, it's a potentially useful feature to consider for large enterprise deployments.

Location-based routing

Location-based routing (LBR) is designed to allow you to manage your compliance with local toll restrictions. For example, your locality may have regulations prohibiting bypassing the public switched telephone network to avoid long-distance service charges.

Location-based routing lets you restrict attempts to bypass tolls by using a policy in conjunction with the user's geographic location. The policy evaluates the user's location while placing or receiving a call.

CAUTION

Care should be taken when configuring location-based routing to ensure that you adhere to your locality's regulations. Location-based routing is an advanced voice routing configuration many organizations won't need to configure. Consult your local telephony regulations to determine if any configuration is necessary.

Survivable branch appliances

Sometimes, a survivable branch appliance (SBA) will need to be deployed to support telephony during outages. Survivable branch appliances are advanced session border controllers that can be used to continue to facilitate calls with the public switched telephone network if the connection to the Teams Cloud Voice service is unavailable.

When connectivity between the Teams client and Teams backend is interrupted, remote user calls are dropped, and further remote calls will not be reachable via a normal SBC anymore. For users inside the corporate network supported by a Teams Survivable Branch Appliance Policy, ongoing calls will be maintained, and further calls will occur via the survivable branch appliance. A Teams client not covered by a Teams SBA policy will display a banner showing it is in offline mode, as shown in Figure 21-3.

Figure 21-3   Teams operating in offline mode

Teams offline voice mode is only supported for desktop clients at this time. Media Bypass must be configured to ensure the Microsoft Teams client at the site can have media flowing directly with the SBA.

TIP

You can learn more about guidance for configuring an SBA from the SBA vendor or through the Microsoft Docs site at *https://aka.ms/drsba*.

Analog telephone adapters

There are several use cases where legacy analog telephony devices are still in use (such as various building alarm systems, point-of-sale fallback authorizations, or legacy fax machines). Many of these devices can't be upgraded with newer digital devices. In order to continue using them, some sort of bridge, connector, or adapter is necessary to enable them to communicate with modern phone systems. Analog telephone adapter (ATA) devices are used to connect analog devices to Direct Routing infrastructures.

Microsoft has certified high-density analog telephone adapters to work alongside session border controllers, should you need to connect analog devices to your Direct Routing configuration.

Operator Connect

Operator Connect is essentially Direct Routing hosted by a service provider or carrier. Operator Connect provides a framework for qualified operators to offer enhanced scalability and integration features into the Teams environment.

One of the benefits of Operator Connect is a much more simplified customer experience over Direct Routing. Certified operators have parity with native Microsoft Calling Plans features and are backed by service-level agreements.

This integration includes services for interconnection, number provisioning, management, reporting, and streamlined support.

Operator Connect–certified carriers connect to the Microsoft Azure Peering Service (MAPS) for Voice. These operators have access to a set of provisioning APIs and a dedicated portal for managing their integration and provisioning of trunks to the Teams Cloud Voice service.

The diagram in Figure 21-4 depicts Operator Connect.

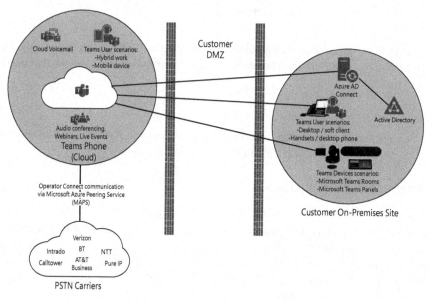

Figure 21-4   Operator Connect

From a day-to-day management perspective, number provisioning and management can be managed within the Teams admin center (as opposed to Direct Routing management, which must be done from PowerShell).

Inside Out

Operator Connect Conferencing

Operator Connect Conferencing allows you to use carrier-provided numbers with Teams Audio Conferencing. Without Operator Connect Conferencing, organizations using Operator Connect can only use phone numbers provided by Microsoft for their Teams Audio Conferencing.

When numbers are acquired through the Operator Connect carrier, they can be added to a Teams Audio Conferencing service just like a Microsoft-provided number.

Now that you understand the capabilities and features of the types of Teams Phone architectures, it's time to shift gears to planning.

Planning network requirements

When planning a Teams Phone deployment, one of the most important design tasks is to ensure your end-users have a well-performing network. Teams Phone relies on your existing network infrastructure to support real-time audio and video network streams. To make these planning tasks easier, Microsoft has released tools, assessments, and planners that can audit an organization's network and identify potential risk areas.

At a high level, the following areas should be reviewed by an organization to ensure their network is ready for Teams voice. Careful validation and alignment with Microsoft's best practices and recommendations will minimize the potential for audio and video quality issues on the platform.

Network requirements

In order to achieve the most reliable performance and experience, certain network requirements should be met. Table 21-2 lists the base network performance requirements to run Teams with real-time voice and video in an organization's environment.

Table 21-2   Minimum network performance requirements

Requirement	Endpoint to Teams service	Customer network to Teams service
Latency (one-way)	< 50 ms	< 30 ms
Latency (round-trip)	< 100ms	< 60 ms
Burst packet loss	< 10 percent for any 200ms interval	< 1 percent for any 200ms interval
Packet loss	<1 percent for any 15s interval	< 0.1 percent for any 15s interval
Jitter	< 30ms for any 15s interval	<15ms for any 15s interval
Packet reorder	< 0.05 percent out-of-order	< 0.01 percent out of order

s (seconds); ms (milliseconds)

As network conditions fall out of compliance with the recommendations, you may notice audio and video degradation.

Bandwidth requirements

Microsoft Teams strives to give you the best audio, video, and content-sharing experience possible, regardless of your network conditions. By using variable codecs, media bitrates can be negotiated in limited bandwidth environments with minimal impact. In situations where bandwidth is not a concern, experiences can be optimized for full-fidelity and quality, including up to 1080p video resolution, up to 30 frames per second (FPS) for video streams, and high-fidelity audio.

Teams can deliver HD-quality video in conditions under 1.2Mbps. The actual bandwidth consumption in each audio/video call or meeting will vary based on several factors, such as video layout, video resolution, and video frames per second from all sources. When more bandwidth is available, quality and usage will increase to deliver the best experience.

Table 21-3 shows the bandwidth requirements necessary to support the following scenarios in Teams.

Table 21-3   Network speed for various communications scenarios

Bandwidth (upload/download)	Example scenario
6KB/s	SILK PSTN voice codec
8KB/s	G.720 PSTN voice codec
28KB/s	Peer-to-peer (P2P) audio calling
64KB/s	G.711 PSTN voice codec
64KB/s	G.722 PSTN voice codec
500KB/s	P2P video calling at standard definition (SD) quality (360p) at 30fps
1.2MB/s	P2P video calling at high definition (HD) quality (720p) at 30fps
1.5MB/s	P2P audio calling with screen sharing
1.5MB/s	P2P video calling at high HD quality (1080p) at 30fps
1.5 / 2.5MB/s	Teams Together Mode
2.5MB/s	Meeting audio calling and screen sharing
2.5 / 4.0MB/s	Meetings video

Kbps = kilobits per second; KB/s = kilobites per second; Mbps = megabits per second; MB/s = megabytes per second; fps = frames per second

In addition to overall bandwidth, it's important to ensure that communications ports are open.

Ports

It is extremely important that all the required and optional ports for the Teams are open outbound on the organization's firewall edge. This is necessary to allow full signaling and media access between the Teams client and Teams Cloud Voice service.

Table 21-4 lists the required and optional network ports.

Table 21-4   Network ports and protocols

Ports	Protocol
80, 443	Required TCP
3478, 3479, 3480, 3481	Required UDP
50000–59999	Optional TCP/UDP

If you are familiar with the Skype for Business Online network configuration requirements, you'll notice that the Teams voice communication ports requirement has been greatly simplified. This should make configuration easier to implement and manage.

Inside Out

Real-time media optimization

While they are listed as *Optional*, it is highly recommended that UDP ports 50000–59999 be opened to ensure the best overall performance. If these ports are not open, media traffic will be forced to travel over port 443 as a fallback.

Real-time media is not optimized to be transmitted via TCP. TCP communications require confirmation of all packets and packet reorder and reassembly to ensure the data has been transmitted successfully. UDP is a broadcast transmission, allowing packets to be dropped or lost along the way with minimal disruption to the audio or video stream.

Microsoft Teams utilizes DTLS, a stream-oriented transport layer security protocol, to provide secure communications.

Network endpoints

When working with cloud services, it's important to ensure your on-premises users can successfully reach all the service endpoints unhindered. Microsoft provides a full list of network endpoints (including network ranges, ports, protocols, and descriptions) for all Microsoft 365 services. An updated list is always available at *https://aka.ms/o365endpoints*.

CHAPTER 21

Split-tunnel VPN

Organizations may deploy virtual private networks (VPN) to facilitate secure communications between off-premises or remote devices and corporate networks. Since Microsoft 365 services are hosted on the public Internet with multiple ingress and egress points, Microsoft recommends that organizations enable split tunneling.

As the name implies, split tunneling allows network traffic to be split into different directions—internal corporate resources can be accessed by traveling the VPN tunnel. In contrast, Internet-facing services are split off and routed directly over the device or site's local Internet connection. Without split-tunneling, traffic from the remote site or endpoint destined for Internet sites or services is routed in through the organization's firewall, back out to the Internet to retrieve data, and then back through the VPN tunnel to the originating site or endpoint.

Some customers have expressed concerns about enabling split tunneling in the past because they think it might present a security risk. It is important to note that all traffic between the Teams endpoint and the Microsoft 365 platform is encrypted using TLS 1.2. Risks can be mitigated using endpoint protection platforms, such as Microsoft Defender for Endpoint.

In addition to adding unnecessary network latency and hops between the endpoint and the VPN infrastructure, the VPN traffic itself is also TCP-based. As mentioned in the "Ports" section, real-time media communications are not optimized for TCP, which may result in audio and video lagging.

Quality of Service

In normal network communications, all traffic is treated with equal weight unless otherwise specified—uploading a document to OneDrive attention as browsing a news site or conducting a Teams voice call. This behavior may result in time-sensitive data packets not being delivered as quickly as they should. Quality of Service (QoS) is a way to ensure Teams voice and video data packets receive priority treatment over other data types in your organization's environment.

You can view your network as a multi-lane highway with all data packets traveling down it to reach their destinations. Just like commuter highways, there are times when the network may become congested—frequently mornings, right after lunch, or during regular business production cycles. As traffic increases, it may take longer to access resources.

Typically, these micro-delays don't have any noticeable impact on most operations, especially asynchronous tasks such as sending an instant message or email. For real-time traffic, however, this congestion can manifest itself as choppy or disjointed audio and video. Insufficient bandwidth can lead to distorted audio or video, freezes during screen or content sharing, or network performance warning messages. Depending on the level of network impact being experienced, the Teams client may warn you of detected poor network conditions. Also, the Teams client might recommend that you disable services like content sharing and video in a meeting; in severe cases, it may even prompt you to join meetings over the PSTN network instead of your data connection.

To limit the impacts of network congestion, you can enable QoS on your devices and endpoints. With the highway comparison, you can think of QoS as a dedicated lane for audio and video traffic. Access to this special lane or queue (called prioritization) is enabled through the use of Differentiated Services Code Point (DSCP) values. Adding these values to packets is commonly referred to as QoS tagging.

Tagging the Teams audio and video packets allows those packets to enter a high-priority queue. This queue prioritizes traffic packets going through the network based on the tag data present in the packet. These tags are set by the Teams clients and devices on each audio, video, or screen-sharing packet transmitted.

Inside Out

Quality of Service Queues

There are three core queues that map to the amount of priority or effort apportioned to the corresponding traffic:

- Expedited Forwarding
- Assured Forwarding
- Default

The Expedited Forwarding (EF) model is used for traffic that is highly sensitive to latency, such as real-time audio or interactive traffic. EF is designated using DSCP marking 46. The Assured Forwarding (AF) model provides priority or weight to different content classes. It is frequently used for content where some latency is tolerated (such as video). AF is designated using other lower DSCP values, such as 34 or 18.

Each queue is characterized by a Committed Information Rate (CIR) and an Excess Information Rate (EIR). These rates describe the minimum bandwidth (CIR) and maximum amount of bandwidth (EIR) that a particular queue is allowed to consume. Network devices may employ one of several weighting algorithms to determine how to handle the traffic that exceeds the specified policy amounts, depending on other simultaneous traffic requirements, to ensure that higher-priority queues don't completely starve lower-priority queues.

Traffic that should receive normal priority is left untagged. You can learn more about the networking specifications behind priority queuing in RFCs 2597 (*https://www.rfc-editor.org/rfc/rfc2597*) and 2598 (*https://www.rfc-editor.org/rfc/rfc2598*).

Figure 21-5 shows a conceptual view of QoS in an environment.

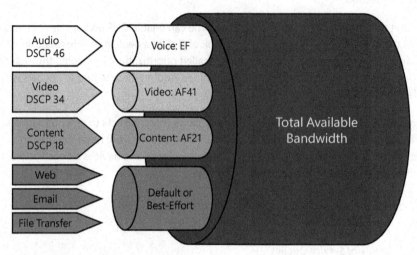

Figure 21-5   How QoS works with Teams

Table 21-5 lists the DSCP marking values set by the Teams client.

Table 21-5   Teams DSCP marking values

Media type	Source port range	Protocol	DSCP value	DSCP class
Audio	50000–50019	TCP/UDP	46	Expedited Forwarding (EF)
Video	50020–50039	TCP/UDP	34	Assured Forwarding (AF41)
Application or screen sharing	50040–50059	TCP/UDP	18	Assured Forwarding (AF21)

As you can see from Table 21-5, each specific type of data gets its own tag. The higher the DSCP marking value, the more priority is given to that type of traffic.

Enabling QoS for Microsoft Teams desktop clients

You can enable QoS tagging on the Microsoft Teams endpoints via Group Policy. To create the Group Policy Object enabling DSCP markings for Teams, use the following steps:

1.   Launch the Group Policy Management console.

2.   In the Group Policy Management console snap-in, locate the Active Directory container where a new policy should be created.

3.   Right-click the container and then select Create A GPO And Link It Here.

4. In the New GPO dialog, enter a name for the new policy object.

5. Right-click the new policy and select Edit.

6. In the Group Policy Management Editor, expand the Computer Configuration node. Expand the Windows Settings node.

7. Right-click Policy-Based QoS and then click Create New Policy, as shown in Figure 21-6.

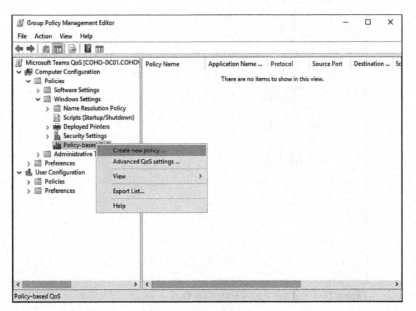

Figure 21-6   Creating a new Teams QoS policy

8. Enter a name (such as Teams Audio) for the new policy in the Name box. Select Specify DSCP Value and set the value to 46. Leave Specify Outbound Throttle Rate unselected and then click Next.

9. Select Only Applications With This Executable Name and enter the Teams executable name, Teams.exe. Click Next.

10. Select the Any Source IP Address and Any Destination IP Address radio buttons. Click Next.

11. Expand the Select The Protocol This Qos Policy Applies To dropdown and select TCP And UDP.

12. Under Specify The Source Port Number, select the From This Source Port Or Range radio button.

13. Enter the port range reserved for audio traffic. Microsoft recommends reserving ports 50000–50019. To use the recommended value, enter **50000:50019** and click Finish.

14. Repeat steps 6-13 to create video and content-sharing traffic policies using the values shown in Table 21-5. When completed, you should have three QoS policies configured similarly to Figure 21-7.

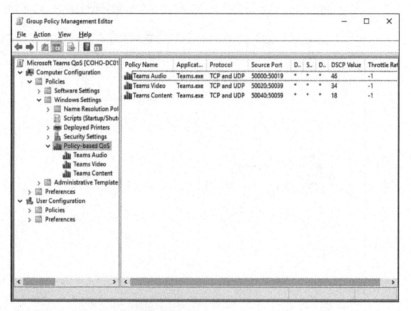

Figure 21-7   Group Policy Editor for QoS

The policy can then be deployed to all the devices that contain Teams clients.

Verifying policy deployment

Once deployed, you can trigger a policy refresh by running the following command from an elevated command prompt on a targeted device:

```
gpupdate /force
```

You can verify that the machine has successfully processed the policy by running the following command from an elevated command prompt:

```
gpresult /H teamspolicy.html
```

Review the `teamspolicy.html` file for the name of the policy you created under the Applied Group Policy Objects section of the report.

Using the Registry Editor, you can also review HKEY_LOCAL_MACHINE\Software\Policies\ Microsoft\Windows\QoS for evidence that the policy has been processed. A registry key should be present for each policy configured and applied, as shown in Figure 21-8.

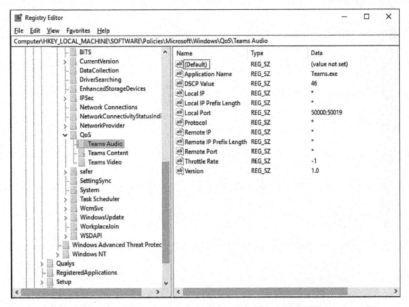

Figure 21-8   Checking for Group Policy settings in the registry

Group Policy is an effective tool for distribution configurations to standard domain-joined Windows computers. However, you may have other dedicated devices that need to be configured separately.

Enabling QoS for Teams devices and mobile devices

The QoS settings are configured through the Teams admin center for Teams devices and mobile devices.

To enable QoS, follow these steps:

1. Navigate to the Teams admin center at *https://admin.teams.microsoft.com*.

2. Expand Meetings and select Meeting Settings.

3. Move the Insert Quality Of Service (QoS) Markers For Real-Time Media Traffic slider to On.

4. Select the Specify Port Ranges radio button and ensure the media ports match your QoS policy for your Teams clients. By default, the Teams admin center has selected the recommended ports, as shown in Figure 21-9. This will enable the markers and ports for Teams Android Devices, Android Mobile Devices, and iOS Devices.

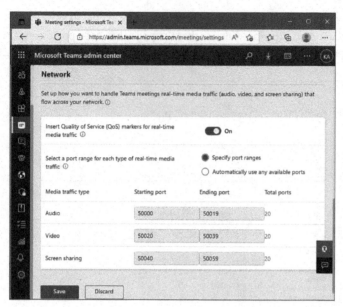

Figure 21-9   Configuring QoS in the Teams admin center

5.   Click Save to commit changes.

After devices refresh policy settings, they will begin tagging packets for QoS.

Enabling QoS for Surface Hub devices

For Surface Hub and Hub 2 devices, you need to use a mobile device management platform such as Microsoft Endpoint Manager to configure QoS. Surface Hub devices must be enrolled in Microsoft Endpoint Manager to configure them.

Once enrolled, you can use the following procedure to configure a custom device configuration profile for Surface Hub 2 devices. Surface Hub and Surface Hub 2 will require different device configuration profiles:

1.   Navigate to the Microsoft Endpoint Manager admin center at *https://endpoint.microsoft.com*.

2.   Select Devices > Configuration Profiles and click Create Profile, as shown in Figure 21-10.

3.   Under Platform, select Windows 10 And Later.

4.   Under Profile Type, select Templates and then select Custom from the list of templates.

5.   Click Create, as shown in Figure 21-11.

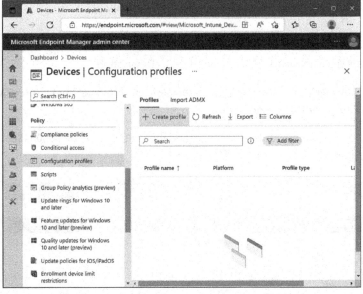

Figure 21-10   Microsoft Endpoint Manager device profiles

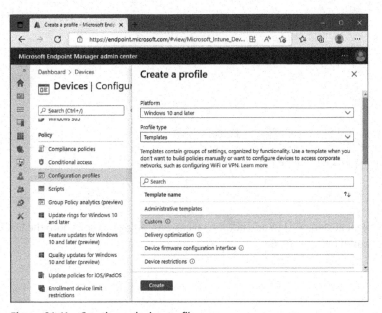

Figure 21-11   Creating a device profile

6. Enter a Name and Description, and then click Next.

7. Click Add to configure a custom OMA-URI setting.

8. Enter a Name, such as Audio Ports, and a Description.

9. Under OMA-URI, enter **./Device/Vendor/MSFT/NetworkQoSPolicy/Audio/ SourcePortMatchCondition**.

10. Configure the Data Type as String, and then enter the value **50000-50019**, as shown in Figure 21-12.

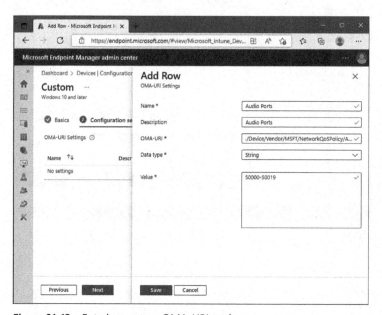

Figure 21-12   Entering custom OMA-URI settings

11. Click Save.

12. Repeat steps 7-11 to add additional custom settings to configure the DSCP markings based on Table 21-6.

Table 21-6 Surface Hub 2 QoS policy values

Name	Description	OMA-URI path	Data type	Value
Audio DSCP	Audio DSCP marking	./Device/Vendor/MSFT/NetworkQoSPolicy/Audio/DSCPAction	Integer	46
Video Ports	Video Ports	./Device/Vendor/MSFT/NetworkQoSPolicy/Video/SourcePortMatchCondition	String	50020–50039
Video DSCP	Video DSCP marking	./Device/Vendor/MSFT/NetworkQoSPolicy/Video/DSCPAction	Integer	34
Sharing Ports	Sharing Ports	./Device/Vendor/MSFT/NetworkQoSPolicy/Sharing/SourcePortMatchCondition	String	50040–50059
Sharing DSCP	Sharing DSCP marking	./Device/Vendor/MSFT/NetworkQoSPolicy/Sharing/DSCPAction	Integer	18

You can create an additional device profile if you have an original Surface Hub device. Follow the same procedure, but use the values shown in Table 21-7 for the OMA-URI configuration.

Table 21-7 Surface Hub 1 QoS policy values

Name	Description	OMA-URI path	Data type	Value
Audio Ports	Audio Ports	./Device/Vendor/MSFT/NetworkQoSPolicy/HubAudio/SourcePortMatchCondition	String	50000–50019
Audio DSCP	Audio DSCP marking	./Device/Vendor/MSFT/NetworkQoSPolicy/HubAudio/DSCPAction	Integer	46
Video Ports	Video Ports	./Device/Vendor/MSFT/NetworkQoSPolicy/HubVideo/SourcePortMatchCondition	String	50020–50039
Video DSCP	Video DSCP marking	./Device/Vendor/MSFT/NetworkQoSPolicy/HubVideo/DSCPAction	Integer	34

Best practices and additional network tools

To ensure the best possible operation and performance, Microsoft recommends the following best practices.

Verify all required outbound network ports

Verify all required outbound network ports for Teams as described in the "*Planning network requirements" section are* allowed to communicate with the Microsoft Teams environment. As a reminder, if UDP is blocked or closed, communications will fall back to TCP, which is not optimized for real-time media and will introduce latency.

CHAPTER 21

Bypass encryption and other filtering devices

Verify that Teams client media and signaling data streams are bypassing double encryption scenarios, VPN tunnels, intrusion detection or prevention appliances, and other traffic shaping applications. If organizations must use VPNs to communicate, configure split-tunneling to allow Teams traffic to bypass the VPN. Routing Teams traffic via a VPN will cause media delays due to encapsulating traffic inside TCP streams.

Microsoft Teams Network Assessment Tool

You can use the Microsoft Teams Network Assessment Tool to see how real-time media traffic will flow between your endpoints and the Microsoft 365 service.

> NOTE
>
> **The Microsoft Teams Network Assessment Tool is available at _https://www.microsoft.com/en-us/download/details.aspx?id=103017_.**

Network Planner for Teams

The Network Planner for Teams is a design tool to help determine bandwidth requirements for your network sites based on user profile types. Additional information about how to set up and use the Network Planner can be found at _https://aka.ms/teamsnetworkplanner_.

Microsoft 365 Network Connectivity Test

The Microsoft 365 Network Connectivity Test tool can determine if the appropriate DNS records are resolvable and if the appropriate network ports are open between the Teams endpoint and the Microsoft 365 platform.

> NOTE
>
> **The Microsoft Network Connectivity Test can be found at _https://connectivity.office.com/_.**

Call Quality Dashboard Report

After deployment, regularly review the Call Quality Dashboard Report to analyze tenant-level reports on the quality of your connectivity from the perspective of the Microsoft Teams service.

What's next?

In this chapter, we discussed the basic Microsoft Teams Phone System terminology, licensing, and general telephony and networking terms. We also reviewed the core Teams architecture designs (Calling Plans, Direct Routing, and Operator Connect), including the advantages and features of each architecture.

You also learned the networking requirements and best practices to achieve the best Teams voice outcomes. These best practices included configuring Quality of Service tagging and enabling VPN split-tunneling. Configuring your environment optimally ahead of time will help limit problems encountered during onboarding.

In the next chapter, you'll be able to use this architectural knowledge as you configure a Microsoft Teams-based phone system.

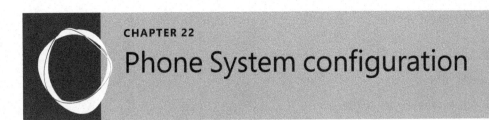

Phone System configuration

Configuring the Teams Phone System is one of the most complex pieces of Microsoft 365 administration. The shift to integrated and unified communications platforms brings previously out-of-scope technology to the Microsoft 365 administrator.

For many organizations, this means connecting a modern collaboration platform with technologies and responsibilities typically assigned to network and telephony engineers.

In this chapter, we'll step through configuring the Teams platform features necessary to get a basic cloud-based phone system fully deployed, specifically

- Emergency dialing

- Phone numbers

- Teams voice policies

By the end of this chapter, you'll be able to set up the most common features associated with the Teams Phone System.

Inside Out

Architecture-specific guidance

In this chapter, we're only going to focus on Microsoft-native Calling Plans architectures. Many configuration tasks overlap between Calling Plans, Direct Routing, and Operator Connect. Still, some distinct differences exist, such as provisioning phone numbers or implementing third-party hardware like session border controllers and survivable branch appliances.

For organizations implementing Direct Routing infrastructures, we recommend you work with a partner or vendor to design a system that best meets your needs. The configuration steps in this chapter for rooms, resources, auto attendants, and other calling policies will still apply to those deployments.

Prerequisites

Some Microsoft Teams options can only be configured via the Microsoft Teams PowerShell module. To install the module, follow these steps:

1. Launch an elevated Windows PowerShell prompt.

2. Run the following command:

    ```
    Install-Module MicrosoftTeams
    ```

3. If you have not previously installed the NuGet package provider and dependencies, you might be prompted to download and install them.

4. If you have not previously trusted the Microsoft PowerShell Gallery repository, you might receive a message that you are attempting to install a module from an untrusted repository. The PSGallery PowerShell repository is owned and operated by Microsoft. You can view the MicrosoftTeams module at: *https://aka.ms/teamsps*. Type Y to proceed with the installation.

After installing the module, you can open a PowerShell window and use the `Connect-MicrosoftTeams` command to connect to the Microsoft Teams management interface.

Emergency dialing

Before any other configurations are put in place, you should configure emergency dialing. Emergency dialing features need to be in place before you begin assigning phone numbers, so it's best to take care of this section first.

Microsoft Teams supports Enhanced 911 (commonly referred to as E911). The Teams platform allows for both static and dynamic E911 configurations.

Completing the emergency calling configuration for your tenant requires five steps:

1. Define trusted networks.

2. Define emergency addresses for each site.

3. Choose identifiers that will be used to add specificity to emergency locations.

4. Create and assign emergency policies to enable notifications to centralized departments, such as the service desk, receptionist, or security desk.

5. Assign emergency policies to locations.

The correct configuration of emergency locations is critical to ensuring Teams can find the caller's location and route the emergency call to the appropriate Public Safety Answering Point (PSAP) or Emergency Call Relay Center (ECRC).

Inside Out

Emergency routing

There are a lot of factors that go into emergency routing. The type of emergency information provided determines where calls get routed, as shown in the following table:

Type of emergency address information	Emergency routing method
Defined by administrator	Direct to PSAP
Derived from a geocode without end-user confirmation	ECRC screened and transferred to PSAP
Derived from a geocode with end-user confirmation	Direct to PSAP
Derived from geocode and edited by the user	ECRC screened and transferred to PSAP
Manually edited by the user	ECRC screened and transferred to PSAP
Edited by map string match with user confirmation	Direct to PSAP
Statically assigned to a user or phone number	Direct to PSAP
No emergency address provided	ECRC screened and transferred to PSAP

As you can see, address detail and method of entry or assignment significantly impact how emergency calls get routed, which, in turn, can impact how quickly first responders are dispatched and can find a location.

With that in mind, let's look at the steps to configuring emergency addresses and routing.

Define networks

The first step in configuring E911 is identifying one or more external IP addresses or networks for an organization. These networks will determine whether a client is internal or external to a particular site.

To configure trusted IPs, follow these steps:

1.   Navigate to the Microsoft Teams admin center at *https://admin.teams.microsoft.com*.

2.   Expand Locations and click Network Topology.

3.   Select Trusted IPs.

4.   Click Add to begin adding external IP addresses. It is recommended that you add both IPv4 and IPv6 ranges. Ensure you configure the correct number of masking bits under the Network Range parameter, as shown in Figure 22-1. To configure a single IP Address, specify 32 (for 32 bits in the mask). If you are unsure of the network mask (entered in the Network Range field), check your router configuration or ask your Internet service provider.

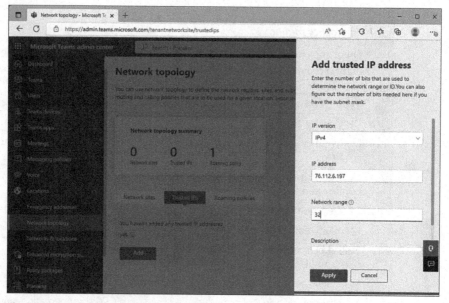

Figure 22-1   Adding trusted IP addresses

5.   Click Apply when finished to save the address.

Repeat this procedure to add your organization's external IP address or range.

Configure Location Information Service

The Location Information Service (LIS) is used to associate defined networks to emergency address locations and emergency policies. The LIS is hierarchical in nature and includes information from emergency locations, civic addresses, and network locations. Together, these data elements specify a user's physical location when placing an emergency call.

Recall from Chapter 21, "Phone system planning," that a civic address represents a physical, navigable address. The location (or place, in Teams vernacular) offers a layer of specificity. You'll define elements such as subnets, network switch ports, or access points in each location to more precisely identify positioning.

Create a civic address

1. Navigate to the Teams admin center at *https://teams.admin.microsoft.com*.

2. Expand Locations and select Emergency Addresses.

3. Click Add to add a new emergency address, as shown in Figure 22-2.

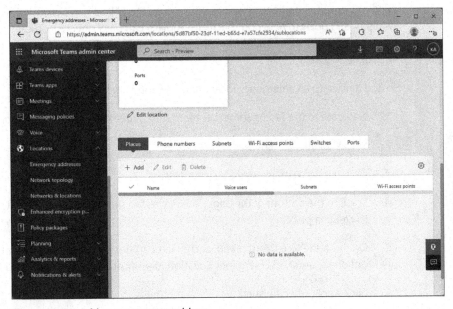

Figure 22-2   Add an emergency address

4. Enter a Name for the emergency address and select a Country Or Region from the dropdown.

5. After selecting a Country Or Region, enter the physical address. The address will be validated against the Azure Map service and plotted on a map with geographic coordinates. You can also manually input the address, specifying those same values.

6. You can also add an Organization Name value if the one pre-populated from your tenant is incorrect.

7. Finally, you can enter an optional Emergency Location Identification Number (ELIN). The ELIN is a telephone number already associated with a physical street address and will be sent to emergency responders. If you add an ELIN, it must match an address already configured with your local exchange carrier (LEC).

8. Select the checkbox for acknowledging the changes and click Save.

After you configure an address, you cannot update it. You will have to delete it and start over.

Add a place

In the Teams Phone System, a *place* is a refinement to an emergency address that helps more accurately describe the actual location. For example, you can use descriptive terminology like buildings or suite numbers, as well as rooms, subnets, phone numbers, wireless access points, switches, and ports to help add specificity. A place can be connected logically to a network element. This additional information will be sent to the PSAP along with the civic address of the emergency address.

To add a place to an emergency location, follow these steps:

1. Navigate to the Teams admin center at *https://admin.teams.microsoft.com*.

2. Select Locations > Emergency Addresses.

3. Click the name of an emergency address.

4. Scroll to the bottom of the page. The Places tab should be selected by default. Click Add to create a place.

5. On the Add Place flyout menu, add a Name to describe the place accurately. You can also optionally enter an Emergency Location Identification Number (ELIN). See Figure 22-3.

6. Click Apply when finished.

You can add as many places as necessary to accurately describe unique locations.

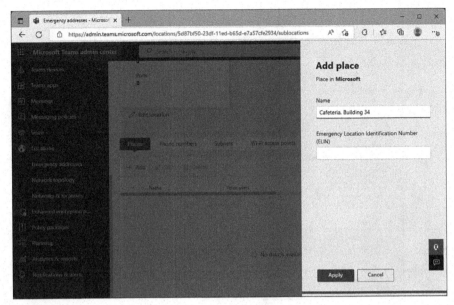

Figure 22-3 Adding a place

Define subnets

Subnets are logical subnetworks where your devices reside. Defining subnets will allow you to map them to locations or places.

To define a subnet, follow these steps:

1. Navigate to the Microsoft Teams admin center at *https://admin.teams.microsoft.com*.

2. Expand Locations and click Networks & Locations.

3. On the Subnets tab, click Add.

4. Choose an IP version (IPv4 or IPv6) on the Add Subnet flyout menu.

5. In the Subnet field, enter a valid network ID. You can calculate this using a subnet calculator. For example, if your network address were 10.1.10.133/24 (255.255.255.0), you would enter **10.1.10.0**. If your network address were 10.1.10.133/25 (255.255.255.128), you would enter **10.1.10.128**.

6. Scroll down to Emergency Location. You can search for locations by address or name. You can select a main location and a more specific place, as shown in Figure 22-4.

CHAPTER 22

Figure 22-4   Adding a subnet

7.   Click Apply to save the subnet.

Inside Out

Subnet creation

There are a number of ways to create subnets. One such way is by selecting Locations > Networks & Locations Or Locations > Emergency Addresses.

Subnets need to be associated with an emergency address or a place, so it's easier to do it all from the Emergency Addresses menu. You can add a subnet directly to an emergency address or edit a place and add it directly to a place.

Repeat this procedure to assign subnets to emergency addresses.

Define an access point

In addition to subnets, you can also use WiFi access points to add specificity.

You can use a similar process to define an access point and associate it with a location or place. To add an access point, you need an access point's basic service set identifier (BSSID) to physically identify it.

Your wireless access point might have the BSSID stamped on it, in which case you can use that value. You also might be able to retrieve it from your access point's configuration interface. If you are connected to the access point, you can obtain the BSSID using the command `netsh wlan show interfaces`, as shown in Figure 22-5.

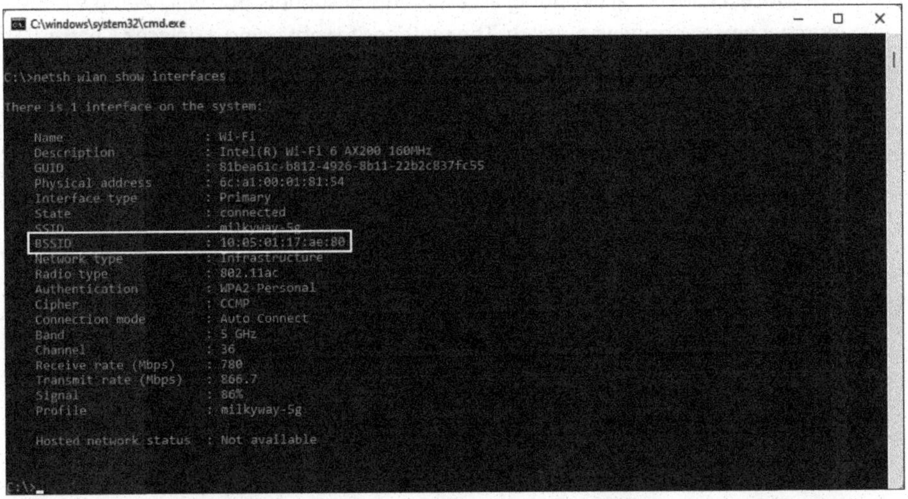

Figure 22-5   Viewing the BSSID of the local network

Once you have the BSSID value, you can add a WiFi access point as an element. To do so, follow these steps:

1. Navigate to the Microsoft Teams admin center at *https://admin.teams.microsoft.com*.

2. Expand Locations and click Networks & Locations.

3. Select the WiFi Access Points tab.

4. Click Add.

5. On the Add WiFi Access Point flyout menu, under BSSID, add the BSSID value of the access point. While `netsh` shows the BSSID value as xx:xx:xx:xx:xx:xx, you will need to replace the colons with hyphens so the value appears as xx-xx-xx-xx-xx-xx.

6. Under Description, add a description of the access point.

7. Under Emergency Location, choose an emergency location (and, optionally, a place) to where you'll associate this access point.

8. Click Apply.

Repeat this procedure to add additional access points.

CHAPTER 22

Switches and ports

Like access points, physical network switches and switch ports can also be used to help pinpoint a physical location. You can add both switches and ports in the Teams admin center.

The process is identical to adding access points or subnets. You will need the Chassis ID or serial number when specifying a switch. The methods for obtaining a device's Chassis ID vary by vendor and model. Often, the Chassis ID is the switch's media access control (MAC) address.

When specifying a port, you will need both the Chassis ID and a Port number associated with the physical ethernet port, as shown in Figure 22-6.

Figure 22-6   Adding a switch port

Repeat this process for every switch or port you configure.

Inside Out

Bulk configuration

If you are configuring the switch or switch port network elements, be sure to enter enough detailed data in the Description field to uniquely identify each location.

It might be better to configure these elements via PowerShell if you have a significant number of switch or port elements to add. You can use `Set-CsOnlineLisPort` and `Set-CsOnlineLisSwitch` in conjunction with the GUID of the location.

To obtain a list of your organization's names and locations, use the `Get-CsOnlineLis-Location` cmdlet, as shown below and in the following figure:

```
Get-CsOnlineLisLocation | Select Location,Description,LocationId
```

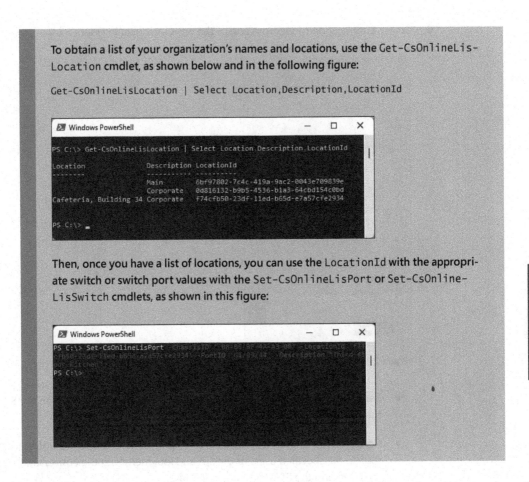

Then, once you have a list of locations, you can use the `LocationId` with the appropriate switch or switch port values with the `Set-CsOnlineLisPort` or `Set-CsOnline-LisSwitch` cmdlets, as shown in this figure:

CHAPTER 22

Configure emergency policies

An emergency calling policy defines how Teams handles an emergency call event. To configure an emergency calling policy, follow these steps:

1. Navigate to the Teams admin center at *https://admin.teams.microsoft.com*.

2. Expand Voice > Emergency Policies and select the Calling Policies tab.

3. Click Add to create a new policy; click Global (Org-Wide Default) to modify the built-in policy.

4. On the Add Emergency Calling Policy flyout menu (or emergency calling policy, if you are editing the built-in one), enter a Name and Description.

5. Set the External Location Lookup Mode toggle to On if you want to enable Dynamic E911 For US Work From Home.

6.   Select a notification mode from one of the options shown in Figure 22-7.

Figure 22-7   Configuring an emergency calling policy

- **Send Notification Only**   This option will send a Teams notification message to the specified users or group.

- **Conferenced In But Are Muted**   This option will send a Teams notification message to the specified users or groups and join them with the conversation between the caller and the PSAP operator (on mute).

- **Conferenced In And Are Unmuted**   This option will send a Teams notification message to the specified users or groups and will join them with the conversation between the caller and the PSAP operator (unmuted).

7.   If you selected either the Conferenced In But Are Muted or Conferenced In And Are Unmuted notification mode, you can enter a value for Numbers To Dial For Emergency Call Notifications. You can specify one or more of the following: a security group, a phone number, or a series of numbers (depending on how calls are routed).

8.   If you selected a notification mode, you will also be prompted to select a user or group from the directory.

9.   Click Apply.

Inside Out

Configuring notification policy

During the emergency policy configuration, the flyout menu allows you to set one of three notification modes. The default, however, is blank.

If you want to return to no notification mode, you cannot do it through the user interface. To make this change, you'll need the Microsoft Teams PowerShell module.

For example, to update the notification mode for the policy with the identity Global, you would run:

```
Set-CsTeamsEmergencyCallingPolicy -Identity Global -NotificationMode $null
```

As mentioned earlier, there are some differences when working with direct routing. Emergency call routing policies for direct routing are configured through the Call Routing Policies menu; select Voice > Emergency Policies > Call Routing Policies menu.

Test the emergency location configuration

If you are using either the Microsoft-native calling plans or Operator Connect architectures, you can validate your emergency location configuration by dialing **933** from a user with an assigned phone number. This special number is routed to a Microsoft-hosted bot that reads back the line's phone number, emergency location details, and whether the call would be automatically routed to the PSAP or be screened first.

For organizations using direct routing, contact your Emergency Service Routing Provider (ESRP) or carrier to validate your emergency routing details.

Phone numbers

Obtaining and assigning phone numbers can vary depending on the type of infrastructure you are implementing and the types of numbers you're requesting or assigning.

With calling plans, Microsoft manages the numbers (either Microsoft-issued numbers or numbers you have ported to Microsoft from an existing carrier). We will focus on the architecture of cloud-native calling plans, though the assignment portion will also work for Operator Connect.

Obtain phone numbers

In this section, we'll cover the two ways you can acquire numbers:

- Ordering numbers from Microsoft

- Porting numbers from an existing carrier to Microsoft

We'll start with the easier (though less common method)—ordering numbers from Microsoft.

Placing an order with Microsoft

Each Microsoft calling plan includes user direct inward dial (DID) numbers. DIDs are user-assignable phone numbers. To obtain numbers, you need to:

1. Obtain at least one Microsoft 365 license (F3, E1, E3) and a standalone Phone System license or a Microsoft 365 E5 license bundle.

2. Obtain at least one calling plan.

3. Assign a Teams license and Phone System license to a minimum of one user.

4. Create at least one emergency address.

Once these requirements are met, you will be ready to place an order for numbers:

1. Navigate to the Teams admin center at *https://admin.teams.microsoft.com*.

2. Expand Voice and select Phone Numbers.

3. Under the Numbers tab, you will see a list of available numbers to assign to users. If you have no numbers, you can start an order by clicking Add, as shown in Figure 22-8.

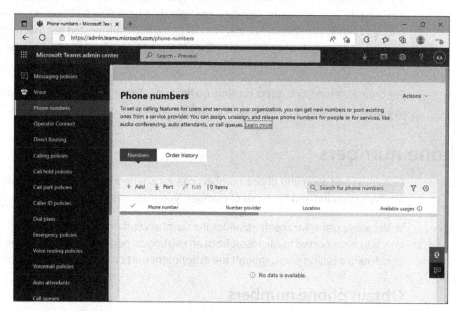

Figure 22-8   Preparing to order phone numbers

4. You will need to populate the following fields on the Select Location And Quantity page, as shown in Figure 22-9.

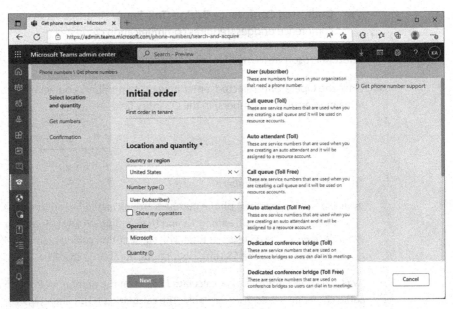

Figure 22-9   Choosing phone number order options

5. Enter a Name for the order, such as `Initial order`.

6. Enter a Description of the number order, such as `First order in tenant`.

7. In the Country Or Region dropdown, select where numbers will be issued.

8. Under Number Type, select from the following options:

   ■ **User (Subscriber)**   Numbers assigned to end-users (included with calling plans).

   ■ **Call Queue (Toll)**   Toll-based service numbers used when creating a call queue with a resource account (included with Phone System)

   ■ **Auto Attendant (Toll)**   Toll-based service numbers used when creating an auto attendant with a resource account (included with Phone System)

   ■ **Call Queue (Toll-Free)**   Toll-free service numbers used when creating a call queue with a resource account (requires communication credits)

   ■ **Auto Attendant (Toll-Free)**   Toll-free service numbers used when creating an auto attendant with a resource account (requires communication credits)

- **Dedicated Conference Bridge (Toll)**   Toll-based service numbers used for conference bridges (included with Audio Conferencing)

- **Dedicated Conference Bridge (Toll-Free)**   Toll-free service numbers used for conference bridges (requires communication credits)

9. Select Microsoft from the Operator dropdown.

10. Once the Operator is selected, enter how many numbers you want to obtain (up to your remaining available numbers) in the Quantity field.

Inside Out

Calculating available numbers

Available user (subscriber) phone numbers are calculated by multiplying the number of calling plan licenses by 1.1, adding 10, and then adding on any pay-as-you-go plans. For example, if you have 25 users in total with subscription calling plans and 15 pay-as-you-go plans, you can acquire 53 subscriber phone numbers ((25 x 1.1 + 10) + 15).

Available service numbers are calculated based on the number of Phone System and audio conferencing licenses available. The calculation is not linear; instead, it is based on tiers. For example, if you have up to 25 phone system and audio conferencing licenses, you are allotted 5 service numbers. If you have 500 Phone System and audio conferencing licenses, your allotment is 90 service numbers. You can review the tiering at *https://aka.ms/maxphonenumbers*.

11. Search for available numbers based on a previously configured emergency address location or area code:

- You can search for your location by selecting the Search By City Name radio button and entering the city name used in a configured emergency location. Choose the location and click Select.

- You can search for an area code by selecting the Search by area code radio button and typing in an area code.

TIP

If the area code or locality you are trying to obtain a number for is unavailable, you can click Get Phone Number Support at the top of the page and request the area code from the Telephone Number Services (TNS) page.

12. Review the selected options and click Next to continue, as shown in Figure 22-10.

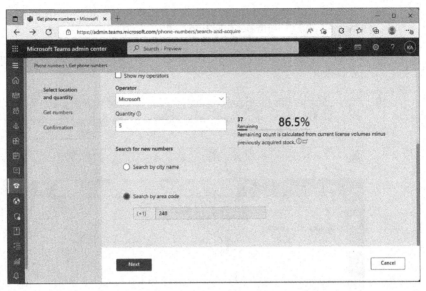

Figure 22-10   Verifying phone number order information

13. Once the numbers are reserved, you will see the selected numbers and have 10 minutes to complete the transaction. As shown in Figure 22-11, you can select

- **Place Order**   To select numbers

- **Back**   To change the search

- **Cancel**   To cancel the number request

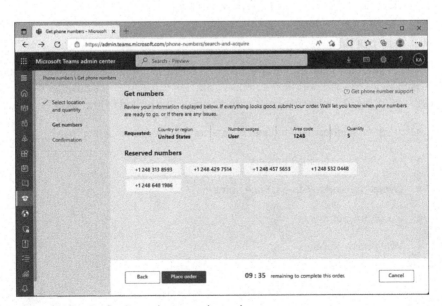

Figure 22-11   Confirming a phone number order

14. If you select Place Order, you will see a message stating that the inventory is being updated and the number selection has finalized to your tenant.

15. Click Finish to exit the ordering process or Create Another Order to restart the ordering process.

16. After an order has been processed, you will be able to find the numbers listed under Voice > Phone Numbers, along with their allotted usage types, as shown in Figure 22-12.

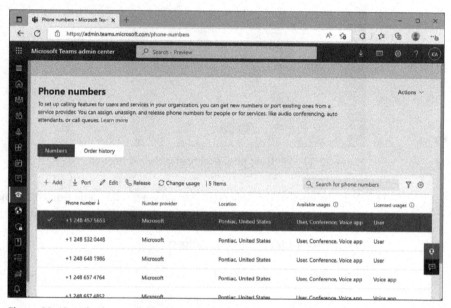

Figure 22-12   Viewing available phone numbers

Number porting

Just as organizations can port (move) numbers between traditional terrestrial or mobile carriers, organizations can also port their numbers from their current service provider to Microsoft for use with Teams. The following types of numbers can be ported to Microsoft Teams:

- Traditional terrestrial (landline) phone numbers for voice or facsimile

- Mobile device phone numbers

- Owned toll and toll-free service numbers

- Fax phone numbers

- VoIP phone numbers

Review the swim lanes flowchart in Figure 22-13 to understand the porting process.

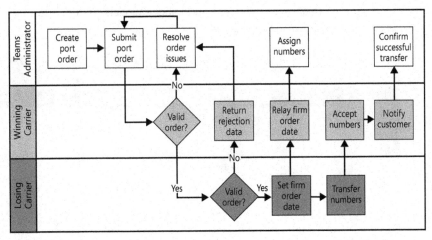

Figure 22-13   Overview of porting process

The porting process beings when a Teams administrator submits a port order (sometimes known as a port request).

TIP

It's recommended that the administrator requests a Customer Service Record (CSR) from the losing carrier. The CSR includes all necessary information regarding the carrier service and phone numbers. This information should be used to ensure the port order is filled out correctly. Even the slightest error or omission will likely cause the losing carrier to reject the request (which will delay the porting process).

The losing carrier must approve the port request for it to move forward. The losing carrier must honor your port request, though there is no service level agreement, regulation, or timeline they must follow. Since you are moving business away from them, many carriers make the process difficult. In the United States, if you experience significant problems porting your numbers, you can file a complaint with the Federal Communications Commission at *https://consumercomplaints.fcc.gov* or call 888-225-5322.

Porting in

To initiate a port request to Microsoft, you need to generate a Letter of Authorization using the wizard located in the Teams admin center. To initiate the process:

1. Navigate to the Teams admin center at *https://admin.teams.microsoft.com*.

2. Expand Voice and select Phone Numbers.

3. On the Numbers table, click Port.

4. Review the information on the screen, including reminders, prerequisites, and suggestions, as shown in Figure 22-14.

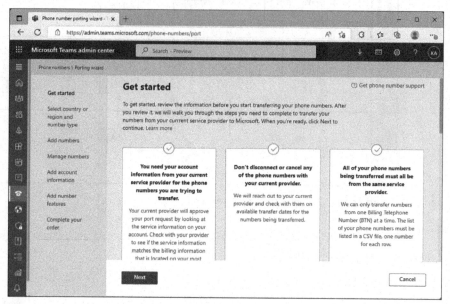

Figure 22-14   Launching the porting wizard

5. Click Next.

6. On the Select Country Or Region And Number Type page, use the dropdown to select the country or region that you are porting from. You'll also need to choose whether the numbers are geographic (local toll number) or toll-free, as shown in Figure 22-15.

7. Click Next to continue.

8. Enter the billing telephone number (BTN) associated with the numbers to be ported. The BTN can be found on the losing carrier's Customer Service Record (CSR). To verify the number, click Check BTN.

9. Select either the Add Phone Numbers Manually or Upload Numbers By CSV radio buttons:

   - If you provide the numbers manually, separate each number with a semicolon.

   - If you submit a CSV, the file should be formatted as a single column with no header information. Enter one number per row in E.164 format. Upload the CSV file into the form.

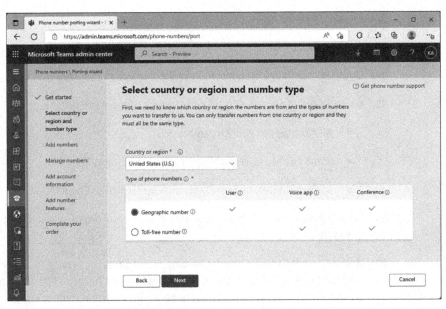

Figure 22-15   Selecting source country or region and number type

10. Click Next.

11. The wizard will validate the numbers. If successful, you can click Next to continue, as shown in Figure 22-16.

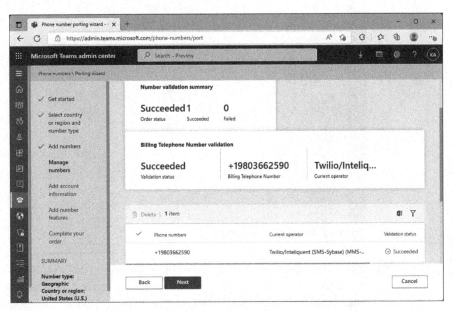

Figure 22-16   Number validation summary

12. Fill out the order form.

13. Enter an Order Name.

14. Under Port Details > Requested Port Date, select a requested port date and time.

15. Under Port Details > Port Type, select which numbers to port:

    - All Numbers In Your Organization

    - Some Numbers In Your Organization, Including The BTN

    - Some Numbers In Your Organization, Excluding The BTN

16. Under Organization Details, enter the name of your organization as it appears on the losing carrier's CSR.

17. Under Current Service Provider Details, enter values for Service Provider Name, your organization's Account Number, and the associated Account PIN. Omit any non-alphanumeric characters in the account number, such as hyphens or periods. See Figure 22-17.

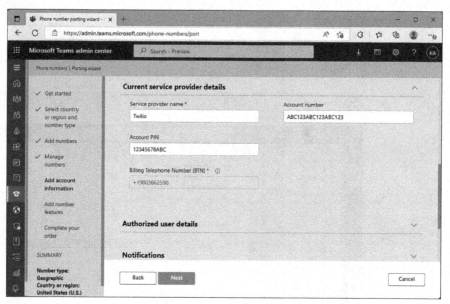

Figure 22-17   Port order details

18. Under Authorized User Details, enter the First Name, Last Name, Title, Phone Number, and Email Address of the user authorizing the port request (typically, someone who is listed as an organizational or billing representative on the account or losing carrier's CSR).

19. Select either the E-Signature or Paper Signature radio button, indicating how you will provide the authorized user's signature for the port request. If you select Paper Signature, you will need to print off the final Letter of Authorization (LOA), have the authorized user sign it, and upload it back to the port request.

20. Under Notifications, enter one or more email addresses for individuals to be notified of the port request, separated by a semicolon.

21. Under Service Address, select the location that maps to the service address listed with the losing carrier. If the service address is not listed, click Add A Location to add the service address.

22. Select either the Yes, Change Usages radio button to update the number usage category for the order or the No radio button to maintain the default number usage.

23. Click Next to continue.

24. If you choose Yes, Change Usages, you'll be prompted to select a number and change its usage. After updating the usage, click Next to proceed to the Complete Your Order page.

25. If you choose No, you'll be directed to Complete Your Order page.

26. On the Complete Your Order page, click the Complete And Send E-Signature Request Button (if you selected to confirm authorization via electronic signature) or Download Template to download the Letter of Authorization for the authorized user to sign.

NOTE

If you cannot complete the online port request form to generate the Letter of Authorization template, you can download a blank template at *https://docs.microsoft.com/en-us/MicrosoftTeams/phone-number-calling-plans/manually-submit-port-order* and then fill it out by hand. After filling it out, you'll have to go back to the Port Request wizard and upload it.

27. Have the authorized user sign the port request:

    - If you choose to use an e-Signature, the authorized user whose email address was specified in the port request will be sent an electronic document to sign, as shown in Figure 22-18. After electronically signing, the port order will be submitted automatically.

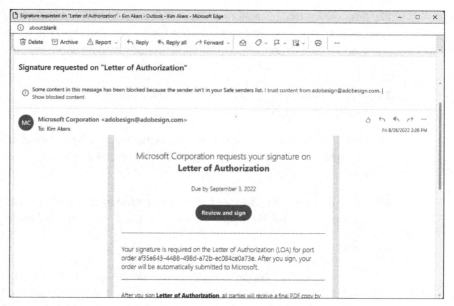

Figure 22-18   Electronic signature request

- If you opted for a physical signature, print the downloaded form and have the authorized user sign in. After it has been signed, scan the document to a file and click Upload A Signed Letter Of Authorization. Click Submit to send the request.

28. After the port request has been submitted, the pending order will be listed on the Order History tab under Voice > Phone Numbers in the Teams admin center.

29. Upon submission, Microsoft will route the request to the losing carrier for approval. If the losing carrier accepts the port request, an approval will be sent back to Microsoft with a target completion date.

30. One week before the port date, the numbers to be ported will appear in the Teams admin center under Voice > Numbers. From here, they can be pre-provisioned to users.

NOTE

Even though the numbers show up in the admin center at this time and can be assigned, the numbers have not been ported and will not impact routing.

At the port date and time specified by the losing carrier, the numbers will be transferred from the losing carrier to Microsoft. The losing carrier will deprovision those numbers from their network, allowing the numbers to route to the Microsoft Teams Phone system infrastructure.

If the port is rejected, the rejection response will be delivered to Microsoft (who will relay it to the port requestor) with a reason. The requestor can remediate the issue and resubmit.

Porting out

At any time, you can decide to port your Microsoft calling plans-based numbers to another carrier. As with the porting-in process, you'll be required to supply a PIN to the winning carrier to confirm authorization of the port request. To configure Teams porting PIN, follow these steps:

1. Navigate to the Teams admin center at *https://admin.teams.microsoft.com*.

2. Expand Voice and select Phone Numbers.

3. Select Actions and then click Manage Porting PIN, as shown in Figure 22-19.

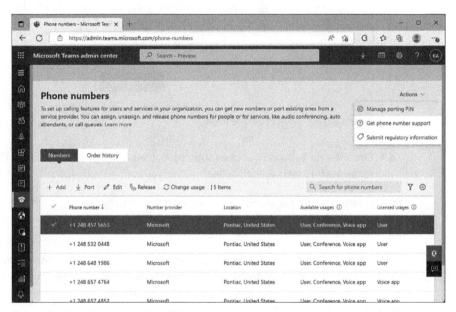

Figure 22-19   Manage porting PIN

4. When prompted, enter a 10-digit number and click Apply.

Failure to configure a PIN before the porting process might result in your request being denied.

Canceling a port request

If you decide to cancel a port request, you can do so at any time through the Teams admin center. To cancel a request, complete these steps:

1. Navigate to the Teams admin center at *https://admin.teams.microsoft.com*.

2. Expand Voice and select Phone Numbers.

3. Select the Order History tab.

4. Click the port request to cancel. Under Actions, select Cancel.

5. Select an option from the Reason For Cancellation dropdown menu and confirm the cancellation by clicking Continue on the Cancel Your Order dialog, as shown in Figure 22-20.

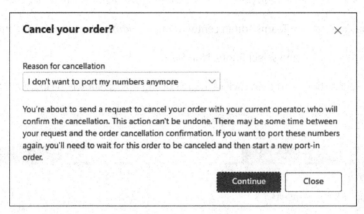

Figure 22-20   Cancel port request

6. Once the cancellation has been submitted, the port request will show as Cancelled on the Order History tab.

You can return to this page and start a new port request anytime.

Troubleshooting issues with a porting request

If you have a problem with the porting process, you can use the Get Phone Number Support Link located in the top right-hand corner of the Phone numbers page. This link directs you to the Phone Number Services Center at *https://pstnsd.powerappsportals.com*, where you can submit a request for assistance.

Assign phone numbers

For a user to receive PSTN calls, they need to have a phone number assigned. Once you have phone numbers available, you can begin the assignment process.

This section will cover assigning phone numbers for both calling plans and Operator Connect-based architectures.

To assign a number to a user, follow these steps:

1. Navigate to the Teams admin center at *https://admin.teams.microsoft.com*.

2. Expand Voice and select Phone Numbers.

3. On the Numbers tab, choose the number to assign and click Edit.

4. On the Assign/Unassign flyout menu shown in Figure 22-21, search for a user by entering the user's name into the Assigned To field and press Enter. When the correct user is displayed in the search box, click Assign.

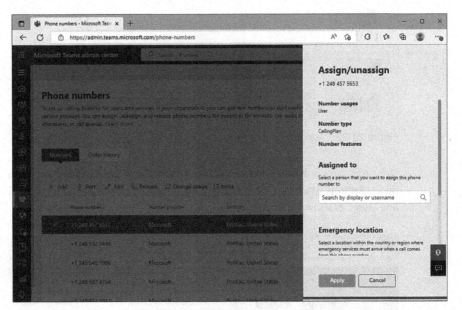

Figure 22-21   Assign/unassign number flyout menu

5. Under Emergency Location, select the user's emergency location.

6. If desired, slide the Email User With Phone Number Information toggle to On to notify the user that they have a new phone number.

7. Click the Apply button to assign the number and associated emergency location to the user (see Figure 22-22).

Figure 22-22   Assign a number to a user

Once the number has been assigned, you can see both the Assigned Phone Number and Emergency Address when viewing the user's Teams profile on the Account tab under Users > Manage Users, as shown in Figure 22-23.

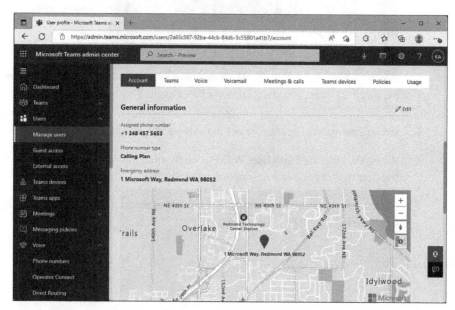

Figure 22-23   Assigned Phone Number and Emergency Address

To update the user's number or emergency location, click Edit next to General Information.

Next, we'll look at working with communications credits.

Communications credits

Communications credits are used to pay for calling services beyond the subscribed plan minutes for calling and audio conferencing plans. Communications are required for toll-free dial-in service numbers. Communications credits can also be used to cover international dial-out minutes.

Communications credits are purchased in bundles from $20 to $10,000.

> # NOTE
>
> **Information on the current pricing for communications credits can be found at**
> *https://www.microsoft.com/en-us/microsoft-teams/microsoft-teams-phone.*

Toll-free dial-in and international dial-out draw down this pool on a per-minute basis. These funds can also be used to cover overages in the event the shared outbound calling pool or audio conferencing minutes are exhausted.

To restate it, communications credits can be used for the following purposes:

- Overages on domestic calling plans and outbound audio conferencing

- Inbound toll-free numbers

- Audio conferencing pay-per-minute

Communications credits roll over month to month and expire one year from purchase. Credits can also be set to recharge automatically. Credits can be purchased via a saved credit card or an Enterprise Agreement.

Communication credits are pooled at the tenant level and are made available to users through license assignment. Users will not be able to leverage communications credits unless they are specifically assigned a communications credit license.

To enable a Communications Credit license for a user, follow these steps:

1. Navigate to the Microsoft 365 admin center at *https://admin.microsoftcom.*

2. Expand Users and select Active Users.

3. Choose a user from the list.

4. On the flyout menu, select the Licenses And Apps tab.

5. Under Licenses, select Communications Credits to enable the user to draw down from the pool of credits.

6. Click Save.

Communication credits usage (along with other PSTN minute usage metrics) can be obtained by reviewing the PSTN Minute & SMS Pools reports in the Teams admin center. To access the report, click Analytics & Reports > Usage Reports, as shown in Figure 22-24.

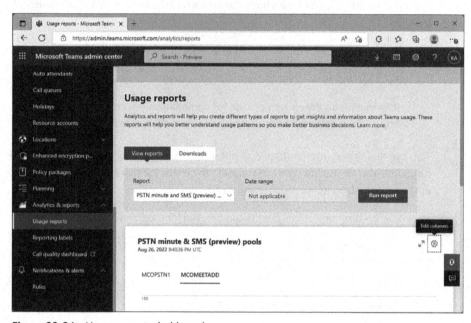

Figure 22-24   Usage reports dashboard

Working with numbers for both native calling plans and Operator Connect is relatively straight-forward. As you've seen, you can request, port, and assign numbers easily inside the Teams admin center.

Teams voice policies

Teams voice policies cover a wide range of calling capabilities, including calling restrictions, parking, and caller ID. In this section, we'll explore configuring the common voice policy settings.

Calling restrictions

Many organizations need to place limits on who can make or receive calls. For example, if you manage a group of direct sales employees, you might need to prevent users from being able to receive inbound calls from competitor phone numbers. You also might need to manage the ability of users to be able to make outbound calls.

Teams Phone allows you to manage features to support both of these scenarios.

Inbound calling

You can manage inbound calling restrictions using the Microsoft Teams PowerShell module. Inbound phone number blocking is configured by creating a regular expression (RegEx) pattern that identifies the number patterns you want to block.

Inside Out

Phone number regular expressions

Regular expressions can be tricky to construct because the syntax is foreign to many Microsoft-platform administrators. However, some tips will help even novice administrators handle this task.

The key to working with regular expressions with Teams calling is learning to match ranges of numbers. Some of the key operators that you'll be working with are as follows:

( )   Parentheses denote a capture group. It's often used to find a particular group of characters in combination with other operators. For example, (123) matches the string 123.

[ ]   The square braces define character ranges. For example, [123] means matching characters 1, 2, or 3, and [1-5] means any character between 1 and 5.

∧   The caret is an anchor operator and denotes that the pattern to match must occur at the beginning of a word or line. For example, ∧123 means that a sequence must start with 123 to be considered a match.

$ The dollar sign is another anchor operator—this time, representing the end of a string. For example, 123$ means a sequence must end in 123 to be a match.

.   The period is a wildcard operator for a single character or space. For example, the regular expression 1.3 could match 123 or 1a3.

*   The asterisk is a wildcard operator that matches any number of characters or spaces.

?   The question mark operator has many functions, depending on where it exists in the regular expression. The most common, however, when working with Microsoft

Teams is making the previous character optional. For example, the regular expression 1?4255551212 would match both 4255551212 and 14255551212.

\   The backslash is an escape character, meaning that it prevents the regular expression evaluation engine from interpreting the character immediately following it as anything but a text character—essentially removing the "special" from special characters or command sequences. For example, \. matches the period character, whereas entering . would match any character (because the period character is a wildcard).

\d   Represents the digit (numeral) character class. It indicates that only a digit (numeral) following this operator should be matched.

{n}   The curly brace operator is a quantifier that says n number of characters must be present for a match. For example, \d{4} means a sequence of four digits is required for a match.

| The pipe operator is an alternation symbol, allowing you to specify an either-or combination. For example, (123|456) would match either 123 or 456.

With those tips in hand, you'll be able to craft regular numerical expressions successfully. You can use tools like RegEx Pal (*https://www.regexpal.com*) and RegEx 101 (*https://www.regex101.com*) to build and test regular expressions.

It's important to note that all the non-numerical characters are stripped from the phone number string before the regular expression engine processes it (so you don't need to worry about entering parentheses or hyphens as part of your expression).

In the following sections, we'll take a look at a few examples.

Blocking numbers

Blocking numbers is accomplished using the New-CsInboundBlockedNumberPattern cmdlet in the Microsoft Teams module. Let's say you want to block any inbound calls from area code 303 and all numbers from the 425-555-0000 to 425-555-9999 range. To do this, you can create a block using this command:

```
New-CsInboundBlockedNumberPattern -Name "Block Range 1" -Description "Block area code `
303 or 425-555-xxxx" -Pattern "^(\+?1?303\d{7}|\+?1?425555\d{4})$" -Enabled $True
```

Unblocking numbers

If you need to unblock a number, you can either use the `Set-CsInboundBlockedNumber-Pattern` cmdlet to set the `Enabled` value to `$False`, or you can use the `Remove-CsInbound-BlockedNumberPattern` cmdlet to remove it altogether:

```
Set-CsInboundBlockedNumberPattern -Identity "Block Range 1" -Enabled $False
Remove-CsInboundBlockedNumberPattern -Identity "Block Range 1"
```

Adding exceptions

If you need to allow a certain number inside a blocked range, you can add an exception with the `New-CsInboundExemptNumberPattern` cmdlet.

For example, to allow 425-555-0123 to be exempted from the block specified earlier, use this command:

```
New-CsInboundExemptNumberPattern -Name "Exemption 1" -Description "Allow 425-555-0123"
-Pattern "^\+?1?4255550123$" -Enabled $True
```

Removing exceptions

Like removing blocked numbers, you can also remove exceptions with the `Remove-CsInbound-BlockedNumberPattern` cmdlet:

```
Remove-CsInboundExemptNumberPattern -Identity "Exemption 1"
```

Outbound calling

Teams Phone can manage outbound calling restrictions for Audio Conferencing and PSTN services. This allows administrators the ability to block things like long-distance or out-of-region calling.

In addition to restriction regions for outbound calling, you can use outbound calling restrictions to disable outbound calling altogether.

Configure outbound calling for a user

To configure outbound calling restrictions or settings for an individual user, follow these steps:

1. Navigate to the Teams admin center at *https://admin.teams.microsoft.com*.

2. Expand Users and select Manage Users.

3. Choose a user to edit by clicking their Display Name. See Figure 22-25.

CHAPTER 22

Figure 22-25   Selecting a user

4. On the user's property page, select the Voice tab.

5. Under the Outbound Calling section, click the Dial-Out Settings For Calling dropdown, as shown in Figure 22-26.

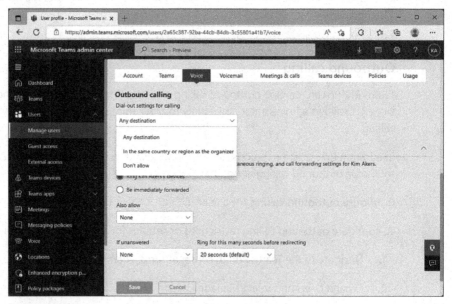

Figure 22-26   Updating the outbound calling options

6. Select one of these options to update the restrictions: Any Destination, In The Same Country Or Region As The Organizer, or Don't Allow. When the selection is made, the policy will be applied.

Configure outbound calling for multiple users

The Teams admin center interface only allows you to configure a single user's outbound calling policy at a time. This is not scalable in an organization with hundreds or thousands of users.

When managing multiple users, you can use the `Grant-CsDialoutPolicy` in the Microsoft Teams PowerShell module to iterate through any number of users.

To manage the policy for a single user, you can use the following command:

```
Grant-CsDialoutPolicy -Identity <username> -PolicyName <PolicyName>
```

You can also use a loop to iterate through a group of users by importing from a text file or specifying them on the command line:

```
$Users = Get-Content users.txt
$Users | % { Grant-CsDialOutPolicy -Identity $_ -PolicyName <PolicyName> }
```

Using the parameter `-Global`, you can also assign a policy tenant-wide:

```
Grant-CsDialoutPolicy -PolicyName <PolicyName> -Global
```

Refer to Table 22-1 for valid `PolicyName` values and descriptions.

Table 22-1   Grant-CsDialOutPolicy values

PolicyName value	Description
DialoutCPCandPSTNInternational	Conference users can dial out to international and domestic numbers. Users can also make outbound calls to international and domestic numbers.
DialoutCPCDomesticPSTNInternational	Conference users can only dial out to domestic numbers. Users can make outbound calls to international and domestic numbers.
DialoutCPCDisabledPSTNInternational	Conference users cannot dial out. This user can make outbound calls to international and domestic numbers.
DialoutCPCInternationalPSTNDomestic	Conference users can dial out to international and domestic numbers. Users can only make outbound calls to domestic PSTN numbers.
DialoutCPCInternationalPSTNDisabled	Conference users can dial out to international and domestic numbers. Users cannot make any outbound calls to PSTN numbers besides emergency numbers.
DialoutCPCandPSTNDomestic	Conference users can only dial out to domestic numbers. Users can only make outbound calls to domestic PSTN numbers.

DialoutCPCDomesticPSTNDisabled	Conference users can only dial out to domestic numbers. Users cannot make any outbound calls to PSTN numbers besides emergency numbers.
DialoutCPCDisabledPSTNDomestic	Conference users cannot dial out. Users can only make outbound calls to domestic PSTN numbers.
DialoutCPCandPSTNDisabled	Conference users cannot dial out. Users cannot make any outbound calls to PSTN numbers besides emergency numbers.
DialoutCPCZoneAPSTNInternational	Conference users can only dial out to Zone A countries and regions. Users can make outbound calls to international and domestic numbers.
DialoutCPCZoneAPSTNDomestic	Conference users can only dial out to Zone A countries and regions. Users can only make outbound calls to domestic PSTN numbers.
DialoutCPCZoneAPSTNDisabled	Conference users can only dial out to Zone A countries and regions. Users cannot make any outbound calls to PSTN numbers besides emergency numbers.

NOTE

For more information on international zones for audio conferencing, see *https://docs.microsoft.com/en-us/microsoftteams/audio-conferencing-zones*.

Calling policies

Calling policies control a number of features for the Teams Phone System, including the following:

- Making Private Calls

- Call Forwarding Options

- Simultaneous Ring

- Voicemail

- Group Calling

- Auto-Answer For Meeting Invitations

- Delegation

- Call Recording

- Busy-On-Busy

- Music On Hold

- Web-Based PSTN Calling

- Transcription

- SIP Device Compatibility

By default, all users are assigned the global calling policy. You can edit the default global policy to apply settings to all users across the tenant or create custom policies to apply to individual users or groups of users.

Configure a calling policy

To create and configure a new calling policy, follow these steps:

1. Navigate to the Teams admin center at *https://admin.teams.microsoft.com*.

2. Expand Voice and select Calling Policies.

3. Click Add.

4. Enter a calling policy Name and Description.

5. Enable or disable calling policy settings by moving the sliders to On or Off, as shown in Figure 22-27.

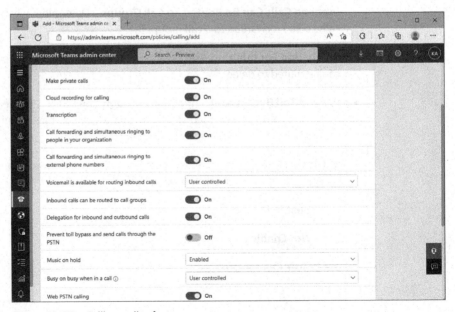

Figure 22-27   Calling policy features

The calling policy settings are explained below:

- **Make Private Calls**   Enables or disables calling capabilities in Teams. Turning this feature off disables all calling functionality.

- **Cloud Recording For Calling**   Enables users to record calls. Recorded calls are saved in the user's OneDrive in the Recordings folder.

- **Call Forwarding And Simultaneous Ringing To People In Your Organization**   Controls whether inbound calls can be forwarded to internal Teams users and whether internal users can be configured to ring simultaneously.

- **Call Forwarding And Simultaneous Ringing To External Phone Numbers**   Controls whether inbound calls can be forwarded to an external number and whether an external number can be configured to ring simultaneously.

- **Voicemail Is Available For Routing Inbound Calls**   Determines how inbound calls will be routed to voicemail. Choose one of the following settings:

  - ▼ **Enabled**   Voicemail will be enabled.

  - ▼ **Disabled**   Voicemail will be disabled.

  - ▼ **User Controlled**   Teams users can enable or disable voicemail for their own inbound calls.

- **Inbound Calls Can Be Routed To Call Groups**   Determines whether incoming calls can be forwarded to a call group.

- **Delegation For Inbound And Outbound Calls**   Controls whether inbound calls can be routed to delegates.

- **Prevent Toll Bypass And Send Calls Through The PSTN**   This feature determines how calls will be routed externally. Some localities have regulations requiring calls to be made on PSTN networks to collect toll charges.

- **Music On Hold**   Determines whether hold music will be available when a PSTN caller is placed on hold. The following options are available:

  - ▼ **Enabled**

  - ▼ **Not Enabled**

  - ▼ **User Can Control**

- **Busy On Busy When In A Call**   Determines how incoming calls are handled with the recipient Teams user is already on a call. The following options are available:

  - ▼ **Not Enabled**   Not configured. Incoming calls will show up for the Teams recipient, who has the option to place an existing call on hold or answer a new incoming call.

  - ▼ **Enabled**   Incoming calls are declined with a busy signal.

  - ▼ **Unanswered**   Incoming calls are handled according to the user's unanswered call settings (Voicemail, New Number Or Contact, Do Nothing, and Call Group).

- **Web PSTN Calling**   Controls whether users can place PSTN calls using the Team web client.

- **Real-Time Captions In Teams Calls**   Determines whether real-time captions can be enabled on a Teams call.

- **Automatically Answer Incoming Meeting Invites**   Controls whether incoming meeting calls invitations are automatically answered and joined.

- **Spam Filtering**   Enables or disables spam filtering for inbound calls. Calls identified as potential spam will be tagged as Spam Likely.

- **SIP Devices Can Be Used For Calls**   Enables or disables the use of third-party non-Microsoft Session Initiation Protocol (SIP) devices.

- **Open Apps In Browser For Incoming PSTN Calls**   Enable the calling platform extensibility option for passing PSTN calls to third-party apps (such as call center or CRM applications).

6. Click Save to save the settings and create the policy.

The policy is now available to be edited or assigned to users.

Assign a calling policy to a user

Calling policies can be easily assigned to users using the Teams admin center. To assign a calling policy to an individual user, follow these steps:

1. Navigate to the Teams admin center at *https://admin.teams.microsoft.com*.

2. Expand Voice and select Calling Policies.

3. Select the Manage Policies tab.

4. Highlight and select a policy to assign. Select Manage Users.

5. From the Manage Users dropdown, select Assign Users, as shown in Figure 22-28.

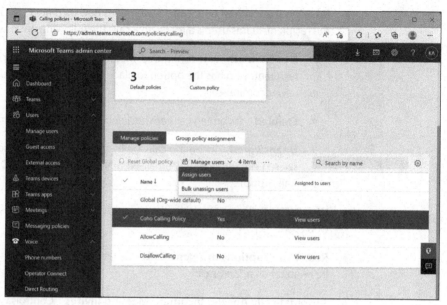

Figure 22-28   Manage calling policy for a user

6.   On the Manage Users flyout menu, search for users and click Add to add users to the policy, as shown in Figure 22-29.

7.   Click Apply to save changes.

Figure 22-29   Adding users to a policy

TIP

You can also assign any policy to a user through the Manage Users interface by selecting Users > Manage Users, selecting a user, selecting the Policies tab, and then updating the policy assignment under Assigned Policies. You can use this interface to review and assign Teams policies to a particular user.

Assign a calling policy to a group

You can also apply policies via a group membership if you create policies that need to be applied to many users at once. For example, you could use group membership to create policies for hundreds of people who work in a call center and need the same policy. Also, policies assigned via a group membership can be ranked.

To assign a calling policy to a group, follow these steps:

1. Navigate to the Teams admin center at *https://admin.teams.microsoft.com*.

2. Expand Voice and select Calling Policies.

3. Select the Group Policy Assignment tab.

4. Click Add.

5. In the Assign Policy To Group flyout menu, select a group that will be assigned the policy.

6. In the Select Rank box, enter a ranking value for the policy. If a user is a member of more than one group with a policy assigned, the policy with the lowest-ranking value will be the winning policy.

7. Choose a policy from the Select A Policy dropdown, as shown in Figure 22-30.

8. Click Apply to save changes.

If you select a value already in use when setting a policy assignment rank, the new policy assignment will take its place. The previous policy at that particular ranking (and all lower-ranked policies) will shift down by one.

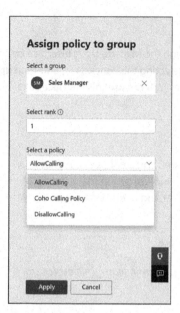

Figure 22-30   Group calling policy assignment

Call parking policies

The call parking feature allows a Teams user to put a call on hold on one endpoint (such as the Teams mobile client, Teams phone device, or Teams client) and then retrieve it. The call might be retrieved from either the same endpoint or another.

Calls might be put on hold for many reasons, including transferring to another Teams user or number, transferring away from an endpoint that is not mobile, or transferring away from an endpoint that is running low on battery.

Park and pick up a call

If a Teams user has a call parking enabled, they can park calls by selecting the More Actions ellipsis in their calling window during an active call and then choosing Park Call, as shown in Figure 22-31.

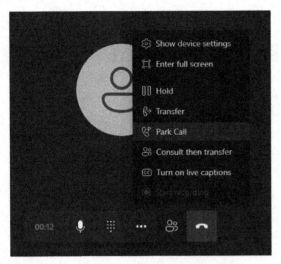

Figure 22-31   Parking a call on web client

If you park a call on the desktop client, you'll receive a notification in the call window that displays the Call Is Parked message with text reading, "Share This Code 47 To Retrieve The Call," as shown in Figure 22-32.

Figure 22-32   Call Is Parked in the desktop client

If you park a call using the web client, you'll be returned to the Calls app, where you can view the parked call code in the call History, as shown in Figure 22-33.

CHAPTER 22

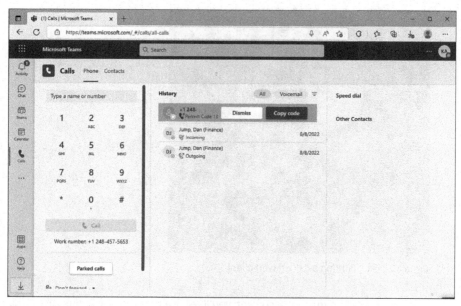

Figure 22-33   Calls app on the Teams web client with a parked call

The Teams user who will pick up the parked call can click the Parked Calls button under the phone dialer and then enter the Teams parked call code.

Configure a parking policy

Now that you've seen how call parking works, let's look at the steps to configure a parking policy:

1. Navigate to the Teams admin center at *https://admin.teams.microsoft.com*.

2. Expand Voice and select Call Park Policies.

3. On the Manage Policies tab, click an existing policy to edit it or click Add to create a new policy.

4. Enter a Name and Description for the policy.

5. To configure a policy with parking enabled, enable the Call Park setting by sliding the toggle to On; to configure a policy with parking disabled, move the Call Park slider to Off. See Figure 22-34.

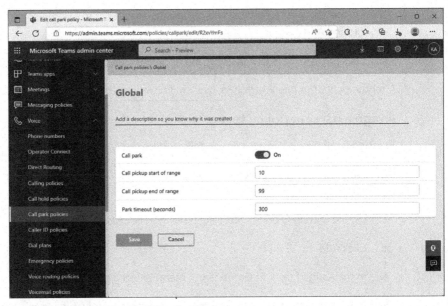

Figure 22-34   Configure a call park policy

6. Configure the range of pickup codes that will be used by entering values in the corresponding Call Pickup Start Of Range and Call Pickup End Of Range fields. The valid range for both values is between 10 and 9,999.

7. Enter a value for Park Timeout (Seconds). This value determines how long a call can stay parked before ringing back to the user who placed the call on park. The valid range is between 120 and 1,800 seconds.

8. Click Save.

The policy can now be applied to users or groups.

Assign a parking policy to a user

Like calling policies, a call park policy can be assigned to users. The process is very similar.

To assign a call park policy to a user, follow these steps:

1. From the Teams admin center at *https://admin.teams.microsoft.com*, expand Voice and select Call Park Policies.

2. On the Manage Policies tab, select the policy to assign, and then click Assign Users.

3. On the Manage Users flyout menu, use the search bar to locate users and select them by clicking Add.

4. Click Apply to save the changes and update the assignment.

After the policy has been refreshed, users will now have the assigned call park policy.

Assign a parking policy to a group

To assign a call park policy to a group, follow these steps:

1. From the Teams admin center at *https://admin.teams.microsoft.com*, expand Voice and select Call Park Policies.

2. On the Manage Policies tab, select Group Policy Assignment.

3. Click Add.

4. In the Assign Policy To Group flyout menu, select a group that will be assigned the policy.

5. In the Select Rank box, enter a ranking value for the policy. If a user is a member of more than one group with a policy assigned, the policy with the lowest ranking value will be the winning policy.

6. In the Select A Policy dropdown, choose a policy.

7. Click Apply to save the changes.

If you select a value already in use when setting the rank of a policy assignment, the new policy assignment will take its place. The previous policy at that particular ranking (and all lower-ranked policies) will shift down by one.

Caller ID policies

Caller ID policies allow you to configure and manage the data displayed to call recipients. Depending on the use case, it might be desirable to display a service number or even no information at all instead of the actual calling line identity information.

Configuring a caller ID policy

To configure a caller ID policy, follow this procedure:

1. Navigate to the Teams admin center at *https://admin.teams.microsoft.com*.

2. Expand Voice and select Caller ID Policies.

3. Select an existing policy to edit it, or click Add to create a new policy.

4. Enter a Name and Description for the policy.

5. To configure a policy to block incoming caller ID data, move the Block Incoming Caller ID slider to On. Blocking incoming caller ID will mask the caller ID data for calls received by internal Teams users. See Figure 22-35.

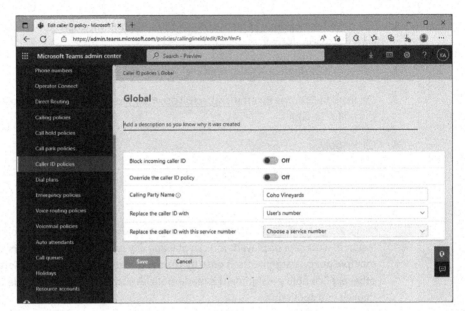

Figure 22-35   Configuring a caller ID policy

6. To allow users to override the caller ID policy applied to them, move the Override The Caller ID Policy slider to On.

7. To send an updated Calling Party Name (CNAM) value, enter a value in the Calling Party Name field. Depending on your locality and the carriers processing the call, this value might not be honored. (Many carriers maintain private CNAM databases that they update on their own schedule.)

8. Select an option in the Replace The Caller ID With dropdown to send a different called ID (calling line identity) value. The default value is the User's number, but you can also choose from Service Number, Anonymous, and Resource Account.

9. If you choose to replace the caller ID with either a service number or a resource account in the previous step, select the appropriate value from the Replace The Caller ID With This Service Number dropdown.

10. Click Save.

After a brief refresh period, the updated policy will be available for assignment.

Assigning a caller ID policy

Whereas calling policies and call park policies are assigned through their respective configuration menus, caller ID policies are applied through the Manage Users interface.

To assign a caller ID policy, follow these steps:

1. From the Teams admin center at *https://admin.teams.microsoft.com*, expand Users and select Manage Users.

2. Select one or more users and then click Edit Settings.

3. On the Edit Settings flyout menu, scroll down to the Caller ID Policy dropdown and select the policy to apply.

4. Click Apply.

The updated policy should take effect shortly.

> ## TIP
>
> While assigning the caller ID policy, you might have noticed that all the policies you can assign to a user are displayed. You can manage any policy assigned to users and update multiple policy assignments at once by choosing Managing Users > Edit Settings. If no other explicit policy assignment is made, policies such as Global (Org-Wide Default) are implicit and applied.

Voicemail policies

Cloud voicemail allows the Teams Phone System to deposit voicemail message data in the user's corresponding Exchange mailbox, whether that mailbox is homed in Exchange Online or Exchange Server on-premises (through an SMTP connector). Voicemail messages are delivered as an email with an audio file attachment containing the message data.

The user's Exchange mailbox also stores any custom greeting information that is played for callers leaving messages. For Exchange on-premises mailboxes, this requires OAuth authentication between Exchange Online and Exchange on-premises (typically configured through the Exchange Hybrid setup process).

> ## TIP
>
> Voicemail counts against a user's licensed mailbox storage (if stored in Exchange Online).

Voicemail configuration falls into two categories: voicemail *policies* and voicemail *settings*.

Configure voicemail policies

Voicemail policies relate to broad configuration items that apply to the service in general. As with other areas in Teams, you can configure multiple policies to apply to different groups of users.

Voicemail policies are accessed via the Voice > Voicemail policies menu in the Teams admin center. By default, new tenants have three built-in policies deployed, as shown in Figure 22-36.

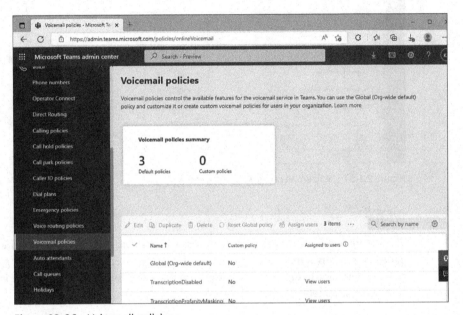

Figure 22-36   Voicemail policies

The `Global (Org-Wide Default)` policy is implicit and applies to all users not explicitly associated with another policy. The other two policies, `TranscriptionDisabled` and `TranscriptionProfanityMaskingEnabled`, have non-configurable settings but can be assigned to users.

To configure a policy, follow these steps:

1. From the Teams admin center at *https://admin.teams.microsoft.com*, expand Voice and select Voicemail Policies.

2. Click Add to create a new policy or select an existing one to edit (except for the two built-in read-only policies).

3. If you want to allow users to change their call-answering behavior, move the Users Can Edit Call Answer Rules slider to On, as shown in Figure 22-37.

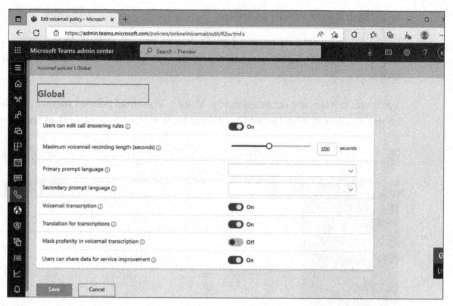

Figure 22-37   Voicemail policy settings page

NOTE

The feature referenced as Call Answering Rules on the Voicemail Policies configuration page in the Teams admin center is referenced as Call Answering Rules in the user's Teams client settings and as Call Answering Mode on the user's voicemail settings page in the Teams admin center.

4. If desired, update the Maximum Voicemail Recording Length (Seconds) by adjusting the slider or entering a numeric value directly. The default is 300 seconds (5 minutes).

5. Choose a primary prompt language from the Primary Prompt Language dropdown.

6. Choose a secondary prompt language from the Secondary Prompt Language dropdown.

7. Enable or disable voicemail transcription using the Voicemail Transcription slider. The transcription will be delivered as text in the email's message body containing the voicemail attachment.

8. Enable or disable transcription translation using the Translation For Transcriptions slider. If enabled, Teams will attempt to translate the voicemail message into the recipient's preferred language.

9. Enable or disable profanity marking in voicemail transcription using the Mask Profanity In Voicemail Transcription slider. If enabled, transcriptions that contain profanity will have the identified words replaced with the asterisk character.

10. If you want to allow users to share data for service improvement with Microsoft, set the Users Can Share Data For Service Improvement slider to On. If disabled, user data will not be shared, regardless of the user's options.

11. Click Save to save the policy.

After the policy has been saved, you can apply it to users.

Assign voicemail policies

Voicemail policies can be assigned to users on either the Voicemail Policies page or the Manage Users page.

To apply a voicemail policy from the Voicemail Policies page, follow these steps:

1. From the Teams admin center at *https://admin.teams.microsoft.com*, expand Voice and select Voicemail Policies.

2. On the Voicemail Policies page, select the policy to assign and click Assign Users.

3. On the Manage Users flyout menu, use the search bar to locate users and select them by clicking Add.

4. Click Apply to save the changes and update the assignment.

After the Teams policy cache has been refreshed, the new policy will be applied.

Configuring voicemail settings

Voicemail settings relate directly to individual users and are mainly used to personalize the service.

To access and configure an individual user's voicemail settings, follow this procedure:

1. From the Teams admin center at *https://admin.teams.microsoft.com*, expand Users and select Manage Users.

2. Select the Voicemail tab, as shown in Figure 22-38.

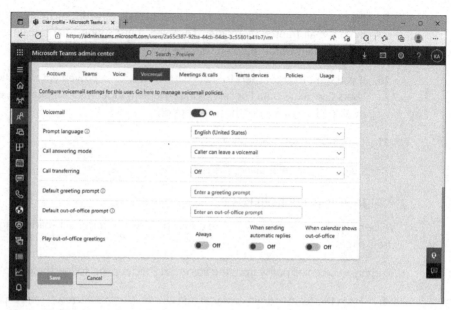

Figure 22-38   User voicemail settings

3. Use the Voicemail toggle to enable or disable voicemail for the user. If you slide the toggle to Off, no further settings can be managed.

4. Use the Prompt Language dropdown to select the language in which the voicemail prompts will be played.

5. Choose a Call Answering Mode (also referred to as the *call answering rule*). The default option is Caller Can Leave A Voicemail. Two other options are available:

   - Play An Outgoing Message To The Caller

   - Service Declines The Call With No Message

6. Set the Call Transferring option. The default setting is Off, but you can also select Transfer To A User or Transfer To A Number. If you select either transferring option, you will be prompted to specify the destination (either a PSTN number or a user selected from the directory).

7. Enter a Default Greeting Prompt to be read as text-to-speech if the user has not set up a custom prompt.

8. Enter a Default Out-Of-Office Prompt to be read as text-to-speech if the user has not set up a custom out-of-office greeting.

9. Set the Play Out-Of-Office Greetings option:

- **When Sending Automatic Replies** This toggle enables Teams to play the out-of-office message if Teams detects that the user has configured an out-of-office automatic reply message.

- **When Calendar Shows Out-Of-Office** This toggle enables Teams to play the out-of-office message when Teams detects that the user has created an out-of-office calendar appointment.

10. Click Apply to save the changes and update the assignment.

The voicemail settings configured will be visible in the Teams user's client after a brief refresh.

What's next?

The Teams Phone platform is an expansive upgrade from the Skype for Business telephony solution. Teams Phone brings new options to replace legacy phone systems as a solution integrated into an already-strong collaboration and development platform.

Now that you understand the basic Phone System configuration, you'll learn about configuring advanced features such as call queues and auto attendants in Chapter 23.

CHAPTER 22

In the last few chapters, we've covered the foundational concepts and core configuration tasks that most organizations will need to deploy a functioning Teams Phone System. Many organizations, however, might have needs for scheduling, room collaboration, automation, or traditional interactive voice response (IVR) features that require more advanced configuration.

In this chapter, we'll discuss the advanced features of Teams Phone System:

- Resource accounts

- Microsoft Teams Rooms

- Holidays

- Call queues

- Auto attendants

By the end of the chapter, you'll be able to configure advanced features enabling the Teams Phone platform to provide parity with legacy on-premises phone systems.

The topics in this chapter are organized to help you progress logically through the configuration items, considering dependencies.

CHAPTER 23

Inside Out

Designing advanced call routing scenarios

There are many moving parts between resource accounts, call queues, and auto attendants. Following are some of the most important points to consider:

- All resources in Microsoft Teams require resource accounts.
- All resource accounts require licenses (either Teams Room licenses or Teams Resource Account licenses).
- Both call queues and auto attendants can have external phone numbers or be internal only with no direct inward dial (DID) numbers.
- Both call queues and auto attendants can have other call queues and auto attendants as routing destinations.
- Some configuration options might preclude legacy Skype for Business clients from fully participating,

Before configuring advanced features in your environment, we recommend reviewing the configuration steps and screens presented and noting the possible settings for each.

You might find it helpful to answer the following questions:

- How many call queues and auto attendants does your organization need? (For example, you might need one auto attendant and call queue per department.)
- How many call queues and auto attendants need external numbers?
- What call queues or auto attendants might be destinations for other call queues and auto attendants?

Also, you should write out scripts for greetings or prompts throughout the call queues and auto attendants. Gathering this information will help ensure you configure all the settings correctly.

Resource accounts

In the simplest terminology, resource accounts are non-person identities (that is, an identity not explicitly connected to a physical person) that are used to facilitate services and features. There are a few Microsoft Teams scenarios where resource accounts are necessary. Depending on your scenario (Microsoft Teams Rooms, auto attendants, or call queues), you might need to acquire and assign licenses or even sign into devices with the resource account.

In this section, we'll look at the types of resource accounts and how you might configure them, depending on your requirements.

Microsoft Teams advanced calling feature resource accounts

Advanced calling features such as auto attendants and call queues also require resource accounts. External-facing advanced calling features will require phone numbers.

Create resource accounts

To create a new resource account for an advanced calling feature, follow these steps:

1. Navigate to the Teams admin center (*https://admin.teams.microsoft.com*).

2. Expand Voice and select Resource Accounts, as shown in Figure 23-1.

Figure 23-1   Resource Accounts page

3. Click Add.

4. On the Add Resource Account flyout shown in Figure 23-2, enter a Display Name and Username and select a Resource Account Type (either Auto Attendant or Call Queue):

   - Choose Auto Attendant if you want to create a navigable interactive voice response menu.

   - Choose Call Queue if you want to create a queue that will be answered by agents.

Figure 23-2   Add resource account flyout

5.   Click Save when finished.

As a reminder, internal auto attendants and call queues do not require phone numbers. If, however, you want your auto attendant or call queue to be able to receive direct inward dial (DID) calls, it will require a telephone number. If the resource account will be configured with a toll-free number, you will also need to assign a Communications Credit license through the Microsoft 365 admin center.

Manage resource account licenses

Just like normal user accounts require a phone system license to enable enterprise voice features, resource accounts also require a type of phone system license. The Teams Phone Resource Account license (previously known as the Phone System Virtual User license) is a no-charge phone system license designated for use by non-person accounts.

Inside Out

Resource account license calculation

You might recall that Microsoft uses a formula to determine how many service numbers you can request for your tenant. Resource account licenses are calculated using a similar methodology.

As soon as at least one paid Phone System license is added to a tenant, Microsoft automatically allocates an initial grant of 25 Teams Phone Resource Account licenses. After that, Microsoft grants an additional resource account license for every 10 paid Phone System licenses.

For example, if a tenant has 500 paid Phone System licenses, Microsoft will allocate 75 Teams Phone Resource Account licenses (25 initial grant + (500 paid licenses / 10)).

Previously, only resource accounts that would be assigned phone numbers required a Teams Phone Resource Account license. However, Microsoft now requires all resource accounts to be licensed.

Acquire resource account licenses

To request the licenses granted to your tenant, you must execute a zero-dollar purchase through the Microsoft 365 admin center:

1. From the Microsoft 365 admin center at *https://admin.microsoft.com*, expand Billing and select Purchase Services.

2. Click View Products and search for **Teams Phone Resource Account**, as shown in Figure 23-3.

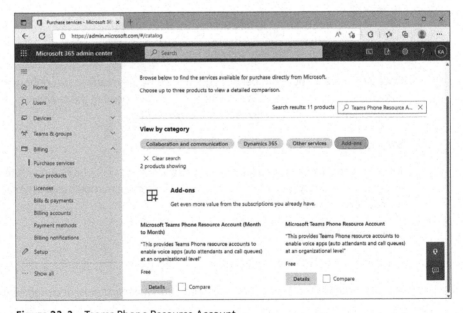

Figure 23-3 Teams Phone Resource Account

NOTE

The Resource Account license was previously called Microsoft Teams Phone Standard–Virtual User.

3. Select the Details button for the purchase options (either yearly or month-to-month) you want to acquire.

4. On the Product Details page, under Select License Quantity, enter the value of the allotted licenses and click Buy.

5. On the confirmation page, click Place Order.

Once the purchase has been completed, the licenses will be available immediately in the tenant.

Assign resource account licenses

Microsoft Teams resource accounts can be assigned licenses using the Microsoft 365 admin center.

To assign the license, follow these steps:

1. From the Microsoft 365 admin center at *https://admin.microsoft.com*, expand Users and select Active Users.

2. Search for the name of a resource account and select it.

3. On the User Account flyout, select Licenses And Apps.

4. Select the Microsoft Teams Phone Resource Account license and click Save Changes.

Once a resource account has been assigned a license, it is ready to be configured as part of an auto attendant or call queue. We recommend that you acquire the resource account licenses ahead of time through the Microsoft 365 admin center.

Service numbers

Service numbers are required for any auto attendant or call queue that needs to be available to external callers directly. You can place an order for service numbers using the same process used to acquire user phone numbers.

Order service numbers

The abbreviated steps are shown here:

1. Navigate to the Teams admin center at *https://admin.teams.microsoft.com*.

2. Expand Voice and select Phone Numbers.

3. Click Add.

4. Enter a Name and Description for the new phone number order.

5. Select Country Or Region.

6. Under Number Type, select from one of the following options for resource accounts:

   - Auto Attendant (Toll)

   - Auto Attendant (Toll Free)

   - Call Queue (Toll)

   - Call Queue (Toll Free)

7. Select Show My Operators to expand providers. To use a calling plans-based number, select Microsoft as the Operator. Select another listed provider if you have configured Operator Connect or Direct Routing.

8. Select the Quantity of service numbers to obtain.

9. Under Search For Numbers, select Search By City Name to search for associated phone numbers, or select Search By Area Code to request numbers in a particular area code. Remember, the city value must be defined as an Emergency Location in your tenant:

   - If you selected Search By City Name, choose the desired Area Code. Click Next to continue.

   - If you selected Search By Area Code, just click Next.

10. Review the details and click Place Order. Like processing an order for user numbers, you will have 10 minutes to complete the process, or the numbers will be released.

11. Click Finish.

After completing the order, you can assign service numbers to resource accounts.

Assign service numbers

Assigning a service number to a resource account will allow that resource account to accept inbound calls. To assign a service number, follow this procedure:

1. From the Teams admin center at *https://admin.teams.microsoft.com*, expand Voice and select Resource Accounts.

2. On the Resource Accounts page, select the resource account that will be assigned a service number and click Assign/Unassign.

3. On the Assign/Unassign flyout, expand the Phone Number Type dropdown, as shown in Figure 23-4, and select one of the following:

    ■   None

    ■   Calling Plan

    ■   Operator Connect

    ■   Direct Routing

4. Expand the Assigned Phone Number dropdown and select from the available service numbers.

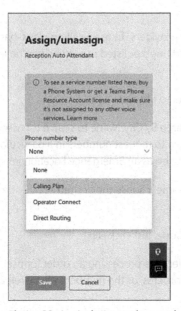

Figure 23-4   Assign a service number to a resource account

5. If the auto attendant or call queue has already been created, you can connect the resource account to the appropriate voice app by selecting it in the Assigned To area of the flyout menu.

6. Click Save when finished.

There are two configuration nuances you should be aware of:

●   You can assign multiple resource accounts to a call queue or auto attendant to allow multiple dial-in numbers.

●   A resource account can only be added to a single call queue or auto attendant at a time.

Next, we'll look at the type of resource account used to configure and manage Microsoft Teams Rooms.

Microsoft Teams Room resource accounts

Microsoft Teams Room (MTR) resource accounts function much like Exchange resource mailbox accounts. In Exchange, resource mailboxes are non-person mailboxes that are provisioned to assist in scheduling resources such as conference rooms (room mailboxes) or other devices like projectors, laptops, or even vehicles (equipment mailboxes).

Microsoft Teams Rooms are dedicated devices that are used to provide collaborative meeting features in a particular designated workspace. An MTR typically features a small compute device (either a tablet or custom PC), a speaker and microphone for telephonic communications, and connectivity to a screen or monitor for shared desktop and whiteboard applications. Each device has its own dedicated resource account that is used to log in to the device, manage room and meeting requests, and join meetings.

Table 23-1 describes the licensing Microsoft Teams Room scenarios for which licenses are required.

Table 23-1   Microsoft Teams Room license details and features

License	Notes
Microsoft Teams Room Basic	The Microsoft Teams Room Basic license enables core meeting experiences, including scheduling, joining meetings, content sharing, and whiteboard on up to 25 devices per tenant. Each license can only be logged into a single device at a time. Any additional licenses must be assigned a Teams Rooms Pro license.
Microsoft Teams Rooms Pro	For organizations with more than 25 devices or advanced needs, such as intelligent audio and video, galleries, multiscreen support, remote device management, conditional access policies, and device analytics.

NOTE

If you want to add audio conferencing to Microsoft Teams Rooms, you can subscribe to Teams Rooms licenses that have audio conferencing enabled.

Deployment scenarios

There are three deployment scenarios for Teams Rooms accounts: online only, Exchange hybrid with Exchange Online resource account, and Exchange hybrid with Exchange Server on-premises resource account.

CHAPTER 23

Online-only

With the online-only configuration, you'll be configuring a cloud-based resource account. This configuration option isn't limited to organizations that only manage identity in the cloud; it can also be used with hybrid configurations where the organizations are comfortable managing MTRs and associated accounts in a cloud-only fashion.

In this example, we'll create a cloud-based resource account for a Microsoft Teams Room device located in an organization's Chicago office.

> **NOTE**
>
> **For this scenario, you will use the modern Exchange Online Management module. You can install it using the following PowerShell script, executed in an elevated PowerShell console session:**
>
> ```
> If (!(Get-Module -ListAvailable -Name ExchangeOnlineManagement)) { `
> Install-Module ExchangeOnlineManagement }
> ```

Remember, you'll need to substitute your own tenant domain name and an appropriate password for your environment. Note the password because you will need it when configuring your Teams Room device:

1. Connect to the Exchange Online PowerShell interface:

   ```
   Connect-ExchangeOnline
   ```

2. Run the following commands in a console session:

   ```
   New-Mailbox -MicrosoftOnlineServicesId ChicagoMTR01@cohovineyards.us -Name `
   "Chicago MTR01" -Alias ChicagoMTR01 -EnableRoomMailboxAccount $True -Room `
   -RoomMailboxPassword (ConvertTo-SecureString -String '4rtR0brx.-#1' `
   -AsPlainText -Force)
   ```

After provisioning the mailbox, you are ready to configure the mailbox. Since it's a normal room mailbox, you can configure room and calendar processing parameters as your organization requires. For this example, we'll use the parameters and values shown in Table 23-2.

Table 23-2 Sample MTR mailbox parameters

Parameter	Recommend value	Description
AddAdditionalResponse	$true	Enables adding additional text to the response sent by the room mailbox.
AdditionalResponse	"Please arrive 5 minutes before your scheduled meeting to verify equipment readiness."	Text value to add to the meeting response.

AddOrganizerToSubject	$false	Prevents the meeting organizer's name from being added to the subject of the meeting request.
AutomateProcessing	AutoAccept	Configures resources account to automatically accept meeting requests.
DeleteComments	$false	Preserves original content in the body of the meeting request.
DeleteSubject	$false	Preserves the original subject of the meeting request.
RemovePrivateProperty	$false	Preserves the original privacy flag setting on the meeting request.

To set these parameters, you can use the Set-CalendarProcessing cmdlet, either individually or using PowerShell splatting. If you are configuring multiple room mailboxes with the same settings, it might be beneficial to save the parameters for reuse with splatting.

NOTE

Splatting is a PowerShell concept that uses a hash table to specify parameter name/value pairs. The hash table is saved as a variable and can be used in place of specifying individual parameters on the command line. For more information on how splatting works, see: *https://bit.ly/3VYicdJ.*

1. From the Exchange Online management shell, run the following command to create a hash table of values:

```
$MTRCalendarValues = @{
'AddAdditionalResponse' = $true;
'AdditionalResponse' = "Please arrive 5 minutes before your scheduled meeting `
to verify equipment readiness.";
'AddOrganizerToSubject' = $false;
'AutomateProcessing' = 'AutoAccept';
'DeleteComments' = $false;
'DeleteSubject' = $false;
'RemovePrivateProperty' = $false
}
```

2. Run the following command to configure the room mailbox, substituting your mailbox name, as shown in Figure 23-5:

```
Set-CalendarProcessing -Identity ChicagoMTR01 @MTRCalendarValues
```

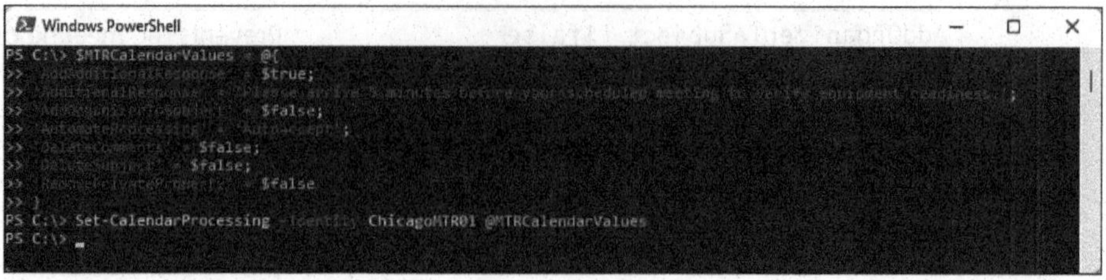

Figure 23-5   Set-CalendarProcessing with splatting

After successfully applying the values and updating the mailbox calendar processing parameters, the resource should be ready to license. You'll need to apply a license that permits the features that you'll be using:

1. Connect to Azure Active Directory using the Microsoft Online Services (MSOnline):

    ```
    If (!(Get-Module -ListAvailable MSOnline)) { Install-Module MSOnline}
    Connect-MsolService
    ```

2. Retrieve a list of valid SKUs:

    ```
    Get-MsolAccountSku | ? { $_.AccountSkuId -like "*rooms*" }
    ```

3. Assign a usage location (where [region] is the two-letter country code representing where the account will be used) and configure the account with a non-expiring password:

    ```
    Set-MsolUser -UserPrincipalName ChicagoMTR01@cohovineyards.us -UsageLocation `
    [region] -PasswordNeverExpires $true
    ```

4. Add a meeting room license (in the format of `tenant:license`) to the resource account:

    ```
    Set-MsolUserLicense -UserPrincipalName ChicagoMTR01@cohovineyards.us `
    -AddLicenses "cohovineyardsus:Microsoft_Teams_Rooms_Pro"
    ```

From here, you'll be able to set up your Microsoft Teams Room device using the account you have configured.

Exchange hybrid

Hybrid deployments (where resource mailboxes are managed through an on-premises Exchange platform) are available for organizations with a configured Exchange hybrid environment. With an Exchange hybrid-based deployment, you can manage the resource mailbox through the on-premises Exchange environment (if desired) using the same commands used to administer remote mailboxes.

The core difference in this scenario is that in an online-only deployment, both the mailbox and the account are created and managed in Azure AD and Exchange Online. With a hybrid deployment, the resource account itself is mastered on-premises and then attached to either an on-premises or a cloud mailbox. However, it is still licensed the same way.

While there are a number of ways to perform the account creation and licensing task, we'll focus on using PowerShell (since it's how the cloud account was provisioned). That will allow you to see both the similarities and differences. Later, if you want to create the account using a graphical user interface (GUI), you can also do that.

Follow these steps to configure the resource account in your on-premises directory:

1. Connect to the Exchange Server Management shell.

2. Store a credential object for the new mailbox, including the new account name and password. You'll need this password later to configure your Teams Room device:

   ```
   $TeamsRoomCredential = Get-Credential
   ```

   ## NOTE

   These steps assume you've followed the procedures in Chapter 9, "Identity and authentication planning," to align your Active Directory domain suffixes with SMTP suffixes. You'll want to ensure that you use a UPN suffix that matches a verified domain address space to prevent issues logging into Teams Room devices.

3. Use the `New-RemoteMailbox` cmdlet to create a new Active Directory account with the appropriate parameters and a cloud mailbox, or you can use the `New-Mailbox` cmdlet to create an on-premises mailbox. If you don't specify a value for `-OnPremisesOrganizationalUnit`, the newly created object will be created in the default `CN=Users` container. You can move it later if you desire.

   ```
   New-RemoteMailbox -Name "Chicago MTR02" -UserPrincipalName `
   $TeamsRoomCredential.Username -Password $TeamsRoomCredential.Password `
   -Room AccountDisabled $false -PrimarySmtpAddress `
   $TeamsRoomCredential.Username -ResetPasswordNextLogon $false -Alias `
   ChicagoMTR02 -SamAccountName ChicagoMTR02
   ```

While the security principal has been configured on-premises, you'll still need to configure either the cloud mailbox or on-premises mailbox with the appropriate calendar processing parameters, just like you did in the online-only section. You can reuse the scripting format to configure the same options, substituting the new mailbox name:

1. Connect to Exchange Online (for a cloud mailbox) or the Exchange Management Shell (for an on-premises mailbox):

   ```
   Connect-ExchangeOnline
   ```

2. From the appropriate shell, run the following command to create a hash table of values:

   ```
   $MTRCalendarValues = @{
   'AddAdditionalResponse' = $true;
   'AdditionalResponse' = "Please arrive 5 minutes before your scheduled meeting `
   to verify equipment readiness.";
   ```

```
            'AddOrganizerToSubject' = $false;
            'AutomateProcessing' = 'AutoAccept';
            'DeleteComments' = $false;
            'DeleteSubject' = $false;
            'RemovePrivateProperty = $false
            }
```

3. Run the following command to configure the room mailbox, substituting your mailbox name:

```
Set-CalendarProcessing -Identity ChicagoMTRO2 @MTRCalendarValues
```

After successfully applying the values and updating the mailbox calendar processing parameters, the resource should be ready to license. You'll need to apply a license that permits the features that you'll be using:

1. Connect to Azure Active Directory using Microsoft Online Services (MSOnline):

```
If (!(Get-Module -ListAvailable MSOnline)) { Install-Module MSOnline }
Connect-MsolService
```

2. Retrieve a list of valid SKUs.

```
Get-MsolAccountSku | ? { $_.AccountSkuId -like "*rooms*" }
```

3. Assign a usage location (where [region] is the two-letter country code representing where the account will be used) and configure the account with a non-expiring password:

```
Set-MsolUser -UserPrincipalName ChicagoMTRO2@cohovineyards.us -UsageLocation `
[region] -PasswordNeverExpires $true
```

4. Add a meeting room license (in the format of tenant:license) to the resource account:

```
Set-MsolUserLicense -UserPrincipalName ChicagoMTRO2@cohovineyards.us `
-AddLicenses "cohovineyardsus:Microsoft_Teams_Rooms_Pro"
```

From here, you'll be able to set up your Microsoft Teams Room device per the vendor's instructions using the on-premises account credential and corresponding cloud or on-premises resource mailbox you have configured.

Work with Teams Room resource accounts

Microsoft Teams Rooms use the Exchange Online or Exchange Server mailbox for calendaring and availability. As such, you can include Teams Rooms in locations and lists to help users locate appropriate meeting room facilities.

Room lists

You can create special distribution groups called "room lists" to group standard conference rooms and Microsoft Teams rooms. Specifically, room lists contain objects of the RoomMailbox type, as shown in Figure 23-6.

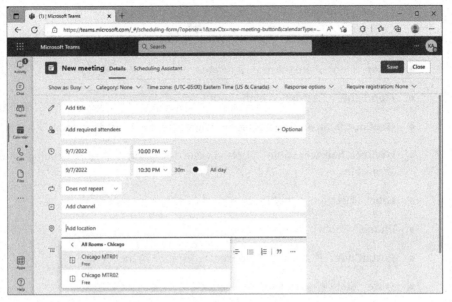

Figure 23-6   Room lists in Teams meeting invitation

Room lists are typically configured geographically, such as all rooms in a certain building or on a certain floor of a particular site.

For example, if you wanted to create a room list called **All Rooms – Chicago** containing the two rooms that were created in this section, you could connect to Exchange PowerShell and run the following command:

```
New-DistributionGroup "All Rooms - Chicago" -RoomList -Members ChicagoMTR01,ChicagoMTR02
```

Room features

A number of additional features can be configured for a room resource (whether it's a Microsoft Teams Room or a standard room). These features can only be configured for cloud-based mailboxes (either in an online-only or Exchange hybrid configuration).

Using the Set-Place Exchange Online cmdlet, you can configure the following additional properties for a room resource:

- **AudioDeviceName**   Name of the audio device located in the room

- **Building**   Description of the building where the room is located

- **Capacity**   Seating capacity

- **City**   City where the room is located

- **CountryOrRegion**   Two-letter ISO code for the country where the room is located

- **DisplayDeviceName**   Name of the video device located in the room

- **Floor**   Floor where the room is located

- **FloorLabel**   Description of the floor

- **GeoCoordinates**   Geographic coordinates for the building or room

- **IsWheelChairAccessible**   Boolean value describing whether the room is wheelchair accessible

- **Label**   Description for the room

- **Phone**   Room phone number

- **PostalCode**   Postal or ZIP code for the location of the room

- **State**   State where the room is located

- **Street**   Physical street address where the room is located

- **Tags**   Comma-separated list of tags for the room, such as "Skyline view" or "Cafeteria access"

- **VideoDeviceName**   Name of the video device in the room

You can specify as many parameters as you like to describe a room more accurately. These features can help filter rooms when searching for an appropriate location in the Room Finder. Set-Place requires an identity but also takes pipeline input.

For example, if you wanted to update all the Chicago MTR rooms you created during the previous example with the -IsWheelChairAccessible, -City, and -Floor properties, you could run the following command from the Exchange Online PowerShell:

```
Get-Mailbox -RecipientTypeDetails RoomMailbox -Name ChicagoMTR* | Set-Place `
-IsWheelChairAccessible $True -City Chicago -Floor 3
```

Currently, the Teams interface does not allow you to search or filter beyond the room list name. To search for rooms matching certain criteria, use the Room Finder in Outlook or Outlook Web App. Figure 23-7 shows the Room Finder in the Outlook Web App.

Next, we'll start configuring the holiday settings that your organization recognizes.

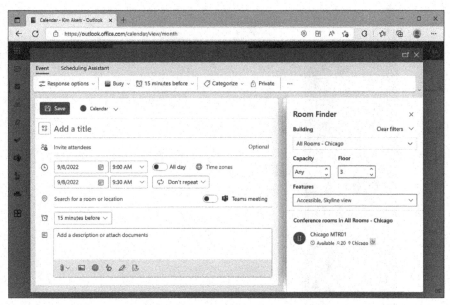

Figure 23-7   Using the Outlook Room Finder

Holidays

The Teams Phone Holidays configuration allows you to establish a list of days or periods that your organization recognizes for time away. The Holidays configuration can be used to direct different behaviors or actions for the auto attendant during the observed periods.

TIP

If you've already explored auto attendants, you might have noticed that you can configure a list of holidays during the configuration wizard. However, if you break away to follow the option to create holidays, all settings in the auto attendant will be lost, and you'll have to start over. To avoid creating more work, we recommend creating holidays before configuring an auto attendant.

To configure a holiday, use this procedure:

1. From the Teams admin center at *https://admin.teams.microsoft.com*, expand Voice and choose Holidays.

2. Click Add.

3. Fill out the Name of the holiday.

4. Under Dates, click Add New Date, as shown in Figure 23-8.

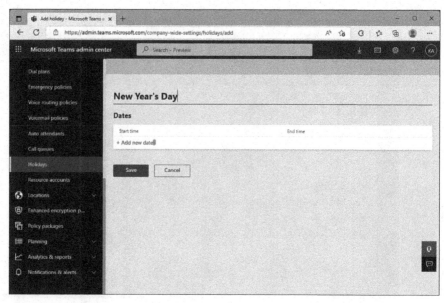

Figure 23-8   Holidays configuration page

5. Under the Start Time column, select +Add New Date to set the start date and the starting time. In the End Time column, select the ending time.

6. Repeat steps 4 and 5 to add as many recurrences as necessary for this particular holiday or observed date. Teams does not currently support automatic date recurrences, so you might want to configure several years of holidays at once, as shown in Figure 23-9.

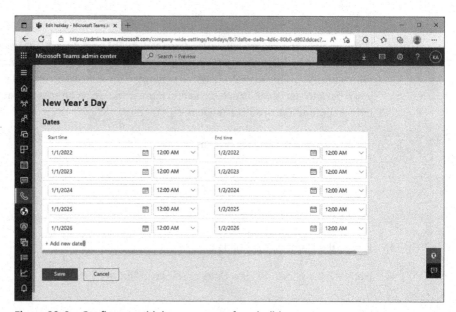

Figure 23-9   Configure multiple occurrences for a holiday

7. When finished, click Save.

Continue creating entries for holidays and other observance days where your organization will not be keeping normal business hours.

Call queues

A call queue is an intermediary waiting area where calls are held to be distributed to a group of Teams users. When an inbound call is directed to a call queue (either by directly calling the queue or being routed there by an auto attendant or another Teams user), the call is placed on hold awaiting pickup by someone known as a queue agent. A queue agent is a Teams user who is part of a call queue.

Configure call queue prerequisites

Like several other services and features in Teams, call queues require resource accounts. You can configure a resource account using the steps provided earlier in this chapter in the "Microsoft Teams advanced calling feature resource accounts" section.

TIP

Remember, you'll need to assign a Microsoft Teams Phone Resource Account license to this resource account if you want to assign it a phone number. And, if the call queue needs to redirect to an external phone number, you will need to assign the resource account either

- **A calling plan license (for Calling Plan or Operator Connect–based architectures)**
- **An online voice routing policy (Direct Routing architectures)**

Configure a call queue

Once you have configured a resource account, you can follow these steps to create a call queue using the Add A Call Queue wizard:

1. From the Teams admin center at *https://admin.teams.microsoft.com*, expand Voice and select Call Queues.

2. Click Add.

3. Enter a Name for your call queue, as shown in Figure 23-10.

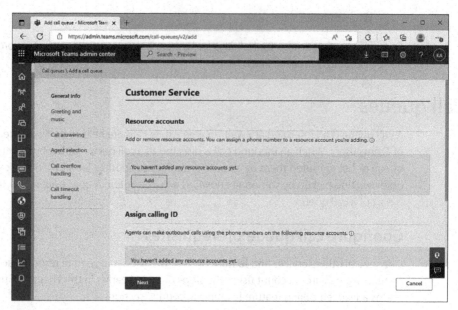

Figure 23-10   Add a call queue wizard

4. Under Resource Accounts, click Add to open the Add Accounts flyout.

5. In Add Accounts flyout, add the accounts that will be connected to the call queue. You can add multiple resource accounts to this call queue if you want to support multiple dial-in numbers. When finished adding accounts, click Add on the flyout to save the configuration.

6. If you want to configure outbound calling for the queue, click Add under Assign Calling ID to assign a resource account. Outbound calls will be able to use the resource account service numbers selected here.

7. Select the resource accounts to assign for calling IDs and then click Add when finished to save.

8. Under Language, select the language used for voicemail transcription and audio playback to callers.

9. Click Next.

10. On the Greeting And Music page shown in Figure 23-11, configure the options that will control the audio experience when callers enter the queue.

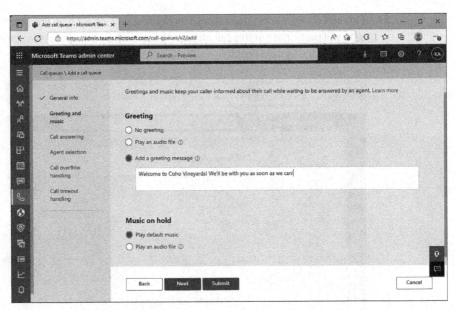

Figure 23-11   Greetings and music page

11. Under Greeting, select from the following options:

- **No Greeting**   The caller will not hear a welcome audio file or message and will be placed directly into the queue. This is the default setting.

- **Play An Audio File**   The caller will hear the supplied audio file before being placed into the queue. The file must be less than 5MB and must be in either MP3, WAV, or WMA format.

- **Add A Greeting Message**   The system will use text-to-speech to read a typed message.

Under Music On Hold, select from the following options:

- **Play Default Music**   Play the default music supplied by the Microsoft Teams Phone platform. This is the default setting.

- **Play An Audio File**   The caller will hear a supplied audio file. The file must be less than 5MB and must be in either MP3, WAV, or WMA format.

12. Click Next to proceed to the next wizard page. (Clicking Submit will save your choices and exit the wizard.)

13. On the Call Answering page shown in Figure 23-12, select how you want to identify users who will participate in this call queue. All users who participate must be licensed with a Teams Phone System license.

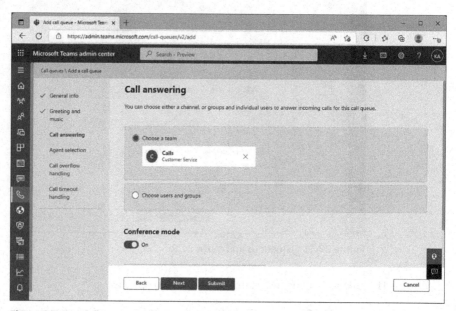

Figure 23-12   Call answering page

- **Choose A Team**   With this option, you choose an existing team and channel to be connected to the queue. The selected channel will become a voice-enabled channel. The maximum number of agents who can participate in a team-based call queue is 200. With a voice-enabled channel, agents can chat and collaborate inside the channel while taking queue calls.

- **Choose Users And Groups**   Select specific users or groups (distribution lists, Microsoft 365 groups, or security groups) to be connected to the queue. You can select up to 20 agents individually or up to 200 agents using groups.

14. Select whether to have conference mode enabled for connecting calls to agents. With conference mode enabled, agents are connected to the call via an ad-hoc conference. With conference mode disabled, agents are connected to the call through a more traditional call transfer process. Ad-hoc conferences provide quicker connection, but Skype for Business endpoints cannot participate in the call queue if conference mode is enabled. Conference mode is enabled by default.

15. Click Next.

16. On the Agent Selection page, under Routing Method, choose how agents will receive calls from the available options:

    - **Attendant Routing**   Incoming calls will ring all the logged-in agents simultaneously. The first agent to pick up is connected to the call; other agents receive a notification that the call has been picked up by an agent. This is the default setting.

    - **Serial Routing**   Incoming calls will ring available agents individually, starting from the beginning of the membership list (depending on how they were added to the queue). If they were added individually, Teams dials the agents in the order they were added. If they were added through group memberships, they will be sorted and dialed by the agents' last names.

    - **Round Robin**   Calls are distributed evenly among agents.

    - **Longest Idle**   Calls will ring agents that have been idle the longest. Configuring call answering for the longest idle will disable the presence-based routing option.

17. Choose whether to enable presence-based routing. If enabled, logged-in agents will only receive calls when their Teams presence state is marked as Available. Presence-based routing also honors a user's Do Not Disturb (DND) status. If disabled, logged-in agents will receive calls regardless of their presence indicator. Presence-based routing is enabled by default.

NOTE

Agents who have signed into a queue with Skype for Business will not receive calls if longest idle or presence-based routing is enabled.

    - By default, the Call Agents Can Opt Out Of Taking Calls slider is set to Enabled and allows agents to opt-out of the call queue. Disable if desired.

    - Configure the Call Agent Alert Time (Seconds) setting, which controls the maximum amount of time the queue will wait for an agent to pick up before moving to the next agent. The default value is 30 Seconds.

18. Click Next.

19. The settings on the Call Overflow Handling page determine how waiting calls are managed in the queue:

    - **Maximum Calls In The Queue**   This setting specifies the maximum number of waiting calls (also known as the Queue Depth) in the queue. The default value is 50.

    - **When The Maximum Number Of Calls Is Reached**   This setting specifies how to handle additional calls once the queue size is exceeded.

- **Disconnect**   Hang up the call. This is the default setting.

- **Redirect This Call To**   Choose from a list of redirect options, including Person In The Organization, Voice App (Auto Attendant Or Call Queue), External Phone Number, Voicemail (Personal), and Voicemail (Shared).

20. Click Next.

21. The settings on the Call timeout handling page determine how to manage calls after a defined wait time has been exceeded:

   - **Maximum Wait Time**   Enter a value for the maximum time that a call should remain on hold before being acted upon. The default value is 20 minutes.

   - **When A Call Times Out**   This setting specifies how to handle calls when the Maximum Wait Time Value has been exceeded.

   - **Disconnect**   Hang up the call. This is the default setting.

   - **Redirect This Call To**   Choose from a list of redirect options, including Person In The Organization, Voice App (Auto Attendant Or Call Queue), External Phone Number, Voicemail (Personal), and Voicemail (Shared).

22. Click Submit to save the call queue configuration.

Repeat these steps for any additional call queues that your organization might need.

Voice-enabled channels

A voice-enabled channel (VEC) is created when you connect a call queue's membership to a team channel.

> ## NOTE
>
> **Voice-enabled channels are only available in the full Microsoft Teams desktop client.**

All members of the channel who have Teams Phone System licenses are automatically included in the call queue. To view a voice-enabled channel, simply navigate to the channel within Teams. Voice-enabled channels will have a Calls tab available, as shown in Figure 23-13.

Inbound calls to the call queue are displayed on the center History pane. The All filter displays all inbound calls, while the Voicemail filter displays only unanswered inbound calls where the caller left a voicemail.

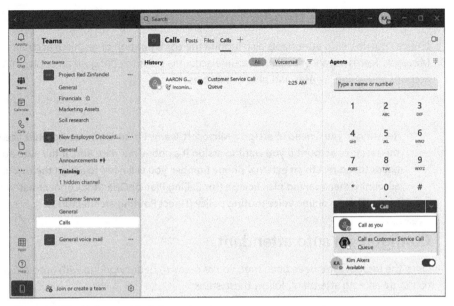

Figure 23-13 Voice-enabled channel

The Agents pane on the client's right side displays the dial pad and a toggle that indicates whether the agent is signed into the queue or not.

When entering a number into the dial pad, agents can choose how they want their outbound number displayed (if the appropriate calling line ID parameters have been configured).

In addition to the special Calls tab, agents have full use of the standard collaboration features available with Microsoft Teams.

Auto attendants

You can think of an auto attendant as a menu of options presented to a caller. Auto attendants provide a mechanism to allow for call routing in the Teams Phone environment based on data received from dual tone, multi-frequency (DTMF) keypresses or through voice input from the caller. Auto attendants can be used to reduce the reliance on human operators for many tasks.

After dialing a number that is connected to an auto attendant, the caller is prompted to select menu options to reach their final destination. An auto attendant configured to route to call queues can provide automated routing for departments throughout your organization.

Configure auto attendant prerequisites

Like call queues, auto attendants also require the configuration of resource accounts. Follow the Microsoft Teams advanced calling resource accounts steps to configure an appropriate resource account and assign licenses and phone numbers.

TIP

Remember, you'll need to assign a Microsoft Teams Phone Resource Account license to this resource account if you want to assign it a phone number. And, if the auto attendant needs to redirect to an external phone number, you will need to assign the resource account either a calling plan license (for Calling Plan or Operator Connect-based architectures) or an online voice routing policy (Direct Routing architectures).

Configure an auto attendant

Once the prerequisites have been met, you're ready to begin working with auto attendants. To configure an auto attendant, follow these steps:

1. From the Teams admin center (*https://admin.teams.microsoft.com*), expand Voice and select Auto Attendants.

2. Click Add.

3. Enter a Name for the auto attendant, as shown in Figure 23-14.

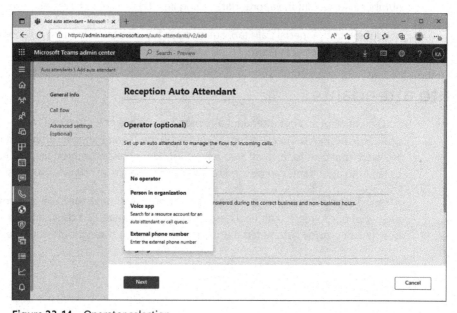

Figure 23-14   Operator selection

4. Under Operator, select from the following options:

- **No Operator**   No operator option will be available to callers. This is the default option.

- **Person In Organization**   Select a person from the Teams directory where operator assistance calls will be directed.

- **Voice App**   The operator option will route to another auto attendant or a call queue.

- **External Phone Number**   The operator option will route to an E.164-formatted PSTN number external to the Teams environment. If you are routing to an internal destination, select either Person In The Organization or a Voice App.

5. Under Time Zone, select the time zone that will be used to determine business and non-business hours.

6. Under Language, select the default language to use when reading prompts, greetings, and dial keys. The default option is the same default language configured for your tenant.

7. Under Language, slide the Voice Inputs toggle to enable or disable voice navigation features. The default setting is off.

8. Click Next.

9. On the Call Flow page, under Greeting Options, select an option for greeting callers, as shown in Figure 23-15.

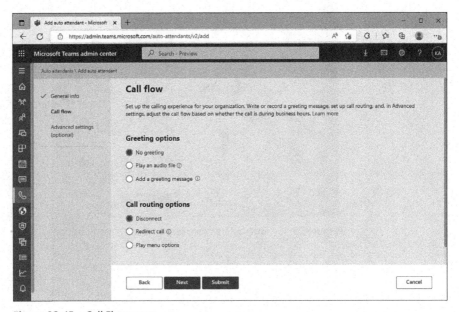

Figure 23-15   Call Flow page

The Call Flow options are explained below:

- **No Greeting**   The caller will not hear a welcome audio file or message and will be placed directly into the queue. This is the default setting.

- **Play An Audio File**   The caller will hear the supplied audio file before being placed into the queue. The file must be less than 5MB and must be in either MP3, WAV, or WMA format.

- **Add A Greeting Message**   The system will use text-to-speech to read a typed message.

10. Under Call Routing Options, select a routing destination for calls from the following options (also shown in Figure 23-16):

- **Disconnect**   Hang up the call. This is the default setting.

- **Redirect Call**   Choose from a list of redirect options, including Person In The Organization, Voice App (auto attendant or call queue), External Phone Number, and Voicemail.

- **Play Menu Options**   Choose this option to build an interactive voice response (IVR) menu.

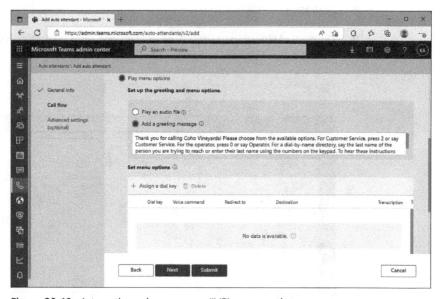

Figure 23-16   Interactive voice response (IVR) menu options

11. Under Set Up The Greeting, you can choose either:

- **Play An Audio File**   Upload a pre-recorded MP3, WAV, or WMA-formatted audio file with instructions for the voice menu.

- **Add A Greeting Message**   Enter text that will be read aloud to the caller in the auto attendant's selected language.

12. Under Set Menu Options, click Assign A Dial Key to begin building the Auto Attendant menu options, as shown in Figure 23-17.

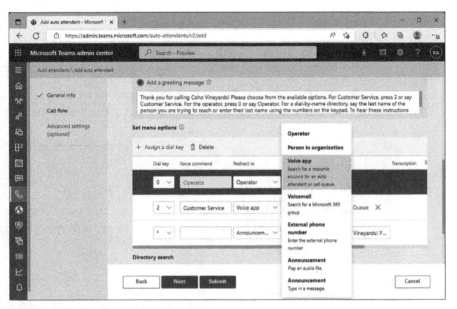

Figure 23-17   Configure AAuto Attendant

13. Under the Dial Key column, select the number that the user will dial or speak to select the option.

14. Under the Redirect To column, select the destination from the following options:

- **Operator**   The operator assigned for the auto attendant.

- **Person In Organization**   A named Teams user in the organization.

- **Voice App**   An auto attendant or a call queue.

- **Voicemail**   Voicemail associated with a Microsoft 365 group.

- **External Phone Number**   External phone number in E.164 format.

- **Announcement (Play An Audio File)**   Select this option to upload and play a specific MP3, WAV, or WMA audio file that will be played for the caller.

- **Announcement (Type In A Message)**   Select this option to type in a text message announcement that the Teams Phone platform will read back to the caller.

15. In the Voice Command column, enter words or a short phrase that callers can speak to activate the option (if voice input is enabled for the auto attendant). You can change all of the voice commands except for Operator.

16. Under Directory Search, choose from the following options:

- **None**   No directory search is available.

- **Dial By Name**   Allow the caller to search for a recipient in the directory using the keypad to spell out the name or voice input (if enabled for the auto attendant).

- **Dial By Extension**   Allow the caller to specify a recipient using the keypad to enter the extension number or voice input (if enabled for the auto attendant).

Inside Out

Working with extension numbers

To use the Dial By Extension option, directory recipients must have an extension specified in their synchronized Active Directory or Azure Active Directory user profile:

- officePhone
- homePhone
- mobile or mobilePhone
- telephonenumber or phoneNumber
- otherTelephone

The phone number must be specified in one of the following formats:

```
+<phonenumber>;ext=<extension>
+<phonenumber>;x<extension>
x<extension>
```

For example, you can set the phone number of the user Dan Jump to the US phone number (425) 555-1234 extension 5678 using one of the following formats in the supported attributes:

```
+14255551234;ext=5678
+14255551234x5678
X5678
```

After the data has been entered in any three of those formats, callers would be able to reach Dan by saying or entering 5678 on the keypad.

17. Click Next.

18. On the Call Flow For After Hours page, under Set Business Hours, you can choose to configure the business hours recognized by this auto attendant. Business hours will be calculated based on the time zone selected on the General info page at the beginning of the wizard. By default, business hours are configured for 24 hours per day, 7 days per week. You can add multiple blocks of time. Calls received outside business hours will be handled by the after hours call flow. To mark a day as being a non-business day, change the Start At and End At times for that day to None, as shown in Figure 23-18.

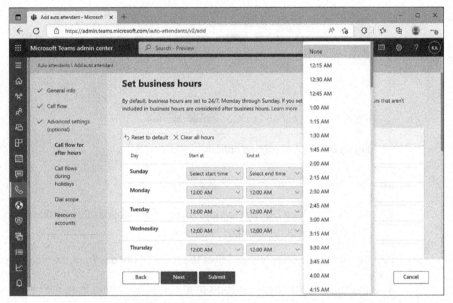

Figure 23-18   Configure business hours

19. Under Set Up After Hours Call Flow, configure the Greeting Options and Call Routing Options, as shown in Figure 23-19. The available options are the same as the ones appearing on the Call Flow page earlier in the wizard.

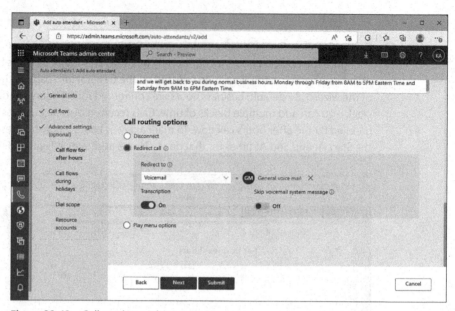

Figure 23-19   Call routing options

20. Click Next.

21. On the Call Flows During Holidays page, under Holiday Call Settings, click Add to add one of the preconfigured holidays to the list.

22. Configure a holiday Name. Select the relevant holiday from the Holiday dropdown.

23. Under Greeting, select the appropriate greeting setting from the following options:

   - **No Greeting**   No greeting is played.

   - **Play An Audio File**   A pre-recorded audio message is played.

   - **Add A Greeting Message**   The Teams Phone platform reads the text of a message to the caller.

24. Under Call Routing Options, select from the following choices (see Figure 23-20):

   - **Disconnect**   Disconnect the call.

   - **Redirect Call**   Redirect the call to one of the following destinations:

      ▼ **Person In Organization**   Redirect to a named person in the directory.

      ▼ **Voice App**   Redirect to an auto attendant or call queue.

▼ **External Phone Number**   Redirect to an external number entered in the E.164 format.

▼ **Voicemail**   Deliver a voicemail message to the specified Microsoft 365 group.

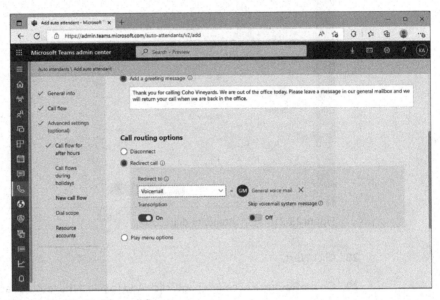

Figure 23-20   Holiday call flow

■ **Play Menu Options**   Use the options to configure an Auto Attendant menu.

25. Click Save to save the holiday configuration.

26. Repeat steps 21–25 to add additional holidays. When finished, click Next.

27. Use the Include and Exclude settings on the Dial Scope page to configure the users that will appear in the directory, as shown in Figure 23-21. If you choose to configure scope restrictions by group, you can use a security group, distribution group, or Microsoft 365 group.

CHAPTER 23

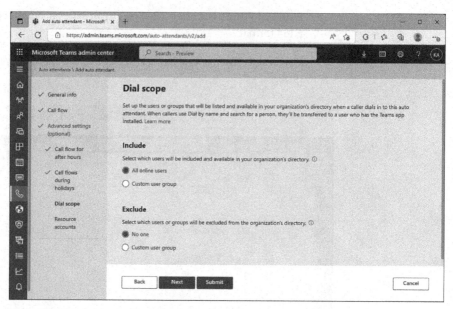

Figure 23-21   Auto attendant dial scope

28. Click Next.

29. On the Resource Accounts page, click Add to select the resource account.

30. Click Submit when finished.

After the auto attendant has been configured, you can begin testing with it to ensure the options work as intended.

Check auto attendant voicemail

While configuring an auto attendant, you might have chosen the option to leave a voicemail message with a Microsoft 365 group.

To check a voicemail message sent to a Microsoft 365 group, follow these steps:

1. Open Outlook or navigate to Outlook Web App at *https://outlook.office.com*.

2. Expand Groups and select the Microsoft 365 group used as a voicemail recipient in an auto attendant.

3. If you have enabled transcription for the voice message, it will appear in the body of the message. The actual audio of the voice message will be attached as an MP3 file, as shown in Figure 23-22.

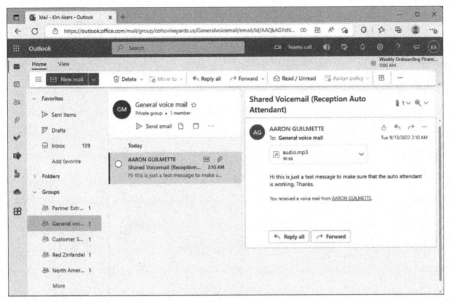

Figure 23-22 Check voicemail for a Microsoft 365 group

Members who are added to the Microsoft 365 group will automatically be able to view and listen to voicemail messages inside the Outlook or Outlook Web App clients.

What's next?

This chapter introduced a number of key advanced features and call routing capabilities, including resource accounts, Microsoft Teams Rooms, call queues, and auto attendants.

Auto attendants provide an interactive voice response (IVR) menu and routing capabilities while call queues enable organizations to distribute calls among groups of users. Both of these features work together to provide automation and scalability for organizations deploying the Teams Phone platform.

In the next chapter, we'll cover administering Microsoft Teams options, features, and security.

Managing Teams

Microsoft Teams has several administration areas, depending on the part of the product that you're configuring and managing.

Up to this point, we've discussed topics such as architecture, governance, and phone system. In this chapter, we're going to explore security and collaboration concepts for external organizations:

- Guest user access

- Private channels

- Shared channels

- Troubleshooting scenarios

By the end of this chapter, you should understand the various control planes available for Teams, policies affecting private and shared channel creation, and common troubleshooting scenarios.

Microsoft 365 Groups and Teams component architecture

In Chapter 19, "Microsoft Teams overview," we discussed the overall architecture of Microsoft Teams. You can review the diagram in Figure 24-1 as a refresher on the Microsoft Teams architecture components and where they fit in the Microsoft 365 ecosystem.

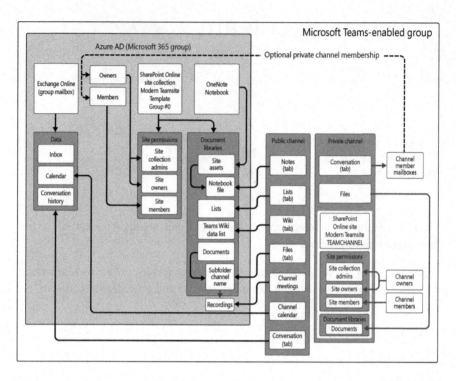

Figure 24-1 Microsoft Teams architecture

As previously mentioned in the book, Microsoft Teams extends the capabilities of the underlying Microsoft 365 group. Since the base security object is still a Microsoft 365 group, you can administer aspects of the group from other shared interfaces (such as Microsoft Exchange, Azure AD, and SharePoint Online).

Teams-specific features, such as channels and tabs, can typically only be administered from Microsoft Teams, though other products may interface with them.

While end users will find themselves administering their own objects in the Teams interface, it might be useful as administrators to interact with the objects through PowerShell.

The Microsoft Teams PowerShell cmdlets replace the Skype for Business cmdlets for voice features and incorporate several new cmdlets and options for managing objects and settings specific to Teams.

You can install the Microsoft Teams PowerShell from the PowerShell Gallery using the following command from an elevated PowerShell prompt:

```
Install-Module MicrosoftTeams
```

> ## Inside Out
>
> *Guest Access*
>
> In the Microsoft 365 environment, an external sharing invitation has traditionally generated a guest identity in Azure AD for the external recipient. With the evolution of Microsoft 365 and business-to-business (B2B) identity federation, the default option for new tenants has been changed to utilize ad-hoc recipients in place of generating guest identities. Ad-hoc users have fewer capabilities but might be less desirable from an auditing and reporting perspective.
>
> Depending on your organization's auditing and security requirements, you can revert to the previous behavior.
>
> You can find the necessary steps to change the behavior under "How external sharing works" in Chapter 26, "SharePoint Online planning and deployment."

Collaboration management

As Microsoft's hub for collaboration and teamwork, Teams provides individuals with several ways to communicate and share data with others—whether those individuals are in the same or different organizations or are external.

Access control planes

The collaboration security controls can be managed in a few places, including:

- Microsoft 365 admin center

- Azure AD portal

- Microsoft Teams admin center

- SharePoint Online admin center

Microsoft 365 admin center

The Microsoft 365 admin center provides some controls for managing external sharing with guests.

Microsoft Teams

To manage the Microsoft Teams settings in the admin center, follow these steps:

1. Navigate to the Microsoft 365 admin center (*https://admin.microsoft.com*), expand Settings, and click Org Settings.

2. On the Services tab, select Microsoft Teams, as shown in Figure 24-2.

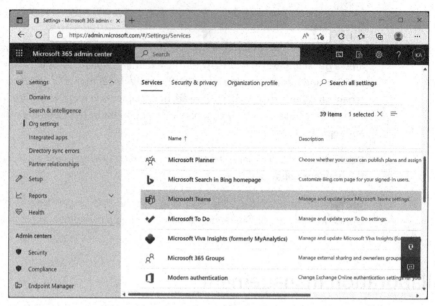

Figure 24-2   Microsoft 365 admin center services

3. Review the options on the Microsoft Teams flyout menu shown in Figure 24-3. Under Turn On Teams For Users With The Following Licenses section, the Business & Enterprise and Other checkboxes are enabled by default in Worldwide Commercial and Government tenants but turned off for Education tenants. These settings control the Enterprise Apps registration setting in the Azure portal. If you disable these settings, users will receive the following error when attempting to access Microsoft Teams:

"You're missing out! Ask your admin to enable Microsoft Teams for <CompanyName>" or "Microsoft Teams Web Client is disabled."

4. Under Guest Access, the Allow Guest Access In Teams checkbox is selected by default. Broadly, this organization-wide setting allows content sharing within Microsoft Teams with external guests. If this setting is disabled, it automatically disables the Allow Guest Access In Teams setting in the Teams admin center.

Changes to the Guest Access checkbox can take up to four hours to take effect.

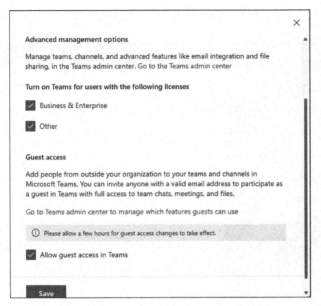

Figure 24-3 Microsoft Teams Service options

Microsoft 365 Groups

Because Microsoft Teams is based on Microsoft 365 Groups, the Microsoft 365 Groups setting also has an impact on how external access is managed.

To manage the Microsoft 365 Groups settings, follow these steps:

1. Navigate to the Microsoft 365 admin center (*https://admin.microsoft.com*), expand Settings, and click Org Settings.

2. On the Services tab, select Microsoft 365 Groups.

3. Under Guests, as shown in Figure 24-4, manage the available options:

   - **Let Group Owners Add People Outside Your Organization To Microsoft 365 Groups As Guests** This setting controls whether group owners can add guest objects to Microsoft 365 Groups and teams. This setting prohibits guests from being added to a team, even if the guest object already exists in the directory.

   - **Let Guest Group Members Access Group Content** If this checkbox is cleared, guests do not inherit the member access to files and content in the team, though they can still access files in the team that have been explicitly shared with them.

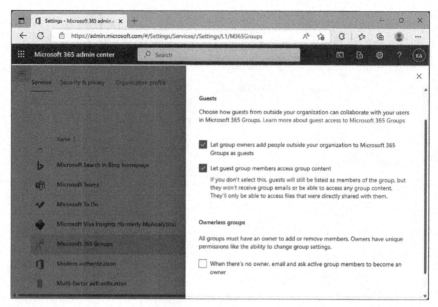

Figure 24-4   Microsoft 365 Groups settings

4.   Scroll to the bottom of the flyout menu and click Save.

After these options are updated, it might take a brief synchronization update to make them fully effective. If you clear either of these options, group memberships will be unchanged, but further external users won't be able to be added to groups, and existing access privileges relying on inherited permissions from the group membership will stop working.

Sharing settings

The Microsoft 365 admin center also provides another sharing management, which allows users to add new guests to the organization. Follow these steps to enable it:

1.   Navigate to the Microsoft 365 admin center (*https://admin.microsoft.com*), expand Settings, and click Org Settings.

2.   On the Security & Privacy tab, select Sharing.

3.   Select the Let Users Add New Guests To The Organization option, as shown in Figure 24-5. Clearing the checkbox updates the guest invitation settings only to allow administrators to invite guests to the environment.

Sharing

When this setting is selected, all users can add people outside the organization as guests, so they appear on the Guest users page. When this setting isn't selected, only admins can add guests. Learn more about guests in your organization.

You can also change the external sharing settings for SharePoint.

☑ Let users add new guests to the organization

Save

Figure 24-5   Sharing guest control in the Microsoft 365 admin center

This setting affects all products, including Microsoft Teams and SharePoint Online.

Azure AD portal

External identity controls can also be managed in the Azure AD portal. To configure settings, follow these steps:

1. Navigate to the Azure AD portal (*https://portal.azure.com*).

2. In the search bar, enter **External identities**.

3. From the navigation bar, select External Collaboration Settings, as shown in Figure 24-6.

CHAPTER 24

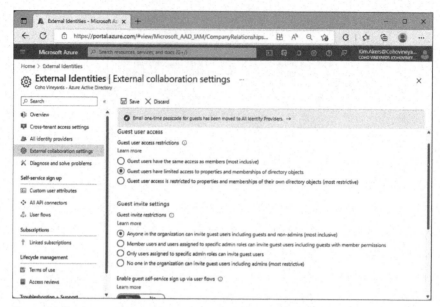

Figure 24-6   Azure AD portal External Collaboration Settings

4. Under Guest User Access, choose the setting that meets your organization's requirements from the following options:

    ■   **Guest Users Have The Same Access As Members (Most Inclusive)**   Guests can view directory object data with the same security restrictions as member objects.

    ■   **Guest Users Have Limited Access To Properties And Memberships Of Directory Objects**   Guests can see the memberships of all non-hidden groups. This is the default setting.

    ■   **Guest User Access Is Restricted To Properties And Memberships Of Their Own Directory Objects (Must Restrictive)**   Guests can't see memberships of any groups, including groups they're in, and they can only view their own user profile data.

5. Under Guest Invite Settings, choose the Guest Invite Restrictions setting to meet your organization's requirements from the following options:

    ■   **Anyone In The Organization Can Invite Guest Users Including Guests And Non-Admins (Most Inclusive)**   Broadest invitation setting, allowing everyone to invite additional guests. This is the default setting.

- **Member Users And Users Assigned To Specific Admin Roles Can Invite Guest Users Including Guests With Member Permissions**   Tenant members, admins, and those who have been granted the Guest Inviter role can invite guests.

- **Only Users Assigned To Specific Admin Roles Can Invite Guests**   This option restricts invitations to the Global Administrator, User Administrator, and Guest Inviter roles.

NOTE

Clearing the Allow Guest Access In Teams In The Microsoft 365 Admin Center checkbox simultaneously configures this option.

- **No One In The Organization Can Invite Guest Users Including Admins (Most Restrictive)**   This option prevents new guests from being added.

6. Choose an option for Enable Guest Self-Service Sign Up Via User Flows. Choosing Yes enables developers to create applications that allow guests to initiate a request for a guest account. Choosing No prevents guests from self-registering. The default setting is Yes.

7. Under External User Leave Settings, choose an option for Allow External Users To Remove Themselves From Your Organization (Recommended). Choosing Yes enables guest users to remove themselves from the organization. Choosing No means guests must ask an administrator to remove their account.

8. Under Collaboration Restrictions, configure the setting to meet your organization's requirement from the following options:

   - **Allow Invitations To Be Sent To Any Domain (Most Inclusive)**   Guest invitations can be sent to users at any domain. This is the default setting.

   - **Deny Invitations To The Specified Domains**   Guest invitations can be sent to users at any domain except those listed.

   - **Allow Invitations Only To The Specified Domains (Most Restrictive)**   Invitations may only be sent to the listed domains.

9. Click Save to finalize the configuration.

After saving the settings, the options configured under the Collaboration Restrictions section will impact the ability for users to generate sharing invitations to new guests from connected applications, including SharePoint Online and Teams.

CHAPTER 24

Microsoft Teams admin center

The Microsoft Teams admin center also has an interface for managing the availability of guest access.

To update the setting, follow these steps:

1. Navigate to the Teams admin center (*https://admin.teams.microsoft.com*).

2. Expand Users and select Guest Access.

3. Under Allow Guest Access In Teams, select either On or Off. See Figure 24-7.

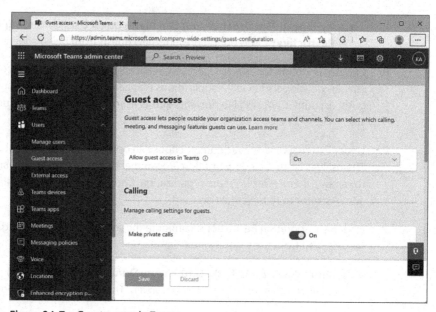

Figure 24-7   Guest access in Teams

4. Click Save.

Enabling or disabling guest access from the Teams admin center prevents users from adding guests from the Teams interface. This setting also extends to other guest user application scenarios with other workloads.

SharePoint Online admin center

Because Microsoft Teams uses SharePoint Online to host content, the access control settings you configure in the SharePoint admin center directly impact sharing capabilities in Teams.

To access the sharing controls, follow these steps:

1. Navigate to the SharePoint admin center.

2. Expand Policies and select Sharing to review the organizational controls, as shown in Figure 24-8.

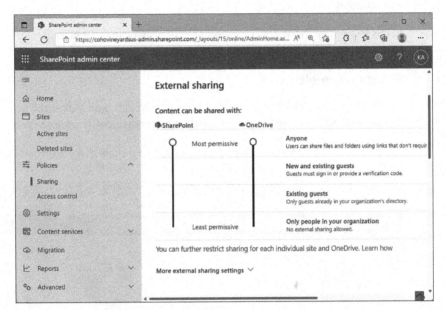

Figure 24-8   SharePoint external sharing controls

3. Adjust the slider controls as desired.

Both SharePoint and OneDrive have individual sharing controls settings. As mentioned elsewhere, OneDrive for Business is a personalized site collection that is part of the SharePoint Online service. As such, you cannot configure a OneDrive for Business sharing control with a more permissive setting than the SharePoint setting.

NOTE

When you move the Most Permissive/Least Permission slider for SharePoint from Anyone to a more restrictive setting, the Anyone With A Link radio button becomes unavailable in the File And Folder Links section.

In addition to managing the tenant-wide sharing settings, you can implement further sharing controls on the individual sites connected to teams. It's important to note that if you block external sharing at the tenant level, settings at the site level have no effect.

For a more in-depth look at the sharing controls and settings available in the SharePoint admin center, see Chapter 26, "SharePoint Online planning and deployment."

Channel controls

As you saw in the previous section, many settings across many control planes are used to manage access to Teams.

In this section, we'll look at two different features that can be used to grant or restrict access to channel content.

Private channels

Private channels have a more restrictive access control list than the overall team. Private channels are indicated by a lock icon and can have members directly added to them.

Figure 24-9 shows a member being added to a private channel named Financials.

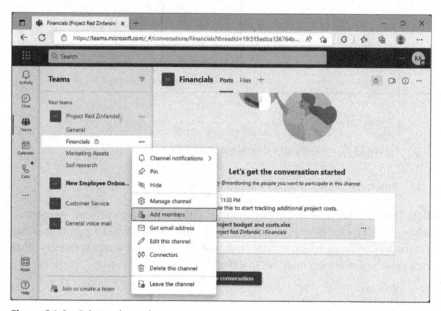

Figure 24-9   Private channels

When adding someone to a private channel, the user interface specifically indicates that the channel is private, as shown in Figure 24-10.

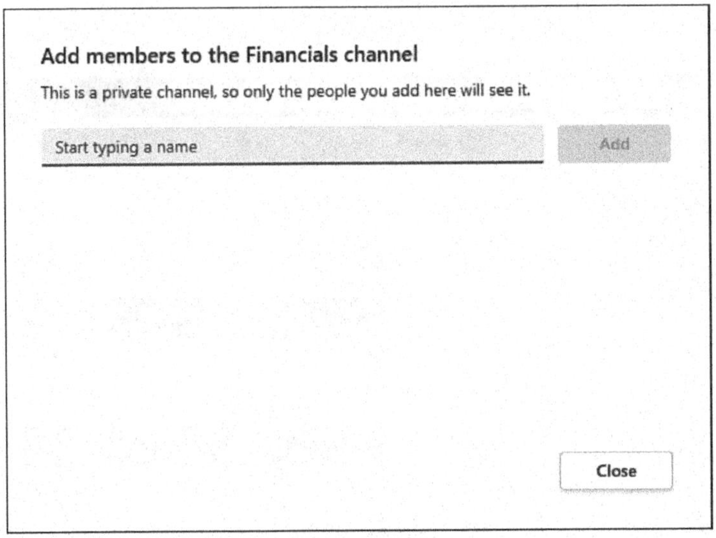

Add members to the Financials channel

This is a private channel, so only the people you add here will see it.

| Start typing a name | Add |

Close

Figure 24-10   Adding members to a private channel

Private channels store their file content in a standalone SharePoint site with its own unique permissions set that contains only the members of the private channel.

TIP

The SharePoint site for a private channel is connected to its parent team by the `RelatedGroupId` property. The `RelatedGroupId` property on the private channel's SharePoint site is mapped to the parent team's `objectGuid`.

The ability to create private channels can be controlled at two levels: the organization level and the team level.

Team-level settings

To manage private channel creation at the team level, a team owner can use these steps:

1.   From Microsoft Teams, select the Teams app on the App bar.

2.   Select a team and then click the ellipsis to open the context menu.

3.   Select Manage Team, as shown in Figure 24-11.

CHAPTER 24

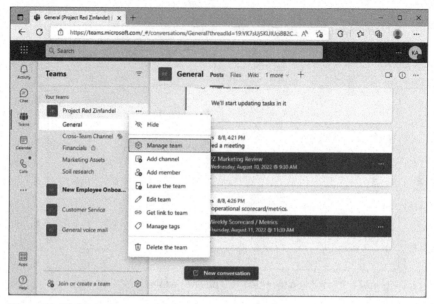

Figure 24-11   Manage team settings

4.   Choose the Settings tab and expand Member Permissions.

5.   Select the Allow Members To Create Private Channels To Enable Private Channel Creation or clear the checkbox for this setting to disable private channel creation, as shown in Figure 24-12.

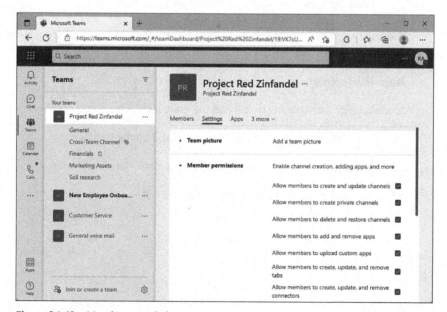

Figure 24-12   Member permissions

The setting for managing private channels at a team level has no effect if the organization-wide setting disables it.

Org-level settings

Private channel creation can also be managed via a Teams policy. To create or edit a Teams policy, follow these steps:

1. Navigate to the Teams admin center (*https://admin.teams.microsoft.com*).

2. Expand Teams and select Policies.

3. On the Manage Policies tab, click Add to add a new policy, or select an existing policy and click Edit.

4. On the Teams Policy flyout menu, slide the Create Private Channels toggle to On to enable private channel creation; slide it to Off to disable the creation of private channels. See Figure 24-13.

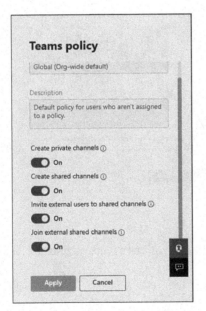

Figure 24-13   Teams policy flyout menu

5. Click Apply to save the policy.

The policy can be applied to individuals by selecting Manage Users > Assign Users or by selecting a group on the Group Policy Assignment tab.

Shared channels

Like private channels, shared channels also maintain a membership unique to the channel. Whereas a private channel contains members from the parent team, a shared channel can contain individuals from anywhere in the organization and external guests.

Shared channels are depicted in the Teams interface with an interlocking loop icon, as shown in Figure 24-14.

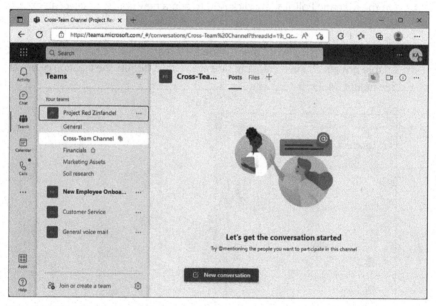

Figure 24-14   Shared channel

Shared channels can be shared with individuals as well as with other teams. See Figure 24-15.

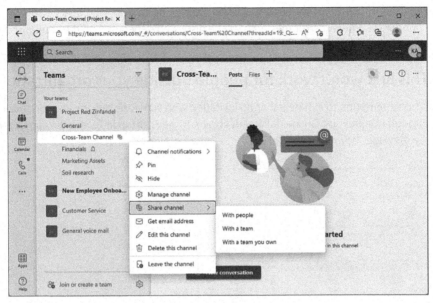

Figure 24-15   Shared channel invitation options

Shared channels are a feature that only team owners can use. The use of shared channels is governed at the org level. To configure a policy for shared channels, follow these steps:

1. Navigate to the Teams admin center (*https://admin.teams.microsoft.com*).

2. Expand Teams and select Policies.

3. On the Manage Policies tab, click Add to add a new policy or select an existing policy and click Edit.

4. On the Teams Policy flyout menu, slide the Create Shared Channels toggle switch On to enable shared channel creation or Off to disable shared channel creation.

The policy can be applied to individuals by selecting Manage Users > Assign Users or by selecting a group through the Group Policy Assignment tab.

Troubleshooting

With so many control planes, it can be difficult to narrow down what can be affected by a particular restriction—especially since many error messages don't give you the necessary information to completely troubleshoot the issue.

End users might report various errors when attempting to work with peers across organizational boundaries. Different error messages will be displayed depending on the configured access control plane.

This link won't work for people outside your organization.

When attempting to initiate a sharing invitation with someone outside your organization (either through a SharePoint Online document library or the Files tab in Teams), an end user might see the message shown in Figure 24-16.

Figure 24-16   SharePoint Online sharing error message

This error message can be caused by configuring the setting under Collaboration Restrictions in the Azure AD portal to either Deny Invitations To Specific Domains or Allow Invitations Only To The Specified Domains (Most Restrictive).

When configuring domain restrictions in the Azure AD portal, those restrictions *are not* reflected in the SharePoint Online admin center.

This error message can also occur if you clear the Let Group Owners Add People Outside Your Organization To Microsoft 365 Groups As Guests checkbox in the Microsoft 365 admin center.

We ran into an issue. Please try again later.

When attempting to add a member to a team, users might encounter the error shown in Figure 24-17.

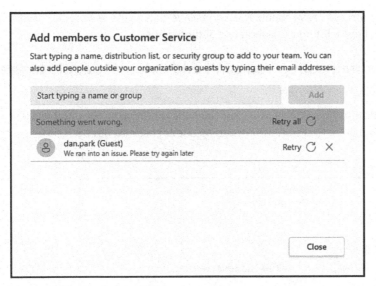

Figure 24-17   Error when adding a guest to a team

This error message can be caused by configuring the setting under Collaboration Restrictions in the Azure AD portal to either Deny Invitations To Specific Domains or Allow Invitations Only To The Specified Domains (Most Restrictive).

When configuring domain restrictions in the Azure AD portal, those restrictions *are not* reflected in the SharePoint Online admin center or the Teams admin center.

This error can also be caused by clearing the checkbox for the Microsoft 365 Groups setting Let Group Owners Add People Outside Your Organization To Microsoft 365 Groups As Guests, located in the Microsoft 365 admin center.

Your organization does not allow collaboration with the domain of the user you're inviting.

When attempting to send a sharing invitation from the Azure AD portal, you might receive the error shown in Figure 24-18.

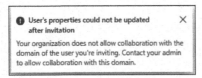

Figure 24-18   Azure AD invitation error

This error occurs if you have configured a domain restriction in the Azure AD portal on the External Identities > External Collaboration Settings page.

Due to admin policy, you can't add external people to the channel.

The error shown in Figure 24-19 can occur when the Let Group Owners Add People Outside Your Organization To Microsoft 365 Groups As Guests checkbox has been cleared in Microsoft 365 Groups.

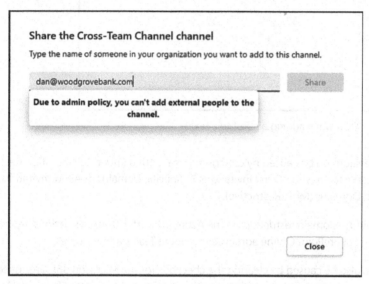

Share the Cross-Team Channel channel

Type the name of someone in your organization you want to add to this channel.

dan@woodgrovebank.com

Share

Due to admin policy, you can't add external people to the channel.

Close

Figure 24-19   Error while creating a shared channel

To resolve this issue, ensure the Let Group Owners Add People Outside Your Organization To Microsoft 365 Groups As Guests checkbox is selected in the Microsoft 365 admin center.

What's next?

The next chapter will explore SharePoint Online, including planning and deployment concepts, hybrid configurations, and data migration.

SharePoint Online is both a collaboration tool and a platform. You can use it to manage documents, lists, and tasks or extend it as a platform with business analytics integrations, dashboards, and third-party plug-ins and applications.

SharePoint Online can function as an intranet or extranet, a document storage and collaboration platform, an enterprise search portal, a social platform, or a workflow engine. In addition, it can be used as a business intelligence platform, bringing in data sets from online or on-premises databases and displaying results in enterprise dashboards, charts, or pivot tables in a browser.

SharePoint Online also provides native storage and integration with a number of other Microsoft 365 applications, such as Microsoft Teams, Power Automate, Power Apps, and Microsoft 365 groups.

SharePoint Online concepts

SharePoint Online is organized into a hierarchy system of site collections, sites, and libraries. If you are familiar with administering SharePoint Server 2007 or later on-premises, you've undoubtedly used the Central Administration web application to manage SharePoint Server farm features.

SharePoint Online has many of the same features as SharePoint Server, although some notable things are hidden, presented differently, or unavailable.

One of the advantages of SharePoint Online (and, indeed, the entire Microsoft 365 experience) is that much of the underlying management tasks are removed, leaving you with purely application-level management. Microsoft handles tasks such as scheduling and updating, and you manage the content, plug-ins, and integration with your on-premises environments.

The following list shows some features that are re-abstracted, hidden, or not available from the user interface:

1. Central administration

2. Service accounts

3. Read-only databases

4. Throttling

5. SharePoint Health Analyzer

6. Timer job management

7. Wizards

8. Individual server management and role distribution

9. Content database management

10. Access to service and web applications

11. Access to server management for updating or service management

One notable exception that has been renamed is the Term Store. In SharePoint Server on-premises, you access this through the Metadata Management Service; in SharePoint Online, the Term Store is directly accessible from the SharePoint Admin Center. You can only have one term store (which can contain 200,000 terms) in SharePoint Online.

SharePoint Online capacities

When it was originally released as part of the Business Productivity Online Suite, SharePoint Online had a number of capacity limitations. As the cost of storage and bandwidth has gone down, the product group has expanded the storage capacity and limits for the service.

Overall service limits

Some overall limits apply to all subscriptions:

1. **File sizes**   The maximum size for a single file uploaded to a library is now 250GB (raised from 15GB). For files attached to a list item, the limit is 250MB per file.

2. **Groups**   A user can belong to 5,000 groups, and each group can contain 5,000 members. You are limited to 10,000 groups per site collection.

3. **Hosted applications**   You can maintain 20,000 instances of hosted applications per tenant.

4. **Items and files**   There are several item limits to be aware of:

   - A list can have up to 30 million items. A library can also have up to 30 million items (combined folders and files). If either a list, library, or folder contains more than 100,000 items, you cannot break inheritance on that list, library, or folder (though you can for individual items).

   - A view can have up to 12 lookup columns.

   - A file name, including the path, must be fewer than 400 characters.

   - A filename stored in SharePoint Online, OneDrive for Business on Microsoft 365, and SharePoint Server 2016 cannot have any of the following characters: " * : < > ? / \ |

   - SharePoint Online has been updated to have no blocked files types. The following executable file types can be uploaded (but won't run unless custom scripting is enabled for the site where they are uploaded): `.aspx`, `.asmx`, `.ascx`, `.master`, `.xap`, `.swf`, `.jar`, `.xsf`, `.htc`.

5. **Sites**   After the release of modern groups, the maximum number of site collections per tenant was raised to 2 million.

6. **Subsites and hub sites**   You can create up to 2,000 sites per site collection. You can create up to 2,000 hub sites per tenant.

7. **Sync**   The OneDrive sync client can synchronize 100,000 items per OneDrive or team site library. The previous OneDrive sync client, Groove.exe, can sync 5,000 items per library.

8. **Users**   You can have up to 2 million users per site collection.

9. **Versions**   Each document can contain 50,000 major versions and 511 minor versions.

Individual service plan limits

In addition to the overall service limits, some limits are imposed on the various service plan levels, as shown in Table 25-1.

CHAPTER 25

Table 25-1   SharePoint service plan limits

Feature	Subscription		
	Microsoft 365 Business Essentials and Microsoft 365 Business Premium	**Microsoft 365 A3, A5, E3, E5, G3, G5** **Office 365 A1, A3, A5, E1, E3, E5, G1, G3, G5** **SharePoint Online stand-alone plans (Plan 1 and Plan 2)**	**Microsoft 365 F1 or F3, Office 365 F3**
Storage	1TB per organization base, plus 10GB per subscribed user	1TB per organization base, plus 10GB per user license purchased	1TB per organization
Terms in term store	200,000	200,000	200,000
Site collection and Microsoft 365 Groups storage	Up to 25TB per site collection or group	Up to 25TB per site collection or group	Up to 25TB per site collection or group Kiosk workers cannot administer site collections. Administration requires one enterprise user license.
Site collections and Microsoft 365 Groups	500,000 per organization, not including OneDrive for Business sites	500,000 per organization, not including OneDrive for Business sites	500,000 per organization
OneDrive storage	1TB per user	1TB per user by default; users with a OneDrive P2 license have unlimited storage.	2GB per user
Number of users	Up to 300	1–500,000+	1–500,000+

NOTE

For updated capacity information, see

- "SharePoint limits" at *http://bit.ly/3XDBA19*
- "Groups overview" at *http://bit.ly/3V8KVMW*

SharePoint Online features

SharePoint Online contains a number of features and product integrations, ranging from very basic to very complex and advanced. It includes the following:

1. OneDrive for Business

2. Office Online

3. Delve

4. Yammer

5. Enterprise search

6. Office Store apps

7. Business Connectivity Services

OneDrive for Business

Formerly known as SkyDrive Pro, OneDrive for Business is a personal SharePoint site collection. Similar in function to a home directory on a file share, a user can use the OneDrive for Business site to create and store online content, sync content between folders on-premises, or provide a collaboration space for external users. See Figure 25-1.

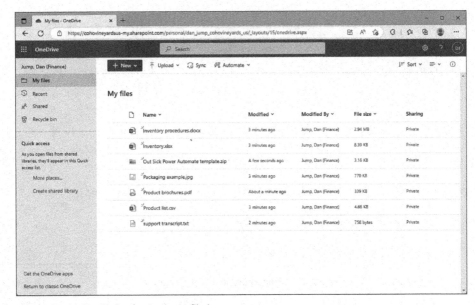

Figure 25-1   OneDrive for Business file browser

CHAPTER 25

A user is enabled for OneDrive for Business when a license for SharePoint Online is assigned. Normally, a user's OneDrive for Business site is provisioned the first time the user accesses the site, although you can provision sites ahead of time by using Windows PowerShell.

NOTE

For more information about configuring and managing hybrid OneDrive for Business, see Chapter 27, "SharePoint Online Hybrid configuration." For more information about deploying and managing OneDrive for Business, see Chapter 30, "OneDrive for Business."

Office Online

The Office Online apps are web-enabled versions of the popular Office desktop software. Applications, including Word Online, Excel Online, and PowerPoint Online, enable your users to create, view, and update documents through any browser, with no desktop software installed.

When a document is stored in either a SharePoint Online document library or a user's OneDrive site, the document is immediately available for co-authoring. Co-authoring is a Microsoft 365 feature that enables multiple people to view and edit a document at the same time. Users can edit documents with a web browser and the Office Online apps or by choosing to open the documents in their desktop application, as shown in Figure 25-2.

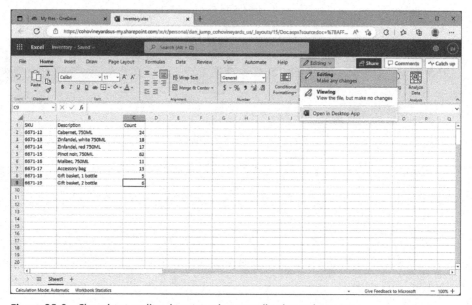

Figure 25-2   Choosing to edit a document in an application or browser

The Office Online apps are enabled automatically when a user is licensed for a SharePoint Online plan. Office Online apps can only open documents stored in SharePoint Online and SharePoint Online storage–backed applications, such as OneDrive for Business and Microsoft Teams. They cannot be used to open files stored in on-premises file shares.

Delve

Delve is an Office Graph API-based application integrated with Microsoft SharePoint and is used to display the contents of your user profile in SharePoint Online. Data in Delve is arranged on cards and displays data based on your usage as well as documents that your peers are working on. Delve cannot change permissions on any content and can only display content that you can access already. Delve discovers and displays information and documents that it thinks might be relevant to your work, based on its analysis of data stored in the Office Graph. You can disable access to the Office Graph in SharePoint settings. Your Delve profile also shows recently accessed documents and generates a list of users with whom you've recently interacted, as shown in Figure 25-3.

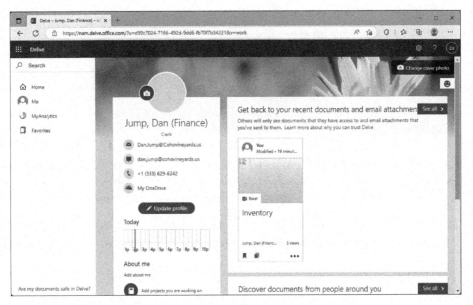

Figure 25-3 Delve

Delve is enabled automatically when a user is licensed for SharePoint Online.

CHAPTER 25

Yammer

Yammer is a post and feed-style collaboration solution, purchased by Microsoft in 2012 and integrated with Microsoft 365. Yammer enables users to post and reply to messages. Users can attach files and polls to posts. See Figure 25-4.

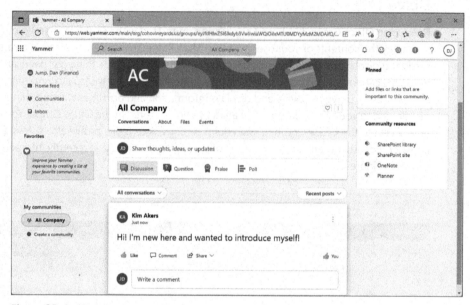

Figure 25-4   Yammer

Yammer is activated and configured outside the SharePoint interface; however, it can be integrated and replaces the Newsfeeds feature of SharePoint Online. Yammer is also used to support the live question-and-answer feature for Microsoft Teams webinars.

Access to Yammer is controlled by assigning an individual user license in the Microsoft 365 admin center. Yammer is administered separately through its own admin center as well.

Enterprise search

Although search is important to organizations of all sizes, it is vital to those with hundreds of thousands or millions of documents scattered among sites and file shares. As documents stored in file shares and sites are moved to Microsoft 365, search indexes them and makes them available for discovery.

If you configure a hybrid search solution between SharePoint Online and your on-premises SharePoint Server farm, you can present a single pane-of-glass view for content—whether your users are looking in the cloud or on the local network.

NOTE

For more information about hybrid search options and configuration, see Chapter 27, "SharePoint Online Hybrid configuration."

SharePoint Store apps

The SharePoint Online platform naturally lends itself to development. Your organization can develop its own application solutions and publish them in an app catalog available to your SharePoint Online users or sell them in the Office.com marketplace. Your organization can also purchase applications from the SharePoint Store (see Figure 25-5) and deploy them to your SharePoint Online users.

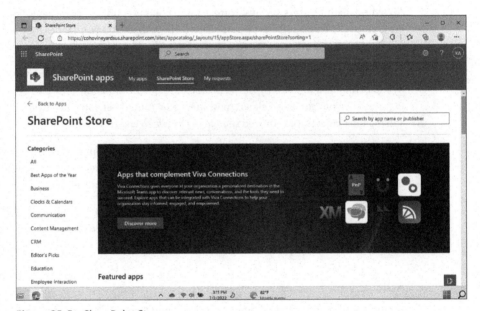

Figure 25-5   SharePoint Store

Business Connectivity Services

Using Business Connectivity Services, you can make data in other locations available in Share-Point Online for consumption, processing, visualization, and updating. External data sources might include another SharePoint Online repository, an OData source on the Internet, or a database instance available in your on-premises environment or a partner's.

Depending on configuration of the Business Connectivity Services data connector, data might be read-only or potentially written back to the data sources. With a Business Connectivity Services connector, SharePoint Online becomes a client to an external data source—whether that content is hosted in a SharePoint Server farm or even a cloud service provider's application.

SharePoint Online hybrid

You can configure hybrid coexistence and integration between an on-premises SharePoint Server farm and SharePoint Online. Some of the features of a SharePoint hybrid configuration include on-premises OneDrive redirection to Microsoft 365 and cross-environment hybrid search.

Inside Out

Hybrid differences

The SharePoint hybrid experience is unique among the Microsoft 365 stack. With Azure AD hybrid identity, users, groups, contacts, and computer objects are synchronized from on-premises to cloud and can be administered in both locations. Changes made to on-premises identities are reflected in the corresponding cloud object.

Exchange hybrid provides cross-platform coexistence and migration capabilities. The hybrid configuration not only allows mailbox users to be either on-premises or in Exchange Online, but it also allows messages to be routed between the environments and mailbox objects to be moved seamlessly between environments.

SharePoint hybrid doesn't really provide either of those functions. It does not allow the migration of content such as documents, lists, or apps between platforms. Also, it doesn't manage the synchronization of content between platforms.

It can, however, be used to provide a single-pane-of-glass user experience for storage content, enabling an easier transition to a cloud-first deployment model.

> **NOTE**
>
> For more information about configuring SharePoint Online hybrid, see Chapter 27, "SharePoint Online Hybrid configuration."

What's next?

This chapter introduced SharePoint Online concepts and features and discussed some of the capacities and limitations of the different licensing options. While SharePoint Online has many of the same features as its on-premises counterpart, SharePoint Server, it abstracts the farm and database management tasks and lets administrators and developers focus on building compelling content experiences.

SharePoint Online hybrid configuration features will be discussed in-depth in Chapter 27, "SharePoint Online Hybrid configuration," while OneDrive for Business administration will be covered in Chapter 30, "OneDrive for Business."

SharePoint Online planning and deployment

SharePoint Online has two core architecture types: the classic site architecture, which goes back to original design patterns of site collections and subsites, and the modern site architecture, which is based on Microsoft 365 groups and hub sites.

While the classic architecture components are still available, we're going to focus on the newer modern site components and structure in this book. Microsoft has pivoted development to the modern site architecture; while the classic will be available for the foreseeable future, Microsoft is encouraging organizations to migrate to the modern architecture, which supports new web parts and responsive page designs.

Planning a modern site architecture

In the classic SharePoint architecture, site collections were typically designated as business boundaries—perhaps based on the organization's regional distribution or business units. Then, sites and subsites would be placed within site collections to further divide and organize content. As the business evolved or reorganized, sites might have needed to be migrated to new site collections, breaking the hierarchical path to content and invalidating existing permissions sets.

With the modern site architecture, every site is a Microsoft 365 group-connected site collection with its own membership and permissions control. Instead of site contents being located within a navigation hierarchy, sites can now be grouped or associated together in a unit called a *hub*. This design allows sites to be reorganized easily by simply changing their hub site association. The links to documents and files in the sites stay the same, as do any of the permissions and sharing settings. This allows for a more dynamic organizing of the sites and helps organizations more easily reflect business changes in their technology infrastructure.

Planning sites and hubs

As you've already seen, with modern SharePoint, the architecture and design shifts from silos and hierarchies to more manageable atomic units.

In addition to manageability, hub site architecture helps drive navigation and manages the search scope. Initially, when users search for content, they can search the sites in the hub for the most relevant resources. They can also expand the search to include other sites outside of the hub.

Figure 26-1 depicts two hub sites with additional sites that are associated with them. In contrast to traditional SharePoint sites, notice how all the sites are individual collections from the main /sites root managed path.

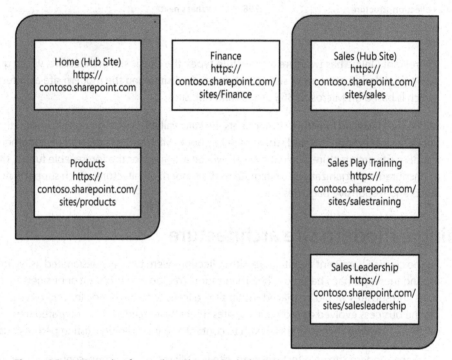

Figure 26-1   Example of a modern SharePoint hub site layout

To designate a hub, follow these steps:

1. Navigate to the SharePoint admin center.

2. Expand Sites and select **Active Sites**.

3. Select a site you want to register as a hub site.

4. From the action menu, select Hub > Register As A Hub Site.

5. On the Register As A Hub Site page, enter the name you want to use for the Hub.

6. Click Save.

Once you have at least one hub site created, you can associate sites to the hub.

Originally, hub sites could not be nested or associated in any way to build a hierarchy. In late 2021, Microsoft introduced features to enable hub sites associations with other hub sites. This feature enables cross-hub relationships for the purposes of searching content.

Associated hub sites help you create groups of related sites that can roll up into a larger set of search results. See Figure 26-2.

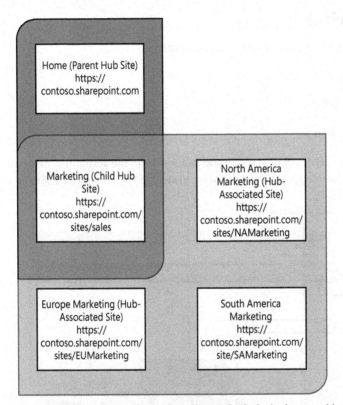

Figure 26-2   Example of a modern SharePoint hub site layout with nested hubs

Using parent and child hubs lends itself to the appearance of a hierarchy like classic SharePoint design, but each site still maintains its own security settings and absolute path. If the operating parameters of the organization change, sites and hubs can be re-associated with new hubs to help manage search without affecting the security of the content or breaking apps and links that depend on the location of documents or other data elements.

To associate a hub as a child of a parent hub, follow these steps:

1. Navigate to the SharePoint admin center.

2. Expand Sites > Active Sites.

CHAPTER 26

3. Select the existing hub you want to associate with a new parent, click Hub on the action bar, and then select Edit Hub Site Settings.

4. On the Hub Site Settings page, under Parent Hub Association, select a new parent hub.

5. Click Save.

Each site can only be associated with one hub at a time.

Planning navigation

Modern SharePoint features three types of navigation:

- Local (site) navigation

- Hub site navigation

- Global navigation

Each type of navigation has its own scope and features. With the addition of associated hubs, you can now expand and update the navigation to include the related hubs. (See Figure 26-3.)

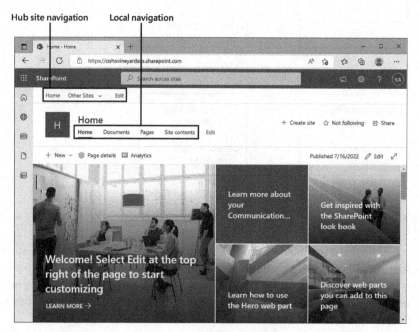

Figure 26-3   SharePoint Online Hub site navigation including associated hubs

Let's look at the various navigation methods.

Local navigation

Local navigation items on a SharePoint site (Home, Conversations, and Documents) are elements that show up on every page of your site. The local navigation is frequently referred to as Quick Launch and is located either on the left side of the page (for sites built using the Team site template) or on the page's header below the site name (for sites based on the Communications site template).

Hub site navigation

Hub site navigation elements can be applied across all sites associated with a particular hub. This enables users browsing related sites to easily navigate to resources or sites that might be common across the hub or enterprise. Hub site navigation appears above the local site navigation, as highlighted in Figure 26-4.

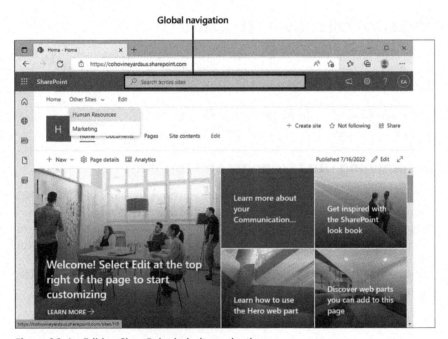

Figure 26-4   Editing SharePoint hub site navigation

Hub site navigation can be edited using the Edit button on the hub site or by selecting Change The Look under site settings and then selecting Navigation. Various theming elements can also be applied across hubs.

Global navigation

Global navigation is, as it sounds, a global navigation method available across all sites, regardless of whether they are classic, modern, or part of any hub association. Global navigation isn't natively available as part of the modern SharePoint experience yet, though it can be created and managed using SharePoint Framework Extensions (SPFx).

> **NOTE**
>
> Navigation construction is outside the scope of this book, as it's a task generally reserved for SharePoint developers. You can experiment with the settings mentioned in this section to see how adding links and displaying hub site associations affects the navigation experience for your users.

> **NOTE**
>
> For more information on configuring the navigation experience, see *https://docs.microsoft.com/en-us/sharepoint/plan-navigation-modern-experience.*

Designing site collection structure

As we've mentioned throughout, Microsoft is recommending customers use the new modern SharePoint experience. However, depending on where an organization is in its SharePoint journey, it might still have a lot of investment in classic SharePoint architecture.

Fortunately, SharePoint Online allows you to host both classic and modern sites, so organizations with highly developed legacy SharePoint environments can use them side-by-side.

Determining site taxonomy and topology

As mentioned earlier, you can decide to create your sites and associate them to hubs based on business units, regions, products, projects, or other design that makes sense. If the structure doesn't adapt well or is difficult to navigate, you can simply reassign hub site memberships to build the navigation and search topology without accidentally compromising security controls.

Managing the association of hubs is really quite simple, as demonstrated in the following example:

1. Navigate to the SharePoint admin center.

2. Expand Sites > Active Sites.

3. Select the site you want to associate to a new hub and then select Hub from the action menu, as shown in Figure 26-5.

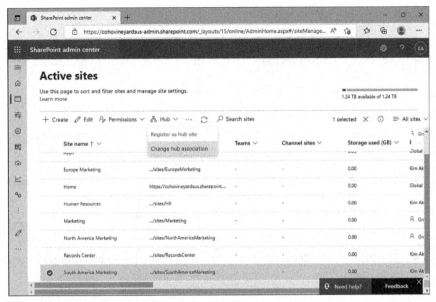

Figure 26-5   Changing a hub site association

4.   Under Hub, select Change Hub Association.

5.   Under Select A Hub, choose a new hub site for association and click Save, as shown in Figure 26-6.

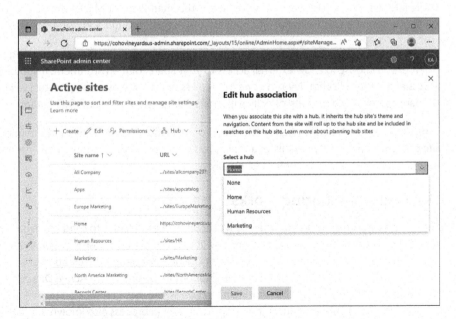

Figure 26-6   Updating a hub site association

Determining site users

Each modern SharePoint site based on the Team template is linked to a Microsoft 365 group. The group membership maps to the built-in SharePoint permissions groups.

The following default permissions exist in each site:

- **Site Owners–Full Control**   This group maps to the built-in SharePoint group Owners group and is granted Full Control over the objects. Microsoft 365 group owners are included in this group.

- **Site Members–Limited Control**   This group maps to the SharePoint group Members group and is granted the Edit permission level. Edit permissions allow users to add, delete, and edit lists, list items, and documents but cannot design the page, customize the site, or change permissions for objects.

- **Site Visitors–No Control**   This group maps to the SharePoint group Visitors group and is granted read access to pages and list items and can download documents.

If you convert the site's corresponding Microsoft 365 group to a Team (sometimes referred to as *Teamifying* a group), additional users who are added as Members or Owners will automatically inherit the corresponding SharePoint permissions.

Planning and configuring site and guest access

While internal site access is easily determined by the SharePoint or Microsoft 365 group membership, external access to SharePoint content is managed through additional controls.

One of the most important decisions to make from a security standpoint in your design is whether you choose to allow external access to your SharePoint environment. If you block access at the site collection level, no one (regardless of their site ownership status) will be able to share content from that site directly with users outside your Microsoft 365 tenant.

External access can be controlled at two levels: organization (tenant-wide) and site (modern) or site collection (classic). By default, external access is enabled organization-wide—meaning any user has the ability to share content externally.

How external sharing works

Sharing is a performative action whereby a user proactively decides to send an invitation to access data (a document, file, list, or other object type). Behind the scenes, when the recipient is external to your organization, SharePoint Online is triggering the creation of an Azure Business-to-Business (B2B) guest account in your organization's Azure Active Directory. When the external recipient receives the sharing invitation email, they can click on the link provided to complete their Azure account signup or provisioning (a process also known as invitation redemption).

Figure 26-7 shows a sharing invitation being created for an external user.

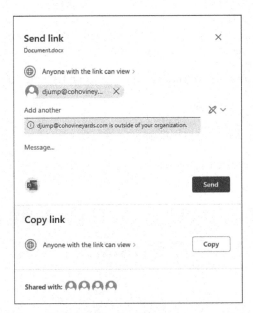

Figure 26-7 Sharing invitation

From the administration side, there are a few different sharing experiences that you can enable in your organization. Depending on the Azure External Identities configuration and the Share-Point B2B and SharePoint B2B integration settings, you might see guest identities provisioned in the Azure portal.

With the email one-time passcode option, a new guest access experience was created that allows external users to simply access content with a passcode delivered to their confirmed email address. This option does not provision a guest user identity in the sharing tenant's Azure AD. Users who are granted access in this manner are known as ad-hoc recipients.

Inside Out

Ad-hoc external recipients

Ad-hoc users are a new feature of Microsoft 365. Previously, all sharing invitations generated an Azure B2B guest user account. With the updated experience, you can choose between provisioning a guest user identity for external recipients or simply providing them access through a link to a specific file or folder.

Ad-hoc recipients have a number of restrictions placed upon them, such as not being able to edit files using Microsoft 365 apps and not being able to be made members of groups or teams. Additionally, ad-hoc recipients cannot have conditional access policies applied to them.

Some organizations might prefer to track and manage guest user identities as part of their security and auditing operations. A guest identity may be granted access to additional resources and assigned licenses for additional services.

To enable the provisioning of guest user accounts during the sharing process, follow these steps:

1. Navigate to the Azure portal (*https://portal.azure.com*) and search for External Identities.

2. Select All Identity Providers from the menu.

3. Under Configured Identity Provider, select Email One-Time Passcode.

4. Ensure the Email One-Time Passcode For Guests option is set to Yes and click Save, as shown in Figure 26-8.

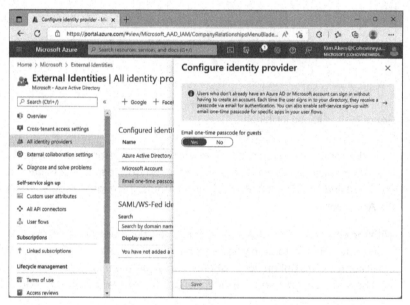

Figure 26-8   Configure identity provider

5. Launch a PowerShell session and connect to SharePoint Online using the Connect-SPOService cmdlet, supplying an appropriate credential when prompted:

```
Connect-SPOService -Url [https://<tenant>-admin.sharepoint.com
```

6. Run Set-SPOTenant to update the service parameters using the following commands, as shown in Figure 26-9:

```
Set-SPOTenant -EnableAzureADB2BIntegration $true
Set-SPOTenant -SyncAadB2BManagementPolicy $true
```

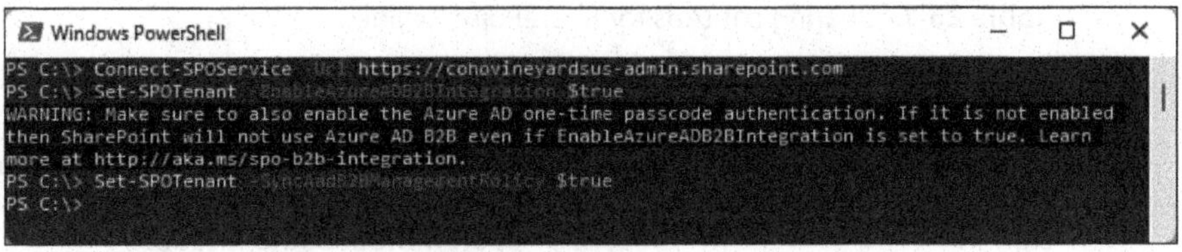

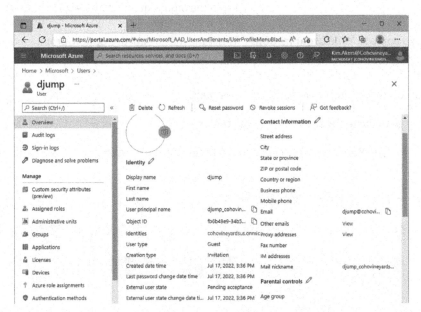

Figure 26-9   Updating the SharePoint tenant settings

When the Azure B2B SharePoint integration is enabled, sharing invitations will trigger the creation of a guest account in Azure AD. Guest accounts created during an invitation show a state of Pending acceptance until the invitation has been redeemed by the recipient, as shown in Figure 26-10.

Figure 26-10   Guest user identity provisioned after sharing invitation

Once the recipient has redeemed the invitation, the External User State Value for their guest object is updated to Accepted.

Planning and configuring sharing and site access

The Microsoft 365 platform allows for management control of external sharing capabilities at both the tenant and site levels.

At the tenant level, settings can be configured with four levels of permissiveness for both SharePoint and OneDrive, as detailed in Table 26-1.

Table 26-1   Sharing controls for SharePoint Online

Permissiveness	Description
Anyone: Users can share files and folders using links that don't require sign-in.	Previously referred to as Anonymous links, this setting allows users to create a shareable link that anyone can open without authentication.
New And Existing Guests: Guests must sign in or provide a verification code.	With this option selected, recipients receive an invitation email that they will use to complete the registration request. Sharing recipients can be new users who have never received a sharing invitation or users who have a provisioned guest identity.
Existing Guests: Only users already in your organization's directory.	With this option selected, users can only send to recipients that already have been provisioned a guest identity in the organization's Azure AD. No new external guests can be added through the sharing interface.
Only People In Your Organization: No external sharing allowed.	This is the most restrictive option, prohibiting external sharing.

To access the sharing controls, follow these steps:

1. Navigate to the SharePoint admin center.

2. Expand Policies and select Sharing to review the organizational controls, as shown in Figure 26-11.

3. Adjust the slider controls as desired.

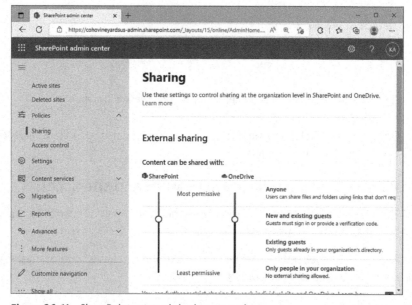

Figure 26-11   SharePoint external sharing controls

Both SharePoint and OneDrive have individual sharing control settings. As mentioned elsewhere, OneDrive for Business is a personalized site collection that is part of the SharePoint Online service. As such, you cannot configure a OneDrive for Business sharing control with a more permissive setting than the SharePoint setting.

TIP

As you move the permissiveness slider for SharePoint from Anyone to a more restrictive setting, the Anyone With A Link radio button is automatically unavailable in the File And Folder Links section.

In addition to managing the sharing settings tenant-wide, you can also implement further sharing controls on individual sites. It's important to note that if you block external sharing at the tenant level, settings at the site level have no effect.

To manage the external sharing settings for a site, use the following steps:

1. Navigate to the SharePoint admin center.

2. Expand Sites and select Active Sites.

3. Select a site to edit.

4. Select the Policies tab.

5. Under External Sharing, click Edit to update the sharing settings for the site, as shown in Figure 26-12.

6. Update the site settings and click Save.

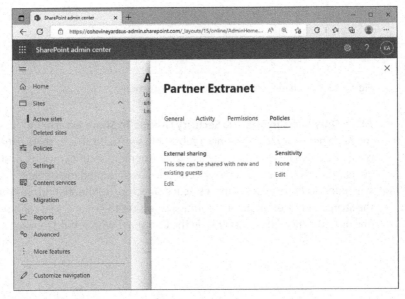

Figure 26-12   Site external sharing settings

If your organization is still developing governance for SharePoint and OneDrive, you might want to block external sharing at the tenant level until you have policies in place to manage the sharing lifecycle.

Planning security options

In addition to the SharePoint and OneDrive permissiveness settings, additional security options can be managed from the SharePoint admin center's Sharing policy:

- **Limit External Sharing By Domain**   When configuring external sharing options, you can choose to configure a list of domains to manage external sharing recipients. See Figure 26-13. The list can be used to either restrict sharing to a list of specified domains or to prevent sharing with the list of specified domains.

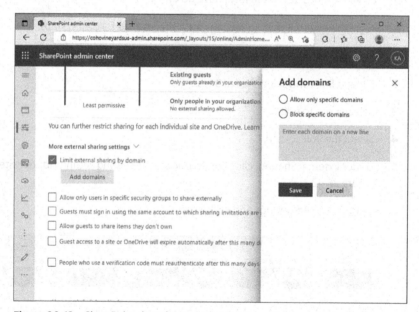

Figure 26-13   SharePoint domain control restrictions

- **Allow Only Users In Specific Security Groups To Share Externally**   In some cases, it might be necessary to allow only a subset of users to be able to share externally. You can configure delegate sharing capability to one or more security groups, as shown in Figure 26-14. You can add one or more security groups (including mail-enabled security groups synchronized from an on-premises Active Directory) to the sharing control. If you have the SharePoint external sharing permissiveness set to Anyone, you can specify either Anyone or Authenticated Guests Only in the Can Share With setting for each security group.

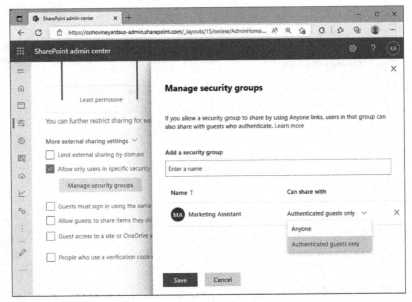

Figure 26-14   Managing sharing through security groups

- **Guests Must Sign In Using The Same Account To Which Sharing Invitations Are Sent**   This option requires that recipients of sharing invitations sign in using the email address to which the invitation was sent. When prompted, recipients must confirm the email address.

- **Allow Guests To Share Items They Don't Own**   By selecting this sharing option, you can enable guests to send sharing invitations for content they do not own.

- **Guest Access To A Site Or OneDrive Will Expire Automatically After This Many Days**   By default, sharing links will last indefinitely. Microsoft recommends configuring sharing links to expire in order to mitigate potential data loss or unintended access scenarios.

- **People Who Use A Verification Code Must Reauthenticate After This Many Days**   This option requires users with a passcode to authenticate to the directory. These users, known as ad-hoc recipients, can be required to re-confirm they are the recipient of the sharing invitation.

File and folder links

In addition to sharing and access controls, you can also specify default settings applied during the sharing invitation creation. See Figure 26-15.

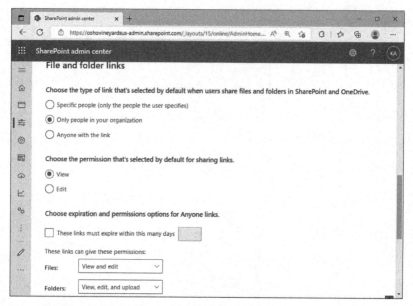

Figure 26-15   SharePoint files and folder links settings

For authenticated sharing, you can choose the default recipient scope and permission set during the sharing invitation. These are only defaults and can be changed by the individual performing the sharing action. Consult your security organization to ensure you have the best defaults set for your business requirements.

If you have enabled the Anyone With The Link permissiveness setting for external sharing requests, you can also manage the permissions assigned to them and the expiration period.

Other settings

Finally, three additional settings can be used to manage the display of links and recipients, as shown in Figure 26-16.

Using these settings, you can enable or disable notifications for file owners to see those who have accessed their shared OneDrive files. You can also choose to enable whether site owners will see who accesses files or pages in SharePoint.

To view the activity of a file in SharePoint, navigate to a document library or the pages library for a site and point to the file. The file card flyout will display access information.

The short links option changes the format of the file sharing link. If you have applications that parse the file path displayed, you might need to update them to work with this setting.

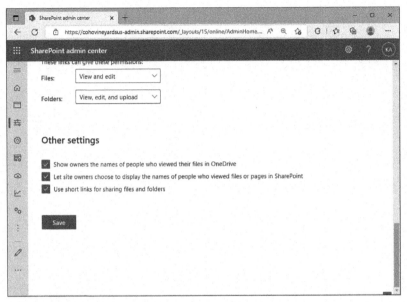

Figure 26-16 Other settings for SharePoint sharing controls

What's next?

In the next chapter, you'll begin extending the SharePoint Server environment into SharePoint Online using a variety of hybrid configuration options. These hybrid options will help you take advantage of your organization's existing SharePoint Server investment as well as provide rich connectivity to the new features and capabilities.

CHAPTER 26

SharePoint Online Hybrid configuration

SharePoint Online, as discussed in Chapter 25, "SharePoint Online overview," is a cloud-based collaboration platform comprised of sites, storage, and apps. SharePoint Online provides the storage backing for a number of cloud services and features, such as Microsoft Teams and Microsoft 365 groups.

In a SharePoint hybrid configuration scenario, you can connect your on-premises Microsoft SharePoint deployment to Microsoft 365 in a number of ways to extend your infrastructure into the cloud.

SharePoint Online Hybrid has four core components:

- **Hybrid OneDrive for Business**   Redirect SharePoint on-premises storage for user files to Microsoft 365 OneDrive for Business.

- **Hybrid Search**   Enable users to search for content in both on-premises and online systems.

- **Hybrid Taxonomy**   Create managed metadata that can be shared and updated between SharePoint 2016 on-premises and SharePoint Online systems.

- **Hybrid Auditing (SharePoint 2016 Preview Feature)**   Configure auditing to provide insights into users' online and on-premises file access activities.

Two additional types of configurations exist to complete a robust collaboration space experience:

- **App launcher**   Configure the Microsoft 365 app launcher to help users navigate between on-premises and online environments.

- **Business-to-business extranet**   Create partner sites to allow external users access to relevant online content in a members-only site.

Planning

In planning any SharePoint topology (including hybrid), the first questions you should be asking are about the business goal you're trying to achieve and how you will manage it. In the case of a hybrid OneDrive for Business configuration, maybe it's transitioning on-premises storage to the cloud. For hybrid search, maybe it's providing an integrated search platform so users can locate content on either platform. After you have identified the organizational goals and capabilities of the platforms, it's important to become familiar with the process and prerequisites of any implementation.

General

After deciding on the hybrid features to implement, ensure you meet the prerequisites for the services you intend to configure. Some services have specific requirements, whereas others are more general and apply regardless.

All SharePoint hybrid configurations have the following shared requirements:

- A supported version of SharePoint Server (2013, 2016, or 2019), where services are running locally on the farm and not federated.

- A working certificate for the SharePoint Security Token Service. By default, the hybrid picker uses the built-in certificate, but you can also use a third-party external certificate.

- Configuring any hybrid service scenario that includes SharePoint Server 2013 requires SharePoint Server Service Pack 1 (*https://go.microsoft.com/fwlink/p/?LinkId=521936*). Without it, site redirection features are unavailable.

- The Subscription Settings service application must be configured.

- The User Profile service application must be configured and Active Directory synchronized with the User Profile service.

- The App Management service application must be configured.

- My Sites must be configured.

- The Managed Metadata service application must be configured.

- Identity synchronization between Active Directory and Microsoft Azure Active Directory must be configured. For more information about configuring identity synchronization, see Chapter 9, "Identity and authentication planning," and Chapter 10, "Installing Azure AD Connect."

In addition, if your organization requires inbound hybrid services (such as hybrid search or Business Connectivity Services), you'll need the appropriate inbound firewall and proxy configurations that meet your organization's security requirements. Any inbound or reverse proxy solution must support client authentication with a wildcard or SAN SSL certificate, support pass-through authentication for OAuth 2.0, and accept traffic on TCP port 443 (HTTPS).

OneDrive for Business

Hybrid OneDrive for Business enables you to shift data consumption and sharing from your SharePoint OneDrive on-premises deployment (if it exists) to OneDrive for Business in Microsoft 365. Hybrid OneDrive for Business enables your users to continue using on-premises SharePoint sites and services in addition to cloud-based OneDrive.

Although configuring hybrid OneDrive for Business does enable you to redirect users accessing their OneDrive to Microsoft 365, it's important to note that the data migration process is *separate*. Data migration must be performed outside of the hybrid configuration process.

For more information on migrating content, see Chapter 28, "Migrating data to SharePoint Online."

Also, because there's no link or synchronization between OneDrive for Business in SharePoint Server and OneDrive for Business in Microsoft 365, the Shared With Me list in Microsoft 365 won't populate with documents shared with a user in the on-premises environment or vice versa.

Hybrid OneDrive for Business configuration also configures hybrid user profiles so that when users view a profile in SharePoint Server, they are redirected to the user's Microsoft 365 profile.

If you want to pilot hybrid OneDrive for Business, consider creating an audience in SharePoint to identify those users or using the Limit OneDrive access feature in the SharePoint admin center.

Search

Two types of search are available in SharePoint hybrid configuration: cloud hybrid search and hybrid federated search:

- **Cloud hybrid search**   Cloud hybrid search is the simplest to configure and stores the search index for all crawled content in Microsoft 365. This single index exposes all SharePoint content (including on-premises) to the Office Graph so your users can discover content inside Microsoft 365 applications such as Delve. Results are ranked based on their relevance, regardless of the source of the content, and presented in a single result.

- **Hybrid federated search**   Hybrid federated search returns content from two indices (Microsoft 365 and SharePoint Server on-premises). Results are grouped and ranked independently according to their source and then displayed in separate result blocks.

CHAPTER 27

For most organizations, cloud hybrid search is recommended. Cloud hybrid search has the following advantages:

- Users see unified search results from multiple sources.

- Your organization can begin using the updated SharePoint experience without upgrading on-premises servers to SharePoint Server 2016.

- You don't need to upgrade on-premises servers past the required updates to enable hybrid functionality.

- You don't have to upgrade your search index.

- Your organization will have a lower total cost of ownership for search, *because* no additional on-premises hardware or capacity needs to be deployed moving forward; the enterprise search index is stored in Microsoft 365.

- Office Graph applications such as Delve can present content to users.

- Cloud hybrid search is simpler to deploy and maintain.

This chapter focuses on configuring cloud hybrid search, although you might want to implement hybrid federated search or use a combination of hybrid federated search and cloud hybrid search (such as for sensitive content sets or unavailable features).

When planning a hybrid search, it's important to understand what's different or unavailable, what has been replaced with newer features, or additional configurations you might need to perform to provide the best experience for your users:

- **Site search**   SharePoint Server does not automatically return results for content that has been moved to Microsoft 365. To return Microsoft 365 results in your SharePoint on-premises environment, you must configure your on-premises environment to retrieve search results from the Microsoft 365 Search service application (SSA).

- **Search verticals**   If you currently use search verticals in your on-premises SharePoint Server environment, you must re-create it in your search center in Microsoft 365.

- **eDiscovery**   eDiscovery for Microsoft 365 is managed in the Microsoft Purview compliance center. Microsoft 365 eDiscovery cannot index or search content in SharePoint Server on-premises; eDiscovery managers might have to perform searches in multiple places to return all relevant data.

- **Cross-site publishing search**   Cross-site publishing search is not available with hybrid search.

- **Custom security trimming**   Custom security trimming is not supported in Microsoft 365.

- **Usage reports**   Usage reports are based on information stored in SharePoint Online. The SSA in SharePoint Server doesn't communicate with SharePoint Online, so the SharePoint Online usage reports do not contain information regarding on-premises user activity.

- **Custom Search Scopes**   Custom Search Scopes is a SharePoint Server 2010 feature. Use result sources in SharePoint Online.

- **Best Bets**   Best Bets is a SharePoint Server 2010 feature. Use result sources in SharePoint Online.

- **Multitenancy**   SharePoint Online cannot preserve tenant isolation in a multitenant SharePoint Server 2013 or SharePoint Server 2016 farm.

- **Thesaurus**   SharePoint Online does not support thesauruses.

- **Content Enrichment web service**   The Content Enrichment web service is not available in SharePoint Online.

- **Custom entity extraction**   SharePoint Online does not support custom entity extraction.

- **Index reset for on-premises content**   It is not possible to clear search results for on-premises content. To remove on-premises content from search results, remove the on-premises content source or create an on-premises crawl rule to exclude the content from the search.

When configuring cloud hybrid search, your on-premises SharePoint server that hosts the cloud SSA needs at least 100GB of storage space. From a cloud planning perspective, SharePoint Online can index 1 million items for every 1TB of space. If you need to index more than 20 million items, you must open a case with Microsoft Support.

Taxonomy

Hybrid taxonomy means you can define a single SharePoint taxonomy to span SharePoint Server on-premises and SharePoint Online. The benefit is that you can use a single metadata set between both platforms.

Unlike other hybrid configurations, taxonomy is different in that it is mastered *online*. With other hybrid solutions (such as Active Directory and Exchange), the on-premises system is the source of authority, and then the cloud derives its data set from what is synchronized from the on-premises environment.

When you configure hybrid taxonomy and content types, you copy your on-premises term store configuration and available content types to SharePoint Online and then configure the on-premises environment to update its taxonomy and content types through a timer job.

App launcher

The hybrid app launcher enables you to create a more seamless experience for users moving between the SharePoint on-premises and SharePoint Online environments. Originally available only with SharePoint Server 2016, the extensible app launcher is available with the July 2016 public update for SharePoint Server 2013. Go to *https://support.microsoft.com/kb/3115286* for more information.

The app launcher experience exposes Microsoft 365 apps through the on-premises SharePoint Server app launcher interface.

Business-to-business extranet

An extranet is a restricted site that enables your organization to share information with external users while prohibiting them from accessing other corporate content. In a SharePoint hybrid configuration, you can direct external users to a members-only site in Microsoft 365.

There are many advantages to configuring extranet sites in SharePoint Online:

- Site collections can be configured to allow all users to invite partner users.

- Site collections can be configured to allow only site owners to invite partner users.

- Admins can control the list of partner domains to which the organization allows sharing.

- Microsoft 365 activity reports can be used to track partner site access and usage.

- Guests or partner users can be restricted to only a single site, preventing access to unauthorized resources.

- Guests or partner users can be restricted to be able only to accept invitations from the address that received the email, preventing sharing with additional accounts or accounts from unapproved domains.

In planning your extranet model, you need to make decisions around three core areas:

- **Invitation model**   This determines how users get access to sites—whether all users or only site collection owners can invite users, or an admin-managed model by which you import partner users from a directory.

- **Licensing**   By default, SharePoint guest users have limited capabilities in SharePoint Online and are limited to the restrictions governing the group into which they are placed.

Authenticated external users can use Office Online to view and edit documents, but further features (such as installing Office ProPlus or being able to create and manage sites) require the assignment of a SharePoint license.

- **Account life cycle management**   At some point, external users might no longer require access to an extranet resource, or the project an extranet site supports will end. In either case, plan for managing and archiving sites and removing partner user accounts and site permissions. If licenses are assigned to some external users, plan for a way that licenses can be assigned to external users (denoted as #EXT# in the directory) and reclaimed when the partner user account is no longer in use.

INSIDE OUT

Is a SharePoint hybrid architecture right for me?

Hybrid deployments can provide a path to the cloud for many workloads. Although this chapter gives you the knowledge to configure hybrid solutions for a variety of scenarios, you still need to work with your organization's service desk managers, call center representatives, application integration specialists, users, or enterprise architects to determine which portions of your SharePoint environment are well-suited for a hybrid topology.

If your organization has developed custom InfoPath forms, configured integrations with other on-premises data sources, or deployed plug-ins to interact with other on-premises applications, you'll need input from the individuals or teams responsible for managing those solutions. Microsoft retired InfoPath in January 2014 but will continue to support it until July 2026. If you want to migrate InfoPath forms, Microsoft recommends redeploying using new technologies such as Microsoft Forms, Power Apps, and Power Automate.

If you have deployed custom solutions but want to explore commercial products, you can explore add-ins and solutions available at *https://aka.ms/sharepointstore*.

However, suppose your SharePoint environment is underused or hasn't undergone a lot of customization. In that case, it might be more worthwhile to migrate content directly to SharePoint Online and bypass hybrid configurations altogether.

CHAPTER 27

Configuration

When the prerequisites have been met for the set of hybrid configuration options you want to perform, you can configure the individual services.

Set up SharePoint services for hybrid integration

You must at least ensure that the base services are configured for all SharePoint hybrid services. The shared services requirements are as follows:

- Managed Metadata service application

- User Profile service application

- My Sites service application

- Apps Management service application

- SharePoint Foundation Subscription Settings service

If you already have a fully deployed SharePoint farm, chances are you've already configured these services and won't have to configure additional instances. However, if your SharePoint farm is new or you haven't provisioned these services, you can use these abbreviated steps to configure them to the minimal level necessary for hybrid configuration. These services are already enabled and configured if you are installing SharePoint 2013 with SP1.

Managed metadata service

The managed metadata service application enables metadata and content type sharing across site collections and applications. A farm can have multiple managed metadata service applications, and each one can publish a term store and content types to be consumed by a managed metadata connection.

For more information about managed metadata, see *https://aka.ms/mmplanning*, "Plan for managed metadata in SharePoint Server."

To configure the managed metadata service, follow these steps:

1. Launch SharePoint Central Administration.

2. Select System Settings and then click Manage Services On Server, as shown in Figure 27-1.

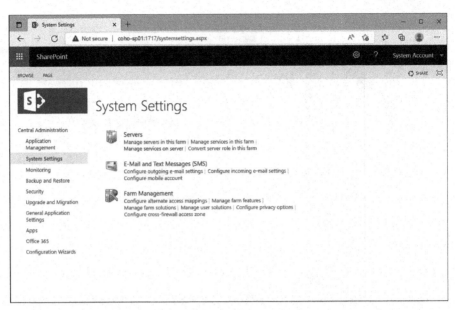

Figure 27-1   SharePoint Central Administration System Settings

3.   If you have more than one server, select the server that you want to run the managed metadata service.

4.   On the Services page, scroll to the Managed Metadata web service and click Start.

5.   In the Central Administration navigation pane, select Application Management and then, under Service Applications, click Manage Service Applications.

6.   If a service isn't currently listed for Managed Metadata, click New from the menu and select Managed Metadata Service from the list.

7.   Type a Name, Database Server, and a new Database Name for the managed metadata database. See Figure 27-2.

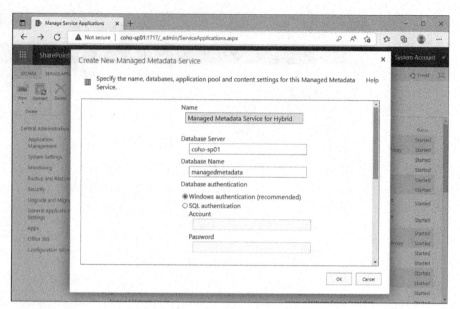

Figure 27-2   Create New Managed Metadata Service page

8. Scroll to the bottom of the page, select the Use Existing Application Pool button, select SharePoint Web Services Default from the dropdown, and then click OK.

My Sites

Use My Sites to provision and store individual user data sites. Users can create sites, store files in My Sites, and synchronize the content through the OneDrive desktop application.

If My Sites is not configured, you can follow these steps to configure the minimum settings necessary to complete the hybrid configuration of SharePoint Server:

1. In Central Administration, select Application Management and then select Manage Web Applications.

2. Select New on the ribbon.

3. Select the Create A New IIS Web Site button and then type a name in the Name box.

4. Under Public URL, type a URL or accept the default (*http://servername:port*).

5. Under Application Pool, select the Create New Application Pool button and type a Name for the IIS application pool.

6. Scroll to the bottom of the page and click OK.

7. Click OK to dismiss the dialog box after the web application has been created.

8. Click Application Management.

9. Under Site Collections, click **Create Site Collections**.

10. Under Web Application, click the dropdown and select **Change Web Application**. See Figure 27-3.

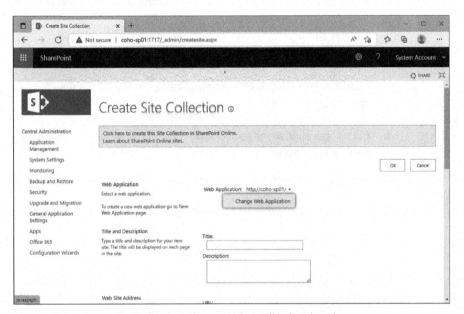

Figure 27-3   Create Site Collection Choose Web Application dropdown

11. Select the newly created web application.

12. Enter a Title and Description for the site collection.

13. Under Web Site Address, leave the default root ("/") URL set.

14. Under Template Selection, select the Enterprise tab and select My Site Host.

15. Under Primary Site Collection Administrator, type a user name or choose one from the People Picker.

16. Click OK.

17. Click OK to dismiss the completion dialog box.

User Profile service

The User Profile service contains individual user data. It must be enabled on at least one server in your SharePoint farm. If you have not configured the User Profile Service, follow these steps:

1. In SharePoint Central Administration, select System Settings and then click Manage Services On Server.

2. If you have more than one server in the farm, select which server to configure.

3. In the service list, locate User Profile Service and click Start.

NOTE

Do not start the User Profile Synchronization Service at this time because it will cause the rest of the configuration steps to fail.

4. Click Application Management, and then, under Service Applications, select Manage Service Applications.

5. Click New and then click User Profile Service Application.

6. Type a Name for the service application, such as User Profile Service, in the Name box.

7. Under Application Pool, select the Use Existing Application Pool button and then select SharePoint Web Services Default.

8. In the Profile Synchronization Instance dropdown, choose the server to run the User Profile Synchronization Service.

9. In the My Site URL Host field, type the URL of the My Site Host site collection you created previously and click OK.

10. Click OK to dismiss the dialog box.

11. Select System Settings from the SharePoint Central Administration navigation pane.

12. Click Manage Services On Server. If you have more than one server in your SharePoint farm, select the server that will run the User Profile Synchronization Service.

13. In the services list, locate User Profile Synchronization Service and click Start.

14. If prompted, on the User Profile Synchronization Service page, type the password for the service account that will be used to run the User Profile Synchronization Service and click OK.

After you configure the User Profile service, connect on-premises Active Directory to the User Profile service. Follow these steps if it has not already been configured in your environment:

1. In SharePoint Central Administration, select Application Management and then click Manage Service Applications.

2. Click the User Profile Service Application.

3. On the Manage Profile Service: User Profile Service Application page, under Synchronization, click Configure Synchronization Connections, as shown in Figure 27-4.

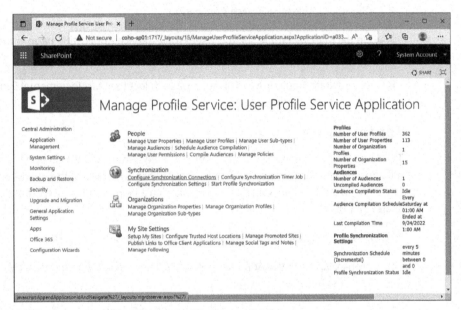

Figure 27-4   Configure Synchronization Connections

4. Click Create New Connection.

5. Type a Name for the new connection, such as `Active Directory`.

6. Ensure the type is set to Active Directory.

7. Under Connection Settings, type your Active Directory fully qualified forest name, such as `contoso.com`.

8. Under Account Name, enter credentials for a user account that is a member of Domain Admins or is granted the Replicating Directory Changes and Replicating Directory Changes All rights (to synchronize secure account details).

9.   Click the Populate Containers button.

10. Expand the domain node and select the containers where your user objects are located.

11. Click OK.

To synchronize user profiles, follow these steps:

1.   In SharePoint Central Administration, select Application Management and then click Manage Service Applications.

2.   Click the User Profile Service Application.

3.   On the Manage Profile Service: User Profile Service Application page, under Synchronization, click Start Profile Synchronization.

4.   On the Start Profile Synchronization page, select the Start Incremental Synchronization button and then click OK.

App Management service

The App Management service stores information regarding SharePoint app licenses and permissions. Licenses downloaded from the Marketplace are stored in the App Management service application. The App Management service must be running on at least one server in the SharePoint Farm.

To configure the App Management service, follow these steps:

1.   In SharePoint Central Administration, select System Settings and then click Manage Services On Server.

2.   If you have more than one server in your SharePoint farm, click Change Server and select the server you wish to configure.

3.   In the service list, locate App Management Service and click Start.

4.   In the SharePoint Central Administration navigation pane, select Application Management and then click Manage Service Applications.

5.   On the ribbon, click New and then click App Management Service.

6.   In the Service Application Name field, type a name for the service, such as App Management Service.

7.   Under Application Pool, select the Use Existing Application Pool button and then select SharePoint Web Services Default from the dropdown.

8. Click OK.

9. Click OK to close the confirmation dialog box.

SharePoint Foundation Subscription Settings

The SharePoint Foundation Subscription Settings service stores configuration information for site subscriptions. It must be configured with SharePoint PowerShell:

1. In SharePoint Central Administration, select System Settings and then click Manage Services On Server.

2. If you have more than one server in your SharePoint farm, click Change Server and select the server you wish to configure.

3. In the service list, locate Microsoft SharePoint Foundation Subscription Settings Service and click Start.

4. Click Start, type SharePoint, right-click Management Shell, and select Run As Administrator to launch an elevated console session.

5. Copy and paste the following commands into the Windows PowerShell window to create the SharePoint Foundation Subscription settings:

```
$AppPool = New-SPServiceApplicationPool -Name SettingsServiceAppPool -Account `
(Get-SPManagedAccount <DOMAIN\SharePointServiceAccount>)
$App = New-SPSubscriptionSettingsServiceApplication -ApplicationPool $appPool `
-Name SettingsServiceApp -DatabaseName SettingsServiceDB
$proxy = New-SPSubscriptionSettingsServiceApplicationProxy -ServiceApplication `
$App
Get-SPServiceInstance | where{$_.TypeName -eq "Microsoft SharePoint Foundation `
Subscription Settings Service"} | Start-SPServiceInstance
```

After the required components for SharePoint hybrid services have been configured, you can begin configuring individual services or settings.

Server-to-server authentication

For a SharePoint Server farm to consume resources and content from SharePoint Online or Microsoft 365, you must configure server-to-server authentication, which enables features to work cross-premises, such as search or other web applications.

Any on-premises application that is currently configured to use Integrated Windows Authentication (IWA) with NTLM can pass claims to Microsoft 365. IWA using NTLM is required for the SharePoint authentication service to pass user claims to SharePoint Online using OAuth. If your existing web application isn't configured to use IWA with NTLM, you can update it or configure a new web application.

CHAPTER 27

For example, you can create a new website in Internet Information Services (IIS) and connect it to an existing content database and web application. You can also create an entirely new web application and an empty content database. For more information about extending an existing application, see *https://aka.ms/claimswebapp*, "Extend claims-based web applications in Share-Point 2013."

OneDrive for Business and Hybrid Sites

Hybrid OneDrive for Business is part of a bundle option that also enables you to configure Hybrid Sites. Hybrid OneDrive for Business performs redirection for users' OneDrive for Business sites, whereas Hybrid Sites configures site-following parameters. Hybrid Sites combines the followed sites from SharePoint Online and SharePoint Server into a consolidated list in SharePoint Online. If a user selects the Followed Sites link in SharePoint Server on-premises, they are redirected to the Followed Sites list in SharePoint Online.

Configuring hybrid OneDrive for Business can be broken down into three main sections:

- Configure Microsoft 365 for SharePoint hybrid

- Ensure proper permissions

- Redirect OneDrive to Microsoft 365

Prerequisites

To configure hybrid OneDrive for Business and Sites, you must meet the following prerequisites:

- Users with SharePoint Online license in Microsoft 365

- Administration account with SharePoint Online admin role privileges

- SharePoint Online My Sites URL

- Administration account with membership in the Farm Administrators group

Configure Microsoft 365 for SharePoint hybrid

To make hybrid services available for SharePoint Online, you must subscribe to a Microsoft 365 plan that contains SharePoint Online and then connect your on-premises directory to Microsoft 365.

NOTE

See Chapter 1, "Jumping into the cloud," and Chapter 2, "Preparing your environment for the cloud" for more information about setting up your Microsoft 365 subscription and domains.

Ensure proper permissions

To use OneDrive for Business in Microsoft 365, users must have the Create Personal Site and Follow People And Edit Profile permissions.

To confirm or configure these permissions, follow these steps:

1. Log in to the Microsoft 365 admin center (*https://admin.microsoft.com*).

2. Expand Admin Centers and then click SharePoint.

3. In the navigation pane, click More Features and then select User Profiles.

4. Under People, click Manage User Permissions.

5. In the Permissions For User Profile Service Application dialog box, select Everyone Except External Users or add a specific audience if you are piloting.

6. Click OK.

PILOTING ONEDRIVE FOR A SPECIFIC GROUP

If you decide you want to conduct a pilot of hybrid OneDrive for Business for a small group of users, you can create an audience for your pilot users. Copy and paste the following script into an elevated SharePoint PowerShell console, editing the values for the variables such as $mySiteHostUrl, $audienceName, and $audienceDescription. If you intend to use that pilot group for other activities in SharePoint Online, you might want to repeat the process by updating $mySiteHostUrl to the SharePoint Online My Sites URL and running this from the SharePoint Online PowerShell console. In this example, you create an audience where the members are in the IT department.

You can also perform this action in SharePoint Server on-premises by going to Central Administration > Manage Service Applications > User Profile Service > Manage Audiences or in SharePoint Online by going to SharePoint Admin Center> User Profiles > Manage.

```
## Settings you might want to change for Audience Name and Description ##
$mySiteHostUrl = "https://www.my.contoso.com"
$audienceName = "OneDrive Pilot Users"
$audienceDescription = "OneDrive Pilot Users"
$audienceRules = @()
$audienceRules += New-Object `
Microsoft.Office.Server.Audience.AudienceRuleComponent("Department", `
"Contains", "IT")
#Get the My Site Host's SPSite object
$site = Get-SPSite $mySiteHostUrl
$ctx = [Microsoft.Office.Server.ServerContext]::GetContext($site)
$audMan = New-Object Microsoft.Office.Server.Audience.AudienceManager($ctx)
#Create a new audience object for the given Audience Manager
$aud = $audMan.Audiences.Create($audienceName, $audienceDescription)
```

```
$aud.AudienceRules = New-Object System.Collections.ArrayList
$audienceRules | ForEach-Object { $aud.AudienceRules.Add($_) }
#Save the new Audience
$aud.Commit()
#Compile the new Audience
$upa = Get-SPServiceApplication | Where-Object {$_.DisplayName -eq "User `
Profile Service Application"}
$audJob = [Microsoft.Office.Server.Audience.AudienceJob]::`
RunAudienceJob(($upa.Id.Guid.ToString(), "1", "1", $aud.AudienceName))
```

7. Verify that the Create Personal Site and Follow People and Edit Profile boxes are selected.

8. Click OK.

Redirect OneDrive to Microsoft 365

Before you begin these steps, ensure that users have a SharePoint Online license in Microsoft 365. (SharePoint Online includes OneDrive for Business.) In addition, you might want to follow the procedure to pre-provision OneDrive for Business sites in Microsoft 365 you find in Chapter 30, "OneDrive for Business."

To perform the redirection, you need the My Sites URL in Microsoft 365. You can locate it through the following procedure:

1. Navigate to the SharePoint Online admin center.

2. Select More Features and then choose Open under User Profiles.

3. On the User Profiles page, under My Site Settings, select Setup My Sites.

4. Under My Site Host, select the value for My Site Host Location, as shown in Figure 27-5, and copy it to the clipboard.

When you have your tenant's My Sites URL, you can follow these steps to configure OneDrive for Business redirection:

1. Log in to Central Administration using a Farm Administrator account.

2. In the navigation pane, select Office 365.

3. Click on the appropriate link to configure OneDrive:

   - If you are using SharePoint Server 2013, click Configure OneDrive And Sites Links (SharePoint Server 2013), as shown in Figure 27-6.

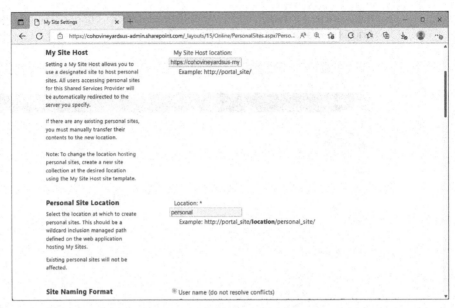

Figure 27-5   Locating the My Sites site collection URL

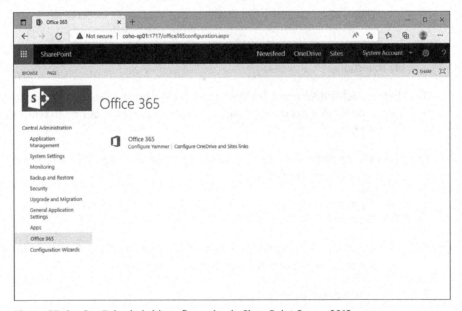

Figure 27-6   OneDrive hybrid configuration in SharePoint Server 2013

- If you are using SharePoint Server 2016 or later, click Configure Hybrid OneDrive And Sites Features, as shown in Figure 27-7.

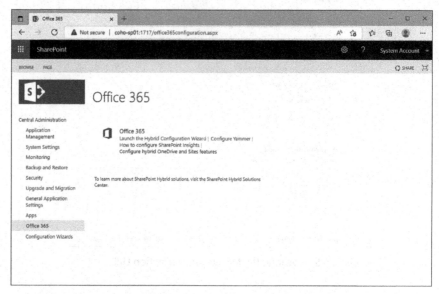

Figure 27-7   OneDrive hybrid configuration in SharePoint Server 2016

4. In the My Site URL box, type the URL obtained from SharePoint Online for the My Sites site collection.

5. Under Select The Audience For The Connection, select the Everyone button to perform redirection for all users or select the Use A Specific Audience button to select a pilot audience group.

6. Select the site redirection feature. Depending on your version of SharePoint server, you might see a different interface:

   - If you are using SharePoint Server 2013, select the Redirect The Sites Page checkbox.

   - If you are using SharePoint Server 2016 or later, select the OneDrive And Sites button to configure both features, as shown in Figure 27-8.

7. Click OK to complete the configuration.

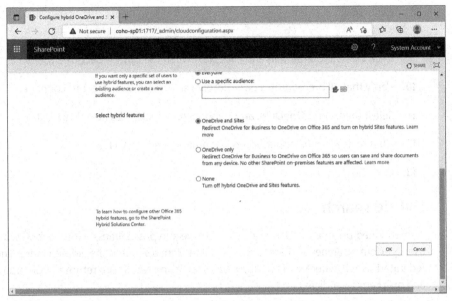

Figure 27-8   Hybrid OneDrive for Business configuration in SharePoint Server 2019

Hybrid Picker

Hybrid Picker is a new option that enables you to configure hybrid OneDrive for Business and Hybrid Sites from a wizard-driven interface. It does not allow the flexibility of the manual configuration option and instead enables hybrid OneDrive for Business for all users.

To use Hybrid Picker to configure hybrid OneDrive for Business, follow these steps:

1. Log in to SharePoint Server. If the SharePoint Hybrid Picker has already been run, you can execute it by double-clicking it on the desktop and skipping to step 9. If the SharePoint Hybrid Picker has not been run yet, continue to step 2.

2. Navigate to the Microsoft 365 admin center (*https://admin.microsoft.com*).

3. In the Microsoft 365 admin center, expand Admin Centers and then select SharePoint.

4. In the navigation pane, More Features and then under Hybrid picker, select Open.

5. On the Hybrid Picker page, click Go To Hybrid Picker Download Page.

6. Click Open to download and launch the SharePoint Hybrid Picker.

7. Click Install.

8. Click Next.

9. Type your credentials for both the local Active Directory environment and Microsoft 365. Click Validate Credentials and click Next when the button becomes available.

10. Verify that all prerequisites pass. Resolve any errors. Click Next to continue.

11. Select the Hybrid OneDrive and Hybrid Sites checkboxes and click Next.

12. After reviewing the configuration summary page, click Next.

13. Click Close.

Hybrid search

As mentioned previously, there are two hybrid search possibilities—cloud hybrid search, where users perform searches and are returned results from a single, consolidated index, and hybrid federated search, where users perform one search and results are returned from both the cloud and on-premises indices.

Microsoft recommends using cloud hybrid search. The default search configuration is recommended for most organizations.

NOTE

For information about hybrid federated search, please see *https://aka.ms/spfedsearch*, "Learn about hybrid federated search for SharePoint."

Prerequisites

Prior to configuring a hybrid search option for SharePoint, verify that you meet the following prerequisites:

- SharePoint Server 2013 Service Pack 1 and the January 2016 Public Update (*https://aka.ms/sppu*)

- SharePoint 2016 RTM

- SharePoint 2019 RTM

- Account with Microsoft 365 Global Administrator role

- Account that is a member of Domain Admins in the on-premises Active Directory environment

- Account that is a member of the SharePoint Farm Administrators group:

    - Account must have the securityadmin server role in the farm's SQL server instance.

    - Account must be a member of the db_owner fixed database role on SharePoint databases.

    - Account must be a member of the local Administrators group on the server where tasks will be performed.

- CreateCloudSSA.ps1 and Onboard-CloudHybridSearch.ps1 scripts, located in the Microsoft Download Center (*https://go.microsoft.com/fwlink/?LinkId=717902*)

- Azure Active Directory Module for Windows PowerShell installed on the search server

- URL of Microsoft 365 SharePoint Online site collection (*https://<tenant>.sharepoint.com*)

Configure Microsoft 365 for SharePoint hybrid

To make hybrid services available for SharePoint Online, you must subscribe to a Microsoft 365 plan that contains SharePoint Online and then connect your on-premises directory to Microsoft 365.

Create a cloud Search service application

The cloud Search service application will be used to configure result sets for SharePoint searches:

1. On the server that will host Search, launch an elevated SharePoint Management Shell.

2. Run `CreateCloudSSA.ps1` and follow the prompts to provide the necessary values, as shown in Figure 27-19. You might need to unblock the script after downloading it before it can be executed:

    - **SearchServerName**   Server that will run the cloud Search service application

    - **SearchServiceAccount**   The Search service account (in `DOMAIN\Username` format)

    - **SearchServiceAppName**   Name for the cloud Search service application that will be created

    - **DatabaseServerName**   Name of the server where the cloud Search service application database will be created

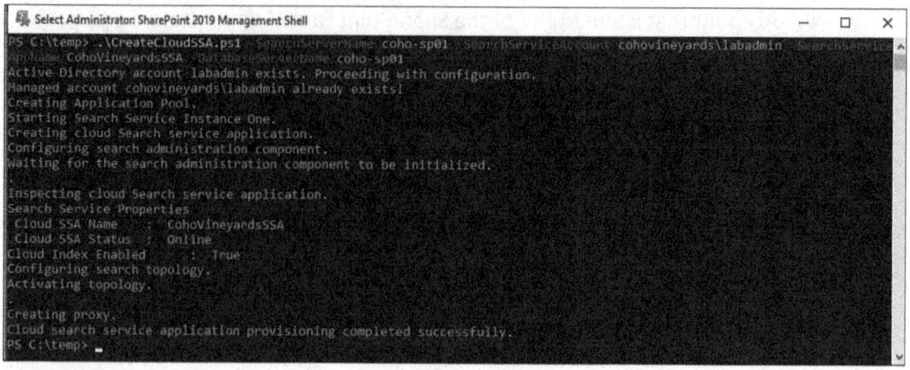

Figure 27-9   Create the cloud Search service application

Inside Out

CreateCloudSSA.PS1 fails because of Internet connectivity

The `CreateCloudSSA.ps1` script requires access to Microsoft 365. If your environment is behind a proxy, please try to bypass the proxy server or appliances to reach Microsoft 365. If bypassing the proxy is not possible, you may need to configure the WinHTTP proxy via NetSh. If you have proxy settings configured correctly in Edge, you can run the following command to import those settings into the WinHTTP proxy configuration:

```
netsh winhttp import proxy source=ie
```

Connect the cloud Search service application to Microsoft 365

After you have created the cloud Search service application, you can proceed with connecting it to Microsoft 365:

1. From the SharePoint Management Shell, run the following command and enter your Microsoft 365 Global Admin credential when prompted:

   ```
   $Credential = Get-Credential
   ```

2. Run the following command, using your organization's SharePoint Online URL and the name of the cloud Search service application you used when running the CreateCloudSSA.ps1 script. See Figure 27-10.

   ```
   .\Onboard-CloudHybridSearch.ps1 -CloudSsaId <CloudSsaID> -PortalUrl `
   https://<tenant>.sharepoint.com -Credential $Credential
   ```

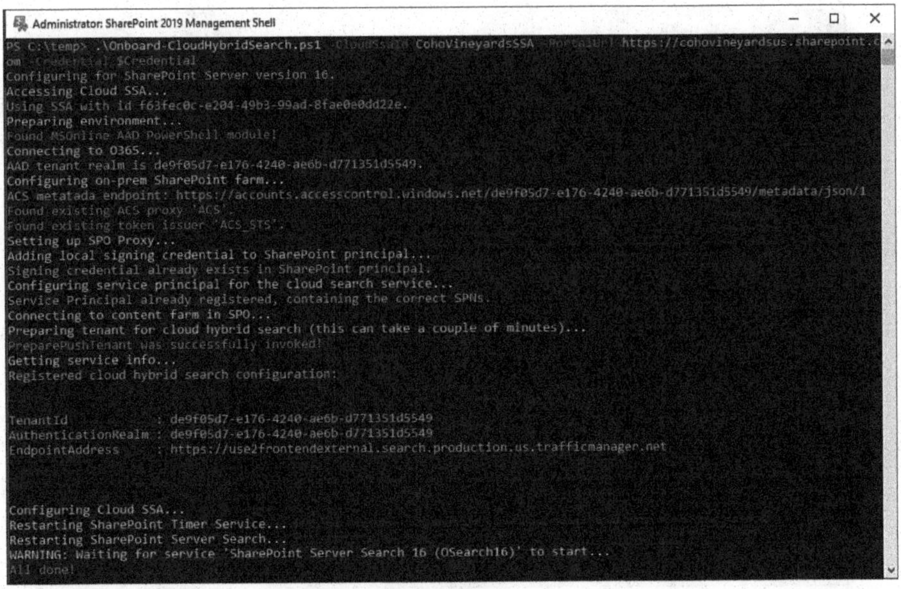

Figure 27-10   Run Onboard-CloudHybridSearch.ps1

Create a content source for cloud hybrid search

After the cloud search application has been created and connected to Microsoft 365, you must create a content source to be incorporated into the Microsoft 365 search index:

1. From Central Administration in your SharePoint Server farm, under Application Management, select Manage Service Applications.

2. On the Manage Service Applications page, select the cloud SSA that you created earlier.

3. Under Crawling, select Content Sources. See Figure 27-11.

4. Click New Content Source to create a selection of content to crawl.

5. Under Name, type a name for the content source.

6. Under Content Source Type, select the type of content that will be crawled. Options include SharePoint Sites, Web Sites, File Shares, Exchange Public Folders, Line Of Business Data, or Custom Repository.

CHAPTER 27

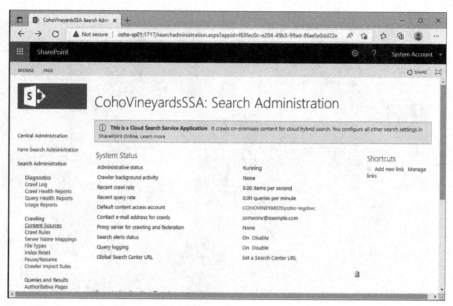

Figure 27-11 Cloud Search Administration page

7. Under Start Address, enter the addresses that will be included in the content search. If you are searching SharePoint Sites or Web Sites, for example, you can type `http://server`. If you intend to crawl file shares, type addresses as `\\server\share`.

8. Under Crawl Settings, select the behavior for crawling—either the folder and all subfolders or just the top-level folder.

9. Under Crawl Schedules, configure a schedule for full and incremental crawls.

10. Under Content Source Priority, configure whether this content source will be High or Normal priority. Selecting High priority prioritizes this content source's processing over content sources with Normal priority.

11. Click OK to create the content source.

12. Right-click the content source and select Start Full Crawl.

13. After the content source crawls are completed, navigate to Microsoft 365 and perform a search for IsExternalContent:true.

    The `IsExternalContent:true` property shows content that is external to the operating environment (in this case, content external to SharePoint Online). In the example in Figure 27-12, a search was executed in SharePoint Online, and the data set shows results from the local SharePoint environment, confirming that the cloud hybrid search is working correctly.

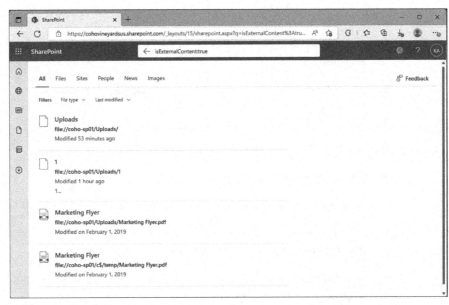

Figure 27-12   SharePoint Online search with SharePoint Server results returned

TROUBLESHOOTING

Why isn't my cloud hybrid search returning expected results?

There can be a number of reasons, but the most common one is that the data source you're indexing on-premises (SharePoint sites, file shares, and so on) only has permissions granted to the Domain Users group. AAD Connect does not synchronize user objects with the `IsCriticalSystemObject` attribute set to True. Domain Users, among other built-in groups, has that attribute set to True, blocking it from synchronization. Check the content sources you're indexing—if Domain Users is the only security principal granted access, update the access control list for the object to a group that is synchronized to Microsoft 365.

Configure on-premises Search to display results from SharePoint Online

When you have configured cloud hybrid search so that SharePoint Online can return results from on-premises content sources, you can configure the on-premises SharePoint Server environment to display results from SharePoint Online. This way, your users get the same results from either environment.

CHAPTER 27

To configure on-premises search results to include Microsoft 365 sources, follow these steps:

1. Using an account that is a member of the Farm Administrators group, launch Central Administration.

2. Under Application Management, select Manage Service Applications.

3. Select the cloud SSA.

4. Under Queries And Results, click Result Sources.

5. Select New Result Source.

6. Under General Information, type a name of the result source, such as `SharePoint Online`.

7. Under Protocol, select the Remote SharePoint button.

8. Under Remote Service URL, enter the top-level URL of your SharePoint Online tenant (*https://<tenant>.sharepoint.com*). See Figure 27-13.

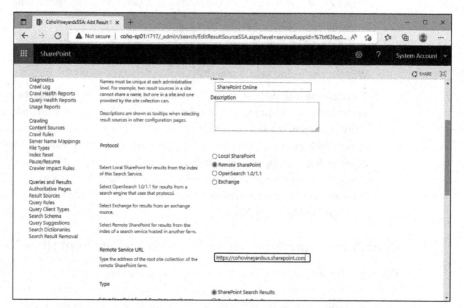

Figure 27-13   Configuring a result source for cloud search service application

9. Under Type, ensure that the SharePoint Search Results button is selected.

10. Under Query Transform, leave the default transform value, `{searchTerms}`.

11. Under Credentials Information, ensure that the Default Authentication button is selected.

12. Click Save.

13. Point to the newly created result source, select the down arrow, and then select Set As Default, as shown in Figure 27-14.

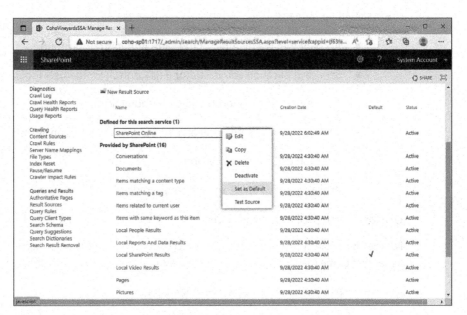

Figure 27-14   Set new result source as default

14. Log in to the SharePoint Server search site with an identity that is federated and licensed in Microsoft 365 for SharePoint Online and perform a search, using the `IsExternalContent:true` search term.

Hybrid taxonomy

Originally available only for SharePoint Server 2016, hybrid taxonomy and content types are available for both SharePoint Server 2013 and SharePoint Server 2016 with the appropriate public updates.

Prerequisites

Following are the prerequisites:

- SharePoint Server 2013 with April 2018 cumulative update (*https://aka.ms/sp2013update*)

- SharePoint Server 2016 with November 2016 or later public update for hybrid taxonomy (*https://support.microsoft.com/kb/3127940*)

- SharePoint Server 2016 with June 2017 or later public update for hybrid content types (*https://support.microsoft.com/help/3203432*)

- SharePoint Server 2019 RTM

- Access to the Copy-SPTaxonomyGroups and Copy-SPContentTypes cmdlets

- Hybrid Picker, which has the following requirements:

  - Account that is a member of the Farm Administrators group

  - Service application administrator (Full Control) for the User Profile service

  - Account that is a Microsoft 365 global administrator

  - Ability to run elevated (local administrator) commands on SharePoint server

  - Appropriate SharePoint version

  - Availability of SPO365LinkSettings cmdlet

Update term store permissions

For the SharePoint Timer job to complete successfully, the Timer service account must be made a member of the Managed Metadata Service administrators. To do this, follow this procedure:

1. Launch an elevated SharePoint Management Shell.

2. Run the following script:

```
$SPTimerServiceAccount = (Get-WmiObject win32_service | ? { $_.Name -eq `
(Get-Service | ? { $_.Displayname -eq "SharePoint Timer Service"}).Name `
}).StartName
$SPSite = "http://coho-sp01" # Replace with server name
$SPTermStoreName = "Managed Metadata Service"
$Web = Get-SPWeb -Site $SPSite
$TaxonomySession = Get-SPTaxonomySession -Site $Web.Site
$TermStore = $TaxonomySession.TermStores[$SPTermStoreName]
$TermStore.AddTermStoreAdministrator($SPTimerServiceAccount)
$TermStore.CommitAll()
```

Copy on-premises taxonomy to SharePoint Online

If you have configured taxonomy groups, terms, and content types on-premises, export and copy those to Microsoft 365 before beginning the hybrid configuration:

1. Log in to SharePoint Server with a Farm Administrator account. The Farm Administrator account should have access by default to view the content stored in the managed metadata service application.

2. Launch the SharePoint Management Shell.

3. Run the following script to copy the non-default taxonomy groups and terms to SharePoint Online.

TIP

The `Copy-SPTaxonomyGroups` command will fail if your group contains special term sets. In this example, the default groups People, Search Dictionaries, and System have been excluded because they contain special term sets that cannot be replicated. If you have additional term sets or the term store is stored in another managed metadata service instance name, you must update those parameters accordingly:

```
$SPOCredential = Get-Credential
$SPOSite = "https://<tenant>.sharepoint.com" # Replace with SharePoint Online URL
$SPSite = "http://<SharePoint Site URL>" # Replace with SharePoint Server URL
$SPTermStoreName = "Managed Metadata Service"
$Web = Get-SPWeb -Site $SPSite
$TaxonomySession = Get-SPTaxonomySession -Site $Web.Site
$TermStore = $TaxonomySession.TermStores[$SPTermStoreName]
[array]$GroupNames = $TermStore.Groups.Name -notmatch `
("People|Search Dictionaries|System")
Copy-SPTaxonomyGroups -LocalTermStoreName $SPTermStoreName -LocalSiteURL $SPSite `
-RemoteSiteURL $SPOSite -GroupNames $GroupNames -Credential $SPOCredential
```

4. Gather a list of the content types you wish to copy to SharePoint Online. To list all of the content types for a particular site, run the following script from the SharePoint Management Shell. Note any custom content types:

```
$SPSite = "http://<SharePoint Site URL>" # SharePoint Server URL
$Web = Get-SPWeb -Site $SPSite
[array]$ContentTypeNames = $Web.ContentTypes.Name
```

5. Review the values stored in $ContentTypeNames. When you have determined the content types to copy from Microsoft 365, use the following script to copy them.

```
$SPOCredential = Get-Credential
$SPOSite = "https://<tenant>.sharepoint.com" # Replace with SharePoint Online URL
$SPSite = "http://<Sharepoint Site Url>" # Replace with SharePoint Server URL
Copy-SPContentTypes -LocalSiteUrl $SPSite -LocalTermStoreName `
$SPContentTermStoreName -RemoteSiteUrl $SPOSite -ContentTypeName @("Content `
Type 1 Name","Content Type 2 Name") -Credential $SPOCredential
```

Configure hybrid taxonomy with Hybrid Picker

When you are ready to set up hybrid taxonomy, you can run Hybrid Picker to complete the configuration:

1. Log in to the SharePoint server with an account meeting the prerequisites. If SharePoint Hybrid Picker has already been run, you can run it by double-clicking it on the desktop and skipping to step 9.

CHAPTER 27

2. Navigate to the Microsoft 365 admin center (*https://admin.microsoft.com*), expand Admin centers, and select SharePoint.

3. In the navigation pane, select More Features.

4. Under Hybrid Picker, click Open.

5. On the Hybrid Picker page, click Go To Hybrid Picker Download Page.

6. Click Open to download and start the SharePoint Hybrid Picker.

7. Click Install.

8. Click Next.

9. Type your credentials for both the local Active Directory environment as well as Microsoft 365.

10. Click Validate Credentials to confirm you have entered credentials correctly.

11. After your credentials have been validated, click Close.

12. Click Next.

13. Verify that all prerequisites pass. Resolve any errors. See Figure 27-15. Click Next to continue.

Figure 27-15   SharePoint Hybrid Configuration Wizard Checking Prerequisites page

14. Select the Hybrid Taxonomy And Content Type checkbox and select the Input Parameters link next to the option, as shown in Figure 27-16.

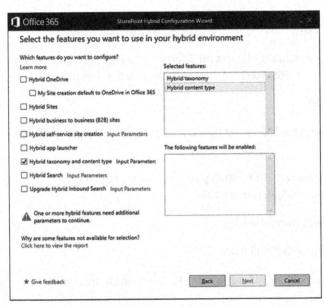

Figure 27-16   Select hybrid features

15. Enter data for the following values:

- **SharePoint Server root site**   *http://<SharePoint Server URL>*.

- **SharePoint Managed Metadata Application**   For most organizations, the default name is Managed Metadata Application. If you are unsure of the Managed Metadata Application Service name, launch Central Administration and select Manage Service Application under Application Management. Look for an entry with type Managed Metadata Service and use the value in the Name column in Hybrid Picker.

- **Groups**   Type the names of the taxonomy groups you wish to replicate. You can use the list from the previous task, where you copied the taxonomy groups to Microsoft 365, or you can leave it blank to replicate all groups except the system and default special groups.

16. Click Validate to confirm the options.

17. Click OK.

18. Click Next to proceed.

19. After reviewing the Configuration Summary page, click Next.

20. Click Close.

App launcher

The hybrid app launcher configures the SharePoint Server App Launcher experience to integrate with Microsoft 365. You configure the app launcher with the SharePoint Hybrid Picker.

Prerequisites

Before configuring the SharePoint hybrid app launcher, you must verify that you meet the prerequisites:

- SharePoint Server 2013 with July 2016 Cumulative Update (*https://aka.ms/spjuly2016update*)

- SharePoint Server 2016 RTM

- SharePoint Server 2019 RTM

- An account with membership in the Farm Administrators group

- An account with Microsoft 365 global admin role

- Local administrator privileges on SharePoint Server where the configuration will be performed

Enable the hybrid app launcher

To configure the SharePoint hybrid app launcher, follow these steps:

1. Navigate to the Microsoft 365 admin center (*https://admin.microsoft.com*), expand Admin Centers, and select SharePoint.

2. In the navigation pane, select More Features.

3. Under Hybrid Picker, click Open.

4. On the Hybrid Picker page, click Go To Hybrid Picker Download Page.

5. Click Open to download and start the SharePoint Hybrid Picker.

6. Click Install.

7. Click Next.

8. Type your credentials for both the local Active Directory environment as well as Microsoft 365.

9. Click Validate Credentials to confirm you have entered credentials correctly.

10. After your credentials have been validated, click Close.

11. Click Next.

12. Verify that all prerequisites pass. Resolve any errors.

13. Click Next to continue.

14. Select the Hybrid App Launcher checkbox and click Next to continue.

15. Review the Configuration Summary page.

16. Click Close.

Business-to-business extranet

Although business-to-business extranets are configured in Microsoft 365, you can configure an optional integration component to enable integrated authentication by using OAuth so that users can navigate seamlessly between local intranet sites on-premises and extranet sites stored in SharePoint Online.

Prerequisites

Before configuring SharePoint hybrid business-to-business sites, you must verify that you meet the prerequisites:

- SharePoint Server 2013 September 2015 cumulative update

- SharePoint Server 2016 RTM

- SharePoint Server 2019 RTM

- An account with membership in the Farm Administrators group

- An account with the Microsoft 365 Global Administrator role

- Local administrator privileges on SharePoint Server where the configuration will be performed

Enable hybrid business-to-business (B2B) sites

Use the following steps to enable the integrated authentication between on-premises Share-Point sites and Microsoft 365 sites:

1. Navigate to the Microsoft 365 admin center (*https://admin.microsoft.com*), expand Admin Centers, and select SharePoint.

2. In the navigation pane, select More Features.

3. Under Hybrid Picker, click Open.

4. On the Hybrid Picker page, click Go To Hybrid Picker Download Page.

5. Click Open to download and start the SharePoint Hybrid Picker.

6. Click Install.

7. Click Next.

8. Type your credentials for both the local Active Directory environment as well as Microsoft 365.

9. Click Validate Credentials to confirm you have entered credentials correctly.

10. After your credentials have been validated, click Close.

11. Click Next.

12. Verify that all prerequisites pass and resolve any errors. Click Next to continue.

13. Select the Hybrid Business to Business (B2B) Sites checkbox and click Next.

14. Review the Configuration Summary page.

15. Click Next.

16. Click Close.

After OAuth has been configured, you can create extranet sites in SharePoint Online and share the sites with external entities.

What's next?

Configuring SharePoint's hybrid options allows your organization to extends is intranet presence into SharePoint Online. In the next chapter, we'll look at the available migration tooling to start transitioning content from on-premises SharePoint server farms and file shares to SharePoint Online, OneDrive for Business, and Microsoft Teams.

Migrating data to SharePoint Online

When preparing to migrate data to SharePoint Online, you'll need to consider several factors from both the source and target perspectives. Migrating the content is fairly straightforward. Making sure you've inventoried all the data sources and permissions and designed an appropriate SharePoint Online structure is the more complex part.

In this chapter, we'll cover the core migration planning and execution steps, including:

- Inventorying data sources' mapping data destinations

- Choosing the migration tools

- Planning network requirements and prerequisites

- Scanning content

- Resolving blocking issues

- Planning for content that cannot be migrated

- Migrating data with SharePoint Migration Tool (SPMT)

Planning and executing a successful SharePoint Online migration can be a lot of work. Fortunately, there are a lot of tools to help you through the transition.

Let's dig in!

CHAPTER 28

Inventorying data sources and mapping destinations

Once your organization has decided to migrate to SharePoint Online, you'll be faced with a list of questions:

- What data is being migrated?

- Where should it go?

- What can't be migrated?

You'll need to work with application and data owners across your organization to get the answers to some of these questions. Once you've identified who you need to talk to, you'll need to work through these questions to establish your overall strategy.

What data is being migrated?

The first step in planning is identifying the data and applications that will be migrated. Source data can include things like:

- Group or team file shares on local servers, NAS appliances, or cloud services

- SharePoint Server document libraries and lists

- SharePoint workflows and applications

- Infopath forms

- Intranet web sites

For each of these content types, you need to evaluate whether this content is truly a fit for SharePoint Online or whether another service or application in the Microsoft 365 suite is a more appropriate destination. While SharePoint Online may indeed be a viable target, it might not be the one that best supports the business's objectives for scalability or integration with other business processes.

Where should it go?

To best map out where your data will go, you should take an inventory of the services you have available in the Microsoft 365 suite. Depending on your licenses, you might have additional services available. And you might also decide to scale up to add additional services.

You can use Figure 28-1 to help evaluate what you have and map it to potential workload services in the Microsoft 365 platform.

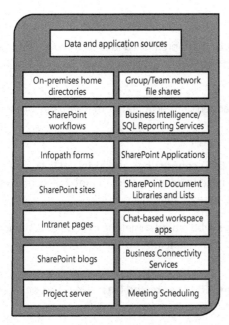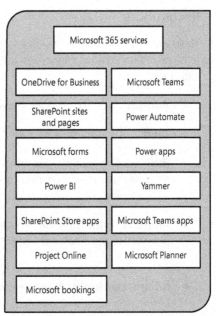

Figure 28-1   Understanding source data and application sources and how they relate to Microsoft 365 services

Some items are easy to map—such as migrating on-premises user home directories to One-Drive for Business or group file shares to Microsoft Teams. Others, like SharePoint workflows, might not have a direct migration path to a comparable service (such as Power Automate) and will require retooling or recreating to take advantage of modern features. And still, others might require significant redesign using new, supported platform technologies like Power BI and Power Apps.

As you inventory your data and applications, it's important to identify the dependencies between applications and the supporting data to ensure you're migrating or redesigning those pieces. Categorizing applications and data in order of difficulty or by dependencies can be beneficial. Doing so allows you to start taking advantage of SharePoint Online and other Microsoft 365 technologies sooner for the easy-to-transition workloads while developing longer-term strategies for workloads requiring more customization or redevelopment.

What can't be migrated?

Configurations, features, and other things that can't be migrated fall into two categories:

- Those that can be reconfigured

- Those that need to be redeveloped

Reconfigure

There are a number of features that exist both on-premises and in SharePoint Online but need to be reconfigured after migrations, as the configuration objects can't be migrated with the native tools:

- **Add-ins**   Add-ins need to be re-added or re-acquired from the SharePoint store.

- **Alerts**   Alerts must be recreated.

- **Business Connectivity Services (BCS) connections and external lists**   Links to external lists and BCS connections need to be re-created, though Microsoft recommends redeveloping them as Power Apps–based solutions if possible.

- **InfoPath Forms**   InfoPath Forms will be retired sometime in 2023, so it's time to start planning to move toward solutions that might include Microsoft Forms, Power Automate, and Power Apps.

- **Information Rights Management (IRM)–protected lists**   IRM must be disabled before migration and then re-applied post-migration.

- **Secure Store applications**   Secure store applications must be re-created.

- **SharePoint Server 2013 workflows**   SharePoint Server 2013 workflows will be retired at some point in the future, though Microsoft has not yet set a date.

Some of the features in this list are slated for deprecation, which might help you evaluate whether you're going to migrate and reconfigure or look toward redevelopment.

Replace or redevelop

In addition to things that need to be reconnected or reconfigured, it's also critically important to be aware of things that will not successfully migrate because the feature is not implemented (or has been deprecated) in SharePoint Online. Those items include the following:

- **Mail-enabled lists and libraries**   This feature is unavailable in SharePoint Online. Sites requiring this feature might be able to use a combination of shared mailboxes, Microsoft 365 Groups, and Power Automate.

- **Full-trust solutions**   Full-trust solutions will need to be redeveloped as SPFx solutions or SharePoint add-ins.

- **Large Excel files**   If you store Excel workbooks larger than 100MB and attempt to edit them in the browser, you will be prompted to use the Microsoft 365 Apps Excel application instead. This size limit has increased from 10MB to 25MB.

- **Sandbox solutions**   Sandbox solutions were deprecated in SharePoint Online in 2014. Sandbox solutions should be redeveloped as SPFx solutions or SharePoint add-ins.

As you can see, features in this list can require more significant effort from a redevelopment perspective to transition to SharePoint Online or other Microsoft 365 services.

Choosing the migration tools

After identifying what content you wish to migrate, where it's located, and mapping out what features or services in Microsoft 365 you'll use as a destination, it's time to evaluate the migration tools available.

Three primary Microsoft methods can be used to facilitate migrations, depending on the location and type of source content:

- **SharePoint Migration Tool**   The SharePoint Migration Tool (SPMT) is used to migrate content from on-premises file shares and on-premises SharePoint environments. SPMT is available at *https://aka.ms/SPMT-LearnMore*.

- **SharePoint Migration Manager**   SharePoint Migration Manager is an agent-based tool originally designed to move file shares into Microsoft 365. It is integrated into the SharePoint admin center under the Migration node.

- **Azure Data Box**   The Azure Data Box is a combination of a storage appliance and service for migrating significant volumes of data into the Microsoft 365 service. You can learn more about Azure Data Box-based solutions at *https://aka.ms/spoazuredatabox*.

Inside Out

What happened to Mover.io?

Microsoft purchased the Mover.io service in 2019. Mover.io is designed for cloud-to-cloud migrations (such as DropBox and Google WorkSpace). While this tool is still available for customers who have already started migrations and configured connectors, its functionality has been incorporated into the SharePoint Migration Manager.

Planning for requirements and prerequisites

Planning for migration will require the coordination of multiple resources and reviewing any hardware, networking, and service prerequisites. In this section, we'll review the prerequisites necessary from the SharePoint Online service perspective as well as on-premises networking considerations.

SharePoint Online planning and prerequisites

In preparing for the SharePoint content migration, you'll want to download a few tools to your environment as well as ensure SharePoint Online settings are configured to allow scripting if your migration includes a custom script.

Downloading the SharePoint Migration Assessment Tool

The SharePoint Migration Assessment tool (SMAT) can help identify potential migration issues. To obtain the tool, follow these steps:

1. Navigate to *https://www.microsoft.com/download/details.aspx?id=53598*.

2. Download the file and extract it to a location on a SharePoint server.

The SharePoint Migration Assessment tool can also map user identities from on-premises to Azure AD and SharePoint Online.

Downloading the SharePoint Migration Tool

The SharePoint Migration Tool (SPMT) is the tool we'll use to migrate SharePoint Server content to SharePoint Online. To obtain the tool, follow these steps:

1. Navigate to *https://aka.ms/spmt-ga-page*.

2. Select the I Agree To The Terms Of Service And Privacy Policy checkbox and then click Install, as shown in Figure 28-2.

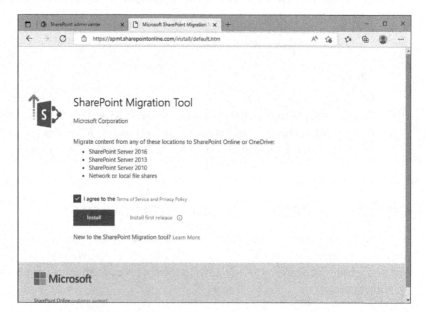

Figure 28-2   Starting the SharePoint Migration Tool

3. After downloading the installer in the browser, click Open File to launch it.

4. Enter a Microsoft 365 Global Admin credential to sign in.

5. Click the X to close the SharePoint Migration tool for now. See Figure 28-3.

Figure 28-3   The SharePoint Migration Tool start page

Now that you've obtained the prerequisite software, it's time to configure SharePoint Online for the migration.

Configuring SharePoint Online to allow custom script

Depending on what components you will be migrating, you might need to enable additional services and components in the SharePoint Online service. If you are migrating and enabling web parts, you might need to enable scripting using these steps:

1. Navigate to the SharePoint admin center.

2. Select Settings, and then scroll to the bottom of the page and click Classic Settings page.

3. Scroll to the Custom Script section. Select Allow Users To Run Custom Script On Personal Sites and Allow Users To Run Custom Script On Self-Service Created Sites, as shown in Figure 28-4.

CHAPTER 28

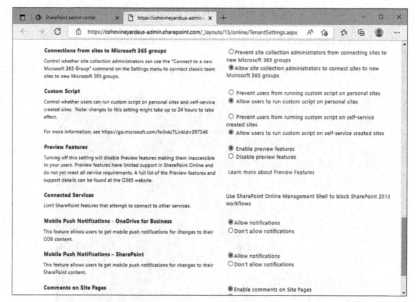

Figure 28-4   Enabling custom script

4.   Scroll to the bottom of the page and click OK to save the settings.

These settings should be updated at least 24 hours before initiating migrations.

Network planning and prerequisites

From a network planning perspective, you need to gather accurate information about how much data you'll be migrating and understand your bandwidth capabilities.

Network migration events sustain a peak load for an extended duration, so you'll want to make sure you've configured everything optimally. Network throughput planning should include the following:

- **Proxy devices**   Microsoft recommends that the traffic destined to the service bypass proxy devices, applications, or services for traffic. If your network utilizes proxy-type infrastructure (including proxy servers or third-party proxy services), you'll want to ensure that the migration traffic is excluded from the path.

NOTE

Microsoft reiterates this recommendation for all migration activities at *https://aka.ms/m365networkguidance*.

- **Intrusion protection systems and intrusion detection systems**   Migration activity can be seen as bulk data exfiltration attempts by these types of devices. It's critical to exclude the internal migration endpoints and the Microsoft 365 service to ensure uninterrupted data transfer to the cloud for the duration of the migration events.

- **Stateful packet inspection firewalls**   All traffic to the Microsoft 365 datacenters is SSL-encrypted. Inspection will require decryption and re-encryption of the data stream, which will significantly impact the firewall performance and transfer speeds. Consider excluding migration traffic from stateful inspection activities.

In addition to configuring your infrastructure to support maximum throughput and performance, you also might need to ensure that your network communications devices allow traffic to and from the required endpoints. See Table 28-1.

Table 28-1   Endpoints for SharePoint Online migration

Endpoint	Description
https://secure.aadcdn.microsoftonline-p.com	Authentication services
https://login.microsoftonline.com	Authentication services
https://api.office.com	Microsoft 365 application programming interfaces (APIs)
https://graph.windows.net	Microsoft 365 APIs
https://spmtreleasescus.blob.core.windows.net	SharePoint Migration Tool (SPMT) installation source
https://*.queue.core.windows.net	Azure migration API
https://*.blob.core.windows.net	Azure migration API
https://*.pipe.aria.microsoft.com	Telemetry data
https://*.sharepoint.com	SharePoint Online service
https://*.queue.core.usgovcloudapi.net	Azure migration API for U.S. Government
https://*.blob.core.usgovcloudapi.net	Azure migration API for U.S. Government
https://spoprod-a.akamaihd.net	User interface CDN data
https://static2.sharepointonline.com	User interface CDN data

CHAPTER 28

Scanning content

To help ensure the smoothest transition possible, you should scan your content before migration. Scanning can identify a number of issues, such as invalid file or path names or permissions discrepancies. Also, you should develop an identity mapping for sites to be migrated.

Generating an identity map

To generate an identity map for the on-premises sites, follow these steps:

1. From the SharePoint server where you downloaded the SharePoint Migration Assessment Tool (SMAT), launch an elevated command prompt, as shown in Figure 28-5.

2. Change the working directory to the location where SMAT was extracted.

3. Run the following command:

```
SMAT.exe -GenerateIdentityMapping
```

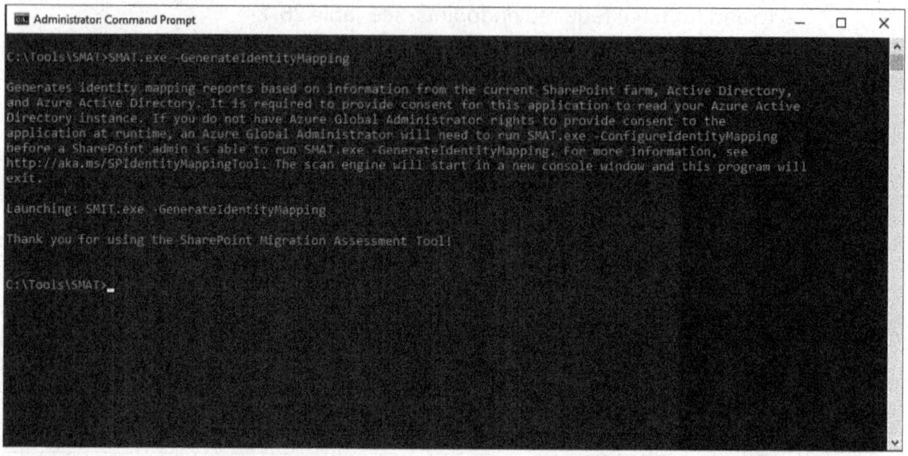

Figure 28-5   Launching the SharePoint Migration Assessment Tool with the -GenerateIdentityMapping parameter

4. When prompted, enter a Microsoft 365 Global Admin credential.

5. Select the Consent On Behalf Of Your Organization checkbox and click Accept, as shown in Figure 28-6.

6. Review the output generated by the tool. Note the location of the output data and press Enter to close the command prompt window, as shown in Figure 28-7.

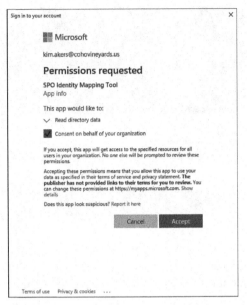

Figure 28-6   Consenting to permissions on behalf of your organization

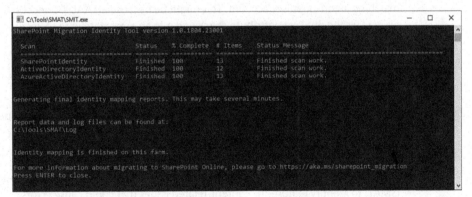

Figure 28-7   The output of the SMIT tool

7.   Review the `FullIdentityReport.csv` output file for identities that are not synchronized to Azure AD. Locate the `TypeOfMatch` column and filter for `PartialMatch` and `NoMatch` values. See Figure 28-8.

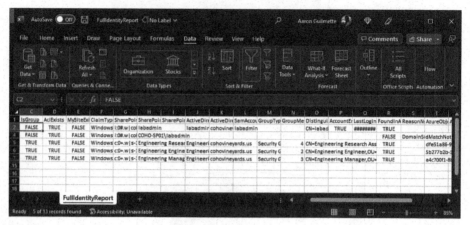

Figure 28-8   The SMIT tool output CSV

8. Make updates in your local Active Directory or Azure AD to ensure all necessary identities are in place. Repeat the identity mapping scan and review the process until you have corrected the errors.

The most common issue you will likely encounter is that there is no target identity in Azure AD matching an on-premises account. This might be because an AAD Connect scoping filter or object fails the duplicate attribute check and is in an error state in the Synchronization Manager.

NOTE

For a complete list of possible error codes, see *http://bit.ly/3F7NaKU*.

With identity mapping complete, it's time to scan the content for potential issues.

Scanning SharePoint content

The next step in preparing for a migration is to use the SharePoint Migration Assessment Tool (SMAT) to identify feature- or content-related issues that could cause errors.

To perform the scanning process, follow these steps:

1. Log in to the SharePoint Server with either the Farm Service account or a Farm Administrator account.

2. Launch an elevated command prompt.

3. Change the working directory to the location where SMAT was extracted.

4. Run the following command:

   SMAT.exe

5. SMAT will detect the installed version of SharePoint and launch an appropriate scan engine.

6. After the scan engine has completed, you will be prompted to enter your SharePoint Online tenant name, as depicted in Figure 28-9.

Figure 28-9   SharePoint Migration Assessment

Choosing to provide your SharePoint tenant information has no impact on the tool results and is only used for telemetry and tracking purposes. As with the SMAT identity mapping process, SMAT saves its report output to the Log subfolder.

Customizing the SMAT scanning process

You can also customize the SMAT scanning process using two files located in the main folder where SMAT has been extracted:

- **SiteSkipList.csv**   This configuration text file is used to list the sites you do not want to scan.

- **ScanDef.json**   This configuration file is used to enable or disable individual scan tasks. Enable or disable tasks by changing the task's Enabled value from true to false.

If you are troubleshooting scanning issues, you can use these customizations to exclude sites that don't need to be scanned or tests that might not apply.

Resolving blocking issues

The purpose of running scans is to identify problems that would prohibit a successful migration. There are many categories of errors, and it's important to determine if the errors listed present any business risk if left unresolved.

The most important log files to review as part of this process are:

- `SMAT.log`   This log file contains information, warning, and error messages. Error conditions should be investigated and resolved because they indicate potential blocking issues that could prevent the migration from completing.

- `SMAT_Errors.log`   This log file contains only the error content. If this file is not present after running the SharePoint Migration Assessment Tool, then no blocking errors were present in the scan.

- `ScannerReports\UnsupportedWebTemplate-detail.csv`   This file contains information about templates incompatible with SharePoint Online. SPMT SharePoint Online only supports transitioning to sites with the TeamSite (STS) and Personal Site (SPSPERS) templates. If your organization has templates other than these, don't worry—SPMT will allow you to map them to new templates.

Using the error logs, resolve any system, permissions, or other configuration issues. You might want to continue re-running the SharePoint Migration Assessment Tool to ensure you've resolved critical errors before proceeding.

Planning for content that cannot be migrated

Finally, before migrating, it's important to make plans regarding the content that cannot or should not be migrated successfully to SharePoint Online. You should have already identified most of this content during the Inventorying data sources and mapping destinations process.

However, after running the SharePoint Migration Assessment Tool, you might have discovered additional sites or applications with errors that will impact the migration. You might be able to ignore some warnings or errors, but doing so could result in certain items or features not being migrated.

If you encounter these issues, it's important to reevaluate the business requirements. Potential courses of action include:

- Mapping the application, content, or feature to a new service in the Microsoft 365 suite

- Update the source application, content, or feature to something compatible with SharePoint Online

- Evaluate if a third-party tool can migrate the source application, content, or feature

- Deprecate the source application, content, or feature

- Exclude the source application, content, or feature from migration and continue to use it as-is

After you have determined the outcome for all content, features, and applications, it's time to begin a migration.

Migrating data with SharePoint Migration Tool (SPMT)

Now that you've identified and resolved potential migration issues, it's time to start migrating data. In this section, we used the native tooling provided by Microsoft to perform SharePoint migrations—the SharePoint Migration Assessment Tool and the SharePoint Migration Tool.

Use the following steps to configure a migration:

1. Log in to the SharePoint Server where SPMT was installed.

2. Launch SPMT from the desktop shortcut.

3. Sign in to the tool using a Microsoft 365 Global Admin account.

4. Click Start A New Migration, as shown in Figure 28-10.

Figure 28-10   SharePoint Migration Tool splash page

5. Select the data source, as shown in Figure 28-11. For this example, choose SharePoint Server.

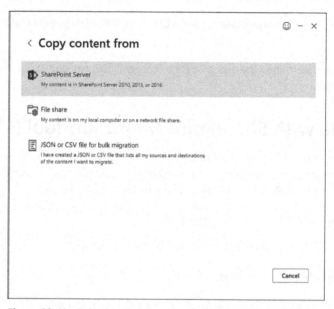

Figure 28-11   Selecting the type of content to migrate

6. Enter the URL for the content to migrate. You can choose a site, subsite, or list. If prompted, enter credentials that have access to the content.

7. From the Content You Want To Migrate dropdown, select the type or scope of content from the Content You Want To Migrate dropdown, and click Next, as shown in Figure 28-12.

8. From the Copy Content To dialog, select the destination—either Microsoft Teams or SharePoint, as shown in Figure 28-13.

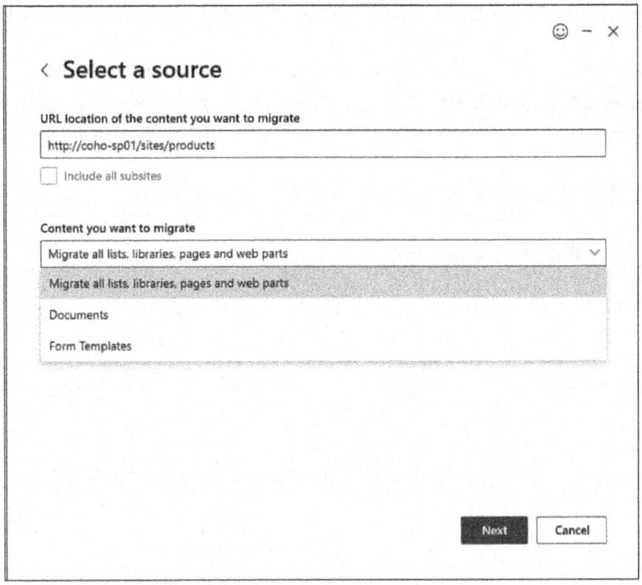

Figure 28-12   Selecting the source path of the content

Figure 28-13   Selecting a destination for the migration

- If you select Microsoft Teams, you are prompted to choose an existing Team.

- If you choose SharePoint, you are prompted to enter a URL. You can select a new or existing SharePoint site. If you select an existing target site and it still needs scripting enabled, you might see the Select A Destination dialog shown in Figure 28-14.

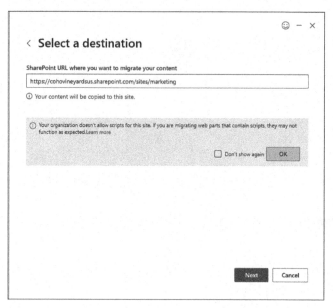

Figure 28-14   Confirming the destination if the target site does not have scripting enabled

9. Review the settings for the migration. You can enter a name for the migration in the Name Your Migration field.

10. If you want to add another migration, click Add Another Migration to restart the selection and mapping wizard. You can add additional migrations of any supported type. See Figure 28-15.

CAUTION

You can't edit the migration mapping that you've created, so if you make a mistake, you'll need to remove the item and then click Add Another Migration to reconfigure it.

Figure 28-15   Reviewing migration sources and destinations

11. When you are finished adding or updating migration mappings, click Next to proceed.

12. Select the settings for the migration from the options shown on the Choose Your Settings dialog (see Figure 26-16).

Figure 28-16   Configuring the settings for the migration

13. Clicking View All Settings opens the All Migrations flyout menu shown in Figure 28-17, where you see additional options, such as filtering by date, excluding files by extension type, options for replacing invalid characters, and migrating managed metadata. If you choose to migrate managed metadata, you'll need to have already configured the appropriate taxonomy and keywords so that items can be tagged.

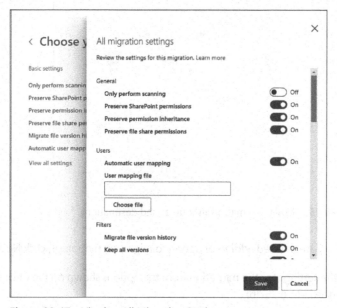

Figure 28-17   Viewing All Migration Settings

14. If necessary, click Save to exit the All Migration Settings flyout menu.

15. Click Migrate to begin the migration.

16. Review the migration progress, as shown in Figure 28-18.

The migration will proceed. At any point, you can click View Reports under each migration thread object to see the details of the particular task. You can also select Migration Details, which will display the reports folder showing two files:

- `GlobalSettings.csv`   The settings selected for this migration.

- `SummaryReport.csv`   A report that describes the sources being migrated, including the status of each.

Once the migration is complete, you'll receive a status update, as shown in Figure 28-19. You can view reports to see successes or failures, and you can start a new migration if desired.

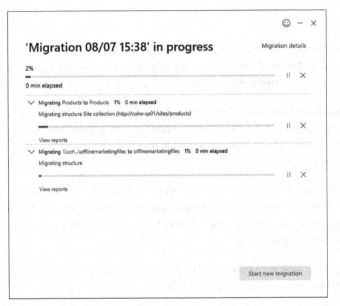

Figure 28-18   Viewing the migration progress

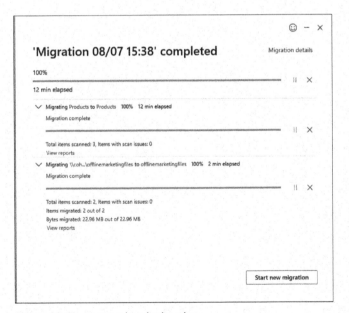

Figure 28-19   A completed migration

What's next?

In this chapter, we reviewed the processes for migrating content to SharePoint Online. Using the native tools provided by Microsoft, the SharePoint Migration Assessment Tool and the Share-Point Migration Tool, you learned how to conduct scanning and migration operations.

The SharePoint Migration Assessment Tool allows you to generate an identity mapping file, useful for determining which on-premises security principals might not have a corresponding Azure identity. It also allows you to scan for potential migration issues, such as invalid characters or unsupported components.

The SharePoint Migration Tool is used to perform the actual migration activities, including con-figuring migrations from file shares and existing on-premises SharePoint sites. While executing the SharePoint Migration Tool, you can select Teams, SharePoint Online, or OneDrive for Busi-ness as targets to receive migrated data.

In the next chapter, we'll look at the tools and capabilities for administering your SharePoint Online instance, including site management and sharing options.

SharePoint Online is a large product with hundreds of settings, features, and configurations ranging from simple deployment to deep enterprise integration. Because it's a service, a repository, and an application platform, there really isn't any limit to what you can do with it.

There are, however, some configurations that help you get the most out of your enterprise subscription.

Unless otherwise specified, you perform all management and configuration changes inside the SharePoint admin center (see Figure 29-1), available by logging on to the Microsoft 365 admin center, selecting the Admin tile, and then navigating to Admin > SharePoint or by browsing to *https://<tenant>-admin.sharepoint.com*.

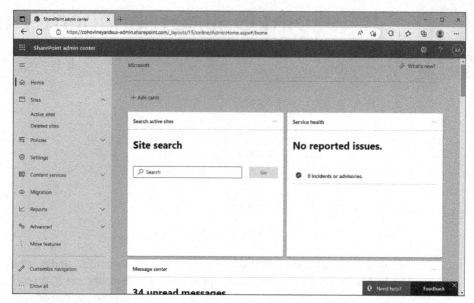

Figure 29-1   SharePoint admin center

The updated SharePoint admin center includes menu navigation for new features, such as usage reporting and migration. In the next few sections, we'll review the high-level navigation elements and what administration features are located beneath each.

Sites

The top-level content storage and administrative unit in SharePoint Online is the site collection. Site collections hold sites, and sites can contain pages, applications, lists, document libraries, and other sites. Sites and subsites are designed to inherit permissions from their parent container.

In the classic SharePoint architecture, administrators typically create site collections based on organizational or geographic hierarchies and then create sites and subsites within those collections.

Microsoft 365's modern architecture introduces the concept of hub sites. Any new sites that are created from the SharePoint admin center are created as site collections and can participate in the hub site architecture.

With classic architecture, a site collection contains a group of related sites. During a site's lifecycle, if you decide to move the site to a different location (for example, moving a product site from one business unit's site collection to another business unit's site collection), many things about the site collection and its references will change. Other links, apps, or documents that referenced items through the site's original location will need to be updated to continue working.

One of the advantages of the modern hub site architecture is that instead of creating hierarchies and risking having to migrate content from site to site, administrators can simply update a site's hub association to update its place in the organizational structure and search. No paths change, allowing links embedded in applications and documents to continue working.

Sites are divided into two main categories: active and deleted. You administer active sites and site collections from the Active Sites page in the SharePoint admin center. The Active Sites page, shown in Figure 29-2, is where you can create and manage the resources for site collections, purchase additional storage, assign ownership, and restore deleted items.

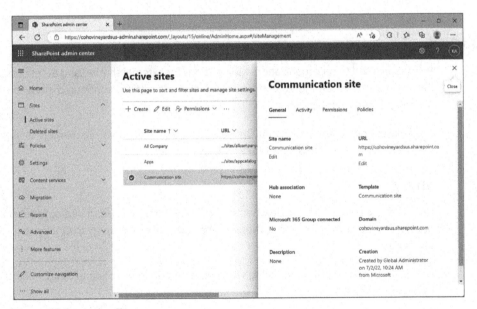

Figure 29-2　Active Sites

TIP

In previous versions of SharePoint Online, you could change the resource quota parameters for a site collection. With the new modern site architecture, the administrators can no longer manage the server resource quota.

Your SharePoint Online tenant comes with two out-of-the-box site collections:

- **https://<tenant>.sharepoint.com**　This is the default site collection. The default team site is created here. You can manage it and create additional sites or subsites inside it.

- **https://<tenant>-my.sharepoint.com**　Users' OneDrive for Business sites are automatically provisioned into the site collection.

Additional SharePoint site collections can be automatically provisioned the first time you access certain features:

- **https://<tenant>.sharepoint.com/sites/appcatalog**   This site collection is created the first time you access the SharePoint Online Store.

- **https://<tenant>-my.sharepoint.com/sites/allcompany<number>**   This site collection is tied to the All Company Yammer group and is provisioned the first time someone in the organization accesses Yammer.

Deleted sites are retained for 93 days; during this time, they can be pulled back and restored to their original locations. You can also permanently delete a site before the automated deletion schedule.

Policies

Policies are used to set organization-wide settings for external sharing and access control. Restrictive controls configured at this level will override settings configured elsewhere in the SharePoint admin center.

The Policies node of the SharePoint Online admin center allows you to manage tenant-wide external sharing and access control settings.

Sharing

Use the Sharing page to manage whether and how content can be shared outside your organization, as shown in Figure 29-3. These settings are global and apply to OneDrive for Business sites as well.

Figure 29-3 shows the Sharing dialog's External Sharing slider for SharePoint Online and OneDrive for Business.

The Sharing dialog allows you to manage the sharing capabilities tenant-wide. Available permissions range from Anyone (Most Permissive) to Only People In Your Organization (Least Permissive). Because OneDrive for Business is part of SharePoint Online, its permissiveness must be set to the same or less than that of the SharePoint Online service.

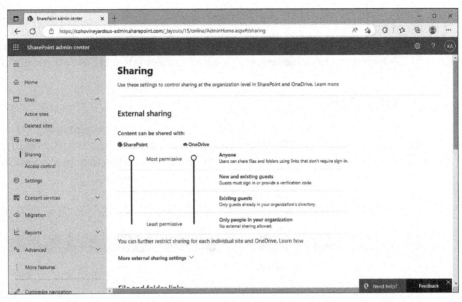

Figure 29-3   External Sharing controls

The External Sharing controls also have additional options to manage who can perform sharing activities and who can receive or redeem sharing invitations, as shown in Figure 29-4.

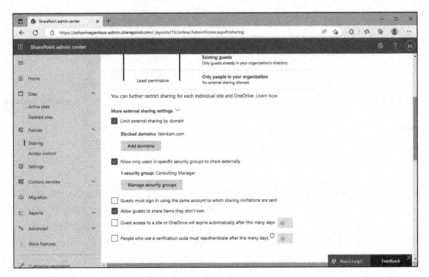

Figure 29-4   More External Sharing Settings

A number of restrictions are available, such as prohibiting all external sharing, only allowing sharing with certain domains, or preventing users from using sharing invitations with addresses other than the intended recipient.

NOTE

Sharing activities can be audited through the Security & Compliance Center. For more information about auditing, see Chapter 6, "Labels, retention, and eDiscovery."

Access control

You can use the settings on the Access Control page to restrict locations, apps, and devices from which users can connect to SharePoint Online–based services. These settings apply to Share-Point, OneDrive for Business sites, and Microsoft 365 groups (because they have a SharePoint component) and the Files tab in Microsoft Teams. See Figure 29-5.

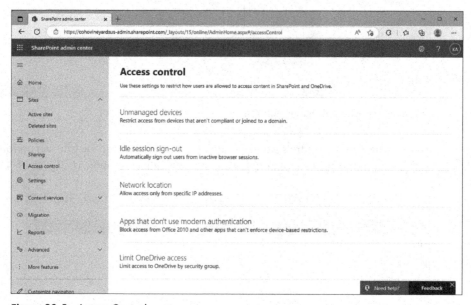

Figure 29-5   Access Control page

There are several configuration nodes here, including:

- **Unmanaged Devices**   This option allows full access from any device, application, or browser and allows web-only access; it allows you to block access altogether. Configuring the service to either web-only or blocking access will also prohibit PowerShell access from working correctly. You'll need to update the setting in the portal if you need to manage via PowerShell. If possible, Microsoft recommends using Conditional Access or Microsoft Defender for Cloud Apps to manage access.

- **Idle Session Sign-Out**   This option lets you sign out inactive users based on activity requests sent to SharePoint. Idle session sign-out applies tenant-wide. To use more restrictive settings, you'll need to configure conditional access.

- **Network Location**   By configuring network location settings, you can restrict what devices are allowed to access the SharePoint Online service.

Inside OUT

Location-based access settings

The location-based access controls apply to all clients, regardless of platform. For example, configuring the IP address restrictions to only an organization's corporate IP address ranges prohibits mobile devices from synchronizing OneDrive for Business content or accessing the Files tab for any team in Microsoft Teams when they are on cellular data networks or WiFi networks not egressing the configured IP ranges.

Depending on your organization's requirements, there might be a number of ways to control access for your environment. You can use Active Directory Federation Services claims to restrict access as well. However, Microsoft recommends using Intune Conditional Access.

- **Apps That Don't Use Modern Authentication**   This option lets you allow or block apps that don't use the modern authentication flows. This includes some third-party apps and legacy versions of Office.

- **Limit OneDrive Access**   This new feature allows you to use a security group to manage who can use OneDrive for Business or access files shared through OneDrive for Business. This feature requires an E5/A5 or E5/A5 Compliance subscription.

Settings

The Settings page contains a number of options that can be configured to change the experience and capabilities of SharePoint Online, as shown in Figure 29-6.

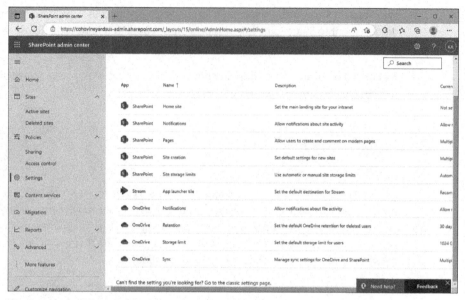

Figure 29-6   SharePoint Online Settings page

There are several configuration options here, including:

- **Home Site**   Use this setting to set a Communications site as your default landing page for SharePoint Online users.

- **Notifications (SharePoint)**   Enable or disable the ability for notifications to be delivered to the SharePoint mobile app.

- **Pages**   Enable or disable the ability for users to create and comment on modern pages using the Add A Page feature by default, tenant-wide. If this feature is enabled, site owners can still disable it at an individual site level.

- **Site Creation**   Allow or prevent users from creating sites from the SharePoint or OneDrive interfaces. With this option disabled, users can still create Microsoft 365 groups (which will provision a SharePoint site as part of the group provisioning). To fully prevent users from creating SharePoint sites from any interface, you will also need to manage the creation of Microsoft 365 groups.

- **Site Storage Limits**   Using this setting, you can manage whether all sites share the storage pool assigned to the tenant or set quotas on individual sites.

- **App Launcher Tile**   This option lets you choose where the Stream App Launcher Tile directs users. Expect this item to change (or be deprecated altogether), as Microsoft is planning on migrating classic Stream infrastructure into a SharePoint-backed platform.

- **Notifications (OneDrive)**   This option enables or disables users tenant-wide to receive notifications about OneDrive file activity. Like the SharePoint app notifications, users can still enable or disable notifications in the OneDrive mobile app.

- **Retention**   You can configure this value to manage how long SharePoint Online will retain OneDrive for Business sites for deleted users (both future and existing deleted users). The default value is 30 days. This only affects the visibility and accessibility of the site contents; it does not prevent users with access from deleting the content itself. To manage the preservation of content, you will need to configure retention policies through the Microsoft Purview compliance portal.

- **Storage Limit**   This option allows you to configure the default OneDrive for Business sites. The default is 1024GB and can be set to a maximum of 5120GB for users with qualifying licenses.

- **Sync**   This option lets you manage the synchronization of data through the OneDrive app. It controls the visibility of the Sync button on the OneDrive site; also, it allows the restriction of synchronization to machines that are members of certain domains (controlled by additing the domain's object GUID to the admin center). You can also prevent the OneDrive client from synchronizing certain file types, though they can still be uploaded to SharePoint Online through the web interface.

As of this writing, you can also still access Classic Settings at the bottom of the Settings page (shown in Figure 29-6). Navigating to the Classic Settings page allows you to configure the options shown in Figure 29-7.

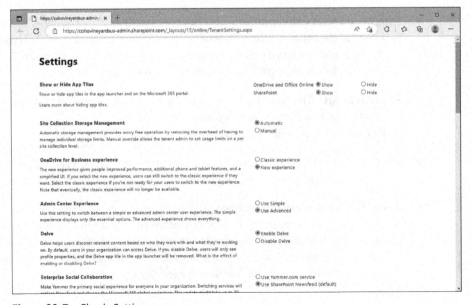

Figure 29-7   Classic Settings page

- **Show Or Hide App Tiles** This option contains buttons to show or hide OneDrive For Business, Office Online, and SharePoint tiles. This setting removes the tiles from the App Launcher but does not disable the services. If users have bookmarked the URLs or know how to navigate them, they can still access them. The default setting is Show For Both Settings.

- **Site Collection Store Management** This setting has two options—Automatic and Manual. Manual storage operation means you, as the administrator, must update quotas for site collections as they grow, whereas the Automatic setting automatically grows the size of the site collection as it nears its limit. The default is Automatic.

- **OneDrive For Business Experience** You can enable the New Experience or Classic Experience user interface. The default is New Experience.

- **OneDrive Sync Button** You can use this option to show or hide the Sync button in the OneDrive user interface. The default is Show The Sync Button.

- **Admin Center Experience** This setting controls whether to show a minimal set of configuration options or all options. The default setting is Use Advanced.

- **Delve** Use this setting to enable or disable access to Delve. Delve analyzes the relationships between users and data in Microsoft 365 and presents it through the Delve profile page. If this option is disabled, users only see their own user profile properties. Previously, this setting was used to control access to the Office Graph application and affected services beyond Delve. Based on customer feedback, this option was updated to only manage Delve and was decoupled from other services.

- **Enterprise Social Collaboration** You can select whether to use Yammer or SharePoint Newsfeed as the social platform. Yammer is currently not covered in the Microsoft 365 Trust Center and requires a service amendment for Government Community Cloud customers. The default setting is Use SharePoint Newsfeed (Default).

- **Personal Blogs** The option still exists to enable or disable the ability for users to create personal blogs. However, Delve blogs were retired in April 2020. You can still create blog pages on modern Communications sites.

- **Site Pages** Modifying this option lets you control whether users can create site pages using the authoring canvas. The default setting is Allow Users To Create Site Pages.

- **Global Experience Version Settings** While this option is still visible, it has been deprecated. This option previously controlled which version of a site collection users could create and whether users could upgrade site collections. The selected option is: Prevent Creation Of Old Version Site Collections, But Allow Creation Of New Version Site Collections. Allow Opt-In Upgrade To The New Version Site Collections.

- **Information Rights Management (IRM)**   Enable or disable Information Rights Management for your tenant. To enable IRM, you must have a subscription that includes Azure Rights Management and enable IRM in your Microsoft 365 tenant before enabling IRM in SharePoint Online. For more information about deploying Azure Rights Management, see *https://aka.ms/activateirm*. The default setting is Do Not Use IRM For This Tenant.

Inside OUT

Information rights management

You can use information rights management to encrypt documents and make them available only to users who have access to the Azure Rights Management Service and have been granted permissions to a file. IRM can be applied to libraries and lists, protecting all documents contained within them. Typical restrictions include making a document read-only or prohibiting the use of screen-capture tools or printing. Using IRM to protect documents can help prevent the distribution of documents outside your organization. SharePoint Online encryption supports PDF, XPS, and Office documents created in Word, Excel, and PowerPoint from version 97 onward. Microsoft recommends leaving this setting disabled and using Azure Information Protection and data governance controls in the Microsoft Purview compliance portal.

- **Site Creation**   There are multiple settings groups under this option:

  - The first settings group is used to hide or show the Create Site command. Only users who have permission to create sites see this command in SharePoint Online. The default option is Show The Create Site Command To Users Who Have Permissions To Create Sites.

  - The second settings group takes effect when a user creates a site. Because Microsoft 365 groups can be integrated with SharePoint Sites, you can control whether the Create Site command still functions normally if Microsoft 365 group creation is disabled. If Microsoft 365 group creation is disabled, the Create Site command will create a site without a connected group. The options are:

    - ▼ **A New Team Site Or Communication Site**   This setting allows the creation of a site using Team or Communications site templates.

    - ▼ **A Classic Team Subsite**   Choose this option if you want to enable users to create only a classic team subsite.

    - ▼ **Create Groups Under**   Set the location for new sites using the available managed paths (by default, `/sites/` and `/teams/`). You can also specify whether to require a secondary site contact.

NOTE

For any option, you can also choose to create the sites using a form using the Use The Form At This URL checkbox. This option will likely be deprecated because custom form capabilities are being migrated to Power Apps.

- **Subsite Creation**   This option manages settings for users who have permissions to create subsites. The available options include disabling subsite creation tenant-site, enabling sub-site creation for classic sites only, or enabling creation of subsites fo all sites. The default option is to disable subsite creation tenant-wide. Microsoft recommends using hub sites to connect related sites instead of provisioning subsites.

- **Custom Script**   There are two settings under this option. Use this option to enable or disable custom scripting on personal and self-service created sites. The default settings are Prevent Users From Running Custom Script On Personal Sites and Prevent Users From Running Custom Script On Self-Service Created Sites.

- **Preview Features**   This option determines whether preview features are enabled in SharePoint Online. The default setting is Enable Preview Features.

- **Connected Services**   This option limits SharePoint Online features that attempt to connect to other services. The Block SharePoint 2013 Workflows checkbox is cleared by default.

- **Mobile Push Notifications – OneDrive for Business**   This setting determines whether users can get push notifications for the OneDrive for Business mobile app. The default setting is Allow Notifications. This setting mirrors the OneDrive for Business notification option configured in Settings.

- **Mobile Push Notifications – SharePoint**   This setting determines whether users can get push notifications for SharePoint content. The default setting is Allow Notifications. This setting mirrors the SharePoint notification option configured in Settings.

- **Comments on Site Pages**   You can use this setting to determine whether users can leave comments on site pages. Users who have access to view a page can leave comments. The default setting is Enable Comments On Site Pages.

After making any changes to settings, click OK at the bottom of the page to commit changes.

Content services

The Content services menu node expands to show the Term Store and Content Type Gallery options.

Term Store

SharePoint Online enables you to tag and categorize data for standardization purposes. You can use data contained in the Term Store to achieve this.

For example, if your organization is a winery that is cataloging products in its inventory, you might want to create a set of standard terms describing flavor characteristics, such as strawberry or vanilla, as shown in Figure 29-8. If your organization produces vehicles, you might want to create categories and terms describing passenger vehicles, trucks, or trailers.

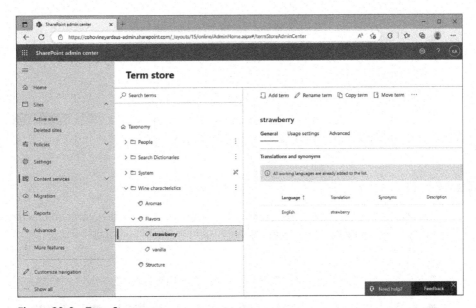

Figure 29-8   Term Store page

To manage the Term Store, you must be granted permissions to do so. Select the top level of the Term Store and add administrators in the Term Store Administrators area.

NOTE

For more information about term sets, see "Create and manage terms in a term set" at *https://docs.microsoft.com/en-us/sharepoint/create-and-manage-terms.*

Content Type Gallery

Content types are used to describe both a data element and information about an item. Content types can be used to associate items with types of metadata, document templates, or policies. The Content Type Gallery page provides an interface to create, edit, and publish content types, as shown in Figure 29-9.

After creating a custom content type, it will be automatically published to all sites. Unlike SharePoint Server, you cannot unpublish content types. To unpublish a type, you must delete it.

CHAPTER 29

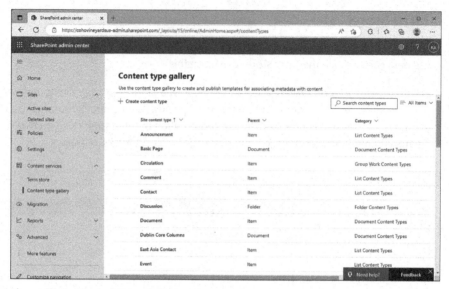

Figure 29-9   Content Type Gallery management page

Migration

The Migration page, shown in Figure 29-10, allows you to start the migration process from a variety of file storage solutions, including on-premises file servers, Box, Google Workspace, Dropbox, and Egnyte.

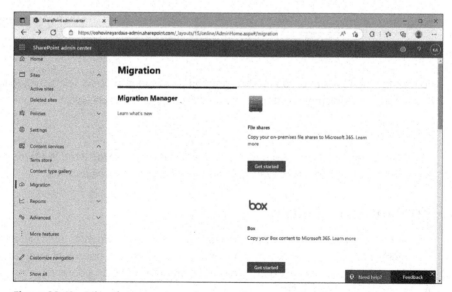

Figure 29-10   Migration management page

Each source option launches a wizard to assist you with the migration effort.

Reports

The Reports node includes features to review content statistics reporting as well as data access governance.

Content Services

The Content Services reports give an overall view of how metadata is created and managed in the organization. See Figure 29-11.

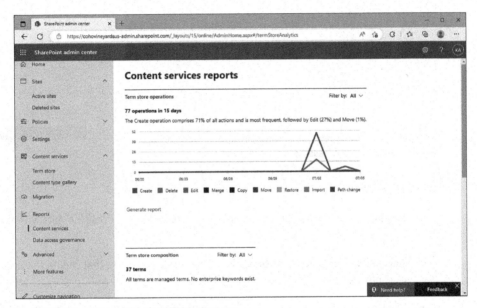

Figure 29-11   Content Services Reports page

From this page, you can generate reports on the metadata operations performed, including creating, deleting, copying, and moving.

Data access governance

These reports focus on common data governance management tasks, such as reviewing the creation of sharing links and which sites have files with applied sensitivity labels. See Figure 29-12.

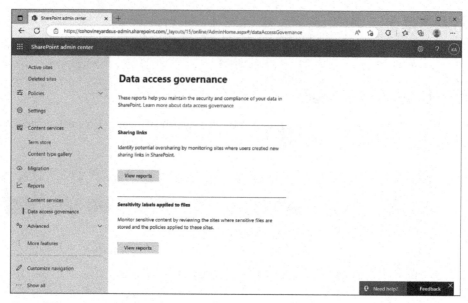

Figure 29-12   Data Access Governance page

Choosing Sharing Links offers three site categories:

- **Anyone Links**   Sites containing links where anyone can access the data without signing in.

- **People In Your Organization Links**   Sites containing links that can be shared with anyone internally.

- **Specific People Links**   Shared externally, focused on sites with sharing invitations sent to named individuals outside the organization.

Each report is limited to the top 100 sites in each category. It's important to note that these reports don't indicate the shared files. Instead, they are focused on the sites with the most sharing activities. The visible reports are limited to the top 100 sites, but you can also download a CSV containing the top 10,000 sites.

Similarly, Sensitivity Labels Applied To Files reports show the top 100 sites containing files with sensitivity labels applied. You'll need to use the Microsoft Purview compliance center to get more detailed reporting on labels.

Advanced

Under the Advanced menu option, there is currently a single node for API access. Figure 29-13 shows the API access requests made for SharePoint Framework components and scripts. On this page, you can approve or reject API requests.

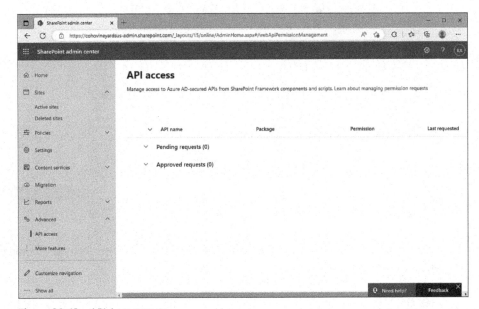

Figure 29-13   API Access page

NOTE

To learn more about building SharePoint Framework solutions that leverage Azure AD–secured APIs, see *https://bit.ly/3FBsf3g*.

More Features

Selecting More Features in the navigation menu displays a number of classic SharePoint management tools that are either infrequently used or are being deprecated in favor of other tooling. See Figure 29-14.

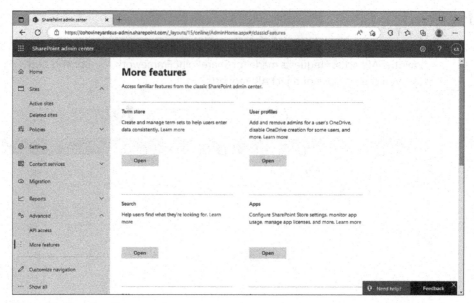

Figure 29-14   More Features page

In the next sections, we'll review the classic SharePoint admin center features that can be accessed from this page.

Term Store

This link provides a path to get to the classic user interface version of the Term Store. It may be removed in future updates to the SharePoint admin center interface since there is already a modern version available in the SharePoint admin center.

User profiles

The User Profiles section is where all of a user's personal information and properties are stored for SharePoint Online. Suppose your organization is synchronizing with Active Directory. In that case, user attributes from the on-premises environment are synchronized into Microsoft Azure Active Directory. Then the User Profile Synchronization Service (which is not exposed in Share-Point Online) synchronizes that data into the individual user profiles. See Figure 29-15.

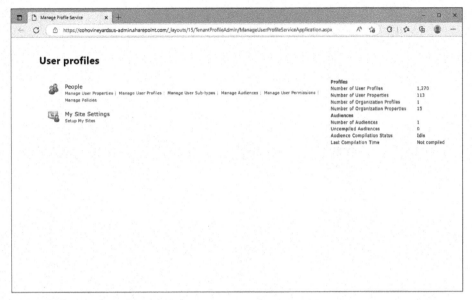

Figure 29-15   User Profiles page

People

The People area of the User Profiles settings contains management tasks related to users. Tasks in this area include configuring additional user properties and audiences—both of which can be used to make SharePoint Online deliver customized value to your organization. The tasks found here are described below:

- **Manage User Properties**   By creating additional property fields, you allow users to enter data in their SharePoint profiles that might not otherwise be captured in other systems. This can be useful for creating *audiences* (SharePoint terminology for groups that can be created based on certain properties) or for enabling user discovery through search. For example, you might create a property field called Previous Departments to provide users a way to indicate what other roles they might have had in an organization. See Figure 29-16.

- **Manage User Profiles**   In this section, you find options to manage the individual user profiles of users in your organization, as shown in Figure 29-17. From this page, you can choose Edit My Profile to modify the individual properties associated with a user. If you are synchronizing data from Active Directory, fields might be overwritten during the next profile synchronization process. You can also delete the user profile or update settings for the user's OneDrive for Business site by selecting either Manage Personal Site or Manage Site Collection Owners.

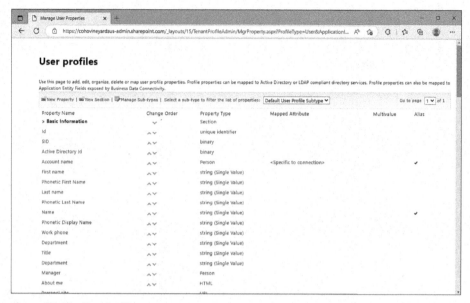

Figure 29-16   User Profiles management

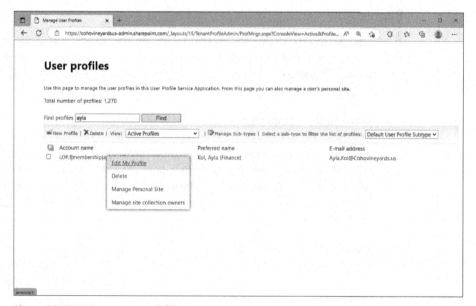

Figure 29-17   Manage user profiles

- **Manage User Subtypes**   User subtypes are classifications that you can apply to user profile properties. You can use subtypes to configure which profile fields are available for various user types. For example, you might create a subtype for employees and contractors and then restrict a profile field such as Office Phone to be available to employees only.

- **Manage Audiences**   Audiences are groups of users that can be created based on user profile properties. For example, you might choose to create an audience that contains all members whose department is Marketing and whose work phone contains the digits 555.

- **Manage User Permissions**   You can use Manage User Permissions to adjust users' permissions for the User Profile service. For example, you can use this to restrict OneDrive for Business provisioning (for more information, see Chapter 19) or access other User Profile Service features.

- **Manage Policies**   You can manage the policies to configure which profile fields are required or optional for the User Profile Service and configure the visibility of those profile fields.

My Site Settings

The My Site Settings area contains settings by which you manage My Sites (OneDrive for Business) sites across your organization:

- **Set Up My Sites**   You can modify the settings in Set Up My Sites to configure the behavior of the sites the User Profile Service application manages, as shown in Figure 29-18. Some of the settings, such as My Site Host and Personal Site Location, cannot be changed because they were configured when the User Profile Service for your tenant was created.

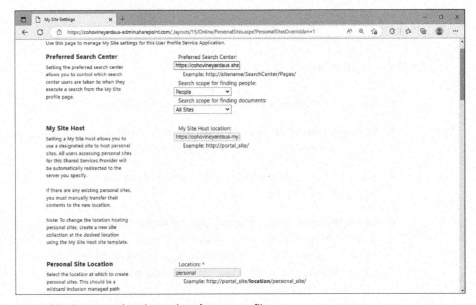

Figure 29-18   Managing site settings for user profiles

NOTE

Management settings on this page, including My Site Cleanup and and My Site Secondary Admin, will be discussed in Chapter 30, "OneDrive for Business."

Search

The Search Administration page enables you to customize Search for your organization. See Figure 29-19 for Search configuration options.

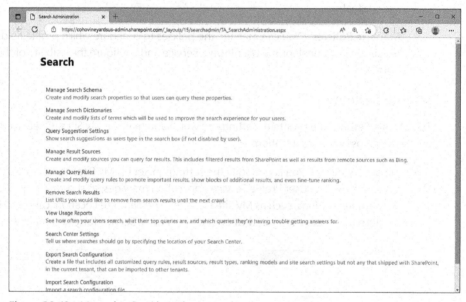

Figure 29-19   Managing Search settings

The Search page provides an interface to many classic SharePoint admin center settings:

- **Manage Search Schema**   The search schema enables you to control which properties of users, documents, and other objects are indexed for search.

- **Manage Search Dictionaries**   This option opens the Term Store, enabling you to create and manage term sets.

- **Manage Authoritative Pages**   Use the Authoritative Pages settings to tune the order and weight of returned documents. For example, if you have a document called `Procedures.docx` in `/sites/active` and a copy from several years ago with outdated historical content in `/sites/archive`, you can choose return results so that the item in `/sites/active` is ranked higher.

- **Query Suggestion Settings**   Use these settings to enable or disable search suggestions. You can also prepopulate common search phrases from a text file.

- **Manage Result Sources**   Configure locations that search queries.

- **Manage Query Rules**   Create rules to promote important or preferred results and tune search ranking.

- **Manage Query Client Types**   Use Client Types to manage the sources of queries and rank them in priority for performance.

- **Remove Search Results**   Use this to remove specific URLs from the search results. URLs are re-added upon the next crawl. To permanently remove a result from search, change permissions on the item or remove it completely.

- **View Usage Reports**   View usage reports to get information about how often your users are using search as well as what types of queries are being run.

- **Search Center Settings**   Use this setting to point to the URL of the enterprise search portal. By default, it points to *https://<tenant>.sharepoint.com/search/Pages*.

- **Export Search Configuration**   Create an export file containing the query rules, ranking models, and settings.

- **Import Search Configuration**   Import a search configuration file.

- **Crawl Log Permissions**   Type the email addresses of users to whom you wish to grant permission to read the crawl log.

You can use these settings to control how the search service works across the SharePoint Online environment.

Apps

You can enable the use of apps in your SharePoint Online environment to further extend the platform's capabilities. See Figure 29-20.

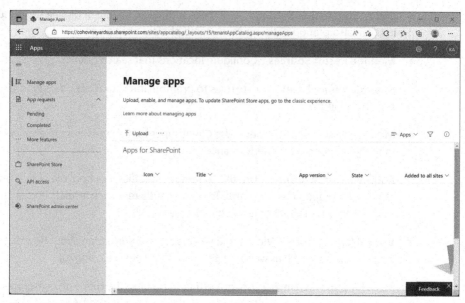

Figure 29-20   Apps page in the SharePoint admin center

You can upload custom apps from the Manage Apps page and make them available to add to SharePoint sites. You can also expand the ellipsis to access additional menu options, such as reviewing Power Apps available in your tenant and Power App forms that have been used to customize lists:

- **App Requests**   Apps that users request to purchase will show up in this area. You can review, approve, and reject app requests.

- **More Features**   The More Features option exposes some additional SharePoint Store and app configuration settings that were available in the classic interface, as shown in Figure 29-21. The options available on the More Features page include:

    - **Tenant Wide Extensions**   Allows you to configure SharePoint Framework solution extensions. This feature primarily targets organizations that develop their own SharePoint app solutions.

    - **App Permissions**   Use the App Permissions page to remove permissions granted to apps. By default, the only app permission listed is Microsoft 365 Exchange Online (listed as Display ID 00000002-0000-0ff1-ce00-000000000000). They appear here as you add more apps to your organization and request access to data on behalf of your users.

    - **Configure Store Settings**   Allows you to manage the ability for users to purchase apps.

    - **Site Contents**   This setting allows you to manage the apps installed on the site.

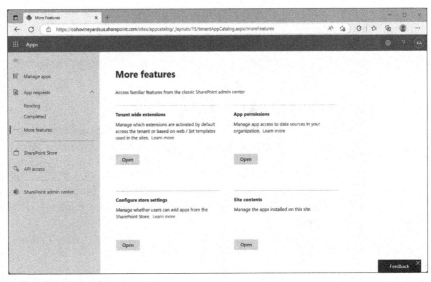

Figure 29-21   More Features

SharePoint store

You can search for and purchase apps directly from the SharePoint store. If purchase details are needed, you can input those. Some apps, such as the one shown in Figure 29-22, require the classic SharePoint store to purchase.

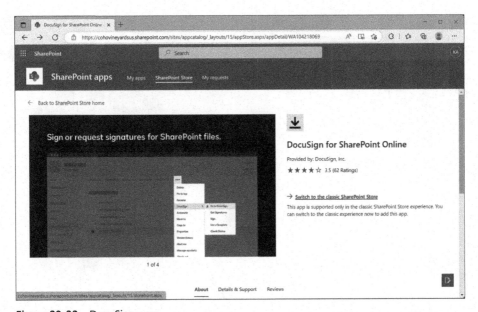

Figure 29-22   DocuSign app

CHAPTER 29

After purchasing an app, you might be prompted to add it to the app catalog or to all sites automatically.

> ## Inside OUT
>
> ### Sorry, this site does not support apps
>
> **If you navigate to the SharePoint Admin site and launch the App Catalog directly, you might encounter an error when attempting to purchase an app.**
>
> **The Sorry, This Site Does Not Support Apps But You Can Still Acquire Them And Add Them On Other Sites error appears because you cannot install apps to the SharePoint admin center site. You can purchase the apps here, but you have to install them directly into sites.**

After you have acquired an app, you receive a notification that the app has been made available to everyone in your organization. Site administrators can then add the app to their sites.

Manage licenses

The Manage license feature has moved to Site Contents. To view or manage licenses (or license administrators) for a particular app, navigate to More Features > Site Contents, expand the ellipsis for the app, and select Manage Licenses. See Figure 29-23.

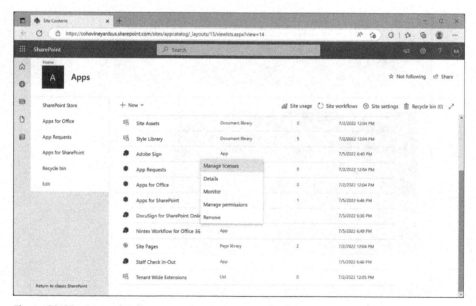

Figure 29-23 Managing licenses

After selecting Manage Licenses for an app, you can view the individual license details, as shown in Figure 29-24. You can also revoke individual licenses and assign a license manager from this page.

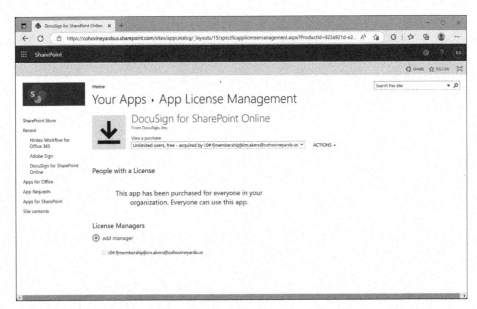

Figure 29-24   App License Management page

Monitor Apps

Like the Manage Licenses page, the Monitor Apps page has moved to the Site Contents. You can expand the ellipsis for an app and then select Monitor Apps. From the Monitor Apps page, you can track the usage of apps across your tenant.

Business Connectivity Services

Business Connectivity Services enables you to connect to data sets outside of SharePoint Online and then make them available. The Business Connectivity Services page enables you to configure connections to external data sources, as shown in Figure 29-25.

CHAPTER 29

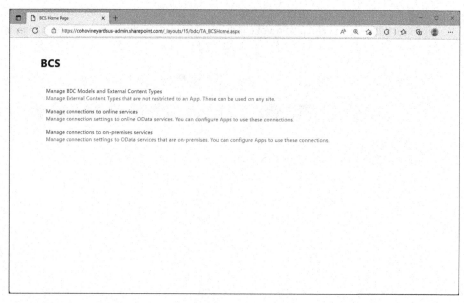

Figure 29-25   Business Connectivity Services page

To fully configure Business Connectivity Services, you must do the following:

1.   Configure permissions.

2.   Configure a Secure Store credential mapping.

3.   Create an external content type.

4.   Configure a connection to a data source.

5.   Create an output (such as an external list).

6.   Grant permissions to view and manage the external content type.

Before you begin configuring Business Connectivity Services, use the Manage BDC Models And External Content Types page to configure permissions on the Business Connectivity Metadata Store.

Select the Set Metadata Store Permissions button on the ribbon and add the administrators for the application to the list, select the appropriate permissions, and click OK. See Figure 29-26.

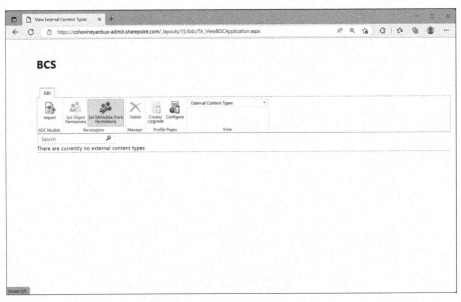

Figure 29-26   Business Connectivity Services manage external content types page

You must create an external content type (ECT) by using Visual Studio or SharePoint Designer 2010.

TIP

SharePoint Designer 2010 is available as a free download from the Microsoft Download Center at *https://www.microsoft.com/download/en/details.aspx?id=16573*.

NOTE

For an example of how to create an ECT and build an external list that retrieves data from a SQL Azure table, see "Make an External List from a SQL Azure Table with Business Connectivity Services and Secure Store" at *https://bit.ly/3uvhgSs*.

You can configure connections to online services by using the Manage Connections To Online Services setting shown in Figure 29-27. Connections might be used by apps that you develop or purchase from the SharePoint Store.

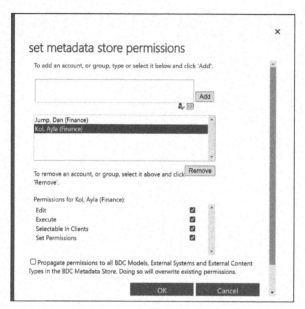

Figure 29-27   Set Metadata Store Permissions

You can configure connections to on-premises data services by using the Manage Connections To On-Premises Services setting. If you configure an on-premises data service, you can use a credential stored in a target application (configured on the Secure Store page).

TIP

Business Connectivity Services is the evolution of the Business Data Catalog, released as part of SharePoint Server 2007. It's been a valuable data interchange tool for thousands of organizations. However, it is limited to being managed by and connecting to SharePoint data sources. For new development efforts, Microsoft recommends building with the Power Platform suite of tools (Power Apps, Power Automate, and Power BI). This next-generation platform allows you to integrate with any REST-based API services, build apps for mobile devices, and create compelling data visualizations.

Secure Store

Secure Store is essentially a trusted credential store for SharePoint applications. Secure Store management is also a legacy SharePoint admin center feature. To use Secure Store, you can create a new target application (see Figure 29-28) and configure which users are mapped to this application and credential.

After a target application has been configured, you can configure credentials. They are encrypted and can be stored in SharePoint Online for use by Business Connectivity Services or apps.

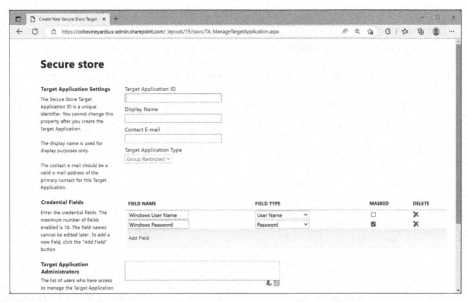

Figure 29-28   Secure Store new target application

Records management

You can configure SharePoint Online to manage records in place or send them to a records management center. The Records Management page enables you to configure a Send To connection for records management that the Content Organizer can use.

Inside OUT

The future of SharePoint records management

SharePoint has long been a robust document storage and management tool. One of the many strengths of the platform is records management. SharePoint records management is a legacy feature. While it is still supported, it can be more difficult to implement than other more modern practices. SharePoint-based records management is dependent upon content types and document metadata— tasks that can be cumbersome for users who are interfacing with SharePoint through other apps (such as Microsoft Teams), which doesn't natively display all of the metadata columns that the SharePoint Content Organizer will be using to route documents.

Microsoft recommends using the more holistic Data Governance tools that are available as part of the Microsoft Purview compliance center for in-place records management.

You can learn more about the new data governance features in Chapter 6.

Before implementing a records management plan, you should work with business owners and content experts to develop a file plan to describe the types of items and documents to acknowledge as records and where the records will be stored.

SharePoint-based records management is dependent upon content types and metadata.

The following example can be used to set up a Records Management site collection and configure a site to route documents there automatically. To do so, follow these steps:

1. From the SharePoint admin center shown in Figure 29-29, expand Sites and select Active Sites.

2. Click Create.

3. Scroll to the bottom of the page and select Other Options to select the classic SharePoint site templates.

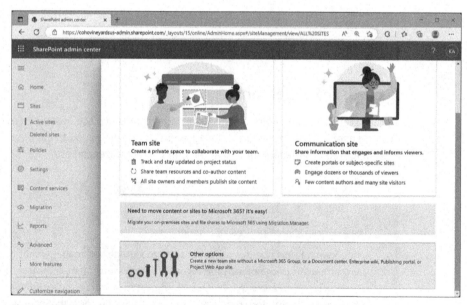

Figure 29-29   Create site wizard

4. Under Choose A Template, select More Templates to be redirected to the classic SharePoint site templates.

5. Fill out the page details, including Title, Address, Template Selection, Time Zone, Administrator, and Server Resource Quota details. For the template, select the Enterprise tab and then select Records Center. See Figure 29-30.

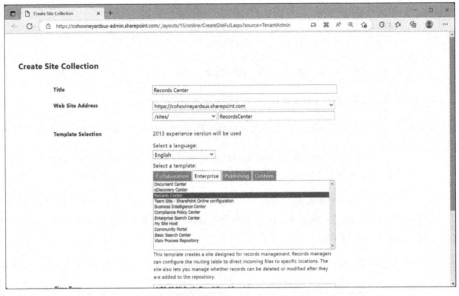

Figure 29-30   Classic SharePoint Create Site Collection

6.   Click OK to create the site collection.

7.   After the site collection has been created, you can navigate to it and examine the structure. See Figure 29-31.

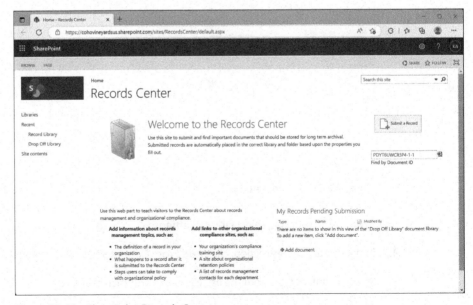

Figure 29-31   SharePoint Records Center page

When your Records Center has been configured, you can configure libraries and lists to manage and contain records. Content types are associated with libraries, which ultimately enable documents to be routed to the correct libraries. Follow these steps:

1. On the Records Center site, click Libraries in the navigation pane.

2. Click New, and then select Document Library.

3. In the Create Document Library fly-out menu, type a name and click Create.

Content types enable the Records Center to process documents automatically. Follow these steps to add content to a library:

1. Select the new library you just created in the navigation pane, and then, at the bottom of the library, select Return To Classic SharePoint to view the Classic SharePoint library controls.

2. On the ribbon, select Library. See Figure 29-32.

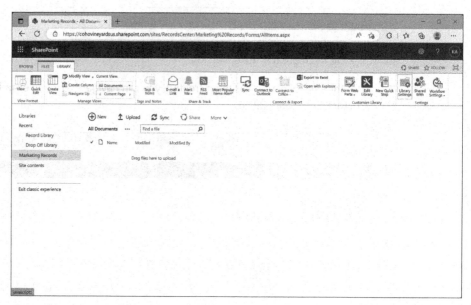

Figure 29-32   Library settings

3. In the Settings group, select Library Settings.

4. In the Content Types section, click Add From Existing Site Content Types.

5. Select a content type from the list, click Add, and then click OK.

TIP

If you cannot see the Content Type settings, select Advanced Settings and then select the Yes radio button under Allow Management Of Content Types. Scroll to the end of the page and click OK. For more information, see "Turn on support for multiple content types in a list or library" at *https://bit.ly/3h8RwbA*.

Finally, follow these steps to create an information management policy to route documents to the library:

1. On the Records Center site, click the gear icon and select Site Settings.

2. In the Web Designer Galleries section, click Site Content Types.

3. On the Content type gallery page, click Return To Classic to navigate to the classic Content Type gallery page.

4. Select the content type to which you want to apply the policy settings, such as Document.

5. Select Information Management Policy Settings.

6. Type a description and a policy statement, enable one or more policy settings, and then click OK.

NOTE

For more information about configuring a Records Center and management policies, see "Implement Records Management" at *https://aka.ms/recordmanagement*.

Now that a Records Center has been created, you can configure the Send To connection in the SharePoint admin center. To do so, follow these steps:

1. In the SharePoint admin center, select More Features, and then select Records Management.

2. Configure Send To Connections by typing a name for the connection and a Send To URL. The Send To URL can be obtained from the Records Center site in Site Settings > Content Organizer Settings under Submission Points. The default value is `https://<tenant>. sharepoint.com/sites/<RecordsManagementSite>/_vti_bin/OfficialFile.asmx`. See Figure 29-33.

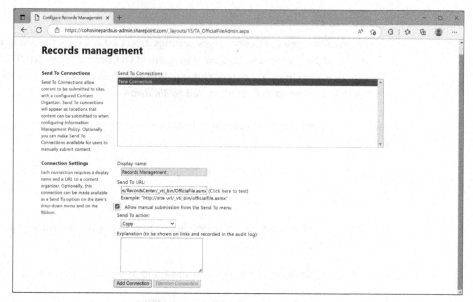

Figure 29-33   Configuring the Send To connection

3.   Click Add Connection.

Your organization might also use the combination of a records management site and preservation or retention policies (configured through the Microsoft Purview Compliance Center) to label and preserve important business data. See Chapter 6 for more information.

Finally, in order to be able to use Send To Connection in a document library, you'll need to enable SharePoint Server Standard Site Features, SharePoint Server Enterprise Site Features, and Content Organizer features on each site collection.

To do it for an example site collection, follow these steps:

1.   Navigate to a site where you wish to enable the Content Organizer to send data to the Records Center.

2.   Select the gear icon, select Site Information, and then click View All Site Settings.

3.   Under the Site Collection Administration section, select Site Collection Features.

4.   Select the Activate button next to both the SharePoint Server Enterprise Site Collection Features and SharePoint Server Standard Site Collection Features options.

5.   Navigate back to the View All Site Settings page.

6. Under Site Actions, select Manage Site Features.

7. Click the Activate button next to the Content Organizer option.

Once these actions have been completed, you can now use the Send To option in the classic SharePoint view of a document library to send content to the Records Center for further review, as shown in Figure 29-34.

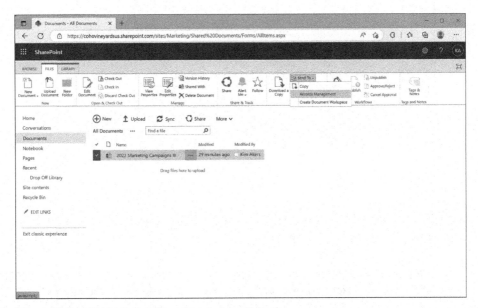

Figure 29-34   Set Metadata Store Permissions dialog box

Infopath

The Infopath page enables you to configure the SharePoint Online Infopath Forms Services. From this page, you can enable or disable browser-based forms (which would require clients to complete forms by using the Infopath desktop application). You can also configure user agent exemptions for indexing. Configuring user agent exemptions causes search indexers with matching user agents to index the Infopath form as XML text instead of as a web form.

Infopath has been deprecated and will be retired on July 14, 2026. Microsoft recommends using Power Apps for creating and delivering custom forms and lists. Power Apps-based forms can be created directly on SharePoint list and library pages.

Hybrid Picker

The Hybrid Picker page, shown in Figure 29-35, provides information about hybrid configuration options between SharePoint Server and SharePoint Online and a link to the Hybrid Picker download. The Hybrid Picker is a wizard designed to assist in configuring SharePoint Server hybrid features.

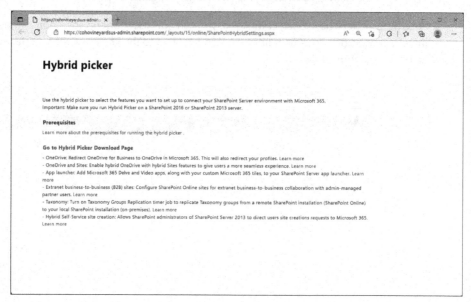

Figure 29-35   Hybrid Picker page

SharePoint Hybrid options include redirecting on-premises OneDrive to SharePoint Online, configuring hybrid taxonomy, and configuring cross-premises search capabilities.

NOTE

For more information about SharePoint Hybrid configurations, see Chapter 27, "SharePoint Online Hybrid configuration."

What's next?

This chapter discussed SharePoint Online concepts and features as well as how to manage many settings in the SharePoint Online admin center—including the SharePoint Term Store and global sharing policies. Some of these settings, such as sharing policies, will be pertinent as you begin working with OneDrive for business in the next chapter.

OneDrive for Business

OneDrive for Business is a personalized Microsoft SharePoint library designed to give you a space to store, share, and synchronize content. It's a multiplatform collaboration tool, accessible through apps for Windows, iOS, Mac OS, and Android devices as well as a web browser.

OneDrive for Business allows synchronization and offline editing of files on Windows and Mac. Because it's built on SharePoint Server, it also provides coauthoring capabilities for documents stored in OneDrive for Business and SharePoint libraries.

Accessing OneDrive for Business

To access OneDrive for Business Online, you must have a license that includes SharePoint Online or OneDrive for Business. Follow these steps:

1. You can access OneDrive for Business Online by opening a web browser and navigating to *https://portal.office.com*.

2. The dashboard appears, as shown in Figure 30-1, and includes a OneDrive tile.

3. The first time you click the OneDrive tile, you will be presented with a splash page while your OneDrive for Business site is provisioned (if it was not automatically provisioned by another administrator). After it's provisioned (which usually takes about 30 seconds), a Your OneDrive Is Ready link appears, and you're ready to start using OneDrive for Business.

4. Click Your OneDrive Is Ready to access OneDrive for Business. If the Welcome to OneDrive Wizard opens, click Not Now to cancel it.

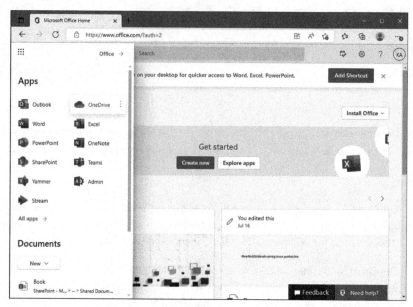

Figure 30-1   Microsoft 365 portal dashboard

5.   The navigation pane on the left enables you to upload and create Office documents (Word, Microsoft PowerPoint, Microsoft Excel, Microsoft OneNote) from the New menu. See Figure 30-2.

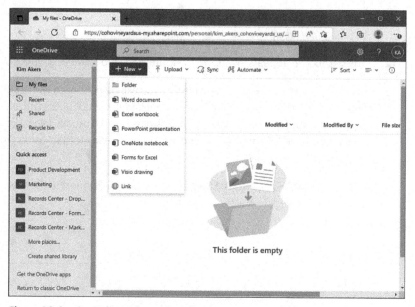

Figure 30-2   OneDrive web user interface

In the navigation pane, you also see links to sites that have been created for any Microsoft 365 groups that you are a member of.

OneDrive sync client for Windows

The new Microsoft OneDrive sync client (sometimes referred to as the next-generation sync client), built for Windows 10, Windows 8.1, Windows 8, and Windows 7, enables you to synchronize content between your computer and OneDrive for Business accounts. The OneDrive sync client also enables you to sync content from SharePoint Online sites.

Although OneDrive is a component of SharePoint on-premises deployments, the OneDrive sync client does not yet support OneDrive for Business when deployed on-premises.

Inside Out

So many sync clients

If you're using a new computer with a fresh installation of Windows 10 or Windows 11 and Office 2016, Office 2019, or Microsoft 365 Apps, you probably have the new OneDrive sync client installed. However, if you're running a previous version of Windows or Office (or upgraded from a previous version), you could have one of the older clients, the new client, or multiple clients.

Because the versions and builds of the sync clients are continuously changing, look at the visual identifiers of the applications in the system tray to determine which client you're running, or check the actual file names.

To check visually, hover over the icon in the system tray and look for the text that appears:

- If you see a white cloud icon that says OneDrive – Personal or OneDrive, and you're running Windows 11, Windows 10, Windows 8.1, Windows 8, or Windows 7, you're using the new OneDrive sync client.

- If you see a blue cloud icon that says OneDrive – <Company>, where <company> is your organization's name, you're using the new OneDrive sync client.

- If you see a white cloud icon that only says Files Are Up To Date, and you're running Windows 8, Windows 8.1, or Windows RT 8.1, you're using the previous OneDrive for Business sync client.

- If you see a blue cloud icon that says OneDrive For Business, you're using the previous OneDrive for Business sync client.

CHAPTER 30

> - To check the file name, locate the shortcut for OneDrive, right-click it, and select Properties. On the Target tab, look for the executable name:
>   - **OneDrive.exe**   New OneDrive for Business sync client
>   - **Groove.exe**   Previous OneDrive for Business sync client
>   - **SkyDrive.exe**   Previous OneDrive personal client
>
> For the purposes of this chapter, you need to be using the new OneDrive sync client.

To begin the setup, you can initiate it from either your computer or the Microsoft 365 portal. If you do not have the newest OneDrive sync client, you can download it from *https://go.microsoft.com/fwlink/?linkid=616514*.

If OneDrive is already installed, you can launch OneDrive setup from your computer by clicking the Start button, typing OneDrive, and selecting OneDrive from the results.

To start OneDrive setup from the Microsoft 365 portal, follow these steps:

1. Sign in to the Microsoft 365 portal, click the App Launcher, click OneDrive, and then click Sync on the Files page, as shown in Figure 30-3.

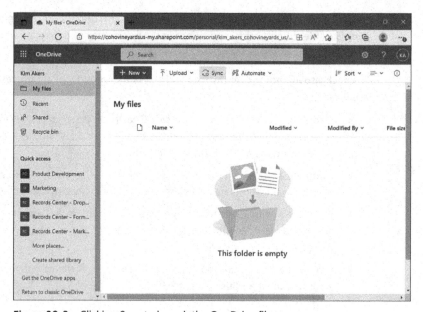

Figure 30-3   Clicking Sync to launch the OneDrive file sync

2. The dialog indicates OneDrive is being configured. However, if the OneDrive client is not installed, you will need to click the Install The Latest Version Of OneDrive link at the bottom of the We're Syncing Your Files dialog box, as shown in Figure 30-4.

Figure 30-4   OneDrive synchronization dialog

3. In the browser's Downloads list or download manager, click Open File on the OneDriveSetup.exe file to launch the OneDrive setup application.

4. Wait while the OneDrive setup application runs.

5. Click Close on the We're Syncing Your Files dialog, and then click the Sync icon on the OneDrive page again.

6. If desired, select the Always Allow SharePoint.com To Open Links Of This Type In The Associated App checkbox, and then click Open. See Figure 30-5.

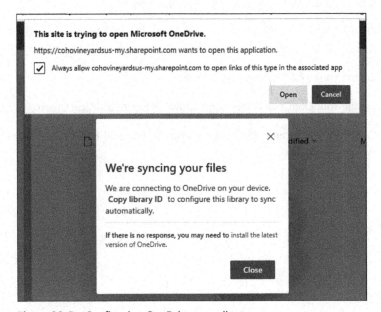

Figure 30-5   Configuring OneDrive sync client

7. To set up OneDrive, if your sign-in address isn't already populated, you will need to select Work Or School Account, type your email address, and click Sign In. See Figure 30-6.

Figure 30-6   Microsoft OneDrive initial setup wizard

8. If prompted, enter your password, and click Sign In.

9. On the Stay Signed In To All Your Apps page, click OK (Recommended) to allow Windows to automatically log you in.

10. On the You're All Set! page, click Done.

11. On the Your OneDrive Folder page, shown in Figure 30-7, click Next.

12. On the Back Up Your Folders page, shown in Figure 30-8, choose the folders you want to sync and click Next.

Figure 30-7   This Is Your OneDrive Folder page

Figure 30-8   Selecting files and folders to sync to your computer

13. On the Get To Know Your OneDrive page, click Next.

14. On the Share Files And Folders page, click Next.

15. On the All Your Files, Ready And On-Demand page, review the icons displayed and click Next, as shown in Figure 30-9.

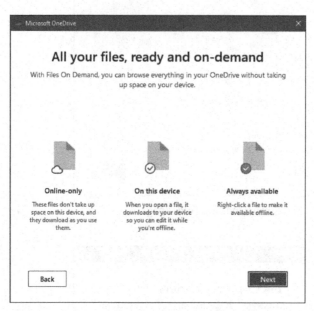

Figure 30-9   OneDrive files on-demand information

Inside Out

Files on demand

At the end of the OneDrive for Business setup, you may see the screen in Figure 30-9 describing how the different cloud icons appear for files included to be synchronized.

These icons only appear for machines that are running Windows 10 Fall Creators Update (version 1709) or later. This is because of the new attributes included in NTFS: Offline, Pinned, and Unpinned.

```
C:\windows\system32\cmd.exe                                    —  □  ×

C:\>attrib /?
Displays or changes file attributes.

ATTRIB [+R | -R] [+A | -A] [+S | -S] [+H | -H] [+O | -O] [+I | -I] [+X | -X] [+P | -P] [+U | -U]
       [drive:][path][filename] [/S [/D]] [/L]

  +   Sets an attribute.
  -   Clears an attribute.
  R   Read-only file attribute.
  A   Archive file attribute.
  S   System file attribute.
  H   Hidden file attribute.
  O   Offline attribute.
  I   Not content indexed file attribute.
  X   No scrub file attribute.
  V   Integrity attribute.
  P   Pinned attribute.
  U   Unpinned attribute.
  B   SMR Blob attribute.
  [drive:][path][filename]
      Specifies a file or files for attrib to process.
  /S  Processes matching files in the current folder
      and all subfolders.
  /D  Processes folders as well.
  /L  Work on the attributes of the Symbolic Link versus
      the target of the Symbolic Link

C:\>
```

The Pinned Attribute corresponds to the solid green Always Available icon. The file is downloaded and available on your device. It is marked to be stored in the Offline Files cache.

The Offline Attribute corresponds to the cloud icon with the blue border, which is labeled Online-only. These files can't be accessed until you are online.

The Unpinned Attribute corresponds to the semi-green On This Device icon. It may be cached on your device, but it can be removed from the cache at any time.

16. On the Get The Mobile App page, click Get Mobile App to be redirected to a webpage where you can enter a mobile number or email address to download the OneDrive app. You can also click Later to skip the download.

17. On the Your OneDrive Is Ready For You page, click Open My OneDrive Folder to open the local staging folder on your computer or click the X icon to close the setup.

After sync setup completes, you can close the We're Syncing Your Files dialog if you initiated OneDrive setup from the Microsoft 365 site. Your OneDrive for Business files appear in File Explorer as OneDrive - <CompanyName>.

CHAPTER 30

OneDrive sync client for Mac OS X

The OneDrive client for Mac OS X is available in the App Store:

1. Launch the App Store from the dock.

2. In the App Store search box, type **OneDrive**.

3. To download the app, click Get.

4. After installation, press Cmd+Space to open Spotlight and type OneDrive to display the OneDrive application. Click OneDrive to initiate the OneDrive configuration.

5. Enter your Microsoft 365 account name (usually your email address) and click Sign In.

6. When the Microsoft 365 sign-in dialog appears, complete the sign-in process by entering your password and click Sign In.

7. On the This Is Your OneDrive Folder page, click Next to accept the default installation location, as shown in Figure 30-10.

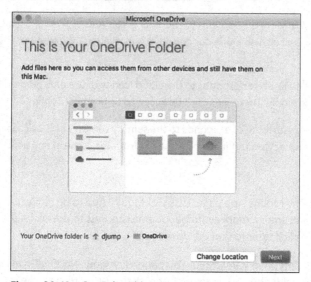

Figure 30-10   OneDrive This Is Your OneDrive Folder page

8. On the Sync Files From Your OneDrive page, depicted in Figure 30-11, select which existing files and folders (if any) in your OneDrive for Business site you want to sync to your computer and click Next.

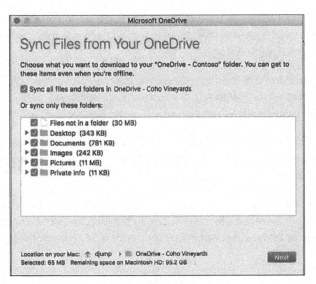

Figure 30-11   Choosing files and folders in OneDrive to sync to your computer

9.   In the Microsoft OneDrive setup wizard, click Open My OneDrive folder to see your files.

OneDrive will maintain synchronized copies of the selected files and folders on your device with your OneDrive for Business library in SharePoint Online.

Collaborating with OneDrive for Business

With OneDrive for Business, you make files available to share inside or outside your organization, depending on your organization's sharing settings. Office document files located in One-Drive support coauthoring and document versioning.

Sharing documents and folders

You can share documents and folders with both internal and external recipients. To share a document or folder, follow these steps:

1.   Navigate to the Microsoft 365 portal (*https://portal.office.com*) and sign in.

2.   Select the App launcher and click OneDrive.

3.   On the Files page, select a file or folder.

4.   Click either the Copy Link or Share buttons.

If you click the Copy Link button, OneDrive creates a link that you can share by pasting into an email or instant message. If you select a file, the link grants the default permissions configured in the SharePoint admin center. By default, this permission is set to Edit. If you select a folder, the recipient can create folders, upload files, and download files in that folder unless you change the permissions in the sharing dialog.

Depending on your SharePoint sharing settings, you may be able to select different security scope options (such as Anyone With A Link, People In <organization> With The Link, People With Existing Access, or Specific People).

If you click the Share button, you can enter email addresses for recipients that you want to share the file or folder with, just as with SharePoint sites. By default, users are granted Edit permissions (based on the default SharePoint sharing permissions).

You can click a file or folder, select the ellipsis, and then click Details to show the details pane of a file or folder. From there, click Manage Access to bring up the access control dialog, which enables you to view or update the permissions for the item. See Figure 30-12 for permissions settings.

Figure 30-12   Modifying permissions for a shared file or folder in OneDrive

Coauthoring

Just like documents stored in other SharePoint libraries, documents stored in OneDrive for Business support coauthoring, so multiple users can work on a document simultaneously.

To coauthor a document from OneDrive for Business, follow these steps:

1. Place the file you want to coauthor in OneDrive for Business or create a new Office document in your OneDrive and distribute a link to other users.

2. Edit the document from the site by using one of the following methods:

   - From OneDrive For Business in the Microsoft 365 portal, left-click the document name to launch the associated Office Online app.

   - From OneDrive For Business in the Microsoft 365 portal, hover over the document to expose the ellipsis (...). Click the ellipsis and then select Open > Open In Browser or Open > Open In <Office Application>.

   - In the following example, because a Word document is selected, OneDrive for Business prompts you to use Word Online or the Word Office application installed on your computer. Figure 30-13 shows the application options.

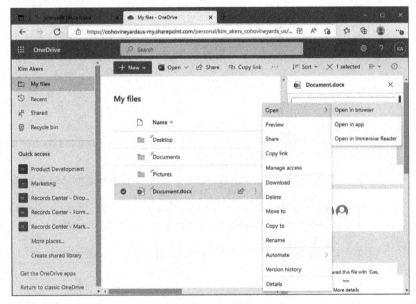

Figure 30-13   Opening a document from OneDrive for Business to enable coauthoring

Document versioning

Versioning in OneDrive for Business should already be turned on, as Microsoft has removed the radio button to disable versioning in the user interface.

However, it's always good to make sure.

CHAPTER 30

To check whether your OneDrive site is configured for versioning, follow these steps:

1. Log on to the Microsoft 365 portal and navigate to OneDrive For Business.

2. Select a document, right-click it, and look for Version History on the context menu, as shown in Figure 30-14.

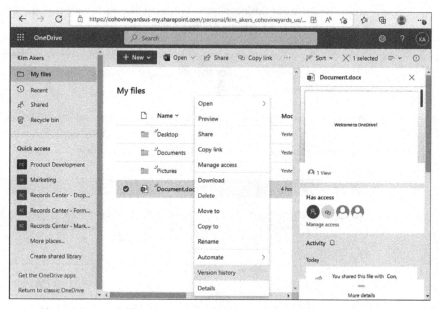

Figure 30-14   Verifying presence of Version History on the context menu

3. View the versions of a file by selecting Version History. See Figure 30-15.

If you don't have the Version History properties for files, then versioning is not turned on for your OneDrive site. To configure versioning, follow these steps:

1. In OneDrive For Business, click the gear icon to open Settings. Click OneDrive Settings.

2. Click More Settings.

3. Click Return To The Old Site Settings Page.

4. On the Site Settings page, under Site Administration, click the Site Libraries And Lists link. See Figure 30-16.

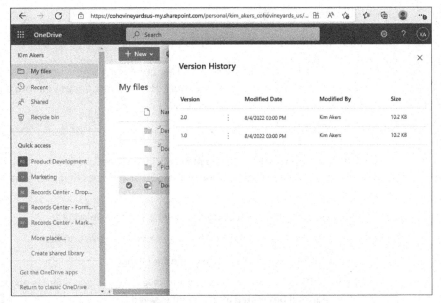

Figure 30-15   Displaying Version History for a document

Figure 30-16   OneDrive for Business Site Settings page

5. Click Customize Documents.

6. Click Versioning Settings.

7. Next to Document Version History, select either Create Major Versions or Create Major And Minor (Draft) Versions. Adjust the number of major versions as your organization requires.

NOTE

Major versions are created as when you manually invoke the Save function on a document or when you open a document for editing. Other activities that create major versions include:

- When a list item or file is first created or when a file is uploaded.

- When a file is uploaded that has the same name as an existing file.

- When the properties of a list item or file are changed.

- When an Office document is opened and saved. After a document is opened again, a new version will be created after an edit is saved.

- Periodically, when editing and saving Office documents. Not all edits and saves create new versions. When saving edits frequently, for example, each new version captures a point in time rather than each individual edit. This is common when Autosave is enabled.

- During co-authoring of a document, when a different user begins working on the document or when a user clicks Save to upload changes to the library.

- Minor versions are created automatically and cannot be controlled by the user. Minor versions can, however, be promoted to major versions.

8. Click OK.

NOTE

Versioning is a per-library setting.

Deploying OneDrive for Business to your users

OneDrive for Business is very simple to deploy—just enable the SharePoint Online license in Microsoft 365, and OneDrive for Business is enabled automatically.

However, turning on OneDrive for Business doesn't necessarily mean it will be used according to your organization's needs. You might need to deploy settings in conjunction with the application and licensing to make sure your organization is getting the most out of it.

Group Policy

One of the best ways to ensure consistent deployment of OneDrive is to use Group Policy. OneDrive for Business can be managed through the Group Policy templates available in the OneDrive Deployment Package (*https://go.microsoft.com/fwlink/p/?LinkId=717805*) or by downloading and installing the OneDrive sync app.

Typically, organizations have several common requests regarding security and data management:

- Preventing changes to the path of the OneDrive folder

- Preventing synchronization with OneDrive personal accounts

- Preventing synchronization with other tenants

- Redirecting the users' Documents folder to OneDrive

- OneDrive silent configuration

The following sections will help you configure your environment to meet those requirements.

Create a GPO for OneDrive for Business to prevent changes to the OneDrive folder path

After you have downloaded the templates, follow these steps to import them into your Active Directory environment and create a policy that prevents users from changing the location of their OneDrive for Business folder:

1. Connect to Azure AD PowerShell by using the `Connect-AzureAD` cmdlet. If you don't have the Azure AD cmdlets, run `Install-Module AzureADPreview` to install them on your computer. For more information about the Azure AD Preview module, see *https://docs.microsoft.com/en-us/powershell/azure/install-adv2?view=azureadps-2.0*.

2. After you're connected, obtain your Azure Active Directory tenant ID by running the following cmdlet:

    `Get-AzureADTenantDetail | Select ObjectID`

3. Copy the tenant ID to the clipboard or a Notepad window.

4. Copy the `OneDrive.admx` file to the `%systemroot%\PolicyDefinitions` folder on a domain controller.

5. Copy the `OneDrive.adml` file to the `%systemroot%\PolicyDefinitions\<language>` folder on a domain controller. For example, if your system is using U.S. English, the folder path would be `%systemroot%\PolicyDefinitions\en-us`.

6. Launch the Group Policy Management console (gpmc.msc).

7. Navigate to the Group Policy Objects folder, as shown in Figure 30-17, right-click it, and select New.

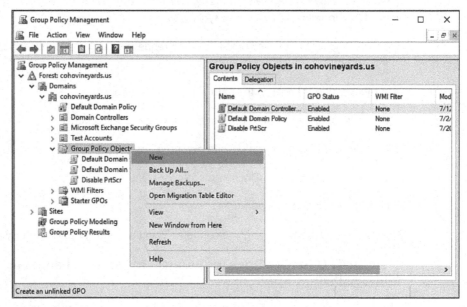

Figure 30-17   Group Policy Management console

8. Name the Group Policy object and click OK.

9. Edit the newly created Group Policy object.

Now that you have a OneDrive Group Policy, we'll configure settings to meet a typical organization's security and functionality requirements.

Prevent changing the path of the OneDrive folder

In this section, we'll configure a policy to prevent users from modifying the path of the One-Drive for Business folder. This is an important step in order for Known Folder Move to work consistently:

1. With the newly configured policy open for editing, expand User Configuration > Policies > Administrative Templates and select OneDrive.

2. Open the Prevent Users From Changing The Location Of Their OneDrive Folder policy object.

3. Configure the setting to Enabled.

4. Next to Change Location Setting, click Show to bring up the Show Contents dialog. In the Value Name column, paste your organization's Tenant ID. In the Value column, enter 1, as shown in Figure 30-18.

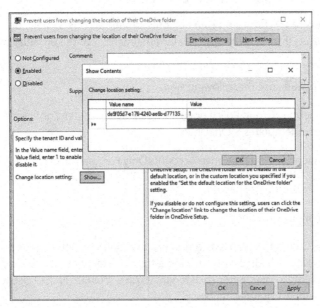

Figure 30-18   Configuring OneDrive Group Policy to prevent users from changing the location of their OneDrive for Business folder

5. Click OK to close the Show Contents dialog.

6. Click OK to close the Prevent Users From Changing The Location Of Their OneDrive Folder policy object dialog.

Next, we'll update the personal OneDrive setting.

Prevent users from syncing personal OneDrive accounts

Many organizations want to ensure work devices are used exclusively for work purposes. To help accommodate this, you can set this policy configuration to prevent the OneDrive client from synchronizing with OneDrive.com personal sites:

1. With the OneDrive Group Policy open, navigate to User Configuration > Administrative Templates > OneDrive.

2. Open the Prevent Users From Syncing Personal OneDrive Accounts policy object.

3. Configure the setting to Enabled and click OK.

Users will be unable to configure OneDrive personal accounts. If they currently have a OneDrive personal account configured, it will stop further synchronization.

Prevent synchronization with other tenants

In addition to prevent synchronizing with personal storage accounts, many organizations also want to prevent users from synchronizing data with tenants that the organization does not own or manage.

To configure this feature, use the following steps:

1. With the OneDrive Group Policy open, navigate to Computer Configuration > Administrative Templates > OneDrive.

2. Open the Allow Syncing OneDrive Accounts Only For Specific Organizations policy object.

3. Configure the setting to Enabled.

4. Next to Tenant ID, click Show.

5. In the Show Contents dialog, paste your organization's tenant ID value into the Value box, as shown in Figure 30-19. If you have more than one tenant that you would like to allow OneDrive clients to sync, enter each tenant ID on a separate line. Click OK when finished to close the Show Contents dialog.

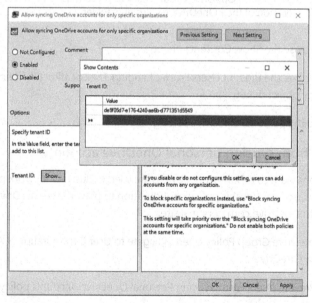

Figure 30-19   Configuring OneDrive Group Policy to users to only sync with listed tenants

6. Click OK to close the Group Policy object.

OneDrive sync clients will now only be able to synchronize with the tenants listed in this policy object.

Configure Documents folder redirection

To take advantage of OneDrive's storage and synchronization capabilities by default for users, you can configure the Windows Documents folder to be stored in OneDrive. To use Group Policy and folder redirection for OneDrive for Business, the OneDrive for Business folder must be installed in the default location.

> # NOTE
>
> **Previously, the Known Folder Move (KFM) used the native Folder Redirection Group Policy Object in conjunction with item-level targeting. The current KFM will not work correctly if you have previously configured native document folder redirection for the Documents folder.**
>
> **To review the legacy Known Folder Move documentation, see *https://aka.ms/LegacyKFM*.**

To configure the modern Known Folder Move solution, use the following process:

1. With the OneDrive Group Policy open, navigate to Computer Configuration > Administrative Templates > OneDrive.

2. Open the Silently Move Windows Known Folders To OneDrive policy object.

3. Configure the setting to Enabled.

4. From your Microsoft 365 tenant, copy the Tenant ID value and paste it into the Tenant ID box in the Silently Move Windows Known Folders To OneDrive policy object.

5. By default, the Desktop, Documents, and Pictures folders are selected. Deselect any desired. You can come back and select additional checkboxes, but once selected and implemented, you cannot undo the policy by clearing the checkbox. See Figure 30-20.

CHAPTER 30

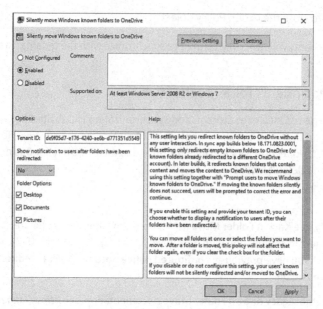

Figure 30-20   Configuring the Silently move Windows known folders to OneDrive option

6.   Click OK.

7.   Open the Prompt Users To Move Windows Known Folders To OneDrive policy object.

8.   Configure the setting to Enabled.

9.   In the Tenant ID box, paste the tenant ID value from your Microsoft 365 tenant.

TIP

It's recommended that you configure both the Silently Move and Prompt Users policy options together. The silent move will take precedence, and if errors are encountered, the user will be prompted to resolve the issues.

Additionally, Microsoft recommends limiting the scope of the folder redirection policy to approximately 4,000 devices per week until your organization is fully on-boarded.

Enable silent configuration of user accounts

Silent configuration of the OneDrive app allows the OneDrive client to automatically populate the credentials and configure the OneDrive app to start up automatically.

Following are the prerequisites for this configuration object:

- Hybrid Azure AD joined devices

- Supported operating system:

  - Windows 7 or later

  - Windows Server 2008 R2 or later

To configure this setting, follow these steps:

1. With the OneDrive Group Policy open, navigate to Computer Configuration > Administrative Templates > OneDrive.

2. Open the Silently Sign In Users To The OneDrive Sync App With Their Windows Credentials policy object.

3. Configure the setting to Enabled.

4. Click OK.

To test these policy objects, link the policy to an Active Directory organizational unit that contains both the user and device objects.

After you have logged on, you can review File Explore for visible confirmation that the policies have been applied, including folder redirection. See Figure 30-21.

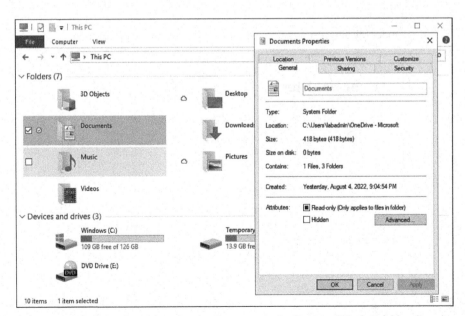

Figure 30-21 File Explorer view showing Documents, Desktop, and Pictures folders have been redirected

When testing and verification are complete, expand the scope of the linked Group Policy to more users and devices.

Manage OneDrive for Business

There are a number of administrative and management tasks that you might need to perform in OneDrive for Business, depending on your organization's business requirements. Some of these might include granting access to other administrators or personnel for eDiscovery or management, preventing apps or clients outside your organization from synchronizing content, or even disabling the provisioning of OneDrive sites altogether.

Granting access to a secondary administrator

Some organizations require administrators to have access to everyone's content. By default, OneDrive permissions restrict access to only the owner. Microsoft 365 automatically designates the owner as Site Collection Administrator.

This process works only for OneDrive sites created after you designate a secondary site collection administrator (and does not work on existing OneDrive for Business sites):

1.   Log in to the Microsoft 365 admin center (*https://admin.microsoft.com*) with an account that has Global Administrator privileges.

2.   In the navigation pane, select Admin Centers > SharePoint.

3.   In the SharePoint admin center, select More Features, and then select Open under User Profiles.

4.   Under My Site Settings, click Setup My Sites, as shown in Figure 30-22.

Figure 30-22   Setup My Sites

5. Scroll to My Site Secondary Admin, select the Enable My Site Secondary Admin checkbox, and type a user or group name to grant Site Collection Administrator privileges to a second security principal. See Figure 30-23.

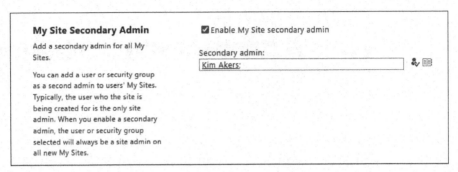

Figure 30-23   Granting My Site Secondary Admin privileges

6. Scroll to the bottom of the page and click OK.

TIP

As previously stated, this configuration only affects new sites going forward. To grant access to existing sites, you will need to use a tool such as the OneDrive for Business Admin Tool (*https://aka.ms/OneDriveAdmin*).

Restricting devices that can synchronize OneDrive content

There are several settings you can use to control which devices can synchronize content, which might be important for your organization.

You can restrict PC synchronization to only PCs that are joined to specific domains. Follow these steps:

1. On a domain-joined computer with the Active Directory Remote Server Administration or Active Directory Domain Services installed, launch a Windows PowerShell session and run the following commands to retrieve a list of domain GUIDs:

```
$domainGuids = @()
[array]$domains = (Get-ADForest).Domains
Foreach ($domain in $domains) {$domainGuids += Get-ADDomain -Identity $domain | `
Select ObjectGuid}
$domainGuids.ObjectGuid.Guid | Clip
```

2. Log in to the Microsoft 365 admin center (*https://admin.microsoft.com*) with an account that has Global Administrator privileges.

3. In the navigation pane, select Admin Centers > SharePoint.

4. Select Settings.

5. Select Sync, as shown in Figure 30-24.

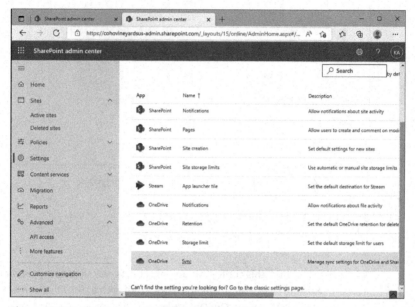

Figure 30-24   OneDrive sync administration

6. On the Sync fly-out menu, select the Allow Syncing Only On PCs Joined To Specific Domains checkbox, as shown in Figure 30-25.

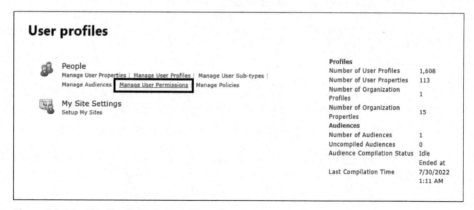

Figure 30-25   The OneDrive Settings Sync flyout

7. Paste the contents of the clipboard from the script in Step 1 into the Enter Each Active Directory Domain As A GUID On A New Line text box.

8. Click Save.

TIP

The combination of the SharePoint/OneDrive domain restriction and the sync client restriction under the Prevent Synchronization With Other Tenants will mitigate unauthorized attempts to synchronize data.

Restricting sharing

OneDrive for Business enables you to restrict sharing outside your organization. Because OneDrive is a component of SharePoint, your OneDrive for Business site cannot have less-restrictive sharing permissions than SharePoint online.

NOTE

To configure OneDrive and SharePoint sharing options, see the "Sharing" section under "Policies" in Chapter 29, "SharePoint Online management."

Disabling OneDrive provisioning

OneDrive is a feature of SharePoint Online. A OneDrive personal site collection (formerly known as My Sites) is provisioned for each user automatically the first time they attempt to access OneDrive.

However, some organizations might want to roll out OneDrive in phases or start using SharePoint right away but haven't yet had time to develop governance of how best to use OneDrive. In those instances, you can disable automatic OneDrive provisioning or restrict OneDrive for Business provisioning to certain individuals or groups. Follow these steps:

1. Log in to the Microsoft 365 admin center (*https://admin.microsoft.com*) with an account that has Global Administrator privileges.

2. In the navigation pane, select Admin Centers > SharePoint.

3. In the SharePoint admin center, select More Features and then select Open under User Profiles.

4. Under People, select Manage User Permissions, as shown in Figure 30-26.

CHAPTER 30

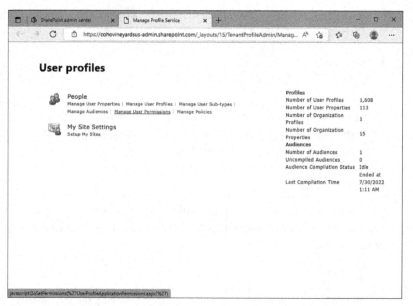

Figure 30-26   OneDrive user profile management

5. To add users or a group of users you want to be able to provision OneDrive sites, type the user or group name and click Add.

NOTE

You can only add groups if they are mail-enabled security groups.

6. After you have added any users or groups you want to have permissions to provision their OneDrive sites to the list, select Everyone Except External Users in the user list and then clear the Create Personal Site checkbox. See Figure 30-27 for an example.

7. For every user or group you have added that you want to enable provisioning for, you must select the user or group from the permissions list and then select the Create Personal Site checkbox. When you are finished, click OK.

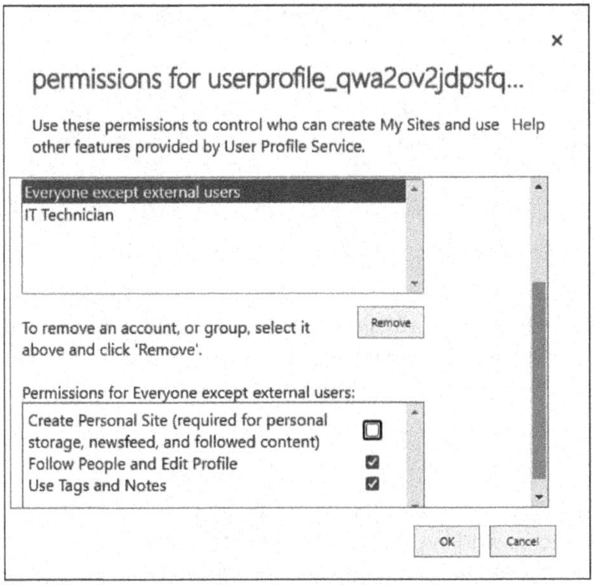

Figure 30-27   Updating permissions for users and groups

These steps affect only new OneDrive site provisioning going forward. OneDrive sites that have already been provisioned are unaffected. To remove user access to those, you must either remove access to the individual user sites or remove the user's SharePoint license. Removing the user's SharePoint license could result in loss of data stored in the OneDrive site.

NOTE

You can use the OneDrive for Business admin tool at *https://aka.ms/OneDriveAdmin* to administer OneDrive for Business site permissions.

Pre-provisioning OneDrive for Business sites

If you are onboarding users in a staged fashion or preparing to onboard a significant number of users, you may want to pre-provision OneDrive for Business sites to help speed the onboarding process.

To pre-provision a list of users, follow these steps:

1.   Enter all of the addresses for the users into a text file such as users.txt, with one address per line:

    User1@contoso.com
    User2@contoso.com
    User3@contoso.com

2. Connect to the SharePoint Online Management Shell using the `Connect-SPOService` cmdlet and the admin site for your tenant:

   ```
   Connect-SPOService -Url https://<tenant>-admin.sharepoint.com
   ```

3. Using the `Request-SPOPersonalSite` cmdlet, import the text file containing the users from step 1:

   ```
   Request-SPOPersonalSite -UserEmails (Get-Content .\users.txt)
   ```

   ## CAUTION

   In order for the OneDrive site provisioning to be successful, a user must be licensed for the SharePoint Online service, and the user account must not be disabled.

Troubleshooting

If you experience OneDrive synchronization problems, you might need to troubleshoot it. If the application seems not to be working, it might be simply a matter of restarting the OneDrive app or checking to see whether some files are preventing it from synchronizing properly.

OneDrive does have some limitations, which are described in the following list:

- Microsoft recommends synchronizing no more than 300,000 files across all libraries or sites (up from 20,000).

- The maximum file size that can be synchronized through the OneDrive sync client is 250GB (up from 2GB).

- Folder name and file combinations can have up to 400 characters after the tenant name and after decoding. File paths longer than this will cause synchronization errors. For example, when examining the length of the `https://cohovineyardsus.sharepoint.com/sites/Marketing/Promotional Materials/handout1.pptx` file, the content starting with `sites` is counted (for a total path length of 41 characters).

- You cannot synchronize file names with invalid characters: `\ / : * ? " < > |`

- You cannot synchronize filenames that begin with a period (`.`) or filenames that have leading or trailing spaces.

- A folder named `Forms` cannot exist in the root of a OneDrive for Business library.

- `_vti_` can't exist anywhere in the filename.

- A folder name cannot have a leading tilde (~).

- OneNote notebooks cannot be synced because they have their own sync mechanism.

- Open files cannot be synced.

- Certain reserved names or words are prohibited: .lock, CON, PRN, AUX, NUL, COM0 – COM9, LPT0 – LPT9, desktop.ini, or files beginning with ~$.

NOTE

Current details about restrictions are available at *https://aka.ms/od4brestrictions*.

CHAPTER 30

Index

Symbols

Plug into learning at

MicrosoftPressStore.com

The Microsoft Press Store by Pearson offers:

- Free U.S. shipping

- Buy an eBook, get three formats – Includes PDF, EPUB, and MOBI to use with your computer, tablet, and mobile devices

- Print & eBook Best Value Packs

- eBook Deal of the Week – Save up to 50% on featured title

- Newsletter – Be the first to hear about new releases, announcements, special offers, and more

- Register your book – Find companion files, errata, and product updates, plus receive a special coupon* to save on your next purchase

 Pearson